THE WHY, WHO AND HOW
OF THE EDITORIAL PAGE

THE
Why
Who
AND
How
OF THE
Editorial Page

SECOND EDITION

Kenneth Rystrom

Virginia Polytechnic Institute and State University

STRATA PUBLISHING COMPANY

State College, Pennsylvania

To Amy, Jennifer and Randall

Second Edition
9 8 7 6 5 4 3 2 1

Published by:
Strata Publishing Company
1124 S. Atherton Street
State College, PA 16801
(814)234-8545

Library of Congress Cataloging in Publication Data

Rystrom, Kenneth
    The why, who and how of the editorial page.
    Includes bibliographic references and index.
    1. Editorials.   I. Title.
    PN4778.R95 1994   070.4'1   93-084254
    ISBN 0-9634489-1-9

Manufactured in the United States of America.

Cover photo: A Newsday article reprinted by permission. Newsday, Inc., Copyright, 1993.

Text and cover design by Leon Bolognese & Associates, Inc.

CREDITS AND ACKNOWLEDGEMENTS

Permission is gratefully acknowledged for use of materials appearing on the following pages:

239: Laird B. Anderson. 289: Reprinted with permission from The Atlanta Journal and The Atlanta Constitution. 211–212: Reprinted with permission from the Beaver County Times. 166–167: Reprinted from The Birmingham News. 82: Copyright 1972 by Warren G. Bovee. 286, 287, 292: ©1990, 1991, 1993 The Charlotte Observer. 193–194: Written by Erwin Rieger, former managing editor of The Columbian newspaper at Vancouver, Wash. 189: ©1992, The Courier-Journal. 179: Daily Press. 135: Daily Tribune. 180: Des Moines Register. 184–185, 242–243, 282: Reprinted with permission: The Detroit Free Press. 231–233: The Editorialist. 228–229: G. Donald Gale. 234–236: Courtesy of Don Gale, Editor, *The Editorialist*, Professional Journal of the National Broadcast Editorial Association, Nov.–Dec. 1983. 165: Copyright The Greenville News. 278: Copyright 1979 The Houston Post. Reprinted by permission. 277: The Idaho Statesman. 40: ©1990, Lexington Herald-Leader. Permission to reprint portions of articles from *The Masthead* appearing throughout the book: National Conference of Editorial Writers. The Masthead. 158, 168: Milwaukee Journal. 49: Reprinted by permission of Montana Journalism Review. 119: National Conference of Editorial Writers. 170–171: Fort Lauderdale Sun-Sentinel. 198: ©The Kentucky Post. 229–231: Editorial Courtesy of KCBS-Newsradio 74. 280: The Norfolk Ledger-Star. 196–197: Copyright, 1979, Los Angeles Times. Reprinted by permission. 279: Copyright ©1978. The Louisville Times. Reprinted with permission. 169–170: The News-Sentinel, Fort Wayne, IN. 44–46: Reprinted from The Orlando Sentinel. 283: Copyright 1992, The Oregonian. 214–215: The Patriot News. 212–213: Philadelphia Daily News. 285: The Phoenix Gazette. 185–186, 217–219: Reprinted from the Pittsburgh Post-Gazette. 284: The Plain Dealer. 178: Roanoke Times & World-News. 191: Reprinted with permission of the St. Petersburg Times. 198–199: ©1991 San Francisco Examiner. Reprinted with permission. 240–241: ©The Santa Fe Reporter, 1990. 213: Scranton Times. 244–245: Reprinted from The Seattle Times, 1988. 216–217: ©The Tribune-Democrat, Johnstown, Pa. 133–134: West Central Tribune. 276: Copyright ©The Washington Post. 175–176: Reprinted from The Washington Times. 148–149, 150, 237–238: By permission of the authors.

Contents

Preface

When I wrote the first edition of *The Why, Who and How of the Editorial Page*, I had two purposes in mind. I wanted to help students and other would-be editorial writers learn how to write editorials and edit an editorial page. I also wanted to help them understand what it is like to be an editorial writer today. I hoped that readers would find that the book spanned the gap between the theoretical and practical aspects of opinion writing.

In preparing this edition, I have retained the basic content and framework of the first edition, but I have also updated and slightly expanded the book to include new thoughts and ideas about editorial writing that editors and educators have expressed since publication of the earlier edition. Most of the examples of editorial writing are new, and so are many of the experiences of editorial writers that I have cited. A new chapter provides an introduction to a broader variety of opinion writing, and one of the chapters on editorial writing has been expanded into two chapters.

DESCRIPTION OF THE BOOK

The suggestion that I write the book originally came from officers of NCEW. They saw a need for a textbook that would appeal to professionals as well as students. Several editors have told me since that they require their new editorial writers to study the book before they try their hand at editorials. The book has also been used widely in college and university courses with various titles: editorial writing, opinion writing, persuasive writing and feature writing. The opening chapter, "The Editorial Page That Used to Be," might be appropriate for a media history course, and the chapter on "Editorials on Elections" for a political communications or a public affairs reporting course. The extensive bibliography should be helpful in any mass media course.

As the title suggests, the book consists of three main sections.

The first, "The Why of the Editorial Page," looks at where editorial writing has come from, where it is today and where it might be headed. The first chapter provides what may be the most extensive account of the history of the American editorial page now in print.

The second section, "The Who of the Editorial Page," contains material not usually found in journalism textbooks. Chapters 3–9 describe how men and women become editorial writers; how they can prepare themselves to become writers, or better writers; and how editorial writers fit into the newspaper organization and the wider community. Included are discussions about relations with publishers, the news staff, the editorial page staff and the community. Chapter 9, on community relations, examines the opportunities and potential conflicts of interest that editorial writers face in participating in public affairs. In all these relationships, the place of the editorial writer has been changing. It continues to change. In many instances, editorial writers are better prepared and are being given more responsibility than in the past, but more also is expected of them in terms of knowledge, commitment and integrity.

The largest section of the book, "The How of the Editorial Page," explains how to write editorials and edit opinion pages. Emphasis is placed on how writers and editors can do their jobs better, whether in writing editorials, handling letters to the editor and syndicated features, bringing diverse opinions to the page or attracting readers through design and layout.

The chapters are liberally illustrated with examples of the ideas, experiences and written products of writers and editors, as well as thoughts, some of them contradictory, about how writers and editors think editorials should be written and editorial pages produced.

As I recount some of my own experiences and state my opinions, I hope readers will catch my enthusiasm for editorial page work. I have enjoyed writing my own editorials and editing other people's. I have found pleasure in seeing the results of editing and arranging letters, columns and cartoons on an editorial page. Probably as much as anything, I have enjoyed the life of an editorial writer as a recognized member of, and participant in, a community. I think that as you read about what other writers and editors have said and done, you will conclude that they too find their jobs fun, interesting and stimulating.

FEATURES OF THE NEW EDITION

As mentioned earlier, Chapter 15, "Other Types of Opinion Writing," is new to this edition. In this chapter, students are introduced to writing broadcast editorials, reviews and signed opinion pieces.

Material that appeared in the first edition in a chapter titled "Subjects That Deserve More Attention" has been expanded into two chapters: Chapter 12, "Subjects That Are Hard to Write About," and Chapter 13, "Subjects That Are Deceptively Easy or Neglected."

Nearly all writing examples in these and the other chapters are new, taken from recent issues of editorial pages from across the country. Many of these editorials have been awarded prizes for excellence.

Chapter 1, on the development of the editorial page ("The Editorial Page That Used to Be"), has been expanded substantially, partly to recognize an increasing awareness of the contributions to opinion writing that have been made by women and African-Americans. The chapter also provides a much more extensive look at the history of the editorial page in the United States.

Several chapters draw on recent scholarly research on the processes and effects of opinion writing, including material from *Journalism Quarterly* and *Newspaper Research Journal*. Nearly every chapter has benefited from new material that has appeared in *The Masthead*, the quarterly publication of the National Conference of Editorial Writers (NCEW).

ACKNOWLEDGMENTS

As this manuscript nears completion, I realize I have been teaching editorial writing and other journalism courses for more than 15 years. It won't be long before these years match the 20 years (17 of them in editorial writing) I worked on newspapers. I suppose the way I write editorials and the way that I teach editorial writing can be traced largely to on-the-job lessons I learned during my first editorial writing job, on the *Des Moines* (Ia.) *Register and Tribune*. The editorial page editor, Lauren K. Soth, had just won the Pulitzer Prize for editorials proposing an exchange of farm delegations between the then Soviet Union and the United States (For the mid-1950s, this was a very daring proposal, but it eventually resulted in Nikita Khrushchev himself coming to the United States with the Soviet group.) As a green editorial writer, I listened eagerly to the editorial wisdom exchanged among the nine people at the morning editorial conferences and not so eagerly for the call to come into Soth's office to discuss my latest editorial effort. The basic message of those lessons was that you try to convince readers, not harangue them.

While still learning how to hold my own and fight for space on a large editorial-page staff, I received an invitation to return to the newspaper (*The Columbian* in Vancouver, Wash.) where I had been a reporter to take over the editorial page. I become a one-person staff. There I learned that it is possible to write two editorials a day, edit the letters and columns, lay out the page, get around in the community and still find time for a family and social life. Looking back, I think those days as a lone voice were the most exciting and rewarding part of my journalistic career. One reason was that I had lucked into a newspaper that was owned by two brothers, Don and Jack Campbell, who were committed to putting out a good newspaper with a strong, independent editorial voice. (I must admit that on days when time ran out before a second editorial was written, or when I was out of town, I could count on contributions from the managing editor, Erwin Rieger, who not incidentally had put me thorough a rigorous training as a reporter during my first stint on *The Columbian*.)

After a few years in which I was the sole script writer for *The Columbian*'s voice, the publishers proposed adding another person to the editorial page staff. By the time I left the paper several years later, the editorial staff had grown to three in number. Elisabet Van Nostrand, Dennis Ryerson and Mike Heywood, at various times, had had a hand in teaching me, as much as I taught them, how to write editorials and put out a lively editorial page.

The name of Nathanial B. Blumberg figures prominently in my more than 40 years as a student or professional journalist. My first journalism class at the University of Nebraska, with Professor Blumberg, helped convince me journalism should be my life's work. Ten years later, he put me on to the editorial writing job in Des Moines. Sixteen years after that, he lined up my first teaching job. While I was teaching at the University of Montana, he and I brainstormed the basic format of this textbook.

I am grateful for the association I have had with countless editorial writers and editors through the National Conference of Editorial Writers. Without the encouragement and contributions of members of NCEW, this book literally would not have been possible. The officers of NCEW allowed, in fact urged, me to draw as much as I wished upon the rich, varied contents of more than 40 volumes of that organization's quarterly, *The Masthead*. I also want to express appreciation to the 50 or so editors, publishers and students who have given me permission to reproduce the editorials, reviews, signed articles, and editorial and op-ed pages that appear in this edition.

My thanks also go to the reviewers whose many substantial contributions helped me refine and improve the book. For the first edition, they were R. Thomas Berner, The Pennsylvania State University; Kenneth Edwards, University of Alabama; Robert C. Kochersberger, Jr., State University of New York, College at Cortland; William McKeen, Western Kentucky University; and Robert M. Ours, West Virginia University. For this edition, they were Sharon Barrett, University of Montana; David Bennett, Indiana State University; Terry M. Clark, University of Central Oklahoma; Martin L. Gibson, The University of Texas at Austin; and Donald A. Lambert, Ohio University.

With the first edition, published by Random House, I was initiated into the book-publishing business with the help of Mary Shuford, Martha Leff and Kathleen Domenig. Then, nearly a decade later, as editors and professors were starting to ask whether a new edition would be coming out, I received a surprising telephone call from Kathleen Domenig. Would I be interested in working on a new edition with her at Strata Publishing Company? The result, from my point of view, has been the smoothest major writing effort with which I have been associated. Kathleen has helped especially in blending the new with the old, in my efforts to bring fresh material and fresh insight to the two "W's" and the "H" of editorial writing.

Kenneth Rystrom
Blacksburg, Virginia
April 1993

Introduction

One of my friend's most fiercely articulated beliefs is that nobody can change anybody else's mind about anything, ever. Now that's an intriguing and ironic point of view—for someone who earned his living writing editorials.

—DAVID SHAW, LOS ANGELES TIMES MEDIA CRITIC[1]

Sometimes an editorial prompts a voter to pull a certain lever, other times not. Sometimes it inspires citizens to ask for reform in the state capital or Washington, other times not. Yet the win-lose ratio of editorials is not the real point. Their role—as lofty as it may sound— is to educate, provoke debate and offer enlightened judgments to their readers. That's enough justification, after all.

—ROSEMARY YARDLEY, GREENSBORO (N.C.) NEWS AND OBSERVER[2]

Readers may not spend much time wondering who writes the anonymous editorials they read in their newspaper. If they did, what image of today's editorial writers would come to mind?

Some readers no doubt would describe editorial writers as simply mouthpieces for their publishers. Others might view editorial writers as idealists, writing from their "ivory towers," far above the nitty-gritty issues of everyday life, or as anonymous, ineffective writers hiding behind the editorial "we." Some readers, perhaps with trepidation, would describe editorial writers as powerful opinion leaders, imposing their points of view on their communities.

Editorial writers have been all of these, but neither one description nor all of them provide a realistic description of today's writers.

Some editorial writers have been, and some always will be, publishers' mouthpieces—"mindless robots with a knack for parroting other people's ideas," in the words of one writer.[3] But publishers, busy with other parts of the newspaper operation, can't be expert enough in most editorial topics to hold their own in discussions with knowledgeable editorial writers. More than ever before, editorial writers are being hired because of their education and experience, and are being given more opportunities to do their own thinking. Instead of worrying about what their publishers may think, most editorial writers are concerned about making sense of complicated issues.

Perhaps on some newspapers editorial writers still possess the power to influence directly what is thought and done in their communities—remnants of the days of the personal journalism of a William Allen White of the *Emporia* (Kan.) *Gazette* or a Ralph McGill of the *Atlanta Constitution.* But today editorial writers are more likely to influence their readers through clear, rational, consistent editorializing over a space of time than mighty pronouncements. What they say is likely to be more persuasive with readers than who they are. "What influence the press retains owes far more to pervasiveness than to persuasion, far more to its role in setting agendas than in stating opinions," *Los Angeles Times* media critic David Shaw has written in evaluating the state of opinion writing today. "The press today may help determine what people think *about,* but only rarely does the press help determine what people *think.*"[4] Even though most people say that they get more news from television than from any other source, research shows that newspapers remain the principal agenda-setter at both local and national levels.

If today's editorial writers can't match the persuasive powers of a White or a McGill, what is it that attracts them to editorial writing? One attraction is the opportunity to help set the public agenda. The power to control the subject matter that a community reads about is no small power. Editorial writers generally have more freedom than reporters to decide what they will write about.

On an increasing number of newspapers, editorial writing is not an anonymous job. While today's editorial writers are not as well known to their readers as they were in the days of personal journalism, they are likely to be better known than their predecessors of a few decades ago. Many editorial pages now offer opportunities for editorial writers to attach their names to signed columns, interpretive articles and other opinion pieces. A few are writing signed articles that dissent from the official policies of their papers. A photograph or a sketch accompanying a signed article brings even greater recognition to a writer.

Another reason journalists are attracted to editorial writing these days is that more than in the past they are getting the chance to have their voices heard in the making of editorial policy. Increasingly policy is being set by a board of editors and editorial writers, rather than by the publisher or a single editor. More and more publishers are opening their editorial and opposite-editorial pages to a variety of points of view, and an increasing number are seeking to include writers of varying views on their editorial staffs. Publishers are looking for younger people, for more women and for more members of racial and ethnic minorities.

Journalists are attracted to editorial writing because they like to dig into and write about subjects in a more thoughtful and leisurely manner than they typically can as reporters. Writing a clear, incisive, informative editorial can provide a great deal of pleasure to the writer (and to the reader).

Finally journalists become editorial writers because the job, on the right newspaper, can be fun, rewarding, exciting and a power trip. Editorial writers have excuses to meet and talk with presidents, governors, mayors, famous scientists, underpaid but wise college professors and the philosophers of the age— then sit back and pontificate on the meaning of things. The cliched "ivory tower" may be just that.

The promotion department of the newspaper that I served as editorial page editor once ran a full-page promotional ad, with a large photograph showing me in a reflective pose. "Jolting the conscience of Clark County" proclaimed a headline an inch high. (Of course, the next day the owner-publishers and I might have had a falling out over something, and I would have been looking for a job as the conscience of another community.)

These are some of the reasons that journalists are attracted to editorial writing. Those reasons also partly answer the question: Why have an editorial page?

One reason is tradition. For a century and a half or so, most American newspapers have set aside a page for the opinions of their writers, their readers, various other contributors. Most editorial pages, in fact, look much alike.

A second reason for an editorial page is prestige. No self-respecting newspaper would dare appear without an editorial page (except maybe on Saturday). If for no other reason than the limited space, on the average more thought probably goes into a column-inch of type on the editorial page than on any other page.

A third reason is that traditionally the editorial page has been set aside as the place for expression, and exchange, of opinions. In recent decades this distinctiveness has been softened, with the appearance on the news pages of analysis, interpretation and personal columns. It still remains the place where opinion is consistently found.

A fourth reason for an editorial page is to provide community leadership. Leadership does not necessarily require that opinions be changed. One role of the editorial is to reinforce and help clarify opinions that are already held. Another role is to call the attention of the community to problems, projects and situations and to press for community action.

We might find part of the answer to the question of why editorial writing seems to be surviving—and reviving—if we look briefly at how editorial pages have changed in the two hundred years or so of their existence. In that time editorial pages have undergone several transformations, staying alive by responding to changing circumstances. In the end, we will find that those editorial pages of today that have not headed for the museum are being transformed into pages quite different from those of the past.

Section

1

THE
Why
OF THE
Editorial
Page

Chapter 1

The Editorial Page That Used to Be

*[Horace Greeley] has done more than any other man to bring slaveholders
to bay, and place the Northern fingers on the throat of the slavery
institution. . . . His influence is now immense.*

—E. L. GODKIN, 19TH-CENTURY EDITOR[1]

*. . . editorials neither make nor mar a daily paper, . . . they do not much
influence the public mind nor change many votes.*

—JAMES PARTON, 19TH-CENTURY BIOGRAPHER[2] (FOLLOWING THE DEATH OF GREELEY)

Editorial writing is not what it used to be.

Now, you may assume that I am comparing today's editorial writers with Horace Greeley or James Gordon Bennett or Charles Dana. And I am. No editorial writer today is blessed with the name recognition or devoted readership of these giants of the days of "personal journalism." But I also have a much more recent comparison in mind. Many of today's editorial writers are different from editorial writers of only a few years ago. They are better prepared for their jobs and better known in their communities than those "anonymous wretches" that one participant described as assembling at the first national meeting of editorial writers in 1947.

Editors no longer thunder in the manner of a Greeley, whose editorials could send a screaming mob to New York's city hall or provoke an ill-prepared Union Army into fighting the Battle of Bull Run. Editors of the first half of the 19th century often spoke with the editorial "I," and when they used "we," they meant "I." Editorials didn't have to be signed; readers knew who wrote the editorials in the papers they read.

Readers usually agreed with editorials in the papers they subscribed to. The large number of newspapers in most cities represented a wide variety of political opinions, and people read the papers they found most compatible with their own views. Consequently, editors could be as dogmatic and vitriolic in their editorials as they wished to be and know that their readers would not only agree with what they said but enjoy every nasty word written against mutual opponents. Editors could find comfort in the fact that, even if they did not know any more about an issue than their own political party's line, they were more knowledgeable than the vast majority of their readers. During the days of the "penny press" (when some papers actually did cost only one penny), many readers were immigrants—new to the country and new to the language—and most of them, as well as readers born in America, were only aware of what they read in their papers.

Those were great days for editors who were sure of what they wanted to say and said it boldly. But, in addition to spreading their views, they spread a great deal of misinformation and fear among their readers. You have only to recall how the circulation war between Joseph Pulitzer and William Randolph Hearst whipped up a frenzy that helped ignite the Spanish-American War.

No editor of today has that kind of power over the emotions of readers. Today journalists may lament the passing of the great days of personal journalism, but they can't lament the shenanigans, the (sometimes self-) deception and outright lying, those great editors engaged in. The days of the "great editorialist" have been gone for a century—or at least since the turn of the century.

Compared to Horace Greeley, today's editorial writers are not well known to their readers. They rarely sign their names to what they write. Their editorials are the anonymous opinions of "the newspaper." Since today's readers have virtually no choice of a local daily newspaper, modern editorial writers know that those who read what they write hold as many varieties of opinion as exist in the community. This diverse readership is one reason that editorial writers no longer roar like Greeley. If writers take a strong stand on a controversial issue, they know they will please those who agree with them but displease those who disagree (if these people read the editorials at all). Today's writers suspect that if they come on too strong in their editorials, they will antagonize the readers they think they have the best chance to influence, those in the middle who have not made up their minds. Expression of a strong editorial opinion also may suggest to readers that the paper is using its news columns to advance that same opinion.

Writers know a lot of their readers are as well educated as they. Readers may not see another daily newspaper, but they have many other channels of communication through which to learn what is happening in their communities and the world. Today's public has a far better chance of finding out whether editorial writers know what they are talking about than did readers of a century ago. If an editorial hands out the party line, those who are unfamiliar with the issue at hand may be swayed for the moment. But, if the editorial has told only half the story, and the readers come across the other half at a later time, they are likely to sway right back again—and will thereafter be warier when the newspaper tries to tell them something.

These are some of the ways in which editorial writing is different now from the way it was in the days of Greeley, Bennett and Dana. How, then, does today's editorial writing differ from that of more recent times?

Personal journalism began to die out in the 1870s. Newspapers became corporately, instead of individually, owned. Publishers became more important than editors. Editorial-writing staffs, at least on larger papers, grew in size. If editorials did not specifically represent the handed-down views of the publisher, they were at least the product of a group rather than the thoughts of an independent editorial writer. When the group of "anonymous wretches" assembled in Washington, D.C., in 1947, the 26 editorial writers, all men, had not previously met one another. The majority had never heard of most of the others. Only a few of the persons whose work appeared on editorial pages then were very well known. Beginning in the early 1930s editorial page columnists such as Walter Lippmann, David Lawrence, Raymond Clapper and Arthur Krock had gained many readers through interpreting national and international events. Their bylines were displayed prominently, generally on the right side of the editorial page. But the opinions on the left side of the editorial page, those of "the newspaper," almost invariably were left unsigned. These writers were not well known, and they were not well paid. If they disagreed with what they were told to write, they could try to find another job. Participants at the Washington meeting speculated that they were among the last newspaper groups to form a national organization because their publishers didn't want them to get any ideas about gaining an independent voice.

Since then, editorial writers on many newspapers have carved out for themselves more secure and more prominent positions in relations with their publishers and with their communities. They have adapted to, and helped to change, the condition in which they work.

Change and adaptation, in fact, have been at work in the evolution of the American editorial page ever since the introduction of the first newspapers on the continent. The changes began long before Greeley, Bennett and Dana appeared on the journalistic scene. The strong editor of personal journalism comes in the third of five general phases through which American newspapers, and editorial pages, have passed since Colonial days. The five phases can be described as follows:

1. During the Colonial era and the period immediately after the Revolutionary War, little effort was made to separate opinion from news. Both appeared intertwined in the columns of the press. Newspapers openly proclaimed that they were partisan voices.
2. With the writing of the new Constitution in 1787 came political parties and the partisan press. Editorials began to appear as distinct forms. Each newspaper was committed to a political party.
3. With the populist ("penny") press that emerged in the 1830s came the strong editor, who initially was concerned with sensationalized news and not with editorials but who, as readers became more literate and sophisticated, began to produce highly personalized editorial pages—and better news products as well. Ties to political parties began to weaken.
4. Following the Civil War, and more so following the turn of the century, anonymous corporate editorial staffs began to replace the famous editors. Writing became more bland. Newspapers, while claiming increasing independence, generally remained committed to conservative editorial policies.
5. In recent years, beginning in the politically active 1960s, a younger, more aggressive and more pragmatic editorial writer has started to emerge. This type of writer tends to be nonpartisan but committed to a general editorial philosophy.

In each of these phases, newspapers and their editorials served different purposes, according to the readers' changing needs. Those papers—and editorials—that succeeded in changing with the times survived; those that did not perished.

The remainder of this chapter will briefly describe the first four phases. The last phase will be discussed in the following chapter and throughout this book.

NEWS MIXED WITH OPINION

During the Colonial period, the first newspapers were heavily influenced by British tradition. The British press was licensed and printers published under the authority of the crown. Licenses could be suspended if the printer published anything that displeased the authorities. The publisher of the first newspaper on American soil, Benjamin Harris, quickly learned what would happen if opinions displeased the Colonial authorities in Boston. In his *Publick Occurrences, Both Foreign and Domestick,* published on Sept. 25, 1690, he said that the English has postponed attacking the French because their Indian allies had failed to provide promised canoes. If that were not a clear enough criticism of Colonial policy, Harris proceeded in his news columns to call the Indians "miserable savages, in whom we have too much confided." Harris had not obtained the required license. Members of the Colonial Council did not like what he had written and shut the newspaper down. It died after one issue.

For a large part of the Colonial period, American readers were more interested in what was happening in Europe than what was happening in the Colonies. Events in the Colonies did not seem very important except as they related to events in Europe. Consequently the Colonialists primarily looked for news from abroad in their early newspapers.

The first generally recognized American newspaper, the *Boston News-Letter,* was started in 1704—14 years after Harris' first attempt—and was a printed version of what had been a written newsletter circulated by Boston postmaster John Campbell. Not much concerned with politics, Campbell avoided Harris' troubles by publishing with the permission of the government. But he did not hesitate to offer opinions, unpolitical though they were. At the conclusion of a news item about a woman's suicide, he said he hoped that the recounting "may not be offensive, but rather a Warning to all others to watch against the Wiles of our Grand Adversary." The reporting of the whipping of a prisoner who had sold tar mixed with dirt was "here Inserted to be a caveat to others, of doing the like, least a worse thing befal (sic) them."

With the *News-Letter* already in existence, the father of James, and Benjamin, Franklin thought James was making a mistake in starting the *New England Courant* in 1721. The continent could not support more than one newspaper, he felt. Franklin not only dared to publish; he dared to publish without the required license. The *Courant,* carrying little news and few advertisements, contained mostly commentary and essays. One of Franklin's targets was a group that advocated smallpox inoculations. He also attacked civil and religious leaders and questioned some of the religious opinions of the day. Franklin so enraged the Rev. Increase Mather that Mather called the *Courant* the work of the devil. If the government did not do something about the paper, he proclaimed from his pulpit, "I am afraid some *Awful Judgment* will come upon this land, and that the *Wrath of God will arise, and there will be no Remedy.*" However, what finally provoked the Colonial Council to charge Franklin with contempt was an allegation that the government had not done enough to protect Boston from pirates. Franklin was thrown into jail and ordered not to publish again. Subsequent issues were listed as being published by his younger brother Benjamin.

Benjamin Franklin began publishing his own *Pennsylvania Gazette* in 1729. He was not averse to inserting opinions into what he wrote, but, being a skilled writer and diplomat, he was able to avoid the trouble that James had encountered. One device that Benjamin Franklin used to help arouse the Colonies was the printing of a snake divided into eight parts representing New England and seven other Colonies, accompanied by the motto "Join or die." It was run with an account of the killing and scalping of frontier Colonists in Virginia and Pennsylvania by the French and Indians.

British tradition also insisted that, in matters of libel, the only task of the jury was to determine whether the alleged words had been published. A comment mixed with news in John Peter Zenger's *New York Weekly Journal* was the first step toward putting an end to that tradition on American soil. Zenger "reported" in a story on election results that voters had been harassed about their qualifications for voting, and in another story that Gov. William Cosby had allowed the French to spy on Colonial naval defenses. In 1734, a year after his first issue had appeared, Zenger was charged with "raising sedition." An elegant appeal by Andrew Hamilton, then an 80-year-old Philadelphia lawyer, convinced the jury that it should ignore English common law, which would have limited the jury to finding Zenger innocent only if the alleged libel had not been published. The favorable decision for Zenger did not immediately change Colonial law, but it encouraged other editors to speak out and finally became accepted practice before the end of the century.

More threatening to most newspapers than the prospect of libel was the Stamp Act of 1765, through which the British attempted to levy a heavy tax on paper to support their military presence of the Colonies. The tax produced vigorous editorial protests. Franklin suspended the *Gazette* for three weeks, during which time he printed as substitutes large handbills headed "Remarkable Occurrences" and "Stamped paper not to be had." The day after the act took effect, William Bradford III's *Pennsylvania Journal and Weekly Advertiser* ran a black border, usually indicating mourning, in the shape of a tombstone.

As the Revolution approached, Colonial papers began to mix more and more editorial comment into the news columns. The papers generally split into three camps: Tory, Whig and Radical. The Tories championed the status quo, continued Colonial relations with Britain. In 1772, one of the most prominent Tories, James Rivington, began publishing *Rivington's New York Gazetteer or the Connecticut, New Jersey, Hudson's River and Quebec Weekly Advertiser.* Rivington tried giving space to all sides of the political issues—an unusual practice at the time. But, to quote Rivington himself, "the moment he ventured to publish sentiments which were opposed to the dangerous views and desires of certain demagogues, he found himself held up as an enemy of his country." In 1775 a party of armed men on horseback broke into his print shop, destroyed his press, carried away his type and melted it into bullets.

The Colonial Whigs represented a rising business class that at first was more interested in protecting itself from economic harassment by the British than in effecting political and social change. One of the most widely published Whigs was John Dickinson, who argued for the preservation of property and for self-taxation in several articles titled "Letters From a Farmer in Pennsylvania." First published in the *Pennsylvania Chronicle* and the *Boston Gazette* in 1767, they were widely reprinted through the Colonies.

One of the most successful publishers of the Revolutionary and post-Revolutionary periods was Isaiah Thomas (who, incidentally, published *The History of Printing in America* in 1810). In 1770 he founded his *Massachusetts Spy,* advertising it as "A Weekly Political and Commercial Paper—Open to All Parties, but *influenced* by None." Thomas tried to open the *Spy* to both Whigs and Tories and to put their respective positions before the public. But he found he could not maintain this stance. The Tories stopped taking his paper, and Thomas concluded that the *Spy* would have to have "a fixed character." Since he was in principle opposed to the British economic measures, he made it a Whig paper. As issues became even sharper, Thomas and other Whigs joined the Radicals.

One of the first avowed Radical publications was the *Boston Gazette and Country Journal.* As early as 1764 publishers Benjamin Eades and John Gill were writing and providing space for anti-British essays. Thomas thought that no other paper or publisher played a greater role in bringing about the independence of the United States.[3]

Samuel Adams, who wrote for the *Gazette,* reasoned that in the cause of liberty events and facts could be twisted and interpreted to help arouse the Colonists against the British. One example, with a slight difference, was the "Journal of Occurrences," in which anonymous authors working for Adams compiled the verbal and physical assaults committed by British soldiers in Boston. In 1768, the "Occurrences" began appearing in John Holt's *New York Journal,* a Radical paper. They were widely reprinted. Although historians have since concluded that some of the "facts" were not quite true, the authors made a point of distinguishing between facts and comments by printing their opinions in italics. This attempt at differentiation between fact and opinion in news columns represented a step toward the use of the editorial as distinct from the news article.

Another Radical opinion writer who helped ignite the Revolution was Tom Paine, more pamphleteer than newspaper writer. His *Common Sense,* which appeared in early 1776, pleaded the cause of independence with an eye to persuading the Whigs who were still on the fence. During the war he published a series called "The Crisis." The papers presented no new facts or arguments but, in the fashion of editorial writers of more than one later era, put ideas into words that could be understood by the less literate.

THE PARTISAN PRESS

The framers of the Constitution in 1787 thought they had achieved sufficient compromises between large and small states, and between the central government and the states, to eliminate the divisiveness that had characterized the late Colonial period. James Madison expressed the hope in "The Federalist," also known as "The Federalist Papers," that under the new government there would be no need for factions. One of the reasons for nominating George Washington, the leader of the Continental Army and symbol of Colonial resistance, as the first president was to rally all Americans around the new government. The "Federalist Papers" themselves, written by Alexander Hamilton, James Madison and John Jay to support ratification of the Constitution, were first published in a newspaper, the *New York Independence Journal.* They were a mixture of fact, argument and opinion.

In spite of the hopes for political unity under Washington, disagreements over how strong the federal government should be began to appear. Hamilton, as secretary of the Treasury, pushed for an active national administration. Since he favored the business community, he wanted firm financial support for the government and, specifically, he wanted a national bank. Thomas Jefferson and others wanted a weaker federal government. The Jeffersonians tended to be favorably disposed toward the French Revolution. Those around Hamilton generally allied themselves with Great Britain. Factions (later called "parties") eventually formed around these two leaders, the Hamiltonians becoming known as Federalists, the Jeffersonians as Democratic-Republicans.

To foster public support for the Washington administration, in which he was a dominant influence, Hamilton provided the inspiration for founding the first partisan newspaper under the new Constitution, the *Gazette of the United States.* It appeared in New York in 1789 under the editorship of John Fenno.

Other Federalist papers followed. *Porcupine's Gazette and Daily Advertiser,* founded by William Cobbett in Philadelphia in 1797, was known for its vitriolic attacks on the opposition. In one instance, calling the French minister to the United States a "blunderbuss," Cobbett lashed out (in part) with these words: "When we see an unprincipled, shameless bully, 'A dog in forehead, and in heart a deer,' who endeavors, by means of a big look, a threatening aspect, and a thundering voice, to terrify peaceable men into a compliance with what he has neither a right to demand, nor power nor courage to enforce, and who, at the same time, acts in such a bungling, stupid manner, as to excite ridicule and contempt in place of fear; when we see such a gasconading, impudent bluff as this (and that we do every day), we call him a *Blunderbuss.*" Cobbett's attacks on the French became such a scandal that President John Adams, a Federalist himself, considered ordering Cobbett to leave the country under provisions of the Alien Act.

A Federal writer of much milder tone was Noah Webster, of dictionary fame. Webster is credited by historian Wm. David Sloan as writing "the first editorial, in the modern sense, ever to appear in an American newspaper."[4] A contribution written by Webster was published under the "Hartford" local news column of the *Connecticut Courant.* Later, while editing a Federalist paper called the *American Minerva* (founded in 1793), Webster placed editorials under the "New York" local news heading, but by 1796 he was placing them under the heading of "The Minerva" (the nickname of the paper). This heading was the forerunner of what we now call the masthead, a box on the editorial page that carries the name of the paper, the names of the main editorial and business persons and other information about the paper. These innovations represented further steps toward differentiating editorials from news.

Once the Federalist press began extolling the virtues of the Washington administration, it was not long before plans were laid to present another point of view. Madison, even though he had contributed to the "Federalist Papers," found himself urging Jefferson, as secretary of state, to provide government subsidies to Philip Freneau to start an anti-Federalist newspaper. The resulting *National*

Gazette was published only from 1791 to 1793, but Freneau's virulent attacks on the Federalists inspired other anti-Federalists to speak up. The anti-Federalists opposed increasing the powers of the central government. They opposed increased taxes. They did not want a national bank. Generally they spoke for agricultural interests, the less affluent, the smaller states and Americans who sympathized with the French Revolution.

For most of American history, American citizens have considered George Washington to be beyond reproach. But some of the anti-Federalist writers did not. One of the most outspoken was Benjamin Franklin Bache, grandson of Benjamin Franklin. Bache founded the *Philadelphia General Advertiser,* widely known as the *Aurora,* in 1790. When he wrote that the nation had been "debouched" by Washington, Federalists wrecked his office and beat him. Of Bache, *Porcupine's Gazette* stated: "This atrocious wretch (worthy descendant of old Ben) knows that all men of any understanding put him down as an abandoned liar, as a tool and a hireling. . . . He is an ill-looking devil. His eyes never get above your knees." One day on the street, John Fenno, editor of the *Gazette of the United States,* hit Bache in the face. Bache struck Fenno over the head with his cane. This started a long tradition of street encounters between rival 19th-century editors. The *Aurora* was the first, in 1800, to make its second page specifically an editorial page. It also used the editorial "we." Other editors began to follow both practices.

Several historians have called this the Dark Age of Journalism because of the scurrility of the press. But others have seen this emotional outpouring, especially among the anti-Federalists, as a venting of stored-up anger against the British and against anything that resembled the imposition of the strong government that the British attempted to impose on the Colonies. Because of their antipathy toward Britain and sympathy for the French Revolution, the anti-Federalists attacked the administration's inclination to support the British and oppose France. This opposition helped account for the passage of the Alien and Sedition Acts of 1798, which forbade "any false, scandalous and malicious writing . . . against the government of the United States, or either house of the Congress . . . or the . . . President . . . or to excite against them the hatred of the good people of the United States. . . ." The vice president (then Jefferson, an anti-Federalist) was intentionally excluded from the act, which was aimed specifically at the anti-Federalists. The administration of the law was so unfair—so obviously against anti-Federalist editors—that the apparent injustice contributed to the defeat of John Adams and to the election of Jefferson. Jefferson pardoned the imprisoned editors, and the laws were allowed to expire.

With the election of Jefferson, the press became less vicious but remained strictly partisan. Now it was the Federalists' turn to establish a press in opposition to the government. In 1801, the year Jefferson took office, Hamilton founded the *New York Post,* with William Coleman as editor. Hamilton wrote many of the editorials. The *Post* pushed Federalist policies—such as a strong merchant marine and navy and an internal revenue system—and defended the Alien and Sedition Acts. Mostly it saw its purpose as ridiculing the Jefferson administration.

Coleman reluctantly acknowledged that the Louisiana Purchase, one of Jefferson's major accomplishments, was "an important acquisition" but suggested that its principal value might be to trade for the Floridas, "obviously of far greater value to us than all the immense, undefined region west of the river."

When Jefferson reported to Congress that up the Missouri River was a mountain of rock salt, the *Post* said:

> Methinks such a great, huge mountain of solid, shining salt must make a dreadful glare in a clear sunshiny day, especially just after a rain. . . . We think it would have been no more fair in the traveler who informed Mr. Jefferson of this territory of solid salt, to have added that some leagues to the westward of it there was an immense lake of molasses, and that between this lake and the mountain of salt, there was an extensive vale of hasty pudding, stretching as far as the eye could reach. . . .

Coleman kept up the Federalist fight against Jefferson and later against Madison, but by 1816, when James Monroe was elected president overwhelmingly during the "Era of Good Will," the Federalist Party had dwindled nearly to obscurity. According to the formerly Federalist *Post*, the Republican-Democrats, soon to be known as the Democrats, had taken over the Federalist principles. The *Post* continued as a voice for the commercial community but began espousing Democratic principles.

Beginning with Jefferson, every president through John Buchanan, elected in 1856, had an official newspaper in Washington. The principal purpose of the administration paper was to serve as a mouthpiece for the president. The party faithful read the official organ to find out the official line of the party in power. Even though the *National Intelligencer* became the official paper of the Jefferson administration, editors Joseph Gales Jr. and William W. Seaton built a reputation for separating their editorial positions from their news reporting and for providing nonpartisan coverage of Congress.

The most effective use of an official newspaper was made by President Andrew Jackson, who became president in 1829. He first made his influence felt with the party faithful through the *United States Telegraph*, founded in 1825 by Duff Green. When Green switched allegiance to Jackson's rival, John C. Calhoun, Jackson brought Francis P. Blair to Washington to establish a new administration organ, the *Washington Globe*. Blair, who had been on the *Argus of Western America*, the official Democratic Party paper published in Frankfort, Ky., came to have great influence on Jackson and came to be one of Jackson's "kitchen cabinet." Another *Argus* editor, Amos Kendall, became Jackson's principal writer.

The Jackson charm also worked to bring editors under "Old Hickory's" spell, allowing Jackson to gain influence over a substantial number of other newspapers throughout the country. He appointed many editors to government positions; local postmasterships were among the most popular.

One of the papers that shifted its editorial policy to support Jackson was the *Post*. William Cullen Bryant, who became editor the same year Jackson took office, supported low tariffs and opposed the national bank, positions also held by Jackson. Bryant was one of the first editors to speak out for the right of free speech for abolitionists and the right of labor to organize. Although he loyally supported the Democrats, his editorials—unlike those of the earliest party press—were not marked by excessively partisan, shrill tones. The *Post*, also unlike most other party papers, was seeking to expand its readership beyond a few thousand politically aware readers and merchants. Bryant, who could write to satisfy the best of literary critics with his poetry, used such techniques as beginning an editorial with a humorous saying or an appropriate story to try to win subscribers from among a new and growing working class.

The *Post* succeeded in making the transition from the era of the party press to that of the populist press. Most of the other party papers did not. One reason was that the vast majority of presidents between Jackson and Abraham Lincoln were weak leaders, incapable of inspiring strong journalistic voices. A more important reason was that, unlike the *Post,* the party papers attempted to remain party papers when the new, growing readership in the country was not much interested in politics. Much of the population was barely literate. Partisan politics became extremely confusing during this time: The Whig Party split apart, then died; the new Republican Party came out of almost nowhere; and the Democratic Party divided along North-South lines.

By the time Lincoln became president, designation of an administration paper had become little more than a formality, and Lincoln didn't even bother to seek an official voice. By then most of the readership was concentrated in the populist press. It was this press, not the party press, that became important for politicians.

THE POPULIST PRESS

The first papers that reflected the nation's interest in something besides party politics were the mercantile dailies, which became prominent in the business community in the 1820s. But like the party papers they found only a few thousand readers sufficiently interested to read them regularly. They offered little editorial comment.

Ignored by both party and mercantile press was a rapidly growing potential readership, resulting partly from immigration, partly from increasing literacy. These readers may not have been especially interested in party politics, but they were interested in what was going on in their communities. Out of this development grew an opportunity to publish papers that would sell to the masses.

Day, Bennett, Greeley and Raymond

The first of the populist papers were called the "penny press" because some of them actually cost only a penny. Others cost two or three cents. In the first years much of the content was crime news and gossip. Courts and the police record were favorite sources for stories, many of them full of sex, blood and drunkenness. The readers loved these new papers, and circulation soared into the tens of thousands.

Editorial pages were slow in working their way into these papers. The first of the penny press papers was the *New York Sun,* founded in 1833 by Benjamin H. Day. He allied himself with no political party and employed no regular editorial writer. The few editorials that appeared dealt briefly with the latest sensations, municipal affairs, and morals and manners. One example: "SUDDEN DEATH— Ann McDonough, of Washington Street, attempted to drink a pint of rum on a wager, on Wednesday afternoon last. Before it was half swallowed Ann was a corpse. Served her right." Another example: "DUEL—We understand that a duel was fought at Hoboken on Friday morning last between a gentleman of Canada and a French gentleman of this city, in which the latter was wounded. The parties should be arrested." The *Sun* had only this to say when the 1843 New York

Legislature adjourned: "The Legislature of this State closed its arduous duties yesterday. It has increased the number of our banks and fixed a heavy load of debt upon posterity."

The *New York Herald*, founded in 1835 by James Gordon Bennett, offered even more sensationalism than the *Sun.* In the early years, Bennett offered little serious editorial comment, but he loved to flaunt his ego and wit before his readers; they loved his swagger and flippancy. He was the first of the editors noted for "personal journalism." Concerning the *Herald*, he wrote: "Nothing can prevent its success but God Almighty, and he happens to be on my side." Although he liked to attack speculators, pickpockets and competing editors for their "crimes and immoralities," his editorials contained more bombast and personal references than solid opinion. Bennett's famous competitor, Horace Greeley, while perhaps not the most objective of critics, accurately characterized Bennett as "cynical, inconsistent, reckless, easily influenced by others' opinions, and by his own prejudices."

Bennett's biting editorial language and sensational news practices earned him occasional physical abuse. Several times he was horsewhipped in the streets. Usually he took advantage of these attacks to parade his fearlessness before his readers. After James Watson, editor of the *Courier and Enquirer*, had pushed Bennett down some stone steps, Bennett reported that he had suffered only a scratch and three torn buttons, but that Watson's "loss is a rent from top to bottom of a very beautiful black coat, which cost the ruffian $40, and a blow in the face, which may have knocked down his throat some of his infernal teeth for anything I know." He concluded self-righteously: "As for intimidating me, or changing my course, the thing cannot be done. . . . I tell the honest truth in my paper, and leave the consequences to God."

Bennett's ego was never more evident than in an editorial announcing his engagement. The heading was: "To The Readers of the Herald—Declaration of Love—Caught at Last—Going to Be Married—New Movement in Civilization." The editorial said in part:

I am going to be married in a few days. The weather is so beautiful; times are getting so good; the prospects of political and moral reform so auspicious, that I cannot resist the divine instinct of honest nature any longer; so I am going to be married to one of the most splendid women in intellect, in heart, in soul, in property, in person, in manner, that I have yet seen in the course of my interesting pilgrimage through human life.

. . . . I cannot stop in my career. I must fulfill that awful destiny which the Almighty Father has written against my name, in the broad letters of life, against the wall of heaven. I must give the world a pattern of happy wedded life, with all the charities that spring from a nuptial love.

In later years, as readers became more sophisticated and Bennett less flippant, the *Herald* developed a serious and thoughtful editorial page. But it is to Horace Greeley that credit traditionally has gone for making the editorial page a significant and respectable portion of the daily newspaper. Greeley might also have been credited with establishing the first penny press. He published his first issue on a snowy day in January 1833, but readers could not get out to buy the paper, and he did not sell enough copies to be able to put out a second issue. His second effort came in 1841 with the founding of the *New York Tribune.*

Tribune editorials, written in a variety of styles but almost always with literary merit, commented on a broad range of topics, generally following a consistent editorial policy. Several writers contributed to the thinking behind the editorials and to the writing of the editorials, but it was customary for readers to think of the *Tribune*'s editorial page, if not the *Tribune* itself, as a one-man show. Subscribers read the paper to see what Greeley thought, and they assumed that every word was his. The *New York Weekly Tribune*, in particular, with circulation across the country, was read with devotion.

With Day's and Bennett's papers appealing mostly to Democratic voters, Greeley's *Tribune* was the first of the populist press with a Whig editorial outlook. But Greeley's philosophy was far more radical than that of most Whigs. He favored high tariffs, as did the Whig party, but not just to protect business; he wanted the creation of an American economy that would benefit merchants, workers and farmers as well. His interest in socialist and utopian ideas reflected the belief that all classes working together in an ideal community could produce wealth and harmony for all. He not only preached this belief in his editorial columns but he traveled the country lecturing to audiences on his ideas.

Greeley strongly believed in Western expansion and supported the march of farmers and merchants westward. But he did not support the methods he saw being used in annexing Texas. The only New York editor to oppose the Mexican-American War, Greeley wrote this editorial after the Senate had voted to annex Texas:

The mischief is done and we are now involved in war! We have adopted a war ready made, and taken upon ourselves its prosecution to the end. We are to furnish the bodies to fill trenches and the cash to defray the enormous expense. Mexico, despoiled of one of her fairest provinces by our rapacity and hypocrisy, has no choice but to resist, however ineffectively, the consummation of our flagitious designs.

Greeley was an early advocate of the abolition of slavery. E. L. Godkin, editor of the *New York Evening Post*, concluded that by the early 1860s Greeley had "done more than any other man to bring slaveholders to bay, and place the Northern fingers on the throat of the institution." Godkin perceived that Greeley had "waged one of the most unequal battles in which any journalist ever engaged with a courage and tenacity worthy of the cause, and by dint of biting sarcasm, vigorous invective, powerful arguments, and a great deal of vituperation and personality."[5]

But, for all that, Godkin accused Greeley of treating his opponents with contempt, of being half-educated "and very imperfectly at that." According to Godkin, Greeley had "no grasp of mind, no great political insight"; his brain was "crammed with half truths and odds and ends of ideas which a man inevitably accumulates who scrapes knowledge together by fits and starts on his way through life." Greeley was saved, Godkin said, by his unflagging enthusiasm, an unshakable faith in principles and a writing style virtually unsurpassed in vigor, terseness, clearness and simplicity. But he was known also for his coarse and abusive language. As Godkin wrote: "He calls names and gives the lie, in his leading articles, with a heartiness and vehemence which in cities seem very shocking, but which out in the country, along the lakes, and in the forests and prairies of the Northwest, where most of his influence lies, are simply proofs of more than ordinary earnestness."

Illustrating both Greeley's penchant for name calling and his devotion to the anti-slavery cause was an editorial titled "Stephen A. Douglas as the Volunteer Executioner," published on Feb. 22, 1854. Greeley depicted a scene in which "a poor, miserable, half-witted and degraded Wretch, who consorted with the negroes," was about to be lynched by a mob. As the execution was about to take place, there was hesitation. He wrote then:

A moment more and there would have gone up in the crowd a cry, "Let him go," "Let him go," but at this moment a person unknown to the crowd was seen to move toward the cart. Springing upon it and rudely seizing the dangling rope, he turned round to the astonished spectators and said: "If none of you will act as hangman, I will. Damn the Abolitionists!" In another instant the fatal cord was adjusted, the cart driven off, and there was suspended between heaven and earth the trembling— the dead—form of an innocent man.

Now who was this hangman? Who was this fierce defender of the peculiar institution? Was he a Southern man? No. Was he a citizen identified with the South? No. It was on the contrary a Northern man, from a free State—in fact, one who had been but two days in the place. It seemed as if, suspecting his own principles, revolting in his heart at slavery and afraid that in the excitement of the hour he might next be arraigned, he took this fearful and terrible office of executioner in order to place himself, as he supposed, on "high Southern ground". . . . And here is to be seen reflected the true picture of Mr. Douglas's turpitude. Southern men may have in the madness of the hour conceived such iniquity as is embodied in the Nebraska bill. They may have prepared the halter for the neck of the Missouri Compromise—but the last fatal act would never have been undertaken had not the Senator from Illinois volunteered to act as executioner, had been willing to mount the scaffold, and call down the infamy of murdering liberty upon his own head.

Greeley wanted desperately to be elected to high political office. He did win one term in Congress, but his self-righteous attitude toward his colleagues made him unpopular. For a time he was one of the three Whig leaders in New York state, but invariably, just as he thought he was about to be nominated for a position on the Whig ticket, his political allies would outmaneuver him, promising him a chance next time. When the Whigs disintegrated, divided in part over the issue of slavery, he became one of the leaders in the formation of the Republican Party. Finally, when he was old and the nomination was not worth much, some of Greeley's fellow editors and others nominated him for president on a coalition Democratic–liberal Republican ticket in 1872. But he was overwhelmingly defeated by Ulysses S. Grant. Greeley died a few weeks later.

Another editor of the populist press era who was interested in holding public office was Henry J. Raymond, who with George Jones founded the *New York Times*. Raymond, like Greeley, helped form the Republican Party when the Whig Party disintegrated. But he was more successful than Greeley in winning office and in fact was nominated and elected lieutenant governor of New York at a time when Greeley hoped to be nominated.

Raymond's goal in establishing the *Times* was to publish a paper that was more objective in its news columns and less emotional in its editorials than were the *Tribune*, the *Herald* and other populist papers. In this he succeeded. The *Times* was less flamboyant and more respectable than its competitors. It was also less exciting to read. Raymond's inability to make up his mind about whether he was more editor or more politician also affected the vitality of the *Times*. If he had not been lured into politics, he would have been a better editor, in Godkin's view "the most successful journalist that has ever been seen." But, to quote Godkin, Raymond had a tendency to hold doubts about his political convictions and lacked the "temper which was necessary to victory" in the political realm; and a "sense of the necessities and limitations of his position as a politician" kept him from being the journalist he could have been.

Other Voices

Historians traditionally have described the journalism of the 18th and 19th centuries, and even the 20th century, as the work of the white male editors, most of them in New York City or Washington, D.C. But there were other voices as well, including women and African-Americans, some of whom are only now being rediscovered.

A number of strong newspapers emerged elsewhere in the country in the mid-1800s (but run by white males). In Chicago the *Tribune*, which had been founded in 1847, achieved a formidable reputation after Joseph Medill assumed control in 1855. This paper took a strong anti-slavery stand, promoted the new Republican Party and pushed fellow Illinoisan Lincoln for the presidency. In the Northeast, the *Springfield* (Mass.) *Republican*, founded by Samuel Bowles II in 1824, earned respect for conservative, enlightened, well-written editorials. In 1884, the *Republican* displayed its political independence by switching its support to a Democrat, Grover Cleveland, in the race for president.

As for women editors and publishers, 17 are known to have taken over operations of newspapers following the deaths of their husbands during the Colonial period.[6] The first was Elizabeth Timothy, who became publisher of the *South Carolina Gazette* upon the death of her husband in 1738. The first woman to start a newspaper on her own (in 1762), with the help of daughter Mary Katherine and son William (who didn't stay around very long), was Sarah Goddard, of the solidly Whig *Providence* (R.I.) *Gazette*.

Seventy years later, declaring she had "no party, the welfare and happiness of our country is our politics," Anne Royall launched *Peter Pry,* which Ishbel Ross described as containing an occasional "gleam of common sense sift[ing] through the thick layers of fanatical upbraiding."[7] She fought against corrupt officials, for separation of church and state and against the Bank of the United States. The bank was the subject that she wanted to interview President John Quincy Adams about when she supposedly (quoting Ross) "sat on his clothes while he bathed in the Potomac River and refused to budge until he had answered her questions." In less flamboyant style, Royall published *The Huntress* from 1836 to 1854, advocating Jacksonian principles, free public education, free speech and justice to immigrants and Indians.

Although not strictly an editorial writer, Margaret Fuller wrote essays, reviews and opinion pieces for Greeley's *Tribune* that advanced radical ideas. From 1846 until her death in a shipwreck in 1850, she wrote for the *Tribune* from Europe as the first U.S. woman foreign correspondent.

In 1870 Victoria Woodhull and her sister, Tennessee Claflin, launched *Woodhull and Claflin's Weekly* to promote "Progress! Free Thought. Untrammeled Lives." But, according to Ishbel Ross, they "plunged [so] boldly into the muckraking field . . . all the banned topics of . . . prostitution, free love, social disease, abortion [that] the very words were shocking to the prim readers of the day."[8]

Using a lighter touch, Kate Field, through the columns of *Kate Field's Washington,* published from 1890 to 1896, supported the rights of women and campaigned for Hawaiian annexation, international copyright, temperance, prohibition of Mormon polygamy, and dress reform.[9]

The first African-American newspaper in the United States, *Freedom's Journal,* was begun in 1827 by John B. Russwurm and Samuel E. Cornish to answer attacks on African-Americans coming from the *New York Inquirer.*[10] Most of the readers were white, since few African-Americans were literate. It lasted three years. Forty more African-American newspapers were founded before the Civil War, but most were short-lived. The second paper, the *Weekly Advocate,* another Cornish paper, lasted from 1837 to 1842, an unusually long time. I. Garland Penn, one of the few historians of African-American journalism, edited the *Lynchburg Virginia Laborer.* Most of these publications were much more oriented toward opinion, advancing the cause of anti-slavery, than toward news.[11]

A journalist who was both African-American and a woman was Ida B. Wells-Barnett. The daughter of slaves, she spoke out against racial injustice as part owner and editor of the Memphis *Free Speech and Headlight.* When the newspaper office was burned and she was physically threatened, she fled to the North, where she continued to write and lecture in the cause of justice for African-Americans. Each year an Ida B. Wells Award is given to a person who has displayed exemplary leadership in providing employment opportunities in journalism for minorities. Sponsors are the National Association of Black Journalists and the National Conference of Editorial Writers.

Abolition and the Civil War

The Civil War and events leading up to it provided editors of the time with plenty of opportunities to express their strong and diverse viewpoints. We have already noted Greeley's conversion to the cause of abolition. The popularizing of the abolition movement began with the publication of the *Liberator,* founded by William Lloyd Garrison in 1831. At first Garrison was ignored and almost forced into bankruptcy. Even those who sympathized with his views found his blunt, coarse language offensive; in some cases it proved counterproductive. The *Liberator* might have failed in its first year if an African-American preacher named Nat Turner had not led a slave revolt in Virginia that resulted in the deaths of 57 whites. Although Garrison had no subscribers in the South at the time, his writings were perceived to have induced Turner to riot. Southern editors, who wished to place blame on abolitionist interference from the North, began reprinting Garrison's writings as examples of inflammatory material. Garrison was immediately thrust into the editorial leadership of the abolitionist movement.

Illustrative of Garrison's work was his response when President Millard Fillmore called for new, tougher legislation after abolitionists had defied the Fugitive Slave Act by rescuing a slave from a U.S. deputy marshal in Boston. Garrison wrote:

Nobody injured, nobody wronged, but simply a chattel transformed into a man, and conducted to a spot where he can glorify God in his body and spirit, which are his! And yet, how all the friends in the pit are writhing and yelling! Not tormented before their time, but just at the right time. Truly, "devils with devils damned firm concord hold!" The President of the United States is out with his Proclamation of Terror, conveying it to us in tones of thunder and on the wings of the lightning; even as though in the old Bay State chaos had come again, and millions of foreign mymidons (sic) were invading our shores! A poor, hunted, entrapped fugitive slave is dexterously removed from the courtroom, and the whole land is shaken! . . . Henry Clay—with one foot in the grave, and just ready to have both body and soul cast into hell—as if eager to make his damnation doubly sure, rises in the United States Senate and proposes an inquiry into the expediency of passing yet another law, by which everyone who shall dare peep or mutter against the execution of the Fugitive Slave Bill shall have his life crushed out!

Abolitionist editors who spoke out strongly risked their property and their lives. Garrison barely escaped an angry mob in Boston in 1835 by jumping out a window and voluntarily spending the night in jail. Threats discouraged abolitionist editor James G. Birney from attempting to organize an abolition movement in Kentucky. When he founded the *Philanthropist* in Cincinnati in the mid-1830s, a mob attacked his office. The abolitionist editor who became the most honored was Elijah Lovejoy. Anti-abolitionists twice destroyed the offices of his *St. Louis Observer*, which had been forced to move from St. Louis to Alton, Ill. When he re-established his paper for a third time, in 1837, a mob destroyed the office and killed him.

One of the editors whom Garrison helped to launch was Frederick Douglass, the best known of the African-American abolitionist editors. Douglass toured the Western states and Europe with Garrison, then went his own way in 1847 to found the *North Star*. The object of the *North Star*, Douglass wrote, "will be to attack slavery in all its forms and aspects, advocate Universal Emancipation; exact the standard of public morality; promote the moral and intellectual improvement of the colored people; and to hasten the day of freedom of our three million enslaved fellow countrymen." Douglass's *North Star*, and his subsequent *Liberty Party Paper,* were not attractive typographically, with mostly solid type, but Douglass's inspired writing and the depth of his convictions made his publications anything but dull. He continued to promote the African-American cause in a series of publications until 1875. By then both he and Garrison were widely honored, at least among African-Americans and Northerners.

The *Post,* under the editorship of William Cullen Bryant, defended the right of the unpopular abolitionists to meet and demonstrate as early as 1833 and spoke sympathetically of John Brown at the time of his raid into Virginia in 1859 to free slaves and incite insurrection. While Southerners were arguing for the extension of slavery, the *Post* foresaw a growing threat of uprising among African-Americans: "But while they speak the tocsin sounds, the blacks are in arms, their houses are in flames, their wives and children driven into exile and killed, and a furious servile war stretches its horror over years. That is the blessed institution you ask us to foster and spread and worship, and for the sake of which you even spout your impotent threats against the grand edifice of the Union!"

Raymond's *Times* characteristically took a more moderate stance, opposing abolition until after the Civil War had begun, even though it had strongly supported the election of Lincoln in 1860. Bennett's *Herald* also remained opposed to abolition until after the war began. It did not favor the election of Lincoln and in fact demonstrated strong sympathy for the South both before and during much of the war. Following the firing on Fort Sumter, the *Herald* contended that "the tempest which now threatens so menacingly" could be entirely dispelled if the Northern states would only call constituent assemblies to ratify constitutional amendments proposed by the South.

At the opposite end of the political and geographical spectrum in the pre–Civil War period were the Southern "fire-eaters." Robert Barnwell Rhett, of the *Charleston* (S.C.) *Mercury*, was ignored in 1832 when he first began writing that the South should secede. In later years, however, he and others not only gained credence but helped convince their fellow Southerners that the North would let the South go.

When the war began, Northern papers supported Union policies; but the *Times* was the only major paper, and only one of three or four of the 17 New York dailies, to consistently support Lincoln throughout the war. On the day after the bombardment of Fort Sumter, the Times editorialized:

> . . . For the first time in the history of the United States, an organized attempt is made to destroy, by force of arms, the government which the American people have formed for themselves—and to overthrow the glorious Constitution which has made us the envy of the world. The history of the world does not show so causeless an outrage. . . . One thing is certain. Now that the rebels have opened the war, the people will expect the government to defend itself with vigor and determination. There is no room for half-way measures now. . . . *The South has chosen war, and it must have all the war it wants. . . .*

By 1864, however, Raymond feared that Lincoln stood no chance for re-election, barring some bold stroke, but he kept his doubts out of his newspaper columns.

The *Herald,* reflecting its sympathy for the South, chided the Union's misfortune whenever it could find cause and became increasingly bitter against Lincoln. A month after Lincoln took office, the *Herald* referred to the "vicious, imbecile, demoralized Administration." Because the *Herald* was the most widely read American paper in Europe, readers on that continent got many of their impressions of the war from the pro-South *Herald.* After initially promoting Ulysses S. Grant for the Republican nomination for president in 1864, the *Herald* gradually softened its opposition to Lincoln. A rumor indicated that Lincoln had offered Bennett the ambassadorship to Paris. Whether he actually had made such an offer, Bennett wrote a note to Lincoln declining the appointment.

Greeley ran hot and cold on both Lincoln and the war in spite of his alleged strong abolitionist beliefs. Shortly after Fort Sumter, he argued for letting the South secede if that was what the Southern people really wanted. But a few weeks after that, the *Tribune* urged immediate action to bring the seceding states back into the Union. As the summer of 1861 approached, the *Tribune* ran a war slogan atop its editorial page every day for a week:

The Nation's War-Cry

Forward to Richmond! Forward to Richmond!
The Rebel Congress must not be allowed to meet
there on the 20th of July! BY THAT DATE THE
PLACE MUST BE HELD BY THE NATIONAL ARMY!

These *Tribune* editorials contributed to the pressures that pushed the Union army to battle prematurely at the First Battle of Bull Run. Casualties were heavy, and the troops retreated in disarray to Washington. The editorials had been written by Fitz-Henry Warren, the *Tribune*'s Washington correspondent, while Greeley was away and Charles A. Dana was in charge of the paper. However, since the slogan ran for a week, Greeley must have known what was being said. In any case, he accepted responsibility for the articles in print and, convinced of the power that he and the *Tribune* had, described himself "as a scapegoat for all the military blunders of the last month." He suffered so much personal remorse that he became physically ill and could not leave his bed.

During the war when things were going well, Greeley was optimistic and tended to speak well of Lincoln. When they were not, he became despondent and blamed Lincoln. In 1864 Greeley suddenly switched to supporting Lincoln after pressing for a substitute presidential nominee. In his case a rumor circulated of a possible postmastership in the second Lincoln administration.

The *Post* strongly supported the war and the administration's measures to wage it, but Bryant became increasingly impatient with Lincoln when the president delayed until 1863 the issuance of the Emancipation Proclamation freeing the slaves. Bryant was also disgusted with newspapers that professed to support the Union but took every possible opportunity to criticize it and taunt it. In fact he published a sarcastic editorial titled "Recipe for a Democratic Paper," which historian Allen Nevins summarized in this fashion:

(1) Magnify all rebel successes and minimize all Federal victories; if the South loses 18,000 men say 8,000, and if the North loses 11,000 say 21,000.

(2) Calumniate all energetic generals like Sherman, Grant and Rosecrans; call worthless leaders like Halleck and Pope and master generals of the age.

(3) Whenever the Union suffers a reverse, declare that the nation is weary of this slow war; and ask how long this fratricidal conflict will be allowed to continue.

(4) Expatiate upon the bankruptcies, high prices, stock jobbers, gouging profiteers and "shoddy men."

(5) Abuse Lincoln and the Cabinet in two ways: say they are weak, timid, vacillating, and incompetent; and that they are tyrannous, harsh, and despotic.

(6) Protest vehemently against "nigger" brigadiers, and the atrocity of arming the slaves against their masters.

(7) Don't advise open resistance to the draft. But clamor against it in detail; suggest doubts of its constitutionality; denounce the $300 clause; say that it makes an obvious distinction between rich and poor; and refer learnedly to the military aristocracies of France and Prussia.[12]

Even more anti-Union than the "Democratic Papers" were the Copperhead papers, which spoke for Northern Democrats who openly sympathized with the South. The most prominent of the Copperheads was Clement Laird Vallandigham, who became co-owner of an anti-abolitionist magazine, the *Dayton* (Ohio) *Empire*, in 1847. When the governor of Ohio prepared to answer Lincoln's call for troops after Fort Sumter, the *Empire* declared: "Governor Dennison has pledged the blood and treasure of Ohio to back up a Republican administration in its contemplated attack upon the people of the South. . . . What right has he to make such a pledge? Does he promise to head the troops which he intends to send down South to butcher men, women and children of the section?"

One effect of the Civil War was to put a premium on news. Readers wanted to know how the war was going more than they wanted to know some editor's opinion. Newspapers that could not afford correspondents of their own pooled their resources and formed cooperative news reporting services. Since these services provided news to papers of widely differing editorial viewpoints, they had to be careful to report in as objective a manner as possible to keep from offending the editors. Reliance on the telegraph for transmission provided further incentive to keep stories factual and short. The line between news and editorials became more marked. The press became more impersonal. Shortly after the war, the great populist editors died, Raymond in 1869 at the age of only 49, both Bennett and Greeley in 1872.

"The prestige of the editorial page is done," wrote James Parton, who might not have been the most objective observer, since he had written a highly laudatory biography of Greeley. With the great voices gone, editorials no longer "much influence the public mind, nor change many votes, and . . . the power and success of a newspaper depend wholly and absolutely upon its success in getting, and its skill in exhibiting the news," Parton wrote.[13]

Woman Suffrage, Indians, African-Americans

Among the editorial topics most written about immediately following the Civil War were woman suffrage, Indians, the newly emancipated slaves and economic development. Within a few years it became clear, to say the least, that the Civil War had barely disturbed the white male power balance, at the national level or on editorial pages. Editors were more interested in promoting prosperous communities than in sharing power with another race or sex.

Women such as Susan B. Anthony, Lucy Stone and Elizabeth Cady Stanton, who had been working for abolition, expected that after emancipation and voting rights for African-Americans, woman suffrage would come next. A few editorial voices, among them Greeley's, supported their cause, but others argued that women didn't need the vote, since, according to the *New Orleans Crescent*, "they are represented at the ballot box, as well as in the halls of legislation, by their husbands, fathers, and brothers." The *Richmond Whig* saw women's "most effective and irresistible weapon [to be] the artillery of her charms, before which the Columbiad, the Brooke, the Armstrong, and all other guns, 'pale their ineffectual fires.'" Some of the editors expressed the fear that allowing women to enter into the evil world of politics would destroy their traditional superior moral capability, which the St. Louis *Missouri Republican* described as "the aptitude and the habit of the soul to distinguish the finest shades of good and evil, and of what is beautiful and decent."

"It will be a pretty spectacle," wrote an editor for the Memphis *Avalanche*, "to see a strong minded woman haranguing a crowd or squabbling at the ballot box, while her husband is at home darning stockings, making night caps, baking bread and rocking the cradle."

As more and more travelers and settlers headed west after the end of the war, the nation faced difficult choices concerning the Indians on the Western

Plains. A few editors expressed the belief that (in the words of the St. Louis *Missouri Democrat*) "the Indian is endowed with many nobel traits of character, which under proper treatment and training might be rendered highly serviceable to humanity." A few questioned whether, as did the Louisville *Courier-Journal*, "civilization must be pushed as far as it will go, that Christianity has to be taught the heathen." But most editors seemed to agree with the *Missouri Republican*, in condemning "the war-path, murdering, scalping and plundering, spreading terror through various settlements and causing mourning in many families." Forget the peace treaties. "Let the Peace Commissioners stand aside for a few months while Gen. Sherman goes in and thrashes these savages till they cry for peace and will be ready to go upon their reservations and stay there." The *Raleigh Standard* was even more blunt: "Let the war of extermination be commenced and followed up until the Indians are either destroyed or driven beyond the limits of the United States."

Most newspapers in the North, but only a few in the South, supported civil and political rights for the newly emancipated African-Americans. Some papers, like the *Memphis Appeal*, lamented that, with the end of slavery, "there. . . never again will be . . . a body of agricultural laborers, so generally contented, so happy, so prolific, with so little disease and deformity among their children, and so little want of common comforts of life among the adults." Some papers, like the Nashville *Republican Banner* (decidedly not a Republican paper), viewed "the Negro [as] indolent by nature, faithless to all their pledges, false to their engagements, deceitful in their contracts, and thriftless and wasteful [and] insolent." The *Charleston Courier* expressed the opinion of many Southern editors concerning the abilities of African-Americans to exercise political rights: "No negro can be so blind as not to know that white men are to be right rulers in this great Republic. Compared with the whites the negros (sic) are as insignificant in numbers as they are deficient in intelligence, and he deceives himself who does not think that intelligence and numbers will not rule."

More sympathy was exhibited toward the African-Americans by the relatively few Republican papers in the South and, of course, by the even rarer African-American papers. Responding to concerns similar to those expressed above, the Nashville *Colored Tennessean* said in August 1865: "One set of people declare we won't work, and must be made to. Another is afraid that a war of races will arise. Another thinks we will abandon our Southern homes, and go North. . . . Another thinks we must be made to emigrate. . . . " To all of these, the writer said: "Now, dearly beloved friends, we can solve your problem. A few words will suffice. *Do justly by the Negro, and then let him severely alone*. . . . We are not exceptional beings, we are human. In these dark bodies run the same red running blood. . . . "

The *Missouri Democrat*, in spite of its name, was one of the Republican papers that rather consistently espoused the cause of the African-Americans. It advised the Southern states to accept the terms of Reconstruction and offer "all Constitutional guarantees," including suffrage, to the African-Americans. It warned that "resistance is useless" and that "the attempt to tire out the North will prove suicidal." The suffrage amendment was adopted over the objections of the Southern states. For a time African-Americans and Republicans wielded modest amounts of power, and won a few elections, in the South. But the *Democrat* was to be proved wrong. It was not long before the Conservatives, and the Conservative editors, of the South carried the day and returned to power. During this time several editors were accused of being local, and even state, leaders of the Ku Klux Klan (which of course they denied).

Dana, Godkin, Watterson

American newspapers were approaching the threshold of corporate journalism, the fourth phase in the development of the editorial page. But, even as most editors were lapsing into corporate anonymity, a few recognizable voices spoke out. Among them were Charles A. Dana of the *New York Sun*, E. L. Godkin of the *Nation* and later of the *New York Evening Post*, Henry Watterson of the Louisville *Courier-Journal* and Henry W. Grady of the *Atlanta Constitution.*

Dana quit the *Tribune* in 1862 after disagreement over Greeley's criticism of the conduct of the Civil War. He felt so strongly about Lincoln's policies that he joined the administration as assistant secretary of war. After the deaths of Raymond and Greeley, Watterson wrote that Dana, then on the *Sun*, was "left alone to tell the tale of old-time journalism in New York." Dana, he said, was as "blithe and nimble" as the young editors in the country, and was "no less a writer and scholar than an editor."

During the early days of this editorship, Dana took editorial swings at the corruption of the Tweed regime in New York and waged campaigns for reforms in government. But as the years went by the *Sun* became more cynical toward reform. Turning a good phrase and enticing readership through humorous, clever writing assumed greater importance. Edward P. Mitchell, later editor of the *Sun* himself, recalled that, before he joined Dana's staff as an editorial writer, he had been told, "Dana's a good teacher for condensation and for saying what you want to say, but as to what he generally wants to say!—"

Dana's sarcasm could be so strong that readers would take him at his literal word. When a public campaign to raise money to erect a statue of Tweed seemed to lag, Dana wrote:

Has Boss Tweed any friends? If so, they are a mean set; it is now more than a year since an appeal was made to them to come forward and put up the ancillary qualities to erect a statue to Mr. Tweed in the centre of Tweed Plaza; but as yet only four citizens have sent in their subscriptions. . . . [T]he hundreds or rather thousands of small-potato politicians whom he has made rich and powerful stand aloof, and do not offer a picayune. . . . [W]e have not decided whether it shall represent the favorite son of New York afoot or a-horseback. In fact, we rather incline to have a nautical statue, exhibiting Boss Tweed as a bold mariner, amid the foretop-gallant buttock shrouds of his steam yacht. But that is a matter for future consideration. The first thing is to get the money; and if those who claim to be Mr. Tweed's friends don't raise it we shall begin the rumor that the Honorable P. Brains Sweeney has turned against him, and has forbidden everyone to give anything toward the erection of the projected statue.

The yacht mentioned in the editorial was one of the luxurious perquisites enjoyed by Tweed but no doubt financed by the public purse. P. Brains Sweeney was Tweed's lieutenant of a slightly different name, Peter B. Sweeney.

Edwin Lawrence (E. L.) Godkin came to the United States to cover the Civil War for English papers. He stayed after the war to found the *Nation* magazine, devoted to discussing political and economic issues. One of his interests was in a more equal distribution of the economic and social benefits of prosperity. Philosopher William James described Godkin as "the towering influence in all thought concerning public affairs" during the 1880s and 1890s. James said Godkin influenced many writers who never bothered to quote him and "determined the whole current of discussion" during that era.

Godkin's style was complex and carefully written, but, when he so desired, lively, humorous and ironic. Concerning the appointment of Elihu B. Washburne as President Grant's secretary of state, Godkin cited the "general, and apparently well-founded belief" that Washburne's "installation in the State Department would be the commencement of his intimate acquaintance with the precedents and principles of international law."

In describing an anarchists' picnic, at which there was a riot, Godkin wrote: "The meeting was a great success in the way of promoting practical anarchy, the rioting being protracted to a late hour in the afternoon. Anarchy, like charity, should always begin at home."

Godkin's successor, Edward P. Mitchell, credited Godkin with being the first in New York to hold daily conferences with his editorial writers. Mitchell recounted that every writer was encouraged to propose his own topic and to comment freely on topics proposed by other writers. But Godkin had no mercy on unsound and commonplace ideas. "If the junior editor had nothing worth while to say, Godkin would cut across his flounderings with 'O, there's nothing in that,' or 'We said that the other day,' or 'O everybody sees that.' " But, when a writer came up with a new idea, "Mr. Godkin's eye would kindle with interest, he would lean forward alertly, and catching up the theme, he would perhaps begin to enlarge it by ideas of his own, search its depths with penetrating inquiries, and reveal such possibilities in it that the original speaker had the feeling of having stumbled over a concealed diamond." Sometimes, Mitchell recalled, Godkin became so enthusiastic about the idea that he would decide to write on the subject himself.[14]

One of the strong, and extravagant, voices after the Civil War was that of Colonel Henry Watterson of the *Courier-Journal*. Watterson had edited a Southern paper during the Civil War but thought that secession was wrong. For half a century (from 1868 to 1918) he preached conciliation between North and South—and both sides listened to him, at least to the extent that either listened.

In 1868, when Kentucky was being criticized for having elected anti-Reconstruction Democrats to office, Watterson reminded the North that Kentucky had not seceded during the war: "Kentucky's head was with the Union and her heart was with the South; for it is in the nature of a generous and manly people to sympathize with the weak in its struggle with the strong." Watterson said that the laws were better enforced and there was less crime in Kentucky than in Indiana and Ohio. He concluded:

We are perfectly honest, and think we have a right, as free citizens of a free republic, to decide for ourselves. For so doing and so thinking we are denounced as traitors to our country and a despotism is sought to be placed over us by those who claim that we ought to be forced to vote for Republican candidates and Republican measures, and who declare that if we do not, we are guilty of rebellion and should be punished therefor.

While flamboyant in style, Watterson usually based his editorials on a thorough knowledge of what he was talking about. Most of his editorials were not brief, but one of his most famous was a one-paragraph piece titled "To Hell with the Hohenzollerns and the Hapsburgs," urging the United States to enter World War I:

Herman Ridder [a German editor] flings Japan at us. Then he adduces Russia. What does he think of Turkey? How can he reconcile the Kaiser's ostentatious appeal to the Children of Christ and his pretentious partnership with God—"meinself und Gott"—with his calling the hordes of Mahomet to his aid? Will not this unite all Christendom against the unholy combine? May Heaven protect the Vaterland from contamination and give the German people a chance! To Hell with Hohenzollerns and the Hapsburgs.

Watterson and Henry W. Grady of the *Atlanta Constitution* have been credited with urging their readers to forget old grievances arising out of the Civil War and to work toward a New South that was more concerned with prosperity than issues.

Promotion and Prosperity

For all his concern for national and international issues, Watterson worked at promoting Louisville, Kentucky and the South, a theme that ran through newspaper editorial pages through the last third of the 19th century and early part of the 20th century. Editors promoted transcontinental railroads, local and regional railroads, canals, ports, agriculture, paved streets, municipal water, electrical and sewer systems, and schools of higher education. In the eyes of the local editor, his community was the one most deserving of success and prosperity.

Henry W. Grady of the *Atlanta Constitution* may been the pre-eminent promoter. He preached a New South ("sunshine everywhere and all the time") up and down the Atlantic Coast (mostly promoting Atlanta). A promotional trip to Boston, when he was ill, resulted in an early death at age 49, at the height of his prominence.[15]

Community promotion was not limited to the cities. Hal Borland recalled in *Country Editor's Boy* that his father used the *Flager* (Colo.) *News* to editorialize for water, electricity and paved streets.[16] A recent biography of William Allen White of the *Emporia* (Kan.) *Gazette*, generally regarded the ideal small-town editor, reveals that he worked some deals to promote his community that today might be considered conflicts of interest.[17]

Pulitzer and Hearst

For every trend, there is an exception. While most newspapers were headed toward corporate journalism, Joseph Pulitzer and William Randolph Hearst exploded onto the journalistic scene. With the purchase of the *New York World* in 1883, Joseph Pulitzer brought to the East Coast the sensational, aggressive style of news reporting that he had developed with the *St. Louis Post-Dispatch*—and a strong commitment to the editorial page.

In St. Louis, Pulitzer had campaigned editorially for the middle class at the expense of the wealthy. In New York, he took on the cause of the more numerous poor, including workers and the millions of new immigrants. The irresponsible rich, he said, had "the odor of codfish and not the mustiness of age." The World's editorial opinion was that "such an aristocracy ought to have no place in the republic." Pulitzer printed the following list of governmental goals for social justice that the *World* would pursue:

1. Tax Luxuries.
2. Tax Inheritance.
3. Tax Large Incomes.
4. Tax Monopolies.
5. Tax the Privileged Corporations.
6. A Tariff for Revenue.
7. Reform the Civil Service.
8. Punish Corrupt Officers.
9. Punish Vote Buying.
10. Punish Employers who Coerce their Employees in Elections.

At the end of the list, Pulitzer tacked this notice: "This is a popular platform of 10 lines. We recommend it to the politicians in place of long-winded resolutions."

The *World* generally supported Democrats, but it reluctantly backed William McKinley for president in 1896 because Pulitzer thought that the Democratic candidate, William Jennings Bryan, was ignorant on important issues and that the mining and coining of more silver (the "free silver" issue) would not solve the problems of economic depression. But, even though he praised McKinley's election, Pulitzer took the occasion to say that some of the problems that Bryan and the Populists had been talking about were real:

There is no doubt that in this Republic, based as it is upon simplicity and ideas of equality before the law, there are growing inequalities of privilege and increasingly offensive encroachments and vulgarities of the rich.

The trust combinations are fostered by tariffs that protect them from foreign competition. They grow every year more arrogant, more despotic, and more oppressive in their exactions. Yet the laws against them. . . .

In the same way the people have seen bargains made in secret between the Treasury authorities and a Wall Street syndicate for the sale of millions of bonds for 15 cents on the dollar less than their open market value. . . .

They have seen State legislatures of both parties dominated by corporations so that no measure of relief from wrong doing by corporations could become law. . . .

In brief, money is too largely usurping power and influence of manhood.

The New York press was further enlivened when Hearst ventured off his home base in San Francisco in 1895 to out-sensationalize Pulitzer with his newly acquired *New York Journal.* Hearst too undertook the cause of the have-nots, but his editorial approach was a more simplistic, emotional, entertaining appeal to readers. On the first birthday of the new *Journal*, Hearst editorialized:

What is the explanation of the *Journal*'s amazing and wholly unmatched progress? . . . When the paper was purchased by its present proprietor, a year ago today, the work contemplated was at once begun. . . . The *Journal* realized what is frequently forgotten in journalism, that if news is wanted it often has to be sent for. . . .

No other journal in the United States includes in its staff a tenth of the number of writers of reputation and talent. It is the *Journal*'s policy to engage brains as well as to get the news, for the public is even more fond of entertainment than it is of information. . . .

To entice readers, some of whom were not very literate, Hearst used large type for editorials, used large headlines to call attention to the editorials, spread editorials over several columns and sometimes published them on page one. Editorial cartoons added further interest to the page.

Arthur Brisbane, one of the many editors and reporters hired away from Pulitzer, became a master at expressing Hearst's views and promoting his causes in clear, direct language that no reader could misunderstand. The *Journal* addressed such topics as "The Existence of God," "What Will 999 Years Mean to the Human Race?" "Crime Is Dying Out," "Have the Animals Souls?" and "Woman Sustains, Guides and Controls the World." Brisbane editorials often had a simple moralistic tone. An example is "Those Who Laugh at a Drunken Man," written during the prohibition movement following World War I:

How often have you seen a drunken man stagger along the street!

His clothes are soiled from falling. His face is bruised. His eyes are dull. Sometimes he curses the boys that tease him. Sometimes he tries to smile in a drunken effort to placate pitiless, childish cruelty.

His body, worn out, can stand no more, and he mumbles that he is going home.

The children persecute him, throw things at him, laugh at him, running ahead of him.

Grown men and women, too, often laugh with the children, nudge each other, and actually find humor in the sight of a human being sunk below the lowest animal.

The sight of a drunken man going home should make every man sad and sympathetic. . . .

That reeling drunkard is going home.

He is going home to children who are afraid of him, to a wife whose life he has made miserable.

He is going home, taking with him the worst curse in the world—to suffer bitter remorse himself after having inflicted suffering on those whom he should protect . . . .

. . . we cannot call ourselves civilized while our imaginations and sympathies are so dull that the reeling drunkard is thought an amusing spectacle.

The trouble with Spain over Cuba in the late 1890s was ready-made for Hearst in his efforts to overtake Pulitzer. Hearst had a new underdog to champion—the Cuban rebels. Sensationalizing news and editorial comment about Spain and Cuba sold papers, and Hearst's circulation soon caught up with Pulitzer's. Pulitzer responded in kind. The battle between the two to see who could find, or invent, the most grisly revelations about Spanish atrocities helped create the political climate in which President McKinley finally concluded he had little choice but to seek a declaration of war against Spain. Following the sinking of the *U.S.S. Maine* in the Havana harbor in 1898, the *Journal* pretended to withhold judgment concerning the cause of the explosion and to urge caution. But it concluded that, no matter how the investigation turned out, there was no reason not to proceed with freeing Cuba. The editorial stated:

To five hundred thousand Cubans starved or otherwise murdered have been added an American battleship and three hundred American sailors lost as the direct result of the dilatory policy of our government toward Spain. If we had stopped the war in Cuba [between Spain and the rebels] when duty and policy alike urged us to do so the *Maine* would have been afloat today,

and three hundred homes, now desolate, would have been unscathed.

It was no accident, they say. Perhaps it was, but accident or not, it would never have happened if there had been peace in Cuba, as there would have been had we done our duty. . . .

The investigation into the injuries of the *Maine* may take a week, but the independence of Cuba can be recognized today. . . . The American fleet can move on Havana today and plant the flag of the Cuban Republic on Morro and Cabanas. It is still strong enough for that in the absence of further "accidents." And if we take such action as that, it is extremely unlikely that any further accidents will appear.

Both Hearst and Pulitzer had political ambitions. Pulitzer satisfied his ambition with one term in Congress and some service in the Missouri legislature. But it look Hearst a long time to learn that he was not destined for high office. Narrow defeats in races for mayor of New York City and governor of the state did nothing to lessen his efforts to become president. Hearst was a serious contender for the Democratic nomination in 1904, but he deluded himself into thinking he was a possible nominee in the three subsequent presidential elections. Few took him seriously as a candidate in those years.

Hearst's editorial urgings toward war, in the case of the Spanish-American War, were not renewed in the periods leading up to World War I and World War II. The Hearst papers took a pacifist and anti-British position in both news and editorials, in 1914 through 1917. Hearst dismissed critics who charged him with being pro-German. When the United States entered the war in April 1917, the Hearst papers scrambled to support the cause. In World War II, Hearst followed a similar pattern of expressing opposition to entering the war, then switching to a strong support, but in this instance a change of policy on the war did not indicate an end to Hearst's growing bitterness toward President Franklin D. Roosevelt. Part of his resentment resulted from a growing conservatism on social issues; part resulted because Roosevelt was not paying as much attention to Hearst as he had in the early days of his administration.

THE CORPORATE EDITORIAL PAGE

We have already noted the change in emphasis from opinion to news that followed the Civil War. The metamorphosis from prominent editors to anonymous editorial writers came gradually. Dana continued for some years to run the editorial page on the *Sun* as he wished, as did Godkin on the *Post*, Watterson on the *Courier-Journal* and Grady on the *Atlanta Constitution.* Most readers of Hearst's papers knew that Arthur Brisbane wrote the editorials that they read, and many knew that Irvin S. Cobb, Pulitzer's handpicked editorial writer and eventual successor, wrote the editorials on the *World* until Cobb's death in 1923. But few names are remembered today from other papers in the last decades of the 19th century and the first decades of the 20th century.

The *New York Times* epitomized the trend toward editorial anonymity of American newspapers. The *Times* had one brief moment of glory following the Civil War before lapsing into journalistic grayness. One of the underlings of W. M. Tweed, boss of New York's Tammany Hall, had been going from newspaper to newspaper trying to interest editors in publishing records that showed the corruption that existed in city government. Finally, after several editors refused, the *Times*, under the late Henry L. Raymond's partner, George Jones, published the revelations. It listed column after column of fraudulent bills, totalling millions of dollars, that had been paid to Tweed's friends and supporters. The stolen money, the *Times* said editorially, went "to meet the expense of the Ring in the matter of fast horses, conservatories, handsome horses and newspaper editors." After news stories had reported that $360,751.61 had been paid to an obscure carpenter named C. S. Miller for one month's work and $2,870,464.06 had gone to plastering work done by Andrew J. Garvey, a *Times* editorial said: "As C. S. Miller is the luckiest of carpenters, so Andrew J. Garvey is clearly the Prince of Plasterers. His good fortune surpasses anything in the Arabian Nights." (Thomas Nast, with his famous cartoons in *Harper's Weekly*, also helped rouse the public to oust Boss Tweed and send him to jail.)

That was about the last that was heard from the *Times.* "The mistake of the *Times* was in lapsing into the dulness (sic) of respectable conservatism after its Ring fight," Dana wrote in the *Sun* in 1875. "It should have kept on and made a crusade against fraud of all sorts." By the mid-1890s, the *Times* had fallen onto hard financial times. A new owner, Adolph S. Ochs, took over the paper in 1896. Primarily interested in presenting a good news product, Ochs was satisfied with a bland, anonymous editorial page. In recounting the history of the *Times,* Harrison E. Salisbury noted that "there were those who felt he would have been happier had there been no editorial page."[18] The page was plain and dignified: small headlines, regular type sizes, one-column measure, no political cartoons. One of the few *Times* editorial themes in the early 20th century was a defense of industrial entrepreneurs against the encroachment of legislation and the attacks of critics.

Newspapers in general during this period were closely allied with the growing business and industrial community. The papers themselves began to grow more prosperous and to become capitalistic enterprises. They became more dependent on advertising for revenue and on increasing circulation to justify higher advertising rates. The business side of journalism overshadowed the editorial side.

The Social Reformers

By the beginning of the 20th century most of the literary effort directed toward social reform was confined to magazines and books. One reason these publications took on the role that might have been performed by newspaper editorial writers and investigative reporters was that they were able to reach a nationwide audience for recruiting readers and building a mass circulation. At the local level readers interested in hearing about the evils of society were a minority in the years before World War I, when the prevalent attitude in America and Western Europe was that the world was making social and economic progress.

The most prominent platforms for the social reform writers, dubbed "muckrakers" by President Theodore Roosevelt, were *McClure's,* Hearst's *Cosmopolitan, Collier's* and Edward W. Bok's *Ladies' Home Journal.* The articles that appeared in these magazines, by such writers as Lincoln Steffens, Ida M. Tarbell and Ray Stannard Baker, were part investigative reporting and part editorializing.

One of Steffens's best known efforts was a series of six articles in *McClure's* on corruption in American cities. His findings later appeared in modified form in a book, *The Shame of the Cities.* One of the assumptions of the reformers of an earlier day, including E. L. Godkin on the *New York Evening Post,* was that municipal corruption arose out of the conditions of the poor, the illiterate and the immigrant classes, who in their ignorance were easily manipulated by the bosses. Steffens tried to show that corruption came from the top of the economic and social order, from the business community and the educated: "Don't try to reform politics with the banker, lawyer, and drygood merchant, for these are business men," he wrote in a letter to his father.[19]

Upton Sinclair, another muckraker, wrote in *The Brass Check*, an expose of American journalism, that "American corruption was the buying up of legislatures and assemblies to keep them from doing the people's will and protecting the people's interests."[20] Sinclair set out to show how the press, even the so-called reform press, had sold out to business. He contended that Charles Dana, on the *New York Sun*, while once "something of a radical," had "turned like a fierce wolf upon his young ideals" and now "had one fixed opinion, which was that everything new in the world should be mocked at and denounced."[21] Sinclair recognized Godkin as "a scholar and a lover of righteousness" but wrong in viewing corruption as stemming from the pandering of venal politicians to an ignorant mob. Concerning the typical municipal reformer supported by Godkin, Sinclair wrote: "The candidate was swept into office in a tornado of excitement, and did what all 'Evening Post' candidates did and always do—that is, nothing."[22]

A Few Noted Editors

Several 20th-century editors have stood out. Walter Lippmann, as much a political philosopher as editorial writer and columnist, earned a reputation as a wise analyst in writing, successively, for the *Nation* magazine, the *New York World* and the *New York Herald Tribune*. His column was widely syndicated. Lippmann did, however, have his detractors. He himself acknowledged that he had made a mistake in opposing the League of Nations following World War I. He had criticized it not because of too much internationalism but because of too little, claiming that President Woodrow Wilson had agreed to too many compromises. Later he changed his mind. Lippmann was also criticized for an ambivalent attitude toward the politically powerful. His seeking of their confidence and favor, in some critics' views, posed a conflict of interest. He earned back some of his critics' respect, when he broke, belatedly, with President Lyndon Johnson over the Vietnam War.

William Allen White became the most famous small-town newspaper editor during the first decades of the 20th century. He had written articles exposing social evils for a time for *McClure's*, but he earned his nationwide reputation initially with an editorial titled "What's the Matter With Kansas?" Written in a satirical tone, the editorial argued that the populists, who were complaining that the state was suffering from bankruptcy and an exodus of population, were wrong. White's editorials were widely quoted for their down-to-earth, yet idealistic, approach to national and regional issues. In Emporia, however, a recent biographer reminds us, White was the epitome of the small-town editor, promoting local economic growth and social harmony.[23]

In the days before World War II, White served as chairman of the Committee to Defend America by Aiding the Allies, one of whose purposes was to encourage newspapers to support the Allied cause. Hearst was one publisher who was not convinced by White's efforts. Others included what Henry Luce's *Time* magazine called "the Three Furies of Isolationism"—the three grandchildren of Joseph Medill: Robert McCormick, who had taken over Medill's *Chicago Tribune*; Joseph Medill Patterson, who had founded the *New York Daily News* in the 1920s, and Eleanor Medill "Cissy" Patterson, who became publisher of the *Washington*

Times-Herald when the McCormick-Patterson interest purchased that newspaper. In an editorial in the *News,* Joseph Patterson contended that the United States had been pushed into World War I, and that "some of the same forces" were pushing the country into World War II. In two editorials titled "Family Portrait," he said that the Pattersons had descended from a Scotch-Irish ancestor "whose great ambition was to get as far away from England and English aristocratic ideas as they could possible get. . . . It is also natural for us, with our midwestern background, to think first of America in times like these, and to hate to see Americans kidded and cajoled into impossible crusades to remake the world. . . . "

In establishing the paper in New York, Patterson had set out to remake the world of journalism. A tabloid, the *New York Daily News*, championed the cause of the poor and the latest immigrants, and offered them sensational, easy-to-understand news and lots of pictures. But the editorial page, with its casual, simplified, often flippant style, seemed incidental. Soon the *News* had surpassed Hearst's papers in circulation.

At the *New York Post*, a simplification of style was also occurring. Godkin's scholarly editorials had given way to short comments on the news and headlines that summarized the editorials that followed them.

20th Century Conservatism

During the first decades of the 20th century most of the press was extremely conservative in its politics. The *New York Sun*, which had had a liberal bent under Dana, warned against the perils of American entrance into the League of Nations supergovernment. Hearst expressed anger with France for not using "some of her German indemnity to pay her honest debts to America, especially because if it had not been for America she would now be paying indemnity instead of receiving it." Many newspapers joined in the "witch hunt" for "subversives" in the 1920s.

During the 1920s Americans were routinely electing Republicans as presidents, and most American newspapers were routinely endorsing them. New doubts about the power of the editorial page appeared in the 1930s when readers saw that the press was attacking and opposing the election and re-election of Franklin D. Roosevelt, a candidate whom the voting public continued to support. Editorials may have been the place readers previously had looked for interpretations of current events and general enlightenment. But with Roosevelt's New Deal and the Depression, the United States faced an economic and social, if not political, revolution. The country required greater quantities and kinds of information and insights. Most of the nation's anonymous editorial writers were unwilling or unable to provide what readers wanted. Many of their editorial pens were stuck with automatic reactions to proposals for change. One result was the sudden growth in popularity of bylined columnists, hired by newspapers and syndicated services to explain to readers what was going on, primarily in Washington, D.C. The columns, generally interpretive in nature, were usually published on the editorial page. They were more lively and informative than most of the unsigned editorials that represented the views of the corporate newspaper.

By the 1950s, most newspapers had shed the formal labels that tied them to one party or the other (usually the Republican), but they did continue by wide margins to endorse Republicans for president and, to a lesser degree,

Republicans for lower-level offices. In 1952 President Harry Truman leveled the charge of "one-party press" at the newspapers in the race between Dwight D. Eisenhower and Adlai Stevenson. A subsequent study found that the editorial pages of the nation had backed Eisenhower by a margin of almost five to one but that partiality had been evident in the news columns in only 6 of 35 newspapers studied.[24]

In that same era only a few editorial voices were raised early against "McCarthyism," the emotional and largely unsubstantiated campaign against "communists" and "un-American activities" that took its name from Sen. Joseph McCarthy, a Republican from Wisconsin. Alan Barth of the *Washington Post* was one of those few voices, but the voice that came through strongest was that of Edward R. Murrow. Murrow put together a documented television program on CBS that showed McCarthy for the demagogue that he was. The broadcast helped move public opinion toward eventual support of censure of McCarthy by his Senate colleagues.

One looks in vain for many examples of strong editorial leadership in the 1950s and 1960s. If the Eisenhower administration was content to let social issues lie dormant, so was most of the press. If editorial writers responded to John F. Kennedy's challenge of a "New Frontier " in the early 1960s, it may have been more because of their fascination with the personality and glamour of the new administration than because of concern for civil and social injustices. On the eve of his assassination in 1963, President Kennedy's programs were in deep political trouble, and he himself faced much antagonism among political leaders and voters. The assassination shocked editorial writers, as it did most Americans. One result was that voters, and editors, rallied around Lyndon Johnson, the new president, and in 1964 overwhelmingly elected him to the presidency. For the first time in the 20th century more newspapers supported a Democrat than a Republican for president. Still feeling the shock of the assassination, editorial writers generally supported a brief flurry of civil rights and social legislation during the Johnson administration.

The euphoria over the Johnson administration did not last long. (Not until 1992, in the Clinton-Bush race, did a plurality of daily newspapers again endorse a Democrat for president.) The high hopes of the "Great Society" proved overly optimistic, partly because funds that might have gone to fight poverty and racial inequality were sent to fight a war in Vietnam. Editorial writers in general, like administration officials, failed to realize that the country was not willing or able to wage full-scale battles on both foreign and domestic fronts, or, in the phrase of the day, to supply both "guns and butter." Only a few editors recognized that the country was unwilling or unable to accomplish what it set out to do in Vietnam. Among the early skeptics over the war were Robert Lasch of the *St. Louis Post-Dispatch* and Lauren Soth of the *Des Moines* (Iowa) *Register and Tribune*. A later skeptic was the *Washington Post*, which continued its support of the war until Russell Wiggins was replaced as editorial page editor by Philip Geyelin.

Editorial endorsements returned to supporting Republicans in the 1968 election when Richard Nixon barely defeated Hubert Humphrey for president. Even though much of the press, and the public, had grown weary of the Vietnam War and become convinced by that time that it could not be won, the war dragged on, at a somewhat reduced level, for Nixon's entire first term. The press eagerly endorsed Nixon for a second term in 1972, even though many of the revelations later to be known as "Watergate" had been published during the campaign. The documented details of Watergate eventually emerged, and Nixon resigned from the presidency—nearly two years after the break-in at the Watergate complex. A few newspapers, notably the *Washington Post*, deserved credit for the early revelations and for keeping public attention centered on the affair. But the Watergate story was essentially a news story, not an editorial page accomplishment.

Since Watergate neither editorial pages in particular, nor newspapers in general, have taken the lead in crusading in national or international matters. Journalists in general were quiescent during the two Reagan terms. In the 1980s the press played no significant role in smoking out the "Irangate" affair, in which Iran bought U.S. military arms with cash that then was sent to support "contra" forces in Nicaragua. In the 1990s editorial writers generally applauded military action in the Iraq war and seemed as overwhelmed and confused by the saving and loan crisis as the rest of the country.

HISTORICAL SUMMARY

In the nearly three centuries in which editors on the North American continent have been commenting on public issues, opinion has taken different roles. For the first century or so, editorial comment was sparse and generally intermixed with (often highly personalized) accounts of news. Then, as tension mounted between the Colonies and Great Britain, editors began to feel called to a cause. As the Revolutionary War approached, journals tended increasingly to be filled with opinion.

In the first decades following the ratification of the Constitution in 1787, newspapers, including editorial pages, served as mouthpieces for political parties. The function of editorials, which began appearing during this era on a designated page, was to argue the party line as forcefully as possible for the party faithful. The stronger and more emotional the tone of the editorial, the more likely it was to please the reader.

Beginning in the 1830s, the new populist press began appealing to a much broader and less political group of readers. At first these penny papers offered mostly crime, sex and gossip. Unsophisticated readers were not interested in editorial comment. But as readers became more literate and editors more concerned about issues, the populist press became more serious. In the two decades before the Civil War the major issues facing the nation got a thorough, if highly emotional and personalized, airing in the editorial columns. Editors did not hesitate to put into print their concerns about the conduct of the Civil War.

The Civil War brought new interest in news, and the day of the great personalized editorialist began to wane. A few voices still spoke out; writers such as Charles Dana, E. L. Godkin, William Randolph Hearst and Joseph Pulitzer raised a ruckus in the late 19th and early 20th centuries. But the trend was clear. Editorial writers were retreating into anonymity on conservative newspapers owned by corporations. One looks in vain for more than a few examples of strong, enlightened editorial leadership on national and international issues during the period dominated by the corporate press.

Only in a few instances have readers had reason to look to editorial pages for insightful examinations of the national and international issues of the day—and to expect to find anything except predictable responses to issues. The picture is brighter at local, regional and state levels. Here at least some editorial writers are speaking out with knowledge and conviction. In the next chapter we will look at what several of these writers and their newspapers have been doing and at what editorial writing could, and should, be in the future.

QUESTIONS AND EXERCISES

1. Why did writers for the Colonial press see little reason to make a distinction between news and opinion in the accounts that they wrote?

2. What brought about the decline and eventual demise of the partisan press of the first years of the Republic under the Constitution?

3. Why were Benjamin Day and James Gordon Bennett not interested in editorial comment during the early days of the populist press?

4. What accounts for Horace Greeley becoming the most famous editor of the mid-19th century? Do you think the esteem in which he was held was fully merited?

5. From examples in the chapter (plus other samples if available) contrast the writing styles of Horace Greeley and William Cullen Bryant. What does the difference suggest concerning readers of their papers?

6. Why has Charles Dana remained better known than E. L. Godkin?

7. Based on material in this chapter and information from other sources, does it seem reasonable to hold the *New York Journal* and the *New York World* primarily responsible for the political atmosphere that allowed the Spanish-American War to occur?

8. Why did most of the writing exposing social problems in the early 20th century appear in magazines rather than in the daily press?

9. What factors contributed to the trend toward anonymity of editors in the corporate newspaper era?

10. Why have recent decades produced no modern-day Horace Greeleys, Henry J. Raymonds, William Randolph Hearsts, Joseph Pulitzers or William Allen Whites?

Chapter 2

The Editorial Page That Should, and Could, Be

Nothing but a newspaper can drop the same thought into a thousand minds at the same moment. A newspaper is an adviser that does not require to be sought, but that comes of its own accord and talks to you briefly every day of the common weal, without distracting you from your private affairs.

—ALEXIS DE TOCQUEVILLE[1]

The first step toward understanding the role that the American editorial page can play today is to understand the nature of the readership of the page. In general, readers today are better educated than readers of the past. They are also probably more sophisticated, although many may not be as interested in public issues as were the faithful followers of editorials in the more partisan papers of the past. Most of today's readers do not read editorials as consistently as readers did when they could subscribe to, and relish reading, a newspaper with which they agreed politically. In most communities today's readers have little or no choice of a daily paper; they take the one that is available or none at all. In fact, a growing percentage of families today does not subscribe to a daily paper. Those who do subscribe represent not the narrow range of the faithful, as in the past, but a diverse political, philosophic, economic and social range. Unlike newspaper readers of the past, most of today's subscribers are exposed to many other sources of information and opinion from media—television, radio, cable, magazines, satellite, fax—and from social, civic, labor and business organizations.

All of these related characteristics of the modern editorial page audience suggest major implications for editorial page editors and writers who want to do the most effective jobs of informing and persuading their readers. The purpose of this chapter is to examine those implications and to see how editors deal with them in an age of a more diversified, more disinterested audience. My major point will be that there is still room for strong editorial leadership—for editorial crusades—but the best chances for editorial writers to achieve credibility and to be persuasive lie in being informed, reasonable, articulate and sensitive to the feelings and opinions of others.

A FEW BUGLE CALLS

"Today's editorial trumpet, when it sounds at all, too often sounds not so much like a trumpet as like a kazoo." That's the judgment of Robert Reid, former editorial writer, now associate professor at the University of Illinois. He sees a need especially for editorials "of an outrageous or even irresponsible" type. "We need loud, clamorous, jarring, persistent voices in our newspapers, hitting people hard enough in their prejudices to make them think and act in the public arena rather than in effect encouraging readers to slouch around feeling as if what they think doesn't matter or won't do any good," Reid wrote in an article titled "More Hell-Raising Editorials."[2]

Editors of *The Masthead* once asked several editorial writers what they thought about hard-hitting editorial campaigns. Several writers questioned the effectiveness, or wisdom, of outspoken campaigning, but others cited specific instances in which they were convinced strong editorials had made a difference in the outcome of public issues. George P. Crist Jr. thought a long, persistent effort by his paper, the *Bay City* (Mich.) *Times*, to stimulate more public awareness of the problems of nuclear power had had an effect.[3] Brian Dickinson of the *Providence* (R.I.) *Journal and Evening Bulletin* said his paper had taken "every possible opportunity to rail against" a court system in which the legislature elected state judges. He thought support of the paper had helped contribute to the legislature's eventual tightening of the selective process.[4] Tom Kirwan of the *Fresno* (Calif.) *Bee* thought his paper's editorials had helped build public understanding of the newspaper's position when they defended the "Fresno Bee Four," staff members who were jailed when they refused to reveal a source for stories about a sealed grand jury transcript.[5]

Over a period of more than a year, the *Lexington* (Ky.) *Herald-Leader* raised hell in a series of editorials titled "To Have and to Harm: Kentucky's Failure to Protect Women from the Men Who Beat Them." In several of the editorials, writer Maria Henson told in graphically horrifying terms what had happened to victims of beatings. A first editorial labeled "A Death Foretold" began in this manner:

Betty Jean Ashby's life was in danger. She knew it. Her family knew it. Her neighbors in Louisville's Shepherd Square knew it.

Louisville police knew it.

The Jefferson County Courts knew it, too.

Had the threat come from a mugger, rapist, or holdup man, the authorities might have seen their duty more clearly. But this was what the law calls a "domestic" case. The man who was stalking Betty Ashby was Carl Branch, her common-law husband and the father of her four children. . . .

In fear, Betty Ashby turned to the law. She went through all the steps. She appeared in court, signed sworn statements, told her story to police. But nothing, it seemed, could keep Carl away. . . .

The neighbor . . . could only hug her 4-year-old daughter and cry "Lord Jesus! Lord Jesus!" as Carl hit Betty in the head again and again until she sank to the floor, dead at 22.[6]

Another editorial began: "Lynn Milam has five metal plates in her head to remind her of the night her former boyfriend nearly beat her to death." Some of the editorials commented on what courts, law enforcement agencies and social agencies could or should be doing. Editors of the *Herald-Leader* reported that the editorials "have led to dramatic improvements in Kentucky's efforts to shield women from violent men." The editorial series also earned Henson and the newspaper the 1992 Pulitzer Prize and the Sigma Delta Chi Award in Journalism.

During the fall of 1991, the *Des Moines Register* published a series of 11 half- to full-page editorials on the front of the Sunday opinion section in an attempt to inspire a state in political and economic doldrums to envision "what a place this could be." The editors urged Iowans to concentrate on quality of life and wrote editorials supporting recreational and environmental green spaces, hiking trails, consolidated school districts, reformed local government and slimmed-down state government.

Between 1955 and 1965 six Southern newspaper editorial writers won Pulitzer Prizes for daring to speak out about civil rights. One of these was Buford Boone, publisher of *The Tuscaloosa* (Ala.) *News.* When the board of trustees refused to allow Autherine Lucy to be admitted to the University of Alabama in 1956, Boone, in a front-page editorial, criticized the board for having "knuckled under to the pressures and desires of a mob" and for making "an abject surrender to what is expedient rather than what is right." He concluded: "Yes, there's peace on the University campus this morning. But what a price has been paid for it!"[7]

Hazel Brannon Smith, editor-owner of *The Lexington* (Miss.) *Advertiser*, knew speaking out on civil rights was risky. She had written: "There was a time, almost a decade ago, when we Mississippians were free . . . we did have the habit of liberty. Newspaper editors were free to write editorially about anything in the world, giving our honest opinions, and there was no fear of economic reprisals or boycott. Today a newspaper editor thinks a long time before he writes anything that might be construed as controversial." That fear did not keep her from speaking out, among other occasions, about the bombing of the home of an African-American man who had tried to register to vote. "This kind of situation would never have come about in Holmes County if we had honestly discharged our duties and obligations as citizens in the past; if we had demanded that all citizens be accorded equal treatment and protection under the law. This we have not done."[8] The Pulitzer Prize was awarded to her in 1964.

Some publishers allowed their newspapers to take a stand on the controversial issues surrounding the Vietnam War and Watergate. A number of editors risked public (and their publishers') wrath by speaking out against the Vietnam War in the middle and late 1960s. One of these editors was Robert Lasch of the *St. Louis Post-Dispatch.* The paper I was working for at the beginning of the war, the *Des Moines* (Iowa) *Register and Tribune*, also spoke out early. The *New York Times* and the *Washington Post*, in spite the federal government's opposition, fought to print the Pentagon Papers, which revealed how the United States had been drawn into the Vietnam War. The *Chicago Tribune*, traditionally a very conservative paper, created a stir when it became one of the first major newspapers to call for the resignation of President Nixon during the Watergate affair.

In most instances in which a newspaper achieves an editorial goal, it is difficult, if not impossible, to determine precisely to what extent an editorial campaign contributed to the outcome. The newspaper is usually only one participant in the process. This was true for the hardest fought campaign waged by *The*

Columbian, of Vancouver, Wash., while I was on that paper. The Port of Portland wanted to expand the runways and parking of the Portland International Airport by dumping a square mile of fill into the Columbia River. The river separates Portland from Vancouver as well as Oregon from Washington. The Portland newspapers and, at the beginning, the major public figures in Portland firmly supported the expansion. Opinion differed in Washington. Some citizens were concerned that altering the course of the river would have detrimental effects, especially on the Washington bank. But others feared that, if the airport were not expanded at its present location, convenient to Vancouver, the port would relocate it on the other side of Portland.

Before *The Columbian* had taken a position on the proposal, two local citizens, both of whom owned property on the river, came to me with research they had done on the hydrological and legal aspects of changing the river channel. They convinced me that building a runway into the river would increase airplane noise in Vancouver and possibly threaten the Washington bank. They were trying to raise enough money to retain a prominent environmentalist as an attorney to press their case in court, and they wanted the paper's support. We gave it. During the next two to three years opponents of the airport plan won not a single court decision, and lost several, at both federal district and court of appeals levels. The project did not get under way, however, because the port had agreed to wait until the last legal hurdle had been cleared.

Our paper was able to make no discernible impact on opinion in Oregon across the river, but in a succession of editorials we made a strenuous effort to shore up community support for the opponents on our side of the river as they carried their battles to the courts and later to Congress. Without *The Columbian* legitimizing their efforts, they would have had a more difficult time raising money. Delay proved the undoing of the project. A new projection of future usage of the airport showed original estimates had been too high. The years of delay coincided with the rise of the environmental movement of the late 1960s and early 1970s. More voices began to express concern over the plan. Finally, a new mayor, Neil Goldschmidt, was elected in Portland, and he began questioning the expansion. Soon the port abandoned the plan and came up with one that would fit on existing land.

If I ever deserved a feather for my editorial bonnet, it was for *The Columbian*'s efforts in this cause. One reason for this lengthy account is that I can think of no other instance in which we waged a similar campaign during my 12 years associated with the editorial page of the paper. We editorialized for home rule, fairer taxes, more money for schools and land-use controls, not so much as concerted campaigns but simply as general comments on daily news topics. I would be hard pressed to come up with evidence of the newspaper's impact on these broader issues, and yet I am certain that *The Columbian*'s persistent support for these causes did produce results with readers, and public officials, over an extended time. I could also cite any number of other instances in which our editorials seemed to have no impact at all, immediate or long term. We couldn't sell residents of adjacent suburbs on annexing to the city, or residents of the county on modernizing county government.

Some of the editors who responded to *The Masthead*'s inquiry about editorial campaigns offered examples of frustrating experiences. Ed Williams of the *Charlotte Observer* recalled that his paper had been pushing "a couple of things for as long as the oldest editorial writer here, roused gently from his slumbers, can remember": a less regressive sales tax system and a liberalizing of the sale of alcohol. He noted, ironically, that that very year "we were rewarded . . . by a legislative attempt to give manufacturers yet one more tax break." On the matter of liquor, in an equally ironic tone, he said that, "thanks, no doubt, to our rational, persuasive editorials," Charlotte residents "can now walk into a bar and buy a mixed drink—if they are willing to drive 25 miles" to South Carolina.[9] Robert Reid, then editorial editor for the Lindsay-Schaub Newspapers of Decatur, Ill., while suggesting that "maybe we just aren't dynamite enough writers," concluded that in his community there probably wasn't much worth accomplishing that could be attained in one or two hard-hitting editorials. "Sometimes it takes a decade or more to get even fairly minor change," he wrote. "So patience and lack of patience, as well as a high tolerance level for the same subject written in many different ways, are important qualifications for a crusading editorial writer."[10]

A number of picturesque images have been used to warn editorial writers against expecting too much from editorial campaigns. Bernard Kilgore, when he was publisher of the *Wall Street Journal*, said he thought it was all right for newspapers to regard themselves as thunderers and for editorial writers to picture themselves "with a bolt of lightning in each hand about to smash down on something." But he urged writers to be "very careful about demolishing a subject with one swoop, because good subjects for the editorial pages are very hard to come by."[11] He was warning editorial writers that most topics require analysis and comment over a period of time, not a single definitive pronouncement. Donald Tyerman, at the time editor of the *Economist* of London, reminded editorial writers at a meeting of the National Conference for Editorial Writers (NCEW) that they are neither Moses nor God. He warned against the Tablets of Stone theory— "that you can hand down the truth or, indeed, that you have it to hand down." Nor did he believe that editorial writers can effect a conversion such as occurred to Saul of Tarsus on the road to Damascus.[12]

At another NCEW meeting Philip Geyelin of the *Washington Post* recalled that James Cain, who served with Walter Lippmann on the *New York World* and wrote *The Postman Always Rings Twice*, had argued that a newspaper ought to fight for its beliefs as hard as it could. He turned to music for an illustration, noting that a piano has eight octaves, a violin three, a cornet two, but a bugle has only four notes. "Now if what you've got to blow is a bugle there isn't much sense in camping yourself down in front of piano music," Cain said. To which Lippmann replied, "You may be right, but goddamit, I'm not going to spend my life writing bugle calls."[13] A bugle call may be appreciated by readers once in a while, and it may mobilize them in a worthy cause, but readers can quickly tire of answering bugle calls. Editorial writers may not have an eight-octave persuasive tool at their disposal, but they ought to be able to play more complex tunes than Reveille and Charge!

A MORE COMPLEX MELODY

Readers look to the editorial page for more than bugle calls. One newspaper survey found that the highest percentage of regular readers followed the page either to feel they were participating in current events or to strengthen their arguments on issues. Others read the editorial page to help make decisions on issues, to use in discussion with friends, to determine what is important, to keep up with the latest events, to agree with editorial stands or to help form opinions. These results suggest that readers use the editorial page more to gain information than to seek guidance in forming opinions.[14]

I am not one to urge editors slavishly to fashion their journalistic products to reflect readership surveys. The decisions that editors face—whether to give readers what they want or what the editors think they should have—must still be made. A wise choice may be a compromise between the two, but if a choice must be made, editorial writers generally ought to come down on the side of facts and logic. The aim of the writer should be toward the mind, editorial writers were advised by Lenoir Chambers, who, while on the *Virginian-Pilot* of Norfolk, Va., was one of the six Southern Pulitzer Prize winners mentioned earlier. Editorial writers had better aim for the mind, he said, "for everybody is better educated now, and the editorial writer has a harder job to stay out in front." If writers don't know what they are talking about, readers soon spot them for phonies.[15]

Columnist James J. Kilpatrick, formerly of the *Richmond News Leader*, has warned editorial writers: "Unless an editorial can add something to what appears in the news columns—something besides mere opinion—it has no business in the paper." He urged writers to use historical background, comparisons of parallel situations, fresh facts from other publications and research sources, interpretive analysis and the setting straight of misinformation.[16]

It is easy to dash off an editorial that merely expresses opinion or rewrites the news. It is harder to find something to say about a subject that has not appeared in the news columns or gone through the minds of readers. Here is where time, previously acquired knowledge, ingenuity and an abundance of resources pay off. Jane E. Healy of *The Orlando* (Fla.) *Sentinel* chose what she termed "a rather unconventional way" when she set out to expose the ineffectiveness of Florida's development laws. "I interviewed dozens of people—politicians, developers, planners and ordinary residents—to gather material," she said. "I pored over dozens of planning documents and developers' plans as well: a touch of investigative reporting applied to the editorial page." Acquiring all this information "made it easier for me to raise hell about the situation," she said. The result was a series that ran six days straight under the title of "Florida's Shame." Development companies pulled $55,000 in ads from the newspaper, but county commissioners took action, and Healy's editorials won the Pulitzer Prize and the Sigma Delta Chi Award.[17]

An Orange going sour?

How would you like to live in a place where:

▶ **(A)** Some elementary school children must eat lunch at 10:30 a.m. because the cafeteria is too crowded to seat everyone during normal lunch hours.

▶ **(B)** All but one high school is overcrowded. Some academic classes have to be held in the school gym or, worse, the gym's storage room.

▶ **(C)** Cars jam up bumper to bumper on dozens of roads, and the worst is ahead. A place where in just seven years half of the major roads will be carrying more cars than the roads were built for.

▶ **(D)** Parks rank so low on priority lists that total park acreage must increase by 60 percent just to meet state standards.

▶ **(E)** All of the above.

Welcome to Orange County, Florida, the 13th fastest-growing area in the country, where you never have to choose between the rotten fruits of unmanaged growth. In Orange County, the answer is always (E), "All of the above."

The Sun Boom? No question. Orange County is right in the thick of it. The economic statistics look jim-dandy on paper, but kids don't go to school on paper. Nor do roads and parks get built on it. Beneath all those rosy data-bank projections, Orange County is being sold out for a quick buck. It's a county in crisis.

Mind you, Seminole, Osceola, Lake and Volusia counties have serious problems as well. But that's a subject for another day. In this series of editorials, we'll concentrate on Orange County, a place still hanging a "For Sale" sign at its border, a quick-buck, bottom-line piece of real estate that's selling its future for a pittance.

Is it the same tired Florida story? To some extent, sure. Taking the real-estate money and running away may be the oldest profession in the Sunshine State. And elected officials here have been managing them, since time immemorial, or so it often seems. But, no, the Great Florida Land Grab of the 1980s isn't the land boom of the 1920s.

Then, developers and land speculators used up Florida for their own purposes and headed back up North to enjoy life. Today's developers and land speculators use up Florida for their own purposes and head to North Carolina to retire.

Then, developers and land speculators stuck the communities they pillaged with all the bills for necessary services. Today's developers share in the cost of growth by helping build roads and sewer systems, but don't worry, they still can meet the Mercedes payments. Oh, yes, today's developments also look prettier, sit back farther from the road and might even have smaller signs.

But, face it, that's window dressing. The land grab continues. And when all is said and developed, the people who live here still are the ones left to fight the traffic, pay most of the bills and live with the eyesore.

Maybe worst of all, the all-consuming greed back in the 1920s was out in the open, where just about everyone who cared to look could see it for what it was.

Today's greed gets to hide behind the illusion that Florida finally is serious about managing its growth.

The illusion? The tough new law the legislature passed two years ago, the one that said services must go hand in hand with growth.

The reality? In the Orlando area, the law won't go into effect for at least three more years. That's a year later than originally scheduled. Too much paperwork for everyone, the state says. Let's wait just a little bit longer, it says. The rest of us can only wonder how many more times this deadline will be delayed.

This means at least three more years of business as usual in Orange County. Hold on to your steering wheel.

As for that thick, serious-sounding growth management plan Orange County has, yes, it exits. But try to get a majority of Orange County commissioners to treat it as anything other than an annoyance. Just look at the pitiful record:

August 1985: Orange County updates its five-year-old plan for growth, leaving enough land in urban areas to accommodate developers for the next 20 to 30 years. In other words, the county says it won't be necessary to leapfrog out to rural areas and waste money building roads, utility lines and schools all over the place. Commissioners even agree that developers won't be able to ask for changes to the plan every time they walk in the door. They now can ask for changes only twice a year. Hallelujah, a new day.

Or perhaps we should say, it looked like a new day. Turns out most of these commissioners are leap-frogging fools.

Spring 1986: County commissioners grab at the first chance they can to leap five miles into the woods. They allow an industrial park in rural southeast Orange County that will employ 40,000 people. That's 5,000 more than work in downtown Orlando now.

Summer 1986: Commissioners allow 525 more rural acres to be developed as urban densities, this time on the west side.

Spring 1987: Commissioners open 3,790 acres southeast of Orlando International Airport to city-like development. They also open 1,200 acres near Windermere to such development.

Fall 1987: Commissioners say "go ahead" to urban development on another 300 rural areas east of Windermere.

By now you must be wondering how much of Orange County isn't on the verge of urban development. Good question. The answer: not much.

Who benefits from this contempt for limiting urban densities to urban areas? Certainly not the typical Orange County resident. Such development only further strains the county's ability to provide adequate schools, roads and parks elsewhere.

No, the people who benefit from all this are the same folks who have been pillaging the Sunshine State for most of this century—the speculators and developers who get rich quick whenever land becomes urban overnight. How? Easy, land costs a lot less in the rural area, but once the county commission declares it urban, values skyrocket. A developer can build at least four times as many houses in urban areas because lots can be smaller.

Sadly, the county commission still refuses to say, "Enough. We won't be stomped on anymore for a quick buck." That is Florida's Shame.

The Orlando Sentinel

When editors of *The Masthead* asked editorial writers for suggestions for improving editorial pages, Al Southwick of the *Worcester* (Mass.) *Telegram* said he thought that 99 percent of all editorials could benefit from just one-half hour more of research. "That one extra fact, that one additional insight" is what makes the difference between a routine editorial and "something that causes readers to sit up and take notice," he said.[18]

Syndicated columnist Neal R. Pierce said he has found that writers on the best editorial pages "have studied issues in depth, so that the commentary offered is neither kneejerk nor shoot-from-the-hip, but rather based on extensive knowledge." To produce a column, he said, he may conduct half a dozen interviews, read scores of background papers and spend hours writing and rewriting. He acknowledged that most editorial writers do not have the luxury, as he does, of writing only one piece a week, but he thought that more hurried editorial writers could achieve similar results by keeping comprehensive files on subjects likely to be written about. His second suggestion was that newspapers should make certain that their editorial writers have time to get out of the office to talk personally with a range of public officials and other experts. One of his favorite techniques was to ask an official or an expert to "name—in his or her own words—the priority subjects that will be coming up in the following months."[19]

Even though editorial writers may be as pressed for time as reporters, their writing needs to give the impression that they are not—that they had all the time necessary to research and to write their stories. "We need to break down that amorphous block of events, slow down the flow of information with explanation and relate these events to the readers," editorial writers were advised by Thomas Williams, professor at the University of Southern Illinois at Carbondale. Print journalism, he said, does the best job of presenting information in depth and in step-by-step analysis—"and the editorial page equals dignity and the page to turn to when you want a little more than just the story."[20]

Not only must editorial writers slow down the news that streams through the news columns, but they also should be constantly seeking topics for comment that never find their way into the news columns. The editorial writer who reads widely—the mail, news magazines, specialty magazines, current fiction and nonfiction, the classics, cereal boxes—is certain to come across ideas worth sharing with readers who are looking for more than the same old commentaries. Robert

Bartley of the *Wall Street Journal* has urged editorial writers to engage in "fresh reporting" and to set their own agendas. "Their reporting needs to be guided not by yesterday's events, but by some kind of intellectual framework that tells them what might be worth learning about the issues of the day," he said. "If they have this kind of curiosity, and go to work developing their own news sources they are going to find a lot of news readers otherwise would never see."[21]

A VARIETY OF TUNES

The diverse composition of today's editorial page audience presents another challenge to editorial page editors. Not only must they recognize, when they write their own editorials, that readers hold a variety of opinions, but they also need to create opportunities for those viewpoints to be presented. Because of time limits and the fleeting nature of messages of film and tape, most of the broadcast media do not find it possible to carry varied viewpoints in depth. That responsibility must fall to the print media. When you are the only newspaper in town, that responsibility falls on you.

Providing opportunities for and encouraging readers to write letters to the editor represents a start in this direction. But providing this forum is not enough. Some readers are less inclined to write than others, or are less likely to write on one side of an issue than another, or are less likely to write on some subjects than on others. So the editor must seek to diversify opinion on the editorial page in other ways. Syndicated columns for 60 years or so have been a traditional source of some diversity. The columnists have their limitations, since most write on national and international news and have their favorite topics. Trying to find provocative non-regular writers requires time and effort, but these offer an opportunity to bring varied and fresh views to the editorial page. The addition of an op-ed (opposite-editorial) page on an increasing number of papers has expanded opportunities for publishing material that can not be squeezed into a single page.

Opinion pieces in one newspaper can't be expected to replicate faithfully all viewpoints of a community's readers. But with a little help from friends, and adversaries, newspapers should be able to create opinion pages that make readers feel their views are being taken into account.

THE TUNE PLAYER

Finally we come to editorial writers themselves, the players of the tunes. What types of men and women are they, and should they be, at a time when audiences are diverse and distracted by other demands on their time and attention? Obsequious, bland editorial writers who are content to mouth a harmless editorial policy, as many did during the corporate era, will not do. They will bore readers to death with platitudes. They may never arouse the ire of their business-minded associates, but they certainly won't arouse the ire, or the enthusiasm, of readers either.

Opportunities to speak out forcefully may not come immediately to beginning editorial writers. Many beginners come from the news side of their papers, where they have been conditioned to keep opinion out of the paper, at least their own opinions. Those with editorial writing experience who come from other papers find themselves working for a new, unfamiliar employer. In both instances, being junior members of a staff, and feeling junior even on a one-person staff, they are not likely to push their bosses toward a more aggressive, outspoken editorial policy or to feel that they are in a very strong bargaining position. But if they allow themselves to remain indefinitely in such a weak position, they ought to change newspapers or change jobs.

Editorial writing is a job for someone who has the ability to dig into a subject and to figure out something meaningful, and often controversial, to say. Now, a novice editorial writer ought not to be given license to put into print anything he or she comes up with. The art of writing editorials is a demanding and subtle one. It can take quite months, or years, for a writer to get the hang of blending fact, interpretation and opinion into a piece that is interesting and convincing—and not too long. Beginning editorial writers are likely to write overly lengthy editorials. They are likely to write editorials that have either weak conclusions or strong conclusions unsubstantiated by facts and arguments. The roots of both problems are similar. The novice suffers from a lack of experience in using facts and arguments to produce and support conclusions. The only way to correct this common failing of apprenticeship is through experience, preferably under the guidance of a competent, demanding editor.

Once editorial writers fully grasp the subject matter they are writing about and get the feel for putting fact and argument together to support conclusions, they should be able to begin strengthening their positions on their editorial page staffs. If editorial writers know what they are talking about, the odds are that they will convince readers, or at least cause them to rethink their opinions, and that they can convince their editors, general managers and publishers that their ideas merit publication.

On many, too many, newspapers editorial writers must restrict their published opinions to narrowly defined policies determined by someone who is not actively engaged in the day-to-day editorial decision-making. The trend in setting short- and medium-range policy, however, seems to be moving from the corporate level to the editorial page staff, or at least to the editorial conference. Ironically, the trend toward group ownership may contribute to an increased autonomy of editorial staffs. Sensitive to charges of monopolization of news and opinion, executives of most of the larger groups have said that they consider news and editorial decision-making as the function of their local newspapers. The group's business representative at the local level, whether called a publisher or a general manager, is likely to be more concerned with profit than with news and editorial policies. On the diminishing number of independently owned papers, editorial writers who can hold their own in policy discussions have opportunities to earn respect and the opportunity to influence policy.

Editorial writers are increasingly strengthening their credibility through public recognition. Anonymous editorial writers are being replaced by men and women whose names appear on the masthead and on bylined interpretive and opinion pieces on the editorial and op-ed pages, and whose faces, either in pictures or sketches, appear from time to time with these pieces. Editorial writers are not only getting out into their communities to find out what is going on, but they also are going out to make themselves known among their readers. They make speeches and appear on panels, belong to civic organizations and show up for public events, where they may be among the most widely recognized persons present. In many communities, the women and men who write editorials are regarded, deservedly or not, as important, influential persons. This recognition, coupled with sound editorials, provides the making of the power to persuade readers and to influence a community.

Because of the unique role that an editorial page plays in a community, it has become fashionable in editorial writing circles to describe the page as the conscience of the community, the soul (or heart or personality) of the newspaper, the moral substructure of the paper. Editorial writers should hope that their pages are all of these and more. But writers who set out to be the conscience/soul/heart of the community/paper risk committing one of the follies of editorial writing. At a time when philosopher-kings and prophets are rare and the credibility of institutions is low, the role of truth-seeker should be a humble one. Modern readers don't want truth through revelation; they want to feel that they are discovering it for themselves. Writers who would lead must become servants of those readers.

The editorial writer is "uniquely equipped to stand at the corner of life and represent us all," somewhat like the person who hangs around in the piazza in the little towns in Italy, Pacific Northwest editorial writers once were told by R. S. Baker, assistant professor of humanities at what was then Oregon College of Education at Monmouth. Baker said he had often wondered how the Italians, who read very few newspapers, could be so well informed. The mystery was solved when he observed the buzzing chatter, the exchange of information and gossip and the constant movement of people in the piazza, the public square. Over a period of days, you could spot the person who is the equivalent of the editorial writer. He described the person in this manner:

> He is usually middle-aged with a face made grave by experience yet softened by flickers of humor. Most of the time his head is inclined in attentive listening while his eyes scan the square, alert and skeptical. But when he speaks he is listened to. He does not orate. He does not preach. He does not even adopt a tone of outraged innocence. Softly but clearly, he suggests how the matter appears to him. In his words there is a ring of wisdom based on his balancing of claims of past, present and future, the claims of the ideal and the actual, the desirable and the probable. If he lived here he would have your job—would, from his station in the piazza, keep one eye on the new-book shelf in the library and the other on City Hall, on the till.

Baker urged the writers to drop the pose of divine authority and accept simple humanity. "Do not aim to be Zeus the Thunderer (your 19th- and early 20th-century crusading editor) nor even Jove the All-seeing (your cool, shrewd commentator on legislative/administrative matters). Rather, you should settle for being wily Odysseus, content to be—in all its terror and glory—a man among men, *primus inter pares*."[22]

CONCLUSION

So how does the editorial writer become the woman or the man in the piazza instead of a publisher's mouthpiece, an ivory tower dweller, an impersonal penman or a judgment imposer? No secret magic will cause such a transformation. The chapters that follow are intended to offer suggestions for writers who may not have all the answers but, like the wise one in the piazza, want to be listened to when they speak.

QUESTIONS AND EXERCISES

1. Examine newspapers in your area for a period of several days. Do you get the impression from reading the editorial pages that the editors are trying to find a wide variety of opinions to present to their readers? In what forms do these opinions appear?

2. Examine the editorial pages of these papers for evidence of the personalities and individual opinions of editorial writers. Are the writers faceless persons, or do their names appear on the masthead or on bylined articles?

3. What seems to be the general tone of the editorials on these papers? Are the writers issuing bugle calls or something more subtle and complex? If a mixture, is the tone chosen for individual editorials appropriate?

4. Put in your own words what you think R. S. Baker meant by likening the editorial writer to the person in the piazza.

Section

THE
Who
OF THE
Editorial Page

Chapter 3

Anybody for Editorial Writing?

Here we are, the practitioners and champions of a profession which, we modestly like to think, assists the sun to rise and set—and we are doing very little, seemingly, either to seek out the young people with brains and judgment who we hope will be our successors or to interest them in the virtues and satisfactions of editorial writing.

—ROBERT H. ESTABROOK, WASHINGTON POST [1]

Why would anyone want to become an editorial writer? What kinds of people make the best editorial writers, and where do they come from? These are some of the questions raised in this chapter, which is intended to give prospective editorial writers some idea of what it is like to be an editorial writer.

In the 1950s and early 1960s, when I was beginning my newspaper career, few young journalists gave much thought to becoming editorial writers, at least not until they had had their fill of walking a news beat. So I was surprised when, at age 28, I was asked by a friend and former professor if I would be interested in an editorial writing job he knew about in Des Moines, Iowa, on the *Register and Tribune.* Having left my native Nebraska and taken a job in the Pacific Northwest only three years before, I was not keen on returning to the Midwest. But the editor of the editorial page in Des Moines, Lauren Soth, had recently won the Pulitzer Prize for editorial writing, and I had enjoyed writing editorials on my college newspaper. So I applied for the job, got it and never looked back. Editorial writing became my new life.

My professor-friend said something else when he was trying to interest me in that editorial writing job. "Someday," he said, "you ought to have an editorial page of your own." I could not possibly have dreamed that five years later the publishers I had been working for in Washington state would hire me back as editorial page editor of their newspaper. I had my own editorial page at age 33.

THE ATTRACTIONS OF EDITORIAL WRITING

What have I and other editorial writers found so attractive about working on an editorial page?

Editorial writing offers the chance to step back a pace, to take a broad view of the stream of news that rushes through the pages of a newspaper. Reporters, from time to time, have opportunities to write interpretive articles that attempt to put news into perspective, but only editorial writers spend their entire working day trying to understand what's happening in the world. To interpret the news, editorial writers must have enough time to do a quality job of researching and writing. Editorial writers, at least on some papers, can take half a day, if need be, to dig out information for an editorial that, when set in type, might be only five or six inches long. Editorial writing tends to appeal to people who take pleasure in careful writing. Of all the duties editorial page people may be pressed to perform, the one they are likely to enjoy the most is turning out the one or two editorials that must be written each day.

Another attraction of editorial writing is having a ready-made "soap box" from which you can explain and persuade. Readers, of course, don't always fall in line with the editorials they read in their local newspapers, but over a period of time an editorial page with credibility will influence the thinking and direction of the community. It is exciting and rewarding to be a part of the decision-making process of a community.

The job of editorial writer may carry more importance at the newspaper and in the community than it did not so many years ago. Editorial writers may not get their names in print as often as star reporters, but the position tends to be one of the most prestigious on the paper. An increasing number of papers are providing opportunities for writers to become known to the public, partly through signed articles on the editorial page. While most editorial writers don't spend as much time out in public as reporters, they do, in fact must, get out and become acquainted in the community.

From a financial standpoint, editorial writing also has its advantages. Editorial writers generally are better paid than reporters and newsroom editors, and their job tenure is usually longer. A survey in 1988 found that 72 percent of editorial writers thought they were paid "very well" or "well" compared to other staff members of their newspapers. Sixty-eight percent said their jobs were "very satisfying," and an additional 29 percent said "satisfying."[2]

Despite these attractions, a survey of newsroom staffs showed that only about 30 percent of news reporters and editors were interested in editorial writing.[3] Interest was expressed primarily by those under age 30 who had pursued more formal education. The most frequently mentioned reason for not going into editorial writing—mentioned by about 20 percent—was personal disinterest. Almost as many saw too many restrictions and a lack of freedom of expression. Smaller numbers saw the job as too removed from reality (too much ivory tower). Some saw themselves as lacking the necessary scholarship or experience.

The survey caused William W. Baker of the *Kansas City* (Mo.) *Star* to conclude that "our little niche in the profession does not command the respect that it might among our fellow workers across the room." He wondered whether news staffs had the impression that editorial writing was "dull, uninteresting and downright boring." To overcome that impression, he suggested that editorial writers come out of their ivory towers and into the newsroom more often, work at creating more stimulating writing and frown "a bit less frighteningly when we tackle our typewriters."[4]

THE QUALIFICATIONS FOR EDITORIAL WRITING

Surveys suggest that it is not just discomfort with the editorial ivory tower, but also the demanding qualifications, that leads newsroom people to shy away from editorial writing. A significant 58 percent of the respondents to one survey thought that the qualifications for a competent editorial writer were different from those for a competent news staff writer, pointing in particular to the need for more education and knowledge. Also mentioned were the need for more analytical skills, more experience, sharper insights, better grasp of issues and trends, and better writing.[5]

What qualities are required for editorial writers?

First, they need a wide variety of interests. Editorial writers on large staffs may have opportunities to specialize in subject matter, but those on most papers need to be able to write on almost any subject on almost any day. Even those who specialize need to understand how their topics fit into the broader world. Writers need to know about economics, politics, history, sociology, the arts and the sciences. In stressing the catholic interests of editorial writers, Warren H. Pierce of the *St. Petersburg* (Fla.) *Times* said that writers "should know more about all these subjects than any except a specialist in one of the fields, and enough of each so that even the specialist will not scoff" at their opinions.[6]

Second, editorial writers need to be good reporters. They must be able to dig out information and to recount accurately what they find. No editorial is stronger than the facts behind it. Previous experience as reporters can help editorial writers know where to go and with whom to talk when they need information.

One might think that, because editorial writers deal with opinion, they require less ability to be objective than do reporters. But the capacity to understand an issue or situation fully may be even more important for editorial writers than for reporters. In arguing for the need for objectivity, David Manning White, then professor at Boston University, said: "To the editorial writer is given the power to exercise the most unrestrained use of language in the name of rhetoric and persuasion," and for this reason editorial writers must check and double-check that what they write "conforms as closely as possible to objective, examinable truth."[7]

A third qualification is good writing. Editorial writers must write succinctly, since the editorial page is usually tighter for space than the news pages. Writers also need to be able to write in an interesting and convincing manner. Newspaper readers may have to read the news columns if they want to know about news, but they don't have to read the editorials, and they won't if editorials are dull or don't say anything.

Fourth, editorial writers need a quality that is sometimes called a sense of fairness or justice, sometimes called a spirit of the reformer, or a commitment to principles, or integrity. The subjects they write about should be approached with a sense of purpose.

A fifth qualification is the desire to express an opinion. Hoke Norris of the *Chicago Sun-Times* saw reporters who became editorial writers as moving "from the sidewalk to the parade, from the press table to the speaker's table." As participants, Norris, said, editorial writers "must study, weigh, deliberate, contemplate, meditate, judge, discuss, talk over, think through and generally know all there is to know about any given subject, and . . . must be capable, at times, of completing the entire process in five minutes."[8]

Another desirable quality is the ability to reason cogently. Warren Pierce, a professor at the University of Oregon, had this in mind when he quoted the philosopher Arthur Schopenhauer as saying that geniuses share one characteristic: an ability to proceed from the particular to the general. Pierce thought that editorial writers need that ability, as well as the reverse ability. Editorial writers must be able to go from one specific case of juvenile delinquency to the general causes of such delinquency, and "from one deep-freeze or white convertible Oldsmobile to a proposition of ethical conduct in public office." Equally they should be able to give meaning to reciprocal trade agreements in terms of a clothes-pin factory in their community or of cotton or corn growers in their state.[9]

One view of an editorial writer's qualities was expressed by Irving Dilliard, editorial page editor of the *St. Louis Post-Dispatch*, who compiled an impressive list in an article titled "The Editor I Wish I Were." His principal points: Editorial writers should know their community, state, nation and world and read a great deal. They should be courteous, treating readers as individual human beings. They should be cooperative, working with associates to produce the best possible newspaper. They should be curious; perhaps they are not the first to learn everything in the community, but they at least should know more new things than anyone else. They should have imagination, seeing opportunities for improving the press in content, service and leadership. They should be persons of conscience and courage, with the ability to stand up to interest groups or a superior editor or publisher. They should have judgment, avoiding "the heavy artillery . . . if a spatter of birdshot will suffice." They should be able to criticize others, but also able to accept criticism. They must take care to avoid activities that might prove embarrassing or detrimental to editorial independence. Writers should be "sparing" in friendships because friendships outside their newspapers "may at any time force the hard choice between personal kindness to a friend and devotion to duty as an editor."[10]

Frederic S. Marquardt of the Phoenix *Arizona Republic* was so overwhelmed by Dilliard's description of the ideal editor that he asked: "Doesn't the guy ever have any fun?" The need to find out about so many places in the world "would give most newspaper auditors acute melancholia," Marquardt said. "I would need at least 72 hours [a day] to keep up with Dilliard, even if I didn't stop for a short beer now and then." Marquardt was especially critical of the admonition to be sparing in friendships. "Show me an editor who bends an elbow in a neighborhood tavern once in a while, or who occasionally sees if he can fill an inside straight, or who goes to a football game without the slightest intention of improving his mind, and I'll show you an editor who knows more about life than all the Ivory Tower boys," Marquardt said.[11]

Who are these journalists who become editorial writers? Surveys show that they tend to be male, white, college-educated, middle-aged and leaning politically toward the Democratic Party. The picture is changing, but more slowly than most editors who are doing the hiring would like.[12]

A survey in 1988 found that only three percent of editorial writers were members of ethnic minorities.[13] In 1989 the chair of the Minority Participation Committee of the National Conference of Editorial Writers (NCEW) wrote: "My own industry—the newspaper business—prides itself in thinking it is progressive, that it provides leadership for the communities its newspapers serve. But the sad fact is that newspapers are belatedly responding to the story they have been covering since the 1960s civil rights movement."[14]

Editorial staffs may be lagging behind news departments in recruiting ethnic minorities and women. A 1992 survey found that news and editorial departments, when taken together, were made up of 11 percent minority workers and 40 percent female employees.[15]

The 1988 survey had found that 16 percent of editorial writers were women, compared to seven percent 10 years before. Another survey the same year, which tallied editors in both news and editorial departments, concluded that women would not "attain levels in newspaper editorships on a par with their level of the population (53 percent)" until the year 2055.[16] My impression, gained from reading newspaper mastheads from across the country, is that women are moving more rapidly into editorial writing than this prediction would suggest. More women are becoming editorial page editors. As of 1992, three of the last seven presidents of NCEW have been women, although the only other woman to serve in the 45 years of the organization did so in 1981.

A survey aimed at comparing women and men on the editorial page concluded that "the hiring of women on editorial page staffs does bring about a more diversified staff. Women tend to offer different expertise, somewhat different motivation, a possibly different generational outlook, and a different political orientation than do their male colleagues."[17] The survey found that women who were editorial page editors tended to be on smaller papers, and that women who were writers tended to be on larger papers. Women tended to be younger, have less journalistic experience but more post-graduate education. They had lower salaries. They were more likely to be Democratic than men, although independent was the largest designation for both women and men. Women were more likely to regard themselves as specialists or experts in specific subject areas, notably science and health, "women's issues" (defined in the survey), education and minority issues.

The first woman editorial page editor of a major newspaper may have been Molly Clowes. She joined the editorial page staff of the *Courier-Journal* of Louisville, Ky., in 1940. It took her 26 years to become editor. When editors of *The Masthead* asked women editorial writers about their professional experiences, all those who responded expressed confidence that their sex had not kept them from meeting all of the requirements of the job, but several told of difficulties in getting to be an editorial writer and in dealing with the public after they became editorial writers.[18]

Jane Reid of the *Burlington County* (N.J.) *Times* thought that the chief disadvantage of having a woman editorial writer on a staff "is the same one which for many years barred women from radio and television broadcasting—the belief that the audience would not accept a woman's voice as authoritative." If readers think about it at all, she wrote, chances are they will assume the writer is a man. Once a member of the National Rifle Association came stalking into Reid's office, "with fire in his eye, ready to take a swing at the fellow who wrote that editorial supporting gun controls." He simmered down when he saw the writer was a woman and meekly asked if she would read some of his literature. Reid said he apparently regarded arguing with a woman as "beneath his dignity." She added: "Frankly, the feeling was mutual."[19]

Elisabet Van Nostrand, then of *The Columbian*, Vancouver, Wash., said that a common response when she answered the telephone was: "I don't wanna talk to no secretary. I wanna talk to the EDITOR!" Hysterical readers who called to complain slowed down when they found themselves talking to a woman. "When they learn that the person responsible also has children, especially daughters, it tends to subdue them somewhat," she wrote, "although I have upon occasion been asked, 'What kind of mother are you?'" Van Nostrand said the big problem for her was not so much being an editorial writer or editor but convincing editors and publishers that a woman could be a competent editorial writer.[20]

WHERE EDITORIAL WRITERS COME FROM

Because editorial writing requires so many skills and qualities, it is not surprising that editors and publishers despair when they face the task of finding an editorial writer. Any publisher or editor who has found the right person will say without a doubt that such success is one of the most satisfying experiences in the field of newspapering. I know; I have experienced both despair and success.

It is infinitely more difficult to predict the potential ability of a would-be editorial writer than it is to decide whether a candidate will make a good reporter. Few guidelines exist for judging whether a former reporter, a college professor, a recent liberal arts graduate or an editorial writer from another newspaper will do the job a publisher or an editor has in mind. For one thing, most people who hire editorial writers, no doubt thinking of some of those qualities mentioned above, are not certain whether editorial writers are born or made. Some editorial writers seem to have it, and some seem not to. James H. Howard, a professor at the University of California, Los Angeles, thought that editorial writers probably had innate talent but that "those not blessed with the talent at birth" could be taught to improve their research, sharpen their writing and "present readable results of logical thinking."[21] Donald L. Breed of the *Freeport* (Ill.) *Journal Standard* said his experience on small newspapers showed that adequate editorial writers were usually found "only by accident."[22]

One of the dilemmas faced by an editor looking for a new writer is whether to look in the newsroom for a person with no editorial page experience or to search outside for a person who has had editorial experience in another community. Most of the editors who were asked in a *Masthead* symposium said they looked first in their newsrooms but were not especially optimistic about finding exactly the right person.[23] An employer identified only as "an editor in the West" said he was discouraged by what happens to good reporters "who can pound out several thousand words of news copy a day" when they sit down in front of the editorial typewriter. "That clear, decent prose becomes stilted, 'literary' or arch. Why can't they relax?" One reporter who started on Monday ran out of things to say by Thursday. Another didn't work out because of lack of background. "I don't think he's read a book since he left college," the editor said.[24]

William D. Snider of the *Greensboro* (N.C.) *Daily News* said he found that good editorial writers often come from non-journalistic backgrounds. He cited Ed Yoder, who had come to the *Daily News* after majoring in English and then studying philosophy, politics and economics as a Rhodes Scholar at Oxford. He had been editor of his college paper. Between stints at the *News* he taught college history. From Greensboro Yoder went to Washington, where he became the last editorial page editor of the *Star* (then a syndicated columnist, and a college professor again). Snider himself had been secretary to two governors before returning to the newspaper world.[25]

I must acknowledge that, in seeking new editorial writers on *The Columbian*, we did no more advanced planning than most papers. My first search represented a classic case of frustration. An ad in *Editor & Publisher* elicited more than 100 applications. Few came close to the person we thought we wanted. Some were "hacks," old-timers looking for an easy chair. Many were acquainted with neither editorial writing nor the territory. Almost in desperation, we allowed a *Columbian* reporter, who eagerly wanted the job, to try out for it. Here was the exact opposite of the reporter who has trouble moving from fact to opinion. After a few weeks of overexuberantly expressing her opinion, she settled down to become a fine, if still flamboyant, editorial writer. In the next search for a writer, we hired a person who had been an editorial writer, in fact the editor, on a small daily newspaper in California. He knew how to write editorials, and it didn't take him long to learn the territory.

My first editorial writing employer hired me when I knew very little about editorial writing and even less about Iowa, where the newspaper was located. But my return to the Vancouver paper represented an almost ideal set of circumstances. I had become acquainted with that community during three years of news reporting. I had had five years of editorial writing experience under a respected editorial page editor and excellent teacher. To make my situation even sweeter, I was brought back to Vancouver six months before the retiring editorial page editor was to leave the paper, enough time to get re-acquainted again in the community and break in slowly. I recommend this combination of experiences but recognize that these opportunities do not arise often.

CONCLUSION AND A WARNING

My comments and the surveys of editorial writers may suggest that editorial writers think highly of themselves. They think that they practice the best of professions. The jobs they hold require all those "fantastic" qualities discussed above. Thus if they hold those jobs, editorial writers reason, they must be fantastic themselves.

Some of this self-esteem is merited. Some of the best informed, most talented, incisive, conscientious people I know are editorial writers. In my experience, nothing can be more stimulating than bringing editorial writers together, at an editorial staff meeting or a meeting of writers from several papers. But as praiseworthy as these wordsmiths generally are, perhaps a warning about too much self-congratulation is in order.

Editorial writers may be well-educated, draw good salaries and have their own offices, but they are still newspaper people. Newspaper people tend to be held in high esteem these days—higher than half a century ago certainly. But much of this esteem comes from the jobs they hold, not from their own individual qualities. Press critic Ben Bagdikian has warned that, with newspapers becoming "a respectable institution and editorial writers the most respected of all," newspaper people shouldn't forget where their journalistic predecessors came from. "Newspapers were born and raised in the bloody arena, kicking and gouging their newspaper competitors in the ring while the crowd screeched. . . . " Now most of the competitors have been "carried out on stretchers" and the few that are left are not scrapping but giving their audiences pompous "lecture[s] on the Manly Art."[26]

Among middle-aged and older members of NCEW, perhaps the best remembered call for humility came from Jonathan W. Daniels, editor of the *Raleigh (N.C.) News and Observer*, who delivered an address titled "The Docility of the Dignified Press" to a convention of the NCEW in 1965. He spoke at an evening banquet at an exclusive country club on the outskirts of Milwaukee, Wis. Daniels told the writers that the editors and publishers who gathered for meetings of the Associated Press and the American Newspaper Publishers Association at the Waldorf-Astoria Hotel each spring were "indistinguishable from bankers." He quickly added: "You look pretty impressive yourselves." He reminded them that they are courted by senators, cabinet members and generals. "You really cannot blame the press for wanting a little dignity," he said. "Its members, as their social positions improved, naturally did not want to seem to be like Horace Greeley, who before he founded the famous *Tribune* was fired from one paper because its owner wanted 'only decent looking men in the office.'" Why shouldn't members of the press like their "pants pressed—sometimes striped?" He acknowledged that, "if [the press] didn't appear full-armored from the brow of Jove, it doesn't twist genealogy more than some other people do in suggesting that it is descended from the Bill of Rights." But he reminded his listeners that there were other ancestors. "There was the guitar player on the back of the patent medicine salesman's wagon. Also there was the ink-stained impertinent fellow who began long ago to put embarrassing reports on paper."

Now it had become more fashionable, he said, to look like Walter Lippmann, the distinguished columnist, than Heywood Broun, the disheveled-looking columnist of the 1920s and 1930s who had rankled publishers by trying to organize labor unions in their newsrooms. Perhaps it was at this point in Daniels' speech that one of the editorial writers suddenly rose from his table, lurched drunkenly toward the right side of the room, uttered a profane epithet at Daniels and staggered out, never to be seen at an NCEW meeting again. Daniels bade him farewell and continued with his speech: "There is, of course, something disreputable about any business devoted to prying into matters," he said. "It is a nosey business. And it should remain so. Anybody who would never wish to hurt anybody's feelings, who never wishes to make anybody mad, should stay out of the newspaper business. The editor who deserves the respect of his community can be no respecter of persons in his community. He must be nosey and often a public scold."[27]

So when editors and publishers want to hire a new editorial writer, all they have to do is find a man or a woman who is a writer, a thinker, a scholar, an objective viewer, a critic, a scold and a person with humility. Is it any wonder that good editorial writers are hard to find—or any wonder that, once found, they think pretty highly of themselves?

QUESTIONS AND EXERCISES

1. What are the reasons for trying to find a new editorial writer in an editor's own newsroom?

2. What are the reasons for looking elsewhere?

3. How do you account for the slowness in opening editorial page positions to women and racial minorities?

4. Are there women editorial writers or members of racial minorities on editorial pages in your area? How long have they been editorial writers? What education and experience did they have when they became editorial writers?

5. What do you regard as the most important qualities of an editorial writer?

6. What aspect of editorial writing would appeal to you most? What would appeal to you least? Why?

7. If you wanted to land an editorial writing position on a major newspaper within 10 years, what route would you attempt to follow?

8. On what newspapers with which you are acquainted could you feel philosophically comfortable writing editorials?

Chapter 4

Preparation of an Editorial Writer

It is hard to imagine any discipline that would not benefit a journalist.
—A RESPONSE TO A QUESTIONNAIRE CONCERNING COLLEGE CURRICULA[1]

Everybody has a sort of reading anxiety neurosis.
—ROBERT B. FRAZIER, EUGENE (ORE.) REGISTER-GUARD[2]

Preparing oneself to be an editorial writer is like preparing oneself for life. Everything that the potential editorial writer thinks, learns or experiences is likely to become pertinent someday in the writing of some editorial. The same is true of journalists who are already editorial writers. Every word they read can provide an idea or information for an editorial. Compulsive readers who find themselves reading the sides of the breakfast cereal box may write an editorial that day, or another day, about the dangers of the sugar content in children's breakfast foods or the lack of meaningful nutritional information. A casual conversation may provide an insight into Social Security or the minimum wage.

In this chapter a discussion of the unending education necessary for editorial writing is limited to five areas: undergraduate education, continuing education, firsthand experiences, reading and culture. A sixth area, professional experience, was discussed in the previous chapter.

UNDERGRADUATE EDUCATION

Bring an editor and an educator—or even two editors or two educators—together and you will have a debate on how best to prepare students for careers in Journalism.

Journalism schools are a rather recent invention, and many editors before World War II saw little need for them. They hadn't gone to journalism school—and perhaps not even to college. Reporting and editing, they knew from experience, could be learned on the job. But the world was becoming more complex, and readers were becoming more knowledgeable and sophisticated. To the GI Bill, which provided educational and other benefits for World War II veterans, must go much of the credit for sending more Americans than ever before to college. Students poured into journalism and every other field of study. Before many postwar classes had graduated, the competition for jobs made a college degree a necessary ticket for many positions.

Skills vs. Liberal Arts

With the legitimacy of journalism programs gradually becoming accepted, the debate turned to skills courses versus liberal arts. How many courses in journalism were necessary to prepare students to write a news story? How many courses in "academic" subjects were necessary to prepare students to know what they were writing about? Out of that debate came general acceptance of the 75/25 ratio set by the American Council on Education for Journalism, the national accrediting agency in journalism. In other words, 75 percent of graduation credits should be in liberal arts and related areas and not more than 25 percent in journalism. More recently this arbitrary rule has been relaxed, but it still remains a reasonable guideline for educators who want to ensure that prospective journalists get a broad liberal arts background.

Green Eyeshades vs. Chi-Squares

Next came arguments over which journalism courses should be offered and required. The protagonists in these arguments were sometimes referred to as the "green eyeshades" and the "chi-squares." Now you hear these disagreements discussed more in terms of "professional" versus "history and theory" courses.

"Green eyeshades" was a reference to the transparent green bills that copy editors used to wear to cut the glare of overhead lights. "Chi-square" is a mathematical procedure used in statistics to measure differences in sets of numbers. The green eyeshades feared that journalism schools were shifting from old-fashioned skills to theory and research. They wanted the schools to concentrate on reporting, news writing, feature writing, copy editing and editorial writing, plus courses in media law and history. They wanted attention paid to spelling, grammar, punctuation and style.

The chi-squares were interested in creating courses in communications theory, communications research, surveys of mass communications, effects of the media, and mass media and society. One of their goals was to make journalism and communications academically respectable among their research- and theory-oriented colleagues in other university departments. Coupled with this emphasis has been a sharp trend toward valuing advanced degrees over professional experience in hiring new faculty members.

Members of the newspaper business and some educators have expressed concern. Hugh S. Fullerton, associate professor at the University of North Florida, in a letter to the newspaper division of the Association for Education in Journalism and Mass Communication (AEJMC), complained: "The 'academic' side has raised barriers against the professionals. I know many professionals who would be happy to teach if they received the respect that they have earned by many years' experience. But instead, we professionals are told again and again that we are unqualified because we don't have Ph.D.'s."[3] Anticipating what concerned Fullerton, when I switched from newspapering to teaching, I immediately enrolled in a Ph.D. program within commuting distance of the school at which I was teaching. Six years and an editorial writing textbook later, I was able to obtain a position at a university that regarded degrees, research and publications as important. Since then, these qualifications have become even more important at most four-year schools. The trend is not likely to be reversed.

Non-Professional Courses

Some critics argue that journalism programs have no place in higher education. "Indeed, a good case can be made for abolishing J-schools," Jake Highton, associate professor at the University of Nevada-Reno, has written. "What journalism students need is an education—not a journalism education. . . . [Time] would be better spent having students take courses in literature, history, political science, fine arts and economics," with some "critical analysis of media performance."[4]

Most editors probably would not go so far as to advocate abolishing journalism programs but would agree with Otis Chandler, then publisher of the *Los Angeles Times*, when he complained that among job applicants "we're getting too many hopefuls who lack a background in economics, literature, philosophy, sociology and the natural sciences" and who "know little of government." He also deplored journalism students' inadequate exposure to ecology, energy, land-use planning and economics, as well as the physical sciences, birth control and bureaucracies.[5] When NCEW members were asked to recommend areas of study, they suggested, in this order: U.S. history, composition, state and local government, introduction to sociology, principles of economics, critical writing, constitutional law, comparative economic systems, geography, history of political thought, political parties, history of modern Europe, economic history of the United States, public financing, urban and regional planning, and philosophy.[6]

Some educators have concluded that, because of the need to know about so many things, the journalism program should be a five-year one. Such a program might lead to a master's degree.[7] Other educators think that four years is enough to produce a working newspaper person, that he or she can grow on the job and later pick up additional education on the side or return for a master's degree, perhaps in another discipline.[8]

Because reporting and commenting on the news are becoming more specialized as the world becomes more complex, the student who comes to a newspaper with training in a particular field—economics, the arts, the health sciences or the criminal justice system, for example—can prove to be a valuable asset to a news or editorial staff, especially when a newspaper seeks to fill a beat or an editorial writing position that requires knowledge in that field.

Practical Experience

One method of impressing students with the need to learn basics—and to teach them at the same time—is through an internship on a newspaper or with another news operation. If interns have at least a couple of news writing and reporting courses, within a three-month internship they can acquire the ability to substitute on several of the regular beats, handle most stories that come into the newsroom and write a simple feature story. The internship experience helps when applying for a job after graduation. The prospective employer knows that the applicant has had some practical experience, and that the internship supervisor can provide an evaluation of the applicant's work. Often a successful internship can lead to a job on the paper on which the student worked as an intern.

Another valuable experience is reporting and editing on a campus newspaper, especially if the work is supervised and criticized by faculty advisers or knowledgeable senior staff members.

CONTINUING EDUCATION

Editorial writers, and would-be editorial writers, should never stop trying to expand their educations. Science, mathematics, agriculture, medicine, politics, geography, education—all have vastly changed from the days that many of today's editorial writers were in college.

Educational Fellowships

The most formal way for writers to recharge themselves intellectually and psychologically is through educational programs. An editorial writer for the *Boston Globe* was given a year's leave of absence to study law at Harvard Law School. "I cannot urge too strongly the desirability, for editorial writers particularly and working journalists generally, a good dose of formal legal education," Anson H. Smith Jr. said. "It sharpens the mind, provides valuable sources of information and advice on legal issues in the news, and generally enhances one's understanding of the legal process."[9] After completing a fellowship at Stanford University, Sig Gissler of the *Milwaukee Journal* said the experience gave him the chance to think about "the big, tough questions that editorial writers seldom have time to dig into deeply." He added: "Think how rewarding it would be to spend nine months at a great university contemplating these concerns—without deadlines, spats with the boss, phone calls from ired readers; without mandatory term papers or exams; without significant restraints on your freedom to explore and reflect."[10]

Probably the most prestigious fellowship is the Nieman Fellowship for Journalists at Harvard University. Information about this and other fellowships can be obtained through most journalism schools. From time to time *The Masthead* publishes a listing of fellowships and other educational offerings.[11]

Seminars

Among programs of a briefer nature, the best known is at the American Press Institute (API) in Reston, Va. For four decades API has provided one- and two-week seminars in almost all phases of newspapering, including sessions on editorial writing and editorial pages. The seminars are financed through tuition fees. Participants meet in small groups to criticize and praise each other's editorials and editorial pages and in larger groups to discuss current issues with experts in journalism and other fields.

From time to time various universities and colleges offer short courses in specific areas of newspapering or in state government or business. (NCEW and the University of Maryland periodically co-sponsor seminars on public issues.) Editorial writers who feel the need for more education can enroll in one or more courses in a nearby college. Evening courses in such areas as economics or public administration can give editorial writers knowledge that might improve their editorials.

Visiting Professorships

One way to learn is to teach. Possibilities exist at several universities for editors and writers to return to the campus as visiting editors or visiting professors. The William Allen White School of Journalism at the University of Kansas, for example, has brought a series of editors to campus. The University of Montana, which from time to time has money for a professional visitor, invited me to teach during the fall quarter of 1976 while I was an editor. The experience was so satisfying that, when a few months later I had a chance to teach an entire year at Washington State University, I accepted the offer.[12] Teaching forces you to think about what you have been doing as a matter of unreflective habit.

FIRSTHAND EXPERIENCES

The editorial writer who hopes to address a changing world must get out of the office. "There is no real substitute in journalism for the face-to-face confrontation," Terrence W. Honey of the *London* (Ontario) *Free Press* wrote in an article titled "Our Ivory Tower Syndrome Is Dead."[13] Unfortunately for some editorial writers it is not dead.

Local Level

Busy editorial writers are often tempted to write editorials on local topics on the basis of what has appeared in the news columns, interpreted in the light of past editorial policy, rather than attend meetings of city councils and local citizen bodies that can become an every-evening job. Most of the time spent at these gatherings may seem boring and unproductive, so writers tend to put off going to local meetings until a hot issue comes along. Attending only at crucial times is better than not attending at all. But most of the work of local government bodies is done in regular, humdrum meetings in the absence of the eyes of the public. Editorial writers who want to know how a council or council member functions under normal circumstances should attend at least some of these dull assemblages. Editorial writers also can boost their credibility with members of local organizations and with anyone else who happens to be at these meetings.

More informative than public meetings are private ones, perhaps over lunch, with key persons. Editorial writers, or the editorial board, may find it advantageous to meet separately with members of opposing sides of issues. On other occasions inviting representatives from all sides to meet together to discuss an issue may prove an effective way to gain information. To make certain that such conferences are not limited to times of crisis—and that lethargy does not win over good intentions—some editorial boards schedule a weekly meeting to which they invite one or more sources. Writers should meet, from time to time, with labor officials (as well as rank-and-file members), Chamber of Commerce leaders, other business groups and individuals, environmental groups, utility officials, energy interest groups, consumer groups, education groups (professional and citizen), religious leaders, social activists, sports people, transportation people and even people from rival media.

It also is important for journalism students to become acquainted with people who are making, or trying to make, public policy. An editorial writing course offers an opportunity to bring speakers to class or to take students out into the community to learn first-hand what they are writing about.

State Level

Face-to-face confrontation can be more difficult at the state level. Unless a newspaper is located in a state capital, legislative sessions and committee hearings are difficult and time-consuming to attend. Most provide little immediate information for editorials, since the legislative process is spread over an extended period of time. But much of what was said about local meetings applies here too. Writers need to get a feeling for the process at its usual slow pace to see how it works and how its practitioners function. Editorial writers need to show their faces and make their presence known, at least among their local legislators. Credibility with the legislators, as well as knowledge, is the goal.

It was easier to follow legislatures when they met for short sessions every two years. Now critical moments in the process are spread out, and opportunities for strategically directed editorials become more difficult to spot. Some of the difficulty can be alleviated if a newspaper has skilled reporters assigned to the legislature who can keep editorial writers informed about the timing of bills as well as track down information for editorials.

Maintaining contact with the executive branch of state government is even more difficult from a distance. Decisions can come at any time and often without public notice. Probably the best approach to establishing contact is through people at the assistant level—governors' aides, assistant attorneys general, the elections supervisor in the secretary of state's office, a key assistant in the state planning office, a high-level career employee of the tax commission. These second-level people are more likely to be expertly informed than their bosses and, even more important, are usually easier to get on the telephone.

Another way to keep abreast of state affairs is to watch for statewide conferences of such groups as county commissioners and city officials and meetings on specific issues, such as taxation, education and legislative or judicial reform.

Students who attend a university in a state capital should find it easy to become acquainted with officials and issues by following the media and dropping in on legislative- and executive-branch meetings. I have found that taking students to the capital (200 miles away) for even a few days helps awaken their interest in state government, particularly when the legislature is in session. It is easier to arrange these visits if the news and editorial people from the capital city newspaper help with the arrangements.

National Level

For national issues, most editorial writers must rely heavily on the news services and newspapers such as the *New York Times*, the *Washington Post*, the *Wall Street Journal*, the *Christian Science Monitor* or the *Congressional Quarterly*. Editorial writers with Washington bureaus that they can call on have access to information at the national level. Close contacts with the offices of the state's two senators and that of the local representative can be useful. Most of these officials will have offices in the district or the state, but sources there are likely to prove beneficial primarily on matters of local interest or subjects relating to the committees on which the senator or representative serves.

Short visits to Washington, D.C., may seem even less productive for an editorial writer than trips to the state capital. But through periodic visits to the capital, a writer can begin to cultivate sources in the federal government, especially in departments that deal with issues pertinent to the writer's own region.

From time to time the Department of State invites editors and editorial writers to Washington for briefings on world affairs. I found the first one I attended fascinating because of the opportunity to see famous personages. But by the second briefing I began to realize that the presentations offered little more than I could have obtained by reading readily available publications.

I have taken some of my students on three-day travel seminars to Washington, D.C., to meet with people of differing opinions, usually on international topics. These have been arranged with the assistance of the local YMCA and some of the campus ministries.

Attendance at national political conventions can benefit an editorial writer, although not as much as it did in the days before television. The principal benefit is probably in getting some of the flavor of the proceedings and watching the home-state delegation.

International Level

The American Association for the United Nations sometimes invites editorial people to meetings and briefings at the United Nations headquarters in New York City. Again, the principal value is in getting a feel for the personalities and the atmosphere. Probably more productive are visits to foreign countries—that is, if the writer has made substantial advance preparation. A quick tourist- or host-conducted visit may distort rather than provide insight into affairs abroad. In recent years NCEW has sponsored a series of overseas tours for members that provide participants with background information about and interpretation of what they are seeing. Of course, these trips are expensive; the cost may be prohibitive for small papers. I found an NCEW trip to Eastern Europe in 1990 and a trip to Mexico and Cuba in 1993 to be exciting and eye-opening. Projected trips usually are announced in *The Masthead*.

Of course personal travel abroad, especially if you are conversant in a foreign language, can be educational and useful to the editorial writer. I benefited from two trips to Central America, arranged by a local campus ministry, that were led by residents of the countries that we visited. They knew the places to visit and the people to see, and could help us with the language and local customs.

Professional Level

Associating with journalists with similar interests can help rejuvenate editorial writers' enthusiasm for their work and challenge them with ideas for doing a better job. One of the main purposes of NCEW is to improve the quality of editorial pages by bringing editorial writers together for sessions of mutual enlightenment and criticism. A valuable and consistent feature of NCEW's annual meeting has been the day- or half-day-long critique session in which participants study the editorial pages before arriving, and analyze, praise and criticize one another's pages. Held at some time in nearly every section of the country, the NCEW meetings have given members a firsthand (though brief) look at other communities. The speakers are almost consistently good. From time to time regional or state versions of these meetings take place.

THE EDITORIAL SHELF

Robert B. Frazier of the *Eugene* (Ore.) *Register-Guard* once surveyed 100 editorial writers to determine their reading habits.[14] Later he wrote an article for *The Masthead* titled "The Editorial Elbow," in which he offered a "more-or-less compleat (sic) listing of reference works useful, day by day, to the editor, reporter and copyreader."[15] From the two efforts Frazier concluded that writers consistently thought they read too little, that probably no other group in the country "read more or more catholically" and that writers on smaller papers, with smaller editorial page staffs, followed a more varied reading diet than writers on larger staffs.

Non-fiction was more popular than fiction. Only about 40 percent said that fiction accounted for a quarter or more of their reading. Half said they read essays, poetry or plays. About 10 percent read often in a foreign language. Some bought only two or three books a year, but one bought 200. Forty percent were regular patrons of libraries. A quarter of them said they read in bed. Two got up to read in the middle of the night. Three read early in the morning. Four admitted to being bathroom readers. One had read Gibbon and one Spinoza. Shakespeare appeared on several lists.

Columnist James J. Kilpatrick thinks that editorial writers do not read enough, and "it shows up with painful transparency in the superficiality, the shallowness, the gracelessness, of our editorial writer."[16] He advised writers to read the Bible and Shakespeare and to read heavily "in the older classics"—Thucydides, Plutarch, Homer, Aeschylus, Disraeli, Gibbon, De Quincey, Spinoza, Voltaire—and then the more recent works of Thorstein Veblen, William James, John Dewey, Alfred North Whitehead and Peter Finley Dunne. To this assignment, Kilpatrick added a list of poets, from Alexander Pope to Edna St. Vincent Millay, and fiction writers, from Charles Dickens to O. Henry. Irving Dilliard of the *St. Louis Post-Dispatch* said an editorial writer should be "familiar with the monumental publishing projects of his time in biography, in history, in the social sciences, regional life, in the messages and papers of the great Americans—Franklin, Adams, Jefferson, Lincoln."[17]

Magazines and Newspapers

In moments when they are not reading the classics, where should editorial writers turn for help in writing their daily assignments? Most probably subscribe to *Time*, *Newsweek* or *U.S. News & World Report*. These magazines give a more comprehensive account of some news than daily news stories and, maybe more important, provide essays and reports on such areas as religion, science and the arts, which generally are not covered well in most newspapers. Back sections of these magazines often provide ideas for nonpolitical editorials.

Writers should seek out varying points of view on public issues, if only to know what the opposition is saying. One way is to subscribe to, say, the *New Republic* or the *Nation* and the *National Review*. *Business Week* publishes easy-to-understand articles on business and economics and well-done editorials that discuss issues beyond a narrow business orientation. *Playboy*'s in-depth interviews sometimes are worth checking. *Foreign Affairs* offers writing by recognized international experts. The *Economist* and the weekly edition of the *Guardian* offer British points of view. Other periodicals worth considering are *Harper's*, *Atlantic*, the *New Yorker*, *World Press*, *Washington Monthly*, *Esquire*, *Fortune*, *Money*, *Consumer Reports*, *Scientific American*, *Omni*, *Science*, *Rolling Stone*, *Mother Jones*, *Village Voice*, *Architectural Digest*, *Columbia Journalism Review*, *American Journalism Review*, *Family Circle*, *Ms*, *Lear* and *Cosmopolitan*. From time to time writers should look at sports and outdoor magazines, computer and medical periodicals and even the supermarket tabloids. Ideas for editorials lurk everywhere.

Editorial writers should be devourers of newspapers. They should read every newspaper in their community, even those that circulate among a small portion of the population, and their own paper meticulously. They should read the local minority press, if there is one, and the *New York Times*, the *Christian Science Monitor*, the *Washington Post*, or the *Los Angeles Times* daily. Another important newspaper, the *Wall Street Journal*, offers not only business news and well-written editorials but also one or two in-depth front-page articles every day on subjects that often are worthy of editorial comment.

Writers should also subscribe to state or regional papers. From time to time they should look at major newspapers, among them *USA Today*, the *Boston Globe*, the *St. Petersburg Times*, the *Chicago Tribune*, the *Philadelphia Inquirer*, the *Miami Herald*, the *St. Louis Post-Dispatch*, the *Oregonian* of Portland and the *Courier-Journal* of Louisville.

Without subscribing to them, an editorial writer can get a glimpse of other editorial pages through exchanges sponsored by NCEW. Some of the editorials reprinted in this book were obtained through the NCEW exchange.

Periodic Research Materials

Available generally on a weekly basis are the following sources of information:

Facts on File, a weekly service that boils down the essential elements of the news into a ready-reference form. It is a good source of elusive facts. Facts on File, 460 Park Ave. South, New York, N.Y. 10019.

The CQ Researcher (formerly *Editorial Research Reports*) provides background material on a variety of current issues 48 times a year. Congressional Quarterly, 1414 22nd St., N.W., Washington, D.C. 20037.

The *National Journal*, published 50 times a year, provides weekly reports on current national issues and more in-depth reports on major topics. National Journal, 1730 M St. N.W., Washington, D.C. 20036.

Published on a daily basis while Congress is in session is the *Congressional Record*, which can be obtained through your senator or representative in Congress. This publication provides a day-to-day account of what happens in Congress (and some things that don't happen but that legislators wish had happened). The *Record* also contains a large amount of reprinted material, including editorials. The daily volumes present a storage problem and far too much material for most editorial writers. One way to use the *Record* is to glance through the index that arrives every 10 days or so. It does not take long to look up your state and district legislators to see what they have said or inserted into the *Record*. Current, and especially regional, topics also can be checked quickly, as can the names of editorial writers' newspapers and the cities in which the editorials are published. It is nice to know when you have been reprinted in the *Record*.

Data Bases

Students at university libraries and some editorial writers through their newspapers' computers have access to large collections of information through computerized data bases. Larger newspapers are likely to be tied in with one of the national news data bases. DIALOG offers access to more than 200 data bases and to articles in more than 40,000 journals and magazines. LEXUS, from Mead Data Central, offers full-text access to more than 160 newspapers, magazines and newsletters. Vu/Text, a Knight-Ridder data base, serves 75 or so newspapers. These three tend to be expensive, but both LEXUS and Vu/Text offer lower cost educational rates for professors and students. Compuserve and GEnie offer access, at moderate cost, to U.S. and international wire services, encyclopedias, electronic mail and other information.[18] Broader bases, still in the less-expensive range, are provided by Knowledge Index (offered by DIALOG) and BRS After Dark (Bibliographic Research Service). Each of these contains more than 100 of the most popular services. Telebase also offers a large selection of resources through EasyNet.[19]

To use these more modest services, a prospective user needs to call the service and ask for a user kit and a password. The kit will explain how to proceed. In general, once on line, users are presented with a bibliography or series of menus to select the subject area to be searched. Costs depend on on-line time and number of articles selected for downloading to the printer. Searches through these data bases can be helpful to editorial writers, but time on the computer can be expensive, especially if they are not proficient in seeking what they want.

You don't need a computer to use the old-fashioned *Reader's Guide to Periodical Literature* (which indexes about 200 magazines) or the *New York Times Index*. The Gale Research Co. produces an annual, *The Directory of Directories*, which provides a guide to nearly 10,000 directories. The *American Journalism Review* annually publishes a "Directory of Selected News Sources." Lois Horowitz has published a book titled *Where to Look*.

Permanent Reference Materials

Every editorial office, and certainly every good-sized library, has a supply of reference materials that include an encyclopedia of fairly recent date, *Webster's Third International Dictionary* (or the Second if the writers are purists), foreign language dictionaries, a thesaurus, a quality atlas, a music dictionary or encyclopedia, a biographical dictionary (or *Current Biography*), a geographical dictionary, a medical dictionary, a legal dictionary (or at least a media law dictionary), one or more annual almanacs, a book of quotations, *Who's Who in America*, probably *Who Was Who*, a regional *Who's Who*, the *Congressional Dictionary*, the *United States Government Manual*, the annual *Statistical Abstracts of the United States*, the *Official Postal Guide* (plus a book of ZIP codes), a state directory usually referred to as the "Blue Book," city directories going back as many years as possible, telephone books from assorted cities, the Bible, perhaps the works of Shakespeare.

Books on Language Usage

Here are a few books on language usage that may be helpful to editorial writers:

The Elements of Style, Third Edition. William L. Strunk Jr. and E. B. White (New York: Macmillan, 1979, paperbound).

Working with Words: A Concise Handbook for Media Writers and Editors. Brian S. Brooks and James L. Pinson (New York: St. Martin's Press, 1989, paperbound).

Dictionary of Modern English Usage. H. W. Fowler. Second revised Edition, by E. Gowers (Oxford: Oxford University Press, 1987). (Paperbound also available.)

Dictionary of Contemporary Usage. William and Mary Morris. Second Edition (New York: Harper & Row, 1985, paperbound).

Modern American Usage: A Guide. Reissue. Jacques Barzun. Wilson Follett, ed. (New York: Hill and Wang, 1966, paperbound).

Writer's Guide and Index to English. Eighth edition. Wilma R. and David R. Ebbitt (Chicago: Scott, Foresman and Co., 1990). (Also available in paperbound.)

Watch Your Language. Theodore M. Bernstein (New York: Atheneum, 1976, paperbound).

The Associated Press Stylebook and Libel Manual (paperbound).

CULTURE

Editorial writers should know something about and be comfortable at a symphony concert, whether the orchestra is playing Beethoven or some composer whose work features only drums, cymbals and whistles. Writers should be somewhat knowledgeable about art and be comfortable at an exhibit of Monet or some local artist. They should know something about various religions and the divisions among religions even though they may not be comfortable at services that are much different from their own, if they attend them.

Editorial writers may scoff at television as trivial and entertainment-oriented. But nearly every family has at least one television set, and one show may be watched by as many as 60 million Americans. If editorial writers want to know what their fellow citizens do and think about in their leisure hours, they had best watch the tube enough to know what's on. They should watch the three network news broadcasts, the talk shows, CNN, a sampling of the cable channels and enough local broadcasts to know the types of news their readers are getting. They will never know when television is presenting quality programs unless they read *TV Guide* or the daily TV listings. Columns by television critics are worth following.

Much of radio is an intellectual wasteland. News is sketchy, except for all-news stations. But writers should know the types of songs the younger generation and not-so-young generations are listening to. They may never write an editorial about any of the top-40 tunes or country music, but they almost certainly will write about the people who listen to this music. Writers ought to tune in from time to time to the call-in programs. Public radio and public television offer more intellectual stimulation, with more extensive news coverage and programs on topics worthy of editorial comment. I would guess that many editorial writers listen to "All Things Considered," an hour and a half or more of news, comment and reports on a variety of topics aired on public radio; and that they watch the MacNeil/Lehrer NewsHour on public television.

Writers also need to keep abreast of the movies—not necessarily seeing every major show but making certain they are aware of what is being seen by their readers. And the newspaper comics should be followed. Most comics may be intended for entertainment, but they often provide insights into what is going on in the younger, or older, or middle generation. Some are works of art. Some carry political messages that are as forthright and controversial as any editorial on an editorial page. Editorial writers should look in on MTV.

CONCLUSION

Perhaps more than anything else, editorial writers must come to editorial writing equipped with curiosity and a good memory. They must want to find out about everything that comes within touch or sight or hearing. Editorial writers who hope to address the human condition must know about that condition in all its aspects. The specific list of books or newspapers or television programs that writers tackle is not as important as the open, searching attitude good writers bring to whatever they approach. If they are restless, energetic and curious, enough material worth examining will come to their attention to keep them on a productive search for information, insight and truth that will last a lifetime.

If what writers find in their quest goes "in one ear and out the other," the time they have spent will have been wasted. Writers must assimilate and remember—or at least remember where they can find what they want. Shakespeare and the Bible may be worth reading and rereading, and so may a few other books. But demands on the time of editorial writers are too great, and life is too short, to have to spend time searching for information and ideas that they should have tucked away in their heads or for materials that they should have at their editorial elbows.

QUESTIONS AND EXERCISES

1. What do you regard as the ideal undergraduate preparation for a potential editorial writer? For a journalist?

2. The American Council on Education for Journalism, the national accrediting agency for journalism schools, is reluctant to allow a school to give more than a minimum number of credit hours for internships because the council considers that most of the journalism credit hours should be earned under close supervision of faculty members. Do you think that this limitation is reasonable? Why or why not?

3. Among the periodicals you are acquainted with, which do you think would prove most beneficial to an editorial writer? Why?

4. What reference books and books on writing do you consider most appropriate for your own personal library?

5. What computerized data bases are available at your school?

Chapter 5

Who Is This Victorian "We"?

Who would not be an editor? To write
The magic we *of such enormous might:*
To be so great beyond the common span
It takes the plural to express the man.

—J. G. Saxe in The Press (1855)[1]

Agood deal of confusion exists among readers, and even among newspaper people, over the identity or identities behind the editorial "we."

That confusion is reflected in a humorous piece that *The Masthead* reprinted from *Quill* magazine. It was written by Fred C. Hobson Jr., professor at the University of North Carolina. Here is a portion of it:

It was not intended this way, but when I started to write we got so pronouely—er, profoundly—confused we changed my mind.

Besides, when we sat down at my typewriter, I first-personally felt singular.

Hopefully now, what I say, you see—in an editorial, why am I we? Enough poetics. Now for how I—er, we—got confused.

We had an interview the other day. It went fine until we wondered if the person I was interviewing were plural too. If so, then I was we and he was they. But if I am we and he is they, then how the hell is *he*?

And should was be were, if I be we? Or is be are, if she be they? . . .

After all this, I've decided to stick to the editorial I. You should too. After all, there is an old adage . . . we Southerners especially like. . . . You can't legislate plurality.[2]

This confusion did not exist in the days of the Popular and Populist press in the 19th Century. When the *New York Tribune* published an editorial in the mid-1800s, readers knew who wrote it, or thought they did. Subscribers read the *Tribune* to find out what Horace Greeley had to say, and, if someone else on his staff wrote it, everyone assumed that it expressed Greeley's point of view.

When the days of the great editors began to pass, following the Civil War, it became less clear who was writing the editorials and for whom the editorials spoke. As the era of corporate newspapers emerged, editorial writers retreated anonymously into their ivory towers and took to writing what a publisher or an editorial board asked them to write. When Greeley had said "we," he meant "I." When these writers used "we," they may have meant the views of "the publisher, the editor, an editorial board, or even a member of the staff or a newspaper reader who has persuaded the board of the rightness of a certain position."[3] The purpose of this chapter is to discuss who are the speakers of editorials on American newspapers today and to examine competing arguments over for whom editorials ought to speak.

THE CASE FOR THE UNSIGNED EDITORIAL

Surveys that show that a large majority of editorials are published anonymously suggest that the owners and publishers of most newspapers want their editorials to speak for someone or something other than an individual writer. One survey found that more than 70 percent of 178 editors and editorial writers said they never signed editorials. Sixteen percent said they signed them occasionally; 14 percent signed regularly. More signatures appeared in smaller than in larger papers.[4]

One reason advanced for unsigned editorials is that, even when written by a specific editorial writer, they reflect policy set by the paper's owner or the publisher. Robert U. Brown, editor and publisher of *Editor & Publisher*, asked: " . . . whose name should be put on the editorial when the owner-publisher—whose prerogative cannot be questioned—says 'tomorrow we will endorse such-and-such candidate and I want a strong editorial endorsing him'?"[5] An editorial writer may write all of the words of an editorial, but the editorial speaks for the publisher. No editorial writer, on the basis of his or her own convictions, "has a right to demand a share of ownership's private forum," Floyd A. Bernard of the *Port Huron* (Mich.) *Times Herald* has written.[6]

But with the trend toward group ownership, publisher-domination of editorial pages may be waning, if results of a poll conducted in 1988 are an indication. Twenty-seven percent of editorial writers on family- or independently-owned newspapers reported that their owners or publishers exerted little or no influence in determining priority given to editorial topics. In contrast, little or no influence was reported by 72 percent of writers on private group-owned papers and by 77 percent on public group-owned papers. The poll also revealed what appeared to be a widening gap between the political views of publishers and editorial writers. In a 1979 survey 62 percent of editorial writers had said that their views and their publishers' were similar on most issues. In 1989 that percentage dropped to 47. The percentage of those who agreed with their publishers only about half the time increased from 24 to 33.[7]

These figures seemed in line with the results of a survey in 1980 that showed that 85 percent of group editors did not ever consult with group headquarters before taking a controversial editorial stand; 11 percent said they did consult. In contrast, 71 percent of editors on independently owned papers said they consulted with owners, compared to 27 percent who did not consult.[8] (Of course, the local owner or publisher was likely to be in an adjoining office.) A symposium conducted by *The Masthead* found that 11 out of 12 groups surveyed reported that editorial policies were set at the local level. A representative of the Gannett

Co., owners of more daily newspapers than any other group, reported that local editors and publishers were free to determine their own editorial policies. He said that Gannett asked local executives a lot of questions about business and technology, "but how the newspapers stand on this or that editorial policy is *not* one of the queries because that would violate the local autonomy that has been a keystone of the Group policy ever since the late Frank E. Gannett began accumulating newspapers. . . ."[9]

Another of the large groups, then known as Knight and later to become Knight-Ridder, "chooses its editors carefully and gives them their heads," an editor reported. He said the group had no "corporate line" or "group line" on editorial policy, "but neither does the top management of the organization have a 'don't-give-a-damn' view of the individual paper's editorial policies." For months editorial writers would not hear from headquarters. When they did, comment was informal, and editors who disagreed with the comment were free to state their views and go on about their business.[10]

The only decidedly different report came from Merrill Lindsay, president of Lindsay-Schaub Newspapers, who said that local papers had full responsibility for policy on local issues, but, on state, national and international issues, a group of editorial writers at a centralized office researched and wrote the editorials.[11]

An article in *Journalism Quarterly* questioned whether local papers were as autonomous as the respondents to the survey had insisted. After studying presidential endorsements from 1960 through 1972, the authors found that the vast majority of groups had generally homogeneous endorsement patterns in those elections—data that "would appear to contradict clearly" the proposition advanced by representatives of the groups that they were independent in their political endorsement policies.[12] The study did not attempt to look at endorsements at state or local levels or at editorial stands on other issues, where group influence might be expected to be less.

If an increasing number of editorials do not reflect policies of the owners, and perhaps not even the publishers', for whom do they speak?

The most often heard explanation for unsigned institutional editorials is that they express more than one person's opinion. *Editor & Publisher*'s Brown pointed out that many times an editorial is not the product of one writer's opinion "but the amalgam of thought pounded out in an editorial conference of several people." He wondered what purpose it would serve to attach to the editorial "the name of the technician (a skilled editorial writer, albeit) who was assigned to express in words the agreed-upon thought or policy?"[13] The opinion might be a general one worked out over time among writers on a paper, or it might be worked out on a single issue during a morning editorial conference. In any case the writer would be expressing a combination of ideas. It might then make as much sense to put every staff member's name on the editorial as that of the actual writer. Sometimes the actual writing of an editorial will end up being the work of more than one person. Most editorials must pass through an editor or a publisher before they go into print. Since the editor or the publisher has the final say, the end product may be slightly, or greatly, different from the original version. Whose name, or names, should go on in this case? The original writer might not want to be identified with the editorial after the editor or the publisher has made substantial changes.

Sometimes institutional editorials are explained as something more than the sum of the opinions of the members of the editorial page staff. "Editorials express the opinion of an institution, sometimes older than the writer," a Florida editor argued in response to a bill in the Florida Legislature that would have required editorial writers to sign their names.[14] "Editorial writers come and go. . . . But The Paper stays in the community for decades, through depression and prosperity," another editor wrote.[15]

Some defenders contend that unsigned editorials carry more weight with readers because they are not just the personal opinion of an individual. "A signed editorial carries about as much punch as a letter to the editor," Ann Merriman of the *Richmond* (Va.) *News Leader* wrote in arguing that signed editorials have no place under the masthead of a newspaper's editorial page, "even though it would be a good thing if every editorial were written as if it were to be signed."[16]

What about the one-person editorial page staff where it is fairly obvious who is writing the editorials? When Michael J. Birkner took over as editorial writer for the *Concord* (N.H.) *Monitor*, he wrote a bylined column introducing himself. He explained that he would become the "anonymous voice" that henceforth would appear every day in the upper-left-hand corner of the opinion page. "The anonymous voice representing the opinion of this newspaper is, of course, not truly anonymous," he wrote. "A fallible, flesh and blood person can be found behind the 600 or so words that fill the editorial space every day. . . . The editorial 'we,' in this case, is me."[17]

EDITORIAL BOARDS

On a number, probably a growing number, of newspapers the editorial "we" is an editorial board. In some cases it remains anonymous to readers, but in other cases the masthead on the editorial page identifies the names and positions of board members. The makeup of boards varies widely. In some instances the board is limited to members of the editorial page staff. In addition some boards include an editor with responsibility for both news and editorial departments, the publisher (or general manager) or representatives of other departments of the newspaper. In some instances not all staff members who write editorials are included on the board. Some newspapers have experimented with asking people outside the newspaper to serve on editorial boards. The *Hartford Courant* has invited readers to spend two to three months as visiting members of its board, and to participate in all deliberations. (The part-time job paid an honorarium of approximately $200 a week.)[18]

The main purpose of an editorial board is to set general editorial policy. In addition, a board might determine editorial stands on major issues and decide on editorial endorsements. The power that boards exert over the day-to-day editorials varies greatly from paper to paper. Meetings may be formal or informal, regular or irregular.

Richard T. Cole, a professor of public relations, has suggested that the editorial board is a "great charade" or at least a "polite fiction" on most newspapers. Citing the two major dailies in Detroit, he wrote in *The Masthead*: "Neither has a formal editorial board, although I would venture to say I could introduce you to dozens of politicians, business, labor, association and public relations leader who would say they have appeared before them. There are no voting members, no quorums, no amendments, no regular meetings, no public notice. Editorial chiefs assemble colleagues and staff to hear a case. My guess is that if an important person insists on meeting the editorial board, the meeting gets called an 'editorial board meeting,' and the innocent fiction lives on. Long live the editorial board."[19]

Cole's experience may reflect the practices, or lack of practices, of some newspapers, but it certainly does not coincide with my perception, based on examining editorial pages from across the country. It seems evident to me that more and more newspapers are establishing formal editorial boards to make clear to policy-setters and readers just who speaks for the editorial "we."

A few newspapers have opened their editorial board meetings to the public. George Neavoll recalled that editorial colleagues around the country were "aghast" when they heard of his open-door policy at the *Wichita Eagle-Beacon*. "It's good for the editorial writers, myself included, to have real, live readers in our midst as we make our editorial decisions," he said. "Their presence reminds us that our editorials are written for people, after all, not for some bloodless amalgam without form and void."[20]

THE CASE FOR THE SIGNED EDITORIAL

The most persistently heard objection to unsigned editorials, and the most frequently heard argument for signed editorials, is that editorials are generally the work of individuals and that, while they may reflect some broad newspaper policies, the thinking and the words that go into them are more important than any general philosophy. A flamboyant argument along these lines, in the form of an attack on "editorial transubstantiation," was made by Sam Reynolds of the *Missoulian* in Missoula, Mont. In Roman Catholic and Eastern Orthodox rites, bread and wine are transubstantiated (or converted) into the body and blood of Christ although the appearance remains unchanged. "I view editorial transubstantiation with less awe," he wrote. "Editorial transubstantiation is the basis for editorial anonymity. It is not a miracle; it is nonsense." He argued that "flesh-and-blood human beings" write editorials, and usually it is only one of them who does so. How does the work of a human being become the product of an institution? "The answer must lie in faith, not fact," Reynolds said. In the end editorial transubstantiation "is merely a lie; a lie eloquently defended by its many priests, but in the end a complete lie."

When Reynolds switched from unsigned to signed editorials he found that he was no longer blamed for editorials that someone else had written and that the advertising staff no longer had to "fend off attacks from persons aroused by my editorials." He also found his editorials had more influence, and he felt that signing editorials was more honest than pretending that editorials represented an institution.[21]

A similarly rewarding experience was reported by George J. Hebert of the *Norfolk* (Va.) *Ledger-Star*, which began attaching writers' names to opinion pieces in 1976. The switch attracted wide attention in editorial writing circles. In announcing the change, the editors said readers had told them that they wanted to know who was writing the editorials. "There will be real people with real names on our end of what we hope will be a continuing exchange of views between us and our readers," the editors said. They hoped to give their writers freer rein and an opportunity to "have more time to probe issues and sharpen their comments."

The change elicited almost unanimous approval by readers. The paper added to this emphasis on its writers by inserting sketches of their faces alongside the editorials.[22]

The most elaborate case for signed editorials was a two-part series in *The Masthead* written by Professor Warren G. Bovee of Marquette University.[23] Bovee set out to debunk what he saw were seven myths about editorial anonymity. The first was that newspapers traditionally have run unsigned editorials. Our look into the history of the editorial page in Chapter 1 has shown that anonymity is only about a century old. The second myth was that editorials represent the views of the paper, not an individual. Bovee argued that, "until the time arrives when editorial positions are decided by the total personnel of a newspaper. . . . it is misleading to attribute those positions to 'The Paper' . . . " While publishers might set broad guidelines, he likened them to "the ball field within which the editorial writers must still decide how to play the game." He said that "editorial writers say more than most publishers would ever think of saying."

The third myth, that editorials represent an editorial conference point of view, could be resolved by all members signing the editorial, he argued. A fourth myth, that "anonymity is necessary to protect the writer from verbal and physical abuses," Bovee saw as the "real, secret reason" why readers think editors do not sign editorials. His comment was that writers ought to be as subject to "phone calls, crank letters, crosses burned on the lawn and stones thrown through picture windows" as readers whose signed letters also appear on editorial pages. My own experience is that this fear of personal abuse figures minimally in editorial anonymity. Most editorial writers I know would appreciate more public recognition.

A fifth myth is that, if an editorial is signed, it becomes only a personal article or column. But Bovee contended that signed pieces by William Randolph Hearst and Jenkin Lloyd Jones were regarded as editorials. As to a sixth myth, that unsigned editorials carry more weight, Bovee argued that the impact depends more on what the editorial says than on who signs it. To the seventh myth, that there are no good reasons for signing editorials, Bovee replied that signing might help overcome reader mistrust of newspapers, giving writers greater freedom to write. "If the occasion demands it," he said, "the signed piece can be as personal and informal as a love letter, or it can be as formal and impersonal as a doctoral dissertation." Finally, he argued, when a paper has a number of editorial writers, there are bound to be occasions on which the writers disagree with one another. By allowing each, with a byline, to offer his or her view, the paper would have a more interesting editorial page.

When editors of *The Masthead* asked 11 editorial writers to describe who was the "we" for whom they spoke, nine remained firmly committed to speaking anonymously for the newspaper, two expressed some interest in departing from anonymity, but only one took a strong stand for signed editorials. That one, Everett Ray Call of the *Emporia* (Kan.) *Gazette*, argued that writers who sign their names are likely to take more pride in their work and make more effort to check their facts than writers who know they will not directly be associated with what they write. He also thought that, in a time when people feel overwhelmed by institutions and readers see newspapers as corporate units, signing editorials helps readers relate more closely to their newspapers. While the *Gazette* had gained a name for personal journalism in the early 20th century when William Allen White had become editor and publisher, the practice of signing editorials came much later, following publication of an anthology that was supposed to include only editorials of William Allen White. After the book was published, White noticed that about two-thirds of the editorials in the last section had not been written by him but by his son, William L. White. "Since then," Call wrote, "initials have been used at the end of editorials that appear in the Gazette."[24]

A case for using initials, at least sometimes, was offered by Robert Schmuhl, associate professor of American studies at the University of Notre Dame.[25] His interest in identifying writers grew out of his students' reports that they found editorials "bland and boring." One answer to "Why?" was: "It's as though there's no one behind what's being said."

"Initialing editorials provides an authorial recognition in an understated yet useful way," Schmuhl wrote. "The writer receives credit for composing the editorial, while the finished product appears in a manner quite distinct from a bylined column or even a signed editorial." He hoped that "this modest attribution" would encourage previously anonymous writers to write in a "more engaging, spirited and possibly more persuasive way." The newspaper would appear to have a human voice. "We" would continue to be used. Editorial writers' names would be listed in the masthead.

A COMPROMISE—BYLINED ARTICLES AND COLUMNS

Some of the fire may have been taken out of the debate over signed editorials by an increasing use of articles and columns bearing the names of editorial writers. Publishers have been able to give their writers public recognition and increased opportunities to express their individual views without giving up the principle of the institutionalized editorial. One survey of editorial writers found that almost all of them wrote signed articles, as contrasted with signed editorials, at least on occasion.[26]

The advantages most cited in the survey were that signed articles help make the editorial page more human, allow for more casual and informal writing and provide more space than editorials for background or firsthand accounts, especially about local matters. Less often mentioned was the function of the signed article as an expression of a writer's views that might be at variance with the paper's editorial policy. This function can provide an outlet for frustrated editorial writers, but it also can cause problems. Some publishers may be willing to allow writers to express contrary opinions; some publishers may not. Some publishers may be willing to allow writers to disagree on some issues but not on others.

Most publishers probably would have no objection to the balance between signed and unsigned pieces that we maintained on *The Columbian*, in Vancouver, Wash. In my later years there, when there were three of us writing for the editorial page, I urged other writers to write bylined articles and on occasion to write pro-con articles, with each person signing one of the articles. We did not use those articles to express opinions directly opposed to the official editorial policy, but through the use of the byline we gained a greater feeling of editorial freedom for ourselves.

If most newspapers have been reluctant to give up the anonymous editorial "we," they have at least largely abandoned the "we" in personal columns and in obvious references to individuals. The change in philosophy on this point can be illustrated by the case of David V. Felts, who wrote a personal column for half a century for the Lindsay-Schaub newspapers. After his retirement Felts wrote an article for *The Masthead* in which he said: "I chose to use first-person plural 'we' in order to avoid the capital I, which seemed at the time . . . to suggest a vanity I did not care to confess, or an arrogance I would deny. So I rejected Teddy Roosevelt's 'I' and instead went along with Queen Victoria's 'We.'" However, Felts acknowledged, logical extension of the "editorial we" can be embarrassing and even ridiculous. He recalled that on one occasion a radio disc jockey, who was a friend of his, quoted from his column. Felts wrote: "I had written, so he read, 'When we stepped on the bathroom scales this morning. . . .' Then my friend observed: 'Oh, well, couples who weigh together, stay together.'" Felts then wrote: "Should I someday be assigned to one of those golden typewriters in the great city room in the sky to write celestial chit-chat, I will use the first person singular pronoun, even if only a modest, chastened lower-case i. Queen Victoria probably will not be amused, but Teddy Roosevelt surely will be 'dee-lighted.'"[27]

There is no historical evidence, or even a suggestion, that Horace Greeley could have done what Dave Felts did—look back years later and laugh at a ridiculous use of "we." Greeley's editorials abounded with "we's." In 1846, for example, Greeley was recalling the first election in which he had taken an interest, the presidential race of 1824: "We were but thirteen when this took place. . . ."[28]

PERSONAL EXPERIENCES

In my 12 years on *The Columbian*, we ran editorials that were not signed, presumably to indicate to readers that they represented the opinions of the newspaper, not just one person. But I would have counted myself as among those who did not consult with the owners in most cases. My co-publishers and I had spent considerable time before they hired me sounding out each others' views. When they decided we were compatible, they, in effect, handed me the editorial "we" to use as I wished (subject of course to cancellation at any time they thought we should go our separate ways). On occasion the publishers were not wholly pleased with what I had written, but for the most part they kept silent. At one point one of the publishers thought the paper should be taking a stronger stand in favor of legalizing marijuana, but he made no attempt to change the policy. On another occasion I found out several months later that this publisher had not been in sympathy with the paper's strident opposition to plans to expand Portland International Airport onto a square mile of fill in the Columbia River. But he had made no effort to soften or change our editorial stand.

You learn who the real "we" is during elections, especially presidential ones. In the 1972 election my publishers had their minds set on endorsing Richard Nixon for re-election, and neither the other editorial writer on the paper nor I could budge them from that decision. We argued no endorsement, since we saw neither Nixon nor George McGovern as meriting our support. I wrote an editorial pointing out the weaknesses of both candidates, but the publishers wouldn't consider it. I suggested that it be published as a signed article elsewhere on the editorial page. The publishers said No; readers might be confused by conflicting viewpoints on the page. Neither the other writer nor I was required to write the

Nixon editorial. A semi-retired former managing editor, who had written editorials over the years, accepted the assignment.

The only other disagreement over who was "we" in those 12 years also involved an election, this one for a local judgeship. The publishers had their candidate. Two other editorial writers and I preferred another candidate, although we would have settled for kind words for both. In this instance the publishers agreed to look at an editorial that said either candidate would be a good judge. What emerged in print, however, was an editorial, using many of the words I had written, that added praise for the publishers' choice and a firm conclusion backing their candidate. That was one occasion when it would have been impossible to have put one person's name on an editorial.

CONCLUSION

The pendulum that had swung so far from the personal journalism of Horace Greeley to the anonymity of the corporate newspaper has begun to swing back. A small, but seemingly growing, number of newspapers publish signed or initialed editorials. Many more promote the identities of editorial writers through encouraging signed articles and columns, and by listing names on mastheads. Some writers are allowed to express opinions contrary to their newspapers' official policies.

Editorial writers are getting out of their offices and becoming better known in their communities. Editorial writers are also strengthening their positions on editorial boards. Editors on group newspapers think they have more independence from management in setting editorial policy than do editors on independent papers. On all papers, personal expertise provides the best opportunity for editorial writers to achieve stronger and more public voices. In an era of complex issues, writers who know what they are talking about stand a good chance of convincing not only their readers but also their editors and publishers. They stand a good chance of getting a piece of the editorial "we."

Whether editorials are signed or unsigned, newspapers perform a service to their readers—and bolster their own credibility—when they spell out exactly who determines editorial policy. Readers should have the right to know who is telling them what to think and what to do.

In even the most compatible relationships between editorial writers and publishers, writers are almost certain to find out from time to time that, as smart and knowledgeable as they think they are, they are not the final boss. If they have too many disagreements, they need to find another boss or try some other line of work.

I asked students in one of my editorial writing classes about the types of disagreement they thought they could tolerate with a publisher. Almost to a person, they said they would quit if asked to write an editorial contrary to their opinions on apartheid or abortion, but they generally would not quit because of disagreement over a president, a local judge or a school bond measure. "I don't think that editorials endorsing presidential candidates really make that much impact on the voters," one student said, but on abortion she would tell her publisher that, "through my religious belief and moral attitudes, I could not write an editorial that supported taking away legalized abortion." She said she would have asked "very nicely" to have someone else write it, and "take the consequences of my actions."[29]

QUESTIONS AND EXERCISES

1. Try to find a newspaper with signed or initialed editorials and read them for three or four days. Compare them in terms of tone and style with unsigned editorials on the same subjects published in other newspapers. Do you think that readers would respond differently to these editorials?

2. Look through a number of editorial and op-ed pages of papers in your area. Try to find bylined opinion articles by editorial staff members. Do these articles express opinions that differ from the papers' editorials? Analyze how a reader is likely to respond to specific editorials and opinion articles that express different views.

3. Select an editorial with which you disagree and write a signed opinion piece expressing your view that would be suitable to publish alongside the editorial.

4. Select several editorials that use the editorial "we" in referring to the newspaper's opinion. Does the "we" clearly convey the impression of a corporate opinion behind the editorial? Rewrite the sentences to make the same point without the use of "we."

5. Can you find a column in which the writer refers to himself or herself with the Victorian "we"? Could "I" have been used just as well?

6. Write a letter to an editorial writer on one of the papers in your area to ask about specific instances in which he or she and the editor or publisher might have disagreed on issues. How were the disagreements resolved? Did the writer end up producing an editorial he or she disagreed with? Was he or she allowed or encouraged to write a dissenting opinion? How often and on what kinds of issues has disagreement occurred?

7. Can you uncover, perhaps by reading *Editor & Publisher*, instances in which editorial writers have resigned or moved to non-editorial positions because of disagreement over editorial policy?

Chapter 6

Relations with Publishers

Editorial-page editors and their publishers should fight. How else can a paper consistently come up with good editorials? "Good" in the sense of researched, definitive, you-can-tell-where-we-stand editorials. Arguing helps clarify positions and quickly knocks down ones that are poorly defended.

—MEG DOWNEY, POUGHKEEPSIE (N.Y.) JOURNAL[1]

When they drew up the Bill of Rights in the late 1780s, the Founding Fathers did not have to worry about whether they intended freedom of the press to apply to publishers or to editors because most of the printers who produced periodicals, books, pamphlets and handbills were owner-editors. The authors of the First Amendment anticipated, in the words of Hugh B. Patterson Jr. of the *Arkansas Gazette*, "that the editor would most likely be the owner whose resources as well as reputation would be at stake; that newspapers would be vigorous critics and advocates on public questions; that newspapers would generally be locally owned and controlled; and that readers would have available from different publications a variety of views, sometimes directly competitive, from which to choose, whether the question was local, regional or national in scope."[2]

Today the editor and the owner (or publisher) most often are not the same person. With the demise of the owner-editor, the relationship between editor and publisher became what Bernard Kilgore called "a new kind of problem." Kilgore experienced the problem from both sides, as editor and then later publisher of the *Wall Street Journal*. "The question which somebody is likely to ask," Kilgore said, is "whether publishers are necessary."[3] In any other industry, he said, the job parallel to that of publisher would be clear: He or she would hire and fire. But in the newspaper business, "that's where we get into all the trouble. . . . A publisher just does not hire and fire editors because our business is not that kind of business." The difference is that the product a newspaper sells is "a completely intangible thing." Newspaper people should remind themselves that all the physical plant and machinery around the newspaper business provide only the package or container of the product, "just something to wrap up the ideas that editors have" and carry these ideas to the public. But the newspaper business has become "a great big manufacturing operation and great big selling operation," Kilgore said. Consequently, "the general management of a newspaper has more and more come to be regarded as a job for a manufacturer or a salesman, and the editorial function . . . has tended to become a secondary consideration."[4]

LOCAL VS. GROUP OWNERSHIP

The era of the local family-owned newspaper may look rosier in retrospect than it actually was. Many papers did not make enough profit to produce a good product. Some of the owner-publishers did not know what a good journalistic product was, and some didn't care. But the publishers were products of their communities and those who wished could do what they wanted with their papers without worrying about satisfying a bigger boss somewhere else. The publisher-editor who runs the whole show "in theory . . . is the happiest of mortals, if he can keep his separate selves from warring with one another," wrote Donald L. Breed, editor-publisher of the *Freeport* (Ill.) *Journal-Standard*.[5] Even those owner-publishers who did not write editorials tended to dominate their papers. Editorial writers tended to be "anonymous wretches," as Ralph Coghlan of the *St. Louis Post-Dispatch* referred to writers who attended the first meeting of the National Conference of Editorial Writers in 1947. Indeed, a survey of editorial writers in 1951 found that fewer than 50 percent thought they could stand up for what they believed without risking financial disaster and 63 percent said they wrote opinions that were not always their own.[6]

Since then, group ownership has come to most cities with daily newspapers. Most publishers are no longer home-grown. Often they are sent in for a few years, then transferred elsewhere. Another publisher from another community is brought in. Many of these group publishers are strictly business people.

Nevertheless, results of a survey sponsored by the American Society of Newspaper Editors suggest that group ownership may offer some advantages for editors and editorial writers. A survey found that editors on group newspapers thought they had more freedom in determining editorial policy than did editors on independently owned papers. Before taking a stand on a controversial issue, 85 percent of group editors said they did not consult with group headquarters, while only 27 percent of independent editors said they did not consult with the owners. Of course one reason may be that the editor on an independent paper has only to go to the next office to find out the views of management, while the editor on a group paper has to contact group headquarters hundreds or thousands of miles away. When asked what happened when they disagreed with management, 32 percent of the group editors said they wrote what they wanted to, while only 8 percent of independent editors did so.[7] These figures suggest that out-of-town ownership and a non-newspaper-oriented publisher may provide opportunities for editorial writers on group newspapers to emerge less cautiously and more outspokenly from publisher's offices and editorial conference rooms.

An editorial page, however, can be restricted as much by financial as by editorial restraints. When a newspaper is locally owned, the publisher can determine the profit levels that seem proper and desirable. But, with group newspapers, budgets and required profit-margins tend to be set at group headquarters. In addition, with groups and major newspapers going public and selling stock on the market, owners are becoming even more concerned about profits. If profits lag, the stock is likely to fall in value. If the newspaper ventures into an area of controversy in its news or editorial columns—and perhaps stakes its reputation in tackling a sensitive public issue—the paper's stock may skid in value. Robert T. Pittman of the *St. Petersburg* (Fla.) *Times* perceived "a basic conflict" between an editor's responsibility to readers and the responsibility of an investor-owned newspaper to its stockholders: "What's good for Media General stock isn't necessarily what's good for the country."[8]

Defenders of groups contend that ownership of several papers allows the groups to use their combined resources to enable an individual paper to stand up to the pressures of advertisers or other special interests. That may be true, if the owners are sufficiently dedicated to the newspaper business to be willing to forgo some of the profits while the paper fights its battle. But, if the publishers and groups must answer to stockholders who are interested in profit, not journalism, it may not be possible to remain so idealistic.

David Halberstam, in *The Powers That Be*, noted that the Washington Post Company had gone public only two days before publisher Katharine Graham had to decide whether to defy the government and publish the Pentagon Papers. "The shadow of the stock hung very much over the editorial deliberations," Halberstam wrote. "The timing for everyone concerned could not have been worse. In addition to everything else, there was one little clause in the legal agreement for the sale of the stock that said that the sale could be canceled if a catastrophic event struck the paper." If the government halted distribution of the *Post*, that might be such an event; so might an indictment for contempt of court. The effect on the stock was one of the matters considered by the *Post* in deciding to follow the lead of the *New York Times* in publishing the papers.[9] Court injunctions obtained by the federal government temporarily halted publication, but a 6-3 decision by the U.S. Supreme Court removed the injunctions and allowed the newspapers to resume publication.

In a growing number of instances newspapers and other media have become only minor parts of corporations with investments in a variety of industries. At best, the media owned by these conglomerates are viewed as business operations that must produce their share of the corporation's revenue. At worst, the conglomerate may view profitable media as sources of funds to shore up its weaker operations—or, as ABC Inc. did with ABC News, a conglomerate may chop funds from a media operation because of weaknesses elsewhere in the system.[10] Corporations that were once primarily newspaper-oriented have become involved in telephone book publishing, timber, cable television, billboards, Bibles, television, radio and magazines. Diversity may help ensure profitability and stability, but it also tends to produce a corporative hierarchy that is primarily business- rather than newspaper-oriented. Basic decision-making is removed farther from the editor and editorial writer. When these large corporations are committed to doing a good job in news and editorial operations they have the resources to do so. But when they are not committed to doing a good job, chances are slim for influencing their editorial priorities.

THE PUBLISHER'S ROLE

Weighing on the publisher's mind almost as heavily as making a profit is maintaining "harmonious relations" among employees. Publishers like to run smooth operations and generally do not like to employ personalities that clash. Publishers dislike friction between news and advertising or between news and editorial operations. Publishers tend to subscribe to the philosophy expressed in a publication titled *The Economics of the American Newspaper*, which suggests to news and editorial people that the entire newspaper staff is in this together and that no one can benefit without everyone helping. So why doesn't everyone cooperate and forget differences of opinion and interest?[11]

One of the threats to the why-can't-everyone-be-friends atmosphere is posed by the publisher's responsibility to negotiate with labor unions. Most editorial writers do not have to worry about coming into conflict with the publisher in contract negotiations, since most are excluded from newsroom organized labor groups. But a publisher who is worried about a threatening strike or angered by what he or she sees as an unfair tilt of federal or state labor relations laws may hold a strong opinion about what editorial writers ought to be saying concerning organized labor. More than one newspaper has departed from its generally moderate-to-liberal social philosophy when the subject of labor has arisen.

Since a publisher's first concern is often to function successfully in the economy, he or she is also likely to have firm views on business topics. "There is one special interest always present, and that is the pro-capitalist bias of a newspaper," publisher-editor Donald L. Breed wrote. "Privately-owned and operated newspapers are expressions of newspaper enterprise, and they must make a profit to survive. . . . Therefore, it must be taken for granted that American newspapers will support the free enterprise system."[12] But the free enterprise system has been made substantially less free by government support and protection of business, direct and indirect government intervention in the economy and increasing control by huge corporations. Commenting intelligently on the economy these days requires a lot more information and sophistication than it used to. Publishers may be up to date on economic matters affecting their own businesses and that of fellow local merchants. They may also be familiar with property and income taxes, state and federal health and safety requirements, unemployment and workmen's compensation, and perhaps local zoning and building regulations. While experiences in these areas may provide publishers with some insights for editorial comment, they need to recognize that they are parties with special interests in these matters.

If publishers have contributions to make in evaluating economic issues, they probably have fewer to make in other areas. It is not that publishers, given time and resources, are not smart enough to hold their own with editorial writers. But most publishers are likely to have neither the time nor the frame of mind for knowledgeable editorial writing. Publishers are often hard-pressed to find time to read their own newspapers thoroughly. (One of my publishers, acknowledging this difficulty, asked that his staff forewarn him about any news or editorial items that were likely to bring him a phone call or personal comment.) Publishers simply do not have the time to be editorial writers. Therein lie the makings of both conflict and a good working relationship between publisher and writer.

If publishers try to act as editorial writers, they are likely to drive the editorial staff out the door, up the wall or into the closet. The result will be a weak, submissive staff that stands no chance of putting out a vigorous editorial page. On the other hand, if publishers allow themselves to be too busy to think about the editorial page or to discuss ideas and issues with the writers, conflict is likely to occur at some point. The publisher should exercise leadership continuously and cooperatively, rather than intermittently and imperiously. Almost as annoying as having publishers constantly breathing down the necks of editorial writers is having them descend suddenly and unpredictably into the editorial department.

Surveys of publishers and opinion-page editors found substantial participation—but not necessarily control—by publishers in editorial policy-making. Sixty-two percent of the publishers said they attended editorial page conferences at least once or twice a week. Sixty-six percent said they express their views at these conferences most of the time. Forty-five percent said they discuss social, economic and political issues with executives once a day; another 33 percent once a week. Fifty-nine percent said they had the final decision on editorials. At the same time, the same percentage of publishers said they were "not concerned" or "only a little concerned" that the writing of editorial page staff members may not be consistent with the newspaper's editorial stands.[13] As noted in the chapter on "Who Is This Victorian 'We'?" about three-quarters of editorial writers on group-owned newspapers reported that owners and publishers exerted little or no influence in determining the priority given to editorial topics.[14]

One of my publishers used to say that he expected disagreements to arise between us, although he expected me to convince him of my point of view most of the time, since I (presumably) knew more about the subject than he did. That usually proved to be the case, or at least he let me think so. The degree of freedom that an editor achieves thus lies partly within his or her own control. As author Robinson Scott has said, the editor owes whatever freedom he or she enjoys to "force of character, . . . knowledge and the strength of [his or her] convictions."[15]

GETTING ALONG WITH PUBLISHERS

Relationships between editors and publishers probably vary as widely as do the personalities of editors and publishers. The relationship depends partly on the rules that are set when a publisher hires an editor. Some publishers and editors are easy to get along with; some are not. Some personalities work better together in an editor-publisher relationship than others. Publishers and editors are almost certain to encounter some differences of opinion. (The survey of publishers and editors mentioned above found that the two groups gave measurably different opinions when asked a series of questions about liberal, conservative and pragmatic issues, but neither group was consistently more liberal or more conservative than the other.)[16]

The first thing that editors need to recognize is that, even in the most congenial relations, an editor and a publisher are bound to disagree from time to time. "Editorial-page editors and their publishers should fight," in the opinion of Meg Downey, editorial page editor of the *Poughkeepsie* (N.Y.) *Journal*. "How else can a paper consistently come up with good editorials? 'Good' in the sense of researched, definitive, you-can-tell-where-we-stand editorials. Arguing helps clarify positions and quickly knocks down ones that are poorly defended."[17] David

Holwerk of the *Lexington* (Ky.) *Herald-Leader* made the point more picturesquely: Conflicts are not inevitable, he said, "if either you or your publisher is a brain-dead cretin who doesn't give a fresh-frozen's rat's rump what your paper stands for."[18]

Of course no editorial writer wants to be constantly battling with the publisher over policy, if for no other reason than that when fights go all the way to the mat, the publisher almost always has the authority to win and usually does.

The first advice for editorial writers is to choose their papers and publishers carefully. Editors need to know enough about the personality of a prospective publisher to have a pretty good idea that they can get along despite disagreements. They need to know enough about the prospective newspaper's editorial policy so that they can, in most cases, feel comfortable writing editorials expressing that policy.

Throughout the country editorial writers looking for jobs may find some middle-of-the-road (apple pie and motherhood) newspapers on which writers of moderate convictions might be able to muddle through a lifetime of editorial writing. Kenneth McArdle of the *Chicago Daily News* may have had these papers in mind when he said, referring to publishers, "Generally speaking, it would be hard to be utterly out of synch with them unless you, yourself, were on the kooky side, because they tend to be rational people."[19] But at least some newspapers, to their credit, have stronger editorial convictions, and, fortunately, so do some editorial writers and would-be writers. Nevertheless, unless a writer's views fall within the middle 50 to 60 percent of the political spectrum, opportunities for signing on with a congenial editorial page are limited.

The task of finding a congenial editorial page may also be more difficult today than in earlier times because journalists don't seem to hop around the country from newspaper to newspaper as much as they once did. They get married, raise a family, buy a house and try to find a decent school system in an attractive community. They put their roots into the community and may develop as deep a concern for it as any publisher. Their concern for and knowledge of the community, in fact, may go deeper than a publisher's because of the newspaper groups' practice of moving their publishers around. The writer may feel that he or she has a bigger stake in the community than the representative of ownership. Such feelings are not likely to ease the working relationship with publishers who have different ideas on editorial policy.

Dialogue helps to keep editors and publishers from suddenly being surprised to learn that they hold differing opinions on important issues. If publishers and editors can talk about issues before it is necessary to make decisions, chances of compromise improve greatly. Bernard Kilgore warned that misunderstandings between publisher and editor sometimes result because of editors. He suggested that editors should "get into the business side of a newspaper and try to see what the thing is all about."[20] Editors who want a bigger slice of the corporate budget might stand a better chance of succeeding if they could convince the business side that they understood the problems of producing income and holding down costs. On occasion my publishers took several department heads out to solicit new subscriptions. My principal memory of those occasions was of all the reasons that people had for not taking the paper. For a greater understanding of the community as well as for purely pragmatic business reasons, editorial writers should keep abreast of circulation and advertising lineage figures. If they have a head for figures, so much the better. (In my experience, journalists and journalism students tend to shy away from anything that sounds like math.) If editorial writers can talk the publisher's and the circulation manager's languages they are more likely to project an image of having their feet on the ground—and stand a better chance of selling their editorial ideas.

One of the principal functions of editorial writers may be to educate their publishers. "If the editor is willing to educate everybody, including the world, and foreign countries, then it is also necessary for the publishers and the owners to be educated," Kilgore said. But the writer must educate the publishers with what Hoke Norris of the *Chicago Sun-Times* called "a certain tact—even a tenderness." Norris described an editor friend who saw his function in "the care and feeding" of the publisher: "His publisher always believes that he originates the ideas and holds his own opinions. This is perhaps a harmless deception and it might even save a publisher, on occasion, from making a damn fool of himself."[21] A writer who is more educated and informed than the publisher must handle the boss with special care. Otherwise, the writer may run the risk of making the publisher feel resentful or intimidated rather than favorably impressed. As Frank Taylor of the *St. Louis Star-Times* put it, "More than one inferiority complex parades the precincts of publishers."[22]

Publishers might feel less intimidated if they availed themselves of opportunities to keep abreast of current events, took time to dig deeply into local issues or enrolled in a course at a local college. Houstoun Waring, publisher of the *Littleton* (Colo.) *Independent*, warned that it is "only partially effective to educate the reporter and the feature writer if the arteries of the man who calls the tune continue to harden. . . . Publishers may feel they are omniscient, but adult education programs are good for them, too."[23] He had in mind such formal programs as the Nieman Fellowship and other sabbatical opportunities, local press councils and discussions over breakfast with local sources. Nathaniel B. Blumberg, professor of journalism at the University of Montana, recalled press critic "A. J. Liebling's essentially accurate aphorism that without a school for publishers no school of journalism can have meaning."[24] The American Press Institute offers sessions for publishers, but establishing a service-oriented editorial policy for a community, if it is done at all, is likely to rank far down the line on the agenda after more business-related subjects.

Methods generally available to editors for educating publishers, however, are likely to be much less formal. Editors can send memos and background articles (although probably not books) across publisher's desks to help them understand issues before decisions are made, although busy publishers may not find time to read the material. Editors can invite publishers to public meetings, speeches, panel discussions and workshops where a variety of points of views are likely to be aired. Editors can invite publishers to lunch to exchange, in a less formal atmosphere than the editorial conference, ideas about what their newspapers should be doing and saying.

Publishers who want a hand in editorial policy should accept as much responsibility as editorial writers to sit and plow through all the material necessary for making intelligent decisions. Publishers also need to understand that editorial writers do not appreciate being descended upon at the last minute, after all the hard work is done, to give an opinion, even if the opinion is a modest one.

To avoid unexpected, last-minute opinions or decision changes, editorial conference members should try to establish the habit of delaying decisions on important matters until every member has aired his or her opinion and the issue at hand has been fully discussed. Once a person—especially a publisher, who could lose face before employees—declares even a tentative position on an issue, moving off that position becomes difficult. An editorial page staff that anticipates disagreement with the publisher might find it advantageous to meet before the editorial conference to plan a strategy. If the writers anticipate that they will not be able to convince other conference members of their opinion, they might try to agree beforehand on a compromise that they would find acceptable.

Editorial writers need to be especially sensitive to editorial topics that touch on activities or causes with which the publisher personally is involved. In a survey of editorial page editors, 94 out of 101 reported that their publishers were active in community affairs. Only about a fourth of them (25), however, reported that the publishers' activities had "affected how editorials were written." Several editors said their publishers voluntarily excused themselves from participating in decisions concerning their activities. One editor said the publisher checked with the editorial board before joining boards of local organizations. Another editor said that the publisher would sometimes suggest editorials "but will ask us not to comment on activities he is involved in."[25] A number of editors thought that involvement of the publisher was good for the newspaper and for the community. "Those who advocate volunteer involvement and shirk it are guilty of the worst hypocrisy," said one editor. Still, the potential conflict of "boosterism" remained a major concern of the editors.

Phil Duff, executive editor of the Red Wing (Minn.) *Republican Eagle*, argued in *The Masthead* that publisher involvement benefits the newspaper and the community, especially in a small community. "There's an inverse proportion at work," he wrote. "The smaller the newspaper and the smaller the town, the more extensively the publisher may legitimately involve himself in civic-political affairs."[26]

How should a writer respond to a special-interest request from a publisher? If the editorial idea is a good one and seems in the interest of the community, the writer should produce it—posthaste. If the request is obviously self-serving or out of character with the paper's policy or contrary to reason and common sense, the editorial writer has a problem. The best course is to dig into the subject, document arguments against writing the editorial and present them to the publisher boldly and positively. Confidence and facts are the best weapons. By no means should a writer ignore or delay action on such a request—even if he or she thinks that an idea is so far out of line that the publisher couldn't be serious about it. Chances are, just as a writer is congratulating himself or herself on successfully having avoided doing anything about the request, the publisher will issue a sharp reminder. At that point the publisher has the upper hand. The writer is embarrassed, apologetic, off balance and in a poor position to convince the publisher of the lack of the merits of the idea. (I found myself in this spot when a publisher asked me to write an editorial on certain practices of labor unions that offended him. In addition to convincing him that the idea was not a good one, I faced the task of convincing him that I had not intentionally ignored him.) A writer stands a better chance of fending off undesirable requests by confronting the publisher and risking an argument than by ignoring the request. Publishers don't like to be ignored.

To the publisher who has a yen to write, editors might be tempted to suggest a personal column. But editor-publisher Donald L. Breed of the *Freeport* (Ill.) *Journal-Standard* warned that publishers who write "should have exceptional capacity for self-criticism" and for evaluating the criticisms of others. "It is perfectly obvious that many publishers who write editorials or 'columns' have no power or will to step aside and look at themselves and their work," Breed said. "Publishers who write columns about their personal friends, their daily lives, their travels can sometimes be interesting, but the balance of experience is against them."[27]

Writers who have a disagreement with their publishers or editorial boards might seek to express their dissident opinions in a signed article or column on the editorial or op-ed page. But many publishers, and some editors, are reluctant to open this avenue for contrary opinions from staff members.

Several articles in *The Masthead* have suggested that editorial writers as a group "take on" their publishers. One of the first rallying cries came in 1970, from Curtis D. MacDougall, professor of journalism at Northwestern University. He quoted with approval a statement that had been made by one of the (unidentified) founders of NCEW a couple of years earlier: "During our first two decades we have educated ourselves. Now let us devote our energies toward doing the same for our publishers."[28]

Over the years editorial writers have carried a lot of ideas back to publishers from conferences of NCEW. At the following year's meeting writers often report that suggestions that emerged from critique groups were accepted back home and that the editorial pages were better for them. That is one way of bringing the collective enlightenment of editorial writers to bear on publishers. But ideas are not always accepted. Editorial writers on some papers receive criticism for the same deficiencies year after year. When asked why they don't change, the answer is usually that the publishers (or editor) "wants it that way."

One editorial writer once issued a battle cry for a full-fledged offensive against the publishers. In 1977 Sam Reynolds, editorial page editor of the Missoula (Mont.) *Missoulian*, wrote: "We must lay down standards of what is good in a publisher, and what is bad. We must, as an organization, sharply criticize shabby publisher performance." Reynolds suggested using *The Masthead*. "It must be done because nothing so retards healthy editorial comment in America as lame-brained, narrow-minded, unimaginative, cowardly, sluggish, dogmatic, and imperial publishers. . . . Until the vital step of ripping up publishers who sit like slugs upon editorial spirit and quality is taken, this organization is simply bird-doggin' it, a representative group of aggressive slaves, or hired guns." He called on NCEW to encourage good publisher practices and to attack the bad. "Growl! Snap!" he wrote; "it's time we blew the whistle."[29]

Reynolds' call for NCEW to "blow the whistle" seemed to go unheeded. *The Masthead* carried no further references to his proposal. Perhaps editorial writers did not know what they wanted to put into a code of ethics for publishers. One survey, of the 101 editorial page editors, found that 56 of their newspapers had ethics codes. In 34 instances the codes applied to the publisher, but only 17 applied to the publisher's involvement in community activities.[30]

What should a code of ethics for publishers contain? For starters, NCEW members might look to their own statement of principles, especially sections dealing with personal favors and conflicts of interest. A code might include a provision emphasizing the integrity of the editorial decision-making process—the need for previously agreed-upon procedures to be followed in setting editorial policy. It might contain some variation of the NCEW statement that says that an editorial writer "should never write anything that goes against his or her conscience." The statement of principles also emphasizes that "sound collective judgment can be achieved only through sound individual judgments," and it implies that editorial policy should evolve through discussion, not be imposed from the top. A code might state that a publisher should participate in editorial decision-making only if he or she has participated in the information-gathering and discussion phases of the process. It might state that publishers (and editors too) should refrain from participating in editorial decisions that involve conflicts of interest.

Perhaps members of NCEW were reluctant to take on the publishers because they faced a tough enough task back home dealing with publishers who didn't pay a lot of attention to them. They might have feared that, if they stirred up trouble, they would end up with a bigger battle on their hands. The way most American newspapers are run today, publishers may lose a skirmish now and then, but they rarely allow themselves to lose the big battles if they are determined to win them.

THE CASE FOR THE EDITOR

A survey of editorial page editors on 82 of the largest daily newspapers found that more than half (45) reported to a news-side editor, compared to 37 who reported directly to a publisher. Those who reported to the publisher tended to argue that their chain of command was better suited to maintaining a wall of separation between news and editorial departments. "If the editorial page is put in charge of an editor who is also in charge of news, that indicates a lack of concern for the opinion function," said one editorial page editor. "It makes it just another so-called function of the newspaper." But those who reported to an editor contended that their structure kept editorials from being tainted by the business side of the newspaper. "The drawback in reporting to the publisher is that in the final analysis the publisher is a businessman," said one of the respondents.[31]

Whether the editorial page editor reports to a publisher or an editor, a strong case can be made for the argument that, once the editorial page editor gets the job, he or she should be entrusted to set a newspaper's editorial policy. Hugh B. Patterson Jr., publisher of the *Arkansas Gazette*, contended that editorial page editors ought to be given room to set policy, and owner-publishers should support them completely. He thought that, just as career politicians are generally best suited to hold high public office, so "career newspaper editors are best qualified to run newspaper editorial pages."[32] Frank Taylor of the *St. Louis Star-Times* saw publishers as "God-fearing, decent men who would much rather push a cash register button than pull a tiger's tail." He thought that "a majority of editorial writers would measure up well on the God-fearing test but would come through 100 percent plus on pulling a tiger by the tail."[33]

Sevellon Brown III, editor of the *Providence* (R.I.) *Journal-Bulletin*, saw three reasons why "the editor *ought* to be the one—and only one—to make final decisions on editorial policy." First, the editor "is relatively uncluttered by other professional duties and responsibilities." The publishers, with all the other duties they must perform, can give only limited time and energy to the editorial page. Editing an editorial page is a full-time job. Second, the editor is the person "in closest, broadest touch with the news," one of the primary ingredients in editorial policy-making. Third, the editor is best qualified because he or she is, or ought to be, "*relatively* disinterested, *relatively* uncommitted to any particular cause or faith or point of view." The publisher, properly so, comes from the business side and represents only a business point of view. With brains, "moxey" and endurance, the editor can become a lightning rod for all points of view—for business, labor, politicians of all parties, enthusiasts for public education or world trade "or what-have-you, do-gooders of all kinds." The editor, in dealing with a specific issue, can sort out and synthesize the varied pressures and interests "into something like a reasoned, intelligent conclusion"—and there is the paper's editorial policy.[34]

An editor who has fortitude and convictions can attain a strong, unique position in relations with a publisher. As Kilgore pointed out, much to the chagrin of some editorial writers, " . . . you cannot make a five-year-old eat. No amount of force or physical violence will work. . . . Authority, you see, does not accomplish things. With editors it is somewhat the same thing." You can't force an editorial writer to write, and even more fundamentally you can't force an editorial writer to think. The relationship between editor and publisher, Kilgore said, is "a case where you have a boss who is not really a boss, and a case where you have a workman who is not really a workman."[35]

Yet, when it is necessary to make basic policy and settle disagreements, someone must assume the final authority, and it is a rare newspaper where that final authority does not rest with the publisher, general manager or representative of ownership. "Ownerships generally last longer than editorships," William H. Heath, editor-emeritus of the *Haverhill* (Mass.) *Gazette*, wrote. "Therefore, policy made by ownership is more stable. There is a rock-of-ages quality about a newspaper that is distinguished by editorial policy. This quality strengthens public confidence in the paper."[36]

CONCLUSION

Publishers do have the final say on most newspapers. But on many papers editors and editorial writers have more say than they did several years ago. Editorial writing is increasingly regarded as a career, not just a job that a news person from some other part of the paper has wandered into at a late stage in his or her working life. The job on many papers is beginning to lose its image as a mouthpiece for the bosses. Publishers are hiring editors and giving them increased editorial freedom. One reason for this new confidence is that editorial writers and editors are better prepared for their jobs. In recent years they have become better educated, more interested in their communities and more willing to speak up for what they know and believe. Knowledgeable, confident writers these days can expect to win a considerable amount of freedom from publishers, at least from those publishers who recognize the value of strong, enlightened editorial pages.

QUESTIONS AND EXERCISES

1. If you were a publisher, what role would you choose to play in regard to the editorial page? If you were an editorial page editor, what would you want the role of the publisher to be?

2. Should the role of publisher vary with the size of the newspaper? Should whether a paper is owned locally, by a distant owner or by a group make a difference in the role of the publisher?

3. Judging from the newspapers with which you are acquainted, what chances do you think you would have to sign on with a publisher with wholly compatible views on issues?

4. Among the group-owned newspapers with which you are familiar, have you detected any evidence of control of editorial policy by the group headquarters? Have you seen any evidence of similar editorial policies among newspapers of the same group?

5. What do you think are the most effective ways for an editorial writer to keep a publisher happy and to achieve a maximum sphere of freedom?

6. If editorial writers were "to take on the publishers," as suggested in *The Masthead* articles mentioned in this chapter, what steps might they take?

Chapter 7

Relations with the Newsroom

Historically the relationship between the newsroom and the editorial page has been a one-way street. The newsroom produces the news. The editorial writers sit back in Olympian reflection, rearrange their dandruff into new patterns, and then write comments on or interpretations of that news.

—CLIFFORD E. CARPENTER, ROCHESTER (N. Y.) DEMOCRAT AND CHRONICLE[1]

American newspapers have grown out of an early tradition that made no effort to keep editorial views or comment out of the news sections. For the last hundred or more years, most newspaper owners have subscribed to a policy, more or less successfully, to keep editorials and news separate. Most provide a separate editorial page and tell readers that is where the newspaper's opinions should go.

Sometimes, intentionally or unintentionally, editorial policies will influence how a news story is written or played in the paper. Sometimes, intentionally or unintentionally, the news side will influence the editorial side. Ideally, news will be written and played in as objective a manner as writers and editors are capable of achieving. Ideally, people on the news side will keep their opinions to themselves, not sharing them with editorial writers, sources or readers. To encourage this separation, most newspapers—certainly large and middle-sized ones—have erected a journalistic, if not a physical wall, between their news and editorial departments. In some extreme cases, an editorial writer in a newsroom is viewed as suspiciously as an advertising sales representative.

But times change. One change, as noted in the previous chapter, is that newspaper bosses have begun to subscribe to the philosophy that, because everyone on the paper is in the same business, everyone should understand and help everyone else. Another change is a growing realization, among news and editorial staff members, that they can help each other without threatening the integrity of either of their departments.

A survey of editorial page editors of 82 of the largest newspapers found that 69 (84 percent) saw the need for a wall between news and editorial, but nearly half of those (32) added that such a wall should not rule out communication between the two departments.[2] Reporters can be especially helpful to editorial writers, providing tips, insights, fact and contacts. Unfortunately, because of the tradition mentioned above, jealousy, antipathy or misunderstanding, much of that potential help never gets past the partition that separates the offices.

"In the eyes of some editorial writers," wrote Edward M. Miller of *The Oregonian* of Portland, "the news department is manned by fugitives from the world of intellect. The news department is notable for misjudging the news. It is concerned with trivialities at the expense of Things that Really Matter." To news people, the editorial page is staffed by "fugitives from the world of reality." Editorial writers "commune with God, and do that with considerable reluctance."[3]

Another source of news-editorial trouble is the resentment sometimes felt by news personnel who disagree with a paper's editorial policy, especially policy involving endorsement of candidates. Readers, they contend, assume that editorials speak for the entire journalistic side of the paper (or the entire paper), when in fact editorials represent the views of only a few policy makers. On occasion newsroom people have been known to purchase advertisements in their own paper to support policies or candidates different from those endorsed by the editorial page.

Sometimes relations between news and editorial people can be soured by an excessive amount of competition. Editorial writers may take delight in scooping the news department—finding a story and writing an editorial before the story appears in the news columns. Once in a while reporters may find sardonic pleasure in reporting a story that makes the editorial staff look as though it didn't know what it had been writing about. Repeated efforts on one side of the news-editorial partition to embarrass the other can be destructive to the morale of a newspaper staff and can harm the credibility of the paper. But a little friendly competition between news and editorial can help keep both departments on their toes. It may provide the only such competition in one-newspaper communities.

Problems of a different sort arise when a firm partition is not maintained between news and editorial content, when a publisher does not insist that editorial writers hold complete responsibility for policies expressed in the editorial columns and that news personnel have complete responsibility for the news columns. The editorial staff must not expect the news department to produce articles aimed at bolstering an editorial viewpoint, and the news staff must not allow its opinions to filter into news articles.

REPORTERS AS SOURCES

Whatever the reason, reporters and editorial writers have tended to go their own ways. In many cases in which editorial comment is called for, editorial writers have no need to talk with reporters. They have their own sources, or the subject of the editorial may already have been fully explained in the news columns. But ignoring help available on the news side is a "recipe for disaster," in the words of one of the editorial page editors included in the survey cited above. "Your perspective can get limited without talking with the beat reporter[s]. . . . You can go off half-cocked if you don't talk to them."[4] Since a newspaper invariably has more reporters than editorial writers, the news people are likely to have more sources of information and spend more time in the community than editorial writers. They may have information, not yet ready for print, that might make a big difference in how editorial writers evaluate an issue.

Clifford E. Carpenter of the *Rochester* (N.Y.) *Democrat and Chronicle* found during his years in the newspaper business that reporters generally knew more about a story than they could put into print. "But much of it isn't always admissible as news in the normal concept of a newspaper," he said. "This unused information can be invaluable to the editorial writer who has much more latitude."[5] Reporters, William J. Woods of the *Utica* (N.Y.) *Observer-Dispatch* pointed out, "are invaluable in keeping the egg of silly mistakes off the editor's chin."[6]

Editorial writers who want to tackle a subject in which they are not experts can ask a knowledgeable reporter to brief them on the subject. If a proposed zone change is coming before the city council, a reporter may be able to recount the history of the case, from the developer through the planning staff and zoning commission. The reporter may also be able to provide technical information on zoning procedures. The editorial writer might ask the reporter to clarify the issues involved—to recap the arguments of the developer, the protesting neighbors and the zoning commissioners.

REPORTERS IN THE OPINION PROCESS

"There's nothing wrong with editorial writers sitting down with news types to get their observations," one editorial page editor said. "You have to be careful, though, because if you carry it too far the reporters begin to articulate your policy, and that's not good."[7] In the case of the zoning case, the editorial writer might ask the reporter for a personal opinion on the issue. The reporter might reply that, in comparison with other similar changes, this one does not seem out of line—or perhaps that the change does seem out of line. In seeking an opinion, the editorial writer should be wary. Reporters are responsible for maintaining the appearance of fairness in reporting the news as well as fairness in their writing. A city editor who is concerned about the credibility of reporters may not appreciate having reporters offer opinions to an editorial writer on subjects that they write about. A reporter's relations with a news source can be adversely affected if it becomes known that the reporter has voiced an opinion. To think public matters through to editorial conclusions is the job of the editorial writer, not the reporter.

Some editors—on both news and editorial sides—are receptive to encouraging reporters to express opinions, in print and personally. Desmond Stone of the *Rochester Democrat and Chronicle* reported that inviting reporters to participate in editorial board meetings for a period of two weeks was one way that his paper and its sister paper, the *Times-Union*, tried to make news personnel feel more a part of the editorial decision-making.[8] Rufus Terral of the *St. Louis*

Post-Dispatch suggested picking two promising writers in the newsroom to contribute editorials from time to time, so that they could fill in when members of the editorial staff were on vacation or ill and possibly become regular editorial page staff members when a replacement was needed.[9] Some papers ask reporters to write editorials or bylined opinions on a regular basis on particular subjects on which they are experts, but this practice runs the risk of the dangers cited above in weakening the wall between news and editorial sides.

In the survey of editorial page editors cited above, a few said they would be willing to undertake joint projects with the news department. "I'd like to be able to send out a reporter and an editorial writer for six weeks to cover a controversial issue and have the reporter write the news story and the editorial writer write the editorials," one said. "Now, when the news side does a big investigation, the editorial page gets left out until the stuff appears in the paper, and then we have to play catch-up."[10]

David H. Beetle of the *Albany* (N.Y.) *Knickerbocker News* once asked several reporters based in Washington to write a 500-word appraisal of the current administration. The reporter from the Albany paper responded that writing a signed opinion article on the editorial page would brand him as biased forever. As a reporter, he dealt only in facts; he was proud that, in public, he had no opinions. Beetle asked other editors what they thought. They were divided. "Ridiculous," said one editor. "Our city hall reporter writes straight news daily and once a week tells what he thinks of it all. No one believes he is biased." But another editor argued, "If a city hall reporter writes opinion, he'll instantly become 'suspect' when he gathers news."[11]

When I was an editor with supervision over both news and editorial sides, I did not encourage reporters to write articles that expressed opinion about the subjects they were reporting. I did, however, encourage them to write in-depth, analytical articles for use in either the daily news columns or the Sunday opinion section. My experience as both a reporter and an editorial writer convinced me that something happens inside a writer when he or she writes a piece that expresses an opinion. As an editorial writer, I often ended up having much stronger opinions on a subject after I had written an editorial. Once a writer has thought through the arguments and embraced one of them, his or her attitude on an issue is likely never to be the same again.

EDITORIALS IN THE NEWS COLUMNS

Two ideas for introducing editorials into the news pages were considered in early issues of *The Masthead*. Neither idea has been given much credence by editors.

The first is the front-page editorial. Such editorials have become rare in recent years, but occasionally an editor or publisher will run an editorial on page one to call attention to a statement considered to be especially important. Fred A. Stickel, president and publisher of *The Oregonian*, wrote a signed page-one editorial urging Oregonians to vote against a ballot measure that would have restricted the rights of homosexuals.[12] Nathaniel B. Blumberg, while a professor at Michigan State University, found enough page-one editorials during the 1952 election that he wrote an article for *The Masthead* titled "The Case Against Front-Page Editorials." Blumberg argued that page-one editorials may confuse readers about what is news and what is opinion and may increase their "suspicions that the news coverage might not be impartial."[13]

Some papers summarize election endorsements in a front-page box, and some editorial page editors use front-page teasers to call attention to editorials on the editorial page. At least some of the criticisms of front-page editorials might apply to these practices as well.

Another suggestion for bringing opinion into the news columns apparently originated in 1935 with historian Douglas Southall Freeman, then editor of the *Richmond* (Va.) *News Leader*. While going through old *News Leader* files in the early 1950s, James J. Kilpatrick found that Freeman had suggested to his publisher that the news needed interpreting when and where it was printed. The reader should not have to wait until the next day, "when his interest in it has been diminished or has been distracted by some new event." Freeman suggested that the editorial page be abolished and that interpretation and comment be appended at the end of news stories that merited opinion.[14] Kilpatrick's resurrection of the proposal prompted the laboratory newspaper at the University of Michigan, the *Michigan Journalist*, to try Freeman's proposal. Students found that one advantage of tacking an editorial on the end of a news story was that the editorial did not require so much space; there was no need to rehash factual information. But the professor who worked with the students said he feared that readers would think that news sources had not been "given a square shake if the newspaper proceeds to bludgeon those views editorially in the same news column." He also feared that the instant editorial would encourage off-the-cuff reactions and discourage double-checking, digging for more information and calm reflecting required for first-rate editorial comment.[15]

EDITORIALIZING ABOUT NEWS POLICIES

One approach to lowering the bar between news and editorial that seems justified is the use of editorial columns to explain news policies and practices—and editorial practices for that matter. An editorial or a signed article on the editorial page can be a proper forum for telling readers why certain types of news and not others are covered in the news columns or why new features have been added and others dropped.

In the last couple of years in which I was on a newspaper, I regularly wrote a Sunday op-ed column, which I usually devoted to a journalistic issue. Some of the columns dealt with my own paper's policies and practices. Others concerned matters of more general interest, such as protecting the confidentiality of news sources, libel, invasion of privacy and the signing of editorials. Reader response seemed good. Subscribers wanted to know more about their newspaper, and the press in general.

Some newspapers assign a full- or part-time person to respond to complaints of readers and to write about media matters. Their work usually is published on the editorial or op-ed page. When the remarks of these media critics have pertained to the newspaper industry in general, they have been given considerable freedom to draw conclusions. On some newspapers, however, when criticism comes too close to home, critics find that they don't have as much freedom as they may have thought.[16]

CONCLUSION

The newspaper that wants to maintain the credibility of its news and editorial columns needs to draw a line between the two and take every opportunity to remind readers of this line. But news and editorial are two parts of a package. It may be possible to produce an outstanding news product without a good editorial page. It is virtually impossible to produce an outstanding editorial page without the support of a good news product. Editorial writers need reporters more than reporters need editorial writers: They simply don't have enough arms and legs and eyes and noses to do their jobs all by themselves.

QUESTIONS AND EXERCISES

1. Why do you think that editorial writers have tended to ignore reporters and newsroom editors?

2. Do reporters, in your opinion, have a legitimate complaint when the editorial page expresses views with which they strongly disagree? What steps should be open to them?

3. Should news persons be allowed to purchase advertising space in the newspaper for which they work to express views contrary to those of management?

4. Should reporters be invited to write editorials on subjects with which they are familiar? Or to write signed opinion pieces for the editorial and op-ed pages?

5. Do reporters on papers in your area write editorials and/or signed articles for the editorial or op-ed pages? How far do they go in expressing their opinions?

6. Do you think that editorial writers should ask reporters for their opinions on issues that the reporters are covering?

7. Are there occasions when a page-one editorial can be justified? What about page-one election endorsements?

8. What do you think of the idea of tacking editorial comments to the ends of news stories?

Chapter 8

The Editorial Page Staff

Many editorial pages in this country's newspapers are wretchedly understaffed.

—LAURENCE J. PAUL, BUFFALO EVENING NEWS[1]

Mine, by damn, all mine.

—DON SHOEMAKER, ASHEVILLE (N.C.) CITIZEN[2]

An editorial page staff, no matter how large or small, never seems to be quite the right size for all members. Ask editorial writers if they need more help in putting out the editorial page, and chances are they will answer Yes. But ask a writer who puts out a page all by himself or herself—or better yet one who used to put one out alone—and chances are you will get a lecture on the freedom and rewards, and misery, of doing the whole job by yourself.

The writer on the one-person staff knows that he or she is overworked and doesn't get enough time to write editorials. Writers on some two-person and three-person staffs, especially on larger papers, think they need more help. On some days, on papers with large staffs, a writer may wish that not so many colleagues were competing for space, promotion and community recognition. Some members of large staffs think back fondly to the days when they wrote all the editorials, handled the letters and still found time for a Chamber of Commerce luncheon. I did when the editorial staff on *The Columbian* grew from one to two, and then from two to three members.

Just as editorial-page people hold a variety of views about staff size, so do they have differences of opinion concerning how much freedom each member of the staff should have and how much members should collaborate through editorial conferences.

THE ONE-PERSON STAFF

A survey of editorial writers in 1979 found that the one-person staff was the most prevalent on U.S. daily newspapers (27 percent of all papers) and that 17 percent had no full-time person at all. Another 17 percent had two persons; 14 percent had three; 10 percent had four; 8 percent had five; 6 percent had more than five.[3] I think there is little reason to think that these percentages have changed much.

Putting out a page by yourself has its advantages. You can write what you wish if you have a good relationship with your publisher. You don't have to worry about disagreements among staff members. You get full credit, or discredit, for whatever you do. Your readers know whom to praise or blame. You can go home at night and point to what you have accomplished.

"I should confess that I still recall with pleasure some of the aspects of those years when I wrote editorials for a semi-weekly and later a small daily newspaper without conferring with anybody in advance," recalled Wilbur Elston, then of the *Detroit News*. "I won't say those editorials could not have been improved. Obviously they could have been. But they were all mine. Whatever praise or criticism I heard from readers was especially pleasant to my ears." Unfortunately, Elston also recalled, most of the editorials "were, I fear, written off the top of my head."[4]

The one-person show is a tough one, and it's not for everyone. In the words of Don Shoemaker of the *Asheville* (N.C.) *Citizen*, it's like being "the keeper of the zoo." Shoemaker, who was the inspiration for the leading character in Jeff MacNelly's cartoon strip, "Shoe," saw the single editorial writer as "more put upon" than any other person in the field of newspapering. The writer had to please "crotchety and sour-bellied" printers, select and edit editorial page features that would complement the locally written editorials and satisfy the publisher—and know all about proofreading, page layout and makeup. The writer had to worry about "any novice journeyman who happens to be around the shop" fouling up the page. At the same time the one-person staff had to "keep a weather eye cocked for the passions and prejudices" of the community, the state and the region. "As any fool kin plainly see, the curator has an impossible, a thankless, a miserable job," Shoemaker wrote. But mostly the "fool" loves it. "I (ugh!) do," he concluded. "But there are moments."[5]

One of the big pluses is satisfaction of the ego. Shoemaker spoke of the "complete identity with a whole product—. . . come gripe or praise." When you are a one-person staff, you don't have to worry about bylines. Readers who are familiar with your page will know who wrote the words they agree or disagree with. The letters to the editor that comment on editorials are written to you. Members of the community who want support from the editorial page know whose door they should knock on.

Michael Loftin was reminded of a scene from the movie *Raiders of the Lost Ark*: "Archeologist Indiana Jones, having captured an ancient artifact, is trying to escape from a giant rolling boulder chasing him through the tunnel. Think of the boulder as the looming daily deadline and the production of 800 to 900 words of (reasonably intelligent) commentary as the goal and you can understand why those of us in this situation were cheering for Mr. Jones."[6]

Turning out the letters, the columns, the cartoons and the page layout, while handling telephone calls and office visitors, can account for a good share of the working day. But, once you get into the swing of it, composing one thoughtful, researched editorial and another quick one every day turns out not to be impossible. Topics always abound. Karli Jo Hunt, of *The Home News* of New Brunswick, N.J., said that she has learned "to get through a five-day week writing seven days' editorials, . . . to read, read, read, clip, clip, clip, and pace my 'production' so that Thursdays and Fridays are only nine- or 10-hour sessions at the tube."[7]

When she finds herself under the pressure of time, Linda Egan, of the *Santa Barbara* (Calif.) *News-Press*, said she "fudges," explaining: " . . . we may publish two live editorials, instead of our customary three a day. We say then that our readers deserve more detailed background on this tricky subject. We mean that we don't have time to write short. Sometimes we don't even have time to write long, so we flesh out the column with a space-eating illustration that dresses up one of the editorials. We call that a treat for our readers."[8]

Some editors—in fact, some editors who also double as publishers or managing editors—are able to produce two, three or four editorials a day and say something significant in each of them. They seem able to cover an unlimited range of topics. But my experience has been that single writers make the best use of talent and time if they concentrate on one major topic a day, a topic they know about.

IF NOT ONE, HOW MANY?

The 1979 survey of editorial writers cited earlier in this chapter did not attempt to compare staff sizes with circulations of the newspapers. But an earlier survey had found that 54 percent of dailies with less than 100,000 circulation had only one full-time editorial writer or a part-time writer. "Is it any wonder that performance occasionally falters?" asked Laurence J. Paul of the *Buffalo* (N.Y.) *Evening News* after reviewing the findings. "Apparently all this ink-stained Solomon is expected to do, in addition to whatever other sideline duties he may have, is to comment stylishly, thoughtfully and consistently on a broadening array of complex subjects in 15 to 25 lucid editorials a week. And after the value judgments are made, Solomon, don't forget the waste baskets before you leave." Paul found it scarcely more reassuring that 16 percent of the writers on papers of more than 100,000 circulation worked on staffs of no more than two full-time members. The deficiencies that he saw included superficial analysis, clumsy style, convenient subject matter, padded editorials and "even the canned editorials (God save us)."[9] (Canned editorials are opinion pieces supplied by editorial writing services or representatives of interest groups that a newspaper passes off as its own editorials.)

One of the tendencies of an overworked editorial staff is to write about national and international issues that have been researched and reported by the national wire services, news magazines, the *New York Times* or other publications. It is no trick to turn out several of these editorials in a few hours. Information is not likely to be so easily available on local, regional and state topics. Fewer editorial voices are easily available to listen to and imitate. Consequently these issues tend to be ignored when deadlines approach.

Paul thought it ought to be possible to set some guidelines for the size of the editorial page staff based on a newspaper's circulation. He suggested that the National Conference of Editorial Writers recommend that papers with circulations between 50,000 and 100,000 should have a minimum of two writers, that papers with 100,000 to 150,000 should have at least three and those with 150,000 to 200,000 at least four.

In one sense, the circulation of a newspaper has little to do with the size of the staff needed to turn out a high-quality editorial page. A column of editorials needs to be written, columns and letters need to be handled and callers and visitors dealt with. An editorial page in a paper with a small circulation is the same size as in a larger paper. One difference, of course, is that a larger paper may produce seven editions a week instead of five or six, may have two opinion pages a day instead of one and publish an opinion section on the weekend. The main reason that larger papers should maintain larger editorial page staffs is that they have greater resources with which to do so. They have more circulation, more advertising and more money to spend, and therefore should be expected to put more resources into the editorial page.

Another reason: Larger papers tend to serve not just a local community but a region or an entire state. These papers thus have the opportunity to provide leadership in public affairs in the areas they serve. They will not make full use of that opportunity unless they provide their writers with the time and the incentive to do their own research and their own thinking on the issues.

DIVISION OF DUTIES

A one-person staff doesn't have to worry much about how to split up the duties of producing an editorial page. He or she does whatever needs to be done. But help, primarily with letters to the editor, might be available from a newsroom secretary, copy clerk or someone with clerical skills. This person could check addresses of letters, enforce rules the paper has concerning letters and retype them on video display terminals. The person might be encouraged to try writing headlines for letters. Assistance with letters is probably the greatest help that a one-person staff can get. Next best is with messages and phone calls.

As staffs increase in size, one person is likely to be assigned the letters to the editors as full- and part-time job, another perhaps the syndicated columns and the layout. They may write editorials as they find time. One person may have responsibility for the weekend opinion section. The editorial page editor usually edits the editorials of other staff members and meets with the public and the newspaper management.

As staffs increase, writers may have their own special subject areas. Specialization can produce a more knowledgeable editorial writer, and thus more knowledgeable editorials. If an editorial is directed primarily toward experts in the subject, it may fully serve its purpose. But specialization has limitations. First, writers may become so engrossed in their specialty that they may turn out editorials that are incomprehensible to the average reader. Second, when a paper's specialist on a subject is sick or on vacation or has left the staff, an editor may find that no one else on the staff is capable of writing on that topic. Ideally, editorial writers should be able to write about many subjects, in addition to their specialties.

EDITORIAL CONFERENCES

Editorial writers and editors divide sharply over the value—or lack of value—of regular editorial conferences. Proponents argue that they provide an opportunity to bring the thinking of several people to bear on topics, that give-and-take discussion can produce ideas that might otherwise not emerge. Discussion can also reveal that a topic needs more research or possibly ought to be dropped entirely as unworthy of comment. John G. McCullough of the *Philadelphia Evening Bulletin* said that when his staff skipped the morning editorial conference he and the other writers missed it. "When the free give-and-take of these conferences is missing, I feel it shows in [the resulting editorials]," he said. "They seem to have a structural narrowness reflecting the absence of other, counter, views. Such editorials come through as a whoosh of heated opinion." He said the editorials lacked the persuasive logic that is provided by "the extra ingredients fed into the mix during the editorial conference."[10]

Some of the critics of conferences contend that this mixing contributes to bland editorials. Hugh B. Patterson Jr. of the *Arkansas Gazette* of Little Rock acknowledged that discussions could help clarify and sharpen arguments but they also could result in "the lowest common denominator of mutual agreement."[11] Pat Murphy of the Phoenix *Arizona Republic* contended that his staff members did not need editorial conferences. "Our staff is made up of self-starters who spin out ideas and suggestions and hit the ground running every morning." he said. Instead of a conference, he made the rounds of staff members first thing in the morning to suggest ideas and listen to their proposals. "Fie on daily conferences," he said. "They're a waste of time."[12]

Various combinations of people involved in setting editorial policy might be tried. Editorial writers might meet each morning with the editorial page editor to discuss that day's topics. At less frequent intervals the editorial page editor might meet with the newspaper editor or the publisher. Daily staff meetings, coupled with the editorial page editor conferring with the editor, were our policy when I was on the *Des Moines* (Iowa) *Register and Tribune*. On *The Columbian*, in Vancouver, Wash., we had a daily meeting of editorial writers and a bi-weekly meeting of the editorial board, consisting of the editorial staff members, the co-publishers and two or three representatives of other departments. Another possibility is for the publisher to sit in on all daily conferences. This arrangement helps assure that the publisher is informed on editorial issues, but it may have an inhibiting effect on discussion of sensitive issues.

PERSONAL EXPERIENCES

The principal purposes served by the daily conference in Vancouver were two: to coordinate assignment of topics and to discuss, perhaps only briefly, the arguments that might be made. After an assignment had been made, the topic sometimes might not be discussed. But because of differences in experience and philosophy—and some friendly competition—one of us might ask, "What do you intend to say about it?" or sometimes more pointedly, "You're not just going to say such-and-such, are you?" Usually the result was that the writer, who may have planned to dash off something that had come quickly to mind, was slowed down enough to take a more careful look at the issue.

After I left *The Columbian*, I sat in one day as an observer at the morning editorial conference. The three staff members conducted the conference in much the same way as when I worked there. Most of the possible editorial topics mentioned concerned national and international events, items that had been in the paper that morning. These topics got very little discussion, partly because staff writers had previously commented editorially on these or similar topics and they all knew the paper's positions. Local topics accounted for most of the discussion. A proposed local expressway did not get much attention; the proposal was not a new one. But lengthy and heated discussion arose over a rumor that congressional redistricting might put Vancouver and Tacoma, 140 miles apart, into the same district. (The writer who eventually was assigned that topic spent almost an entire day tracking down a reliable source on the subject and writing the editorial.) Some discussion focused on a local weekly open-air market that was about to fold, a topic that seemed of interest to two of the writers. At the end of the conference the editorial page editor said that, since the writer who had suggested the subject already had a topic for the day, he, the editor, would write about the market. A story in a rival newspaper prompted discussion about the county auditor's charges that unforeseen costs justified a re-evaluation of a proposed new county jail. The project got a thorough airing at the conference, but the writer who was assigned the topic, one he had written on before, eventually concluded that the project was merited and that these were not likely to be the only unforeseen costs in the project.

The national and international topics were not addressed in editorials that day, although several of them might have been if all the writers had not met later in the day with a subdivision developer who had a project he wanted to discuss and with the editorial board in one of its bi-weekly meetings.

The editorial page editor reported that the board meeting had gone well. No major disagreements had arisen. He said that one reason he had been satisfied with most of the board meetings was that he made a point of establishing the agenda and researching his topics thoroughly ahead of time. I know from my experience with the board that, when the agenda was not set, some of the non-editorial members were likely to bring up matters of interest to them, topics that the editorial writers often were unprepared to address. In such instances the editorial writers were likely to find themselves agreeing to look into subjects that they were not interested in or on which their views differed from those of the non-editorial members. We counted ourselves fortunate when we emerged from the meetings without being saddled with these topics. The board meetings hardly ever provided the real thrashing out of issues that took place in the smaller morning sessions.

Editorial writers, even those who hold regular meetings, need to step back a pace or two from time to time. Gilbert Cranberg of the *Des Moines Register and Tribune* found that putting out two editorial pages a day kept his staff so occupied that it had no chance to examine how it really operated or how the pages could be improved. Cranberg tried a 90-minute luncheon for the writers and found that the session produced ideas for improving use of syndicated features, increasing locally written material for the pages and instituting a proposed sabbatical leave program.[13]

When I was on *The Columbian*, the three of us left the office early on a couple of afternoons, with a six-pack of beer, to talk about the broader issues, some details and the inter-workings among our personalities. The result was a clearing of the air that could not have taken place in a hurried morning meeting and some ideas for improving the page that did not spring full-blown from the mind of any one of the participants.

THE TYPICAL DAY

A "typical day" for editorial writers on most papers is a contradiction in terms. Editorial writers who have contact with the outside world, or with other members of the staff, are not likely to *have* a typical day. It is hard for writers to plan their day and stick to that schedule. The smaller the staff, the greater the difficulty. Here is the day that John Sanford of the *Reno* (Nev.) *Evening Gazette* would like to have had:

First thing, the stack of newspapers to be scanned—all the Nevada papers, representative Western ones, with the *Wall Street Journal* and the *Christian Science Monitor* for topping. Then there's the morning mail, but that doesn't take long. Most of it hits the wastebasket.

Then along comes the day's editorial proofs, followed by close watch on the editorial page make-up, and a page proof for a double check.

Selection and editing of features and columns for tomorrow's page follow, for this material has to be in the backshop by noon.

That should leave the afternoon open for editorial meditation and writing. This *is* a beautiful schedule—if it would ever work. It hasn't for the last 20 years.

Sanford said that, with interruptions and other demands, only an hour or two a day was left for editorial writing, and the trick was to find that free hour or two.[14]

Interrupting this ideal schedule are phone calls from everyone (from pests to big shots), unanticipated talks and conferences with other staff members and the boss, a cry of anguish from the composing room about missing copy, people who wander off the street to talk or sell an editorial idea. Then there are speeches, lunches, meetings, the stroll down Main Street (dreamer!) and afterhours cocktails that help keep the ivory tower from becoming too isolated—but may keep a spouse waiting at home with a no-longer-hot dinner. Some hard-pressed editors find they have to wait until most of the staff has gone home to find time to write editorials.

CONCLUSION

The staff size that editorial writers are likely to regard as ideal may depend on their own prior experience. To writers who have run a one-person show, a two-person staff may look like a luxury. To writers who have worked on a larger staff, two persons are likely to seem wholly inadequate. Although some attempts have been made to prescribe staff sizes for papers of varying circulation sizes, the circulation of a newspaper has little correlation with the work that needs to be done on an editorial page. The page must come out every day, whatever the circulation; columns and letters must be edited; a certain number of editorials must be written; visitors and callers must be dealt with; meetings, editorial conferences and research must be attended to.

All things being equal, a larger editorial page staff should be able to turn out a better product. If writers have an opportunity to spend time thinking about one or two areas of editorial writing, instead of having to render the judgments of Solomon on all issues, they ought to be better editorial writers. If they write only one editorial a day, they should be able to do a better job than if they have to write three. However, if they overspecialize, they may work themselves out of their jobs. Editorial writers must never stop being generalists.

QUESTIONS AND EXERCISES

1. Editorial page staffs on the average apparently have not been growing in size. What does this seem to say about the attitudes of publishers and other holders of the newspaper budget purse strings?

2. What are the advantages of a one-person editorial page staff? The disadvantages? Do you think the disadvantages outweigh the advantages?

3. Determine the number of editorial page persons on papers in your area. How do these staffs compare in size with the staff sizes mentioned in this chapter?

4. How are the editorial duties distributed among the staff members of these papers?

5. How do the editorial conferences—if any—work on these papers? Who attends? How often do they meet? How are assignments made? Does the editor, the publisher or the editorial board make the final decisions?

Chapter 9

Relations with the Community

In general, I think it is acceptable to contribute money to organizations whose purposes are endorsed by one's paper.

—Susan Hegger, St. Louis Post-Dispatch[1]

I choose to remain virginal.

—Norman A. Cherniss, Riverside (Calif.) Press-Enterprise[2]

S
ome of the toughest decisions faced by editors and editorial writers involve the degree to which they allow themselves to participate in, or contribute to, civic, business and political causes. Involved in these decisions is the question: How can editorial writers be a part of a community without becoming biased, or appearing to be biased, through associations with groups with special interests? Closely related to this aspect of maintaining integrity and the appearance of integrity is the problem faced by all journalists: To what extent, if any, can you accept drinks, meals and trips from persons with whom you deal without compromising yourself? These questions have provoked a lot of conscience-searching among editorial writers and have led several organizations in the newspaper business to conclude that consciences need help through codes and guidelines.

TO PARTICIPATE OR NOT TO PARTICIPATE

Those who defend participation in community affairs contend that editorial writers should recognize that they are part of their community and should feel a responsibility to help make it a better place in which to live. But others contend just as strongly that, if writers become involved,

If editorial writers were to subscribe wholeheartedly to either philosophy, decision-making would be easy. If they thought that working through organizations was as appropriate for them as molding opinions through their writing, they would say Yes when asked to participate in a worthy cause. If they thought they should undertake no obligations, they would say No. Most editorial writers, however, seem to think that there are some occasions when they can or should become involved and some occasions when they cannot or should not. Places for drawing the line are almost as numerous as editors and writers themselves. When 13 editorial writers participated in a 1966 *Masthead* symposium on the question of proper community involvement, they gave 13 different answers.[3]

Political and Civic Activities

Editorial writers generally agree that they ought to avoid public partisan politics. A poll in 1988 found that 89 percent of editorial writers said that they agreed or strongly agreed that they should avoid partisan political organizations. Only 9 percent (down from 19 percent in 1979) reported that they had given money or bought tickets to help a party or a candidate; a similar percentage had urged individuals to vote for a party or candidate; only 7 percent had attended meetings, rallies or dinners not required by their jobs. The poll revealed that 46 percent of the newspapers, in fact, prohibited political participation by employees and that an additional 37 percent discouraged or strongly discouraged participation. These percentages marked a sharp increase over polls taken in 1971 and 1979, when 0 (!) percent and 29 percent of newspapers, respectively, prohibited participation.[4]

When asked about professional and civic organizations, however, the editorial writers were not so clearly in agreement. Sixty-six percent said that they participated in professional journalism societies; 46 percent in civic, religious, fraternal and veterans groups; 31 percent in non-profit, non-governmental organizations. Thirteen percent had participated in public issue groups (foreign policy, civil liberties) and 6 percent in governmental boards or agencies. Only 12 percent said they had not participated in any civic or professional groups.

The principal argument against joining and participating in political and civic activities is that association with organizations and causes may cause "conflicts of interest, real or apparent," in the wording of the Basic Statement of Principles of the National Conference of Editorial Writers. Conflicts, or at least the appearance of conflicts, can sneak up on you when you least expect them. Paul Greenberg, editorial page editor of the *Pine Bluff* (Ark.) *Commercial*, agreed at one time to serve as president of his local temple. He thought that certainly that position would present no risk of conflict with his editorial duties. But within two months the temple became involved in a zoning controversy. Since then, he said, he has been more cautious about volunteering for causes. "I would say that serving spaghetti at a fundraising dinner is the highest role to which the editorial writer ought to aspire," he told a panel on ethics at an NCEW convention.[5]

For David Boeyink, one-time editorial page editor of the *Owensboro* (Ky.) *Messenger-Inquirer*, a personal friendship led to a potential conflict of interest. As a newcomer to Owensboro, Boeyink renewed what had been a casual acquaintance with a fellow student at Harvard Divinity School. The families of the two became friends. They attended the same church. As staff member of the Owensboro Chamber of Commerce, the friend "was a great source of insights into local political figures," Boeyink recalled. Then the staff member moved up to become chief administrative officer. "His new prominence . . . provided a few moments of concern, particularly on rare editorials involving the chamber," Boeyink wrote in an article in *The Masthead*. "But with our principal focus on government and education, the problem of possible favoritism never became acute." Then the friend decided to run for mayor and at the same time became executive director of a citizens committee on education, of which Boeyink was a member. Boeyink immediately resigned from the committee. The two stopped talking politics in any informal setting. The families saw each other less and less frequently. To have cut off all ties, he said, "would have meant leaving the congregation we loved and virtually all the best friends we had in Owensboro," a price that was "too high." Boeyink said he was certain he could have written editorials critical of the new mayor's policies, although the newspaper generally supported the programs he was proposing. Boeyink, however, was never put to the test, since, in a decision that had nothing to do with this situation, he changed careers and left Owensboro.[6]

While he was on the *Richmond* (Va.) *News Leader*, James J. Kilpatrick accepted an appointment to a state commission that seemed at first to be innocuous but that eventually came to embarrass him. For eight years he served on the state Commission on Constitutional Government, an agency organized to encourage states to defend their reserved powers under the federal government. He also was chairman of publications for the commission. But when the commission came under attack in the Virginia General Assembly, Kilpatrick said he found himself in a trap. "I could not defend the Commission's publications without appearing to be saying what a great guy am I." In the end, he said, he wrote a "lame piece" to the effect that the incident ought to have taught him a lesson about becoming involved with boards and commissions.[7]

Kilpatrick said that he recognized that, while a newspaper's policy may admonish editors and editorial writers to avoid positions with groups that might be the subject of editorial comment, "in actual practice it tends to get bent around the edges." What is an editor to do when asked to serve on the board of the local library, or the symphony orchestra, or the community college or the art museum? Or perhaps a committee on public parks or race relations? Sometimes, he said, editors can get away with saying No, but inevitably requests catch up with them. Accepting some of these requests may leave the editor's "editorial purity something less than that of Ivory soap," he said, but they also are likely to make the editor "a better informed and more useful citizen of the community on which the paper depends."[8]

In the same vein, Laird B. Anderson, professor at American University, has expressed concern that, in overreacting to disconnect themselves from public people and events, editorial writers and other journalists have become second-class citizens. "In following this road to second-class status so that we can be viewed as more ethical and credible, we have righteously denied ourselves equality with the citizens whose consciousness we want to reach," Anderson said. "Our offices have all too often become havens, a refuge to scurry back to after dipping a toe in the vast sea of public affairs and then writing about what we've seen or learned. Many of us, I suspect, like this protective buffer. It uncomplicates our lives."[9]

Some of those who try to draw a line between the acceptable and unacceptable differentiate between reporters and opinion writers. Don Lowery, editorial director of WHDH-TV in Boston, told an NCEW convention panel that he had chaired a portion of the local United Way campaign, served on the board of a Special Olympics organization and participated in a public policy group. "As a reporter, I would have declined all such activities," he said. "But my role as an editorialist is different. As an advocate for editorial positions, I see nothing wrong with promoting activities we support."[10]

When editorial writers were asked in a *Masthead* symposium about the ethics of contributing to charities, several drew the line between what Lewis A. Leader of the Monterey (Calif.) *Herald* called "joining a non-profit group and contributing to one."[11] Susan Hegger of the *St. Louis Post-Dispatch* said she thought it was generally "acceptable to contribute money to organizations whose purposes are endorsed by one's paper" but not to organizations "whose platforms or principles run counter to one's editorial page."[12] Van Cavett of the Allentown (Pa.) *Morning Call* reported that, because his paper "supported policies advocated by Planned Parenthood," he and his wife Caroline saw no conflict when she was asked to serve on the local board of the organization. "We realized going in that financial contributions and participation of fundraisers would be necessary," he said.[13]

Other writers took a harder line. Charles J. Dunsire of the *Seattle Post-Intelligencer* said he limited his contributions to the local United Way (payroll deduction), his church and a non-profit hospital foundation. He admitted, however, that he contributed annually to his alma mater, the University of Washington "because such contributions have become necessary to retain the privilege of buying season tickets to the games of one of the nation's most successful and popular football programs."[14]

Business Interests

The business, as well as civic, interests of publishers and other non-news, non-editorial executives on a newspaper also can make credible editorial writing more difficult for staff members and hurt the overall credibility of the newspaper. Nor can editorial writers themselves expect exemption from the effects of economics. For one thing, the newspaper is a business; one of the first concerns of the owners is to make a profit. One of the editorial writer's concerns is to make enough money and have a steady enough job to live securely and comfortably.

To a larger extent than many businesses, the profitability of a newspaper is tied to the growth and prosperity of its community. When a community expands, a local supermarket may find its monopoly challenged; another supermarket (which incidentally becomes a potential new advertiser) moves in. The same can be said about service stations and real estate offices, even radio stations. But for the newspaper the result is likely to be more circulation and more advertising, not a new competitor. The temptation to ally a newspaper with whatever brings growth and income to a community has been a fairly consistent one in most communities. This temptation may have proved easier to resist in recent years, with growing evidence of the financial and environmental costs of unplanned growth. Still, it remains difficult not to get excited editorially when a major industry, especially a "clean" one, is considering your town for a new plant.

The *Greensboro* (N.C.) *News & Record* faced that situation when local business leaders seemed about to convince the Carolina-Virginia Fashion Exhibitors to move from another North Carolina city to Greensboro. The local leaders hoped that the new headquarters would provide a catalyst for lagging downtown renewal. The newspaper gave the story major front-page coverage. Initial editorials praised the community's efforts and urged the organization to move. But, "when the price tag for city tax contributions in support of the effort fluctuated, the newspaper editorialized that campaign leaders should keep the citizenry better informed and 'lay out the facts as quickly as possible,'" John Alexander, editorial page editor of the *News & Record*, said. Meanwhile, the other community, including the newspaper, waged an all-out, eventually successful, effort to keep the organization. "The contrast in approaches has been a sore point with many business and government leaders ever since," Alexander said. "Asked to give examples of the newspaper's purported 'negativism' and lack of enthusiasm for community projects, these leaders still point to the *News & Record*'s restrained coverage, to that editorial questioning aspects of the proposal's financing, and to the [publisher's] lack of personal involvement in the recruiting effort." Alexander saw no perfect solution for situations such as this, but he concluded: "Whatever the newspaper's involvement as a corporate citizen, the editorial page must be free to state its opinions freely, consistent with its own philosophy—even if it means not backing a favored project, or raising questions about it."[15]

Closely related to the temptation to look favorably on growth is a tendency among editorial writers toward what might be called local or regional provincialism. Writers should take pride in their city, their state and their region and should want to see their area prosper and become an attractive place in which to live. But it is hard sometimes for them to see beyond their own circulation areas—and such provincialism can become a vested interest. For example, a writer may condemn a proposed federal dam halfway across the country as a congressional boondoggle but praise a proposed local dam as an economic necessity. An editor in Southern California may look with longing toward what appears to be an excess of water flowing into San Francisco Bay. But an editor in Northern California is likely to argue that water located in the north should stay there. One of the challenges for editorial writers is to lift their sights and those of their readers beyond the city limits and the near bank of the next river.

Another concern for editorial writers in the economic arena involves the ever-present threat of a clash between business interests and news or editorial policy. What does a newspaper do when a major advertiser threatens to withdraw advertising because of something that has appeared or might appear in the paper? Does the publisher stand firm and let the advertiser pull out? What does a newspaper do when it learns that an advertiser has been caught in an unfair trade practice or a sex discrimination practice? Does it publish its findings and condemn them on the editorial page? What happens when a local supermarket wants to build a new store, a football stadium, in an area that the community had previously designated as non-commercial? Do the editorial writers feel free to come out against the promoter if they think the proposal is wrong?

Taking a strong stand against business interests can be tough, especially if the financial well-being of the newspaper itself is at stake. In the long run, newspapers probably serve themselves best if they take a firm stand at the beginning of a confrontation. A publisher who refuses to back down to an advertiser's threats will let it be known to other potential threateners that the paper will stand firm against them as well. A paper that can take an editorial stand against its own immediate financial interests can gain public respect that may eventually help not only its credibility but its economic condition as well.

Personal Experiences

In the nearly two decades in which I was associated with editorial pages, I tried to limit my civic activities to those that required little time and seemed to pose little risk of conflict with editorial policy. Looking back, I think I should have limited myself even more. I inherited a Rotary Club membership from my predecessor on *The Columbian*, faithfully attended luncheon meetings for nearly 12 years and never encountered any conflict of interest that I recognized. I was never asked to serve on the publicity committee. I never had an occasion to write an editorial either praising or criticizing the club or its activities. Membership benefited me, I thought, because it brought me into contact with leaders of the business community whom otherwise I might have found difficult to get to know. I allowed myself to think my membership benefited the newspaper too. Instead of being an unknown person in an ivory tower, expressing opinions more liberal than most of those of the club's members, I was a fellow member whom they could poke fun at over typographical or other errors that appeared in the paper. I tried to avoid such activities as clerking at the club's rummage sale and selling tickets for its travel series.

An organization in which I was not so successful in avoiding conflict was Design for Clark County. It consisted of civic-minded citizens who wanted to ensure good government and a good environment for the community. The conflict began when I agreed to head one of four goals committees, the one on government. The committee proved to be the most active of the four, perhaps because goals can be expressed more specifically in government than in other areas of the community. Because of the attention the committee received and because the goals generally coincided with *The Columbian*'s editorial policies, some members of the community began to think that the newspaper and I were running Design. I later backed off sharply in my participation, but the association between the paper and the organization had been established so strongly in people's minds that it was several years before the effect of my initial involvement was forgotten. Design might have been more effective if it had been perceived as a voice more independent of the newspaper.

I served for a short time on the board of the Washington Environmental Council, a private non-profit organization. No problems resulted as long as the council remained concerned with general environmental policies, but when it began to talk about supporting and opposing candidates for the legislature, I got out fast. I found myself in Kilpatrick's shoes, however, when I agreed to serve on the Washington State Planning Commission. It was not a real planning commission. I would not have served on an official state policy agency. It was a two-year ad hoc committee of citizens and officials charged with proposing a new state planning act. Mostly it held hearings on what other people thought the state should do. Eventually the staff, with some help from commission members, drew up a model act to submit to the legislature. The act didn't get very far—or I probably would have encountered greater conflict than I did. I thought I should not comment editorially on the proposal, although I did write an article for the op-ed page trying to explain the model act (with an editor's note pointing out my connection with the commission). Participation on the commission made for two interesting and informative years, but if the act had been seriously considered for adoption a conflict of interest would have prevented me from commenting editorially on it and probably would have hurt the credibility of anything *The Columbian* said, even if the writing had been done by someone else.

I felt less concern about the four years that I served on the Washington Commission for the Humanities, a private, non-profit organization that awarded money mostly to local groups to bring the ideas of humanities scholars to bear on public issues. Some of the awards were controversial among the commission members, but I don't remember any award that would have called for editorial comment in my newspaper. (This was before the National Endowment for the Arts and, to a lesser degree, the National Endowment for the Humanities, became matters of public controversy.) One reason I enjoyed the commission was the chance to know and associate with the other members. It was a stimulating group and one that was concerned with projects that generally were far enough away from my circulation area to present few chances for conflict. Besides, I told myself, an editorial writer needs to have some stimulating, continuing associations beyond those of family, religion and the Rotary Club. Editorial writers aren't supposed to be hermits.

TO ACCEPT OR NOT TO ACCEPT

Another potential conflict of interest concerns what to do about "freebies," the gifts, large and small, that people with views to push are only too willing to share with newspaper people. In recent years government and business, including the newspaper industry, have tended to become more sensitive to possible conflicts in this area. Tighter codes have been written for public officials, and in many instances editorial writers have written in support of the tougher restrictions. If newspapers expect public officials to observe a higher standard, should not newspapers themselves observe an equally high one?

In the mid-1970s, following the lead of other journalistic organizations, NCEW tightened its Basic Statement of Principles. The conflict of interest portion of the original statement, adopted in 1949, had merely said: "The editorial writer should never be motivated by personal interest, nor use his influence to seek special favors for himself or others. He should hold himself above any possible taint of corruption, whatever its source." The revised statement now reads:

The editorial writer should never use his or her influence to seek personal favors of any kind. Gifts of value, free travel and other favors that can compromise integrity, or appear to do so, should not be accepted.

The writer should be constantly alert to conflicts of interest, real or apparent, including those that may arise from financial holdings, secondary employment, holding public office or involvement in political, civic or other organizations. Timely disclosure can minimize suspicion.

Editors should seek to hold syndicates to these standards.

The writer, further to enhance editorial page credibility, also should encourage the institution he or she represents to avoid conflicts of interest, real or apparent.

The Professional Standards Committee and the Executive Committee of NCEW had wanted more specific language on freebies: "Gifts, free travel and other things of value can compromise integrity. Nothing of more than token value should be accepted." A majority of NCEW members, however, preferred to rely on their own consciences, rather than on a strict rule, to tell them what was acceptable and what was not.

Free Trips

The wording in the statement regarding travel was softened partly because NCEW officers at that time were hoping to arrange a trip for members to the People's Republic of China and a trip partly paid for by the Chinese was seen as the only way to get there. Similar concerns were expressed by all six editorial writers who responded to invitations to participate in a *Masthead* symposium on junkets. Basically they argued that the benefits of subsidized trips abroad outweighed any dangers that might arise from possible conflicts of interest. H. Brandt Ayers of the *Anniston* (Ala.) *Star* said he never would have been able to travel to the then Soviet Union and meet leaders firsthand if the trip had not been subsidized. "What we wrote is a better standard for judging independence, intelligence and integrity than who paid for the trip," he said.[16] John Causten Currey of the *Daily Oklahoman* and *Oklahoma City Times* said that familiarization trips offered by the armed services provided the only way that editorial writers could see what the defense budgets bought. He said a paid trip to Israel as an official guest provided him a picture of the Middle East he could not have obtained as a private citizen.[17] Smith Hempstone, then a syndicated columnist, contended that any problems involved in accepting a subsidized trip could be overcome by letting readers know who paid for the trip.[18] Richard B. Laney of the *Deseret News*, Salt Lake City, wondered how free travel could be compromising to those who accepted it, since he suspected that invitations are extended only to those known, or thought to be, friendly. "The persuasion of those already persuaded may not be gutsy PR," he wrote, "but it's hardly an attack on editorial morality either."[19]

One of the earliest, and strongest statements concerning the dangers of accepting free trips was made more than 20 years before NCEW tightened its code. In 1952 Robert Estabrook of the *Washington Post* wrote:

At least a respectable argument can be made that the public interest is served in making available to newspaper readers more information about governmental programs, particularly programs abroad. The plain fact is that many newspapers, if left to their own resources, would neglect these areas and their readers would be the poorer for it. . . .

If we expect to persuade our followers there is something wrong with unreported political funds or junkets by Congressmen at the taxpayers' expense, then we have an obligation, it seems to me, to pay our own way. We properly criticize "influence" with public officials, but I wonder if our readers, if they knew of the all-expense tours, would see much difference.[20]

Stricter codes, unless one stays home and makes no junkets, cost more money. However, in general newspapers and the media are more prosperous than they were when Estabrook wrote. If editors and publishers think their staff members should be sent off somewhere for a story, they should pay as much of their way as they possibly can. What they pay out in money they will regain in credibility with readers.

Gifts

When newspaper salaries were notoriously low, some reporters reasoned that free liquor and tickets to shows and games helped make up for the bucks they didn't get. Today salaries are up, and gifts are down. Some newspapers have attempted to stop the flow of gifts, however inconsequential. "We no longer see cases of Scotch arriving for the sports staff at Christmas," Catherine Ford, associate editor of the *Calgary* (Alberta) *Herald*, wrote in a *Masthead* symposium on ethics. "The shopping columnist does not furnish his house with presents from retailers; the fashion editor buys her own clothes. No newspaper with any sense of ethics at all accepts free trips, considerations from advertisers or free gifts to staff members. Only rarely will an editor approve of staff participation in media events offering prizes, or accept complimentary tickets for staff."[21]

Some editors contend that, if writers can be bought for a bottle of whiskey or a lunch, they have no integrity worth buying. Mark Clutter of the *Wichita* (Kan.) *Beacon* has asked: Why should newspaper people "be offended by gifts of whiskey, ham or similar items?" Sometimes the gifts are a matter of "public relations routine"; sometimes they are "expressions of genuine friendship or admiration," he said. "Whatever the motive, it would be churlish to refuse. . . . No one can give payola to a man of integrity. To a man who has no integrity, practically everything is payola."[22] Jack Craemer of the *San Rafael* (Calif.) *Independent-Journal*, however, said everyone on that paper sent everything back to donors, even though they "look upon us as goof-balls."[23]

CONCLUSION

Probably few editorial writers, and newspaper people in general for that matter, are directly influenced by the gifts, travel and other favors they receive. The publicity over tougher codes has made many of them sensitive to the most blatant forms of handouts. They know that they are not being influenced by the ticket or the drink. But do their readers know? Editorial writers may know that they have made every effort possible to report objectively on a free trip they have taken. But do their readers know? If they were told, would they believe it?

When conflict of interest is involved, appearance can be as important as reality in maintaining credibility.

QUESTIONS AND EXERCISES

1. As an editorial writer, where would you draw the line on participation in political and civic affairs? Would the size of the community make a difference?

2. Does an editorial writer or editor have a responsibility to participate in the life of the community in addition to contributing through work on the paper? Again, might the answer depend on the size of the community?

3. Should an editorial writer feel freer to accept a civic task that is less likely than other tasks to affect the community in which the paper circulates? Does distance, in other words, make a difference?

4. Should an editorial writer feel freer to contribute to causes supported by the editorial policy of the newspaper than to other causes?

5. Should newspaper management people feel freer to participate in community affairs than news and editorial people?

6. Should a newspaper establish a code that spells out what freebies, trips and other perquisites news and editorial people can accept? If so, where should the paper draw the line?

7. If a newspaper does not establish a code, how should it avoid conflict of interest or the appearance of conflict of interest?

8. How do you respond to the argument that, if journalists are not honest and trustworthy, no code will make them so?

9. If you were an editorial writer, what trips would you regard as acceptable?

10. Have you seen evidence in the columns of newspapers in your area that indicates the writers do or do not accept free trips? If they do, do they explain the circumstances to their readers?

11. Do the papers in your area have official codes concerning professional conduct? If so, what do they prescribe?

Section 3

THE
How
OF THE
Editorial Page

Chapter 10

Nine Steps to Editorial Writing

I would not suggest that writing editorials can be codified like a law book or that anyone can learn to write good editorials by learning a few rules. But . . . it would be possible, I submit, for editorial [writers] to advance their craft by giving a little more thought to . . . what would . . . not be rules but intelligent guides.

—VERMONT ROYSTER, WALL STREET JOURNAL[1]

No magic formulas exist for writing editorials. No two editorials are ever exactly alike. Editorial writers have their own styles. Newspapers have different editorial policies. Each day brings new topics for comment. In spite of all the many possible ways to approach writing editorials, the editorial-writing process is basically the same.

An experienced writer may be able to turn out a prize-winning editorial in an hour or so. A beginner may struggle all day long. But each, consciously or subconsciously, proceeds through a succession of steps to produce the journalistic writing form that we call an editorial. The purpose of this chapter is to walk the editorial writer or would-be editorial writer through these steps, one by one. The steps can be defined in different ways, but for our purposes let us identify these nine:

1. Selecting a topic.
2. Determining the purpose of the editorial.
3. Determining the audience.
4. Deciding on the tone of the editorial.
5. Researching the topic.
6. Determining the general format.
7. Writing the beginning of the editorial.
8. Writing the body of the editorial.
9. Writing the conclusion.

To provide an illustration, we will select a topic for an editorial and follow the writing of the editorial through the nine steps.

SELECTING A TOPIC

Selecting a topic usually involves deciding among a variety of subjects that might seem appropriate on any one day. Editorial writers typically scan the morning newspaper, which usually carries international, national, regional, state and local stories that might be worthy of comment, plus off-beat stories that can provide topics for change-of-pace editorials.

On a several-person staff, where writers have their own specialties, some of these topics automatically may fall to certain writers. Selecting a topic may be more difficult on a small, especially a one-person, staff. Writers with limited time for editorial writing are likely to select subjects that they know about or that they can research easily. When time runs short, it is often easier to write about a national or international issue than about a regional or local one, on which you are likely to have to do your own digging for information. Even where writers are few, they should try to select topics from day to day that will provide readers with a variety of subjects at different levels, from local to international.

Questions a writer might ask in deciding on a topic: Can I make a significant contribution to public understanding on this topic? Do I have information or insights that are not generally held among my readers? Is discussion of the topic timely; does it come at an appropriate time for public discussion? Some of these questions may overlap with our next steps, determining the purpose and the audience of the editorial, but they are part of the process of picking a topic.

For the example in this chapter, let us decide that among the topics available to write about on this day we will select a story about a U.S. Supreme Court decision that struck down a "hate crime" law that banned cross burning and similar expressions of racial bias. The judges, by a 9-0 vote, held that a St. Paul, Minn., law violated First Amendment protections of free speech. The topic seems especially interesting, since cities and states across the country have faced a similar problem of how to suppress inflammatory words and actions without infringing on rights of free speech. The decision might be expected to arouse concerns among those who think the courts have been soft on crime.

The picking of editorial topics by itself is an important part of the process of trying to persuade readers. Communications research shows that the mass media exert their strongest influence through helping set the agenda for public discussion. *What* the media choose to write and talk about is seen as having a more significant effect on the public than what the media *say* about the chosen topics.[2] Selecting also is the first step toward getting readers to read what you write. You should not pick topics solely to attract the most readers, but if you write about obscure, technical or dull topics, potential readers are certain to move on to other parts of the paper.

DETERMINING PURPOSE AND AUDIENCE

Determining the purpose and determining the audience of an editorial are interrelated. The purpose of an editorial is to convince a certain audience to think or do something. The purpose may not be to persuade all of our readers. We may want to urge all readers to vote for a certain candidate for office, or we may want to direct our editorial primarily toward convincing readers who are not inclined to be favorable to this candidate. We may want to urge readers in general to turn out for a public hearing on a proposed freeway through the city, or we may want to convince members of the highway commission that the freeway is not a good idea.

We may have more than one audience in mind for an editorial. We may want both to convince the highway commission and to get people to turn out for a hearing. On occasion an editorial, addressed to readers in general, will contain sufficient technical information to speak to the experts as well. On other occasions an editorial will be directed specifically to the narrower group. In a two-level editorial, writers should be careful not to become so involved in the fine points that they lose their general readers.

"Name Check Bouncers" is an editorial, from *The Oregonian* of Portland, that, while aimed at pressuring the House of Representatives to release the names of all members who had written bad checks, also tries to explain why "the House bank matter still merits public interest." At the conclusion the editorial tells the House to tell all and let the voters decide how they want to deal with the guilty ones.

Name Check Bouncers
Public and members who didn't kite checks at House bank deserve full disclosure

The House of Representatives has a chance this week to do something about Congress' sorry image. Whether that something helps or hurts the institution's reputation will depend entirely on the House itself.

If the House votes to release only the names and account histories of the 24 worst rubber-check writers at the House bank, the people's body will deserve all the scorn the people will heap upon it. If members vote to identify the 355 current and former members who banked on the House (overdrawing their accounts and paying no penalties or interest on these loans), the House will regain some measure of public credibility.

Only full disclosure might stop the ongoing public abuse of the House on the check-kiting scandal.

In fact, the House bank issue has always been more symbolic than real. Although the now-defunct House bank was run by public servants and on public property, its funds, the members' pay, were private.

Check bouncers were causing other members, not taxpayers, a financial hardship. That said, the House bank matter still merits public interest—full disclosure. These are, after all, the guys and gals who are supposed to be keeping the nation's finances in order. Moreover, lawmakers were essentially receiving interest-free loans—in some cases, very large ones. Was such "income" reported on members' tax returns? If the "loans" totaled more than $10,000, did members report them on their financial disclosure forms, as required?

In the end, three reasons argue for spotlighting more than the 24 worst offenders, as the House Ethics Committee voted to do Thursday.

First, this determination is arbitrary.

Second, identifying only 24 would let off the hook those other members who overdrew their accounts by more than their next paycheck. There are said to be 200 such cases. Why cover up these cases?

Third, not identifying all offenders would keep on the hook members who have never bounced a check at the House bank. Lawmakers who kept their finances in order would remain guilty by association. That's unfair to these innocent colleagues.

The House should tell voters all, and let the chips bounce where they may.

The Oregonian[3]

The purpose of an editorial and the audience for it will depend partly on our understanding of how persuasion through editorials takes place. Half a century ago mass communications were thought to exert a strong, direct influence on audiences. The Bullet Theory, or Hypodermic Needle Theory, popular then suggested that information and opinion from the media flowed directly into the heads of recipients. Editorials, presumably, would be read and acted upon by readers. Then in the 1940s researchers began to find that audiences were not paying as much attention as had been thought and were not being persuaded to the degree anticipated.[4] To explain this apparent inattention, researchers came up with the Two-Step Flow Theory. It maintained that ideas tended to flow from the media to a select group of opinion leaders, who in turn passed ideas on to the general population. Thus, if only 20 percent of readers read editorials every day, this theory suggested, that was all right, since presumably these few were the opinion leaders. But that theory didn't last long either. Further research showed that information flow is much more complex. The population is not neatly divided into leaders and followers. Much information goes directly to users of the media, not through a middle level.[5] Reader surveys show that relatively large percentages of readers read editorials at least once in a while.[6]

Current theory suggests that it is upon this general audience that a newspaper's editorials have the most effect over a long period. The effect is produced not so much by the persuasion of specific editorials as by the day-to-day dripping of the editorial writer's ink on the stone of the public consciousness. It is the members of a community who decide elections, decide whether to stay or move to another city, or feel good or bad about their community. All these people are the editorial writer's principal audience, even when an editorial calls on a school board to fire a superintendent or criticizes a city manager for a mistake. Public officials are as likely to be motivated by an aroused public as by an editorial's eloquent logic.

In selecting our topic on the "hate crime" decision, we already have indicated at least one purpose for our editorial: to help the readers understand how the ruling might affect them. We have identified an audience: the general, non-expert public. It is not likely that the editorial can be expected to have a direct effect on the lower courts, law enforcers or lawmakers, although it is possible what we write might have some effect when local and state officials consider whether existing laws need to be changed. Since we are not legal experts or writing for a law journal, our principal audience will be the general public and our principal purpose will be to help lay persons understand the issues involved.

DECIDING THE TONE

At least as far back as Aristotle, writers have been concerned with how they can best persuade their audiences. Aristotle identified three avenues available to the persuader: the character of the persuader, the attitude of the hearer and the arguments themselves.[7] The more credible the persuader, the more likely it is that an audience will be persuaded. If an editorial page has attained credibility with its readers over the years, editorials on that page are likely to be viewed favorably. Aristotle thought the communicator needed good sense, good will and a good moral character—appropriate prescriptions for an editorial writer.[8] Concerning the attitude of the audience, Aristotle saw that "persuasion is effected through the audience when they are brought . . . into a state of emotion." For example, "pain or joy, or liking or hatred" can have an effect in changing attitudes. Concerning the third avenue, he saw that "persuasion is effected by the argument themselves."[9] Thus, at least from the time of Aristotle, persuaders have recognized that they have a choice: They can appeal to the emotions or to the rationality of their audiences.

When editorial writers select a tone for an editorial, they have many choices, ranging from deeply serious to satirical and humorous. As for the choice between an appeal primarily to emotion or one primarily to reason, some recent research suggests that emotion and reason may not necessarily be in opposition to each other and that simultaneous appeals to both may serve to reinforce persuasion.[10] For the purposes of most editorials, however, writers choose between making an appeal based mainly on feelings, values and symbols and making one based mainly on information, evidence and logic. The decision will depend on the subject matter and the occasion as well as the writer's own preferences. On the day following the assassination of a prominent political figure, a writer might use an emotional tone to express outrage and grief over the tragedy. The next day the writer might take a more rational approach to talk about what contributed to the killing and how to prevent such incidents in the future. An emotional approach might be appropriate to provide entertainment, to arouse readers to action, to chastise or to praise someone. A rational approach might be more appropriate to explain to readers something they don't know or to convince them of the correctness of the editorial writer's conclusions.

Emotion undoubtedly plays a smaller role in editorial writing today than several decades ago, when daily newspapers were numerous and subscribers could take the paper that came closest to expressing their own opinions. Readers relished reading emotional, partisan appeals, and, if opinions were not changed, they were at least reinforced. Today's editorial writers must appeal to readers with a much broader spectrum of opinions. A rousing editorial based mostly on bombast may please a small group of partisans but leave other readers unconvinced or repulsed. Today's readers are better educated than readers of a hundred years ago and people as a whole are better informed; they should be better able to recognize incorrect or incomplete information. It may be more fun to dash off an editorial that attacks a person or policy without mercy, and perhaps without much thought; such an editorial may draw the strongest, most immediate response from readers. But what value does the editorial have beyond giving a momentary emotional high to some readers and long-term pain to others? Henry M. Keezing of the *New Britain* (Conn.) *Herald* said that one of his prized possessions was a letter to the editor lauding a flamboyant editorial he had whipped up in a matter of minutes. The letter was highly complimentary but it "was written in pencil, in a scrawling longhand, on a piece of paper which a beer distributor gives to cafes and taverns for use for menus." Keezing had made a hit with someone in a tavern. But he said he would have much preferred to hear from a community leader, a legislator or a person of influence.[11]

Columnist James J. Kilpatrick, who writes with about as much indignation as any American newspaper writer, has described how the complexities of today's world have inhibited him from just sounding off. He noted that writing about something you know nothing about is easy; "when research fails, prejudice is there to prop you." But "what raises the sweat and paralyzes the fingers on the keys is to grapple with an issue in which the equities are divided," he said. "It is a maddening thing, but damned little in the editor's world is all white or all black; the editor's world is full of mugwump grays."[12]

The time has come now for us to decide on the tone that we will take in our editorial about the courts. That should be an easy decision after the discussion above. Subjects relating to First Amendment rights might, on occasion, be written in an emotional manner. It might be necessary to raise a public outcry against the trampling of journalistic or religious freedoms. If a newspaper reporter has been held in contempt of court and jailed for trying to report a trial, we might sound off in loud protest against the actions of the judge. The subject we have picked probably will require considerable explanation. While we will hope to convince readers of our point of view, we will not be asking them to take up pickets and march around the courthouse. A rational approach seems to be needed here.

RESEARCHING THE TOPIC

When we decide whether our editorial will be primarily emotional or rational in tone, we also determine the type of research we will have to do to write the editorial. If we can write the piece off the tops of our heads, we can skip research. If we are going to present only one point of view (about which we will say more when we discuss the next step) we can limit our research to the arguments on one side. The amount of research conducted by writers depends to some extent on how much time they have and the availability of resource materials. Very few writers have the luxury of going to the public library or a law library or the city hall or the courthouse to dig out information for that day's editorial. A telephone call—to an office across town or to the state capital—may provide a writer with the only opportunity to obtain information that is not immediately available in the newspaper office. So the kinds of reference materials mentioned in Chapter 4 need to be nearby.

In our court decision example, we start with the story in the morning paper. It seems to provide most of the details we will need to talk about this particular case. The Associated Press story noted that Robert V. Viktora, then 17, had been charged with burning two makeshift crosses in the yard of a black family's home. The Minnesota Supreme Court ruled that he could be tried under the local law if the law were limited to banning only "fighting words" and speech likely to incite disorder or lawless conduct. The U.S. Supreme Court held that even that limited application could "handicap the expression of particular ideas." A closer reading of the story reveals that, while all judges agreed to strike down the law, four of them were concerned primarily that the law was too sweeping, that it would forbid expression "that causes only hurt feelings, offense or resentment."[13]

Readers are likely to want to know whether the decision has put in jeopardy laws in their community and state and whether other (constitutional) means are available to fight "hate crimes." Perhaps the news side of your newspaper already has raised these questions with legal authorities. On the day the original story ran, *The Oregonian* published a separate story saying that the ruling probably would not affect existing Oregon law because of the way it was written but might affect the State of Washington. If the news department has not done the legwork on questions such as these, you would need to contact your own sources. You probably should do so in any case. The local city attorney and attorneys in the state attorney general's office may be able to tell you about laws that apply in your community and about court decisions in your state. A check of your newspaper's clippings files or computer base may turn up news stories about similar cases.

DETERMINING THE GENERAL FORMAT

Deciding whether to be basically emotional or rational in our editorial does not determine how the editorial will be written, especially if we decide on a rational tone. Communication researchers have devoted a lot of effort to trying to discover how arguments can be presented in the most persuasive manner. Among their concerns have been (1) one-sided versus two-sided arguments, (2) the ordering of arguments and (3) the degree to which opinions can be changed.

Research going back to soldiers in World War II suggests that the one-sided versus two-sided decision partly depends on the audience being addressed. One-sided arguments were found to be more persuasive when the receivers of messages were in agreement with the arguments or when receivers were of lower intelligence or less educated. This approach was also found to be more effective when the receivers were not familiar with the issue being discussed and were not likely to be exposed to opposition arguments in the future, and when the topic was not controversial.[14] Presentation of opposing arguments was more effective when the receivers were initially hostile to the persuader's view, were highly educated, were accustomed to hearing both sides of an argument or were likely to hear the other side eventually.[15]

Researchers have come up with contradictory findings about the order of arguments. Both primacy (the favored argument first) and recency (the favored argument last) have been found to be persuasive. The primacy approach has the advantage of drawing an early favorable opinion from the audience, an opinion that may remain unchanged during the remainder of the presentation. The recency approach has the advantage of giving the last impression a better chance of being remembered. One line of reasoning suggests that, if you have arguments that are likely to be received favorably by your audience, you should present them first to establish a favorable setting for less favorable arguments later. If you have a solution for a problem or a need, it may be better to present the problem or the need first, then suggest your solution.[16] Researchers agree that the weakest spot for an argument is in the middle of the message, so you might put arguments unfavorable to your position there.[17]

The third aspect of communication research involves the extent to which readers can be persuaded to change their opinions. It seems clear that readers' first inclinations are to seek and perceive information that reinforces their present viewpoints. Some studies suggest that reinforcing opinions is about all that can be expected of editorials. Readers, they point out, tend to ignore, disbelieve or reinterpret information that does not conform to their own beliefs. Still, some research shows that readers sometimes seek out information that is contrary to their beliefs and, within limits, are willing to modify their beliefs. A person presumably is able to feel comfortable with a different opinion if it is perceived to fall within a certain comfort zone. The closer the offered opinion is to the outer edge of that zone, the greater the change that will have to occur in the person's opinion. If the offered opinion is even barely outside the zone, however, it is likely to be perceived as more divergent than it actually is, and therefore unacceptable. The trick for the editorial writer is to know enough about the newspaper's readers to be able to push for a maximum amount of opinion change without going so far as to antagonize readers with demands for too much change.[18]

In deciding whether to present one or two sides in our editorial on the St. Paul case, we might keep in mind that the initial reaction of a substantial number of readers is likely to be shock and disbelief that the court seemingly could condone such a horrible crime. If we wanted to support that point of view, a one-sided, indignant argument might be appropriate. But, if we want to persuade readers who react in this manner that a free-speech issue is involved here, a two-sided argument probably is called for. The editorial would recognize and sympathize with their concerns but then try to convince them that free speech needs to be protected and that other lawful means are available for dealing with hateful actions.

In writing an editorial that presents opposing arguments, we have another basic choice: whether to tell our readers at the beginning what our conclusion will be or to wait until the end of the editorial after the two sides have been considered. The first approach might start out by assuring readers that they have nothing to fear from the ruling. Their concerns might then be examined, followed by evidence and arguments intended to reassure them. If we follow the second approach, and do not reveal our editorial position at the beginning, we might better be able to convince readers that we understand, and give credence, to their concerns. This type of editorial might also benefit from keeping readers in suspense, not knowing until the end how we will come down on the issue.

In teaching editorial writing classes, I have found it helpful in explaining these, and other, formats, to designate types of editorials using formulas that look like something that might come out of a chemistry course. SA_1A_2DC describes a two-sided editorial. S stands for the statement of the *situation* that prompted the editorial. A_1A_2 indicates the presentation of the *argument* on one side of the issue followed by *argument* on the other side. D is *discussion*, following by the *conclusion* (C). SAC indicates a one-sided editorial with the conclusion at the end; CSAC, a one-sided editorial with the conclusion stated at the beginning. Not many editorials are written strictly according to these formulas, but they give the beginning editorial writer an idea of the options that are available.

WRITING THE BEGINNING

The beginning of an editorial may be the most important part. The first few words must prove sufficiently interesting to attract readers to the editorial. Although we have noted types of editorials that start by stating the conclusion, the most frequently used beginning is a brief statement of the proposal, incident or situation that has prompted the editorial. It may be a simple restatement of information that has been reported in the news columns. This approach is especially appropriate for readers who have no previous knowledge of what the editorial writer is talking about. It also provides a way into the editorial without antagonizing readers who may hold views different from the editorial writer's.

Sometimes a writer needs to present an even broader approach than a statement of the facts of the situation. Starting with some background (designated B in our editorial-writer formula) might help readers understand how the immediate topic relates to more general information with which they may be familiar. Sometimes an effective way to get readers to modify their opinions is to begin with the statement of a generally accepted point of view. After readers have become comfortable with what the editorial writer is saying, the editorial can take what I call a "Yes, but" switch to try to convince readers that another point of view makes even more sense. This approach might be particularly effective in an editorial that seeks to debunk commonly held views or takes a stand that may surprise readers. This approach is not the same as building up an artificial argument to be knocked down. The opening argument need to be credible. "Yes, but" might be useful when a newspaper wants to change or modify an earlier editorial stance on an issue. This type of editorial can be readable and persuasive, especially if the writer sneaks up on the reader and presents the counter-argument unexpectedly.

An editorial sometimes can be started with a question (Q). This can serve to focus the point of an editorial immediately and tell readers that they can expect to find the answer by reading the editorial. A question that arouses curiosity can be effective in attracting readers. But, if a question simply asks, "What should be done about such-and-such?" and the reader answers, "I don't care" or "I don't know," the editorial writer has lost a reader. Questions need to be real, not rhetorical.

If we were to write our editorial that stated our opinion at the beginning, we might open the editorial in this manner, as did the *West Central Tribune*, in Willmar, Minn., in "Supreme Court Made Right Decision on Hate Crimes Law": "As deplorable as burning a cross and other hate-inspired messages are, the United States Supreme Court made the right decision declaring St. Paul's hate crime law unconstitutional earlier this week." This editorial is basically a CBAC editorial with only a brief paragraph (the fourth) touching on the justification for such a law.

Supreme Court Made Right Decision on Hate Crimes Law

As deplorable as burning a cross and other hate-inspired messages are, the United States Supreme Court made the right decision in declaring St. Paul's hate crime law unconstitutional earlier this week.

The law attempts to impose special penalties against the racist thugs and mindless bigots who terrorize people because of their race, ethnicity, religion, sex or sexual preference.

Specifically, the lawsuit dealt with two white youths who allegedly burned a two-foot-tall cross on the lawn of a black family in St. Paul's east side. The cross is an obvious reference to the hatred portrayed by the Ku Klux Klan activities.

The idea behind the law is understandable: In a time when Neo-Nazis, Skinheads and the likes of David Duke appear to be making a comeback with their hate-inspiring messages, society feels a respon-sibility to protect the targets of that hate.

But, like the flag burning controversy before it, sometimes the Supreme Court has to make tough decisions that benefit goons in the short run but, in the end, protect the society in which we live.

The protection comes in the form of free speech and free expression. Without it, as George Washington once said, "dumb and silent we may be led, like sheep, to the slaughter."

When limits are placed on free speech and expression, the Constitution is under-mined.

Freedom of speech is and should continue to be a paramount consideration for any Supreme Court decision. To over-ride the right of free speech, overwhelming circumstances should be present and, in the case of the St. Paul hate crime law, clearly they were not.

As Justice Antonin Scalia wrote, "The First Amendment does not permit St. Paul to impose special prohibitions on those speakers who express views on disfavor-able subjects."

The white supremacists who terrorize blacks and other people with non-European ancestry have an ugly message that should continue to be rebuked by the larger society, and it is hoped that St. Paul will find an appropriate law to charge these hoodlums.

But even if these young men escape without being punished, the larger society will benefit by the Supreme Court's deci-sion not to infringe upon the freedom that is the centerpiece of our Constitution and our society: The freedom of speech.

West Central Tribune, Willmar, Minn.[19]

The *Owatonna* (Minn.) *People's Press* took a similar approach but began with a quotation from the lawyer for the accused Viktora: "What's being said by the court is that all sides have a right to express themselves. . . . you can't make a law on the books that simply makes the expression itself illegal." The editorial writer then stated: "And that, we suppose, is the whole point in the U.S. Supreme Court's decision Monday striking down a St. Paul hate crimes law that prohibited the burning of a cross on a black family's lawn."

A CBAC editorial that expressed a contrary view of the decision might start: "The U.S. Supreme Court has extended the right of free speech beyond reason and common sense by applying it to a man who burned a cross in a black family's yard." Or possibly: "The U.S. Supreme Court Monday made it more difficult for communities to fight racial hatred by extending the right of free speech to a man who burned a cross in a black family's yard."

If we were to open the editorial by posing the issue as a question, we might do as the *Daily Tribune* of Hibbing, Minn., did in "Free Speech" (reprinted on the following page): "Should somebody be allowed to burn a cross on a lawn as a means of exercising free speech?" The writer then expressed concerns over such reprehensible acts, sketched the case involved in the decision and noted that the Supreme Court was faced with a dilemma. Then came the first hint of the direc-tion the editorial would take: "The Constitution, however, is pretty clear that freedom of speech must be tolerated in a democracy. Over the years, the courts have ruled again and again in favor of that freedom." The editorial is basically a CA_1BA_2C editorial with a weak A_1 (second paragraph, where the writer condemns bigoted, hateful attacks).

An editorial might start with background, perhaps in this manner: "Robert A. Viktora was accused of burning a cross in the yard of a black family in St. Paul. The Minnesota Supreme Court ruled that it was proper to prosecute him under a law that bans 'fighting words' that are likely to incite disorder. Monday the U.S.

Supreme Court disagreed. Viktora's actions, the court ruled, are protected by the First Amendment."

Free Speech

Should somebody be allowed to burn a cross on a front lawn as a means of exercising their free speech?

Cross burning is a reprehensible act. It's a sign of bigotry and hatred that attacks the very core of the founding principles of this nation, that all people are created equal. Historically it conjures up decades of overt racism, lynchings and 200 years of pain for black Americans.

St. Paul tried to stop cross burnings and swastika paintings and other signs of hatred with a hate-crime ordinance. Under this law, a St. Paul man who had a cross burned in his front yard was able to go after the perpetrator. Eventually the case reached the U.S. Supreme Court where the justices declared the St. Paul law unconstitutional this week.

The Supremes were faced with a dilemma, as they often are. Few people support cross burnings or flag burnings. The Constitution, however, is pretty clear that freedom of speech must be tolerated in a democracy. Over the years, the courts have ruled again and again in favor of that freedom.

In this case, the court members said there were probably other ways to stop people from performing obscene acts of bigotry, and we agree. Some cities use arson laws. Others use terrorist threat laws.

In the great scheme of a democracy, all voices must be free to express themselves. It's quite possible, and, as we've seen in the Eastern European nations, probable, that at some point the government gets too strong, too dominant, and it fails to represent the people. Protection of freedom of speech is a check and balance against tyranny.

But do we only protect some free speech? Do we draw the line at some point?

The Supreme Court has been unable to find that gray line and so it almost always comes down hard on the side of the freedom of the people. That's good, even though it hurts at times.

Cross burning is a threat to someone's well being and should be prosecuted as such. A city ordinance that prevents people from doing symbolic actions to express their viewpoint, however, no matter how different that viewpoint might be, is contrary to the spirit of the nation.

Daily Tribune, Hibbing, Minn.[20]

An editorial that began with a statement of the situation (S) might start: "The U.S. Supreme Court has decided that nothing in the First Amendment can keep someone from burning a cross on someone else's lawn." This might be a fairly provocative beginning. It is a dramatic way of describing the decision. It hints that perhaps nothing can be done to keep someone from burning crosses. But it also sets the stage for us to suggest later that the First Amendment does not provide the only possible recourse for fighting hate crimes.

WRITING THE BODY OF THE EDITORIAL

The steps we have discussed thus far, starting with picking a topic, have covered a number of pages and involved quite a lot of explanations. Except possibly for research, most of the steps could have been taken quickly. Not more than a few seconds may be required for an experienced editorial writer to select a topic, decide on the purpose and the proper audience, determine the tone and select the general approach. Much of the process takes place without conscious reflection. After writing editorials for a few years, editorial writers get a feeling for the right way, for them, to write an editorial. With the beginning determined, at least tentatively, and all the other steps behind them, they are ready to write the body of the editorial—the explanations, the arguments and the analysis. Here is where they either will or will not convince their readers. Here is where they win or lose in the battle to persuade.

If we decide to use the opening sentence that appears in the last paragraph of the previous section, we will need to compose an editorial based on the SBA_1A_2DC model. That opening, being somewhat a teaser, needs to be followed by a brief explanation of the burning incident and the contradictory positions of the two supreme courts. One long paragraph and one short one then will constitute the background (B). Since our editorial starts with a concern over prosecuting such crimes, it seems natural to use the first set of arguments to expand on this concern. The victimized family expresses dismay. How can the First Amendment be interpreted to protect people who do these hateful things? Shouldn't cross burning fall under the same category as shouting "Fire!" in a crowded building? Isn't a burning cross a clear mark of prejudice and hate?

To move into the second set of arguments, we use a transition sentence: "These questions were not ignored by the court." This gives us an opportunity to report that the court does not think that these are not reprehensible acts. Furthermore, a near majority of the court thinks that constitutionally-sound "hate crime" laws can be devised, and several local and state attorneys think that other existing laws may meet the standards. The effect of the ruling may not be as drastic as it might seem at first. We suggest that the lawyers examine these laws when more information is available.

Then we turn to our major argument, noting that the Supreme Court itself stated that St. Paul had other means than the First Amendment to fight these kinds of crimes. We suggest laws against destruction of property and trespassing. In the discussion (D) we say that authorities should find it easier to prosecute people for their actions than for their expressions and that Americans need reassuring that they can say whatever they wish as long as they don't libel or physically harm someone.

At this point our basic position should be clear to readers. We are more concerned about the threat to free speech than about letting bigots burn some crosses. In the final paragraph we point out that, while it may be tempting to crack down on the speech of white majority bigots today, this type of crackdown has been used more in this country to persecute minorities who have tried to speak out. (Our completed editorial "Burn the First Amendment?" follows.)

Burn the First Amendment?
Has the Supreme Court made it impossible to fight "hate crimes"?

The U.S. Supreme Court has decided that nothing in the First Amendment can keep someone from burning a cross on someone else's lawn.

In a unanimous opinion Monday, the court ruled that "hate crime" laws that forbid expressions of racial bias violate the free-speech rights of even the most maliciously motivated bigots. A 17-year-old, Robert A. Viktora, had been charged with burning two makeshift crosses in the yard of a black family in St. Paul, Minn. The state Supreme Court approved prosecuting Viktora under a local ordinance that banned "fighting words" and speech likely to incite disorder or lawless conduct.

The U.S. Supreme Court disapproved, on the ground that such a law may "handicap the expression of free ideas."

A member of the victimized family said she was dismayed by the ruling. No doubt many other people across the country are equally dismayed. Citizens who are concerned over the evil effects of racial prejudice may wonder what kind of interpretation of the First Amendment permits a hate-inspired young white man to terrorize a black family who had caused him no wrong. In earlier cases, the justices ruled that the First Amendment does not give a person the right to give a false alarm of "Fire!" in a crowded theater or the right to use language to provoke a riot that endangers the public safety. In the St. Paul case, was not the safety of the black family in peril? Has a burning cross not been the symbol of white violence against blacks since the days of Reconstruction? What could constitute stronger evidence of racial prejudice and hate?

These questions were not ignored by the court. "Let there be no mistake about our belief that burning a cross in someone's front yard is reprehensible," Justice Antonin Scalia wrote in an opinion joined by four other members of the court. The other four members, while agreeing to kill the St. Paul ordinance, indicated their belief that a narrowly drafted "hate crime" law could pass the First-Amendment test. Attorneys in several states, including Oregon, have expressed their belief that the stricter laws in their states will not be affected by the ruling.

When details of the ruling become known, lawmakers would be well advised to examine state and local laws to determine if changes are needed to meet the court's standards.

In the meantime, the court itself has suggested how crimes such as the one in St. Paul can be handled without a threat to anyone's free speech. According to Scalia, St. Paul, in fact, "has sufficient means at its disposal to prevent such behavior without adding the First Amendment to the fire." Viktora could have been prosecuted under laws that forbid destruction of property or even simple trespassing.

Prosecuting bigots for their actions ought to be an easier task than trying to prosecute, or persecute, them for their statements, spoken or symbolic. Cracking down on actions rather than on expressions would help reassure all Americans that they ought to be able to say anything they want so long as they don't libel other people or pose a physical threat.

Those who would use "hate crime" laws today in a "just" cause to prosecute members of the racial majority should recall that in this country's history laws limiting free speech have been used much more frequently in *unjust* causes against members of racial and other minorities.

WRITING THE CONCLUSION

Well-written beginnings help attract readers. Well-written endings help convince readers. Possible conclusions for an editorial are as infinite in number and variety as the manner in which the editorial is written. Conclusions vary according to the purposes of an editorial, but a conclusion should express what the writer intends the editorial to accomplish. Conclusions also vary according to the degree of firmness that is intended by the writer. I have found it helpful in acquainting would-be editorial writers with possible varieties of conclusions to think of them as coming in six general forms. Within each form are variations that primarily reflect degree of firmness. In order of descending firmness, the six categories are: urge, approve, disapprove, conclude righteously, take consolation and come down softly. Explained below are the categories, ranked in that order. The examples within each category are also ranked in descending order of firmness.

Urging

The most specific and direct conclusion is one that urges readers, a government official or a private party to do something. An editorial may urge voters to support or oppose a candidate or ballot proposition; it may urge the president or Congress to compromise on tax cut proposals; it may urge a city council to lower the speed limit on a street or fire the city manager; or it may urge readers in general to support something, such as a nuclear arms freeze.

1. *Do*—write or vote or give (to the United Way, for example). This conclusion urges readers to perform some specific action. When the *Missoulian* of Missoula, Mont., decided that a development proposal called Ski Yellowstone "would court disaster," the editorial writer concluded: "Protests against this potential boondoggle should be written today (the deadline) to Lewis Hawkes, Forest Supervisor, Gallatin National Forest, P.O. Box 130, Bozeman, Mont. 59715."

2. *Must*—intended to leave no doubt in the mind of the reader what the editorial writer wants done. The *Daily News* of Newport News, Va., ended an editorial on the need for the community to become involved in fighting crime in this manner: "The police, in turn, must let the public know what to watch for."

3. *Ought*—less forceful than "must" but still a firm stand. A *Montana Kaimin* editorial contended that a state constitutional provision requiring reclamation of mineral lands was not being enforced, then concluded: "Someone ought to tell the legislature about this law, unless perhaps there is a confidentiality clause prohibiting politicians from learning the exact location of the document." (There is, of course, a little satire here, too.)

4. *Should*—slightly less emphatic than "must" and "ought." The *Courier-Journal* of Louisville concluded that, once Kentucky got out of a recession, the governor and the legislature "should set up a rainy day fund to help us weather the next one." Another firmly stated example comes from the *Minneapolis* (Minn.) *Tribune* in an editorial arguing for state control of dredging by the U.S. Army Corps of Engineers: "What should be done? One: The state should pursue the issue to the U.S. Supreme Court. Two: The next Congress should amend the Water Pollution Control Act to force the corps to observe the high standards set by states like Minnesota. At the same time, Congress should provide funds so that the corps can do the job correctly."

   "Should" can have two meanings, and editorial writers need to make certain their readers know which they intend. The manner in which "should" was used in the two preceding examples implies obligation, necessity or duty. The other usage implies expectation or anticipation of an occurrence. "The sun should come out tomorrow" is an example. To avoid possible confusion, some writers prefer to stick with "ought" to express obligation and reserve "should" for expectation.

5. *We urge*—appropriate, if not overused, when urging voters or public officials to take specific actions. The *Kentucky Advocate* of Frankfort, Ky., concluded an endorsement editorial in a governor's race in this manner: "We urge our fellow Kentuckians to vote for change on Tuesday."

6. *Needs to*—similar to "ought" and "should" but framed more in the manner of a statement. *The Oregonian* said that the Oregon governor needed to persuade the Washington governor to take joint action to protect the Columbia River.

7. *We hope*—much overused phrase that seems to temper a recommendation by suggesting that it is only the newspaper's opinion. Some newspapers try to avoid, or even forbid, the use of "we." Usually the point can be made without "we." However, when the *Miles City* (Mont.) *Star* noted that a "significant dent [had been made by Congress] in the OSHA [Occupational Safety and Health Administration] statute which American businesses have found so difficult to comply with," the editorial concluded: "We hope the fight to trim OSHA's autocratic reign is renewed in the next Congress." The writer could easily have said: "The fight to trim OSHA's autocratic reign must be renewed in the next Congress." (Note: Although you will find "hopefully" in the conclusions of editorials, it is not an acceptable substitute for "we hope." "Hopefully" is an adverb and, as such, modifies a verb or an adjective.)

Approving

Sometimes no specific action is expected on a public or private issue. Perhaps some action has already been taken that deserves praise, such as a contribution an individual has made to the community or a decision by a governmental body. Sometimes an editorial writer may want to commend a proposal without going immediately to the next step to urge its approval; additional study or changes may be needed. The following, in descending order of enthusiasm, are variations of positive editorial endings.

1. *Deserves credit*—an appropriate phrase when the writer wants to compliment someone for some action. The *Wichita* (Kan.) *Eagle* said that, in backing away from a proposal that would harm the Arkansas River, the City Council deserved credit. The *Montgomery* (Ala.) *Advertiser* said that civilian employees of Anniston Army Depot "deserve[d] the thanks of the nation for their patriotism" in volunteering for overseas duty in Operation Desert Shield.

2. *Should be grateful*—sometimes used when a community or a group has received some benefit. The *Charlotte* (N.C.) *Observer*, citing the contributions of "a number of generous families" to the state university system, said: "To those families and their foundations, all North Carolinians should be grateful."

3. *Good* or *best*—a solidly positive label to indicate a paper's approval of something. A *Billings* (Mont.) *Gazette* editorial approved everything about a downtown redevelopment proposal, concluding on this note:

"Let's keep Billings downtown area a viable asset. It's good for everyone." The *Richmond* (Va.) *Times-Dispatch* said that the strategy originally adopted in the Iraqi conflict offered "the best way" to minimize casualties.

4. *Makes sense*—indicates approval without much enthusiasm. The *Seattle Times* concluded that encouraging school boards to explore a year-round school calendar "makes financial and academic sense."

5. *We agree*—indicative of a positive, though not wildly enthusiastic, reception. The same Billings paper disagreed with some of the recommendations of the Commission on the Review of National Policy Toward Gambling but concluded: "We do agree that the states should determine what gambling will take place within their borders."

6. *Step in the right direction*—appropriate when the action to be praised is positive but less than desired. The *Eugene* (Ore.) *Register-Guard* described as "a step in the right direction" a truce between proponents and opponents over the issue of open field burning of seed grass.

7. *Deserves a hearing*—suggestive of only lukewarm approval. The *Minneapolis Tribune* examined some proposed changes in the rules of the state senate and concluded: "The proposed rules deserve a favorable hearing when the majority DFL caucus meets next week."

8. *But in the long run*—a phrase useful when a writer thinks that the immediate effects of something don't look very good but that eventually things will work out for the best. The *Minneapolis Tribune* sympathized with the legislative majority's reluctance to tackle a lot of difficult issues that tend to get lost in debate: "That kind of work might not make headlines—but in the long run it would be a major service to the state."

9. *Despite the difficulties*—an expression that suggests that something deserves approval in spite of major deficiencies. This is illustrated in the next example.

10. *Taken as a whole*—an indication that the good outweighs the bad, but maybe not by much. A *Minneapolis Tribune* editorial noted that, while black enrollment in colleges had increased dramatically, recruiting of minorities in the highly selective private schools was waning. The conclusion stated: "We think that, despite occasional difficulties, minority-recruiting programs and education-opportunity programs, taken as a whole, have given solid support to minority hopes of 'catching up.'"

11. *Better than*—a suggestion that something is only the lesser of two evils, not such a good thing in itself. A *Billings* (Mont.) *Gazette* editorial argued that high standards should be imposed on new coal-fired steam plants and that customers who buy the electricity should pay the additional cost. Having all users pay, the editorial concluded, was "better . . . than dumping the crud on those who happen to live downwind."

12. *But at least*—a sense of approval that is getting quite weak. A *Livingston* (Mont.) *Enterprise* editorial noted that a new congressional measure would put severe tax limitations on out-of-country business meetings. "There will be new loopholes, there always are. But at least the new law plugs a couple of the old ones for a little while," the *Enterprise* said.

13. *But only if*—approval only under certain conditions. A *Denver Post* editorial, commenting on federal financing of political campaigns, concluded: " . . . the federal reform effort . . . can only be fully effective if congressional elections are also brought under the law."

Disapproving

The types of editorials that end in disapproval are basically the same as those that end in approval; the editorial writer decides to come down on the negative rather than on the positive side of an issue. My search through a large number of editorials suggests that disapproving editorials are not nearly so abundant as approving editorials and that they come in only a few identifiable forms. Here, in descending order of disapproval, are five examples.

1. *Outrageous*—only one of many words that might indicate strong disapproval. The *Albuquerque* (N.M.) *Journal* said it would be "outrageous" if the Public Service Company of New Mexico were to pass on to ratepayers the costs of a litigation settlement bill.

2. *A disservice*—a controlled but absolute statement of disapproval. When a Washington state senator was arrested on a charge of soliciting for prostitution, *The Columbian* of Vancouver noted that he might have been making only an off-hand remark, as he claimed, but it concluded that the public expects "the highest form of behavior from a man in [his] position" and that he "has done a disservice not only to himself, but to the Washington State Legislature as well."

3. *Makes no sense*—a fairly strong suggestion that something generally lacks merit. The *Missoulian* editorialized in favor of shorter presidential and congressional political campaigns. The conclusion: "Campaigns which last close to 300 days and campaigns which require every major candidate to raise enormous sums to win office make no sense. They do not, in the end, serve the public interest." Using different words with similar meaning, *The Herald-Dispatch* of Huntington, W.Va., concluded that "limiting the terms that a member of Congress can serve, tempting though it may be, simply isn't the answer."

4. *Must be a better way*—suggesting that the idea may not be all bad but not good enough. The editorial may conclude that there must be a better answer even though the writer may not have it. A *Washington Post* editorial that examined the state of automobile liability insurance came to this conclusion: "There has to be a better way of compensating those to whom reparations are due than the clumsy and expensive mechanisms that exist today. . . . "

5. *Would have been wiser*—suggesting that a better idea does exist. A *Minneapolis Tribune* editorial raised questions about an all-expense-paid trip to Taiwan by members of Congress and their aides. Concerning the Minnesota member of the delegation, the *Tribune* said: "It would have been wiser—in the view of the questions being raised—if he had listened to a colleague on the House Ethics Committee. . . . "

Concluding Righteously

One of the ministers I knew in Vancouver, Wash., used to call me "the village preacher." Being a preacher himself, he must have intended this epithet as a compliment. I accepted it as such, since I thought I was upholding the moral standards of the community. But the adjectival form of "preacher," when applied to an editorial, is not particularly complimentary; readers may resent preachy editorials.

Still, one of the purposes of an editorial page is to serve as a community conscience, and one of the duties of an editorial writer is to protect and promote the public good, as he or she perceives it. So, if editorials take on a high moral tone from time to time, perhaps no one should complain about a little preaching.

1. *The public's rights*—a favorite touchstone for the editorial writer in making a case against government secrets or private interests. Writers find particularly gratifying the invocation of rights involving the First Amendment and freedom of information. Newspapers can perform a worthwhile function speaking up for these rights, but it is easy to allow them to become a cliche. The public gets tired of being preached to about rights, especially when these may seem to benefit editors and reporters more than most readers. In Montana the Bureau of Land Management released the names of persons and companies that had "nominated" (proposed) various federal lands for coal leasing but refused to reveal who had nominated what lands. Concluded the *Missoulian*: "The public has a right to know who wants to glom onto what public coal. It has a right to have coal development carefully controlled." In this instance, the paper was contending that the public should know these names, but some of those who opposed publication might have argued that the *Missoulian* wanted the names for the purpose of publishing an interesting news story.

2. *Preservation of liberties*—another strongly righteous conclusion. In an editorial entitled "Freedom's Protector," the *Los Angeles Herald Examiner* noted "the never-ending assault on liberty itself by powers that protect themselves—or seek to—by forbidding public criticism of their actions." The editorial saw "the best protector of existing human liberty as a free press, whose importance cannot be overstated," then concluded: "Preservation of these liberties is critical to the health and even the survival of any true democracy. Keep that in mind the next time another judge tries to interfere with full press coverage of a public trial."

Taking Consolation

When events don't go exactly the way an editorial writer wishes, an alternative to disapproving is taking some consolation that the outcome isn't all bad. Here are four specific types of these endings.

1. *Yes, but . . .*—a conclusion acknowledging that something untoward has occurred but insisting that things aren't so bad as they seem. When Montana voters turned down an initiative that would have restricted nuclear power plant development in their state, the *Missoulian* concluded: "Industry beat Initiative 71. That means people do not want a ban. But that does *not* mean the people want nuclear power development."

2. *But heartening*—suggesting that things are bad but may improve. This is exemplified by an editorial in the *Denver Post* that noted increasing enrollment of minority students in the nation's colleges: "The Civil Rights Office's statistics do not touch on the quality of educational offerings, and on the rise in academic performance, which certainly must be an essential goal. But for now, the rising minority enrollment is heartening indeed for the students and for the nation."

3. *Not a trend, but . . .*—pointing to a bright sign but warning not to make too much of it. The *Denver Post*, after noting the political instability of many African nations, pointed to "a few hopeful signs that this gloomy picture may be brightening" and concluded: "These are modest gains, to be sure, and should not be interpreted as indicating a trend. But they do suggest that the democratic spirit will not forever be denied in independent Africa, if and when the conditions are right."

4. *Not without faults, but . . .*—a way for editorial writers to indicate that something is less than might be desirable. The *Danville* (Va.) *Register and Bee* described a health care plan as "not without its faults, but at least it opens debate on [the] issue. . . . "

Coming Down Softly

As any reader of the editorial page knows, not every editorial reaches a firm or clear conclusion. In fact, many editorials purposely remain inconclusive. (Others, unfortunately, arrive at no conclusion in spite of the writers' efforts to reach conclusions.) Writers might use this type of ending when they want to interpret what is happening or bring their readers information and insights that have not appeared in the news columns. Writers may also resort to this form if they can envision no solution to the problems at hand. Editorial writers, after all, don't have to know all the answers. Here are some examples in decreasing order of firmness.

1. *It appears*—a fine phrase to weaken any conclusion an editorial writer might feel less than certain about, as in an editorial in the *Morning Advocate* of Baton Rouge, La. After viewing the Middle Eastern situation, the newspaper concluded that "it appears there never can be unity among the Arab states."

2. *We think*—suggests that readers might draw a conclusion different from the editorial writer's. On the question of whether revenue from casino gambling might solve Detroit's financial problems, the *Detroit Free Press* said: "We think the evidence doesn't exist to support that conclusion."

3. *Might*—used to indicate an uncertain conclusion. Concerning a proposal that the Canadian prime minister visit South Africa, the *Calgary Herald* concluded: "A formal visit by Mulroney might be in order, but only if he can be sure it would help, not hinder."

4. *These are the questions*—a fitting conclusion when an issue raises only questions for which the editorial writer has no answers. Even when writers do have an opinion, they sometimes will seek to raise an issue merely for community discussion. They may be trying to avoid the reaction of "That paper can't tell me what to do!" This reaction is not uncommon when a newspaper from a larger city tries to tell a nearby smaller town, or a neighborhood within the city, what it should do. Sometimes editorial writers recognize that a community has to work its way slowly to answers that may seem self-evident to the writers themselves. Answers can't often be handed down on tablets of stone, even by writers who believe "Truth" has been revealed to them. In a *Chicago Tribune* editorial the conclusion notes that the deaths of eight tannery

workers raised questions about what steps should be taken to prevent future disasters: "These are the questions that federal and local officials, manufacturing and business associations, and labor unions should address jointly in the wake of the tannery tragedy and in the hope of preventing other fatal accidents in the future."

5. *No easy solution*—when no answer seems to be a good one. For example, when sheriff's deputies were searching students attending concerts at the University of Montana, the *Montana Kaimin*, the student newspaper, said that "people should be safe from injury [from thrown bottles and cans], but they also have the right to be safe from a random search without a warrant." The editorial concluded: "There is no easy resolution to the problem. UM students and officials should attempt to devise an equitable way to ensure safe concerts."

6. *No solution*—when an editorial writer has no solution at all to offer. Lamenting previous studies aimed at eliminating duplication in the Montana college system, the *Helena* (Mont.) *Independent Record* concluded: "We thus hesitate to advocate another study. Nor do we offer any solutions. Meantime—uneasy rests the head wearing the crown."

7. *No issue*—the final step toward softness. These are editorials that don't even attempt to present an issue. Noting changing fashions in slang, the *Montana Standard* of Butte said that things used to be cool and neat but now were weird, and that "type" is being attached to a word to create an adjective. "Many newspapers today use a photo-printing process that yields something called 'cold type,' to distinguish it from the actual 'hot metal type' of days gone by. So far, we haven't heard anybody refer to cold-type type, but it's bound to happen. We've got no particular reason for discussing these things. We just did it to be weird."

CONCLUSION

Editorial writers are not likely to turn consciously to such devices as those listed in this chapter each time they decide how to start, organize or conclude an editorial. The categories mentioned here are not intended to provide a stock of elements from which editorial writers can choose to come up with effective editorials. Form cannot substitute for logic, facts and insight. But editorial writers who pay attention to form—their own and that of other writers—can become more aware of their own writing. By being aware of the elements of an editorial, writers ought to be able to organize editorials in a manner that is clear to their readers. And by becoming sensitized to a variety of beginnings, middles and endings used by others, writers can provide themselves with many more options for attracting and convincing readers.

QUESTIONS AND EXERCISES

1. Find editorials on the same subject that are written in at least three different formats. How are the facts (background information, etc.) handled differently by the writers? What seem to be the writers' assumptions concerning the pre-existing attitudes and prior knowledge of their readers? In what ways are these assumptions different? The same?

2. Find editorials on the same subject that are different in tone. How would you describe the tone of each? Would the approach of any tend to antagonize readers? Cause readers to identify with the writer? Put readers to sleep?

3. Pick a topic and write two editorials using distinctly different formats, for example, SA_1A_2DC and CSAC. Which do you think would be more convincing to most readers in this instance?

4. Select an editorial on a topic that interests you. Then rewrite it in an entirely different tone. Use any of the formats you like. Which editorial is likely to convince more readers?

5. Find several examples of each of the six major types of editorial conclusions. Can you find endings that would fall into categories other than these six?

6. Without substantially changing the editorial, rewrite a coming-down-softly ending to create a conclusion expressing firm approval or disapproval. Do the reverse with an editorial that has a firm conclusion.

7. Select an editorial that is directed toward a single audience and rewrite it as a two-level editorial (addressing a dual audience). For example, pick an editorial that seems directed primarily toward a city council and rewrite it so that general readers will understand how the issue being discussed will affect them and what they ought to do about it.

Chapter 11

Nine Steps to Better Writing

By "good writing," I mean writing that is first, clear; and second, clear;
and third, clear. I would have sentences that go snap, crackle and
pop. . . .[Unless] they convey meaning, and add something affirmatively
to the development of an idea, I would strike them out.

—JAMES KILPATRICK[1]

Now that we have taken a look at the basic steps in writing an editorial, let us turn our attention to some of the finer points of turning out an editorial that is convincing, terse and well written, concentrating on the following nine areas:

1. The right amount of fact.
2. Logical conclusions.
3. Consistent point of view.
4. Clear referents and antecedents.
5. Sentences of appropriate length.
6. Economy of words.
7. Correct grammar.
8. Absence of cliches and jargon.
9. Proper use of individual words.

To provide examples of how editorials can be improved in these nine areas, I will use editorials written by students in my editorial-writing class. The occasion for the writing of these editorials was an announcement that *Playboy* would be sending a photographer to the Virginia Tech campus to take pictures of women students for a future issue. Two of these editorials, "The Playboy Option" and "Sex Objects," appear here in their entirety. I also will cite portions of some of the other editorials to help illustrate these nine points.

"The Playboy Option" appears on pages 148 and 149 with a critique based on principles discussed in this chapter. "Sex Objects" appears on page 150.

Following it is an edited and partly rewritten version of this editorial ("Sex Objects—II"), which also reflects the points made in this chapter.

THE RIGHT AMOUNT OF FACT

Editorials should contain only those facts that are necessary for the purposes for which the editorials were written. "Facts are precious things, and to be thoroughly enjoyed must be tasted sparingly and drooled over leisurely," Vermont Royster of the *Wall Street Journal* advised editorial writers.[2] Usually the detail required in an editorial is less than that needed in a news story on the same topic. In many cases editorial readers will have read the news reports and will not need a repetition of all the facts before finding out what the editorial writer has to add. Still, editorial writers cannot assume that all readers have seen, or remembered, the original story. So a compromise between a brief reference and a full factual account must be worked out. Editorial writers must rely on their judgment, but should try for brevity. Space in editorial columns is far more limited than in news columns.

The two editorials included here are fairly brief (340 and 388 words) and seem not to be overburdened with unnecessary information. The announcement that prompted the editorials, the coming to town of the *Playboy* photographer, requires little explanation. "The Playboy Option" goes into a little more detail about the tryout procedures, but these details will tie in with the conclusion that the editorial writer draws.

The Playboy Option
Women have a choice in how they would be photographed

(ORIGINAL)

Playboy magazine visited the Virginia Tech campus last week in search of young women to pose in their October 1992 "Women of the Big East" issue.

Female students were invited to the Blacksburg Marriott Hotel to be interviewed and to complete a questionnaire. They were also asked whether they would like to be photographed fully clothed, semi-nude or nude.

Students and faculty members believe that such exposure to a well-known magazine would be a beneficial experience for the young women who choose to appear. Many students also view the paycheck as a

(CRITIQUE)

Playboy magazine is singular; use "it"

"Students and faculty" implies "all students and faculty"; use "Some"

Use "benefit from" instead of "would be a beneficial experience for"

"Many" is vague; also what may seem many to one person may not to another person practical way to pay for the rising cost of tuition.

However, many feminists on campus expressed their displeasure at the thought of *Playboy* visiting Virginia Tech. They solely believe that students attend college in order to receive the best education possible, not to take off their clothes for a national magazine. Many believe the magazine will feature the women in a degrading light, thus harming their reputations.

"Solely" is misplaced; it should modify "receive"

"In order to" is wordy; "to" is sufficient

"Believe" implies faith in something; use "think" here

We as students of Virginia Tech have the right to decide whether we would like to participate in this experience. As with the issue of abortion, a woman has the sole right to do as she pleases with her body. The same principle is applied to this case. If a struggling, young student needs help with tuition costs and decides to pose only for the money, don't look down upon her. Yes, there may be other ways in which to earn extra money, but it is up to her to decide how she will go about it.

With "we," a sudden switch from third person to first; keep the same person

You should say "Women *should* have the sole right" and "the principle *should* be applied"

With ". . . don't . . .," you switch to second person

"There may be" is weak construction; try "The student has other ways to . . ."

The young women are also given the option as to how they would like to be photographed. This is to assure them that they do indeed have a voice in the matter. This further implies that the layout will be presented in a tasteful manner. If Playboy wished to degrade these women, then they wouldn't be given so many opportunities in which to voice their opinion.

They "were" given the choice; that was last week

Use "option of," not "option as to how"

"This" doesn't refer to anything specific; try: "Offering them a choice assured them . . ."

You need "had wished"

You need "wouldn't have been"

"Opinion" not right word; try "options for posing"

LOGICAL CONCLUSIONS

It is not always easy to judge whether an editorial presents logical arguments that lead to an appropriate conclusion. To a large extent, whether the arguments work depends on the point of view of the person doing the judging.

For the class assignment on the *Playboy* incident, students were instructed to write an SA_1A_2DC editorial (see Chapter 10), presenting opposing arguments before reaching a conclusion. In "The Playboy Option" the writer first argues that women students could benefit, from a paycheck and from something vaguely

Sex Objects
Playboy photographs feed on exploitation of women

(ORIGINAL)

A photographer from *Playboy* magazine was in town last week to recruit women for their upcoming Big East college issue.

Women were asked to go to the Blacksburg Marriott prepared to have pictures taken of them, preferably in a bathing suit. The incentives given for trying out for this issue were exposure in a best-selling magazine and a large sum of money.

Just a few days after the announcement of the photographer being in town, letters to the editor started appearing in papers of the region every day. The first group of letters to appear in the *Collegiate Times*, the Virginia Tech newspaper, consisted of angry women, condoning such activity going on in a college atmosphere. The degradation of women was an argument, with women being viewed only as sex objects. Some people consider *Playboy* a pornographic magazine that exploits women. In the letters, women were asked to not degrade themselves and to boycott the tryouts.

The responses to the letters from women were mostly from men, who thought it was a great advantage to Tech to be featured in such a famous magazine. They felt that Tech needed the exposure, as well as deserved it. They felt that women have the freedom to choose to do this so it is perfectly justified. Many felt that *Playboy* is a quality magazine and the women of Tech should take advantage of the opportunity.

What these men, as well as the women who went to the tryouts, did not think about is how much their way of thinking contributes to sexist beliefs. When women are treated as sex objects, as they are in *Playboy*, the men reading the magazine believe that what they see is what they get. The women are in the magazine only for the sexual pleasure of men. The women in the pictures are usually the perfect exceptions of nature, or the object of plastic surgeons that fool men into believing what the perfect woman's body is. They are also fooled into believing what the perfect woman wants, judging from her provocative pose and her lack of adequate clothing.

Women should be lucky that they have the freedom of choice. They should explore this freedom of choice, and choose not to contribute to sexist beliefs created and fed by the exploitation of women in the pages of *Playboy*.

referred to as "beneficial experience." Then the writer, using "however" as a standard transition to the opposing argument, notes that opponents were concerned about women students degrading themselves and harming their reputations. At that point the writer drops the A_1A_2 arguments and abruptly takes a new tack, pursuing neither the beneficial nor the degrading lines of reasoning. The issue now is a woman's right to decide what she wants to do with her body. Since *Playboy* has given her some options (fully clothed, semi-nude or nude), she is free to make a choice. The editorial then jumps to a conclusion, which I don't follow, that this choice suggests that the *Playboy* layout will be tasteful. So it seems to me that the writer starts out with one set of arguments, switches to another line of argument and then arrives at an unsubstantiated conclusion.

In "Sex Objects" the writer draws on letters to the editor to provide the arguments. Those opposed to posing contend that *Playboy* is a magazine that exploits women and that women who participate will be degraded. Women are asked to boycott the tryouts. The letters on the other side, mostly from men, say that

Sex Objects—II

Playboy photographs feed on exploitation of women

(REVISED)

A photographer from *Playboy* magazine provoked a debate over sexual exploitation when he came to town to recruit women for the fall Big East college issue.

Women were invited to the Blacksburg Marriott to have their pictures taken, preferably in bathing suits. They were offered the incentives of exposure in a best-selling magazine and possibly large sums of money.

Protesting letters to the editor immediately began appearing. The first group of letters, in the *Collegiate Times*, the Virginia Tech newspaper, came from angry women, condemning such activities in a college atmosphere. Some of the letters described *Playboy* as a pornographic magazine that exploits women. They asked students not to degrade themselves by posing. They called for a boycott of the tryouts.

In response came letters, mostly from men, who argued that Tech could benefit from being featured in such a famous magazine. They contended that *Playboy* is a quality magazine and that Tech needs, and deserves, the exposure. They urged women to take advantage of the opportunity but pointed out that they had the freedom to choose whether to pose.

What these men, as well as those who went to the tryouts, did not think about was how much their way of thinking contributes to sexist attitudes. When women are treated as sex objects, as they are in *Playboy*, men reading the magazine believe that what they see is what they get. The women are in the magazine only for the sexual pleasure of men. The women in the pictures are usually the perfect exceptions of nature, or the products of plastic surgeons who fool men into thinking that these are the perfect woman's body. They are also fooled, by the provocative poses and lack of clothing, that these are what the perfect woman wants.

Women should feel lucky that they have the freedom of choice to pose for *Playboy*. They should exercise this freedom, but they then should choose not to contribute to the sexist atmosphere created and fed by the exploitation of women in the pages of *Playboy*.

women should take advantage of the opportunity to appear in a quality magazine, that women are free to choose whether to participate and that Tech could use the exposure. The writer then uses an effective transition to move into the discussion section. "These men" refers back to the male letter writers of the previous paragraph. The "as well as women who went to the tryouts" quickly enlarges the group to whom the discussion is addressed. "What these men . . . did not think" also allows the writer to move from the letter writers' arguments to the points the writer wants to make. The writer then launches into a full-scale attack on the sexual stereotypes that *Playboy* is perceived to be encouraging. The final paragraph, citing "freedom of choice," also harks back to the language of the A_2 argument. Women should feel fortunate that they have a choice and should explore it. But it turns out in the writer's view that there really is no choice at all for anyone who does not want to contribute to the exploitation of women. Some may question whether this wording has misled the reader concerning the matter of choice, but it seems clear to me that the writer's basic point is clear and that the conclusion follows from the points made in the arguments and in the discussion.

CONSISTENT POINT OF VIEW

The editorial writer should use a consistent point of view in an editorial: the first-person ("we"), second-person ("you") or third-person ("he," "she," "they"). Some papers discourage or forbid the use of "we" in editorials. Other papers regard it as appropriate. In any case, care should be taken to use "we" infrequently. If you use "we" to refer to the paper, do so consistently; don't switch back and forth between "we" and the name of the paper.

On occasion writers find it appropriate, especially when writing on informal topics, to address editorials to the readers in the second-person "you." Once adopted, this form of address should be maintained throughout the editorial. Use of "you," of course, can be overdone. Writers must be careful not to switch suddenly to a "you" point of view in the middle or at the end of an editorial.

I detect no switching of persons in the two editorials cited. But an example of what I am talking about occurred in another student editorial. The editorial asked why people are so offended by *Playboy*: "Why don't they just accept the fact that some people think of the human body as an art form and are going to pose for *Playboy* no matter what they say? And in response to the statement that women are in it just for money, we ask you what is wrong with making some extra money doing something you see nothing wrong with and possibly even enjoy?" The writer, after using the third-person "they," suddenly and for no apparent reason switches to "we" and "you." The remainder of the editorial is third-person again. The wording can be changed easily, and trimmed: "What is wrong with women making some extra money doing something they see nothing wrong with. . . ."

Another inconsistency to avoid is a shift in the intended audience. Unless there is a clear reason, a writer should not start an editorial talking to one audience, then switch to another. For example, a writer should not begin an editorial addressing the general readership about the city's potholed streets and then at the end switch to talking directly to the mayor: "Mr. Mayor, we think you should do something about this."

CLEAR REFERENTS AND ANTECEDENTS

To avoid repeating words in a boring fashion, writers sometimes use pronouns to take the place of nouns. To avoid repeating phrases and sentences, even whole paragraphs, they use "that" or "that idea" or "that concept" or "that development." Sometimes readers become confused by this shorthand. Professor R. Thomas Berner of The Pennsylvania State University referred to pronouns as "those unemotional, ambiguous, spineless parasites we use to refer to other parts of speech somewhere else in the same sentence, or, on occasion, in another sentence in the same paragraph, or, the worst of all possible contortions, in another paragraph." Berner cited the following sentence as an example of what he was talking about: "The city collects only swill from the university, and because of it, it has determined that the rate was higher than it should have been."[3] The only unambiguous "it" in the sentence is the last one, referring to the rate. But to what do the first two refer? According to the rules of grammar—a pronoun should refer to the nearest preceding logical referent—both of them should refer to university. But the first "it" apparently stands for the whole idea that only swill comes from the university, and who knows whether the second "it" means the university or the city?

The two reprinted editorials provide no examples of this problem, but one of the other students wrote: "Whatever the reason for accepting the fact that someone will be chosen and indirectly represent Tech in *Playboy*'s 'Women of the East,' it will not stop the exploitation of women that will occur in that and every issue of the magazine." "It" seems to refer all the way back to "whatever the reason," but can a reason for accepting participation be expected to stop exploitation? The same editorial uses the sentence "This may sound harsh" to start a new paragraph with "this" apparently meant to refer to rambling thoughts in the previous sentence. Another student wrote: "If a student appears in the issue, it would mean publicity for Tech." No referent exists for "it."

SENTENCES OF APPROPRIATE LENGTH

You might expect to find that sentences in editorials would tend to be longer and harder to understand than those in news stories. Yet at least two studies made 20 years apart have shown that readers have found editorials easier to understand than news stories. Professor Galen R. Rarick, who did the second study, speculated that this apparent anomaly occurred partly because most editorial writers have been in the writing business longer than most reporters. Another reason, he suggested, was that news writers may be better at reporting and investigating than at writing. Editorial writers also have a longer time to rewrite and polish their products than most reporters, and so should produce better writing.[4]

The earlier of the two studies was based on a book called *The Art of Readable Writing* by Rudolph Flesch. This book and a subsequent one by the same author, *How to Test Readability*, attracted considerable attention in the late 1940s and 1950s.[5] Since longer sentences were considered harder to understand than short ones and longer words were considered more abstract than short ones, Flesch came up with a scale based on two factors—average sentence length (number of words) and average word length (number of syllables per 100 words). Using the scale, a "standard" rating of 65 (seventh- or eighth-grade level) could be obtained by various combinations. If sentences were short, words could be longer; if words were short, sentences could be longer. A "standard" rating could be obtained by sentences that averaged 15 words in length if 100 words had no more than 149 syllables, but by sentences that averaged only 10 words if 100 words had 157 syllables.

Although Flesch himself warned against taking the scale too seriously, the response to his books was such that Francis P. Locke of the *Dayton* (Ohio) *Daily News* felt moved to write an article for *The Masthead* titled "Too Much Flesch on the Bones?" "We have created a cult of leanness," he wrote. "The adjective is packed off to a semantic Siberia. The mood piece, if tolerated at all, must be astringent and aseptic." He feared "the growing pressure to water everything down to the thinnest possible pablum for the laziest possible minds."[6] So simplification can be overdone.

Writers should realize that readers, even of editorial pages, are usually in a hurry. Today's readers are not likely to labor over the type of heavy prose that an E. L. Godkin or a Charles Dana gave to readers a century ago. Yet simplistic writing can be boring, and if a writer has a fairly complex thought to express, a complex sentence may be necessary. The complexity of the writing should depend on the editorial and the concepts discussed. A good rule is to try to keep the writing simpler than you are at first inclined, since it is still likely to be perceived by most readers as more difficult than you expect.

So how do the students' editorials rate on the Flesch scale? "The Playboy Option" (324 words) has sentences that average 19 words in length, with 147 syllables for every 100 words. On Flesch's scale this would earn a rating of 65 (right on the "standard" mark). "Sex Objects" (388 words) has sentences that average 20 words, with 151 syllables for every 100 words, earning it a rating of only 60 (half way between "standard" and "fairly difficult"). The revised version, "Sex Objects—II," with 340 words, has the same averages as "The Playboy Option" (19 words and 147 syllables), so it also rates as "standard." Notice that, in addition to receiving a more readable rating, the edited editorial also is 48 words shorter than the original. (The Flesch scale should be regarded as only one indication, and a rather arbitrary one, of writing quality.)

Neither of these editorials has a problem with long sentences, but examples can be found in some of the other students' work. A long, complex sentence (40 words): "It seems as though *Playboy* is playing on the fact that (1) college students are willing to try just about anything, (2) college students always need money and (3) careers in modeling are seen as big opportunities for a lot of college women." A shorter, clearer rewrite (28 words): "*Playboy* seems to be taking advantage of college students, willing to try anything once, who are lured by promises of always-needed money or of careers in modeling."

Another confusing example: "While proponents for *Playboy* agree [with opponents] that one's body is sacred, their view diverges in that posing nude for millions to view is a matter of free expression." The writer could have said: "Proponents agree that one's body is sacred, but they believe that exposing one's body for millions to view is a matter of free expression."

ECONOMY OF WORDS

Long or confused sentences are a tip-off to wordiness. But wordiness also can show up in words and phrases that may be part of short sentences.

A phrase that often signals wordiness and the use of the passive voice is "there is" and its various forms (there are, there will be, etc.). Usually you can strike "there is" and insert a stronger verb elsewhere in the sentence. An example from one of the unprinted editorials:

There were a number of sorority women who were interested in auditioning:

Improved:

A number of sorority women were interested in auditioning.

Usually "the fact that" can be chopped out:

Why don't they accept the fact that some people think of the human body as an art form. . . .?

Improved:

Why don't they accept that some people think of the human body as an art form. . . .?"

"Whether" sometimes can be similarly chopped out:

[They] were given the option on whether they wanted to pose nude, semi-nude or clothed.

Improved:

[They] were given the option of posing nude, semi-nude or clothed.

(Also notice the awkward use of the preposition "on" with "option." You should say "option of posing." "Option on" would be appropriate if you had an option on a piece of property. Prepositions give many students lots of problems. They apparently have a deaf ear for prepositions.)

Here a repetition of words can be avoided:

Many argued that posing nude is degrading. Those arguing this feel that. . . .

Improved:

Many argued that posing nude is degrading. They feel that. . . .

An extreme case of wordiness:

She should also consider the ramifications of what this decision will mean to those around her.

Improved:

She should consider what this decision will mean to those around her.

CORRECT GRAMMAR

A person who attains the august position of editorial writer should not have to worry about correct grammar. Agreement of subject and predicate can be tricky, however, when the two are separated by a prepositional phrase such as one from "Sex Objects": "The response to the letters from women were mostly from men. . . ." Response, of course, is the subject and requires a singular verb.

Agreement of nouns and pronouns is another problem. One of the writers wrote: "As Virginia Tech changes their conference. . . ." The writer properly provided Tech with a singular verb but a plural pronoun. Another writer referred to *Playboy* and "their" October 1992 issue.

Everyone and anyone (both singular) can be troublesome. ". . . everyone is the master [hardly the right word when referring to women] of their own body," one person wrote. In this case, since only women were involved, "her" would have been appropriate. Sometimes the plural form solves the problem: "People have control over their own bodies."

I am chagrined by how often comma splices occur in student editorials. The previous example was part of a sentence with a comma splice: "Whether someone wants to pose is not really the issue, after all everyone is the master of [her] own body." Two sentences are needed.

ABSENCE OF CLICHES AND JARGON

Cliches and jargon, in a sense, are at opposite ends of the spectrum in terms of comprehensibility by the general reader. Cliches tend to be used in everyday conversation by the sophisticated and the unsophisticated, the educated and the not-so-educated. Jargon is a special set of words used by a specific group of people. Everyone understands cliches; only the in-group fully understands jargon. The editorial writer must resist the easy temptation to use both—jargon, because many readers will not easily understand what the words mean, and cliches, because good writers need to make clear that they are thinking their own thoughts, not echoing someone else's. Cliches may be appropriate on occasion if they truly are appropriate and no better way can be found to make a point. Some of these expressions have been around for a long time, and they do "ring bells" with readers, but in most cases a little more thought can produce a more exact phrase than the cliche. Instead of "ring bells," I could have said "are easily understood by readers."

Problems with jargon tend to increase with the specialization of editorial writers. When writers associate with educators, lawyers, doctors, sociologists, government bureaucrats, politicians or farmers, they pick up their language and tend to forget that many words full of meaning to these people are either incomprehensible or lacking in meaning to many readers. Writers must constantly be on guard against such words sneaking into their writing.

The two editorials printed here seem to be clear of cliches and jargon. I was pleased to find that I had to look hard to find cliches in this batch of editorials. One of the other writers said the *Playboy* incident was one of the "hot topics" on campus. Another said that we should think of "the big picture." I consider these so minor that I didn't call attention to them when I returned the editorials to the students.

Some of the overworked words and phrases that I have come across over the years include:

alarming trend	broadly speaking
amazing	factor
basic	gratifying

incredible	program
in fact	remains to be seen
in order ("A new examination is in order.")	responsible observers
in terms of	the economy
major ("major event")	thoughtful people
obvious	to be deplored
on closer examination	underlying ("underlying causes")
only time will tell	unquestionable
problem	would seem

In 1955, long before the widespread use of computerized machines, the *Wall Street Journal* suggested that editorial writers might find a use for an IBM gadget called a Wordwriter. It could store up to 42 words or phrases and all the writer would have to do was punch a letter on the machine and out would come the word or phrase. The *Journal* cited the following list as possible entries:[7]

"A": will be for "As we have reminded our readers time and time again. . . ."
"B": "Both sides of this question have merit. . . ."
"C": "Considering all the factors involved. . . ."
"D": "Doubtless some will disagree with this view. . . ."
"E": "Except for the particular circumstances surrounding the case in question. . . ."
"F": "Fortunately, things are not always as they seem. . . ."
"G": "Generally speaking. . . ."
"H": "However, the public believes the facts are. . . ."
"I": "Indeed, there is no gainsaying. . . ."

And so on, to the inevitable conclusion that must follow.
From a short stack of editorials, I came across these cliches:

"It'll soon be time to fish or cut bait."
"Montanans can breathe a sigh of relief. . . ."
"Inflation has reared its ugly head."
"Time marches on."
"The country went absolutely bananas. . . ."
"That's a real can of worms."
". . . time to stir the pot again."
". . . the computer . . . coughed up the latest . . . report."
"A natural tendency to 'let George do it.' "
"Into the breach leapt the Jaycees."

Even less defensible than the use of the cliche is the use of the jargon of government, education and any other field with its own vocabulary. Noting the efforts of the National Council of Teachers of English to fight government jargon, the *Milwaukee Journal* published the following editorial to poke fun at bureaucrats.

Gobbledygook

It's good to know that somewhere in the sprawling government bureaucracy is an employee with a sense of humor. That useful commodity often withers in the criticism heaped on public officials, or is buried in the jargon with which such people often communicate.

Take as a modest example the terms face-value consensus, content validity, concurrent validity and predictive validity that recently fuzzed up an HEW memorandum. They probably mean something to someone, but who knows what to whom? In an effort to get officials to say what they mean in terms everyone can understand, the National Council of Teachers of English presents Public Doublespeak awards, whose wry purpose is to uncover the absurdity of communication that doesn't communicate.

The latest honor went to the State Department for an announcement that its consumer affairs coordinator would use the consumer communication channel to review existing mechanisms in order to improve linkages of consumer input, thruput and output. Its author, surprisingly, stepped right up to claim the award. It was a compliment, he said, considering the "normal inability of the bureaucracy to do anything in a manner which would merit an award for anything." Maybe the answer to gobbledygook is requiring bureaucrats to talk with their tongues in their cheeks.

Milwaukee (Wis.) *Journal*[8]

PROPER USE OF INDIVIDUAL WORDS

After all of these potential writing traps have been checked, we also need to check for weak or inappropriate words.

Beginning editorial writers (and some non-beginners) often misuse "hopefully" to mean "we hope." "Hopefully" is an adverb meaning "full of hope." It needs to modify a verb. To suggest how "hopefully" might be used, I tell my students: "I am looking at you hopefully to see that you have understood my explanation of 'hopefully.'" One of my student writers, referring to family, friends and professors of a student who decided to pose for *Playboy*, began the conclusion of an editorial: "Hopefully they will support her, because it is her decision." Why not: "They should support her" or "They need to support her."

"Think," "feel" and "believe" create problems for writers of news stories as well as editorials. In most instances writers should use "think," when they are recounting the thoughts and ideas of their sources. "Feel" should be reserved for statements concerning feelings and emotions. "Believe" implies a faith or conviction about something.

In "Sex Objects" the writer uses "felt" three times: "They felt that Tech needed exposure. . . ." "They felt that women have the freedom to choose. . . ." "Many felt that *Playboy* is a quality magazine. . . ." "Feel" did not seem the proper word in any of these cases. Several possibilities exist for changes: "They thought that Tech needed exposure. . . ." "They said that women have the freedom to choose. . . ." "Many saw *Playboy* as a quality magazine. . . ."

The same writer had this sentence: "They ['many feminists'] solely believe that students attend college in order to receive the best education possible, not to take off their clothes for a national magazine." "Believe" seems fine here, since that is their conviction. (With "solely" where it is, the sentence implies that this is their only belief. "Solely" belongs before "to receive," and "in order" can be dropped.) Another writer offered this: "Students and faculty members believe that such exposure to a well-known magazine would be a beneficial experience." This seems borderline to me, but I prefer "think."

A possible use of "feel": "The administration felt embarrassed [or didn't feel embarrassed] by the *Playboy* dispute."

Earlier I mentioned not-quite-right prepositions. Here is another example: "What will her family, friends or professors think about her when they find out she has been in a 'skin' magazine." To think "about" is to remember her. To think "of" her is what the writer meant to say.

In "Sex Objects" we have this sentence: "The first group of letters . . . consisted of angry women, condoning such activity going on in a college atmosphere." Obviously the writer meant to use "condemn" instead of "condone." Letters do not "consist of" women but "come from" women. In the same editorial: "The degradation of women was an argument. . . ." Degradation of women is "a concern" not an argument; degradation of women might be *used* as an argument. The writer referred to the "perfect" woman as being "the object of plastic surgeons. . . ." Such a woman might have been the "object" of those who regarded her as a sex symbol, but she was the "product" of the plastic surgeon.

"Many" is a word much abused by editorial writers. With their license to state opinions, perhaps they think they can get away with using the word when they would not think of using it in news columns. Too often editorial writers use this ambiguous word to support a point when they have no idea how many "many" is. What may seem "many" to supporters of a proposal may not seem "many" to opponents. In one editorial the writer said: "Many feminists on campus expressed their displeasure at the thought of *Playboy* visiting Virginia Tech." In the first place, "many feminists" sounds like a lot more feminists than I have been aware of at Tech. "Many" is certainly more than the number of voices that had been heard in public. Third, the writer implies that only "feminists" had expressed displeasure and that those who had expressed displeasure were "feminists." Neither assumption seemed justified under the circumstances.

Somewhat similarly, the same writer stated: "Students and faculty members believe that such exposure to a well-known magazine would be a beneficial experience for the young women who chose to appear." This suggests that all students and faculty members believe this. "Some" may be an appropriate word in cases like this. "Some" seems to put more emphasis on what the group thinks than on the specific or relative size of the group.

Avoiding Biased Words and Phrases

Editorial writers—all writers in fact—need to be especially sensitive to words and phrases that reflect or imply bias toward one sex or the other; toward members of a race, religion or nationality; or toward persons of a certain age, physical condition or lifestyle.

Nouns and pronouns that refer only to males, and thereby suggest that females are not included should be avoided. Frequently a sentence can be recast to change "he" or "his" to the plural "they" or "them." Sometimes that can create problems too. For example, in one of the editorials about *Playboy*, a student wrote:

... everyone is the master of their own body.

In this instance, since the "everyone" being talked about was a woman, "his own body" would make no sense. The writer turned to the plural "their," but of course "everyone" is singular. In addition, if the writer had thought about it, no doubt some word other than the male "master" would have been used. One way to solve both problems:

People (or women) should have control of their own bodies.

Generally recasting the sentence in plural form is the simplest solution. "Himself or herself" sounds awkward and should be avoided.

Words containing "man" often introduce gender bias. Here are several possibilities for alternatives:

Biased	*Alternative*
man-made	manufactured
man-hours	hours
layman's terms	lay terms
man-on-the-street interviews	on-the-street interviews
manhole cover	utility cover
policemen	police officer
fireman	firefighter
founding fathers of journalism	pioneers of journalism
Founding Fathers of the nation	Founders of the nation
foreman	supervisor
workman's compensation	worker's compensation

In the area of race, to refer to "non-white" students may suggest that white students are standard and others are not. Writers should specify the racial groups they have in mind. To refer to someone as "culturally" disadvantaged suggests the inferiority of the cultures of other people. Writers should refer to specific cultural groups.

Some objections were raised to the Washington football team's name "Redskins." Assigned to write an editorial on that topic, one student wrote that those who objected "perceive 'Redskins' to be a relic of white frontiersmen who judged the various tribes they encountered to be wild, uncivilized and violent—none of which is the type of self-image anyone would like to possess, especially a traditionally oppressed race in American society." But another student wrote that "proponents of the nickname say that they, indeed, are honoring Native Americans, and, if they didn't have the utmost respect for the group, they wouldn't waste their beloved team's moniker on the Indian."

The American Society of Newspaper Editors has distributed a card that contains a guide to "acceptable" and "unacceptable" terms to use in writing about the disabled. A person who is "disabled" or "handicapped" ("acceptable") is not necessarily "crippled" or "deformed" ("unacceptable"). A person "uses" a wheelchair, not "is confined to a wheelchair."[9] Also a person "resides in," and is not "confined to," a nursing home.

These are only a few suggestions that might be made for the improvement of writing. Additional suggestions on how to avoid bias in writing can be found in *Without Bias*: *A Guidebook for Nondiscriminatory Communication*.[10] Several books on writing in general were suggested in Chapter 4, "Preparation of an Editorial Writer."

CONCLUSION

Simply following all of these steps, and those described in the preceding chapter, will not guarantee a good editorial. Thought, imagination and lively writing, none of which can be reduced to a simple how-to formula, are even more essential than the format of the editorial or the correctness of the words. No matter how technically correct or skillfully organized, an editorial is not likely to be effective unless it also carries hard-to-define qualities that attract and persuade readers.

James J. Kilpatrick has described the goal of the editorial writer "to be, in 300 words or less, temperate, calm, dignified, forceful, direct, catchy, provocative, stimulating, reasoned, logical, literate, factual, opinionated, conclusive, informative, interesting and persuasive. And put a live head on it."[11]

That's all it takes to write an editorial.

QUESTIONS AND ANSWERS

1. Find an editorial with what you regard as an overabundance of factual information. Rewrite the piece using only those facts that are necessary to make the subject understandable.

2. Apply a heavy editing pencil to an editorial to remove unnecessary words and phrases.

3. Try to find an editorial in which the arguments and evidence presented do not support the conclusion. With the information that is contained in the editorial, can it be rewritten to bring the conclusion into line with the supporting material?

4. Count and average the number of syllables for every hundred words and the number of words per sentence in the editorials of several newspapers. How do the editorials compare in terms of word and sentence length? Are the editorials with longer words and sentences more difficult to understand? If not, why not?

5. In examining these same newspapers, do you find a general trend in individual papers toward long sentences and long words, or short sentences and short words, or do editorials vary within the papers?

6. Find an editorial in which the simplified style of the writing seems condescending to readers. Can you rewrite the editorial to overcome this problem?

7. Scan a handful of editorials for cliches. Which—if any—can you justify? How could you eliminate the remainder?

8. Rewrite an editorial that relies excessively on government or other types of jargon. Translate the offending language into understandable English.

9. Examine several editorials for euphemisms and for more difficult words and phrases than are necessary to convey meaning.

10. Find improper and ambiguous uses of "it" and "that" as referents. Rewrite to clarify the meaning.

11. Find several sentences that begin with a form of "there is" and rewrite them in a clearer and more direct manner.

Chapter 12

Subjects That Are Hard to Write About

Is it necessary or desirable to fill the editorial columns with pieces on government and politics to the virtual exclusion of all else . . . ?

—Creed Black, Nashville Tennessean[1]

Any survey of American editorial writers would reveal that government is the favorite topic of editorial writers. This shouldn't be surprising, since the news business seems concerned primarily with public affairs, and much of public affairs involves government. Writers also may follow this tendency as a matter of least resistance, since their own interests are likely to lie in this direction. The non-political subjects may not get written about, or taken seriously, for at least three other reasons. First, writers may regard some subject areas as too difficult to write about—at least in the time available to them. Second, they may regard a subject as so easy to write about that they dash off an editorial devoting little time or thought. Third, they may regard a non-government topic as not sufficiently serious to warrant taking time from the "great issues of the day." This chapter will look at the first of these editorials: subjects that are tough to write about. The next chapter will look at subjects that are deceptively easy and subjects that editorial writers often ignore.

Any subject can be hard to write about if you don't know what you are writing about. Over the years, I have found that, because of the fear of not knowing enough about the topic, writers have tended to shy away from seven subject areas: economics, legal issues, international affairs, culture, medicine and health, religion and sports.

ECONOMICS

For the writer who wants to write more than cliches, the editorial on economics is one of the hardest to write. Of all the topics that I assign my students, economics is the one that they resist most. The minds of those who have taken introductory economics courses seem bewildered by theories, laws and graphs. The minds of those who have not taken these courses are filled with horror at the thought of writing about what has been called "the dismal science." Part of the reluctance of both groups stems from their impressions that editorials on economics are boring and filled with numbers. If they have read editorials on the subject, they probably think of them as dealing with taxes (too high), government spending (too much), unemployment (too high) or inflation (too rapid). Or they think that editorials on economics deal with the theories of John Maynard Keynes, Milton Friedman or Arthur Laffer. None of this seems to have much to do with daily life.

But economics does relate to how readers live. The supply and price of gasoline affect nearly every American, so editorials about decisions made by the OPEC nations stand a good chance of being read if they talk about how these decisions will be reflected at the gas pump. Editorials about the easing of the capital gains tax, extending the sales tax to food and drugs or boosting the gasoline tax can be written about in a manner that will make readers understand how and why they are affected. So how does a writer produce an editorial on economics that does not end up simply saying the government shouldn't be spending so much money or employees should, or shouldn't, pay a larger share of medical insurance premiums?

Several suggestions have been offered by Lauren K. Soth, veteran at writing editorials on economics as editorial page editor of *Des Moines Register* and as a syndicated columnist. Economics editorials, according to Soth, should explain and interpret, not merely spout official newspaper policy. They should discuss "what is happening here and now" and concentrate on how current economic phenomena actually affect people's well-being. This means avoiding the temptation to "pontificate on every little economic event in terms of. . . . grand ideologies." Soth emphasized that organization of the subject matter is extremely important, that the writer needs to proceed in a manner that seems logical to readers—from the known to the unknown, spelling out each major step of reasoning from the beginning to the conclusion. Each editorial should concentrate on one central idea and drive it home, avoiding getting involved in side issues.

While Soth did not contend that economics can be made simple and entertaining, he believed that the writer can, and should, arouse interest by talking in terms of what people are interested in—people. "Instead of saying, 'Wheat acreage increased to 10 percent,' why not say, 'Farmers planted 10 percent more acres of wheat'?" Without oversimplifying complex issues, the writer can make them understandable. For instance, instead of stringing facts and figures together in prose comparisons, data can be organized in tables and rounded off for easier comprehension.[2]

What Soth was espousing—that the writer should speak in specific, not general, terms—is illustrated in the opening of the editorial titled "Counting Up Costs, Benefits of Clean Air," from the *Greenville* (S.C.) *News*. Rather than referring to impersonal coal companies, the editorial cites the "playful" message on the T-shirt of the A.T. Massey Coal Co. The catchy beginning draws readers into the editorial. The title is not nearly so inviting, and it is not until the sixth paragraph that the writer gets around to talking about benefits to the public. The editorial clearly draws on two sources: the *Wall Street Journal*, for information about the clean air act, and the *New York Times Magazine*, for research about health dangers. In the conclusion, the writer brings these together to conclude that the act will benefit both Massey and the public. The editorial is of moderate length (399 words). The sentences are relatively short—an average of 19 words. There are about 150 syllables for each 100 words, placing the editorial between "standard" and "fairly difficult" on the Flesch readability scale. (See Chapter 11 for explanation of the scale.) An additional note about the editorial: the overuse of "lot," which appears in the fourth, fifth and sixth sentences.

Counting Up Costs, Benefits of Clean Air

"Massey Lite Coal," the T-shirt reads in a parody of the beer commercials, "Burns Great, Less Polluting."

A.T. Massey Coal Co.'s playfulness helps illuminate an aspect of the new clean air law that is common sense, but which often is overlooked in the lamentations over the law's cost, estimated to be $25 billion a year by 2005. Massey, according to *The Wall Street Journal*, is the largest producer of low-sulfur coal in the eastern United States. And Massey is going to sell a lot more coal as the law kicks in.

The law will be costly for a lot of companies—for electric power generators, for chemical manufacturers, for car makers. But a lot of companies that make products needed for pollution control are going to clean up. If somebody pays, somebody has to collect.

Cleaner air could be the most long-lived legacy of the 101st Congress, which was distinguished mostly for a chaotic effort to cut the federal deficit. President Bush is due much credit also. More than a year ago, he proposed the first serious revisions in the Clean Air Act in a decade, and signing the law will put substance behind his campaign promise to pursue an environmental agenda.

It is the nature of things that consumers will pay the costs of cleaner air through higher prices for electricity, automobiles and other products. But it happens as well that the public will collect benefits.

Clean air is not merely an aesthetic ideal found in azure skies and mountain vistas that now often may be obscured by haze. It can be a matter of health.

An article in the Oct. 7 issue of *The New York Times Magazine* discussed research showing the relationship between dirty air and heart disease, cancer and immune system disorders. Even otherwise healthy adults, the article says, can suffer respiratory harm from ground-level ozone, a byproduct of automobile exhaust. *The Wall Street Journal* noted estimates that air pollution is a contributing factor in 50,000 premature deaths annually. The new law, *The Journal* says, is likely to mean fewer cancer deaths and fewer cases of such diseases as asthma and emphysema.

It's much more difficult to assign value to these benefits than to count the costs to car makers and utilities. But like the Ford Motor Co., the public will pay the higher costs of clean air. And like A.T. Massey Coal Co., the public will benefit.

The Greenville News[3]

The *Birmingham* (Ala.) *News* won the 1991 Pulitzer Prize for a week-long series of editorials titled "What They Won't Tell You About Taxes." Three editorial page staff members worked almost three months, examining documents and interviewing experts, to produce editorials that told readers what was wrong with Alabama's tax system and what ought to be done to change it. One of the editorials, which, with the names and numbers changed, might have been written about more than one state, was titled "The Cheap Date." The state's low-tax promises were likened to that of "a painted woman who expects the cheap evening she offers to attract potential dates"—an alluring way to entice readers into an editorial about taxes.

The Cheap Date

Like a painted woman who expects the cheap evening she offers to attract potential dates, Alabama has for decades used its promise of low taxes to lure business and industry.

It's about time this state learned what all cheap dates eventually discover: That they get taken advantage of.

Too many businesses attracted to Alabama's low taxes have packed up and left after having a good time.

Others remain, but refuse to make the same commitment they made in other states. Even companies that do extensive business in Alabama won't put their headquarters here. Our low taxes aren't enough to provide the services and quality education they want for their employees' and executives' families.

Why are we so wedded to these low taxes that do us more harm than good?

Because for decades our state government was not in tune with the needs of the majority of our people. Even when it did try to act in our behalf, like a child who can't stand the taste of medicine, we often refused to acknowledge the benefits of a larger dose.

Instead of doing the right thing, our lawmakers provide whatever taxes and services they can without disturbing ancient tax taboos. Then we try to put enough rouge and lipstick on the result to make it attractive.

Our property tax system is a prime example.

Alabama has, by far, the lowest property taxes in the nation. They got that way over a long, slow route along a path controlled by special interests.

Alabama's 1901 constitution placed caps on the rate, but it did allow 100 percent of the property's appraised value to be taxed. That only stayed on the books until the Revenue Act of 1935 set a 60 percent assessment rate.

But even that was not seriously collected. Alabama Power Co. eventually refused to pay it, saying non-utility taxpayers were "systematically and intentionally" assessed at only 40 percent. Elected county tax assessors knew which side their bread was buttered on.

The Alabama Supreme Court concurred and ordered Alabama Power's property tax assessment rate reduced to 40 percent.

In 1967, L&N Railroad used the Alabama Power argument to have its rate reduced to 30 percent. The state then began assessing all utility and railroad property at 30 percent.

Later that year lawmakers passed Act 502, which said that instead of 60 percent, the slice of a property's value to be taxed was "not to exceed 30 percent."

That much latitude increased the inequities. The amount charged ranged from 8–28 percent, depending on the county.

A lawsuit filed in 1967 sought uniform assessments, saying the out-of-kilter system robbed schoolchildren in the lowest counties of the same chance for school funds the higher counties had.

After a few rounds in litigation, in 1971 the court decided Act 502 was unconstitutional since it had originated in the Senate instead of the House, where revenue measures must begin.

In 1972, voters adopted the 325th amendment to the state constitution, which created three property tax classes. It lowered the assessment rate to 15 percent on most property. But it also formed a barrier to raising taxes on huge timber and agri-business tracts by placing them in the same category as private homes.

Shortly after, the Alabama Farm Bureau used the public's fear of high taxes on homeowners to campaign for passage of a "lid bill."

The 1975 lid bill was supposed to limit to 20 percent the additional revenue a county could collect after reappraisals.

The Alabama Education Association, pointing out the lunacy in putting a lid on what were already the lowest property taxes in the nation, successfully fought the Farm Bureau proposal.

But in 1978, Gov. George Wallace, threatening to expose certain legislators as tax hikers in an election year, steered a new "lid bill" through the Legislature.

Told by Farm Bureau and timber companies that it would save homeowners tax dollars, voters approved it in a statewide referendum.

The Lid Law lowered the assessment ratio on most property to 10 percent and set a cap on how much tax could be collected overall. It also made sure cities and counties would face one tough time raising property taxes. They had to call a public hearing, get permission from the Legislature and then gain local voters' approval to do so.

Wallace's 1978 "Tax Relief Package" also installed a "current use" provision, which lets property owners have their land assessed without consideration of its real value, supposedly to protect the small farmer from taxes on higher land values caused by urban encroachment.

But it also cut in half taxes paid by huge timber, agri-business and corporate land-owners in its first year and shields their land against increases brought by re-evaluations today. The lid bill, current use: Sprinkle them with the various exemptions to the tax code and you can see why property taxes in Alabama are so low.

How low? According to the Advisory Commission on Intergovernment Relations in Washington, in the U.S. in 1988 the average property tax paid per person was $538; in Florida, it was $537; in Georgia it was $396; in Tennessee it was $272; in Mississippi it was $266.

In Alabama, it was $132.

That deprives our schools of local money, because property taxes are the mainstay of local school support. Only 18.3 percent of our school revenue came from local levies last year. The national average was 43.7 percent.

Ridiculously low property taxes also tell large landowners to develop their lands elsewhere first; that they can afford to leave them alone here while the value increases, but taxes do not.

What incentives do we use to bring businesses into the state? We give them property tax breaks, of course.

Industrial property tax exemptions are primarily the result of the Cater Act of 1949, authored by Sen. Silas D. Cater of Montgomery, and the Wallace Act of 1951, authored by a young state representative from Barbour County named George Wallace.

The Wallace-Cater Acts give cities and counties authority to set up industrial development boards that may exempt industries from local property taxes as a way to entice them to locate in the state.

Of course, these exemptions erode the tax base. And since they are for limited periods, they encourage industries to do business in Alabama only for as long as the exemptions are in effect.

Allowed to raise their taxes to a level adequate to provide the quality of life all Americans covet, Alabamians would soon discover that this state doesn't have to be a cheap date to make others want to live and work here.

For too long, we have resembled one of those poor, backward Third World nations we ironically look at as beneath us.

Too often, others use our cheap labor to take our cheap natural resources, and then they sell the finished products back to us at a much higher price—as though we were some conquered colony.

If low property taxes are so good for us, why is it that despite paying by far the lowest taxes here of any state in the union, not one national timber company has located its headquarters in Alabama?

Birmingham News[4]

Economics editorials—in fact all editorials—should raise questions that may not seem obvious to most readers. In noting a report that U.S. chief executives were paid up to 150 times more than the average production worker, no doubt several editorials across the country asked whether such salaries were excessive. The *Deseret News* in Salt Lake City asked: "Are executives of large U.S. corporations being paid too much?" But it also immediately asked a second question: "And are top salaries going to the right officials?" The editorial cited a second report that the biggest paychecks in the United States tend to go to "financial officers, which is consistent with the 'bottom line' mentality of quick profits." In Japan, however, larger salaries go to personnel managers, and in Germany to executives in charge of research and development. The two reports prompted the editorial writer to ask (the title of the editorial) "Do Pay Plans Promote U.S. Growth?" and to conclude that American business had a lesson to learn.[5]

Editorials on economics do not have to be long. "Free Lunch," from the *Milwaukee* (Wis.) *Journal*, is an example. The editorial identifies one specific aspect of a proposed change in the capital gains tax and argues that the social benefits of the tax savings would be lost. The editorial seems to be directed at one audience, the House of Representatives.

Free Lunch

There's sense in using the tax system to stimulate investment as a way of creating new jobs and increasing productivity. The House Ways and Means Committee lost sight of that goal in one proposal to reform the capital gains tax.

Homeowners, once in their lives, would be allowed to pocket the profits—up to $100,000—on the sale of a home without paying any tax. That's unjustified.

We agree that a case can be made for not taxing a capital gain at all if the gain is reinvested, if the tax exclusion serves a larger social purpose. But the logic for special treatment disappears when a gain is simply converted into spending money. The full House should remedy the committee's extravagance.

Milwaukee Journal[6]

Writing about taxes of any kind can be touchy, since taxes affect individual interests more directly than most other economic matters and can become highly partisan, as, for example, with the Bush administration's proposals for reducing the capital gains tax. Writers must be fair, and they must know what they are talking about. Information about proposals for changes in federal taxes can be obtained from sources noted before, including *The CQ Researcher* and the *National Journal*. Information about the effects of taxes on state and local levels may be difficult to find. The writer often must dig out information, digging that may make the editorial all the more convincing and worth while. At the state level people working in the tax commission or for such groups as the state labor organization or state business association are possible sources. At the local level the county assessor is likely to be a good source for information about property taxes.

LEGAL ISSUES

Discussion of a legal issue can become so involved that readers may stop trying to understand what an editorial writer is talking about. Writers need to keep in mind that most readers know little about legal matters, so legal terms should never be used when plain English will do. If a legal term is used, it should be defined in the simplest language possible. Writers should keep a pocket law dictionary handy. Simplifying complex and technical legal matters, however, may distort information or mislead readers. So care must be taken to include enough of the complexities to persuade those knowledgeable of the subject.

In an editorial that won a Knight-Ridder "Excellence Award," Leo Morris of the Fort Wayne (Ind.) *News-Sentinel* enticed readers into an editorial on a Supreme Court decision by talking about stray dogs and cats. His point was that the court had about as much business considering a class action suit involving dogs and cats as it did considering nude dancing. The editorial recognized that the issue was a divisive one for communities, but that communities ought to deal with it.

Is Nude Dancing Really a Constitutional Issue?

It's gotten to the point where no one should feel safe feeding a stray dog without wondering what the Supreme Court would say about it.

Am I really helping this dog, or creating false expectations for it? By feeding it, am I assuming some kind of ownership that will make me legally liable? Am I being unfair to all the other stray dogs who didn't get fed today? And what about stray cats—is a class-action suit possible here? Good Lord, I'd better call a constitutional lawyer.

The court hasn't yet taken up the question of stray rights, or how many angels can dance on the head of a pin, but it ventures into ever sillier territory. On its first day this term, it agreed to review an Indiana case to determine whether nude barroom dancing should be given freedom-of-expression protection under the First Amendment.

Now, nude barroom dancing is a divisive issue over which communities may legitimately differ. It may truly be a morally corrosive perversion that will lead to the destruction of American as we know it; Fort Wayne may want to ban it on that basis. Or it could be totally harmless, a free-spirited ode to the joys of being alive; let it rip, Indianapolis. Such is the rich diversity of American life. Nobody expects Las Vegas and Boise to be the same, and we are all the better for it.

By elevating the dispute to the status of "constitutional issue," the Supreme Court makes nude barroom dancing of critical importance to American life, a distinction it surely does not deserve. If it *is* ruled constitutionally protected, nudity becomes almost sacred; woe to the mother who protests the nude beach next to her daughter's elementary school. If it *isn't*, then the very concept becomes legally repugnant; woe to the person who walks around naked at home but is inadvertently observed by a passer-by. Those are the ultimate outcomes, of course; it will require 15,000 more lawsuits and increasingly delicate judicial fine-tuning to get there.

The Constitution has endured because it outlines broad principles and assumes people have the good sense to look out for themselves and each other most of the time. In constructing the laws we live by, we should consider the Constitution as the general contractor's statement of principle. It's up to us—state by state, city by city—to go out and hire the architects to draw blueprints for the structures we want. Not all of us will build the same thing—and we shouldn't want to.

By trying to make the Constitution itself the blueprint, we deny ourselves the right to make choices. By living in a state of perpetual constitutional crisis, we move further away from the rule of law and to the rule of whim: whatever nine justices decide is right for us.

Not everything should be a constitutional issue. *Most* legal questions shouldn't be, in fact. By turning to the Constitution for resolution of every dispute, we trivialize the concepts it embodies and make ourselves less free.

Much has been written about how the newest justice, David Souter, will vote on this or that issue, and whether he will be a "liberal" or "conservative" or "moderate." He could do the greatest service for his country if he simply said, on 999 out of 1,000 cases that reach the Supreme Court, "This is not a constitutional issue, and we should not even take it up."

The News-Sentinel, Fort Wayne, Ind.[7]

Newspaper writers are especially likely to become involved in issues concerning the press and "the people's right to know" about government. "Courtroom Camera Ruling Benefits the People's 'Right to Know'" is an editorial on a decision of the Florida Supreme Court to allow television and newspaper cameras in the courtroom. The headline and the first sentence echo the familiar slogan. Does the editorial live up to the promise of the headline to explain the benefits for the public of cameras in the courtroom? In the second sentence, the editorial makes its bold assertion supporting the court's ruling: Cameras and microphones serve as the public's eyes and ears. Then the editorial explains and justifies that assertion: First-hand exposure can correct the incorrect impressions that much of the public has about trials and allow voters a better opportunity to judge the officials they must elect, without interfering with a fair trial. At the end the writer suggests that putting court officials on camera might also improve the business of justice. One problem in editorials that show readers how open meetings and open courts help the public is the appearance of self-interest. In "Courtroom Camera" the writer does try to convince readers that they have a stake in the issue; the press is barely mentioned.

Courtroom Camera Ruling Benefits the People's 'Right to Know'

In a victory for open government and the people's right to know how their public officials and criminal justice system operate, the Florida Supreme Court has unanimously ruled that TV and newspaper cameras and tape recorders belong in the courtroom.

Cameras and microphones serve as the eyes and ears of members of the public who don't attend in person.

Winners of this legal battle are not the newspapers and TV stations who will use the cameras in court, but the people themselves—for they will get a close-up view of the reality of a trial in action.

The public's perception of how a trial is proceeding, or how the criminal justice system operates, is twisted by lack of first-hand views.

Real trials are greatly unlike how most TV shows portray them. When voters choose judges, prosecutors, court clerks, and public defenders; when they are asked to support a bond issue for a new jail; when they form their opinions of a jury verdict or a judge's decision, the more knowledge they have, the better.

A year-long experiment, ending last July, showed that the presence of cameras could be controlled so that it did not interfere with a fair trial and distract trial participants.

A survey showed that two-thirds of the jurors, one-half the witnesses and many of the lawyers and judges involved felt cameras were not a problem.

The new court ruling provides strict rules to prevent the kind of disruptive "circus" coverage that marked trials years ago.

Some trial participants may "play to the camera," but the experiment shows this behavior is not widespread. After the initial novelty wears off, cameras are largely ignored.

Any potential for distraction could easily be removed if cameras and photographers were placed behind partitions with one-way glass, so no one could see them.

One result of the presence of cameras—in addition to educating and informing the public—could be to improve the performance of both judges and attorneys, make them stop playing courtroom games and tend more to the business of determining guilt or innocence of the defendant.

Sun-Sentinel, Fort Lauderdale, Fla.[8]

INTERNATIONAL AFFAIRS

International subjects may be both the hardest and the easiest topics to write about. They are easy in the sense that, when you write about a far-away country, you will not have your mayor, governor and next-door neighbor calling to say you don't have your facts straight, as they might on a local topic. Writers used to say that the safest editorial was a hard-hitting one about Afghanistan. That led to the term "Afghanistanism," a label generally thought to have originated in a speech that Jenkin Lloyd Jones, of the *Tulsa* (Okla.) *Tribune*, gave to the American Society of Newspaper Editors in 1948. He said that local readers "bark back, and you had better know your stuff." But you can pontificate on a situation in Afghanistan, he said, since "you have no fanatic Afghans among your readers," and nobody knows or cares about what you write.[9] The term "Afghanistanism" stood for more than 30 years—until the 1979 Soviet invasion of Afghanistan. As events in Afghanistan have shown, we live in an age when no country is totally unconnected with any other country. Now editorial writers are likely to find themselves writing about Kazakhstan, Kirgizstan and Uzbekistan.

A writer for the *Atlanta Constitution*, in fact, found himself or herself writing about those very countries in an editorial with a not-easily-understood title of "Tending to Overlooked Ex-Soviets." The writer faced the task of trying to interest readers in these countries when even the United States government "took it in stride" while Saudi Arabia and Pakistan offered them lavish attention. That wording, hinting that there was more to the story than had been revealed so far, no doubt was intended to draw lackadaisical readers into the next paragraph or two, where the real point of the editorial began to appear. After wading through six strange "stan"-type names, the reader is rewarded with the more familiar names of Iran and Turkey. The editorial serves to introduce readers to some of the players in the former Soviet areas. But it does little to explain why Iran is such a dangerous model and Turkey ("not without its [unspecified] flaws") is such a good one.

Tending to Overlooked Ex-Soviets

When Saudi Arabia and Pakistan, both sternly Islamic, lavished attention on the new republics of what used to be Soviet Central Asia, Washington took it in stride.

Oh, sure, it might have wanted more modern models for newcomer nations like Turkmenia, Azerbaijan, Kirgizstan, Uzbekistan, Tajikistan and Kazakhstan, but Saudi/Pakistani tutelage was not considered threatening.

The possibility of Iranian penetration into the region, however, most definitely was. Diplomatic and religious overtures by Teheran had to be countered, especially considering that several of the new countries still have nuclear weapons stationed on their soil.

After some hesitation, including an arguably justified delay in recognizing these republics, Washington has taken a partner and a most fitting one at that in an effort to steer the new nations right—namely Turkey.

In more ways than one, the Turks and the Central Asians speak the same language. That's right, save for the Tajiks, they all speak variations of Turkic. But in addition, the Central Asians admire Turkey's relatively stable and open politics, its market economy, its moderation in religion, its ties to the West.

So the initiative announced recently by President Bush and Prime Minister Suleyman Demirel of Turkey to begin directing short-term humanitarian aid and longer-term technical aid toward these new countries is a winner on two counts:

▶ It joins Washington and Ankara in a constructive effort at a time when Turkey, still less than a full-fledged member of the Western club, needs to feel respected and wanted.

▶ It signals a serious Western interest in this isolated region, potentially one that will speed its modernization, a point underlined recently by Secretary of State James A. Baker III in his tour of these new countries.

Granted, we haven't always seen eye to eye with our longtime NATO ally, and it is not without its flaws. Still in all, if the people of Central Asia are looking for a neighbor to emulate, Turkey's the one, far and away.

Atlanta Constitution[10]

Except for the hottest topics of the day, writers are faced with the problem of how to interest readers in foreign subjects. Most surveys show that foreign news ranks well down the list of readers' preferences. The issues have to be made extremely clear. Interesting details—specific events, personalities, colorful quotations—can help attract and hold the reader. One enticement can be a strong headline. "Diplomacy by Assassination" was the title the *Star Tribune* of Minneapolis–St. Paul gave an editorial about Israel. The opening sentence was equally strong, and certain to draw a strong response from both those who agreed and disagreed: "If Israel wants to humiliate and infuriate its Middle East opponents, alienate them from the United States and invite reciprocal barbarities, then the execution of Sheik Abbas Musawi goes a long way toward those foolish goals."[11]

One way to ease the way into an international topic is to set a scene to which the reader can relate. This can be especially useful in an opinion column or op-ed article. In a piece that I wrote on El Salvador for *The Oregonian* following a visit to Central America, I began in this manner:

A few weeks ago I was among a group of Americans who attended the first legal political rally of the El Salvador guerrilla group, the FMLN.

More recently a news story reported that former guerrillas had been brought to El Salvador, from asylum in Cuba, to receive a hero's welcome.

These events might suggest that the FMLN (Farabunde Marti National Liberation Front) and the Salvador government are traveling hand-in-hand down the path toward carrying out peace accords the two sides agreed to early this year.

Nothing could be farther from the truth. . . .[12]

How can a writer know enough to comment intelligently without parroting someone else's opinion? Writers must read a lot—and not just the daily press and the weekly news magazines. *The Economist* of London provides reliable reporting and perspectives on all parts of the world. *Foreign Affairs*, a quarterly journal, provides background and perspective. *Atlas* and *World Press Review* show what the press around the world is saying. Listening to speeches by visiting persons from other countries and talking personally with them can provide new points of view. Local world affairs councils can provide information programs and opportunities to meet knowledgeable visitors, as well as local citizens who are concerned with international affairs.

ARTS AND CULTURE

Surveys show that newspaper readership of news about the arts ranks low compared to most other features. Few daily newspapers have good arts and music coverage, even though the surveys have encouraged papers to expand and beef up their "life style" sections. As for opinion pages, according to a former editorial writer turned art-center director, Aubrey Bowie, "[e]ditorial writers seem to turn their attention to the arts only when something very good or very bad grabs the headline and catches their eye, [and] in either case, they are forced to shoot from the hip without the day-to-day research that they do routinely on other community issues."[13]

The funding of the arts should get as much careful attention as the funding of more traditional public programs. Bowie noted that changes in federal tax laws have reduced the tax advantages for contributions to non-profit organizations, that federal government support for the arts has been decreasing and that direct government involvement in the arts is a growing issue. Policy-makers, and editorial writers, have been asking: Should the government be supporting the arts? And, if so, under what circumstances? These questions were raised, for example, when John Frohnmayer was forced to resign as chairman of the National Endowment for the Arts in 1992. The *Washington Post* took the occasion to go beyond the immediate issue of the firing to suggest that changes needed to be made to preserve the "delicate mission" of the NEA.

Curtains for Mr. Frohnmayer

I am deeply offended by some of the filth that I see into which federal money has gone and some of the sacrilegious, blasphemous depictions that are portrayed by some to be art. And so I will speak strongly out opposed to that. But I would prefer to have this matter handled by a very sensitive, knowledgeable man of the arts, John Frohnmayer, than risk censorship or getting the federal government into telling every artist what he or she can paint. . . .

—President George Bush, March 1990

THAT WAS then. This is now: John Frohnmayer, chairman of the National Endowment for the Arts, is out. He was deposed early in the first act of the post–New Hampshire political play in which Mr. Bush tries to best bad boy Patrick Buchanan and like-minded conservatives who endlessly ridicule a federal agency they would abolish. It was a craven performance by the administration, and no sooner did it happen than it was being redirected, re-produced: Patrick Buchanan and the disappointing results in New Hampshire had nothing to do with it . . . Mr. Frohnmayer was on his way out the door anyway . . . He was simply "called in" after submitting his resignation . . .

But whatever the spin, whether it was a clumsy, slow-motion exit or a swift kick, there's no disputing the absolutely untenable position of the man responsible for granting money to artists and their organizations. "Embattled" came to be John Frohnmayer's given name. He tried simultaneously to appease implacable political foes, to mediate between a vocal and at times outrageous arts community that deems public funding an entitlement and an equally pumped-up conservative establishment led by Sen. Jesse Helms and direct-mail crusader Donald Wildmon, who get considerable money and attention by attacking taxpayer support for a handful of projects they and probably most other Americans too rightly perceive as offensive and salacious. He was damned by artists whose grant applications he rejected, and he was damned by Helms et al. for some he approved—namely, those two celebrated and highly controversial "performance artists." Observing all this was an easily terrorized Congress, whose members perennially sought political cover, dodged and hid but (usually behind conference doors) continued nonetheless to fund the NEA with carefully orchestrated language about decency and community standards and so forth.

Mr. Frohnmayer, an arts-loving lawyer and political novice from Oregon, tried his best to prop up all the people slouching toward the NEA—the artists and their detractors. In the end it was he who fell flat. Who wouldn't? The chairmanship of the NEA is a near-impossible job as long as this country's cultural polarization exerts such influence on the agency and its chairman. But it ought to be possible to rise above the poseurs and exhibitionists and present the NEA as the entirely worthy agency that it is, an agency that distributes most of its money to mainstream orchestras, dance groups, civic operas and folk artists, not to artists who urinate on stage. It will take someone who understands the NEA's central purpose, which remains compelling: to encourage artistic expression for the benefit of the American people, to nurture the arts by maintaining the public's confidence. The NEA's natural constituents, as Leonard Garment points out on the opposite page, are the people, the audiences, not the feuding parties. There was a time when the NEA's peer review panel, its national advisory council and its chairmen understood this better than they do today.

We persist in believing that some sense and restraint can be restored within an agency whose very existence is threatened. Mr. Garment's 1990 commission on the NEA suggested reforms, some of which Congress adopted. More procedural tinkering might be in order. But something's got to change in order for the NEA to carry out its delicate mission without all the mindless provocation and answering demagoguery.

The Washington Post[14]

Editorials on the arts have not been limited to "drawing-room" subjects or "drawing-room" language. An illustration, on the same general topic as the previous editorial, was written by *Washington Times* editorial writer Sam Francis, who writes with one of the sharpest pens in the opinion trade. The title of the editorial itself is a shocker, and so is the comparison that Francis makes in the first paragraph. In addition to his main target, the "parasites" of the art world, Francis along the way works in some sharp digs at Congress. This editorial was one of several of Francis's editorials that were included in *The Best Writing of 1990*, published by the Poynter Institute for Media Studies.

Urine the Money

North Carolina's Sen. Jesse Helms may not look much like Jesus Christ, but some of America's artists have done him the honor by putting him in the same place they put the Man from Galilee. This summer in Phoenix, an "alternative" art center called the MARS Artspace displayed as an exhibit a photograph of Mr. Helms immersed in a Mason jar of the urine of an artist known only as "Cactus Jack." The MARS Artspace, it turns out, is funded by the National Endowment for the Arts—in other words, by you and your tax dollars.

Of course, Cactus Jack, whoever he is, didn't mean to honor Mr. Helms. His creation was a spin-off of artist Andres Serrano's "Piss Christ," a photograph of a crucifix submerged in Mr. Serrano's own liquid offal. That creation too was funded by $15,000 from the NEA, and Mr. Helm's response to what he considered a blasphemous use of the taxpayers' money and a waste of human waste was to sponsor legislation cutting off public funds for obscene and indecent artworks.

MARS art director Jason Sikes says his "immediate reaction" to Cactus Jack's inspiration "on a personal level was that it was hilarious. . . . My second reaction was that if we put it up, it could cause us problems." Even "alternative" artists have to eat and pay rent, you see, and even as he was chuckling over how clever Cactus Jack's *piece de resistance* was, Mr. Sikes was beginning to worry whether the yokels might get fed up with him and his whole stupid center.

In the event, Mr. Sikes proceeded with the display and kept it on exhibit until Aug. 17, despite protests from philistines who just don't appreciate genius and clearly have no sense of humor. "We decided," proclaims Mr. Sikes valiantly, "an artist's freedom of expression was more important." But the belly laugh Mr. Sikes and his friends may have gotten from their calculated insult to Mr. Helms may cost them. Rep. Sidney Yates, chairman of the subcommittee that reviews NEA funding, says he doesn't think it's funny when artists make sport with members of Congress. "I don't think any member of Congress should be treated like that," says Mr. Yates of Cactus Jack's masterpiece.

Actually, a good many members of Congress probably deserve treatment far worse than even Cactus Jack's morbid imagination could conceive. It's ironic that at the same time many members of America's freeloading artistic establishment are furious because taxpayers are getting bored with picking up the check for the insulting, obscene, and blasphemous junk that artists create, many members of Congress also are furious that Americans are growing tired of congressional pomposity, hypocrisy, and outright corruption. It seems to be fine with Mr. Yates if whacked-out aesthetes smear their bodily fluids over mainstream American beliefs and values, but they better not even think about poking fun at congressmen.

The Senate was right to pass Mr. Helm's amendment. Cactus Jack's micturitions ought to be carried to the nearest sewer. The Mason jar can serve to hold Mr. Sikes's income after Congress transfers his gallery to the free marketplace of ideas. And American taxpayers ought to put Mr.

Helms's picture on their mantels for his courage in pushing an arrogant gang of parasites off the public dole.

The Washington Times[15]

Public broadcasting (funding and content) has been another controversial cultural topic. When two West Virginia public television stations refused to show a "too graphic" program about black homosexuals, the *Charleston Gazette* carried a highly critical editorial titled "Prim Public TV," apparently a play on "prime-time TV."[16]

Editorials on culture need not involve great principles of major public policy. The *Herald-Times* of Newport News, Va., found "distressing" the prospect of losing a string music program in the public schools: "Not merely for the sake of the youngsters who will be deprived of the exposure and training, but for the memory of a very charming, dedicated woman—Elizabeth Chapman—who was such a vital part of the Peninsula's music life when the area was essentially a cultural wasteland." The writer pointed out that the Hampton Roads area had made great progress toward "achiev[ing] a semblance of cultural stature," partly because of "public television's live and filmed broadcasts of operas, concerts, ballet, orchestras and drama from the great halls of the world. . . . But we also think the seeds were planted far earlier by the likes of Elizabeth Chapman, who believed music and culture is appreciated at very early ages, especially when there is actual participation. We regret sincerely the likelihood the string program will be cut back, perhaps eliminated, in Hampton's schools."[17]

MEDICINE AND HEALTH

The health sciences represent another area in which editorial writers may feel ignorant. "Few issues more readily trip the typical editorialist into silence, drivel or pompous balderdash," D. Michael Heywood of *The Columbian* of Vancouver, Wash., wrote in a *Masthead* symposium on health care. "Anything deeper than a turf battle between ambulance companies involves chopping through layers of increasing complexity. Burrowing through a vein of valuable explanation or suggestion for public action can seem as daunting as attempting heart surgery with kitchen cutlery."[18] Writers need to display not only knowledge of what they are talking about but also an understanding of and sympathy for those who hold different opinions, on abortion, AIDS, euthanasia, artificial insemination, life-preserving treatment, organ transplants and holistic medicine. Heywood's admonition to the opposite sides on abortion: "Our pro-choice position gains strength and validity if we've troubled to keep on talking after we've been branded baby-killers. Our antipathy for *Roe vs. Wade* ought to have its corners rounded by sympathy for survivors of the back alley."

In another symposium, editors of *The Masthead* asked writers in 21 communities with a relatively low incidence of AIDS to describe how they were treating the disease.[19] Several writers said that commentary was difficult because of conflicting medical evidence. Some suggested that the emotion and confusion aroused by AIDS issues could be minimized by treating AIDS as a public health epidemic that demanded governmental attention and public education. The writers indicated that they detected less hysteria among the public than previously, but a substantial amount of ignorance resulting more from self-deception than from misinformation in the news media.

It was a rare newspaper that did not comment on basketball star Magic Johnson's revelation in 1991 that he had been infected with the virus that causes AIDS. But for writers interested in helping readers understand how they might be affected, Johnson was hardly a typical model. In addition to commenting on the Johnson case, the *Detroit Free Press* published an editorial that told the story of the daughter of a well-known local financier and philanthropist. "She is heterosexual and was faithful within her marriage," the editorial said. "But none of that protected her from infection with the human immunodeficiency virus (HIV), which causes AIDS, she presumes as a result of intravenous drug use by her now former husband before their marriage." The editorial concluded: "Those who still try to deny that this is a disease that can touch anyone had better pay attention." The newspaper not only named the woman but also published a 4-by-3-inch photograph in the editorial columns.[20]

In an editorial titled "Right AIDS-Scare Reaction," the *Salt Lake Tribune* tried to assure readers that proper steps were being taken by authorities after a 12-year-old girl pricked her finger on a syringe that a teacher's aide had told her to pick up. It quoted health authorities as saying that "her chances of contracting AIDS from the needle are remote." It asked readers not to "too harshly" judge the school district nor "the hapless teacher's aide" for the "scary episode." It commended school officials for a "quick response [that] should reasonably shield others from the kind of anguish that the . . . student and her parents are now enduring."[21]

RELIGION

Most editors assiduously avoid allowing readers to become involved in denominational or scriptural arguments in the letters columns. Some editors have assiduously avoided religious topics in their editorial columns. But editors today will find it impossible to avoid religious controversies if they expect to comment on such issues in this country as abortion, homosexuality and prayer in the public schools or such events abroad as religious war in the Balkans. Writers, by necessity, are being required to talk about religion and religious differences. Citizens are facing controversies over religious observances in the schools, the placement of crosses and manger scenes on public property, solicitations by Hare Krishnas in public airports, the rights of women and homosexuals in the churches. The question of whether churches and income-producing properties of churches should be taxed raises issues involving the First Amendment as well as tax equity. When a pope or a popular evangelist tours a nation and draws crowds in the tens of thousands on the streets, in the parks and in public arenas, a religious and media event takes on national significance. When groups hold foreign hostages in the name of Allah, the event becomes an international one. Writers presumably can discuss all these subjects without becoming embroiled in a denominational morass—but only if they use a great deal of care, accuracy and charity.

Michael McGough, editorial page editor of the *Pittsburgh Post-Gazette*, has argued that a line cannot be reasonably drawn between public and sectarian issues. "It doesn't take a lot of deconstruction to conclude that an editorial opposing Israeli annexation of the West Bank implicitly rejects the religious views of those Jews who believe Israeli sovereignty over those territories is divinely ordained," he wrote in a *Masthead* article.[22] "Likewise, when a newspaper supports birth control initiatives in this country or as part of U.S. foreign assistance policy, it is telegraphing its disagreement with the Roman Catholic assertion (unpopular as it may be with Catholic laity) that artificial contraception is a moral evil." Why, then, McGough asked, do "editors who as individuals are religiously observant" ban "even minimal celebration of religious truths and impulses . . . from editorial columns"? He said he was not certain whether this "aversion to religious appeal" reflects the feelings of readers and editorial writers or only the "secular ethos" of editorial writers. He recognized, in any case, that "[a]n editorial that explicitly invoked God or doctrines devised to explain this operation certainly would affront secularized readers; might it also offend believing ones?"

If editorial writers have remained reluctant to discuss specific sectarian doctrines, in recent years they have found that they had little choice but to editorialize about the activities of specific church leaders. They have written about televangelists who have swindled their believers and (to quote the *Roanoke* (Va.) *Times & World-News*) "succumb[ed] to the temptations of the flesh." They have commented on a Presbyterian study report that, along with addressing other sexual issues, condemned ministers who have abused counseling relationships. They have also commented on a report from the Roman Catholic Church about instances of pedophilia among priests. All have been considered fit subjects for editorial comment. Concerning televangelists, the Roanoke newspaper offered this comment as part of an editorial titled "Another Televangelist Falls":

The televangelist is more than an ordinary preacher. He is at once a show-business personality and a business tycoon. He is the custodian of tens of millions of dollars. His contributors send him the dough in complete trust. That kind of money conveys power. And power can be an aphrodisiac. The celebrity feasting on the adulation of his followers finds that the forbidden fruit is readily available. And it takes fortitude to resist.

But "Thou shall not commit adultery" is only one of the rules of conduct laid down in the book the televangelist waves before his audience. There are other passages that deal with greed and deception and the worship of material goods.[23]

SPORTS

The sports world seems to be becoming more and more regarded as an appropriate subject for editorial comment. One reason is that sports pages have broadened their coverage far beyond the mere reporting of the outcome and description of events. At the high school level, local citizens argue whether athletes need to maintain passing grades in all subjects. Colleges issues involve minimal scholastic standards, illegal payments to athletes, the professionalization of college athletics and imbalance in women's and men's sports. At the professional level are heard arguments over "instant replay," player salaries, foreign ownership of golf courses and baseball teams, exclusion of countries from the Olympic Games. Many times, of course, sports editorials praise teams and individuals for outstanding performances or offer condolences over losses. Expressing pride in the hometown team is an appropriate editorial function, but sports editorials, like other editorials on the page, serve readers best when they seek to enlighten or evaluate. The topic for discussion is not always good news, as the *Daily Press* of Newport News, Va., pointed out in the following editorial, but the writer tries to foresee a positive effect. (The editorial followed a series of news stories exposing the infractions.)

HU Pays the Price

A sad chapter in the history of Hampton University has been closed with the decision, announced by the National Collegiate Athletic Association, to place the school's football team on probation for two years and to ban it from post-season play in 1991. The penalties follow an investigation of HU's football program and the discovery that the team used an academically ineligible player in 1986 and two ineligible players in 1987.

In addition, the NCAA said, the school showed "a lack of appropriate institutional control and monitoring in the conduct and administration of the athletics program." Its penalties also include the forfeiture of 12 victories in the '86 and '87 seasons and various other sanctions that, together, largely mirror the self-imposed penalties announced by HU President William Harvey in 1990.

In August 1988, the Daily Press reported on apparent improprieties involving HU athletes' grades and course credits. The newspaper's investigation, which prompted the internal inquiry and broadened the NCAA investigation, was criticized by some HU supporters as unfair and motivated by racism. The university and

NCAA actions validate the newspaper's original findings. It is unfortunate that Hampton was not immune to the disease that infects intercollegiate athletics today. At too many schools, how well a student blocks or runs is more important than how well he thinks or how hard he studies.

The self-imposed penalties announced by Harvey indicate that Hampton may be a better school for this episode, but such steps are not unusual when universities have been caught breaking the rules. HU broke the rules. That fact may have helped bring the school some momentary glory on the football field, but it also brought trauma and embarrassment and, in February 1989, a court trial in which the university's dirty laundry was displayed for all to see.

It is perhaps wishful thinking, especially in light of the excellent season the University of Virginia's football team enjoyed, but HU's experience can serve as a stern reminder to all of the colleges and universities in the state that their first business is to educate men and women. Games should never be allowed to interfere with that task.

Daily News, Newport News, Va.[24]

Sports editorials are not necessarily limited to activities that involve teams or individual performers. Hunting, fishing, bicycling, backpacking and mountain climbing can be worthy of comment. A bill that would have banned airboats on Virginia's tidal waters during duck-hunting season prompted an editorial titled "Of Noisy Airboats and Shooters of Shotguns" from the *Free Lance–Star* of Fredericksburg, Va. Expressing a concern about the real beneficiaries of the legislation, the newspaper said, "Nobody has thoroughly considered a duck's point of view. Would a duck rather be frightened by an airboat or killed by a shotgun-toting hunter? Whose environment would be protected by [the] bill?"[25]

Sports editorials offer opportunities for satire and fantasy, as illustrated by "When Baseball Went Wrong," by Bill Leonard of the *Des Moines Register*, who won the "Best of Gannett" award for editorial writing in 1991.

FIELD OF NIGHTMARES

When Baseball Went Wrong

Baseball historians traced the beginning of the collapse to 1991, when Roger Clemens' single-season salary topped $5 million. The Boston Red Sox front office had Clemens' pitching arm insured for $10 million, and because of his tendency to pop off, insured his mouth for another $5 million.

The complexion of the game changed—imperceptibly at first, then dramatically. The players' organization won a provision that no batter making more than the combined salaries of all the bleacher fans had to run out routine grounders.

Then came the unfortunate incident in Dodger Stadium in which $4-million-man Darryl Strawberry was beaned with a peanut, on the very day that Oakland's $3-million Ricky Henderson had his feelings hurt by a heckler. That brought the moat to baseball. A lagoon dug completely around the field pushed fans another 50 feet away from the playing field.

The resulting drop in attendance caused some owners to compensate by putting some floating gambling casinos in the moats to draw fans. Wasted effort; fans soon were abolished as superfluous. TV revenue, not tickets, made baseball rich.

Fans were replaced by movie extras, whose responses to "on-premise interaction syndromes," as baseball plays came to be known, were carefully choreographed for TV consumption.

When the leagues expanded to four, each containing eight divisions comprised of nine teams, the regular season was cut to eight games by each team. The last-place team in each division was eliminated, narrowing the playoffs to 256 teams. Playoffs began on July 4 and were completed on Super Saturday in January.

Then finally, somebody remembered that former cornfield out near Dyersville, Ia., where "Field of Dreams" was filmed, where you could go and imagine baseball in the days of hot dogs and beer and dust and sunburns and fun.

And TV sports gave way to a new pastime, and soon there were ballparks in which people played for the sheer joy of the game.

And million-dollar players were excluded as overqualified.

And fans, despite what the consultants had promised, lived happily ever after.

Des Moines Register [26]

CONCLUSION

Editorials on the subjects discussed in this chapter are not hard to write if you do enough homework to know what you are writing about, and if you write in a manner that enables readers to understand what you are writing about.

QUESTIONS AND EXERCISES

1. Find an editorial on an economic topic. Compare the writing and approach to the suggestions offered in this chapter. Does the editorial follow these suggestions, especially concerning the use of figures and the personalizing of the writer's points? If not, how could it be improved?

2. Analyze an editorial that talks about taxes, property taxes if possible. Is it easy to understand? Could it be simplified? Should more points be spelled out?

3. Find an editorial that relies excessively on legal terms. Rewrite it using more common language.

4. Can you find an editorial that formerly would have been labeled an "Afghanistanism"? Does the editorial seem to have absolutely nothing to do with the interests of the readers most likely to read the editorial? Could the subject have been made more pertinent to readers?

5. Find an editorial on an international topic that stands a good chance of catching the reader's attention—one that is not on a current hot topic. What is it about the editorial that makes it readable?

6. Compare several editorials on cultural subjects. Which seem to have been written simply to get promoters of causes off the backs of the editorial writer? Which are most likely to attract readers? Could the run-of-the-mill editorials have been made more interesting or pertinent?

Chapter 13

Subjects That Are Deceptively Easy or Neglected

If you don't like people, you're called a misanthrope. And if you detest holidays, you're called an editorial writer. [If you decide not to run an editorial on Columbus Day], stand by for irate calls and letters from what seems like every Italian-American for miles around.
—JAMES E. CASTO, HERALD-DISPATCH, HUNTINGTON, W. VA.[1]

Like many journalists with a non-science degree . . . , I previously thought of science as dry and boring. In working with scientists, however, I have learned that science lies at the heart of many of our most important news stories: AIDS, Star Wars, the Challenger disaster, Chernobyl and many others.
—DAVID JARMUL, NATIONAL ACADEMY SERVICE[2]

In continuing the previous chapter's exploration of non-governmental editorial topics, this chapter looks at subjects that may seem so easy to deal with that they appear to be hardly worth writing about as well as subjects that may be neglected because they don't seem sufficiently "editorial" in nature.

THE TYPES THAT ARE DECEPTIVELY EASY

Although the lines between the subcategories in this group of editorials may not be absolutely sharp, I will discuss four deceptively easy areas: obituaries, the local pride piece, the favorite subject (or "easy shot") and the "duty" piece.

Obituaries

De mortuis nil nisi bonum is not a good rule for writing editorials about persons who have died. Speaking nothing but good of the dead may be fine for funeral orations, but telling readers only some of the facts has no more place in an obituary editorial than it has in any other kind of editorial. Relating the full story is relatively easy when you write about a national, or even state, figure. Information is often readily available and indisputable. The family of the deceased is not likely to see the editorial, at least not immediately after publication, so the writer can feel free to tell the good and the not-so-good. But when the person is a local figure, inhibitions take hold. The temptation is to stick with the favorable facts and throw in a dash of "she'll be missed." This is no time to add to the family's bereavement, the reasoning goes. Yet undeserved praise is no praise at all, since those likely to care the most about what is written will know that the words are hollow.

In my experience, families often respond favorably to obituary editorials that mention the human, less-than-perfect side of the deceased. When I wrote that a civic activist had a booming voice and had been something of a glad-hander (not quite in those words), his widow told me, "That was Bob, all right." Another time I wrote that a woman who had been involved in many activities was something of a character and that she sometimes said things that other people didn't understand. Shaking his head, her son told me, "That's the way Mother was, and we loved her for it." Of course, in small and medium-sized communities, if not in larger ones, there are limits to telling the full truth. You would not want to dig up something especially embarrassing from a person's past, particularly something that the person had lived down.

The trick to writing an obituary editorial is to catch some detail—words, behavior, description—that makes the person seem unique and human, something that distinguishes him or her from everyone else, something for which the person can be remembered. You don't always have to write about a widely known person. Fitting subjects might be a person who had taught a long time in the local schools, someone who had been quietly helpful to neighbors and friends, a mail deliverer, someone who had clerked in the same store for many years, a person who had sold newspapers on the same corner ever since anyone could remember.

When Alex Haley died in 1992, typical editorials said that his book *Roots* and the 1977 television version had (to quote one editorial) "earned Mr. Haley a place in the hearts of millions" and had provided African-Americans with roots with which they could identify—nothing very incisive in those comments. The *Detroit Free Press* made these same points, but aspects of the editorial set it apart: First, the editorial graphically describes the "clear views" that Americans got of "the hell that was slavery, of the purgatory of humiliation, of the unfair necessity of the struggle for freedom and dignity. . . ." Second, instead of stopping with the widely accepted *Roots*, the writer makes a major point of calling attention to "an even more important book," one that represents a widely different view of Malcolm X than that held by most Americans. The writer suggests readers look at this book to really understand a "wrenching period in America."

Alex Haley:

He opened eyes to America's past, and gave us hope

Most notably through his wondrous book "Roots," Alex Palmer Haley gave voice to the generations of Africans who, through the crime of slavery, were plunged into a cruel and involuntary process of becoming Americans. Through his art, he gave African-Americans the family story most had been denied.

There have been few moments of shared reality in this country to rival the television version of "Roots" broadcast in 1977 and seen by nearly two-thirds of Americans. America together got a clear view of the hell that was slavery, of the purgatory of humiliation, and of the unfair necessity of the struggle for freedom and dignity that has been the lot of Africa's sons and daughters here. After "Roots," almost no one in America anymore denied what the essence of that history is.

That would be an impressive enough legacy for Mr. Haley, who died Monday at age 70. But he wrote an even more important book: "The Autobiography of Malcolm X." In it, as that crucial 20th Century analyst evolved, we see anger transformed into cool thought. It is one of the best works for understanding a wrenching period in America.

A kind and gentle man, Mr. Haley seemed to have time enough and heart enough for all. Like us, his princely ancestor Kunta Kinte would be proud of what he gave us, sad to see him go.

The Detroit Free Press[3]

Local Pride

Second cousin to the obituary editorial is the local pride editorial, which comments on the activities of local people, local teams or local organizations. As with obituaries, there are ways to make these editorials more than sheer puffery. Sometimes, for example, an editorial may be called for to boost the spirits of someone or some organization in the community after a disappointment. Sometimes residents of a community need to take a realistic look at how they appear to others. Is the community as friendly as its promoters say it is? Does it have residential areas that those concerned with its image do not talk about much? Are residents going elsewhere to shop because they can't find what they want in local stores? Are building and development restrictions keeping out all but a selected, privileged class of citizens?

Editorial writers cannot be expected to be able to view their communities completely objectively. After all, if these writers didn't think their communities were pretty decent places, why would they be living there? Writers should take pride in their communities and should work hard to make them better places. But without a true understanding of the limitations, as well as the advantages, of the area, no writer can help his or her community deal with its problems and successes.

The perennial surveys that rate cities as the "best" places to live invariably draw editorial comment, from "winners" and "losers." In "Staying 'Livable,'" the *Pittsburgh Post-Gazette* discusses how it feels to have been a former winner.

Staying 'Livable'

Any Pittsburgher who feels disappointed that this community's short-lived "most livable" designation didn't bring greater returns should heed the plight of Pittsburgh's successor in that Places Rated Almanac category—Seattle.

"Seattle: Too Much of a Good Thing?" is the title of an article in *The New York Times* describing that city's ambivalent feelings about the aftermath of receiving that designation. The gist of the story: "The notion of the 'livable' city has drawn waves of migration to this Northwestern hub. It's become a victim of its own appeal."

During the late 1980s, a quarter of a million people have moved to the Seattle region (its 1980 population, 1.6 million, is about what Allegheny County remains). That influx rode a tide of newcomers that began early in the decade when Seattle succeeded Denver as "the place to be."

But there has been a price. "Demand drove the housing market wild; last year the average selling price of a house in Seattle was 40 percent higher than the year before, and it was not unusual for anxious buyers to line up three and four deep and make offers on the stoop," the *Times* article said.

Therefore, the rising cost of living is making it harder for the middle class to live within the city limits, and there is an emerging clash between rich and poor. Cocaine dealers have also discovered the city and crime has risen.

"Tolerance, moderation, the small-town virtues that attracted people, are in short supply," the *Times* article relates. "Seattle is no longer a quaint frontier town but a booming metropolis teetering precariously on the brink of becoming something it did not particularly seek to become: a big urban city, with all the advantages and headaches that accompany that designation."

Yes, Pittsburgh's population has declined. It might benefit from a large infusion of newcomers.

But since that hasn't happened, our community should take comfort in the fact that the factors that shot Pittsburgh to the top in an earlier survey haven't deteriorated as a result. Fortunately, being designated "most livable" hasn't proved to be too much of a good thing here.

Pittsburgh Post-Gazette.[4]

A test of the credibility of local-pride editorials comes when something occurs that reflects negatively on a community. Aimed at local private clubs that still discriminate (and members that support them), "Public Affairs, Private Clubs" was one of the editorials that won a Knight-Ridder "best editorial" award for the *Charlotte* (N.C.) *Observer.*

Public Affairs, Private Clubs

There is an odd idea in circulation among some members of Charlotte's social, civic and financial elite. It is that even though they support or belong to country clubs that discriminate on the basis of race, gender and religion, they are not themselves supporters of racism, sexism and religious bigotry.

They try to create a distinction where none exists. They support those policies with their presence and their money. If they support racist, sexist, anti-Semitic clubs, they are supporting racism, sexism and anti-Semitism. It's that simple.

They may argue in their own defense that *they* are not bigots, it's just that someone else makes club policies. It seems fair, then, to conclude that they are

willing to tolerate a little racism, sexism and anti-Semitism rather than cause a fuss or lose access to private tennis courts, golf courses and dining rooms. Apparently, pleading that they are tolerant of bigotry, rather than practitioners of it, makes them feel better. It shouldn't.

There always will be people who see others through blinders of bigotry. Clubs whose policies reflect that view might serve some useful purpose if they were identifiable as havens of the self-professed bigots. But when community leaders are members, they give those clubs patina of respectability.

We would propose this policy for every person and every business, professional and civic organization that does not support racism, sexism and anti-Semitism: Do not support racist, sexist and anti-Semitic clubs with your presence and your money. Do not use their facilities.

It makes no sense to argue that you oppose bigotry while you are supporting organizations that practice it. You may be fooling yourself about where your priorities are. You are not fooling anyone else.

Charlotte Observer [5]

Favorite Subject

Editorial writers cannot be expected to produce fresh wisdom, certainly not on every topic, each day. Reiterating a message is one solution to the lack of more inspiring topics. Since most readers don't read the editorial page every day, remaking a point is not likely to seem repetitive. Another, and less defensible, solution is writing on a subject on which the writer has to do little or no research and do little or no new thinking. Sometimes the subject is a favorite target. I call this type of editorial "an easy shot."

An example of an easy shot taken every year by some editorial writers is the editorial that appears on the day that average taxpayers have stopped "working for the government" and started earning money to keep for themselves. Every year some tax association notifies newspapers of this date and usually points out that it falls one or two or three days later this year than last year. The first time that editorial appeared it had merit; the idea is clever as a piece of propaganda. Since then, the editorial has become a cliche.

Another perennial piece is the one that criticizes the salaries being paid state legislators or members of Congress. This editorial is usually accompanied by an attack on the legislative body for not doing its job and for letting personal interests and pleasures interfere with the public's business. The editorial writer often adds something to this effect: "It is no wonder the voters have lost faith in government." No doubt some legislative bodies deserve criticism for the sneaky ways in which they slip benefits for themselves into legislation and for the seemingly petty politicking that frustrates the legislative process. But an editorial written to condemn a specific misdeed should stick to the particular subject and avoid generalizing about all the wicked ways of government officials. One strange thing about this tendency of editorial writers to pick on legislative bodies is that when it comes time for endorsement of candidates all past sins seem forgotten. Congress is bad, it seems, but our own local member is good enough to merit another term.

Closely related to the let's-jump-on-Congress editorial is the pork-barrel piece. It is not uncommon for an editorial page that persistently calls for cuts in the federal budget and in unnecessary federal projects to issue a stirring defense of a desperately needed local project. A project that would be labeled as "pork barrel" if proposed for another part of the country becomes a fully justified investment in a home community, an investment needed to provide jobs or to prevent floods.

If editors are pressed for a topic, they can pull out the old national-debt piece, or the how-much-is-a-billion bit. That is always good for helping readers understand the complexity of the political issues of the day! It may get a rise out of readers who think the government is spending too much money, but if they want less spending, what are they willing to give up in government benefits? This type of editorial never seems to address the latter question.

Some editors like to pick on the courts: Lenient judges are the cause of today's criminal-infested society. Some like to pick on the schools: No wonder kids can't read; the teachers are just interested in easy jobs and high salaries and don't know how to spell themselves. Some like to pick on environmentalists: If it weren't for these Sierra Club do-gooders, we would have a more viable economy and a lot more jobs. Some like to pick on the oil companies: Big oil wants to force prices up so that it can profit from all that oil it has stashed away. Some like to pick on developers: All they are interested in is the fast buck.

This fault-finding with "easy shot" editorials about the deficiencies of government, or about anything else, must not be misinterpreted. One of the responsibilities of a newspaper, and of an editorial writer, is to keep an eye on the government and public activities in general. If some agency or some activity deserves criticism, the writer should speak out clearly. But the editorial should stick to the subject at hand, should be fair and should make some attempt to enlighten readers, not just inflame them.

The "Duty" Piece

"For tomorrow's page we're going to need an editorial on _____. Who's going to write it?" Fill that blank with "Thanksgiving," "the Fourth of July," "the annual United Way campaign," "the state high school basketball championship" or "a highway safety campaign," and you will understand what is meant by a "duty" piece. It is an editorial that you think you ought to run to mark an occasion or boost a good cause, but it is almost impossible to think of anything more to say than you did the last time you wrote on the subject.

"If you are deathly afraid of tall buildings and other high places, you're called an acrophile," James E. Casto of the *Herald-Dispatch* of Huntington, W. Va., has written. "If you don't like people, you're called a misanthrope. And if you detest holidays, you're called an editorial writer."[6] If you decide not to run an editorial on Columbus Day, he said, "stand by for irate calls and letters from what seems like every Italian-American for miles around." As for holidays such as Easter, he asked, "do you write about the Resurrection or do you confine comments to the Easter Bunny, colored eggs and such?" In either case, "you run the risk of offending a segment of your readers."

At least two points ought to be made on behalf of editorials that support worthy causes. The first is that, while an endorsement of an annual fund drive may be repetitious to the veteran editorial writer, whatever is said is usually appreciated by the promoters. If an editorial doesn't actually raise any more money, it at least serves to legitimize the cause. Second, an editorial writer can regard a duty editorial as a challenge to say something creative or imaginative on an old topic. If a newspaper does publish editorials endorsing causes, it should know what it is backing. Lauren K. Soth of the *Des Moines Register* said that when readers see an editorial supporting a drive for contributions, they ought to be able to assume that the editors have studied the cause and found it to have merit.[7]

Richard B. Childs for the *Flint* (Mich.) *Journal* said that his first rule for handling "the drudgery aspects" of "duty" pieces was "to evade." If you are lucky, someone else on the staff will get the job. But if you can't evade, he advised, "relax and enjoy it." Childs said he actually had begun to look forward to Abraham Lincoln's birthday: Each year he tried to find something new to say. He had written about Lincoln's concept of the Constitution, his role as a politician, his faith in people and democracy, his literary abilities, his defense against black writers who sought to picture him a racist and his continuing image as a national hero despite changing national moods.[8]

In a *Masthead* symposium on holiday editorial pages, Jim Wright reported that the *Dallas Morning News* cut back on "well-here-it-is-again editorials, not only for minor holidays like Arbor Day but for annual charity events and the like." Two exceptions were "the opening of Our State Fair (which is a Great State Fair) and the United Way campaign, the sole regular charity event we note." When a need is felt for "inspirational editorials for holidays," the task usually went to new staff writers, "who tend to have less treadwear on their similes, metaphors and quotations dealing with the occasion."[9]

One Christmas the *Fort Worth Star-Telegram* ran a "wish list" discussing what the editorial writers would "ask Santa" for at each of four levels of government: city, county, state and nation.[10] The *Richmond News Leader* has filled its editorial columns with Christmas poems, carols and stories and the right side of the page with a Christmas sampler of Thomas Nast drawings.[11] For the Fourth of July, the *Hartford Courant*, "the oldest daily newspaper in continuous publication," has dug back in its files of 200 or more years and reprinted contemporaneous accounts of the Revolutionary War.[12] The *Miami Herald* has reprinted the Bill of Rights and the Preamble to the Declaration of Independence.[13] The *Courier-Journal* of Louisville published an editorial titled "Love Letters" on Valentine's Day, apparently not because of a traditional "duty" to commemorate that day but because of a newly noted untraditional method for expressing sentiments.

Love Letters

For those who have been around the block a few times—and for those who have been married so long they can't even remember what a trip around the block was like—Valentine's Day is less an opportunity for warmth and love than a time of intense pressure.

The problem is, it's hard to keep coming up with imaginative ways to demonstrate your love. How many boxes of chocolates or bouquets of flowers or pairs of heart-patterned Jockey shorts can you give before your love is looking like a very tired, very old, very taken-for-granted thing?

The inadequacy so many of us feel has spawned a new business—a California business, of course: Love Letters Ink. For a fee, the company will send a letter "done in calligraphy, personalized just for you." And the letters—being from California—are for moderns. Consider letter #3 ($16.95): "We've gone through some rough times. I believe those to be bridges of growth, and we have emerged with a bond that burns brighter."

That's quite a mixture of metaphors, but what do you expect for $17, Elizabeth Barrett Browning? The world is a busy place, as letter #1 (also $16.95) acknowledges: "Since we've been together, there have been times when my schedule has been overwhelming. . . . Though I seem distracted, you are always there in my heart. . . ."

Not exactly warm, not exactly tender—and is it reasonable to think a canned, calligraphed confession could restore romance to love? Only time, attention and a little imagination can do that.

And, in lieu of imagination, revert to chocolates, flowers or heart-patterned Jockey shorts. Call yourself a traditionalist, then use them in imaginative ways.

Courier-Journal, Louisville[14]

Hoke Norris of the *Winston-Salem* (N.C.) *Journal-Sentinel*, with tongue in cheek, once offered *Masthead* readers a generic "duty" editorial that could be used on almost any occasion. All the writer has to do is fill in the blanks. Unfortunately too many of the cliches in this piece ("The Utility Editorial") show up in editorials that are dashed off without much thought.

The Utility Editorial

_____ is an issue which is a challenge to us all. Every right-thinking person in _____ will (view with alarm)
(state, nation, world, universe)
(point with pride) (be puzzled by) (be gratified by) (be alarmed by) this latest development, which comes at a time when _____ faces the darkest days
(state, nation, world, universe)
in its history.

All men of good will should band themselves together to (see that it doesn't happen again) (perpetuate it) (encourage it) (discourage it) (deplore it) (praise it). Only in this way can we assure continued (progress and prosperity) (justice and freedom) (peace and joy) in a _____ fraught with crisis as
(state, nation, world, universe)
never before.

We must all (get behind) (oppose) this latest development in the ever-changing rhythm of time, in order that the _____ may continue to _____ . On the other hand, _____ . As _____ has so well said, _____ . The future of _____
(state, nation, world, universe)
hangs in the balance. We must not fail!

Hoke Norris, Winston-Salem (N.C.)
Journal-Sentinel[15]

THE TYPES THAT GET NEGLECTED

In this category are editorials on science, the world of nature and the everyday lives of people, and those that are written in a humorous or satirical manner. No doubt others could be included.

Science

Science has not been viewed as a popular or easy subject for editorials. A former newspaperman whose current job was to get articles on science placed on op-ed pages told *Masthead* readers: "Like many journalists with a non-science degree (my own in history), I previously thought of science as dry and boring." But he found, he said, that science "lay at the heart of many of our most important news stories: AIDS, Star Wars, the Challenger disaster, Chernobyl . . . "[16] Writing about science in the abstract may indeed be dry and boring, as well as incomprehensible to the non-science reader. But as the short list cited above suggests, plenty of science topics affect readers directly or involve public policy. An editorial in the *St. Petersburg Times* ("An Ozone Hole of Our Own") was concerned with both effects.

An Ozone Hole of Our Own

Our government's failure to respond quickly or forcefully enough to the spreading destruction of the Earth's protective ozone layer is a perverse extension of the "not in my back yard" syndrome. As long as Americans could reassure themselves that the potentially disastrous effects of ozone depletion would not be felt until the distant future in some distant corner of the globe, it was easy to delay dealing with the issue.

Now, though, it has become almost impossible to ignore the growing evidence that the damage from ozone depletion has begun to affect our lives right here, right now. The incidence of skin cancer in the United States, including potentially deadly melanomas, already is increasing at an alarming rate. Ultraviolet rays, no longer sufficiently blocked by the atmosphere's ozone layer, are the primary culprit. Other effects—crop damage, cataracts, immune system disorders—are being felt in parts of the world where huge holes in the ozone layer already have become a fact of life for part of each year.

As if that weren't enough to accelerate this country's effort to eliminate the man-made causes of ozone depletion, last month's discovery of a developing ozone hole directly over New England and eastern Canada should capture people's attention. The levels of chlorine monoxide over that part of North America were the highest ever recorded anywhere in the world.

Chlorine monoxide, which destroys ozone, is a byproduct of the chlorofluoro-carbons (CFCs) contained in refrigerants, aerosol sprays and other common U.S.-made products. The United States and other Western nations have agreed to eliminate their production of CFCs by the year 2000, but that's not nearly soon enough. Current evidence of ozone depletion is the delayed effect of the widespread use of CFCs years ago. Even if CFCs were eliminated tomorrow, the ozone layer would continue to deteriorate for several more years because of the propellants already released into the atmosphere.

During John Sununu's stormy tenure as White House chief of staff, the Bush administration generally obstructed efforts to establish meaningful international policies to reverse ozone depletion. Now that it is free from Sununu's ignorant intrusions into environmental policy, the administration may finally be ready to play a more responsible role in ending the world's dependence on CFCs and spurring the development of new technologies to correct the atmospheric damage already done.

Environmental Protection Agency chief William Reilly, whose earlier efforts were blocked by Sununu, said this week that U.S. officials are now prepared to move up the elimination of CFCs by three or four years. American industry already has developed adequate substitutes for CFCs in virtually every product that ever contained them, so the technology already exists to end the production of CFCs in this country well before the end of the century.

Unfortunately, science has not yet developed feasible technologies for undoing the damage already done to the ozone layer. In addition to ending our own production of CFCs, the United States should take the lead in supporting innovative research and in aiding developing nations' transition to CFC substitutes.

Now that the immediate threat from ozone depletion has moved from the South Pole to our own back yard, the White House and Congress may finally feel the kind of political pressure that can spur the government toward those overdue commitments.

St. Petersburg Times.[17]

The World of Nature

Editorial writers who would never hesitate to tread where angels fear to go will turn and flee when asked to venture where the wood nymphs dance. They would rather tackle religion or sports.

Al Southwick, who found himself the house nature writer on the *Worcester* (Mass.) *Evening Gazette*, suspected that much of the trouble was psychological. In addition, Southwick wrote, "many newspaper writers shrink from using 'flowery' language," since "it seems to suggest looseness of form and insincerity of purpose." But he saw writing about a setting sun or the delights of picking blueberries as offering him more freedom to use imagination and picturesque phrases than did writing about election returns. It gave him a chance to loosen up metaphors, to let himself go and "to return to the long valley of remembrance." He wrote: "A quiet millpond at dusk, shingled with flat lily pads, may prod your senses into creation. . . . A field of corn wilting in the broiling August sun may recall to memory long hours you spent as a boy weeding and hoeing."[18]

Southwick suggested that a writer who has trouble getting into the mood should go out in the backyard and gaze about, or on a sunny afternoon take the family on a picnic to a secluded spot. He urged the writer to lie back on the grass, look at the sky, the puffs of sailing clouds, the hazy, distant hills. "This is the fabric from which you can weave beautiful things at your typewriter," he wrote. "It is all a matter of seeing and hearing what nature has to offer. Once you catch that, the words will come easily." He was convinced that the same talent that writes an editorial on a school bond issue can describe a babbling brook. "And the chances are that more readers will read about the brook than about the bonds. Furthermore, if they do read about the brook, they may just tarry long enough to dip into the bond disquisition."

Southwick's nature writings proved so popular that 10 of his seasonal pieces were published in a booklet titled "New England Around the Year." "Cider—the Nectar of October," one of these pieces, may appeal more to older than to younger readers and probably more to residents of New England. But its strong feelings of nostalgia should appeal to a broad readership. One of the strengths of the editorial is the specificity of its images: cider presses; apple-laden wagons pulled by patient, plodding horses; square dances in the old barn.

Cider—the Nectar of October

Cider and October go together like Santa Claus and Christmas. There are few experiences in this life to equal the first glass of dark amber cider in the fall.

Cider is a blend of apple varieties, October air, fond memories and stout, wooden casks. A sip of cider will bring a man back to his boyhood, when the height of childhood enjoyment was centered around the old cider press and its squeezings. It recalls apple picking, and slow, apple-laden wagons pulled by patient, plodding horses, and golden autumn sunsets. It recalls October evenings by the fireplace, when the chestnut logs snapped and crackled and tossed their sparks on the hearth, throwing a flickering light on the contented people gathered around, each with a glass of cold cider in his hand.

Cider brings back the memory of gloomy, dusty cellars, with kegs of ripening apple juice in one corner. It recalls doughnuts, and square dances in the old barn, and fall nights lighted up by the ghostly radiance of the moon.

Cider is more than a beverage; it is an institution—a tradition redolent with significance. When a man takes his first drink of cider in the fall, he is renewing a ritual that was old when the country was born.

Worcester (Mass.) *Evening Gazette*[19]

One of the best known writers of nature editorials was Hal Borland, who for many years contributed the last item in the editorial columns of the Sunday *New York Times*. His writings were collected in several volumes, including *An American Year*.[20] When I was on *The Columbian* in Vancouver, Wash., I could count on exquisitely done pieces—both short and long—on the outdoor world from Erwin Rieger, managing editor of the paper. His steady supply spared me the frightening task of having to switch from bonds to brooks. His "Romance of Clouds Invites Mountaineer," as printed here, is a condensed version of a selection from *Up Is The Mountain*, a collection of Rieger's writings.[21] Part of the success of this piece stems from its highly personal writing. The readers know that the writer is a person who is sharing his own feelings and appreciation of the experience. It isn't only because I have known "Mr. Rieger" (as we always have called him) for 35 years that I feel the personality of the writer shining through in the first few paragraphs; throughout the piece, he seems a friendly guide to places most readers have never been to.

Romance of Clouds Invites Mountaineer

Mountain climbing has had many facets for me. I must feel that one of the more delightful has been my encounters with, and my feeling of intimacy with, the clouds.

I say that despite occasional harsh, often disagreeable, sometimes dangerous experience with clouds.

Most of us look up to see the clouds. Mountaineers may look down on clouds. At other times they meet them face to face and at arm's length. . . .

Volatile indeed is the mountain environment. For mountains are stand-up land, and they thrust their immovable and often-serrated bulk up to interfere with the air currents where live so many of our clouds. Not only that, but some of them can and often do make their own weather. . . .

I am afraid I am a romantic about the clouds in my beloved highlands, even though as a climber I have endured their malevolences many a time and would have cursed them in seven languages had I been able.

I have loved to watch cloudlets a-borning, and even dying. One cannot do that intimately at my home. But on a mountain, or on a mountain top, one can be glancing idly through clear air when for no reason at all, puff! there is a baby cloud; a little tossing handkerchief of visible moisture drifting by. It may grow bigger; it may join with other little puffs as turbulence spawns the right conditions; or—pfft! it may be gone without trace.

Occasionally it is a signal to the climber to be long gone from there. The cloud formation may grow and spin and flatten to a streaming compressed mass of dense vapor, an evil vortex of wind and storm inhabited by seven devils.

I have perhaps never seen a more beautiful birth of the cloudlets than on the lovely day we were relaxing in cloudless sunlight on the summit of Mt. Olympus.

Olympus is scarcely a single mountain in the sense of how we usually think of a mountain like Hood. Its broad sub-top culminates in a series of relatively short, sharp peaks arranged not unlike the upturned fingers of an open hand. West Peak, the summit, is only slightly higher than its brothers or sisters.

And as I looked that day down into the scenic snow-filled "palm of the hand" with the sun already above and behind me, puff! a cloudlet appeared. Over there another. Yonder a third—it went on without end. And the wind began to rise; and the cloudlets closed ranks and gathered mass; and they reached to take hold of the lesser tips of the "fingers." It was time to descend.

I have loved to be in the scenic alplands as the morning sun burned off the condensed water vapor and turned it invisible again. It does that at home too. But in the alplands the weakening wisps will cling stubbornly and beautifully to the pointed spires of the alpine firs, and the gradual parting will open vistas of unguessed slopes and crags above and just ahead; and of the clear sky so blue up there. It is a world apart. . . .

I have loved to toil, maybe for hours, up through a cloud blanket to emerge finally topside into brilliant sunshine as far as the eye can see. Riding airplanes, I have come topside also, the easy way. I suppose because I like to climb I have never felt in an airplane the sweetness of the accomplishment nor felt the sense of "other world" insulated from mundane care beneath the all-stretching silvery sea.

I have loved to be above the cloud sea even at night when there has been a full moon. No place I have ever been has been lovelier than the summit of Pinnacle Peak in the Rainier country, where valleys radiate from the spire in several directions.

It has been my fortune to be on that summit under full moon not once but eight or nine times—most of them with the silver cloud sea filling all the valleys three or four thousand feet below me, and the awesome bulk of Rainier across the way somehow gentled and softened. It has been quiet up there on the pinnacle. The spirit of benediction was upon the peak like a spell.

Yes, I have loved the clouds of the mountains and the high country. Even as I have cursed them in concert with fellow climbers. Even as they have wet me to the bone with their penetrating wind-driven fingers. Even as they have iced me with sleet or stung me with ice pellets driven like needles.

Even as they have pervaded all in the incredible density of the whiteout, where one has difficulty keeping his balance and where travel is tolerable only by compass. . . .

Of all my memories none is more distinctive than one I carry from that hoary giant, Rainier. Forty-six years ago one summer I was pushing up alone from Paradise Valley before daylight, headed for Camp Muir at 10,000 feet. The cloud sea was all-enveloping. But as has so often happened, I came out on top of it at about 8,000 feet—only to realize that a second cloud layer, of which I was seeing the bottom, enveloped the mountain top perhaps 5,000 feet higher. It was a quiescent version of the Mt. Rainier cloud cap I have mentioned earlier. I was "sandwiched" in a most unusual formation.

An hour later and a thousand feet higher, the sun rose—to such a spectacle as I had never seen before. Deep rose color suffused the ceiling above me—and reflected for a few moments on the surface of the sea below me. And not only did the visible portion of the great mountain glow softly pink, but a rainbow-like band of light, parallel to the sunward profile of the mountain, framed the profile. That I have never seen again.

The Columbian, Vancouver, Wash.[22]

Lives of People

Editorial writers tend to forget that most readers are more interested in their personal lives than they are in public affairs. Except for letters to the editor, they are not likely to find anything on most editorial pages that speaks to them about their daily lives. The editorial that may have received more favorable response than any other I have written was one I hastily typed for use after a Labor Day weekend. My second daughter was to enter kindergarten the following Tuesday. The result was "To a Barefoot Girl," written in the form of a letter to her. At a session of NCEW later that year, other editorial writers questioned whether it was an editorial, since it was written in the first person and did not comment on an issue. But readers of *The Columbian*, especially mothers of small children, didn't care whether it met the requirement of an editorial. One woman, several years later, told me she still carried a copy of it in her purse.

To a Barefoot Girl

Letter to a daughter who went to school for the first time today:

By the time I get home from work tonight, you will have experienced your first day of kindergarten. You'll be bubbling over with stories about the excitement of school—that is, if you aren't already worn out answering questions from your mother, your big sister and the girls next door.

If I know you, you weren't even a little bit scared today. An article in the paper the other evening said parents should expect their five-year-olds to be a little scared the first day, scared of spending two or three hours away from home in a new place. But that's nothing new to you. You've been gone from home longer than that this summer—without telling your mother where you were going. She was the one who was scared.

If your teacher let you paint or color today, I hope she kept a close eye on you. You can do a good job of staying within the lines when you want to. But your mother tells me that every time she turns her back there's a new mark on the living room carpet or your pillow case. How your teacher is going to keep track of you and 29 other children is beyond me. I wish her luck.

I also wish her luck in getting you to stay on your rug when it's rest time. If she has to stand over you the way your mother and I have to when it's nap time at home, 29 other children are going to be up and around and doing whatever they want to.

I hope you came home wearing your shoes, or at least carrying them. You are a big school girl now, and it's time to start learning to keep track of your shoes. It's all right sometimes to take them off, but you've got to stop forgetting where you left them. The tennis shoes you lost this summer didn't cost too much, but those big saddle shoes we bought you for school cost a lot of dollars, a whole lot more than the six cents you charged me yesterday for lemonade. Maybe it would help if you wrote your name on the inside of your shoes.

I hope you're not going to be disappointed with kindergarten. You have been looking forward to school ever since you knew where your big sister went to school. You always thought she was so smart. She could read and write and do numbers. I've heard you tell people that as soon as you went to school you'd be able to read and write and do numbers, too. It will take you quite a while to learn enough so that you can read a book, or the funny papers, or this letter. Kindergartners these days don't get much chance to learn to read. Maybe it's just as well. Maybe kindergarten should be a time only for enjoying your new friends, playing games and painting pictures.

The most important thing about school is being able to enjoy it. A lot of big boys and girls are scared of school—boys and girls who are bigger than your sister. Most of them aren't doing very well in school either. They aren't learning what they should be. Maybe they started out being scared from the first day. But maybe what happened was that somewhere along the line they forgot that school ought to be fun. Maybe they had some cranky teachers. Or maybe their parents put too much pressure on them.

I'm not sure you know what I'm talking about by this time. But I guess what I'm saying is that I hope that, even though you are now a big school girl, you will still be that smiling, laughing little kid who has a mind of her own and who is interested in more important things than keeping track of a pair of shoes. We can always buy another pair of shoes or clean the pillow case. But it's not so easy to repair the damage if you let the big people in the world who have forgotten how to smile and laugh keep you from smiling and laughing.

I hope you have fun in school—even if you come home barefoot.

The Columbian, Vancouver, Wash.[23]

Included in this group of editorials could be pieces about the weather, Christmas shopping, summer vacations, new hair styles or clothing trends, the computer game rage and what to do with a stack of old newspapers. These editorials may not contribute to the solution of any of the world's problems, but they might help solve some of an editorial writer's problems in getting more people to turn to the editorial page.

Humor and Satire

When press critic Ben H. Bagdikian critiqued the pages of editorial writers attending an NCEW convention, he found few examples of humor and the humor that he found was not very good. "Funny" people are hard to find, he said. "Perhaps it isn't a funny world."[24] When columnist Andy Rooney was asked about humor writing in a *Masthead* symposium, he concluded that "[g]enerally speaking . . . editorial pages, like the Bible, are better off without humor." He said he had found that "[a]lmost every time someone sets out, deliberately, to write something funny, the effort falls flat."[25]

Other participants in the symposium were not so pessimistic. "[B]adly executed humor can decapitate an argument faster than a guillotine," but "humor can smooth the way to making [a] point," Nordahl Flakstad of the *Leader-Post* of Regina, Saskatchewan, wrote. "After all, some of the most persuasive writing—running back to Jonathan Swift and earlier—has used a light touch to make a sometimes heavy point." But Flakstad thought it was a wrong use of limited space to "drop a funny piece into editorial pages merely for entertainment and comic relief."[26] Columnist Rick Horowitz saw an "occasional light touch" as the best way to get readers to the page and keep them there. "Being funny doesn't mean you aren't being serious," he said; "it's simply a different way of making points."[27]

Rena Pederson reported that the *Dallas Morning News* sometimes ran occasional short editorials, "some whimsical, some barbed," on Sundays. "One of my favorites was about the effort by Senator Howard Metzenbaum to get American Airlines to drop its weight policy for flight attendants because it was biased against older women," she wrote. "The concluding paragraph read, 'Instead of throwing Margo into cargo, it's time for American to lighten up. In return, the attendants and Mr. Metzenbaum ought to plead the case for passengers, who are being squeezed into seats so cramped that there's not even room to complain.'"[28]

Often a humor piece depends on the clever use of, and a play on, words, exemplified here in "A Shaggy-Fish Story." The writer tosses in as many disagreeable-sounding words as possible, shifting from fish to other foods to alcoholic drinks. This list sets the reader up for the final gagline, which probably provided the motivation for writing the editorial.

A Shaggy-Fish Story

Many very edible fish have very unappetizing names, among them the gagfish, the ratfish, the dogfish, the rattail and the grunt.

This worries the National Fisheries Service to the point where it is considering a new system for labeling such fish in the supermarkets and on restaurant menus. The lowly gagfish, for example, has much the same texture and taste as the popular red snapper, and the new labeling would point that out.

We think the National Marine Fisheries Service is wasting its time. A nation that stuffs itself on hog maw, scrapple, pigs feet, grits, souse, gumbo, head cheese, tripe, gruel, blood wurst, mush, hangtown fries and rutabagas is not likely to reject a mess of ratfish.

To the contrary, we probably would celebrate our discovery of this new epicurean delight by throwing down a couple of extra wallbangers, bloody marys, grasshoppers, slings, screwdrivers, fizzes, rusty nails, boilermakers or the hair of the dogfish that bit us.

Los Angeles Times[29]

One of the risks in writing humorously is that readers might take what you write seriously—and not get the point. That risk is even greater with satire.

In a *Masthead* symposium on satire, Mark L. Genrich on the *Phoenix Gazette* said that, as a person who hates fruitcake, he sometimes writes editorials calling for its abolition. In one editorial he suggested that the state police "establish roadblocks at Christmas time to intercept the transportation of the distasteful stuff." Violators would be "punished by forcing them to eat, on the spot, the fruitcakes they were caught transporting across state lines." Some readers thought he was serious and wrote long letters describing the wonderful taste of fruitcakes. Others accused him of harming the fruitcake industry. On another occasion he wrote an editorial opposing the extension of daylight-saving time, "pointing out that the time change means more hours of sunlight in the afternoon, drying crops and grasslands," leading to the need for farmers and suburbanites to use more water to keep fields and lawns green. Dutifully a number of readers wrote to "explain carefully and patiently that the sun is not controlled by earthly clocks."[30] Satire had gone awry with these readers.

Joseph Plummer of the *Pittsburgh Post-Gazette* said that he saw the opportunity for "an occasional alliance between the generally understood mission of the editorial page as a vehicle for biting criticism and the intent of sarcasm, which is to deride and taunt," but he wouldn't use it often, "because sarcasm is truly a blunt instrument." He suggested that sarcasm could be appropriate in "criticizing the egregious misbehavior on the part of a public official" but "unsuitable when some point of public policy is being weighed in an editorial."[31]

Dave Cummerow of the *Modesto* (Calif.) *Bee* said in a *Masthead* symposium that satire "works best with an overstuffed shirt, a distended balloon, a house of cards" and "the path to successful satire is narrow, with pitfalls on each side."[32] Cummerow occasionally used a character he called Wink van Ripple "who wakes up every once in a while to remark, often sardonically, on the changes in the community and the performances of its leadership."

The behavior of a public official was the focus of a satirical editorial in the *Kentucky Post* of Covington ("Fund-Raising Primer"). The writer, Shirl Short, said that satire works best "when our readers have been exposed to an issue for a long time and when we are certain they are aware of the folly involved." She explained that this was the case when the aides of the state superintendent of public instruction "started selling pens to state non-merit workers to raise campaign funds for her." The agricultural commissioner was doing the same thing with baseball caps. "While not illegal," Short said, "such activities certainly raised some basic ethical questions." Her satire was a takeoff on an elementary school reader.[33]

Fund-Raising Primer

Look.

Look, look.

See Alice.

See Alice run.

Run, Alice. Run, run.

See Alice run to the lieutenant governor's office.

Oh, oh.

See Alice stop. Why did Alice stop?

Alice needs money to run. What can Alice do?

Oh, oh. Look at Alice now. Alice has a pen. Alice has an idea. Maybe her workers can help.

Now Alice looks sad. She must do the right thing. She must choose the right workers.

Look, look. See Alice smile. Alice's name is on many pens. See Alice give the pens to her non-merit workers.

See the workers sell the pens. The pens cost $100.

See Alice run. See Alice smile.

Wait. Look, look. See Alice's non-merit workers. Some are smiling. Others are not. Why are some not smiling? They don't want to sell pens. They don't think it's right.

Alice still smiles. Alice has found the right way to raise money. She has done nothing wrong.

See Alice's non-merit workers. Some still smile; others still do not. Each worker has 10 pens to sell.

See Alice. See Alice run. See Alice run fast. Alice has money to run fast. Alice is smiling.

The primer on raising campaign funds was based on recent activities related to Kentucky's superintendent of public instruction, Alice McDonald.

What is the moral of the story? Choose one of the following:

To raise campaign funds by what you sell, choose your workers well.

If you are a non-merit worker, it is better to sell pens on the job than to sell pencils on a street corner.

Now, if you didn't get the lesson this time, we could tell you another story.

This one is about David Boswell and some $100 baseball caps. He's the agriculture commissioner and he's running in the same direction as Alice.

See David run. See David run to the lieutenant governor's office. . . .

The Kentucky Post [34]

The *San Francisco Examiner* used satire and exaggeration to make a point about big-time collegiate athletics at the University of California–Berkeley ("Pay for Play at Berkeley").

Pay for Play at Berkeley

Here's one we'd sooner not hear: UC-Berkeley is considering a plan to become the University of Oklahoma at Berkeley. After years of unbearably crummy sports teams, Cal wants to go big time. And win.

Well, Bears' fans, why stop there? Drop the pretense that college jocks are "amateurs" and pay them what they're worth. Then change the school colors from blue and gold to green.

Instead of shelling out $60 million for a new gym and underwriting new scholarships, how about some fat signing bonuses and four-year, no-cut contracts? Salaries need not be as high as the pros. A Cal quarterback might expect $200,000 plus $20,000 for beating Stanford or guiding the team to the Rose Bowl. A defensive tackle might get $80,000 a season—unless he disables USC's tailback, which would mean a $5,000 bounty. Basketball players could be paid $10 thou for every point on their per-game averages. Minor sports would get much less—on a par with professors.

College is supposed to be preparation for life. What better training for a jock than haggling over contracts? Actual academic classes would be optional.

In the 32 years since the Bears last went to the Rose Bowl, Cal has graduated a higher proportion of its players than most other universities. Academic excellence, of course, can in no way make up for the mediocre sports teams. Three cheers for the University of Oklahoma at Berkeley. Go Bear$.

San Francisco Examiner [35]

CONCLUSION

The purpose of this, and the previous, chapter has been to suggest a few of the ways in which editorial writers can offer a heartier, more varied diet of comment to their readers.

They can tackle tough subjects, such as economics and religion, that they might prefer to avoid. They can do a more imaginative job on editorials, such as duty and obituary pieces, that they can't avoid. And they can try their hands at other types of editorials, on nature and everyday happenings, that they may have been avoiding.

QUESTIONS AND EXERCISES

1. Clip several "easy shot" editorials. What makes them fall into this category? What could save them from this category?

2. Find several "duty" editorials. Would you have published them? If not, what could you have written on the same subjects that you would have felt comfortable writing? What angles could the writers have taken that they missed?

3. Find an obituary editorial that is mostly factual and another that goes beyond the facts. What is the difference in the effect of the editorials? What makes the difference?

4. Examine an editorial that expresses pride in the community or some aspect of community life. Is the editorial sheer puffery, or has the writer made an effort to put the event in perspective?

5. Find an editorial dealing with nature and ask yourself if it has genuine editorial value or value only to bird-watchers or professional naturalists. If the former, what is it about the editorial that will appeal to readers in general? If the latter, what could be done to the editorial to make it more appealing to readers?

6. Find a humorous or satirical editorial. Is the humor or satire likely to be misunderstood? Is the use of humor or satire appropriate in this editorial?

7. Find several editorials dealing with everyday life. Does the writer succeed in making the commonplace seem interesting? Might the space have been better used for comment on some public issue?

Chapter 14

Editorials on Elections

[E]ditorial writers should be concerned not because they are failing to influence, but because they may be failing to inform their readers fully.
—ELIZABETH BIRD, UNIVERSITY OF IOWA STUDY[1]

[T]o comment on issues between elections and then to duck the tough choices [concerning endorsements] would be irresponsible.
—EDITORIAL, EUGENE (ORE.) REGISTER-GUARD[2]

Some editorial writers, some scholars and some lay readers think editorial endorsements have little impact on elections. Other writers, other scholars and other readers worry that endorsements carry too much weight with voters, that newspapers control elections. Among the writers who think that they have influence, some worry about making mistakes in making endorsements through lack of information about or prejudice toward a candidate.

The endorsement process is a difficult and time-consuming process, if done right. It involves conducting research into backgrounds and political stands of the candidates, conducting interviews, perhaps attending candidates' meetings and then sitting down to figure out whom to endorse. In a local election with several positions on the ballot, or an election that involves statewide and legislative district candidates, scores of candidates may have to be researched and interviewed. Before an election is over, because of this burden, editorial writers may begin to wonder whether newspapers ought to be in the business of endorsing candidates at all. They may wonder even more if they find themselves disagreeing with their editors or publishers about whom to endorse.

The hell that editorial writers feel that they go through during endorsement season may be one reason why some newspapers—although still a minority—forbear from endorsing candidates in some or all races.

WHY ENDORSE?

The question of why newspapers endorse candidates is much more controversial than you might conclude from the endorsement practices of the papers. Surveys generally have found that approximately 90 percent of daily newspapers endorse candidates in at least some elections.[3] Some make recommendations from president all the way down the ballot to local judges and school board members. Others will endorse in all the way from a very few races to nearly all races. Substantially fewer than the 90 percent endorse in presidential elections (the most visible endorsements but probably those with the least impact on voters), but the number varies sharply from those election to election, apparently depending on the choice of candidates. One survey indicated that smaller papers were less inclined to endorse than larger papers. Those who conducted the survey speculated that small staffs have fewer and less specialized editorial writers, who have less time and less opportunity to evaluate candidates and issues. The survey also found that independently owned papers were less inclined to endorse presidential candidates than were papers owned by groups. No explanation was suggested.[4]

Both non-newspaper and newspaper people argue about whether newspapers should endorse candidates and ballot propositions. Among readers, probably the most frequently heard argument against endorsing is that a paper has no right to use its position of influence to impose its views on the voters. A reader accused the editor-owner of the *Daily News* of Longview, Wash., of inflicting on the community "a slanted and one-sided opinion or recommendation" that "could affect the lives of many people." The letter writer feared that people would "take that recommendation as an easy way out for the solution of their undecided vote." The writer thought that if the editor-owner wanted to express his views, he should take out a political advertisement and label it as such, just like anyone else.[5] A letter writer charged the *Eugene* (Ore.) *Register-Guard* with "meddling into the political affairs of the people of Lane County, dictating to Republicans and Democrats alike." The selection of candidates "belongs to the people. . . . It's their vote," the writer said.[6]

One of the assumptions apparently held by these critics is that endorsements carry a lot of weight with voters. We will discuss the apparent effect of endorsements later in this chapter, but it might be said that, in general, most newspapers in most elections do not have the overwhelming power that these critics fear. One response to these concerns, then, is that the press does not greatly affect the ultimate outcome of many elections.

To the charge that newspapers have no right to tell voters what to do, some editors reply that elections are just one aspect of public affairs and should not be treated differently. In answer to the letter writer in Eugene, an editorial in the *Register-Guard*, noting the paper's practice of commenting on public matters throughout the year, contended that for the paper "to comment on issues between elections and then to duck the tough choices would be irresponsible." When *Newsday*, based in Long Island, N.Y., reversed a former policy of not endorsing, the editors said that "a substantial amount of remarkably articulate and persuasive mail chiding us for failing to endorse" had helped convince them that the paper had a responsibility to its readers to make a clear statement of where it stood on political races.[7] Nelson Poynter of the *St. Petersburg* (Fla.) *Times* thought that by not endorsing an editor "risks taking a lot of fun away" from readers. "They want to kill the editor, whereas a punch in the nose of an unfriendly sports writer is usually enough vengeance for honest disagreement."[8]

Defenders of endorsements contend that the local newspaper is unique in most communities in that no other institution, aside from government and political parties, devotes as much attention to political affairs. Aside from professional politicians, political reporters and editorial writers probably know more about the qualifications of candidates and the merits of ballot propositions than anyone else. They have the added advantage of being less partisan and hence better able to evaluate candidates and issues with some measure of detachment. The editorial columns of a newspaper are among the few places in a community where the pros and cons of the issues can be discussed at length and in a logical, factual manner.

Editorial staffs appear to be devoting more time, and bringing more sophistication, to the process of making endorsements. Bringing candidates into newspaper offices for interviews has become a common, but heavily burdensome, practice. Mary Ann Sharkey reported in a *Masthead* symposium on endorsements that the *Plain Dealer* in Cleveland had to face 140 candidates, from governor down to metropolitan races. To speed up the process and to get a comparison of views, the newspaper tried to get all the candidates in the same race together at the same time, with at least two of the eight board members sitting in on each session. The candidates "gave somewhat coherent presentations and quizzed each other with great enthusiasm, not to mention with great theatrics," Sharkey reported. "What we have learned procedurally is to start out a bit free-form, then ask a series of issue-oriented questions, followed by a period of give-and-take by the candidates, and wrap up with an open-ended question. . . . "[9]

Some newspapers have asked candidates to fill out questionnaires, in lieu of or in preparation for interviews. Thomas W. Still reported that the *Wisconsin State Journal* in Madison once tried to ease the endorsement process by substituting a questionnaire for the traditional full-dress interview. "Well, I might as well have sent out letters that read, 'Dear Candidate: We have decided to interview everyone but YOU.' The amount of time I spent reassuring candidates that the die wasn't cast—and grudgingly inviting them in for a chat—wasn't worth the time saved on the other end."[10] The newspaper subsequently combined questionnaires with interviews.

Even if editorial staffs do know more about the candidates than anyone else in town, some critics of endorsements contend that editorials should be used to share information with readers, not tell readers how to vote. In surveying editorial writers about their opinions of the purposes of endorsements, Elizabeth Bird of the University of Iowa concluded that a large share of editorial writers agree with that point of view. She found that only a third of those surveyed checked either or both of "to advise your readers how to vote" and "to help determine the outcome of the election." Eight out of 10 checked "to define and clarify the issues"; just over half picked "to meet a responsibility to comment on any issue of relevance to your readers." (Writers were asked to rank three preferences.) She concluded that "editorial writers should be concerned not because they are failing to influence, but because they may be failing to inform their readers fully."[11]

Another argument against endorsing is that readers will think that if a paper supports a candidate in its editorial columns, it will be biased in that candidate's favor in its news columns. When the *Los Angeles Times* announced a partial shift away from endorsing, *Times* editors said they hoped to allay suspicions among readers that "editorial page endorsements really affect the news columns," especially in races that arouse the sharpest political passions.[12] A study of newspapers in Chicago and Louisville found some evidence that endorsements do affect how readers perceive the news coverage of a newspaper. Reagan supporters tended to think that the papers that endorsed Mondale favored Mondale in their news coverage; Mondale supporters tended to think that the single paper that endorsed Reagan favored Reagan in its news coverage. (An analysis of the news columns of the major newspaper in each of the cities found that, indeed, each of the two newspapers gave slightly better coverage to the candidate that it endorsed.) A major finding of the study, however, was that less than half of the readers surveyed were aware of which candidate their newspaper had endorsed.[13]

In the years in which I was engaged in writing editorials, the papers on which I worked consistently endorsed candidates and ballot propositions. I was not unsympathetic to the concerns of those who contended that *The Columbian* was trying to impose its candidates on the community. After all, over the years a large majority of the candidates that the paper endorsed were elected. Some critics argued that since *The Columbian* was the sole source of political reporting in the community, the editors should keep their editorial preferences to themselves. But my publishers and I thought that, precisely because we were the only consistent source of political information, we had a responsibility to dig into the backgrounds of candidates, present the arguments for and against propositions and tell our readers what we found and what we had concluded.

WHAT EFFECTS?

Whether endorsement editorials do in fact influence voters has been a matter of speculation and argument for a long time, especially since Democrat Franklin D. Roosevelt began winning elections in spite of overwhelming opposition from the writers of editorials on predominantly Republican newspapers. By 1952 journalism historian Frank Luther Mott, in an article titled "Has the Press Lost Its Punch?" concluded: "There seems to be no correlation, positive or negative, between support of a majority of newspapers during a campaign and victory in a presidential canvass."[14] Following the 1952 election, Professor Nathaniel B. Blumberg noted in a study reported in *One-Party Press*? that "in the 37 presidential campaigns preceding the 1952 election, the winner had the editorial support of a majority of newspapers 18 times and did not have it 19 times."[15] In the 11 elections in the period between 1952 and 1992 the press accumulated a better record, with a majority of newspapers supporting the winning candidate in nine elections, for an improved record of 27 wins and 21 losses. Of course, this tallying proves nothing.

Another way to look at this record: With the exception of the election of Lyndon Johnson in 1964 and Bill Clinton in 1992, the majority of papers has endorsed a Republican for president at least since the Civil War. This tells you more about the newspapers themselves than it does about their power to influence elections. The presidential race is only one of thousands of contests that take place in the country on a regular basis—and the presidential vote may be the one least influenced by editorials. Voters have many other sources of information in presidential elections. Newspapers may have more impact in state and local races, if only because their editorial endorsements are less predictable. Newspapers are more likely to endorse Democrats in these races.

In spite of the popularity of television news, surveys suggest that the public still tends to look to the print media for guidance in setting the public agenda. Studies show that voters look in particular to newspapers for information about elections at state and local levels.[16] One nationwide study of how much voters knew about the qualifications of candidates for the U.S. Senate found newspapers superior to television "as agents of information to help people identify assets and liabilities of important political contenders." The authors concluded: "If reasoning about political choices depends at all on the features of an area's media system, those characteristics will be found in the newspapers that circulate there, not in television coverage."[17] These studies suggest that voters do look, and in fact must look, to newspapers for help in judging candidates.

Endorsements appear to have more effect on some types of elections and ballot choices than on others. Fred Fedler has concluded that endorsements are most effective when:

▶ An election is local.

▶ An election is nonpartisan.

▶ The candidates are unfamiliar.

▶ The ballot is long and complicated.

▶ Voters have received conflicting information or have conflicting loyalties.[18]

Studies that I conducted in California suggested that endorsements have more effect:

▶ On ballot propositions than candidate races.

▶ In primary than in general elections.

▶ On governmental issues (taxes, schools, constitutional amendments) than on emotional issues (death penalty, abortion, gun control, homosexual teachers).[19]

In addition, I found that smaller newspapers seemed to have more influence than larger ones and independent newspapers more than group newspapers.[20] In all of these instances, effects appeared to be modest (from 1 to 5 percent), and hard to measure and prove. Of course, in a close election, a few percentage points can make the difference.

Editorial-writing literature includes several examples of the apparent influence of editorials. During one election, 47 percent of voters leaving the polls in Orlando, Fla., said that they had considered the local newspaper's endorsements "very" or "somewhat" helpful; about half of those (23 percent) went a step farther and said the endorsements actually had helped them decide how to vote.[21] A study of the campaigns of congressional candidates found that newspaper endorsement editorials were "the strongest predictor of percent of vote for . . . non-incumbent[s]"—but that incumbents were much more successful in obtaining endorsements.[22] In Cleveland the endorsement of the *Plain Dealer* in a five-way race for mayor was credited with "propell[ing] a longshot . . . into the run-off and to an eventual win."[23] A study concluded that in a series of elections the *Toledo* (Ohio) *Blade* influenced between 4 and 12 percent of the voters in a governor's race but only 2 to 4 percent in a state senate race.[24]

WHOSE VIEWS?

If an editorial should ever represent more than the views of the specific person who wrote it, that time should be during elections. But whether the editorial should be the voice of the owner (publisher), editor or a consensus of staff members is an issue being fought out in newspapers across the country. In most instances the publisher has the power to win in any dispute. But each year an increasing number of newspapers seem to be allowing staff members to influence, if not decide, endorsements.

Conductors of a 1980 survey of endorsements found some evidence disputing the "critical stereotypes [that] show authoritarian editors and publishers [deciding on endorsements], often on the basis of their own prejudices and in opposition to the wishes of their staffs." (Twenty-one editors in the survey volunteered the information that their papers' endorsements were made by the editorial boards.)[25] Nevertheless, publishers probably still exercise their final editorial prerogative more strongly and more often on endorsements than on any other type of editorial page decision. One survey found that, while 46 percent of publishers played an active role in determining editorial positions on major political issues, 81 percent exercised a strong voice in endorsements.[26]

John J. Zakarian, then of the *St. Louis Post-Dispatch*, described what he called "the publishers' four-year itch" and the "editorial writers' agony." For 47 months many papers carry moderate-to-liberal editorial policies but "on the 48th month of reckoning turn conservative." He described presidential elections as "sacred cows of the highest order."[27] Byron St. Dizier, professor at the University of Alabama–Birmingham, found evidence of this 48th-month turnaround in a study of newspapers in the 1984 presidential election. Newspapers that supported the Democratic Walter Mondale showed "unswerving loyalty" in support of Democratic positions on issues. Among newspapers that supported the Republican Ronald Reagan, however, more than half opposed his position on six out of nine key issues. "The findings may help to explain why some endorsement editorials fail to mention issues when endorsing a candidate," St. Dizier wrote. "In the case of most of the newspapers supporting Reagan, any discussion of the campaign's issues would make the paper's editorial page appear inconsistent at best."[28]

As might be expected, the 57-to-33 percent ratio of Reagan and Mondale endorsements by the newspapers in the survey (10 percent not endorsing) did not coincide with the opinions of the editors of those papers. The editors supported Mondale over Reagan 55 to 43 percent. Of the Mondale backers, 43 percent said they wrote editorials for newspapers that endorsed Reagan. (They did not say that they themselves wrote the Reagan endorsements.) Only one Reagan supporter worked on a paper that backed Mondale. Although 70 percent of the editors said their publishers were more conservative than they were, and 13 percent said their publishers were more liberal, nine out of 10 editors said they were satisfied with their newspaper's endorsement process. Three out of four said they voted for candidates endorsed by their paper at least three-quarters of the time. These findings suggest that it is principally, if not entirely, in presidential elections that newspapers take stands that run contrary to the preferences of editorial page staffs.

Supposed differences between publisher and editorial page staff became a campaign issue when the *Star-Tribune* of Minneapolis–St. Paul endorsed

Democratic Gov. Rudy Perpich for re-election in 1990. A columnist in a rival newspaper had claimed that the editorial staff had preferred write-in candidate Arne Carlson 8–2. Robert J. White, editorial editor of the *Star-Tribune*, reported in a *Masthead* symposium that "we were called undemocratic . . . [a]nd were said to have caved in" to the publisher's wishes. He explained that among all editorial page staff members (including copy editors, artists and the op-ed editor), the preference was for Carlson, but among writers only the split was even, with White and his deputy for Perpich. "But in the end," White said, "the decision was mine, and it was my job to make the recommendation to the publisher. He accepted it."[29] (Carlson won.)

This case, while perhaps not typical, may help make the point that it is not always easy to explain how endorsement decisions get made and who ultimately is responsible for them. Douglas J. Rooks of the *Kennebec Journal* in Augusta, Me., reported that his readers were confused and "felt betrayed by an endorsement they saw as arbitrary and undemocratic." Three years before, the newspaper had created an editorial board that interviewed candidates and made endorsements for the state legislature, city council and school board. The editors felt that their paper and the daily and Sunday papers under the same ownership in Portland, Me., should be responsible for their own endorsements. "But the publisher has decided to continue the previous system," Rooks said, "which—as we were to discover—was poorly understood by many readers." After the *Journal* editorial board had narrowly voted to endorse former Gov. Joseph Brennan, "[w]e were all taken aback when the chairman, acting on previous instructions from the publisher, who did not attend, announced that we would endorse [John] McKernan." Rooks said the board could remember no similar action. "The story of the board's deliberations was quickly out on the street," Rook said, "and was a prominent issues in the waning days of the campaign."[30] (McKernan won by about 2 percent.)

Another variation on disagreement between publisher and editorial page staff was described by Mindy Cameron of the *Seattle Times*. Opponents were seeking to repeal a city ordinance that extended to domestic partners the same sick and bereavement leave benefits provided to married persons. "Not surprisingly, the initiative was vigorously opposed by Seattle's sizable gay community," Cameron wrote. "Much of the support for Initiative 35 smacked of gay-bashing, though proponents consistently denied it was an anti-gay measure." Several editorial staff members "were outspoken in our opposition," and "others felt less strongly or had mixed views," but "the publisher had made up his mind [to support the initiative] for practical and symbolic reasons," Cameron said. He thought the policy, if carried out throughout the city, would be too costly and he feared that Seattle was becoming too much associated with the image of embracing alternative lifestyles. But in this case, the publisher encouraged staff members who disagreed with him to write signed columns expressing their views. One writer wrote a sharp dissent. Then on the Sunday before the election, below a summary of endorsements, Cameron wrote a column that explained to readers "the endorsement process, the internal disagreement, the publisher's role, my unsuccessful efforts to dissuade him." She concluded: "I'm voting 'no' on the initiative. I hope you will, too."[31] (The initiative was defeated.)

One of the questions raised in recent studies has concerned the role of newspaper groups in making endorsements. Most of the studies have looked only at presidential endorsements and, not surprisingly, found a good deal of homogeneity among endorsements, since most newspapers, group-owned or independent, endorse Republicans for president. But some studies have found differences among groups. Cecilie Gaziano, president of Research Solutions, Inc., of Minneapolis, had divided the groups into three categories: consistently homogeneous in their endorsements, somewhat homogeneous and consistently heterogeneous. The homogeneous groups tended to be regional in nature. Papers in this category tended to be smaller, evening papers with no competition, and Republican. The heterogeneous groups tended to be more national in scope, and to be larger, morning papers with more competition.[32]

Gaziano found that homogeneous newspapers outnumbered heterogeneous papers, but that heterogeneous papers had a larger total circulation. She speculated that in future elections "[t]he growth of the large, heterogeneous groups may reinforce tendencies [of voters] to vote Democratic."

Noting that the largest groups own a wide variety of types of newspapers, John C. Busterna and Kathleen A. Hansen of the University of Minnesota suggested that "[i]t may be that region of the country, circulation size, metro vs. rural, or some other local characteristics have more influence on endorsement decisions than chain ownership per se." They also suggested that group endorsement patterns may result, not from directives from the group, but through other, more subtle, forces: "The socialization of newspapers and newspaper executives, the pressure to conform to professional and industry norms, the need to meet superiors' expectations within the organization, and the desire to please powerful sources outside the organization are recognized as forces that may affect media content." They concluded that "chain ownership may play no role, or only a minor one, in affecting the content performance of daily newspapers. . . . "[33]

One study, concerned with the group homogeneity of Gannett newspapers, examined their stands on three national issues (none of them endorsements). It found a higher uniformity of editorial positions on all three issues among Gannett papers than among other papers included in the study. The authors of the study concluded that "a homogenizing effect on editorial position and policy results from chain ownership" but that "the outstanding question . . . concerns the process through which such uniformity results." The authors expressed the concern that "[a]ny tendency on the part of large newspaper chains to orchestrate editorial opinion on national issues would seem to represent one of the most serious threats posed by chain ownership to freedom of information in a democratic society."[34]

WHAT APPROACH?

One Candidate vs. All Candidates

Writers generally employ one of two basic approaches to endorsement writing. A form that goes back to the early days of the Republic involves making the strongest possible case for your chosen candidate and either ignoring or criticizing the opposition. The second approach presents the good and the bad points of all candidates and then, on the basis of the points made, concludes that one of the candidates is the best. On occasion an editorial will conclude that one candidate is not significantly better than the others.

The endorsement that evaluates all the candidates is similar to the SBA_1A_2DC editorial described in Chapter 10 ("Nine Steps to Editorial Writing"). We noted that this type of editorial offers a chance to persuade the reader who may have started out disagreeing with the conclusion, in this case the endorsement. It also is appropriate for races in which readers have received little information from other sources. The editorial that basically presents the case for only candidate, similar to an SAC editorial, might be appropriate if the arguments are overwhelming for a candidate, if voters have previously been fully informed on the issues or if the editorial writer is mainly concerned with encouraging readers who already agree with the endorsement position.

Attributes vs. Issues

Endorsement editorials also can be categorized in another manner: those that primarily discuss the qualifications and personal attributes of candidates versus those that primarily discuss issues and the stands that candidates have taken on these issues.

For some time political experts have been saying that American voters pay more attention to the personality and character of candidates than to issues during political campaigns. With these voters the 30- or 15-second sound-bite and the talk shows have driven out discussion of the issues. These voters are more likely to be attracted to a personality-character editorial than an issues editorial, but a personality-character editorial need not be limited to what one editorial writer called "character assassination." Participating on a *Masthead* symposium during the 1992 presidential election on the question of "How important are character issues," the writer, Nancy Q. Keefe of the Gannett Suburban Newspapers in Westchester County, N.Y., recognized that editorial writers and columnists "have to take on the character issue" but that writers should not expect "really [to] get to know a candidate's character in a political campaign."[35] "There often are occasions when we would be derelict in our duty if we avoided comment [on character issues]," wrote Clarence Page, editorial writer and columnist for the *Chicago Tribune*, but he added, "We can unwittingly add substance to frivolous allegations simply by commenting on them."[36] A consensus of the symposium participants was expressed by William E. Rone Jr. of *The State* in Columbia, S.C.:

A character issue must be based on something firmer than rumor before it is given weight, and even then positions on substantive issues might well prevail over personal shortcomings.

Each case is different. Each judgment has many parts.[37]

The first of these two endorsement categories may appeal more than the second to the interests of these voters, but an editorial that fully and fairly evaluates candidate's qualifications and attributes can offer more insight than a sound-bite or a few minutes of a talk show. An editorial that discusses issues may not be as easy to read and may attract fewer readers, but if issues are not to be completely lost in a campaign someone must provide the space or the time for extended discussion. The editorial columns are the logical spot.

To illustrate these types of endorsements, I have selected a sampling of editorials written during the 1991 U.S. Senate race in Pennsylvania. The Republican, Richard Thornburgh, had earlier served as governor of the state and more recently as attorney general of the United States in the Bush administration. It was generally assumed early in the campaign that Thornburgh, as the more prominently known candidate, would defeat the Democratic candidate, Harris Wofford, who had not previously been elected to public office and had been appointed to the Senate only months before upon the death of Republican Sen. John Heinz.

Our Candidate Only

In its pure form, the our-candidate-only endorsement is not found as often in U.S. newspapers as it was in the past. Papers are not so partisan as they once were. Editors recognize that readers who do not agree wholly with an editorial are likely to resent having an endorsement rammed down their throats.

Yet Professor Peter Clarke reported that a study of congressional endorsements in 1978 found "that in half of the editorial endorsements, it was possible for the editorial writer to come out in support of the incumbent without even mentioning the challenger's name." Clarke concluded that many of these editorials were "crafted, it would seem, by an extremely adolescent mind." Most of the contents of these editorials, Clarke found, discussed the campaign as an event: "The competence of the campaign that the candidate was waging, the adequacy of funds he or she had raised or how good were the TV spots—if they were using TV spots—or billboards, or what have you." The major portions of editorials endorsing incumbents described the incumbents' experience, while the major portions of editorials endorsing challengers described the candidates' personal characteristics. Only a rare editorial referred to issues.[38]

Editors interviewed by Clarke's researchers acknowledged that the candidates tried to emphasize issues, but these editors said they didn't think that voters were interested in issues or that the issues would affect the outcome of the election. "And that," said Clarke, "spells, in my mind, a giant self-fulfilling prophecy. If you believe this stuff doesn't make any difference, and you don't write about it, what is the very likely outcome? It ain't gonna make any difference! People are not going to know about it."

Talking about only one candidate may be appropriate on occasion—perhaps when the candidate stands far above any of the others, or perhaps when one of the candidates is seen as the main issue in the campaign. In the Pennsylvania race, more attention, certainly early in the campaign, was focussed on Thornburgh. For some editors his record became the most important factor in deciding whom to endorse. Although most of those who endorsed Thornburgh also wrote about Wofford, at least one editorial was an almost pure our-candidate-only editorial, "Mr. Thornburgh: We Endorse You, But . . . ," in the *Beaver County Times*. As the title suggests, the editorial was not a 100 percent endorsement of Thornburgh and expressed serious reservations, but it meets our requirements as a one-candidate editorial, since Wofford is mentioned in only two places, and then only in passing.

OPEN LETTER

Mr. Thornburgh: We Endorse You, But . . .

THE ISSUE: *Pennsylvania and the U.S. need effective, decisive legislators to revitalize democracy.*

WE SUGGEST: *Dick Thornburgh offers voters the best chance to do that, but he must prove himself equal to the challenge.*

Dear Mr. Thornburgh:

When your formal efforts to obtain our votes for a U.S. Senate seat began several weeks ago, you promised a campaign that would focus on issues and solutions.

You also promised a term as senator that would build upon what many agree was a distinguished record of service as Pennsylvania's governor.

You and your opponent in Tuesday's election, Harris Wofford, failed miserably for the most part to deliver on the first of those promises. Your campaign, put simply, provided more dismal reminders of our problems than creative answers about how to solve them.

Despite that, we are endorsing your candidacy. By the slightest margins, we believe you offer better potential than your opponent to begin solving the daunting agenda of problems facing this state and this nation. Your ideas on trade and the prospect of national healthcare programs make more sense and offer better vision than Mr. Wofford's.

But we come from a region of Pennsylvania that is tired to death of hearing about potential. We come from a region of Pennsylvania that cares infinitely more about continuing economic disorder than the so-called "New World Order."

Therein lies your challenge.

We endorse your candidacy because we think you have a better chance than Harris Wofford to make an immediate impact in the U.S. Senate for Pennsylvania and this region.

If elected, you should wield clout beyond your Senate seniority. You have been inside the Bush administration. Its officers respect you. Your voice means something to them. You will be on familiar turf.

But for several weeks, you have trod on the turf of half-truths that campaigns often map out. It's time you heard some whole truths.

If you bask in Republican party-line pride about George Bush's foreign policy accomplishments, you will fail us. We need you to use your clout to help turn the administration's attention to our own nation, our own state and our own region.

Pennsylvania is bleeding, and it is beyond caring whether Bob Casey, Ronald Reagan, Dick Thornburgh or the man in the moon wielded the knife. Economic revitalization has come slowly or not at all, especially in our region. If you do not place the economic recovery of this region and this state at the very top of your agenda, you will fail us. We need you to be a burr under the president's saddle, constantly reminding him about domestic priorities and chastising him when he forgets.

Pennsylvania is aging, and you must not forget the legacy of John Heinz if you succeed in occupying the Senate seat so tragically available because of his death. Heinz understood, listened to and helped elderly Americans. The 1990 U.S. Census predicts that by the year 2010, people 65 and over will make up 13.9 percent of the nation's population. Heinz realized that his western Pennsylvania constituency exceeded that percentage already. If you don't realize it as well, by protecting Social Security and enhancing benefits to the elderly, you will fail us.

Pennsylvania is angry, and you must not forget that balancing our nation's checkbook is a bigger concern here than the world's balance of power and all the globe-trotting summits combined. Heinz knew that and he often confronted the farcical finger-pointers in the Senate on just that point. If you don't continue his effort, you will fail us.

We are endorsing you because we believe you can rise to those challenges. It places us in the unusual position of recommending a "Beltway Insider" to voters who have read our chastisement of that characteristic.

We are endorsing you because we believe you can rise above the temptation to become yet another administration loyalist interested more in the next election than the next generation.

Among the many eulogies delivered for Heinz, one is particularly telling and perhaps offers a mission statement for you if voters send you to Washington, D.C.

U.S. Sen. Timothy Wirth, D-Colorado, said John Heinz "really believed he could make the world a better place. Such a contrast to the jaded resignation of our times."

Wirth also said Heinz was a most stubborn adversary when fighting for the citizens of Pennsylvania. "He could send the Senate leadership up the wall faster than anyone else I've seen."

Three years hence, if people say the same about Dick Thornburgh, you will have succeeded.

If not, you will fail us.

Beaver County Times[39]

Mostly the Other Candidate

As mentioned earlier, Thornburgh came to be viewed as the principal issue for some editors. In the case of the *Philadelphia Daily News*, the newspaper endorsed Wofford but devoted more space to criticizing Thornburgh.

Say No to Thornburgh
For U.S. Senate: Harris Wofford

If you want to see the Pennsylvania race for U.S. Senate clearly, consider the recent Dick Thornburgh ad that tries to link Harris Wofford to the BCCI scandal.

Thornburgh, who as attorney general stands accused even by other investigators of ignoring the problem until it got too big, is trying to pin his own problem on Wofford. His ad says that because Wofford accepted a campaign contribution from an old friend who is a law partner in a firm that had represented the bank, Wofford is somehow tainted.

It won't wash. Thornburgh's still the one with the BCCI credibility problem. He's also the one who ran the Justice Department like a ward clubhouse and the one whose crime bill is packed with anti-constitutional crowd pleasers. He is a man who went from a progressive prosecutor (complete with American Civil Liberties Union membership) to knee-jerk supporter of every nutbag idea higher-ranking Republicans want.

"Philosophically flexible" might be a polite way to put it. Ambition does strange things to people. Thornburgh is no longer the man this newspaper endorsed for governor. He's adjusted so thoroughly that he's become a slogan in contact lenses.

Wofford is something else again, a man whose principles have remained intact for more than 30 years. His long, honorable history includes time spent assisting and advising John F. Kennedy and Martin Luther King. His tenure as Pennsylvania secretary of labor and industry was creative, coordinating with other state department to provide services to displaced workers and workers on welfare that provides them with genuine opportunity rather than a simple dole.

Wofford was a founder of the Peace Corps, one initiative of the Kennedy administration that even the most moss-backed conservative wouldn't question. He has been president of both public and private universities and a scholar who has written four books.

After his appointment to the U.S. Senate following the heartbreaking death of Sen. John Heinz, he proved himself to be both tough and courageous, taking the point in a drive for national health insurance. His televised semi-debate with Thornburgh proved he's not one of those pushover Democrats willing to be cowed by mere repetition of sound-bite cliches. This guy is real.

Compare all that to his opponent. Asked about plans for reforming the nation's dreadfully unfair tax system, one that rewards rich hustlers at the expense of both real industrial growth and the finances of working people, Thornburgh only repeats the standard Bush administration line about cutting capital gains taxes, which would only make the disparity worse. His response to Wofford's health proposals is to go on and on about how complicated the problem is.

It is not the responsibility of the voters of Pennsylvania to maintain Richard Thornburgh in a big important job that comes with a limo and a staff. He has no apparent plan for what he's to do should he win, other than to follow the Republican program no matter what and be a really important guy. We deserve better than that.

We deserve a senator with ideas of his own, one who will work at his job of legislating instead of sniffing at the wind to see what will sell at the next election. We deserve a scholarly, tough, smart man who has never let go of the idea of doing what's right. We deserve Harris Wofford.

Philadelphia Daily News[40]

Both Candidates

In endorsing Wofford, the *Scranton Times* ("Wofford for Senate") devoted approximately equal amounts of space to arguing for Wofford and arguing against Thornburgh.[41] By the end of the first two paragraphs, however, the *Times* made it clear that it was endorsing Wofford:

SEN. HARRIS WOFFORD has spent most of his political career ably supporting the careers of others he has admired, whereas former Gov. and U.S. Attorney General Richard Thornburgh has build an impressive resume of elected and appointed office.

Wofford's brief tenure in the Senate and the conduct of his campaign to fill the remainder of the late Sen. John Heinz' term demonstrate that he should have taken the limelight for himself much sooner. He should be elected to fill Heinz' seat.

This approach, arguing for and against candidates, tends to make for a long editorial, as it did in this case. Even in the concluding paragraphs, both candidates receive extensive comment:

Thornburgh, as chairman of Bush's Domestic Policy Council, has an opportunity to influence the president on important domestic matters but, with the exception of an education proposal that has some merit, the panel has done little to address the problems facing average Americans.

Wofford's supporting roles over the years—civil rights adviser to President John F. Kennedy, college president and state secretary of labor and industry—have

placed him in touch with some of the basic problems facing Americans. He seems to have listened and to have resolved to seize the opportunity of his senatorial appointment to do something about them.

That is more impressive, in this election, than his opponent's resume. Wofford deserves election so he will have the chance to pursue that agenda for the people of Pennsylvania.

If You Agree With Us . . .

Some endorsement editorials are written so even-handedly that the reader may not know until the end, if then, who is receiving the endorsement. In "Wofford Deserves to Complete Term," the *Patriot-News* of Harrisburg tells its readers why both candidates "have impressive credentials." In the end (and of course in the headline, too), the paper makes clear that Wofford is its choice but leaves open the possibility that readers might disagree: "If you think the country is pretty much on the right course, Thornburgh is your man. If you think the nation has to address a number of serious domestic issues soon or face further economic and social deterioration, Wofford deserves your vote."

Wofford Deserves to Complete Term

SEN. JOHN HEINZ was one of the few politicians in Washington who bridged the chasm of recent years between conservative Republican administrations and a Democratic-controlled Congress. His moderate views, basic decency and good sense reflected the best characteristics of the people he so ably and devotedly represented.

He will be difficult to replace, but Pennsylvania is fortunate to have two distinguished and capable individuals running to be his successor.

Sen. Harris Wofford and Dick Thornburgh each have impressive credentials. Wofford is a former aide to President John F. Kennedy, co-founder of the Peace Corps, president of two colleges, author of four books and Cabinet secretary in the Casey administration.

Thornburgh is a former U.S. attorney who served in the Ford administration as assistant attorney general in charge of the Criminal Division. After two terms as governor, he headed up Harvard's John F. Kennedy School of Government and was appointed U.S. attorney by Ronald Reagan.

While each candidate's experience is broad and impressive, neither one's is necessarily superior. So in the end, the focus of the Patriot-News Editorial Board was on each candidate's ideas and proposals to determine which would best serve the state and its citizens in the Senate.

A GOOD election campaign, it seems to us, manages to float a few ideas for work-able answers to real problems. This campaign already has achieved some of that.

Thornburgh has proposed that abandoned industrial sites be utilized again, an idea we find particularly attractive, perhaps because we too have advocated recycling sites of past industrial activity.

Thornburgh has suggested that the federal government adopt a capital budget to separate annual operating expenses from the government's long-term investments. We agree that is long overdue. We are less certain about the workability of a balanced-budget amendment and a line-item veto for the president, but we agree the federal budget must be subjected to a more rigorous process if the deficit is ever to be brought under control.

Though by no means a novel idea, Thornburgh has called for the establishment of a revolving loan fund to help college students and their families. He rightly links that with greater discipline on the part of colleges themselves.

But the question arises: Are these and other Thornburgh proposals any more than campaign window dressing? Where were they—where were any domestic initiatives of consequence—when Attorney General Thornburgh headed up the Bush administration's Domestic Policy Council?

It is fair to ask how much influence Thornburgh will have in shaping policy in the Senate, if he can't persuade his former boss, who is actively campaigning in his behalf, to sign legislation extending unemployment compensation to those who have exhausted their benefits.

ONE OF THE most striking contrasts for us in evaluating the two candidates came in connection with the issue of health care. In an interview with the editorial board, Thornburgh described this as "the issue of the 1990s," with which we wholeheartedly agree. But on this most important issue, Thornburgh had no plan of his own to offer, seemed to have little understanding of the issue and preferred to take pot shots at Wofford's advocacy of a national health insurance plan.

It is fitting that this campaign, the nation's only Senate race this year, should feature health care as a pivotal issue. Sooner or later the country will have to come to grips with it. Wofford took a calculated gamble in making the call for national health insurance the centerpiece of his campaign because it is a complex issue that is easier to attack than explain in a 30-second television spot.

While we don't necessarily buy every one of the 11 principles and seven ingredients of the plan he fleshed out last week, most of them are right on target and represent what is probably the best set of guidelines on the subject yet offered in the political arena. Two of those principles are that any system be universal in its coverage and that it cost no more than the existing system, indeed, that it cost at least $50 billion less.

Those, such as Thornburgh, who argue that this is impossible, have to explain how countries such as Japan, West Germany and Canada can provide universal care of high quality at a substantially lower price than the United States. Wofford is absolutely right when he says that to do nothing is really to support "a health-care inflation plan for the American people."

WHAT SETS WOFFORD apart from Thornburgh, it seems to us, are certain guiding principles that have stood the test of time, that were valid 50 years ago when his political philosophy was shaped and remain valid today. One is that programs designed with everyone in mind are better than programs shaped to satisfy a few. He notes that overwhelming success of Social Security and the G.I. Bill, that, unlike so many other government initiatives, are programs that work, that deliver benefits that more than justify their cost.

Another principle is that government efforts should help people become self-sufficient, not make them dependent on those very programs. "There is nothing I want to do more," he told the editorial board, "than end the welfare dependency system."

Wofford says he would support necessary budget cuts and freezes across the board to tackle the deficit, which may be the only practical remedy left to deal with it. He would like all government agencies to be as lean as the Peace Corps.

He advocates reversing the recent trend in tax cuts that is reducing the burden on the wealthy at the expense of the middle class. In face, he proposes a middle-class tax cut of $500 to $600 a year, which also would give the economy a lift.

IN THE END, the decision really comes down to this: If you think the country is pretty much on the right course, Thornburgh is your man. If you think the nation has to address a number of serious domestic issues soon for face further economic and social deterioration, Wofford deserves your vote.

We fall among the latter group. Dick Thornburgh was a good governor for the 1980s, but Harris Wofford is the senator Pennsylvania needs for the 1990s.

Patriot News, Harrisburg, Pa.[42]

Candidates' Attributes

As mentioned earlier, while some endorsement editorials concentrate on issues, others emphasize the personalities and experiences of candidates. "'Hire' Thornburgh as U.S. Senator" in the *Tribune-Democrat* in Johnstown does that.

'Hire' Thornburgh as U.S. Senator

If the people of Pennsylvania were the personnel office of a major corporation and were seeking the best-qualified person for an important position, they would have the responsibility of scrutinizing closely the resumes of the individuals being considered.

That is the type of responsibility before state voters in the days leading up to the Nov. 5 general election, when Pennsylvania will elect a United States senator to complete the remaining three years of what would have been the late Sen. John Heinz' third term.

Although it is an awesome responsibility to elect the right individual for the federal legislature's upper chamber, it will not be as difficult a decision this time as some state residents might think.

It is obvious that former Gov. Dick Thornburgh has the best credentials, and we hope he will be given the nod over Sen. Harris Wofford, who was appointed to the Heinz position on an interim basis last May by Gov. Casey.

Although Wofford, a former Pennsylvania labor and industry secretary, has been a visible figure in Washington in the five months since his swearing-in, it is Thornburgh who has the broadest experience and ability to deal with every level of government.

Even though Thornburgh would be 100th in seniority in the 100-member Senate—the same seniority ranking Wofford now holds—in terms of stature and an ability to gain the ear of President Bush and the president's cabinet, it is Thornburgh who has the obvious edge. In fact, he'll have an edge over many more senior senators from other states.

On Jan. 13, 1987, a week before Thornburgh turned over the reins of Pennsylvania government to Robert P. Casey, a Tribune-Democrat editorial lauded the Thornburgh governorship. The editorial said Pennsylvania could look back on the Thornburgh years as a time of progress, hope and good government.

While governor, Thornburgh was committed to solid economic decisions, and his Senate campaign has shown he remains committed to such a goal, although his responsibilities as a senator would differ markedly from his state service.

Even in Johnstown, the troubled economic situation of the 1980s might have been worse if the Thornburgh administration had lacked the ability to control state spending.

Pennsylvanians received assurance that they had a capable administrator at the helm almost from the beginning of Thornburgh's first term. Seventy-two days after taking office, crisis struck the Three Mile Island nuclear generating station near Harrisburg.

With no precedents to guide his actions, Thornburgh averted panic while nuclear experts averted a catastrophic meltdown.

As a U.S. senator, Thornburgh could not work miracles—at least not initially. Every senator is only 1 percent of the Senate body, and Thornburgh, like every other senator, would have to work in cooperation with others to get things done.

However, the foundation he has built in Washington by virtue of his service with the Bush administration—an administration that seems destined to remain in power for another five years—puts Pennsylvania in a position to reap benefits that the state might not be able to achieve through Wofford.

And it is not wrong for residents of the western part of the state to want one of their own in the Senate, since the state's other senator, Arlen Specter, is from Philadelphia. Thornburgh is from Pittsburgh. Wofford is from Bryn Mawr, Montgomery County.

Wofford is no stranger to Washington. In fact, he was a civil rights adviser to President Kennedy and helped form the Peace Corps.

His work in Washington thus far has shown him to be knowledgeable of the issues facing the upper chamber, and the first bill he introduced would help more middle-income homeowners obtain federal student aid to help their children go to college.

He also has supported legislation extending unemployment benefits, opposed Bush's proposed "Fast Track" for the U.S.-Mexico free-trade agreement, testified against proposed Army cutbacks at Fort Indiantown Gap, urged new federal legislation to establish tougher control on interstate waste and voted for the Senate Highway Bill, which would give Pennsylvania a $1 billion increase in funds for highways and mass transit.

In addition, he has cosponsored legislation to create the Police Corps program, which is aimed at making it possible for local communities to get more police out on street patrol at a relatively low cost. He has introduced a bill to impose tougher fines and longer jail terms for polluters convicted of serious environmental crimes and voted against a $23,000 Senate pay raise.

Wofford, who lists 47 items on his "The First Hundred Days" fact sheet, has been busy. There can be no disputing that.

However, over the long term, we believe it is Thornburgh who would make the bigger impact for Pennsylvania in Washington. It is Thornburgh who would have the more formidable clout to help guide the course this nation should take.

Thornburgh is prepared to serve and to serve well. Why would he resign the U.S. attorney general position if he did not have a commitment to serve people?

If the people were trying to hire someone, they would hire Dick Thornburgh. You can do that by voting for him on Nov. 5.

The Tribune-Democrat, Johnstown, Pa.[43]

The Issues

In contrast to editorials that emphasize the background and personal qualities of the candidates, "For the Senate: Wofford," from the *Pittsburgh Post-Gazette*, focuses almost entirely on the public-policy issues of the campaign. The editorial decries the "caricatures of the candidates" that have been presented to the voters, acknowledges that both are "men of substance and accomplishment" and concludes that "the important difference between them is on the issues."

For the Senate: Wofford

You wouldn't know it from their respective campaign commercials, but in Dick Thornburgh and Harris Wofford Pennsylvania voters have two candidates for the U.S. Senate who overshadow many members of that body in intellect and experience.

For that reason, Tuesday's special Senate election poses a difficult choice for the Post-Gazette. We admire Mr. Thornburgh's poise and purposefulness, which were shown to impressive effect in his two terms as a reform governor and in his more controversial tenure as U.S. attorney general. But we also are impressed by Sen. Wofford's idealism and intellectual curiosity and by his diverse background as a civil-rights activist, college president and government official.

The tie-breaker for us has less to do with the personal qualities of the candidates than with their views—and the votes in the Senate that those views can be expected to produce.

By that measure, our choice is **Harris Wofford** for the simple but significant reason that we agree with him more than we do with Mr. Thornburgh—not only on specific issues but also on the need for the federal government to attack domestic problems with the same sense of urgency that has characterized American foreign policy in recent months.

Dick Thornburgh long has been the subject of amateur psychoanalysis about his evolving political identity. How, it is asked, did a Rockefeller Republican and one-time member of the American Civil Liberties Union metamorphose into a supporter of conservative positions enunciated by Ronald Reagan and George Bush?

Some of the positions Mr. Thornburgh has taken on criminal and constitutional questions were arguably foreshadowed in his earlier incarnation as a tough prosecutor. Others, like his opposition to civil-rights legislation that had been supported by the man he would succeed, John Heinz, can be explained as loyalty to the administration in which he served. And still others, like his extreme position on abortion (he would see it outlawed except for cases of rape or incest or to save the life or health of the mother) are more obscure in their origins.

Whatever the explanation for these positions, they place Mr. Thornburgh to the right not simply of his opponent but also of this newspaper, as readers of our editorials will recognize. And these differences have more significance in a race for the U.S. Senate than they did when Mr. Thornburgh occupied the executive position of the governor and when his agenda, much of which we endorsed, dealt with state issues like the abolition of the state liquor monopoly, judicial reform and the promotion of economic development through the Ben Franklin Partnership program.

Even before the recent recession, a debate had been joined in Congress about whether the federal government should take advantage of the "peace dividend" from the end of the Cold War to address inequities at home.

Many of the specific initiatives that have been proposed—from a cut in the Social Security payroll to more consideration for children in the tax code to some form of national health insurance—would cost the federal government money, or else require a readjustment of the relative tax burden on upper- and middle-income Americans. Other initiatives, like legisla-tion requiring employers to grant unpaid family or medical leave to their employees, would not draw on federal revenues.

The Post-Gazette has supported these initiatives and their underlying rationale: that the federal government should play a major role in ameliorating inequities that can be traced, at least in part, to the Reagan-inspired social and tax policies of the 1980s.

Mr. Thornburgh takes a more cautious approach to an activist role for the federal government, although he does offer some interesting proposals to promote economic development, such as his plan for federal "enterprise zones" modeled on those created in Pennsylvania when he was governor.

By contrast, Mr. Wofford is eager to have the federal government mobilize to address crying domestic needs, even at the risk of being labeled a "tax-and-spend liberal." But on some issues, his call for America to "look homeward" leads him to wrong conclusions. An example is the senator's opposition to "fast-track" authority for the Bush administration to negotiate a free-trade agreement with Mexico.

Even on the issue that he has made the centerpiece of his campaign—health insurance—Sen. Wofford is guilty of oversimplification. Like Mr. Thornburgh, we are skeptical of Sen. Wofford's suggestion that health coverage can be dramatically expanded at no cost. But if the senator's health proposals can't be taken literally, they should be taken seriously as identifying a problem that belongs on the top of the national agenda. Mr. Thornburgh has not convinced us that he shares that sense of urgency.

Even if this newspaper disagrees with Mr. Thornburgh on national priorities, some would argue that a Pittsburgh newspaper should support a candidate from Pittsburgh over an Eastern Pennsylvanian. After all, the late John Heinz was often described as the senator from *Western* Pennsylvania. It is not a ridiculous argument. But we find it hard to imagine an initiative of importance to this region that a Sen. Thornburgh would support and a Sen. Wofford would dismiss.

As in most political campaigns, the voters in this race are being presented with caricatures of the candidates which are distorted further by the funhouse mirror of television "attacks ads." Both Sen. Wofford and Mr. Thornburgh are men of substance and accomplishment. The important differ- ence between them is on the issues. For us, the difference suggests a vote for Harris Wofford.

Pittsburgh Post-Gazette [44]

Unendorsements

Once in a while a newspaper will make an endorsement, then discover new infor- mation and rescind the endorsement before election day. Such was the case with the *Rochester* (N.Y.) *Times-Union*. The paper endorsed a 34-year-old Republican lawyer for city council, along with two other Republicans and two Democrats. Then, six days before the election, the lawyer began making charges of favoritism in city assessment of buildings owned by a prominent Democrat and one of the city's most influential business leaders. The two Rochester papers published a story investigating the charges three days before the election. An editorial on the same day concluded that the charges were groundless and called on the candidate to withdraw them. Instead, Calvin Mayne of the *Times-Union* reported, the candidate and his supporters "counterattacked with accusations against the newspapers that attempted to show [the candidate] as a brave long crusader fighting a big press monopoly." On Monday an editorial withdrew the paper's earlier endorsement. In the election, four of the five Republicans won. The lawyer was the one who lost. Mayne concluded that the paper's unendorse- ment should "guarantee that no candidate of either party will ever try such a tactic so blatantly again."[45]

OTHER APPROACHES

Endorsement editorials are not the only devices used by editorial page editors to help readers become acquainted with candidates and issues. Noted earlier was the practice of asking candidates to fill out questionnaires before coming for interviews. Some newspapers publish the information provided through the questionnaires.[46] Some newspapers tape interviews with candidates and publish full or excerpted transcripts. The comparative stands of candidates on campaign issues might be presented in a table. The *Herald Telegraph* in Dubuque, Iowa, devised a set of standards to rate candidates on experience, background, qualifi- cations and aspirations, which the newspaper shared with readers.[47] The *St. Paul Pioneer Press* organized a community group that sponsored televised political debates for president, U.S. senator, governor and mayor.[48]

CONCLUSION

Following an election, editors are likely to find themselves in as untenable a situ- ation as before the election. If most of the candidates they have endorsed win, the editors and their newspapers are accused of controlling the election and influ- encing the election of the candidates of their choice. If more than a few of the endorsed candidates lose, the newspapers are perceived to have lost credibility.

I have often had voters say to me on election night that the newspaper was, or was not, right in its *predictions*. Somehow these voters seem to think that a newspaper is calling a horse race—waiting to tie its endorsement to winners.

Election time also can be hazardous for editorial writers. The heightened emotion of a political campaign, plus the black-and-white nature of endorsement decisions, can produce crises and magnify differences of opinion between writers and publishers that might be reconcilable at other times. Perhaps these periodic crises serve a purpose in forcing publishers and writers to re-evaluate whether they still see eye to eye on major issues. Perhaps such crises keep writers from being lulled into writing whatever they know will get by their publishers and will not infringe too deeply on their consciences. But in these tense situations both publishers and writers can overreact and later regret that they acted precipitously.

Credibility is the only thing a newspaper has to offer in its editorial endorsements. If a staff thinks that it can fairly and knowledgeably endorse one candidate over another, it should be able to do so in a credible manner. If, on the other hand, the staff does not know enough about the candidates or does not see one candidate as better than another or lacks the fortitude to risk the wrath of unhappy readers, it should not endorse. A major task of the editorial page is to comment on public issues, whether you prefer to call that *urging* voters or merely *informing* them. An editorial page staff that sits out an election loses out on a big part of the political process.

QUESTIONS AND EXERCISES

1. What do you think should be the role of the editorial page in an election? Should a newspaper endorse candidates?

2. How do you evaluate the argument that endorsements exert undue and undesirable influence on voters?

3. How do you evaluate the argument that the credibility of the news columns is jeopardized when newspapers endorse candidates?

4. Do you think a presidential nominee has legitimate grounds for complaint when newspaper endorsements are lined up four or five to one against him? Why or why not?

5. Could you work on an editorial page that had "publishers' four-year itch"—a congenial editorial policy for almost four years and then for a month or two a policy with which you did not agree?

6. Ask editors of newspapers in your area or state how editorial endorsements are determined on their papers. Who is involved in the decision-making? Who has the last say if there is disagreement?

7. Ask editors to evaluate the comparative impact they think their editorials have on ballot issues vs. candidate races and on local vs. state and national races.

8. Have any of the papers in your area allowed dissenting editorial staff members to disagree in print with the papers' endorsements? If so, how were the dissents presented? How did the paper explain the presence of more than one opinion? Did publication of the dissent draw comment from readers in the letters column?

9. Find two or more editorials from different newspapers on the same ballot issue or candidate race. Compare their approaches. What type of reader is most likely to be influenced by each approach? For the particular race or issue involved, which editorial do you regard as more appropriate or more likely to influence readers? Why?

10. Write an endorsement editorial that equitably compares two candidates and avoids making a choice between the two until the conclusion. Then rewrite the editorial to make clear from the beginning your choice of candidate. Which was easier to write? Which types of voters are likely to be influenced by each of them?

Chapter 15

Other Types of Opinion Writing

If [stations are] doing editorials, it's risk taking. . . . If you're going to criticize whomever, and it's people with power and influence, they can give you a hard time.

—JOHN BEATTY, KGTV, SAN DIEGO[1]

Ultimately reviewers' opinions may matter less than the agendas they set.

—WILLIAM L. RIVERS, WRITING OPINIONS: REVIEWS[2]

Newspaper editorials are not the only type of opinion writing that journalists are likely to have the opportunity to write. In this chapter we will look briefly at:

1. Broadcast editorials
2. Reviews
3. Signed articles

BROADCAST EDITORIALS

Should broadcast station owners feel the same responsibility that newspaper publishers feel to provide for exchanges of opinion on issues of the day?

A strong "yes" was the answer given by Boyd A. Levet, the last president of the National Broadcast Editorial Association, even as his organization was preparing to disband because of a decline in broadcast editorial writing across the country. "Opinion is part of the full venue of journalism," Levet, of KGW-TV, Portland, wrote in *The Editorialist*. "I know of no newspaper that earned community respect without opinion. Clearly stations diminish their journalistic influence if they do not air opinion."[3]

Broadcast editorials "show that the station is directly involved in the commu-nity—sufficiently involved to be willing to share management's opinions about community issues and events," G. Donald Gale of KSL-TV in Salt Lake City wrote in a *Masthead* article titled "The Need for Broadcast Editorials."[4]

"The editorial is the most mature form of journalism," Daniel W. Toohey wrote, referring specifically to public broadcasting. "Without the right to edit-orialize, public broadcasting will be relegated to permanent adolescence."[5] He could have said the same about private broadcasting, although public stations are more reluctant to editorialize than private stations are.

In spite of these admonitions, broadcast editorial writing seems in decline. In 1982 a survey of U.S. radio and television stations found that approximately 1,400 aired broadcast editorials. Five years later a survey identified only 339 stations that regularly aired editorials. The second survey was not as extensive as the first, but the trend seemed clear: Fewer stations were presenting their listeners with editorial opinion.[6] In 1981, the National Broadcast Editorial Association had 188 members. The number had declined to 65 in 1991, when NBEA was disbanded and surviving members were urged to join the National Conference of Editorial Writers.[7]

One of the reasons for fewer broadcast editorials seems to be financial. "[M]ore and more stations weigh community service against the bottom line, and find the bottom line more important," Gale wrote. "Apparently, fewer and fewer stations believe editorials are worth the effort."[8] Admittedly, if editorials are done properly, they can add a substantial expense to the tight budget of a station. The station owner or manager who might think of cutting, but never cutting out, the budget for news may see an editorial at the end of a news broadcast as little more than frosting.

The owner or manager who is mostly concerned about profit may believe tough-talking editorials are no way to win advertisers and listeners who may be offended if they disagree. "If [stations are] doing editorials, it's risk taking," John Beatty, editorial director of KGTV in San Diego, has pointed out. "If you're going to criticize whomever, and it's people with power and influence, they can give you a hard time."[9] A study recently showed a slight tendency for viewers to react negatively toward a station's newscaster when they listened to a strongly-worded editorial with which they disagreed.[10]

The demise of the Fairness Doctrine has been cited as another reason for the decline in broadcast editorializing. In 1941 the Federal Communications Commission (FCC) ruled in the "Mayflower Decision" that a station should not be an advocate (state an opinion). In 1949 the FCC changed its mind but admon-ished stations to provide a reasonable opportunity for airing all sides of contro-versial issues. That was the beginning of what became known as the Fairness Doctrine. As part of their public service requirement, stations were expected to provide a balanced presentation of views (including their own) over the course of their broadcast schedule. In 1987 the FCC dropped the Fairness Doctrine. Consequently, "[a]s the regulatory touch grew lighter, and as stations look for ways to cut cost, cutting editorials was a way to save money," Nicholas DeLuca of KCBS-AM of San Francisco told *Quill* magazine.[11]

One of the strongest statements supporting broadcast editorializing came from Frank Stanton, one-time president of NBC: "Any station manager worth his salt will learn the law, hire the people, sacrifice the time, explore the issues, risk corporate or governmental intervention and welcome adverse public opinion to have said on his station what he thinks needs to—and ought—be said. And if he does not care enough, perhaps because he is afraid of losing sponsors, offending public opinion, or creating problems with stockholders, then he does not deserve the job."[12]

Gale recalled that at earlier conventions of the NBEA, members could count on hearing similar "encouraging words from officials at CBS, NBC and other group owners," but no longer. "When Cap[ital] Cities took over ABC, KABC-TV stopped doing editorials and released its editorial writer of many years," he wrote. "Other ABC stations also discontinued editorials. KNBC ceased broadcast editorials late last year [1987] when editorials became superfluous in the eyes of NBC officials. . . . Support by CBS for editorials began to fade two or three years ago. It virtually ended last year. KCBS-TV released its editorial director and his staff."[13]

Broadcast vs. Print

Journalists who write in broadcast style are admonished to

- ▶ Keep it "short and simple."
- ▶ Write in a conversational style.
- ▶ Make points quickly and clearly.
- ▶ Use short, easily comprehended words.

The result of this type of writing, in the view of a surveyed group of newspaper editorial writers, is likely to be a broadcast editorial that is superficial, over-simplified and lacking in guts. But the broadcast editorial writers who were surveyed expressed a different view. They contended that brief editorials were not necessarily superficial, and that broadcast, especially television, offers a more personal, more dynamic approach to offering opinion than the print media do.[14]

Representative of the newspaper writers' views were those of Marcia Sielaff of the *Phoenix Gazette*. She thought that time restrictions and legal restraints push television toward going for "attention grabbers" and aesthetics in lieu of in-depth news and analysis, and that television is not as demanding of its audiences or its writers.[15] One television writer, Phil Johnson of WWL-TV in New Orleans, contended that because television writers face strict time limitations and must make every second count, broadcast editorials are "just the opposite" of superficial. Television writers "must condense the issue and get more meaning in less time," he said.[16] Television does, he added, tend to emphasize personality over content. "Television elevates the [person] with a great personality," Johnson said. Even though "dumb as a piece of wood," if the figure before the camera "smiles at the people, they think it's nice." Lesley Crosson of WCBS-TV in New York noted that television audiences often pay as much attention to inflections, apparel and personality as to the message itself. Another characteristic of broadcast, she said, is that listeners preoccupied with other matters may miss something that was said.[17] With broadcast, they have no second chance to fill in what they missed. They can't reread a paragraph that they failed to understand on first reading or return to a vaguely-heard editorial at a more convenient time.

William P. Cheshire, who has written editorials for both television and news-papers, said he had found television to be "an extremely hot medium," provoking a more visceral reaction than newspapers. Consequently, television editorials tend to be less robust. He speculated that broadcast editorials also could be more robust "if TV station owners were more courageous and had more convictions."[18] Another writer who has had experience in both media, Robert McCord, then of the *Arkansas Gazette* in Little Rock, described brief broadcast editorials as "one of the hardest things to do." He saw television as an ideal place for commentary, "particularly on local issues, [where] they can really have a great effect." He warned, however, against television's overemphasis on pictures over the content of an editorial.[19]

Broadcast and print editorials differ most sharply in the manner in which they are presented. A television editorial is likely to include film footage and to be delivered by an identifiable person. Even though the opinion expressed may be that of an editorial board, one person (often the station's general manager) makes the presentation. I know of no research that indicates whether this type of delivery is more or less persuasive with viewers than anonymous print editorials. Probably the range of persuasive effects differs more within each type than between types. As is the case with print editorials, some broadcast editorials are far more effective than others.

Preparing the Broadcast Editorial

Until the time of actual writing, the editorial preparation process for broadcast is basically the same as for a newspaper. As with newspaper editorials, the broadcast editorial presumably represents the views of the management. Similarly, whether the editorial is specifically the opinion of the owner, the general manager, the news director, the editorial director or an individual editorial writer, it must be written by one person, perhaps with editing by one or more others.

The person assigned to write a broadcast editorial should go through the same nine steps of editorial writing described in Chapter 10: selecting a topic, determining the purpose of the editorial, determining the audience, deciding on the tone of the editorial, researching the topic, determining the general format, writing the beginning of the editorial, writing the body of the editorial and writing the conclusion.

In selecting a topic and determining the audience, broadcast editorial writers probably are more limited than newspaper writers. Newspapers usually publish more than one editorial each day. A reader who is not attracted to one editorial may be attracted to another. Even if none of the editorials appears interesting, the reader can quickly move to other parts of the editorial or another part of the paper without "wasting" more than a few seconds between items of interest. Broadcast viewers and listeners have no such choices, unless they switch chan-nels, which of course no editorial writer wants them to do. Listeners don't enjoy sitting through dull one-minute editorials on topics in which they are not inter-ested. So the first task of the broadcast editorial writer is to pick a topic that is likely to appeal to the vast majority of listeners.

Broadcast writers also have a more limited range of options for the tone of editorials. Long expository pieces are clearly out. Editorials that require exten-sive or complex arguments are difficult to present over the air, at least in the framework of a typical news broadcast. Thoughts presented in a subtle or ironic manner may be misinterpreted or missed completely.

Broadcast writers, like print writers, have a choice of starting their editorials with stating their conclusions or reaching conclusions after arguments have been presented. Broadcast writers, like newspaper writers, may sometimes find it more appropriate to present opposing arguments or arguments on only one side. Of course, the time limitations of broadcast preclude the presentation of more than a few arguments, whether on one side or more than one.

Writing the Broadcast Editorial

Here are a few general rules for writing broadcast editorials:

▶ Writers should remember that they are writing for the ear, not the eye. A broadcast editorial should rate as "easy to read" on the Flesch readability scale mentioned in Chapter 11.

▶ A broadcast editorial must be brief, clear and interesting. An editorial of 150 to 250 words is typical.

▶ Sentences should be short and presented in a straightforward manner. Subjects and verbs should be close together.

▶ The writing should be free from hard-to-pronounce or easily misunderstood words.

▶ Strings of modifying words should be avoided. Instead of saying "Virginia Tech Communications Studies Professor Valerie Speer," say: "Valerie Speer, professor of communication studies at Virginia Tech." The latter uses more words but gives listeners a much better chance to comprehend the four separate ideas (name, position, department, university).

▶ Contractions, such as "The mayor's embarrassed by this," may sound more natural than "The mayor is embarrassed by this."

▶ Incomplete sentences may be used effectively. Some may start with a conjunction, and even without a subject. Referring to the example with the mayor: "And should be."

▶ Verbs also may be dropped: "Good news on the economy today."

▶ "That" and "which" often are dropped if the meaning is clear.

Broadcast news writing places a lot of emphasis on "today," to make listeners think they are getting the latest information. Use of the present tense also helps to give listeners the feeling that they are hearing the news as it happens. Editorial writers need to keep these listeners in mind, but they should not feel that they have to strain for the "today" angle.

In broadcast writing, it is even more important for writers to outline what they intend to say, to make certain that points are made clearly and in the appropriate order. Broadcast writers may find it helpful to clarify what they mean to say if they apply the designations suggested in Chapter 10: S (statement), A_1 (argument on one side), A_2 (argument on the other side), D (discussion) and C (conclusion).

To provide an example of how broadcast editorial writing differs from newspaper editorial writing, the editorial written in Chapter 10, "Supreme Court Made Right Decision on Hate Crimes," has been rewritten in broadcast style by G. Donald Gale (of KSL-TV, Salt Lake City), vice president for news and public affairs for Bonneville International Corp. Gale said that the first thing he did to cut the original editorial (370 words) down to broadcast length (approximately 250 words) was to eliminate names and other details that could easily distract the listener. "For example, when you mention a name, listeners automatically begin thinking about whether they know that individual," Gale said. "It may distract for only a second or two, but by then the whole thought process can be disrupted."

After these first cuts, Gale found that the editorial still had 300 words. He cut "a few good sentences," adjectives, "that," "the" and as many "other convenience words as could be ruthlessly killed without changing the meaning." He also recast several sentences to make them shorter. The result is an editorial of 255 words, about what a fast reader can deliver in 90 seconds.

FIGHTING 'HATE CRIMES'

THE SUPREME COURT TOOK ONE WEAPON FROM THE HANDS OF WELL-INTENTIONED CITIZENS FIGHTING "HATE CRIMES," BUT THE COURT CLEARLY PRESERVED ENOUGH WEAPONS TO WIN THE WAR.

A ST. PAUL, MINNESOTA, "HATE CRIME" ORDINANCE FORBIDS MALICIOUS EXPRESSIONS OF RACIAL BIAS LIKELY TO INCITE DISORDER. UNDER THAT LAW, THE CITY SUCCESSFULLY PROSECUTED A TEEN-AGER WHO BURNED CROSSES IN THE YARD OF A BLACK FAMILY. THE STATE SUPREME COURT REAFFIRMED THE JUDGMENT.

BUT THE UNITED STATES SUPREME COURT REVERSED THE STATE COURT ON GROUNDS THAT SUCH LAWS MAY "HANDICAP THE EXPRESSION OF FREE IDEAS" GUARANTEED BY THE FIRST AMENDMENT.

CITIZENS OFFENDED BY RACIAL PREJUDICES—AND THAT INCLUDES MOST OF US—WERE SHOCKED BY THE COURT RULING. IT SEEMED AT FIRST GLANCE AS IF THE COURT USES THE FIRST AMENDMENT TO CONDONE HATRED, CROSS-BURNING AND ETHNIC PREJUDICE.

QUITE THE CONTRARY. IN THE TEXT OF ITS RULING, THE
COURT GIVES AMPLE EVIDENCE THAT THE JUSTICES SHARE
OUR CONCERN. THEY CALL CROSS-BURNING
"REPREHENSIBLE," AND THEY CLEARLY INDICATE PROPERLY
DRAFTED "HATE CRIME" LAWS CAN PASS CONSTITUTIONAL
MUSTER—IMPLYING THAT STATES SHOULD PROCEED WITH
LAWMAKING.

IN ADDITION, THE RULING EMPHASIZES THAT ST. PAUL
ALREADY HAS LEGAL AUTHORITY TO PREVENT SUCH
BEHAVIOR WITHOUT CHALLENGING THE FIRST AMENDMENT.
FOR EXAMPLE, THE CITY COULD USE TRESPASSING LAWS OR
PROPERTY LAWS TO PUNISH OFFENDERS.

THE FIRST AMENDMENT GUARANTEE OF FREE SPEECH IS
CRITICAL TO THE WELL-BEING OF ALL AMERICANS,
ESPECIALLY MEMBERS OF MINORITY GROUPS. THE SUPREME
COURT WAS CORRECT TO PRESERVE THE FULL POWER OF
THAT CONSTITUTIONAL PROTECTION.

A station that has consistently won awards for its thoughtful yet straight-forward editorials is KCBS Radio in San Francisco, which won the Sigma Delta Chi Award for broadcast editorial writing in both 1991 and 1992. One of the editorials honored in 1992 was "A Time to Every Purpose," which urged listeners to ask President Bush to delay entering the Gulf War. This editorial contains relatively short sentences (an average of 15 words, not including the quotation) and few multi-syllable words (only 132 syllables for every 100 words). On the Flesch readability scale (see Chapter 11), this combination would be rated between "easy" and "fairly easy." The use of pauses, indicated by ellipses (. . .), also should help comprehension.

A TIME TO EVERY PURPOSE

(HERE IS KCBS GENERAL MANAGER FRANK OXARART WITH AN
EDITORIAL OPINION.)

TWO THOUSAND YEARS AGO AND SIX THOUSAND MILES AWAY,
THE CHINESE PHILOSOPHER LAO TZU WROTE THESE WORDS:

WHEN PEOPLE ARE BORN, THEY'RE SUPPLE AND SOFT;
WHEN THEY DIE, THEY END UP STRETCHED OUT FIRM

AND RIGID . . .
IF A SOLDIER IS RIGID, HE WON'T WIN;
IF A TREE IS RIGID, IT WILL COME TO ITS END.

RIGIDITY AND POWER OCCUPY THE INFERIOR POSITION;
SUPPLENESS, SOFTNESS, WEAKNESS, AND DELICATENESS
OCCUPY THE SUPERIOR POSITION.

NOW ON THE EDGE OF WAR, KCBS BELIEVES THAT THIS IS
THE TIME FOR SUPPLENESS AND DELICATENESS, NOT
RIGIDITY AND POWER. IF WAITING A FEW DAYS ALLOWS
SADDAM HUSSEIN A CHANCE TO SAVE FACE AND WITHDRAW
. . . A CHANCE FOR A PEACEFUL SOLUTION . . . WE THINK
THAT'S FAR BETTER THAN WAR TODAY.

WAR IS EASILY STARTED . . . BUT ONCE BEGUN, IT WILL
NOT BE EASILY STOPPED. ONCE THE FIRST SHOT IS
FIRED, EVEN IN THE BEST OF CIRCUMSTANCES, THOUSANDS
WILL DIE BEFORE THE FIRING STOPS.

AND WHY WILL THEY DIE? WHY WILL THOUSANDS OF
AMERICANS AND IRAQIS, EUROPEANS AND ARABS DIE?
PERHAPS SOMEWHERE THERE IS A CAUSE WORTH DYING FOR
IN THE PERSIAN GULF . . . BUT THERE IS NO CAUSE THAT
WILL BE HARMED BY WAITING A LITTLE LONGER, BY GOING
AN EXTRA MILE FOR PEACE BEFORE GOING TO WAR, BY
TAKING ONE LAST CHANCE TO SAVE THOSE LIVES.

WE ARE NOT OBLIGATED TO FIGHT TODAY, TOMORROW OR
THE DAY AFTER. WE ARE WALKING INTO THIS EYES WIDE
OPEN . . . AND WE CAN STOP WALKING. THE WHITE HOUSE
SAYS THAT THE CHOICE OF WAR OR PEACE IS UP TO
SADDAM HUSSEIN . . . BUT THE WHITE HOUSE IS WRONG.
PRESIDENT BUSH MUST ALSO MAKE THAT CHOICE.

NO ONE SHOULD BE SILENT NOW. PRESIDENT BUSH MUST
HEAR FROM EACH OF US. KCBS URGES YOU TO CALL THE
WHITE HOUSE AND TELL THE PRESIDENT NOW IS THE TIME

FOR SUPPLENESS AND DELICATENESS, NOT RIGIDITY AND
POWER. THE NUMBER TO CALL IS 202-456-1414. THAT'S
202-456-1414.

KCBS-Radio, San Francisco[20]

Notice that in this editorial KCBS not only is urging listeners to call the president but also is providing his telephone number. On the third anniversary of Ayatollah Khomeini's death sentence on writer Salman Rushdie, an editorial urged listeners to call the station's number to find out how they could contact their representatives. The editorial wanted listeners to tell their representatives that Rushdie's sentence should be lifted as a condition of U.S. recognition of Iraq. Some broadcast stations end their editorials with a statement inviting listeners to call or write to express their views. One purpose is to ease feelings listeners might have that the station is trying to force its opinions on them. Another purpose is to enlist opposing or supporting opinions for use on the air, either as letters that are read by a station member or as videotaped responses. In either case, of course, the station must make available the time and the resources needed for their responses. A station committed to helping provide a public forum in its community will make the time and resources available.

Writing Better Editorials

While the NBEA's magazine, *The Editorialist*, was alive, Professor Richard Elam of the University of North Carolina–Chapel Hill conducted a series of critiques of broadcast editorials. He pointed to faults and good points and suggested how the editorials could be rewritten. One critique was a lesson in "how to sound conversational, but waste words."[21]

"When we 'write as we talk,' that doesn't mean we write as people talk," he wrote. "Heaven forbid. We mean 'create a conversational tone, but not rattle.' Sounding 'folksy' isn't a license to waste words." Eleven "fatty" phrases identified by Elam in the following editorial are indicated in bold type. Six uses of the vague word "it" appear in italic. Elam eliminated seven of the "fatty" phrases and five of the six "its" in his rewritten version. The "it" that remains is clear in the rewritten version. The four unchanged "fatty" phrases, or the remaining parts of them, might have been cut out with additional editing, but the same could be said about most editorials.

ORIGINAL EDITORIAL

OUR COUNTY BOARD OF WATER SUPPLY COULD'VE **SAVED
ITSELF A LOT OF GRIEF** LAST WEEK. **THOSE PEOPLE FROM**
THE OUTLYING AREA WANTED THE BOARD TO DECLARE THE
OUTLYING SLAUGHTERHOUSE MATTER A CONTESTED CASE.

NOT AN UNREASONABLE REQUEST, SINCE *IT* IS, **IN FACT**, BEING CONTESTED. BY OFFICIALLY DECLARING *IT* CONTESTED THE BOARD WOULD THEN BE OBLIGATED TO HEAR THE ARGUMENTS OF THOSE PROTESTING THE ISSUING OF WATER PERMITS TO COMPANY PACKERS, AFTER WHICH *IT* COULD RULE **ANY WAY *IT* PLEASED**.

HAD THAT BEEN DONE, EVERYBODY WOULD'VE HAD A CHANCE TO **SPEAK HIS PIECE, AT THE VERY LEAST**. AND WHILE THAT WOULD PROBABLY NOT MOLLIFY THE LOSING SIDE, *IT* CERTAINLY WOULD'VE TAKEN SOME OF THE PASSION **FROM ITS CAUSE**.

AS *IT* IS, THE OUTLYING RESIDENTS HAVE MORAL INDIGNATION ON THEIR SIDE. IN EFFECT, THEY HAVE BEEN TOLD **TO SHUT UP AND GO HOME**, WHICH THEY ARE NOT LIKELY TO DO **AT THIS POINT**.

REWRITTEN EDITORIAL

OUR COUNTY BOARD OF WATER SUPPLY COULD'VE SAVED SOME GRIEF LAST WEEK. THOSE PEOPLE FROM THE OUTLYING AREA ASKED THE BOARD TO DECLARE THE OUTLYING SLAUGHTERHOUSE MATTER A "CONTESTED" CASE. CALLING THE CASE "CONTESTED" WOULD HAVE OBLIGATED THE BOARD TO HEAR PROTESTS AGAINST ISSUING WATER PERMITS TO COMPANY PACKERS. AFTER HEARING THE ARGUMENTS, THEN THE BOARD COULD RULE ANY WAY IT PLEASED.

IF THE BOARD HAD RULED THE CASE CONTESTED, THEN EVERYBODY COULD HAVE SPOKEN HIS PIECE. TALKING PROBABLY WOULDN'T MOLLIFY THE LOSING SIDE, BUT DISCUSSION MIGHT HAVE REDUCED SOME OF THE PASSION.

BUT INSTEAD, THE OUTLYING RESIDENTS ARE MORALLY INDIGNANT. THE BOARD, IN EFFECT, TOLD THEM TO

SHUT UP AND GO HOME—WHICH THEY ARE NOT LIKELY TO DO.

Other changes:

Passive voice in the original:

. . . THE BOARD WOULD THEN BE OBLIGATED TO HEAR. . . .

Active voice:

CALLING THE CASE 'CONTESTED' WOULD HAVE OBLIGATED
THE BOARD. . . .

Wordy in the original:

. . . TO HEAR THE ARGUMENTS OF THOSE PROTESTING THE
ISSUING. . . .

More succinct:

. . . TO HEAR PROTESTS AGAINST ISSUING. . . .

Vague and wordy:

HAD THAT BEEN DONE, EVERYBODY WOULD'VE HAD. . . .

Improved:

IF THE BOARD HAD RULED THE CASE CONTESTED, THEN
EVERYBODY. . . .

Wordy:

. . . THE OUTLYING RESIDENTS HAVE MORAL INDIGNATION
ON THEIR SIDE. . . .

Improved:

. . . THE OUTLYING RESIDENTS ARE MORALLY INDIGNANT.

A different type of critique, more concerned with content than with wordiness, also was published in *The Editorialist* ("No Liability Insurance").[22] The anonymous critiquer faulted the editorial for a negative opening and advised against overuse of "we" and confusing use of "they." Among other suggestions were that the writer answer questions (not raise them), take a tougher stand on the insurance companies and reach a stronger conclusion. Following these suggestions, the critic wrote a revised version.

No Liability Insurance

(ORIGINAL)

No one really knows how many drivers in this state have no liability insurance.

We do know that over one hundred and twenty-five thousand drivers have been caught without insurance the law requires. The State Department of Motor Vehicles suspended the licenses of those drivers following accidents in which they were involved. They also found that these drivers had three times as many traffic violations, committed eight times as many other serious offenses, and had 72 percent more accidents than insured drivers.

So why, we might ask, can't there be a crackdown on such people? Why can't we take them off the road?

We were amazed to learn that proof of insurance is not now required to get a driver's license or register a vehicle. Fifteen percent of the state's drivers simply have no insurance.

We find that legislation has often been introduced in recent years to require proof of insurance to get a license. Those laws have all been defeated. It seems that insurance companies have opposed such laws, as they do not want to be forced to cover irresponsible drivers such as we have described.

This major problem, however, is not going to go away until we get tough laws to stop the uninsured motorist.

(CRITIQUE)

This begins with two negatives. Negatives are weak. Turn it around and personalize it to give it more power.

The editorial "we" is okay, but it should not be overused. In this case, it serves only to add to the confusion of the sentence.

Turn this sentence around to build on the strength of the previous sentence.

The reference to "they" is confusing, since the Department is an "it," not a "they."

It would help your general manager to use commas on series, especially lengthy series.

An editorial should answer questions, not ask them.

Why were you amazed? Editorial writers should know such things. This weakens your hard-won credibility.

Again, the editorial "we" distracts in this case.

The laws were not defeated; the proposed laws or bills were.

You let the insurance companies off the hook too easily.

Hardly anyone uses "however" in conversational speech.

This is a weak ending. Call for specific action.

NO LIABILITY INSURANCE

(REVISED)

THERE'S A GOOD CHANCE THE DRIVER IN THE CAR NEXT TO YOU HAS NO LIABILITY INSURANCE—EVEN THOUGH STATE LAW REQUIRES IT.

LAST YEAR, ONE HUNDRED TWENTY-FIVE THOUSAND DRIVERS WERE CAUGHT WITHOUT INSURANCE. THEY WERE CAUGHT ONLY BECAUSE THEY HAD ACCIDENTS, AND THEY COULDN'T COVER THE LOSSES THEY INFLICTED ON THEIR LAW-ABIDING VICTIMS.

VIOLATORS HAD THEIR DRIVERS LICENSES SUSPENDED. THAT'S ALL.

IN THE PROCESS, THE DEPARTMENT OF MOTOR VEHICLES LEARNED SOMETHING ELSE. COMPARED TO INSURED DRIVERS, VIOLATORS OF THE STATE INSURANCE LAW HAD THREE TIMES AS MANY TRAFFIC CITATIONS, EIGHT TIMES AS MANY SERIOUS ACCIDENTS AND 72 PERCENT MORE ACCIDENTS. IN OTHER WORDS, THOSE WHO IGNORE THE INSURANCE LAWS ARE LIKELY TO IGNORE OTHER LAWS AS WELL.

BUT THE STATE DOES NOT REQUIRE PROOF OF INSURANCE TO OBTAIN A DRIVERS LICENSE OR TO REGISTER A VEHICLE. AS A RESULT, AT LEAST 15 PERCENT OF THE STATE'S DRIVERS DO NOT HAVE INSURANCE—ONE OF EVERY SEVEN.

THE FAULT LIES PARTLY WITH THE INSURANCE COMPANIES. EVERY TIME THE LEGISLATURE CONSIDERS A BILL TO ENFORCE THE INSURANCE LAW, THE INSURANCE COMPANIES FIGHT AGAINST IT. COMPANIES ARE AFRAID THEY WILL BE FORCED TO INSURE IRRESPONSIBLE DRIVERS.

```
IT'S TIME TO PUT TEETH IN THE LIABILITY INSURANCE
LAW. PROOF OF INSURANCE SHOULD BE PART OF EVERY
LICENSE RENEWAL AND EVERY TRAFFIC CITATION CHECK.
```

REVIEWS

Reviews can range from A to Z, from art exhibitions to the opening of a new zoo. Most commonly reviewed by newspapers are books, television, films, theater, dance, music and art. Writers associated with the editorial page are most likely to be called upon to write a review of a book.

The task of the reviewer is basically no different from that of the editorial writer. All of the advice about opinion writing offered in Chapters 10 and 11 applies to review writing. Reviewers have two responsibilities: briefly describing to their readers the subject of their review and then commenting on the subject. Beyond that, writers basically are free to organize their reviews as they wish.

In writing reviews, a writer should keep in mind both the background and sophistication of the reading audience as well as the level of professionalism of the artists, authors or performers being reviewed. Reviews are likely to be more elaborate and scholarly in the weekly book section of the *New York Times* than on the book page of the *Roanoke Times & World-News*. Similarly, amateur performances should not be expected to meet the standards of professional productions.

As with editorials, reviews must immediately attract the attention of readers. If the subject matter itself is likely to catch the reader's eye, the reviewer might begin with a description. Otherwise, the reviewer might begin with a provocative comment or evaluation. In most instances, before proceeding more than a sentence or two, reviewers should provide a description of what they are reviewing. Reviewers should not devote too much space to description. Newspaper reviews generally are kept short.

Readers expect reviewers to comment on the subject matter covered in the book, the organization of the book, the comparative emphasis given to parts of the book, the quality of the writing, the qualifications of the author, and the adequacy and reliability of the contents. Reviewers should try to explain what the author intended to accomplish with the book and evaluate how well the author accomplished this purpose.

To be persuasive, reviews should appear to be fair and logical. Scathing reviews, like flamboyant editorials, may be fun to read, but emotion is less likely to be convincing than statements of fact and careful evaluations. In the case of reviews, writers should be especially careful not to overreact negatively. In warning reviewers against "heavily negative reviews," William L. Rivers wrote: " . . . whatever the value of a book, be aware that the author has suffered agonies of the creative process that you could not possibly know. Think of the author as an individual who, in the middle of writing, may spend 'endless' periods scratching deep grooves on the table before him or her, waiting for the right words to present themselves."[23]

Reviewers should write with at least some humility, recognizing that the quality of a book, a play or a musical is likely to be perceived differently by different people. That lesson is often illustrated by the reviews written by my students. For example, four students reviewed a performance by the Virginia Tech Dance Company titled "One Magical Night of Dance." The four offered sharply contrasting views of the professional magician who also served as master of ceremonies. One student wrote:

> [He] provided a great complement to the dances. His act was humorous and certainly entertaining. [He] kept the audience mystified by his magic and provided a good break between dances.

A second student wrote:

> Although [he] was a little goofy at times, his efforts rounded out the show and served as a light transition between some of the more intense ballet pieces.

Another comment:

> The disappearing-dancer-in-the-box trick received loud applause. But this turned out to be the most "magical" part of the whole evening. [He] turned out to be the emcee who performed common card and rope tricks. No zip, no zing. . . .

The fourth comment:

> [He] had the dancer crawl into a glass box, and after he spun the box around a few times the girl disappeared. (Some may have wished [he] had disappeared himself.) . . . [He] was not much. He did a few card tricks and told a couple of bad jokes. The audience would rather have stared at the closed curtain than have "Mr. Magic" stall for time.

One of the reviews (" 'One Magical Night of Dance' More than Bargained For") is reprinted here in its entirety. The review overall is sympathetic and complimentary, but still realistic in its evaluation of a student production. The opening, "tall ones, short ones, skinny ones, fat ones, talented ones and not so talented ones," suggests that the reviewer is not going to judge this production by professional standards. Yet she quickly notes that it did well by the audience. In the third paragraph she explains that the dance company is open to all students and suggests that varying talents are to be expected. She was not impressed with the magician but was not excessively negative in her comments. She notes some problems in the dancing (" . . . some other dancers muttered around in the background"), but overall her evaluation is positive.

'One Magical Night of Dance' More than Bargained for

There were tall ones, short ones, skinny ones, fat ones, talented ones and not so talented ones. The Virginia Tech Dance Company's final show of the year, "One Magical Night of Dance," was full of variety.

From the dancers' abilities to the types of dances, the audience got more than it bargained for from the lengthy two-hour-and-45-minute show.

Although most of the dance numbers were modern funk dance, there were also jazz, classical ballet and even some tap dancing.

There was also one that was hard to figure out. Guest choreographer D—— W—— was going for the shock effect when he choreographed the number titled "Rituals." The abstract composition never got started even though it lasted for about seven minutes. It was like a poor rendition of "follow the leader."

The Virginia Tech Dance Company, offered as a class at the university, is open to anyone who is interested in dance. It was obvious that some of the women had been studying dance professionally. Likewise, it was obvious that some of the women were very new to the dance scene.

Those with more talent than the others should have been in numbers that complemented their level of skill and vice versa. The less skilled ones seemed to have trouble keeping up, and the very talented seemed to be held back by the moderate skill level of the dances.

One of the disappointments of the event was master illusionist E—— A——. To start the show, he performed his first illusion surrounded by silhouetted dancers. The lighting and the music were dramatic as were the moves of the performers. The disappearing-dancer-in-the-box trick received a loud applause. But this turned out to be the most "magical" part of the whole evening. As emcee, A—— performed only common card and rope tricks. No zip, no zing—just dance after dance after dance.

A lot of hard work was put into the production of this show. The costumes, which were the most spectacular part of the evening, were made by the dancers. Some looked homemade, but, for the most part, they added that extra touch that the numbers were often lacking.

"The Play of the Waves" was a classical ballet piece that made the audience ooh and aah. The costumes were simple and elegant, looking as though they were from "Swan Lake." Soloist J—— C—— gave a professional performance while some other dancers muttered around in the background.

The overall performance, however, was appealing, and well worth the 3 dollars.

In some instances it may be more appropriate to begin a book review with a reference to the author, rather than the subject matter. Professor Laird Anderson took this approach in reviewing *Great Editorials: Masterpieces of Opinion Writing* for *The Masthead*. Anderson reminded readers that the lead author, William David Sloan, had previously edited a Great American Editorials series in that magazine and had published a selection of Pulitzer Prize editorials. This approach could be expected to attract readers familiar with Sloan's name or his published works. It also served to establish Sloan's credentials for co-editing the new book. Anderson almost immediately begins his praise ("tremendously valuable anthology"), but in opening paragraphs he concentrates on describing the organization of the book and giving readers a hint of some of the specific contents. Anderson then discusses what he sees as the purpose of the book (to "push" and "shove" writers toward editorial excellence) and his own suggestions on how the book might be used (in recruiting, seminars, etc.). The book does not get a fully glowing report. Anderson suggests that the design, though a minor matter, needed "more vision." Rather than end on a negative note, Anderson adds a strong positive conclusion.

Secrets of the Masters

By Laird B. Anderson
Professor of Communication
American University

Great Editorials: Masterpieces of Opinion Writing. By William David Sloan, Cheryl Watts and Joanne Sloan. Vision Press. $16.95 paperback.

You remember William David Sloan, professor of journalism at the University of Alabama. For years in *The Masthead* he brought us his wonderfully edited Great American Editorials series. His analysis of each piece was penetrating. Then he brought us his collection of *Pulitzer Prize Editorials: America's Best Editorial Writing, 1917–1979*, again each piece carefully analyzed.

Now he and two colleagues have brought us a new and tremendously valuable anthology of classic works by more than 40 masters of the editorial writing craft, among them Charles Dana, Paul Greenberg, Ben Hur Lampman, Henry Watterson, Hazel Brannon Smith, William Cullen Bryant, William Allen White, Hodding Carter, Mrs. T.M.B. Hicks, and Samuel Francis.

The authors consider each a master of something: the political attack, the literate style, editorial influence, the analytical essay, word painting, human interest, personal journalism, the editorial crusade, the forceful style, the narrative style, versatility and—you've got to love this one— editorial poetry.

They have grouped together these masters and their editorials into three historical eras: the Partisan Era, 1690–1833; the Popular Era, 1833–1900; and the Professional Era, 1900–present. Once again, using Sloan's previous technique, the writers have dissected each editorial with an illuminating point of view. Their observations are the most important part of the book: "People are not interested in an editorial writer's opinion!" With that principle in mind, say the authors, writers would "avoid one of the most common causes of poor writing."

What, then, makes a superior editorial? Four standards: "effectiveness, artistry, thematic significance, and truth." I can't imagine that any of us would disagree. What follows in this volume is an elaboration on these standards. But this volume does more. It captures the cacophony of the frequently battered thoughts of the daily editorial writer with quiet reflection. If you want to learn more, the opening chapter, "Learning from the Masters," will provide you with tantalizing answers illustrated by what follows.

Sloan, the pilot behind the controls of this book, is clearly a leading proponent of excellence in editorial writing. He does not nudge in his observations; he pushes and shoves.

The thoroughly developed and well-written comments, which each of us would yearn to emulate if we had time from the daily grind, are inspirational. I've adopted this book for my editorial writing course.

Editors, in my view, must be educators. If I were an editorial page editor, I would make a copy of this book available to each of my writers. I would use it as a recruiting device. I would hold seminars to discuss the observations. I would use historical perspective as the driving force in considering any editorial. But then, what the hey, I'm just a teacher whose day doesn't require 500 words of editorial excellence worthy of master status.

My criticism of this paperback volume is not of its content, but its presentation. The authors also are the publishers and printers. Vision Press, their creation, needs a bit more vision in designing future publications. But overall this is a minor nit to pick.

Want to be a master of opinion writing? Read this book. Maybe the next generation of editorial writers will then read your masterly essays in the next edition.

The Masthead[24]

SIGNED ARTICLES

Editorial writers probably have more opportunities than ever before to write signed interpretive and opinion pieces. One reason is that more newspapers are providing a full or partial additional page for opinion articles and artwork. This page typically is referred to as the op-ed page (the page opposite the editorial page). Another reason for an increase in signed articles is that publishers seem more willing to allow previously anonymous writers to put their names on articles that are not intended to be institutional editorials. These articles range from writings that express personal opinion or dissent from the newspaper's editorials, through interpretive and analytical articles, to media criticism.

Personal Opinion

An article that expresses a personal opinion on an issue may differ little from a signed editorial, aside from being written in the first-person singular. But the article is quite likely to be more personally oriented than a regular editorial. In "NEA Under Fire," Hope Aldrich of the *Santa Fe* (N.M.) *Reporter* wrote a defense of the National Endowment for the Arts in the context of an experience that she had as a child. Except for the opening four paragraphs and the last paragraph (and an occasional "I") the article differs little from an editorial. (This piece won one of the 1991 "The Golden Dozen" editorial-writing awards made by the International Society of Newspaper Editors.)

NEA Under Fire

The painting hung in our dining room. It fascinated me as a child. Called Karl, it portrayed a farmer with blunt features, receding hair, a grim mouth and weary eyes, set low in the right corner of the canvas. In the upper left, drilled into the cracked ceiling, loomed a black meat hook caked with small remnants of the last chicken or pig that had hung there to cure.

I understood from this painting that death is a basic part of a farmer's life; that a farm is not just a place of picturesque barns and ripening orchards, but also a place where people must kill in order to survive. Karl's tense face revealed the toll of this lifestyle, and the bold hook seemed to convey an ever-present struggle within him. Because of this painting, a farmer's life took on a new and harsher meaning for me.

As I grew up, I depended more and more on moments like this, when art jolted me into new ways of seeing old subjects.

Good artists jolt and probe. They raise uncomfortable questions about whether life really is the way it seems on the surface.

One reason I've been proud of the American way of life is that we've had the guts to listen to the critique of the people who stand out on the edge of society—our artists, writers, dramatists and dancers. We've believed this was so important that, starting in 1965, we funded them with tax dollars through the National Endowment for the Arts.

Now that funding is in question. The NEA's very existence will be debated in the next few days in Congress. Enraged by a handful of bold and provocative projects funded by the NEA, a frightened, very vocal segment of Americans is fighting to destroy the organization.

The issue at stake here is not censorship. It is a battle about Congress using tax dollars to influence taste and artistic expression. It's about creating a more restrictive climate for the arts in America.

For nearly 25 years, the NEA went about its business in relative obscurity. As government agencies go, it's not a major player. Its annual budget, a mere $193 million, is not one that fuels the deficit, and until recently, its decisions did not make front-page news.

Then suddenly last year, the NEA hit the headlines along with an uproar over the extreme works of Andres Serrano and Robert Maplethorpe, artists who at one time benefited from the NEA.

In recent months, the NEA has been making major news again. In response to intense pressure on Congress from conservative groups—and from within, led by Republican Sen. Jesse Helms of North Carolina—the endowment has adopted a new set of rules that prohibit its grant recipients from depicting any form of obscenity, "including but not limited to depictions of sadomasochism, homoeroticism, the exploitation of children, or individuals engaged in sex acts."

Anti-obscenity laws affecting local communities have been on the books for years. The language in these new regulations seems hardly earthshaking. In fact, it seems to reaffirm standards most of us would accept in other instances.

But not instances where federal dollars go to the arts. I believe these restrictions are dangerous and should be rejected. I applaud artists who could not bring themselves to sign this new "oath" and so risked losing their grants. Once we accept government regulation of artistic content, we have established a new and dangerous precedent. It is an ominous first step toward greater government intervention in the arts.

Ironically, while Eastern Bloc countries are now throwing off government restric-

tions, the U.S. seems to be moving toward a new and narrow orthodoxy.

NEA grants are currently awarded by panels of experts who are supposed to apply standards of professionalism in evaluating applicants' work. Their job is to determine whether the artist's work is worthy of support, not whether the panelists approve of its political or social content.

This system has its problems: It often seems to select large, established, "safe" groups rather than individuals. Even so, it is a more valid system than imposing a grid of arbitrary rules on every application.

For New Mexico—and especially for its artists and arts institutions—the loss of NEA funding would be extremely serious. Perhaps most threatened would be the rich diversity of our state's culture.

In the last five years, the NEA has granted the state $12,719,536. More than 1,500 artists and institutions have applied for grants, and in this period 335 have been recipients of NEA money. They range from large, traditional institutions like the Santa Fe Opera to individual artists like Frederico Vigil, Terry Allen, Emilio Romero and Michele Zackheim, to name a few.

Without NEA backing, small, professionally staffed organizations would probably be reduced to dependence on volunteers, and many new artists might never get exposure.

For all of us in America, there is a great deal at stake. I, for one, am extremely grateful that when I was a young girl staring at Karl and his butcher's hook, nobody was there to put a hand over my eyes and tell me whether or not this was appropriate art. We as a nation are strengthened by the kind of artistic diversity that until now the NEA has fostered.

Hope Aldrich, Santa Fe (N.M.) *Reporter* [25]

Interpretive and Analytical

Frequently much longer than an editorial, an interpretive or analytical article may reveal the point of view of the writer, but its primary purpose is to provide readers with information and insights, and perhaps to raise questions. In "Where Is Strategy to Make This City Whole?" Joe H. Stroud of the *Detroit Free Press* used a signed article to recount meetings that his staff had with state legislators, to question city officials about their strategy for urban renewal and to defend the raising of these questions. The article does not take the next step, which an editorial might have done, to tell city officials what they ought to be doing. The writer, in fact, expresses the hope that officials will not interpret the criticism as coming from a racist point of view. (This piece won a Detroit Press Club Foundation Award for a signed column.)

Where Is Strategy to Make This City Whole?

A foreign journalist came in to talk to me the other day, having walked down Woodward Avenue from the Cultural Center to downtown. It seemed a good way, he said, to get a sense of the place.

What was his sense of the place? "Pretty depressing," he said. And he began to ask me about whether there was now, or had been earlier, a real plan to redeem the once-glorious old Victorian homes along the way.

His question focused again for me the truth that I do not understand how the mayor's strategy is going to redeem the city any more. I wish I could understand how the huge commitment of energy and money to the City Airport project is going to revitalize the northeast side. Maybe much of the area to be condemned deserves to die, though I doubt it. But what will be gained by the addition of three times as much acreage as is now incorporated into the airport? What economic development will be triggered that will replace the taxes paid on the 3,600 homes, the 52 industries, the 160 small businesses that are to be wiped out by the expansion? Once again, that's the equivalent of a small city.

At Metro Airport, where there is some displacement and some disruption, you have at least enough undeveloped land to provide real opportunities. With City Airport, will the city administration have to clear out even more people to make room for industrial parks? And if there are industrial parks, will there be anyone willing to come unless the city tax rates

can be brought down, or the area can be made to feel secure, or the schools can be made demonstrably better?

I know the mayor and his friends think I—and others—ask such questions only out of malice. The mayor welcomed the return of Charles Beckham, who was convicted of a felony in the Vista case, by talking about the same old unsubstantiated charges. I found that party deeply troubling, the message sad and disturbing. It is one thing to welcome Mr. Beckham, now that he has served his time. It is quite something else to assert that even the conviction of one of the mayor's lieutenants constitutes unsubstantiated rumor.

My staff and I went to Lansing last week for one of a periodic set of meetings with legislators. This time we were meeting with the Republican Caucus. One of the questions inevitably raised was about the utility tax that, according to a Wayne County Circuit judge, had been permitted to expire in 1988. The Senate majority leader, John Engler of Mt. Pleasant, told us that he had been prepared to help pass the extension of the tax in 1988 as a precaution but that the city had advised against doing so. The failure to extend the tax, in other words, was not simply an oversight but a conscious decision.

And although I see from some Republican legislators an attempt to link the utility tax with extraneous issues, and to risk turning a $102-million problem into something even bigger, what I also see are honest people trying to get honest answers to honest questions. I see a city that says it should have exclusive say about the tax. I see a Democratic governor who hasn't really chosen to take a clear position on the utility tax issue and whose party cluttered the issue with a clumsy, partisan set of ads attacking Republican legislators.

Where is the leadership at either the state or local level? Where is the strategy for solving the utility tax problem or the larger problem of how to revitalize the city? Can we do no better than these 1950s-style slum clearance/massive urban renewal projects? Is there absolutely no way to face the reality that the utility tax is, however justified by the exigencies of the moment, not good tax policy? Is there no place in the mayor's grand design for anyone else to make a suggestion about tax policy, or how to achieve accountability?

After I wrote about the state of the city a few Sundays ago, a number of people wrote to express their concern that I was giving up on the city. I don't believe that was what I was saying.

But I do say—and I think we must say again and again—that the strategy now being pursued is too arbitrary, too autocratic, too contemptuous of almost everyone at the city level and too utterly unengaged at the state level. I think the policy changes that were a part of the Reagan revolution have played an important role in bringing Detroit to its present condition. I also believe, though, that the leaders of the city and the leaders of the state are now powerless to fashion a better, more hopeful strategy.

Is that then racism? I search my soul constantly against that awful possibility. I think it isn't. I think it is trying to tell that a more accountable city administration would long since have been called to task for the emptiness of its strategy for making the city whole again.

Joe H. Stroud, Detroit Free Press[26]

Media Criticism

Media criticism is a form of opinion writing in which the microscope is turned around, with the focus placed on the job that the newspaper and other media are doing. Relatively few newspapers have full-time media critics; they are expensive, and free-wheeling critics sometimes raise embarrassing questions. But if newspapers and other media are genuinely concerned about maintaining credibility with their customers, the job of explaining and responding to listeners and readers is essential, whether performed by a media critic, a reader advocate or a senior editor.

One of the responsibilities of this person is to respond to questions and criticism from readers. A second responsibility is to comment on, and criticize if necessary, the media business in general. A third is to tell readers about their newspaper.

Frank Wetzel, ombudsman for the *Seattle Times*, had the second responsibility in mind when he wrote

I have come to realize that newspapers' defects are not for the most part the product of staff dereliction. Rather, they are part of the structure of the American press, and are threefold: 1. Concentration of ownership. 2. Inflated expectations of profitability. 3. Lack of access by the public.[27]

He told readers that they generally get the newspapers that they deserve, but "[e]ditors who simply dish up what they think the public wants are remiss." Newspapers should try to stay "a half-step ahead of the public most of the time; that's what makes them good papers."

Another Wetzel column, representing the third responsibility, is especially appropriate for this chapter. In it he explains the "labyrinth" of the varieties of opinion that appear in a newspaper, from editorials to comic strips.

OMBUDSMAN

Newspapers Should Separate Facts and Opinion

Reading a newspaper isn't as simple as it may seem. With innocent cunning, editors fool even sophisticated readers by mixing fact with opinion, opinions with fact. Then editors complain that readers can't decipher the difference.

Newspapers better get that fixed straightaway. Not just for the convenience of readers but because the courts have decided that opinion, no matter how vitriolic, is protected from libel. That makes it a dollar-and-cents issue, something editors watch closely these days.

The precedent was set in 1984 when a University of Maryland professor sued columnists Rowland Evans and Robert Novak. They had called the professor a Marxist. In reviewing the case, an appellate court set four criteria for distinguishing fact from opinion. One criterion was the location of the statements in the newspaper. They are presumed to be opinion and carry special libel protection if they are on the editorial or facing (op-ed) pages. Academicians, swift with the apt phrase, call this "page environment."

Despite the presumption of the courts, shadings of opinion appear in the paper almost everywhere. For inexplicable reasons, newspapers seldom bother to help readers identify opinion and fact with a road map. What follows is a rough guide through the labyrinth.

▶ **Editorial and op-ed pages:** The implicit contract between editors and readers is clear. It is here, avowedly, opinion is found. The paper's own opinions are expressed in the unsigned editorials. The bylined local and syndicated columns, editorial cartoons and letters to the editor express opinions, too, but they re not necessarily those of the paper. . . .

▶ **General columns:** These are blithely sprinkled through the paper. . . . Columnists express personal opinions. Their boundaries are broad. Occasionally a column that is particularly outrageous will be killed by an editor. But generally the writers entrusted with a personal column are permitted great latitude.

▶ **Criticism:** The arts and entertainment pages frequently contain articles of criticism, expressions of opinion by a critic on [music, art, books, TV, film, pop rock, theater and dance].

▶ **Sports section:** Expression of opinion is more subtle here. Stories focus on the home team. Sportswriters generally are given more leeway than in other departments. Writers characterize outstanding players or game-turning plays on their own authority, for instance—expressions of opinion. . . .

▶ **Bylined news stories:** Bylines have become ubiquitous as earthworms but in some cases they signify that the reporter speaks with greater-than-usual authority. Stories by specialists . . . carry additional weight if not opinion.

A study commissioned by the American Society of Newspaper Editors in 1985 found that readers tend to equate a byline with opinion. But a recent experience at Stanford University . . . contradicts that finding.

The Stanford study also found, incidentally, that articles perceived as opinion appeared to influence readers more than articles perceived as merely factual. I did not find that reassuring.

▶ **Labeled stories:** Occasionally newspapers will label news-page stories "Analysis" or "Commentary." The distinction between the two is not readily understood. ("Commentary" is more opinionated.) Labels ought to be more widely used. Properly employed, labels could serve as the useful equivalent of street signs.

▶ **Comic strips:** Six days per week, Doonesbury, chockfull of creator Gary Trudeau's opinion, is banished from *The Times*' comics page to the Scene section (do not ask me why there). This exile is lifted on Sunday, although Doonesbury is no less opinionated then, when it appears in the colored comics section.

▶ **The front page:** Placement here represents the opinion of the editors of what are the day's most important or most interesting stories. The Stanford experiment showed readers are more likely to perceive an article as opinion when it appears on the op-ed page than the front page—an accurate perception. Still, selection for page one carries a powerful message to readers, more powerful than editors sometimes realize. Otherwise, however, front-page stories are as factual and objective as journalists can make them.

This, of course, is just my opinion.

Frank Wetzel, Seattle Times[28]

CONCLUSION

By no means is the anonymous newspaper editorial the only outlet for opinion. In daily or weekly newspapers, new opportunities are opening in reviewing literary and cultural productions, partly because newspapers are seeking ways to provide more information for consumers. New opportunities also lie on the growing number of op-ed pages, which are open to bylined pieces that range from interpretation to media criticism to personal opinion More and more publishers and editors are relaxing the old rule that editorial writers should remain anonymous.

Until a few years ago broadcast editorial writing seemed to have a bright future. Then editorial writing jobs began shrinking. Budgets got tight. Broadcast people have always been nervous about having to provide equal time for opinions expressed by themselves and others. But why should broadcast stations allow newspapers to hold a monopoly on opinion in a local community? If owners of broadcast stations were to recommit themselves to offering opinions to their listeners and viewers, radio and television could provide not only jobs for opinion writers but also leadership for their communities.

QUESTIONS AND EXERCISES

1. Find a newspaper editorial on a topic that interests you. Rewrite it in broadcast style. Read it aloud to see if any of the wording is awkward or difficult to enunciate clearly. Rewrite to clear up these spots.

2. Keep your ear open for editorials during radio and television news broadcasts. Write to the station manager to ask for a copy. When it arrives, read it aloud. Are there any awkward or difficult spots? How does the editorial approach the subject? Is it analytical or outspoken, one- or two-sided? Is the conclusion at the beginning or the end? Would listeners be convinced?

3. Pick a topic, conduct the necessary research and write an analytical article that would be appropriate for an op-ed page. Then write an editorial based on the article that could run the same day.

4. Write an op-ed piece based on an experience that you have had. Try to make it appeal to as broad an audience as possible.

5. If you can find a media criticism column in one of the newspapers that you read, write the media critic. Ask about the newspaper's policies relating to media criticism and the responsibilities of the media critic.

6. If you spot something that you think merits attention in a newspaper that has a media criticism column, write or call the media critic about it.

7. Select a recent book on a media or current events topic. Write a book review that might be suitable to a book section of a newspaper or an op-ed page. Before writing it, you might read several reviews in newspapers that have strong book departments.

8. Watch for a cultural event that interests you: an art exhibit, a play, a concert, a musical or movie. Write a review for the arts and entertainment section of the paper. Again, it is good advice to read several reviews before you start writing, and in fact before you attend the event.

Chapter 16

Letters to the Editor

If tails ever wag dogs, the letters column of a daily newspaper is a likely candidate for the job.

—PETER G. FRADLEY, PROVIDENCE (R.I.) JOURNAL-BULLETIN[1]

Letters to the editor are about the only part of the editorial page that comes free. But in terms of time, effort and headaches, a good letters column is probably the most expensive part. It's quicker and easier for an editorial-page person to knock out a couple of paragraphs of prose than to prepare a letter of equal length for print.

"Letters give life to an editorial page," Barry Bingham Sr. of the Louisville *Courier-Journal* said. "They also come near to beating the life out of the fellow who has to handle them. Many are illiterate. Others are long, rambling and inchoate. Still others are so abusive in tone that they recall the Turkish proverb, 'Letters written after dinner are read in Hell.' Some of the ones that come to us must be written in the fine frenzy of after-dinner dyspepsia." Then he added: "Letters are worth every bit of trouble they cause, however."[2]

WHY LETTERS?

Editorial page editors put up with—and encourage—letters for one reason: Letters help give readers a better feeling about the newspaper. Letters give readers, as citizens, one of the few chances they have to speak their mind in public. Letters also help create interest in the editorial page and increase readership.

Surveys consistently show that letters are among the best-read parts of the paper. "Some writers put their hearts and souls into one letter of a lifetime, then frame the printed copy and proudly present it as their 'editorial,'" Diane Cole of the *Salt Lake Tribune* wrote in a *Masthead* symposium on letters to the editor. "This process creates a bond between subscriber and newspaper that only a week of late deliveries could break." But the letter column also has its dangers. "Fail to run a writer's masterpiece (or disaster) and you weaken an avid reader loyalty," Cole said. "Get a name wrong or drop a 'key phrase,' and you court alienation."[3]

Letters give readers a chance to talk about what they want to talk about, which is especially important in a one-newspaper town with no built-in voice of opposition. Readers are not stuck with the editor's agenda; they have their own agendas.

Some readers, as well as some legal scholars, think that the public should have a right of access to the letters column and the right to express themselves in any way and at any length they wish. Although the U.S. Supreme Court, in *Miami Herald v. Tornillo*, held that they have no legal right of access, readers still react vigorously when their letters are shortened, altered or not printed. Editors and publishers, especially in monopoly situations, have a good deal of self-interest, if not legal interest, in helping readers feel that they do have access to the printed page.

BUILDING A LETTERS COLUMN

Scholarly studies and reports from editors indicate that readers are increasingly turning to the letters column to express their opinions. A survey published in 1992 found that three-quarters of the newspapers had increased the size of their letters columns since a survey taken 10 years earlier. The editors reported receiving more letters—and publishing a greater percentage—according to the survey authors, Suraj Kapoor and Carl Botan.[4]

In spite of the apparently thriving health of the letters column, most editors would be delighted to receive more letters, especially high-quality letters. Editors on 41 percent of the newspapers surveyed said they received from zero to 50 letters a month, with 13 percent receiving 51 to 100. Most newspapers published more than 80 percent of letters they received, according to the survey.

In the *Masthead* symposium referred to earlier, Keith Carter of the *Desert Sun* in Palm Springs, Calif., offered nine suggestions for building a stronger letters column.[5]

- ▶ Localize.
- ▶ Print as many letters as possible.
- ▶ Encourage debates.
- ▶ Set up rules and follow them.
- ▶ Identify letter writers.
- ▶ Run letters quickly.
- ▶ Verify, verify, verify.
- ▶ Stay flexible.
- ▶ Stimulate interest.

It is clear what Carter had in mind in offering most of these suggestions. The "localize" advice was directed toward urging strong editorials on local topics as a means to stimulate letters. The "stay flexible" advice was intended for editors who seem more concerned with enforcing rigid rules than with printing good (but perhaps excessively long) letters. Probably for as long as there have been letters to newspapers, editors have been concerned with two of Carter's points: stimulating more letters and setting rules for deciding which ones to print. These two areas are discussed at length in the following sections.

STIMULATING INTEREST

In seeking ways to stimulate more and better letters, editors have experimented with ways of displaying letters, methods for speeding the delivery of letters and ideas for encouraging readers to write.

Display of Letters

Giving letters prominent and attractive display is one way that editors can indicate to readers that the newspaper takes letters seriously. Letters typically are placed on the right side of the editorial page, beneath the editorial cartoon. When Professor Robert Bohle of Virginia Commonwealth University examined a series of editorial pages, he found no fault with this placement of letters, but he thought that editors underplayed individual letters. Headlines tended to be small, consisting of one line with few words ("terse and enigmatic," he called them). He preferred two lines to let the reader know what the letter was about.[6]

Bohle applauded papers that worked illustrations or political cartoons into their letter columns. (He might have added photographs.) He urged editors to place the how-to-submit-a-letter box at the top of the column. He thought that a letter could be made more understandable if a summary of the article or editorial that prompted the letter could appear at the top of the letter. Bohle also suggested creating a box (perhaps an entire page) that included a news summary of a topic, editorials, letters to the editor and perhaps columns (somewhat on the order of *USA Today*'s theme editorial page).

Transmission of Letters

Editors have been trying for years to improve on the mails for speeding up letters to the editor. A lively letters column requires that letters appear in a timely manner. One clear indicator of a good letters column is a lot of reader response to editorials, news stories and other letters.

A few years ago some newspapers experimented with allowing readers to call in letters on the telephone. At first readers dictated their letters to a clerk. Later letters were tape-recorded and transcribed. Now many newspapers are receiving letters from readers by facsimile.

Encouraging Writers

To stimulate letters, some editors have staff members call people on the telephone to ask for opinions on topics. Some editors send several letters a day to a sampling of subscribers, asking them to read specific editorials and write their views about them.[7] Some newspapers announce topics and ask readers to submit letters by a certain date. A few editorial pages even carry coupons on which readers can write their opinions. The coupons can be cut out and mailed.[8]

To encourage quality letters, one newspaper put stars next to the signatures on letters of merit. Some papers pay a few dollars for outstanding letters. Some newspapers hold appreciation banquets for frequent contributors. Some run pictures of regular contributors.[9] The *San Bernardino* (Calif.) *Sun* at one time reproduced one or two letters each day in the original typewritten or handwritten form.

Special efforts may be needed, if a letters column has been neglected, to get readers to start looking at the column. But if editors also offer readers stimulating editorials and other editorial page material, the column should soon begin sustaining itself. James Dix of the *Moline* (Ill.) *Dispatch* said his formula for keeping the letters column fired up was to create "a crossfire of disagreement between us and a column, or between us and a letter."[10] The incoming mail took care of itself.

SETTING UP THE RULES

How readers view a newspaper's letters column and how they in turn respond to it can depend on how the editors of that newspaper handle the letters they receive. Both the quality of the column and the readers' perceptions of it can be affected by the policies of the paper. By no means do all editors agree on how best to run the letters column. Policies generally concern seven areas: use of names and addresses, verification of names, subject matter, length and frequency, editing letters, editor's notes and political letters.

Names and Addresses

Whether the publication of writers' names should be required has been debated among editorial page editors for a long time. Most newspapers now, however, require that names appear with letters. A few newspapers will allow a name to be withheld under unusual circumstances, but require that the name of the letter writer be known to the editor. When revealing a person's name might deeply embarrass that person or endanger that person's life, some newspapers will run a letter with no name under a separate heading. The *Waukegan* (Ill.) *Sun-Sentinel* published an anonymous letter from a mother who described how she reacted when she discovered her son was using drugs. Editors on the *Ogden* (Utah) *Standard-Examiner* thought they might withhold the name of a student who was critical of a teacher for valid reasons, but would append an editor's note explaining the reasons for the deletion.[11]

If editors are more insistent on publishing names than in the past, they may be less insistent on publishing addresses. Some readers have been subjected to harassment. Persons who disagree with them have been known to knock on their doors, throw trash on their lawns, make anonymous phone calls and resort to other ways of annoying them. To protect letter writers, some newspapers have stopped publishing street addresses; some have omitted the city as well. Some newspapers leave out the street address but indicate the section of the city. *The Oregonian* of Portland, for example, indicates the city for letter writers from outside of Portland but "Northwest Portland" for a writer from that section of Portland.

Verification of Names

Editors undoubtedly spend more time verifying the authenticity of letters than in the past. Editors seem less inclined to presume the good will of letter writers. They also have become more knowledgeable about the legal dangers posed by letters. A survey by Suraj Kapoor and Carl Botan found that editors were about equally divided between those who verified the authors of all letters and those who verified only when their suspicions were aroused. To verify, almost all relied on the telephone, but one-third also used the mails.[12] The policy of the *Desert Sun* of Palm Springs, Calif., is typical of newspapers that want to avoid all possible mistakes: "Ask for letters to include phone numbers and then assign a news clerk to verify each and every one."[13]

Once in a while an editor will be burned. The *Cleveland Press* once printed a seemingly harmless letter about a streetcar accident. After the first edition appeared on the street, a woman called to say that the professed family name signed to the letter was "an obscene Hungarian word" too nasty to repeat.[14]

James J. Kilpatrick told how a Mr. Stuart Little of New York seduced space from the *Richmond News Leader* with a request for help in finding authentic stories about old crows. His hobby was old crows, he said, the older the better. Many people responded to his requests, including one who sent a package "containing a bottle of an old-time beverage." Another volunteered to send "an elderly female relative by marriage." Kilpatrick reported: "Smiling fondly at the quirks of the amateur ornithologist, we published Mr. Little's letter." Then came a second letter. "But we are not running any more of Mr. Little's crow: We are eating it," Kilpatrick told readers. "For right in the second sentence and in the fourth paragraph was another reference to that 'Kentucky beverage,' and down in the last sentence was still a third mention of this estimable product, and the whole business had about it the faint but unmistakable aroma of the gag, the gimmick, the phonus bolonus." Little turned out to work for a public relations firm that had the account for Old Crow bourbon whiskey. Fifty newspapers had apparently run the first letter.[15]

Subject Matter

Once you decide that a letter is legitimate, you must determine whether the subject matter is appropriate. Most newspapers have rules, stated or unstated, concerning what they will run. Most will not run poetry. "Print a bit of amateur verse and the next day's mail brings a deluge because everyone is a poet at heart if not in pen," M. Carl Andrews of the *Roanoke* (Va.) *World-News* warned.[16] Most papers refuse religious pitches or arguments over the meaning of biblical verses. But some will allow Bible references if they relate to public issues. Most will not publish a letter unless it pertains to an issue of some public interest. Many try to avoid thank-you letters, especially those thanking an individual. Some will weed out publicity seekers who try to get their names in print by praising editorials lavishly. Some are tough on politicians who try to find excuses for getting their names in the letters column (more on this later). Many editors will not publish letters from outside their general circulation areas unless they pertain to a local issue or something that appeared in the paper.

Editors need to be aware of the possibility of an inspired letter-writing campaign. Sometimes they can tell that several letters have been written on the same typewriter or computer, or have the same wording. Some writers make a hobby of sending the same letter to scores or hundreds of papers. Editors can also be trapped by letter-writing assignments in the schools. A letter from a young person may show up one day and get printed. The next day a letter on the same or a different subject may arrive and be put into the column. Then, perhaps on the third day, 20 letters arrive; the other members of the class had been a little slower than their two classmates.

Closely related to this problem is deciding when to call a halt to a continuing series of letters on the same topic. At some point editors find that they simply must call a halt to letters on a subject unless something new is said.

Editors are not in agreement on what to do with letters that don't fall within the customary range of apparent rationality. "How do you handle hate letters?" one editorial writer asked in an article in *The Masthead*. Carol Suplee of the *Burlington County Times* of Willingboro, N.J., recounted that she had a letter writer who was "blatantly inaccurate and unnecessarily inflammatory when he relate[d] his version of history," especially concerning the Jews. She said she sometimes wrote a letter explaining her reasons for not publishing his letter. "But there have been other times when I felt that exposition of his amazing bigotry might serve the community well," she wrote. "That has sometimes backfired. I have received delegations from Jewish organizations questioning why the newspaper chose to give this rather well-known Nazi sympathizer any space."[17]

Hap Cawood of the *Dayton* (Ohio) *Daily News* raised the question of "what to do with madmen who learned to write but, unlike us, do not get to make a living out of that combination." Many letter writers may be crazy, he said, but they keep the column interesting. He said he had tried writing on all kinds of significant subjects in an attempt to get readers to write letters. "Then a letter was published saying one-eyed drivers should not be licensed," he said. "The flood gates opened. We heard from every one-eyed driver in metropolitan Dayton."[18]

While on *The Columbian*, I was blessed with a persistent letter writer who could start writing on almost any subject but within a couple of handwritten pages would wend her way to talking about sublimating sex as a means of delaying marriage, births and population crisis. She would write several times a week for awhile, then not write for several months. She had been writing to the paper for several years when I took over the editorial page. She was still writing 12 years later when I left. One of her letters consisted of 125 six-by-nine-inch pages; many others were long but not that long. I sometimes could use the first few paragraphs before she headed off into sublimation.

Length and Frequency

Most papers have policies on maximum length and frequency of letters from a single writer. The Kapoor-Botan survey found that nearly half of all papers set a limit between 201 and 300 words, with about a third permitting longer letters.[19]

Limiting length encourages readers to write succinctly and saves the editor some work, but it also may prevent a reader from making as complete an argument as editorial writers allow themselves in the editorial column. To meet this problem, editors sometimes will publish a long communication from a reader under a different label, such as "In My Opinion."

Many newspapers limit the frequency with which a letter writer may appear on the editorial page. Once a month may be the most typical limit. Limiting writers has advantages. When the same names appear again and again, letters become predictable, and other prospective writers are discouraged. But the limit also works against writers who may have something significant to say more often than once a month. A one-month rule may also give perennial writers the idea that they have a right to appear once a month. Also, what do you do when a writer attacks another writer and the first writer wants to respond?

Editing of Letters

Editors disagree on what is desirable or permissible in editing the letters they decide to run. Most newspapers reserve the right to trim letters to make them more succinct. Most editors will edit letters to clean up spelling, punctuation and grammar, at least to some extent, on the ground that what writers have to say is more important than the writing mistakes that they make. About half of the editors in one survey said they edited letters "sparingly." Of the remainder somewhat more were inclined to edit heavily than to edit lightly.[20] Of course, whether editing heavily or lightly, editors must make certain that the letters say what the writers intended them to say.

In *The Masthead* symposium on letters, Geoff Seamans recalled that the *Roanoke Times & World-News* once experimented with the no-editing approach. Letters were shortened for reasons of space or redundancy. When words were removed, ellipses were used to indicate excisions. "Our readers noticed," Seamans said. "Complaints? In the dozens, at least. Compliments? To the best of my recollection, zero. The experiment was scrapped." The paper went back to the "laborious pain [of editing letters] from raw into publishable."[21]

Editor's Notes

Editor's notes at the ends of letters used to be more popular than they now are. A clever note that sets a letter writer straight may be fun to write, but Charles Towne of the *Hartford* (Conn.) *Courant* said he suspected that "some editors, too many if there are any, publish caustic rebuttals out of a feeling of superiority—of being so far above such savage assaults as to be immune."[22] Letters columns are meant for exchanges of opinion among readers. If writers have the feeling that the editor is going to have the last word, they are likely to stop writing. If a statement in a letter is clearly wrong in its facts, perhaps a note is justified if the letter is judged important enough to run. But often the truth of a statement is not easy to determine—one person's perception of truth is another person's misperception—and the editor is best advised to print it and let other readers try to set the writer straight. In addition to the one letter, the paper may end up getting several in response.

What does the editor do when a critical letter misstates an editorial? Geoff Seamans of the Roanoke newspaper posed that question. He saw no easy answer:

Run it, and leave the impression with readers that our position was indeed as the writer characterized it?

Don't run it (or edit out the offending but crucial parts), and leave ourselves open to the charge that we're arrogantly stifling dissent?

Run it, but with an editor's note or same-day editorial? Maybe OK if it's a simple correction of a misquoted phrase or figure. Not so OK if it involves more extensive explanation: Here we are, arrogant again, always having the last word.[23]

Political Letters

Policies vary widely about what to do with letters relating to elections. Practices run all the way from treating political letters, including candidate endorsements, like other letters, to telling writers who want to speak for a candidate to buy an ad.

In a *Masthead* symposium on "The Politics of Letters," Wally Hoffman of the *Salt Lake Tribune* said his paper treated campaign letters like other letters except for being more strict in not allowing anonymous letters. A signature might be withheld, he speculated, in "a case in which the writer's job might be jeopardized by disclosure of his or her identity." Hoffman said that the *Tribune* tried to make "a good-faith effort" to balance between Democratic and Republican supporters for president and U.S. senator.[24]

At the other extreme, Phil Fretz reported that the *Amarillo* (Texas) *Globe-News* had no trouble with endorsement letters, since it had a policy against running them. "If you run endorsement letters, you're a masochist," he wrote. "You open yourself to the charge that you didn't run somebody's letter because you endorsed his opponent. And chances are, the letter takes up a lot of space without adding much substance to the discussion."[25] If letters raise a new issue, the news side should deal with it.

Somewhere between these policies was that of the *Omaha World-Herald*, which opened its letters columns to politicians who were not candidates but discouraged letters from candidates themselves. Frank Partsch reported, however, that his paper considered requests by candidates "to set the record straight regarding something that has appeared on the editorial page." The *World-Herald*, like most newspapers, tries to screen out "sweatshop" letters that clearly come from the same source.[26]

To head off last-minute accusations that can't be properly answered, most newspapers set a deadline for election letters. A typical policy was described in *The Masthead* symposium by Robert A. Pierce of *The State* of Columbia, S.C. Readers are told that they must have their letters into the paper by 5 p.m. on the Wednesday before an election and that letters will appear no later than Sunday.[27]

LIBEL IN LETTERS

Mark Franklin, a law professor at Stanford University with expertise in First Amendment issues, has argued that "editors should be protected against libel suits for published letters so long as the letters are authentic and the writers are correctly identified." Letters already serve as a sort of community bulletin board; exempting them from the threat of libel suits would make them even more so, in Franklin's view. Such a bulletin board would "provide access to the media and the community for many who have no other opportunity to get their thoughts before the public," Franklin has written. This access is especially important "as more newspapers become local monopolies." He estimated that about one out of eight letters that are rejected by editors is discarded because of concerns over libel.[28]

For now, however, courts treat letters no differently from the way they treat any other published material in a libel suit. "A long line of case law has held that the author of a libel bears the ultimate responsibility for it, and that everyone who takes part in publication of a libel may be held responsible for it," Professor Steve Pasternack of New Mexico State University warned editors in an article in *The Masthead*. Pasternack noted that a survey had indicated that editors were allowing the use of harsher language in letters columns than elsewhere in their newspapers. He attributed this laxity to the editors' misinformation or lack of knowledge of libel law, and to a reluctance to consult attorneys.[29]

THE LETTERS EDITOR

The job of handling letters is not one for the novice—or for an impatient, careless or uncaring editor. Cliff Carpenter of the *Rochester* (N.Y.) *Democrat and Chronicle* saw some newspapers handling letters lovingly, but he saw others handling them ineptly, casually, and with fear or disdain. "Some pages handle letters as if they were ashamed of them," he said. "And by handling them that way, they get only mediocrity to use as letters—and a vicious circle is created."[30] A person who handled letters on the *Kansas City* (Mo.) *Star* was said to have done it "with a certain amount of tender loving care, a bit of prayer and some tearing of hair." Handling letters can take about as much time as an editor can find to work on them, if a paper receives a strong flow of mail. Carpenter reported that his paper used two full-time assistants and a secretary. Murray Moler of the *Ogden* (Utah) *Standard-Examiner* said that on his one-person staff he spent as much time with letters as with editorial writing and he thought the time was well spent. The Kapoor-Botan survey found that half of the newspapers spent up to 10 hours a week on letters and that a quarter spent between 11 and 20 hours. Presumably the remaining quarter spent more time.[31]

The letters editor needs a thick skin—literally, at times. Palmer Hoyt of the *Denver Post* told of one letter that began: "Dear Palmer Hoyt: We want you to know that we are going to boil you in oil." A week later Hoyt got a letter that said: "Dear Palmer Hoyt: We want you to know that we are not going to boil you in oil after all. We got bigger turkeys than you to boil."[32] A woman brought to the office of the *Burlington* (Vt.) *Free Press* a three-page letter, typewritten, single-spaced, with a pen name. Franklin Smith tried to explain that the letter was too long for publication and pen names were not permitted. "Finally, after a long, long pause, she looked at me," Smith said, "and said plaintively, 'You don't like me, do you?'"[33]

Letters editors, faceless as they may be to the public, can build special relationships with readers. M. Carl Andrews of Roanoke said that some of his best friends were regular letter writers who had never met him. Three of his most delightful contributors over the years, he said, had been "dear old ladies who always found something good to say about people or things." He reported that two of them had died. One of them had requested that he be one of her pallbearers.[34]

CONCLUSION

A good letters column can be a lot of work for an editor. Deciding what letters to print and what should be done to get them ready for print requires skill and judgment. Dealing with letter writers requires tact. The editing of letters requires sensitivity, a sense of fairness and a heavy editing pencil. But efforts put into the letters column are usually worthwhile in terms of the readability and credibility of the editorial page. Letters bring readers to the page. They also help readers believe they have a voice in their newspaper. Perhaps the clearest sign of a good editorial page is a good letters column, especially one in which readers respond to the editorials, columns and other letters that appear on the page. Such a page is truly a community forum.

QUESTIONS AND ANSWERS

1. Examine the letters columns of the newspapers in your area to determine their policies on the use of names and addresses, condensation and frequency of publication. Are these policies spelled out for readers?

2. Compare the letters columns of these papers for quantity and quality of letters published. Which papers seem to have the best letters columns? Is there evidence available to explain the success of these columns?

3. Examine the letters specifically for references to previously published editorials or letters. Such references often indicate that the letters column is providing a lively community forum.

4. Can you find letters that sound as though they were produced by a letters mill that sends the same letter to many newspapers?

5. Can you find political letters that sound as thought they were produced by a letters "sweatshop," letters supporting a cause that sound as though they came from the same source?

6. Do the editor's notes seem fully justified in the columns you have examined? Do you think an editor might have been wiser not to have written one or more of the notes? Why?

7. Do any of the papers request letters on specific topics, perhaps in a weekly roundup or in answer to a question? If so, what kind of responses do the papers get?

8. Write a letter to one of the papers. See if any effort is made to verify your name and address. If it is printed, see what changes are made. If you think the changes altered the meaning of the letter, call and inform the editorial page editor. If it was not published, call to ask why.

Chapter 17

Columns and Cartoons

As syndicated columns arguably become less influential, . . . more and more people seem to want to write them.

—EDWIN M. YODER, JR., SYNDICATED COLUMNIST[1]

. . . the syndicate hacks . . . violate the columns of our newspapers and rob them of credulity with bias and distortion.

—DONALD P. KEITH, EASTON (PA.) EXPRESS[2]

Most newspapers devote more space and less attention to syndicated columns and cartoons than to any other element on the editorial page. These features are relatively inexpensive, undemanding of editorial attention and extremely useful for plugging editorial holes of any size and number. Some editors have streamlined their editing to the point that every day they slap a regular liberal columnist in one position on the page, a regular conservative columnist in another spot and maybe an interpretive columnist in a third spot. A cartoon by the same artist sits atop the page every day.

The editorial writer on a one-person staff may be thankful that syndicated features are still available. With these features, the bulk of the editorial page can be filled with a few minutes' work, and the writer can move on to do what most editorial writers prefer to do—write editorials. But even writers who have little time for handling columnists serve readers poorly if they do not give careful attention to which columns and cartoons are selected for print. Deciding which columnists and cartoonists to subscribe to and which to run on any single day can make a difference in how readers regard the page. In this chapter we will talk about the role that columns and cartoons play on the editorial page, how editors decide which ones to use and how they handle the syndicated material. We also will look at efforts to make syndicated writers more credible with editors and readers.

ROLE OF THE COLUMNIST

Syndicated editorial page columnists date back only to the early 1930s. One reason cited for their rise is that, with the coming of the New Deal, editorial page editors were eager to publish interpretive writers who, because of their inside sources, would be able to tell readers what was going on in Washington, D.C. At least some editorial page editors realized that they were unaware of what was going on in the federal government and out of touch with the new trends in policy. The syndicated columnists moved in, Robert H. Estabrook of the *Washington Post* said, because newspapers were not doing a "good enough job providing background and interpretation in their news columns . . . and not doing a good enough job of providing informed comment in their editorial columns."[3] Readers wanted to know what was going on, and the columnists fulfilled this function.

Many of the early columnists, more in sympathy with the New Deal than most editors, provided contrasting opinions to the editorials with which they shared pages. Noting that most newspapers were editorially against President Franklin D. Roosevelt, Mark Ethridge of *Newsday* on Long Island wrote: "Rather than rouse the natives, or maybe to silence their protests, publishers thought it the better part of wisdom to let the columnists fight it out on their editorial pages."[4] The columnists who appeared about that time included Raymond Clapper, Tom Stokes, Drew Pearson, the Alsop brothers, Robert Allen, Marquis Childs, Dorothy Thompson and Frank Kent.

Although not the earliest columnist, David Lawrence followed a career that typified what Ethridge called "both the rise—and . . . fall—of the columnists." Lawrence had been a favorite of Woodrow Wilson and Bernard Baruch, a prominent financier and presidential advisor. "He had the ears and confidence of the mighty, besides the energy to dig," Ethridge recalled. Columnist Walter Lippmann had also been a confidant of Woodrow Wilson and in fact was to pride himself in his close ties with public leaders through more than half a century of editorial and column writing. Robert Allen and Drew Pearson, with their "Washington Merry-Go-Round," provided readers with inside stories. Westbrook Pegler, sometimes published on the editorial page, became known for "reporting" demeaning things about public figures.

Columnist Ed Yoder has recalled that at the end of World War II Lippmann was still "the philosopher-journalist of Jovian perspective," Arthur Krock was "only slightly less Olympian in tenor and tone" and Joseph Alsop, teamed with his brother Stewart, was calling himself a reporter, "even when he was most opinionated." "Just below" (Yoder's description) were figures like Pearson, "who specialized in gossip," and Lawrence, "who specialized in indignation."[5]

Eventually the popularity of these columns declined. The David Lawrence columns I edited for the *Des Moines* (Iowa) *Tribune* in the early 1960s were mostly a rehash of the daily news with a little conservative interpretation thrown in. Joseph Alsop was stuck on assuring readers that the war was being won in Vietnam. The news from Washington was well reported in the news columns, and the syndicated columnists knew little more inside information than most reporters. The editorial policies of newspapers had also become more moderate. Editorial writers were more informed about, and more sympathetic toward, what was going on in Washington. Readers also were more informed about the federal government and not satisfied with what Ethridge called the "pontificating, . . . griping, . . . off-the-cuff reflections" that came from the traditional columnists.[6]

But columnists have persisted, even though on most newspapers they probably are allotted somewhat less space now than when they first became popular. A new generation of columnists has emerged.

Columnists today serve as more than opinion and information pipelines for public officials and offer more than knee-jerk reactions to the day's news. Looking at changes in column writing, Yoder concluded that busy readers don't particularly care what a columnist thinks about this or that. "My own sense of the columnist's usefulness now is—or some would find it—shockingly esthetic, in the broad sense of that word," Yoder said. "In its new but limited form and function, the column is at best a chance to watch a mind and style at work, through time, on the topics of the day." Columnists, he suggested, should be considering such questions as: "Did the Supreme Court suffer a microbiologist to patent a man-made bug, or discover to the astonishment of many citizens that nude dancing is a form of free speech? . . . Did medical technology raise new questions about the nature of life and death?"[7] Walter Lippmann and Joseph Alsop, mostly concerned with politics and international affairs, would never have raised those kinds of questions.

SETTING POLICIES FOR COLUMNS

Editing syndicated columns involves more than merely placing them in predetermined positions on the editorial page. Editors must decide on the columns that they want to buy and, on any given day, on those that they want to run that day. They must make decisions about how extensively they will edit the columns and about how they will identify the columnists that appear on their pages.

Selecting Columnists

How does an editor go about deciding which columnists to subscribe to? Editors must first decide whether to offer readers a variety of viewpoints or a fairly consistent point of view, or whether to select the columnists on another basis. One survey found that 60 percent of the editorial people who responded sought to balance columnists. Only 12 percent said they selected columnists with philosophies similar to the newspaper's, while 27 percent said they picked columnists for their ability to draw readers, regardless of their philosophies.[8]

Diversification can go too far. More than a quarter of the editors reported that they ran such columns as "health" and "medicine" on their editorial pages. Even in a smaller newspaper, surely these columns belong in the lifestyle section. I once tried to convince a publisher in Washington state to move "Dear Abby" from his editorial page. His response was that the column attracted readers who otherwise would not read the page. He may have been right, but I suspect those readers quickly moved on to other pages to find fare more in tune with Abby rather than remaining to read the rest of the editorial page.

My opinion is that columnists should be selected because they write interesting, challenging, even surprising things. Writers are not as predictable politically as they used to be, and writers of the same general persuasion are likely to offer ample diversity if their writing is of high quality.

Readership surveys and syndicate lists show that traditional Washington columnists continue to rank high on editorial pages. Among these, James J. Kilpatrick, William Safire and George Will will tend toward conservatism. Mary McGrory tends toward the liberal side. Others, such as David Broder and William Raspberry, are not so easily categorized. Charles Krauthammer has been called neo-liberal, which probably means conservative. Anthony Lewis and Richard Cohen, who are not thought of as Washington columnists, usually speak up for liberal causes. Art Buchwald's humor-laden column carries a liberal slant. Dave Barry's would have to be characterized as iconoclastic. Ellen Goodman writes about social issues more than about straight politics, with views that sometimes are hard to label. Ed Yoder writes a column that often takes a broader, more historical view than most columns. Back in the early days of column writing, Anne O'Hare McCormick of the *New York Times* and Dorothy Thompson of the *New York Herald Tribune* wrote columns on international affairs. Today Georgie Anne Geyer and Flora Lewis report and comment on foreign matters.

So who are the most popular columnists with editors today? In looking through a stack of 136 editorial (or editorial and op-ed) pages that I collected in 1990 through 1992 as possible sources of material for this book, I found 68 writers whom I would consider syndicated. These writers appeared a total of 180 times, an average of 2.6 times each. Only nine appeared five times or more. They were: William Raspberry (15), James J. Kilpatrick (11), Mike Royko (9), George Will (9), Cal Thomas (7), David Broder (6), Ellen Goodman (6), Anthony Lewis (5) and Richard Cohen (5). Thirty-one of the 68 appeared only once and 14 only twice.

The 68 columnists were overwhelmingly male and white. Ten were women: Ellen Goodman, Mary McGrory, Anne Quindlen, Georgie Anne Geyer, Flora Lewis, Joan Beck, Meg Greenfield, Cynthia Tucker, Jean Kirkpatrick and Jessica Matthews. Five were known to be African-Americans: William Raspberry, Robert Maynard, Clarence Page, Carl Rowan and Claude Lewis. Two apparently were Hispanic: Jose Armas and Roger E. Hernandez. The search turned up one environmental columnist (Alton Chase), one business writer (John Cunniff), one economics columnist (Robert Kuttner) and one foreign columnist (Michel Gorbachev). Humor columnists were Mike Royko, Art Buchwald, Mark Russell, Dave Barry and Andy Rooney.

Not all columnists are available to every editor. Some metropolitan papers purchase the right to the exclusive use of syndicated features within what they regard as their circulation areas. The editor of the *Waukegan* (Ill.) *News-Sun*, in the shadow of the Chicago papers, was one of the first to protest publicly. "The smaller paper can wail about a 'monopoly of thought' and sometimes pry concessions from the big ones," he said, "but this charity is composed largely of columnar has-beens whose prose is as appetizing as the floor of a parakeet's cage and whose message is as common as a telephone pole."[9]

A partial victory for the smaller newspapers came in 1975, when, in response to threatened action by the Justice Department, the *Boston Globe* gave up its rights to the exclusive use of syndicated columns in Maine, Vermont, New Hampshire and eastern Massachusetts, claiming instead only a 12-city Massachusetts area. The agreement put pressure on other metropolitan papers to restrict some of their exclusivity practices. Suburban newspapers in particular have faced problems. The *Daily Journal-American* in Bellevue, Wash., a paper published across Lake Washington from two Seattle papers, had trouble obtaining syndicated materials when it went to a daily schedule. When one of the Seattle papers bought the exclusive rights to a column but then ran it only infrequently, the Bellevue editor asked: "How can the editors of those papers argue for a free flow of information when they are selfishly impeding it?"[10]

The paper that I worked for, *The Columbian* in Vancouver, Wash., across the Columbia River from two Portland dailies, had the same problem. The only solution we found—a partial one, at that—was to decide immediately to buy a new feature, if it seemed to be a reasonably good one, before the editors on the bigger papers reached their decisions.

Frequency of Appearance

Columnists would like their writing to be run every day that they produce a column. In describing the "new but limited" role of today's columnists, Yoder argued that "continuity is important" if readers are to see the columnist's mind at work.[11] William F. Buckley Jr. once said that his principal complaint about editors was their erratic scheduling of his column. "I believe," he said, "that a columnist tends to communicate with his audience in virtue of his more or less continued presence on the scene."[12]

It probably is true that, if a columnist is to build a following, columns must appear on a regular basis. If a columnist who writes three times a week gets published once or twice during that period, that should be sufficient to establish and keep a following among readers. Some columns are bound to be duds. Yoder acknowledged that columnists are "apt to be as streaky, at best, as baseball hitters."[13] Some columns will have lost their timeliness, or others will be on the same subject that other columnists are writing about that day.

Editing Columns

One way to bring more opinion onto the page is to edit columns for tightness or even run only portions of columns (being careful, of course, not to distort the points being made). If columnists dislike being run erratically, they hate being cut even more. "I weep," Buckley said, "on seeing here and there columns cut without thoughtful reference to what the excisions do to what is left over."[14] Most editors feel free to cut a column to fit the space available, or to fit the space the column seems to merit.

While I was on the *Des Moines Register and Tribune*, the writer of a philosophical, non-political column expressed displeasure over our cuts. He said that he had written the column as tightly as possible and asked us not to use it if we had to cut it. We abided by his wishes for a while, but before long we went back to our old practice. We had only so much space on the page and we disagreed with him about the supposed impossibility of trimming the column. We didn't hear from him again.

A problem that may be tougher than deciding whether to cut the length of a column arises when an editor thinks that all or part of what a columnist is saying is inaccurate, unfair or biased. Editors of *The Masthead* asked several editors what they would do in such a circumstance. Some argued that the column should be published as the columnist wrote it; that the writer, not the newspaper, was responsible for what was said, and the writer should have an opportunity to speak. But other editors contended that they would not want to foist material onto their readers that they thought would mislead or misinform them. They felt as much responsibility for what appeared on the columnists' side of the page as for what appeared on the editorial side. My experience is that columnists can be given much freedom in expressing their views without hurting the credibility of the page, but that columns with obvious misstatements of fact should be discarded without any effort to correct or cut them. If a columnist consistently writes columns that are not usable, for any reason, the editor should drop that column and subscribe to another one. (More about this later, when we discuss the credibility of columnists.)

Identifying Columnists

Another decision for editorial page editors concerns how to identify syndicated columnists. It is important that readers understand that these writers are not on the local staff and that they are distributed across the country. (It is even more important for readers to know when a columnist is a local writer.) One standard device is a syndicate credit line at the top or bottom of each column. A more elaborate device is a short note about the writer's syndicate, area of expertise or background. Some editors attempt to describe their columnists as "liberal," "conservative," "satirical" or whatever. But, as suggested earlier, it's not easy to categorize most columnists these days.

KEEPING COLUMNISTS CREDIBLE

Because columnists are distributed on a nationwide basis, far beyond the scrutiny of editors and readers, these writers tend to operate in a vacuum. It is not easy for readers to reply to a syndicated column if they have complaints. Readers can't simply write to one editor to set matters straight, as they can with a local editorial. Furthermore, it is difficult to know whether writers are writing about subjects on which they may have conflicts of interest. An editor can keep an eye on local staff members to see that they avoid such conflicts, but who knows what hidden ties a national columnist may have?

The National Conference of Editorial Writers (NCEW) on several occasions has taken steps toward encouraging syndicated columnists to accept more responsibility in the areas of reply and conflict of interest. One problem has been that most syndicates will not release the names of subscribing newspapers to a reader (or an editor) who might want to send a reply to a columnist. Because of the added cost, syndicates have also resisted distributing letters to subscribing papers. Some syndicates leave the decision about distributing letters up to the columnists themselves. NCEW members, during their convention in 1974, voted overwhelmingly in favor of a resolution that urged syndicates "to provide mailing lists on request and/or distribute replies by targets of syndicated criticism." Columnist Kilpatrick dubbed this resolution the Cranberg Rule, after Gilbert Cranberg of the *Des Moines Register and Tribune*, who had been NCEW's leading advocate of increased responsibility by the syndicates. Kilpatrick liked the rule, commenting: "Its even-handed observance is bound to help our own image of fairness and right conduct."[15] In 1977 the National News Council cited the rule in a case involving charges against columnist Jack Anderson and United Features Syndicate, which had disregarded the resolution and refused to provide mailing lists.[16] An NCEW report in 1980, however, found that "a dramatic transformation is visible in the industry's attention to affording a day in print to victims of demonstrated unfairness." It found that the Cranberg Rule had raised the consciousness of editorial page editors as well.[17]

At the same time NCEW also was attempting to get the syndicates to adopt conflict-of-interest standards for columnists. The issue arose during the Watergate hearings in 1973 when Jeb Stuart Magruder, former deputy director of the Committee to Re-elect the President (CRP), told an investigating committee that among cash distributions he had made was $20,000 to a writer named Victor Lasky. One editor's inquiry to the North American Newspaper Alliance (NANA), for which Lasky wrote, brought the reply that Lasky had received the money for speeches he had written for Martha Mitchell, a neighbor of Lasky's, and also the wife of the head of the Nixon re-election campaign and former attorney general in the Nixon administration. NANA had not notified any other subscribing newspapers about Lasky's role as both a political columnist and a speech writer paid by CRP.[18] NCEW filed charges with the National News Council, alleging that Lasky had engaged in a conflict of interest and had "abused his position as an editorial page columnist," and claiming that NANA had failed to accept responsibility to inform its clients of the conflict of interest. The council upheld the complaints and concluded:

> It is our view, first, that a syndicated editorial page columnist is under a responsibility to disclose to the syndicate for which he writes the fact that he benefits financially from an organization active in an area on which he regularly comments and, second, that the syndicate is under a responsibility, once it learns of that relationship, promptly to inform its subscribers. Syndicates are urged to consider establishing guidelines for their columnists on possible conflicts of interest.[19]

NCEW members also adopted a resolution in 1974 that called on syndicates to adopt conflict-of-interest guidelines for columnists. At first most of the syndicates dragged their feet, but the 1980 report found that all major syndicates had at least announced that they would hold "their talent to avoidance of undisclosed conflicts of interest in their subject area."[20]

In cases in which editors suspect that conflicts of interest exist, they have a responsibility to their readers to check those conflicts, if possible, and express concern to the syndicates if their efforts to obtain information are frustrated. The credibility of their editorial pages, as well as that of the columnists, is at stake.

THE ROLE OF THE CARTOONIST

When *Masthead* editors asked *Detroit News* cartoonist Draper Hill to take a look at the development of political cartooning in America, he started with Benjamin Franklin.[21] In 1847 Franklin provided an illustration for the pamphlet *Plain Truth* that, in Hill's view, was "clearly the invention of a wordsmith rather than a draftsman." Both editors and cartoonists are still divided over whether form or content is more important for cartoons, and over whether satire or whimsy is more appropriate.

Hill credits Thomas Nast with initiating the "rough-and-tumble era" of the late 19th century, which "petered out with the death of Homer Davenport (1912) and the taming of Art Young." After cartoonists had been exhorted to "bash" the Huns during World War I, the 1920s began an era of "Good Taste." "Information, education and the nurture of consensus" replaced ridicule and satire, Hill wrote. By the end of World War II, and for another decade, cartoonists tended to take a "high-minded, generally predictable, over-labeled, under-caricatured tack . . . more bark than bite."

In 1946 the dominant cartoonists were Daniel Fitzpatrick (*St. Louis Post-Dispatch*), J. M. "Ding" Darling (*Des Moines Register*), Vaughan Shoemaker (*Chicago Daily News*), Herbert L. Block (*Washington Post*) and Bill Mauldin (*St. Louis Post-Dispatch* and, later, *Chicago Sun-Times*). Nearly all cartoons appeared in a vertical format (narrower than they were high).

Then, using the same format, but with more bite and fewer words, came the first wave of younger cartoonists, whom Hill identified as Paul Conrad, Ed Valtman, Hugh Haynie, Jules Fieffer, Bill Mauldin (who had retired and returned) and Bill Sanders. The second was mostly Australian Pat Oliphant, who introduced the horizontal format and a more detailed, more artistic style that did not necessarily rely on humor. The third wave was led by Jeff MacNelly, who also drew in the horizontal, more artistic style, but who used more humor. Hill noted that when MacNelly won his first Pulitzer Prize, in 1972 at the age of 24, Oliphant referred to the cartoonists who had adopted the horizontal style as "those bastards." "Before long the epithet 'clone' achieved a certain popularity," Hill said, and as the MacNelly style became popular, the epithet became "clone of a clone."

In spite of these disparaging labels, Hill concluded that Oliphant's and MacNelly's styles (which he called the phenomenon of "Oliphany" or "MacStyle") "energized committed, aware, talented, college-educated types in unprecedented numbers and propelled them into the profession" of editorial cartooning during the years between the Vietnam War and Watergate. This new generation, Hill said, was younger and more diverse and had "at least as much editorial freedom as they [knew] what to do with."

Cartoonists Today

Today's editorial page editors and cartoonists partly, but only partly, see eye to eye on what the role of the editorial cartoonist should be. Cartoonists, more than editors, tend to think of cartoonists as artists. They also tend to think that they should be given more editorial freedom than editors generally would like them to have.

A survey of cartoonists and editors found that both groups rated "critic" as the first role of the cartoonist.[22] "I believe the fundamental role of an editorial cartoonist is to kick fannies—to convey one's opinion forcefully, graphically and unapologetically," said one cartoonist. The editor's second most mentioned choice (third among cartoonists) was "opinion leader." One cartoonist who thought "opinion leader" was an inappropriate role wrote: "Editorial cartoons do not persuade. They affirm a reader's perhaps hazy stance on a subject by making concrete and graphic their positions. Readers say 'Aha! That's what I mean.'" Among cartoonists the second choice (fourth for editors) was "artist." "Too many editors are poor judges of what is good cartoon art," one cartoonist wrote. The same cartoonist also complained that editors "sometimes rewrite a cartoon caption, thus taking away some of the cartoon's punch." Cartoonists had somewhat more of an image of themselves as "entertainer" (third choice) than did editors (fourth). Both agreed that "reporter" and "teacher" ranked last among expectations for cartoonists.

Who's in Charge?

The survey found that editors and cartoonists have somewhat different ideas about who should have the final word on editorial cartoons.[23] The largest groups of editors and cartoonists (56 percent in both instances) agreed editors and cartoonists should confer in deciding on cartoons. The remainder had different ideas, with 43 percent of the cartoonists saying that they should make the decisions and 35 percent of editors saying that they should. The survey also showed that cartoonists and editors don't necessarily agree politically. Cartoonists tended to consider themselves as more liberal than their newspapers, but apparently most thought that cartoonists should conform to the editorial policies of their papers. "Editorial cartoons reflect opinions of the paper and the skill of the cartoonist, and, if not, the cartoons don't belong in the paper," one cartoonist wrote. "If he doesn't see things in the same way the publisher does, the cartoonist should look for another publisher," another cartoonist said.

Another pointed out, however, that "An Oliphant, for instance, should never be restricted," but to reach that status, a cartoonist had to be "good, well-versed and responsible enough to tell good slams from cheap shots."

The everyday working relationship between editors and cartoonists probably lies somewhere between these two extremes of freedom and subservience. A *Masthead* symposium titled "Getting Along With Your Cartoonist" found that these relationships are complex and vary greatly from newspaper to newspaper.[24]

When, as a beginning cartoonist, Jim Borgman started drawing for the *Cincinnati Enquirer* in the mid-1970s, he drew what was expected of him. At that time the *Enquirer* regarded its editorial cartoon as "an editorial in graphic form," Associate Editor Thomas Gephardt recalled; "[i]t reflected the paper's policy." Through a transformation that Gephardt attributed to artistic skill and professional integrity, Borgman attained a position similar to that of a writer of a signed column, reflecting his, and not necessarily the paper's, view. Gephardt noted that Borgman always brought one or more rough drafts, "mainly to see if I get the point," or to ask him to suggest A, B or C. "But he knows, and I know, that he is the ultimate determiner of what appears on our page over his name."[25]

Borgman said that it had become clear to him that he could do his best work only if he had that kind of freedom: "I couldn't sign my name to work that didn't represent my beliefs." Recognizing that the editorial page belongs to the publisher, he said he "wouldn't have blamed a soul if those were terms with which *The Enquirer* couldn't live." The result, he said, is "that the paper gets my very best ideas expressed with a clear ring to them, and none of that debilitating trench warfare that takes half the energies of other cartoonists and editors."[26] Not many cartoonists have this honey of a deal.

Perhaps a more typical relationship was described as existing at the *Lincoln* (Neb.) *Journal*. Editorial Page Editor Dick Herman reported that cartoonist Paul Fell usually offered three or four rough drafts early in the morning. "We confer. We parlay. Sometimes I bounce Satanic counterproposals at him," Herman said. "But increasingly, his own commentary stands. It becomes a finished product by noon or early afternoon."[27]

Fell reported that it was his idea, not Herman's, to submit the several drafts. "Dick goes through the roughs and selects the one he'd like finished for the next day's page. His picks are usually in line with my preferences, but if he passes on an idea I'm not particularly taken with, I can lobby for my choice with fair success." He "admit[ted], though, that a period last winter where I had two finished cartoons spiked in as many weeks did leave me a bit paranoid." He said that other cartoonists might find the situation too confining, but he didn't. "The *Journal* allows me to draw what I want and I allow it to print what it wants. So far, so good."[28]

Charles J. Dunsire, editorial page editor of the *Seattle Post-Intelligencer*, reported that he rarely rejected a cartoon drawn by David Horsey "because he is very much in harmony with our editorial philosophy which, when pressed hard, I define as pragmatically progressive, or vice versa." He noted that Horsey usually sat in on daily editorial-board discussions of issues and, as a result, "cartoons that complement and support editorials are frequent."[29]

Horsey said he saw the editor's job as hiring a cartoonist with "distinctive abilities and powerful, intelligent opinions," and as being "the cartoonist's defender and intellectual colleague." On the occasion when a cartoon is tossed back, the cartoonist "should, first, think about whether the editor has a good point, second, remember who owns the newspaper and, third, decide if this is the one worth fighting for." If a cartoonist chooses these battles carefully, Horsey said, "your editor may take you more seriously when you do stand up for a truly important opinion."[30]

SETTING POLICIES FOR CARTOONS

Editors face two policy questions when they select cartoons for the editorial page: Should cartoons, especially those at the top of the editorial, reflect only the editorial policies of the newspaper? In buying syndicated cartoons, should editors seek a broad or a narrow array of opinions?

To Support Editorials?

Some newspapers (the *Seattle Post-Intelligencer*, for example) have a policy that encourages editorial writers and cartoonists to focus on the same subject for a particular day's editorial page. Some studies have indicated that cartoons are more persuasive if they are published in conjunction with editorials expressing the same point of view. On other newspapers that have their own cartoonists, the cartoonists and the editorial writers may have their own agendas, and only by chance hit on the same subject. On papers that depend on syndicated cartoons, editors must rely on whatever comes in the mail that day. Saving unused—and even used—cartoons can provide a backlog from which to draw when a cartoon is needed to go with an editorial or column. Most cartoons, however, quickly become dated.

A Variety of Opinions?

A more serious question is whether editorials and cartoons on the same page should express the same editorial philosophy. One line of thought among editors is that any cartoon at the top of an editorial page should conform, or at least not conflict, with the policies of the paper. According to this reasoning, a cartoon at the top of the page will have the most impact if it reflects the paper's position. Some publishers and editors think that readers will be confused about the paper's policy if they see a conflict between editorials and the lead cartoon. Other publishers and editors consider cartoons as they do political columns, as intended to present a variety of opinions.

Most editors who subscribe to syndicated cartoons probably take a middle ground. First, they are not likely to subscribe to cartoons that are completely out of synch with their papers' policies. Second, unless editors subscribe to a large number of cartoons, they must take on a daily basis what they are sent by the syndicates. Contemporary layouts of editorial pages have encouraged editors to publish more cartoons. When cartoons are used to illustrate columns or articles, the reader may be less likely to ask, or care, whether they reflect the paper's policies.

In deciding which cartoons to subscribe to, the editor must decide whether to limit the selection to those that generally agree with the newspaper's policies, to choose from a wide political range, or to seek the best cartoonists. My perusal of editorial pages suggests that a minority of newspapers subscribes strictly to cartoons of one political stripe. Editors may place their favorite cartoonist or cartoonists in the lead spot on the page, but most pages allow for the display of other cartoons. Just as editors are likely to want to provide readers with a variety of columnists, they are likely to want a variety of cartoonists.

In an unscientific look at which cartoonists are most popular today, I examined the same stack of editorial pages that I used in tallying columnists. I found 47 (apparently syndicated) cartoonists appearing a total of 161 times, for an average of 3.4 times. (I counted only those cartoons that did not appear in the cartoonists' own newspapers.) Thirteen appeared four or more times. The leaders were: Doonesbury (24), Jeff MacNelly (17), Patrick Oliphant (9), Don Wright (8), Jim Borgman (8), Berry's World (8), Dunigan's People (7), Dick Wright (5), Henry Payne (5), Bill Day (4), Mike Luckovich (4), David Horsey (4) and Steve Benson (4). As far as I could tell, none of the 47 cartoonists was a woman or of a racial minority. The white male barrier apparently is even harder to break for cartoonists than columnists.

YOUR OWN CARTOONIST?

Surveys show that about 10 percent of daily newspapers have a regular editorial cartoon. Editors who can't afford a full-time cartoonist are sometimes tempted to turn to free-lance artists or artists on their own newspapers. Some successes have resulted. Jim Borgman had done only one cartoon a week for his college paper and wasn't particularly interested in public affairs when he went to work for the *Cincinnati Enquirer*.[31] Paul Fell was teaching art in a small college when he started sending an occasional cartoon to the *Lincoln Journal*.[32] (When Fell later was laid off by the *Journal*, he turned to photofax and radio. He faxed his daily cartoons to 200 local citizens, then went on the air to take calls from his subscribers.)[33]

Skilled local artists can bring life and controversy to a page, especially when commenting on local topics. But they must be more than artists or clever gag writers. When asked for ideas on how to get editorial cartoons from a good artist who didn't follow the news, A. Rosen of the *Albany* (N.Y.) *Knickerbocker News*, then president of the National Cartoonist Society, advised: "Give up on that person; you'll never make him or her an editorial cartoonist. Instead, seek out a young person who may not draw well but who is interested in public affairs. Hire that person."[34]

CONCLUSION

Rosen's point was that the message is more important than the medium. Editors should not run syndicated columnists and cartoonists only because it is the standard thing to do, because these features spruce up the page or because they bring wandering eyes to the page.

They should use these syndicated features—and their own local columnists and cartoonists—to present ideas to their readers. They should try to make their readers think—not just entertain them or present them with writers and artists who express opinions and ideas that readers already have. An editorial page should be a place where readers find some familiar faces and names, but also unfamiliar ways of looking at the local community, the state, the nation and the world.

QUESTIONS AND EXERCISES

1. Keep track of the syndicated columns in the newspapers of your area to determine whether they tend to run columnists that agree with their own editorial policies, that disagree or that express a variety of opinions.

2. Do these papers run a few columnists consistently or a variety of columnists infrequently? If they run a few, do these columns have something new and different to say each day? If they run a variety, do columns appear often enough to build regular followings among readers?

3. How would you judge the overall quality of the columnists published by the various newspapers you have studied? Do some of the papers seem to spend a lot of money on columnists and others only a little?

4. Do any of the newspapers label the columnists they carry, or attempt to describe the columnists' political positions? If so, are the labels accurate and appropriate?

5. Can you find letters to the editor concerning columns that have been distributed by the syndicates?

6. Which cartoonists seem to be most popular?

7. Do any of the newspapers have their own political cartoonists? Where do they appear on the editorial page? Does the local cartoon always agree with the editorial policies of the paper?

8. Ask editorial page editors in your area whether they have had trouble purchasing a column or cartoon because of territorial exclusivity.

9. While you have the editors' attention, ask them how often they receive letters from syndicates in response to columns, and whether they always publish those letters.

10. If you still have the editors' attention, ask about their policies on trimming columns.

Chapter 18

Innovations in Makeup
and Content

Too often page patterns never vary. While this provides the reader with a familiar page, it often is boring, especially if editorials are not noteworthy.
—RALPH J. TURNER, MARSHALL UNIVERSITY[1]

When editorial page editors sit down to plan the following day's editorial page, and the op-ed page if there is one, they must select editorials, letters, columns, cartoons and other materials. They must also decide on the layout that will best accommodate those features. Some editors, by their own choice or someone else's, are stuck with editorial pages that look the same every day and contain the same mix of features. But the trend among daily newspapers seems clearly to be in the direction of varying the editorial page, from one day to the next, in appearance and content. Varied makeup of a page can help attract readers; varied content can provide pleasant and rewarding surprises for readers. The purpose of this chapter is to trace efforts to transform the editorial page and the op-ed page from among the most stodgy-looking pages into spritely, stimulating pages.

THE "GRAY" TRADITION

For most of the 175 years of the American editorial page's history, editors attempted to gain distinction for their pages through gray respectability. When Professor Robert Bohle of Virginia Commonwealth University was asked to look back over 40 years of newspaper design in 1986, he found that editorial pages had changed the least.[2] The guru of newspaper typography, Edmund C. Arnold, agreed. "The page is still locked into a static page pattern," Arnold said. "It's more interesting than it was 40 years ago, but it's still static."[3]

Except for William Randolph Hearst, who jazzed up his editorial pages 50 years before nearly everyone else, most editors continued through World War II to make up their pages much as their 19th-century predecessors had. Although the editorial page began to emerge as a separate page, or as a portion of a page, during the first decades of the 19th century, the page was hard to distinguish from other pages. All the type, news and editorial, was set one column in width. News and editorials ran from the bottom of one column to the top of the next column and sometimes from the bottom of one page to the top of the next.

Aside from content, about the only distinguishing mark of an editorial, evident as early as 1835 in the *New York Sun*, was slightly larger type with lines spaced (leaded) a little farther apart. The only headlines were three or four words in italics of the same size and on the same line as the body type. (The *Sun* for Aug. 11, 1835, is displayed in Figure 1, page 273.) This page measured 11 by 15 inches, about the size of the modern-day tabloid, but the type was considerably smaller than the type used in most newspapers today. The size of the *Sun*'s type is hard to measure, but type on the editorial page of the *New York Times* of 1859 was probably 8 points high, compared to $6^{1}/_{2}$ points in the news columns. (Most news columns today are set in $9^{1}/_{2}$ or 10-point type, and editorials are set in 12-point or larger type.) It takes 72 points to make an inch, so you can see that reading 19th-century newspapers was a strain.

The pages of most of those papers were also wider and longer than today's pages. A typical editorial page in Horace Greeley's *New York Tribune* in 1871 had more than 6,000 words on it, while the 1992 page of the *Charlotte* (N.C.) *Observer* (Figure 13, page 287) contains only about 2,800 words of body type. A cartoon and other artwork account for a portion of the difference. Most of the difference results from larger headlines, more white space, larger type and a smaller page.

Editors were shocked when Hearst and Arthur Brisbane began to set editorials in larger type and wider columns, to run the editorials across several columns (perhaps the original horizontal makeup) and to introduce huge illustrations to the page. Hearst's clouded reputation may even have delayed the brightening of American editorial pages, since "respectable" editors did not want their pages to look like his. An example of the Hearst style, the *New York American* of Oct. 27, 1933 (Figure 2, page 274), uses a banner headline the width of the page for the lead editorial. Above the headline is a scriptural quotation. Columns are separated by white space and wavy lines, unlike most editorial pages of that day, where the columns traditionally were run close together with a thin rule between them. The *American* page is made even more dramatic by a large cartoon.

A textbook copyrighted in 1936 warned editorial page editors:

> In these days, when the average newspaper reader has less time for reading than formerly—when he does more glimpsing than reading, and confines most of that glimpsing to the headlines and leading news stories or entertaining features—he seems to care little or nothing for newspaper editorials. If his attention is to be captured and held by the editorial page, that page must be unusually attractive physically. It must be even more inviting looking than the general-news pages, and even easier to read.[4]

But editors generally ignored this advice. Traditional editorial page makeup in the 1940s, 1950s and 1960s was usually built around a vertically shaped 3-column cartoon at the top of the page. The newspaper's own editorials were

FIGURE 1 NEW YORK SUN

THE NEW YORK SUN.

TUESDAY MORNING, AUGUST 11, 1835.

Distress in Ireland.—Accounts from Ireland, received by the Sheffield, represent many districts of Ireland as suffering great distress from famine. In one parish, consisting of thirty-four families, in the county of Galway, only three possessed provisions for a week. In another, comprising 322 families, only 37 were provisioned till harvest; and, should they extend relief to their famishing neighbors, the whole stock would not hold out a week. "From an authentic source, we have discovered that upwards of 6,000 persons in the barony of Erris, county Mayo, alone, have, on an average, but five days' provision on hand; and in that number there are 106 persons who can command but half a hundred of potatoes amongst them, and 300 without any, whose sole dependence is on chance shell-fish and sea weed, a sample of which we have seen."

Foreigners, and Foreign Influence.—It cannot have escaped the notice of even the most casual observer of what is passing about him in the moral and political world, that within a very short time past, the patriotism of certain of the presses of this city has become most suddenly and most afflictingly sensitive to the appalling dangers which they affect to have discovered overshadowing the liberties and institutions of our republic, by reason of the great influx of emigrants from foreign countries, and the overwhelming influence they are pretended, by these newly fledged patriots, to possess over the judgments and opinions of our native citizens, and the character and destinies of our government. We should do violence to our own imperfect discretion, and to the judgment which our observation of the progress and fruits of the alleged monstrous evil has compelled us to make upon the subject, were we to pretend that we have not ample testimony on every side of us, that the laws of our country, in the premises, do not stand in need of revision and restriction, and that they have entailed upon the country a train of troubles and evils which she could happily dispense with.

But it is not our object now to speak particularly of those evils, or their prospective consequences. Our more immediate purpose, at this time, has been incited by the very recent, and it would seem, almost miraculous discovery, by the presses above referred to, of the stupendous mischiefs against which they are now incessantly harping, and the tremendous and all-devouring force with which this Saul-like conviction has come over them. And, what is most remarkable of all, those very presses which are amongst the loudest in stirring up the bile of native against adopted citizens, are themselves either entirely controlled, or essentially managed by persons coming within the range of their own animadversions, and their most eminent editors are foreigners!

The Courier & Enquirer, for instance, one of the fiercest journals in the city in denunciations of foreigners and foreign influence, numbers among its stipendiary caterers no less than *three* to whom America was a stranger, except by reputation, till within a very few years past; and one of those, the notorious Hoskins, has the supreme control of its course and contents, not excepting even a supervision of the mad ebullitions of Webb himself, who seldom knows, for weeks together, what his paper contains, till it arrives to him at some distant place.

The Evening Star, too, which, under the management of the "King of the Jews"—the dentAmerican Noah, pretends to a sensibility to foreign encroachment which seems at times half frantic, is indebted for full four-fifths of its editorial matter to the pens of a couple of English scribblers—one of whom sits in the shadow of his principal's huge frame, and bespatters alike the venom of his master's disappointment upon American freemen, and his own spite and petty malice upon his own fellow emigrants, much of which perchance, is engendered by the fact that most of them left home with less sullied reputations than he did himself.

Indeed, almost every large paper in the city which has taken sides with the two above named in this sudden crusade of extermination against foreigners, is in a greater or less degree under the management of men who owe to other hemispheres their birth, breeding, principles, and education; and it is the greatest scandal they can utter against American character, that there is in its composition so great a share of gullibility and sycophancy that *themselves* have obtained the control of so large a portion of the mightiest engine of the land, the public press, hnd wield it with impunity against our purest patriots and most sacred interests and institutions. More hereafter.

Coroner's office, No. 118 Wooster street.—On Saturday evening the Coroner was called on to view the body of Martha Ann Finn, aged 23, born in Massachusetts, who was living as a prostitute at the house of Sallome Blanchard, over Ridgeway's grocery at the corner of Little Water and Anthony streets. It appeared in evidence before the jury, that the deceased was on Friday night in a state of gross intoxication, and that between the hours of 11 and 12 that night, fell out of the second story window of the house upon the side-walk, by which fall her skull was so badly fractured that she died in consequence on Saturday afternoon about half past 5 o'clock. Verdict of the jury: death by falling from the second story window while in a state of intoxication and fracturing her scull.

March of the Drama.—"Who saw the sun to-day?" exclaimed a votary of the sock and buskin, as he passed Park Row a few days since. "Here it is, sir," replied a sprightly little vender of a well-known and interesting penny diurnal, at the same time advancing towards the stage-stricken gentleman. "Begone, fellow—thou troublest me," returned the hero; "do you not readily perceive that I am spouting the immortal ——" "Immortal d—l," reiterated the urchin; "you are spouting three-centers!"

Caution.—It has been the practice, for some time, for a great mass of well-grown boys, from 14 to 19 years of age, principally the sons and apprentices of respectable mechanics, to assemble, between 7 and 8 o'clock every night, and to continue, frequently, almost all night, at and about engine house No. 40, in Mulberry street, between Grand and Broome, and to insult and annoy the neighbors and persons passing by, as also to indulge in noise, and riotous and disorderly conduct. The other evening, they broke the windows of Mr. Bogardus, a gentleman residing hard by the place of their assemblage, and enveloped his hired servant girl in a cloud of flour they procured and threw over her. As these boys are known to the police officers, it will be well for them to desist, in future, from their riotous and disorderly assemblages and conduct, unless they wish to be honored with imprisonment, as it is the intention of the officers and some of the neighbors united, to arrest and punish them with the utmost severity, if they continue to indulge in their infamous practices any longer.

Troubles in Baltimore.—Passengers from Baltimore, who arrived here yesterday, state that they were witnesses to a serious riot which took place in that city on Saturday night and Sunday morning.—The mob attacked the houses of Reverdy Johnson and John Glenn, esquires, formerly directors of the bank of Maryland, and caused great destruction in the house of the latter. The citizens flew to arms, and *rumor* says eighteen lives were lost—a great many more were severely wounded;—among the latter Mr. Findlay, Mr. Cheeves, and Mr. Adams. As the passengers left early in the morning, they are not able to state minute particulars.

The Philadelphia papers of yesterday contain corresponding statements, brought by the Baltimore steamboats, and there is strong and lamentable probability that the above account is not exaggerated.

A Small Deluge.—The immense water tank of the gas works on Eighteenth street, which held 30,000 gallons, burst on Saturday last, when nearly full of water, and deluged the premises. At the time of the occurrence, one of the workmen was on a ladder looking into the tank, and another was standing near it on the floor; they were both swept to a corner of the yard as much as sixty feet distant. A horse and cart, the latter loaded with bricks, were lifted from the ground, and the cart turned bottom side up. Poor Dobbin looked perfectly astonished, and snorted loud his wonderment; but fortunately he was more scared than hurt.

A rumpus at Lynn, Mass.—Thompson, the abolitionist, held forth at Lynn on Thursday evening last. There was a large assembly (mostly females, as usual) in the house, and a still larger one, of men, without. There was a continual hallooing and noise, [illegible] and presently the ringing of the bell at the other end of the Common, created much confusion and affright for a few moments—some persons fainted. After the alarm had subsided in some degree, the cry of fire was again heard, but the audience kept their seats. The crowd and noise outside increasing, Mr. T. closed his harangue. The whole congregation then rose and sung the doxology, and the meeting was closed by prayer. The mob exasperated by the expressions of defiance used by Mr. T. in his discourse, closed round the steps and doors of the house, so as effectually to prevent the egress of the audience. Presently there was a rush at the doors by the mob, who threatened Mr. T., but by the prompt exertions of those within, the doors were closed. Rotten eggs were thrown and a missile came near hitting Mr. T.'s head.

The Wave at Boston.—A few days since we copied from the Boston Transcript a paragraph giving some account of a second race between Capt. Stevens's Wave, and the Sylph of Boston, in which the latter beat the former on rough water. Captain Forbes, of the Sylph has contradicted that assertion, in the Transcript, and states that his boat was fairly beaten both times. He however talks of further experiments.

Mortality among Children.—The deaths among the children in Baltimore have been very distressing. The weekly bills of mortality present more than three children to one adult.

Mrs. Hayes' Syrup.—The numerous instances which have within a few weeks past come to our knowledge, in which afflicting and apparently inveterate cases of dysentary and cholera morbus have been effectually relieved and ultimately cured, by the use of Mrs. Hayes' Syrup, induce us again unsolicitedly to call the attention of our readers to her advertisement on our last last page. A perfect conviction that we are but doing our duty to the community, in this age of quackery and humbug, alone induces us to press this invaluable preparation upon the attention of our readers and the public, to whom we recommend it as being, in our estimation and in the estimation of hundreds of others, who, like ourselves, have experienced its salutary effects, decidedly the most efficient and innocent remedy for complaints incident to the present season, of which we have any knowledge.

A Case of Conscience.—A mate of an East Indiaman, named Dennis Carter, aged 36 years, put an end to his life in London, on the first July, under the following extraordinary circumstances:—Since the return of the deceased from his last voyage, he addicted himself to drinking. Meeting with a Bible, he was struck with his bad conduct, and in it wrote the words as follows: "I promise from this day never to drink grog or blaspheme in the name of the Almighty.—Dennis Carter." In a very short time his passion for liquor overcame his resolution, and he got intoxicated; the next morning he was sadly grieved at having broken his vow, and the circumstances preying on his mind, in the evening he cut his throat.

The London Courier says the talked of marriage of the Queen of Portugal with the Duke de Nemours is now wholly given up on account of the known aversion of England to such a match.

The Office of the Sun has been removed to the corner of Nassau and Spruce streets, opposite the City Hall.

Trieste, June 18.—Shocking Calamity.—We have received the following melancholy intelligence from Malta:—An Austrian merchantman, which had taken in a cargo of cotton and gum at Alexandria, had already arrived off Malta, on its voyage to Leghorn, when three of the crew died of the plague, on which the remainder of the sailors were seized with such alarm that they unanimously declared that they would not continue their voyage in that ship. The captain, therefore, went into Malta, landed his crew, and took another that was not so fearful, with which he proceeded on his voyage to Leghorn. But they had not gone far when some men were seized with the plague and died. The captain adopted the usual precautions, such as fumigation, &c. and already entertained hopes of arresting the disorder, when fire broke out on board, and destroyed the ship and cargo; the captain escaped. It is not stated whether the whole or part of the crew had arrived at Malta.

From Jamaica.—By the arrival of the ship John W. Cater, Capt. Moncrieffe, we are put in possession of Kingston (Jam.) papers to the 17th July.

Previous to the sailing of the Comus, which arrived at Kingston, Jam., on the 15th, from the Caymanas, the island was perfectly quiet. Commander Hamilton brings the intelligence of the wreck of the American ship Atlantic, Balley, belonging to New York.—She went on shore on the east point of the Grand Cayman on the morning of the 23d June—the master, crew, passengers, and the whole of the ship's stores and cargo were saved, and sold with the hull by auction to the inhabitants of the island. She was out fifty-two days from Havre de Grace, bound to New Orleans. The master has freighted a small schooner belonging to the island to convey himself, crew and passengers to New Orleans.

A proclamation has been issued calling on the house of assembly to meet and proceed to business on the 4th of August. [Commercial.

Ship Launch and Dreadful Accident.—On Thursday an immense crowd assembled on the banks of the Dry Dock, Lincoln, to witness the launch of a schooner. Upwards of 100 persons were on board the vessel, which had scarcely entered the water when she turned completely over, and all the persons on board, among whom were several women and children were precipitated into the water and against the banks of the dock. By the praise-worthy exertions of the spectators most of the drowning persons were rescued in a few minutes, and numbers escaped by swimming. The bodies of two children, quite dead have been dragged on shore, and other persons are still missing. [Lincoln Gaz.

More Walloping.—Finnell, of the Lexington Observer, and Vanderslice, of the Georgetown Sentinel, had a battle in Georgetown, on Sunday week. Out of respect to the day, they left their pistols at home and fought with fists; Vanderslice, who was the assailant, is said to have come of second best. We are no friend of Mr. Justice Lynch, but he would certainly do a good thing for these ruffian editors of Kentucky, by rendering them *hors du combat* for a time.

Again.—Charles P. Green, the editor of the Boydstown, Va. Expositor, was attacked a few days since in Warrenton, N. C. by two individuals, named Bragg, one of whom he had assailed in his newspaper. A bloody combat ensued. Green was beaten to the ground with a heavy bludgeon, but rising, he drew a dirk, cut the upper lip of one of his assailants nearly off, stabbed him also in the arm, and buried the weapon in the throat of the other, who is expected to die. A Mr. Somerville, who interfered to keep the peace, was severely wounded by the explosion of a pistol. At the termination of the fight, Green invited two others of the Bragg family to come on, and take a hand, if they felt disposed! Our civilization goes backward like a crab.

Mutiny.—In September last, the crew of the Halcyon, whale ship from New London, mutinied while she was prosecuting her voyage in the Indian Ocean, in consequence of which the captain was obliged to put into Port Louis, in the Isle of France, where he delivered up the mutineers, twenty-one in number, to the custody of the American consul. There they remained in prison sixty three days, during which one of them died, and the American consul sent the remaining twenty to England in the British ship Bencoolen. The American consul at London sent home ten of them, whose names are annexed, by the Toronto which arrived here two or three days back, and on Saturday they were brought to the police office, and temporarily committed to bridewell until they can be handed over to the authorities of the United States. Their names are Isaac Wood, Jason Goodrich, David Kenny, Erastus P. Cartwright, Isaac Delon, Henry Joseph Dower, Patrick M'Keever, and Patrick Cosgrane. [Jour. of Com.

The body of a man, named William Moody, a carpenter by trade, was found dead in the street by the city watch on Wednesday night last. There were no marks of violence on it—and the verdict of the coroner's jury, called by Justice H. T. Cox, was, that the deceased came to his death by intemperance. The deceased was supposed to have been a citizen of Portland, Maine, from his having in his pocket book a letter from his wife, addressed to him from that place. [Mobile Register.

Flood and Loss of Life.—We learn by letter from Mercer, Pa. that on the night of the 12th ult. the rain fell to the depth of fourteen inches in the neighborhood of the country north and west of the Broken Straw Creek, in Warren county, producing an unprecedented rise in the smaller streams, and swelling the Alleghany to a degree heretofore unknown for the season of the year. A number of mill dams were swept away, and the bridges of Broken Straw from its mouth to Sprigh Creek, a distance of thirty or forty miles, were entirely destroyed. Above, the flood was equally destructive. The Mercer Luminary states that at Linzora an accident of a most distressing nature occurred. On Sugar run, in this township, a mill-dam was constructed, part of which ran some distance across the flat; and on this flat, below the dam, the owner had erected his dwelling-house. On the night of the storm he discovered that the water was rising very fast, and opened the flood gate: but finding this did not afford a sufficient outlet, he went a short distance to procure help. On returning, he found, to his utter consternation and distress, that his dam had broken, and swept away his house and its contents with his wife and two children! He arrived in time to hear their screams, but could afford them no relief. The bodies were found on the evening of the ensuing day, some distance below.
Philadelphia Inquirer.

The Cincinnati Whig, of the 30th, states six victims of cholera in Green township, Hamilton county, in that state.

Jackson Mahon, indicted in Baldwin, Superior Court, for the murder of Martin Smith on the 1th inst., has been found guilty.

[Reported for the Sun.]

Police Office—Yesterday.

MORNING RETURNS.

Lawrence Clark, for intemperance and rioting in the street, was fined $1 and costs and committed.

Archibald Madden, for rioting and assaulting Elizabeth Leacroft; was committed.

Mars Kneas, of No. 9 King street, a young insolent piece of flesh and blood, who because of his name being *Mars*, conceived himself, no doubt, to be the very God of war; was brought up charged with abusing his father Michael Kneas, and the family, he being an inmate of the same house. As his father was not present to prosecute the complaint, he deported himself with the utmost insolence and haughtiness before the magistrate, endeavored to throw the entire blame upon his father, and proved by his own language that if he was not put in prison for abusing his father, he deserved to be for his impudence in the office; but was necessarily discharged.

Susan Sarles, Anthony Dow, a boy from Long Island, and Michael Hogan out of the alms-house, were brought up for lodging in the watch-house habitually; and discharged, the latter to return to the alms house.

Mary Byrnes, a sick vagrant, was sent to the Penitentiary for 3 months.

Frederick Steneck, a German, in a state of inebriate exhilaration, got his ideas raised so high, that he attacked Charlotte Johnson, a well dressed colored woman, of 93 Christie street, in the street, in a most indecent and ruffianly manner; struck her twice in the face, and on her resisting, tore her silk dress almost off her, seized her bonnet and reduced it to a wreck, and was pursuing her with other acts of violence, when he was arrested and brought in. For all of which he was committed to prison.

William Brown was brought in by James Ward, keeper of the Washington Hotel, who found him up stairs in bed in one of the rooms, under suspicious circumstances, and who, when attempting to be ejected, made a stout resistance, for which he received a black eye, was lodged in the watch-house, and in the morning committed.

Hugh McClean and Owen McClean, committed for riotous and disorderly conduct.

Francis Sheridan came in himself, in a state of supposed derangement, but in the morning was deemed sane enough to be discharged.

Juvenile Thieves.—Yesterday, George Burns, who keeps an old iron and junk shop at No. 127 Washington street, discovered three boys named Phillip King, John King, and Peter Coen, enter his premises and steal about 40 pounds of scrap iron, which they placed in a cart, and were conveying away to sell, when he pursued, overtook and arrested one of them, the first named, whom he brought to the police office, the other two escaping. These boys appeared to be not more than from 12 to 13 years old, and Mr. Burns stated, that during the last week, he had had stolen from him, by these and other boys, above 200 pounds of scrap iron, part of which had been taken and sold at the junk shop of his neighbor, Michael Klone, in Carlisle street. The young thief was committed to prison for examination.

Thefts.—The cabin of the brig Cyrus, of Portland, Maine, lying at the foot of Duane street, was entered on Saturday night, and robbed of a frock coat, pantaloons, and three vests. A white merino shawl was stolen from No. 14 Spring street, and a dark green overcoat from No. 4 Forsyth street; and from No. 34 Cedar street, five thick and thin coats, and two pairs of pantaloons.

On Saturday, Mrs. Margaret Navarra, widow, of No. 40 Avenue D, was robbed of a small black silk purse, containing $103 in bills and silver, which was stolen out of a small basket in her possession, and carried away.

Robbing a Sweetheart.—Yesterday about 6 o'clock, a girl of the town named Sarah Rocket, of 57 Orange street, met a young Englishman, named John Johnsoe, in Chatham street, and charged him with robbing her of $7, and a purse worth 50 cents, for which he was committed.

Land Operations.—We learn that a company of gentlemen from this city have recently purchased the principal part of the land at Elizabethtown point, N. J., including the privileges of the ferry, and intend laying it out in streets and lots; and encouraging the speedy settlement of the place as a new city. For manufactures there are great facilities; there is an excellent back country, and by the way of Amboy vessels of large burthen can come up to the dock.—The Sommerville rail road, already chartered, will terminate at this point. [Commercial.

Shocking Affair.—On Friday afternoon a man by the name of Reuben Amadon, Jr. of Sandlake, was in the act of going with his team, on the lands of one of his neighbors, by the name of William Briggs, when he was forbidden by the latter. Some altercation ensued. Amadon threw down his whip, seized a club, and struck Briggs a violent blow on the head, which killed him instantly. Amadon is committed to jail to await his trial. [Troy Whig.

Gen. William Brady, and Henry Bridly, Esq., died of cholera at Murfreesborough on the 23d, after a few hours' illness.

Two criminals escaped form the gaol at Haddam, Middlesex co., by sawing off the grates of their windows. A reward of $60 has been offered for their apprehension.

Cholera.—There has been no case of cholera at Nashville since the 24th.

The Fire Fly locomotive performed a trip from Ballston to Schenectady, N. Y. and back again, last week, in one hour and three minutes. Distance *thirty-one miles!*

Tunnel under our Harbour.—A few days since we gave notice of the commencement of a new entrance to our harbour, we have now to notice that arrangements are being made for the construction of a tunnel under it at the foot of Main street. Such a work when completed will do credit to those engaged in it and be useful to our citizens, there being now a large tract of land in a business part of the city lying almost entirely useless on account of the difficulty of access to it. The work it is thought can be accomplished with a double track, for from $30,000 to $40,000, leaving 12 feet of water on the arch. [Buffalo Trans.

A volume, written and compiled by two of the crew of Captain Ross's late Arctic expedition, has appeared in London; it brings charges of an unparalleled nature against the captain, and gives all the credit to commander Ross; the captain is declared to have monopolized all the trade with the Esquimaux, selling them the presents sent by government, and retaining the proceeds for their own use, &c. They state that the Esquimaux make sledges of salmon sewed in skins, having cross pieces of deer's bones, and in time of scarcity eat their sledges! It is stated in Ross's Narrative that one sledge was seen made of ice.

Practical Knowledge.—A young girl was presented to James I. as an English prodigy, because she was deeply learned. The person who introduced her boasted of her proficiency in ancient languages. "I can assure your Majesty," said he, "that she can both speak and write Latin, Greek and Hebrew."—"These are rare attainments for a damsel," said James, "pray tell me, can she spin?"

New York Sun, August 11, 1835

FIGURE 2 NEW YORK AMERICAN

TRUTH JUSTICE — FRIDAY—New York American Editorial Page—OCTOBER 27, 1933 — PUBLIC SERVICE

Published Every Day in the Year at 220 South Street, New York City, by the New York American, Inc. President, William R. Hearst, Jr.; Secretary, Austin W. Clark.

Jesus Christ, who hath abolished death, and hath brought life and immortality to light through the gospel.—II Timothy, I, 10.

(The text for today is suggested by Rev. L. D. Woodmancy, D.D., pastor of Grace Methodist Episcopal Church, Manhattan. The next text will be suggested by Rev. Cornelius Greenway, pastor of All Souls Universalist Church, Brooklyn.)

Recognition of Soviet Russia Will Aid World Peace and International Justice

PRESIDENT ROOSEVELT'S effort "to end the present abnormal relations between the 125,000,000 people of the United States and the 160,000,000 people of Russia" ought to commend itself to the thoughtful citizens of both countries. It is a wise act on the President's part and advisable from every point of view.

"It is most regrettable," as Mr. Roosevelt truly says in his cordial message to Mr. Kalinin, president of the All Union Central Executive Committee at Moscow, **"that these great peoples, between whom a happy tradition of friendship existed for more than a century to their mutual advantage, should now be without a practical method of communicating directly with each other."**

To find such a method and to remove the difficulties that have given rise to this anomalous situation are the laudable purpose of the conversations soon to take place in the White House between the President and Mr. Litvinoff, the Russian Commissar for Foreign Affairs.

Mr. Roosevelt does not deny that these difficulties have been serious, but he shares with the American people the hope and the belief that they are no longer "insoluble."

If this free country could continue diplomatic relations with Russia under the government of the old regime, which was opposed to every principle and every ideal on which this nation was founded, we ought to be able to find a way of resuming relations with Russia under the present government, which, although not in accord with our own policies of government, is nevertheless not as diametrically opposed to our ideals as the former despotic autocracy that ruled Russia was.

Nor can we longer question the fact that this form of government is Russia's choice, because it has been firmly established there for fifteen years and there is every indication that it will continue to represent the conceptions of government held by the Russian people.

One of the reasons for this country's refusal to resume diplomatic relations with Russia was the present government's repudiation of pre-war and war-time debts.

This reason seems at present rather ridiculous, as we not only maintain diplomatic relations with France and England, but co-operate in close intimacy with these debt repudiators in regulating the affairs of Europe.

In fact, we have even appeared to be more friendly with these welching nations as they have not paid their just debts and obligations to this country.

• • •

RUSSIA from early days has been the friend of the United States, and a very important friend in past history, and there is every political reason why the two countries should resume this traditional relationship which has proved mutually advantageous in the past and may prove mutually essential in the future.

Japan has of late taken publicly on more than one occasion a very menacing attitude toward the United States.

Some of her less wise but leading statesmen and military commanders have made public utterances which appear to be most menacing in their character.

Furthermore, the moves of Japan, on the diplomatic chessboard, toward absorbing the mandated islands of the Pacific, and her activity in populating the American Territory of Hawaii, and her apparent intention ultimately to take over both the Hawaiian Islands and the Philippine Islands, are developments which would seem to indicate a temptation, if not a disposition, on the part of Japan to disrupt the friendly relations between Japan and this country and to disturb the peace of the Pacific.

Certainly the American people have no desire to see their relations with Japan other than friendly or to be called upon to defend against aggression the peace of the Pacific.

As a great nation and a peace-loving people we cherish nothing but sentiments of friendship for Japan just so long as Japan minds her own business and does not intrude upon American affairs.

But if it be the purpose of Japan, now or later, to dominate the Pacific, violate American rights or menace American territory, insular or continental, America should have an ally or at least a friend in Russia.

Therefore, for the peace of the world and for the establishment of justice among nations of good will, and for the sake of fair dealing and common sense in our international relations, it would seem to be mutually advantageous for the United States and Russia to renew that "happy tradition of friendship" which characterized their relations for more than a century.

We have said little about trade relations because these are, perhaps, the least important consideration. Nevertheless, friendly political relations promote trade relations, and trade relations, when on a basis of fairness, promote friendly political relations, so that the trade aspect of the situation should not be altogether ignored.

• • •

OF THE questions outstanding between Russia and the United States, the most serious is one that can best be removed "by frank, friendly conversations" of the sort that are soon to take place in the White House.

This is the revolutionary activity on American soil against the government and the institutions of the United States, which has been apparently fostered in the past by the government now in power at Moscow.

The American people will share with the President the hope that the Russian Commissar for Foreign Affairs, who is now on his way from Moscow to Washington, will begin his conversations by eliminating, once and for all, this obstacle to the dawn of a new and better day in the relations of these two great nations.

Jobs for Millions

WORK for millions of people would be made possible through a revival of building construction.

It has been estimated that some six million workers are affected by prosperity or lack of prosperity in the building industry. Eighty-five cents out of every building dollar is eventually paid to labor.

Building construction employs thousands of skilled mechanics and laborers. Hundreds of mills and factories employing more thousands of workers must be operated to meet the demand for clay products, woods, metals, cement, paints, textiles, glass, stone and equipment essential to the modern building.

Transportation by rail, air, ship and automobile must be employed to move raw and fabricated materials. Every new building requires new furniture, carpets and rugs, hardware and lighting fixtures. To convert raw material into use for buildings requires tools, machinery and power.

Every building erected means work for architects, engineers, draftsmen and workers in the fields of finance and real estate.

When the amount of direct and indirect employment affected by building is fully realized, the importance of the building industry as an agency for providing jobs for workers is apparent.

• • •

PUTTING men to work is a national and fundamental problem. To quickly accomplish this desirable end it is essential that we concentrate on stimulating those industries which affect the greatest number of workers.

The textile industry excepted, building is responsible for the employment of more persons than any other single industry. Building construction consumes a greater variety of materials produced throughout the United States than any other single industry. Building construction has a greater influence on the trend of general business than any other single industry. The building industry is a barometer that shows the upward and downward movement of all business. Private building construction is the major product of the industry, and therefore is of vast importance in our national economic welfare.

In addition to its Public Works Program the Federal Government should stimulate PRIVATE building construction. The Government should take such steps as may be necessary to remove the obstacles to building, unite forces, and stimulate construction.

To do so will permit employers of labor throughout the United States to put millions of workers back to work.

Keep the Air Clean!

Copyright, 1933, by N. Y. American, Inc.

LIBERTY is not LICENSE. Freedom of the press, which the Constitution guarantees, does not mean that irresponsible or malicious persons may defame others by misuse of the public prints.

Libel laws, which all good publications favor and obey, provide redress when such wrongs are committed.

We also have laws to punish slander (which is unwritten libel), but slander is often difficult or impossible to prove. There remains no written record of a conversation, which would be evidential.

Radio is like the press in its access to the public, and should be like the press in responsibility. But such is not the case, because radio is too often merely disseminated conversation. And slanders sometimes occur with little or no redress.

Out in progressive California they have a law to deal with radio slander. Of that law Governor Rolph has said:

"There should be no difference between a newspaper and a radio station as concerns libel. It makes no difference whether a person is slandered in a newspaper or over a radio; he should have recourse by law in either case."

The Governor proposes to amend the law so as to require every radio station in his State to keep a permanent written record of every radio speech.

Not only California but every other State should have such a law.

Your November Ballot

PERSONALITIES and bossism are not the only issues on which voters of this city are to pass judgment on November 7th.

The ballot will contain, besides its array of nominees for offices, six referenda, consisting of one State-wide proposition, four proposed amendments to the State Constitution, and a charter revision proposal affecting New York City only.

Little has been said of these referenda amid the wild polemics of an excited local campaign. Nonetheless, all are important.

The proposal that will appear on the ballot as "Proposition No. One" represents the public's inevitable duty to destitute families and other victims of the long depression.

It is a proposal to authorize the issuance of State emergency unemployment relief bonds to the sum total of $60,000,000.

Recommended by Governor Lehman and approved by the Republican leaders in the Legislature, there is no opposition to the measure. It MUST be approved. It should be approved UNANIMOUSLY.

Vote YES on Proposition No. One.

• • •

AMENDMENT NO. ONE to the State Constitution will permit a salutary reform in property condemnation procedure in New York City.

Under the amendment a special court will be established, presided over by competent and experienced judges; trials will be expedited, abuses eliminated and "a harmonious body of law and principles of valuation will be developed."

Vote YES on Amendment No. One.

Amendment No. Two proposes to extend "veterans' preferences" in civil service appointments and promotions, preferences now restricted to veterans who were both American citizens and residents of this State when they entered military service.

Without injustice to deserving veterans and their meritorious claims it is doubtful, indeed, if this proposal would do the public service any good and not do it considerable harm. "Veterans' preferences" are a form of class legislation. The civil service should be based upon ability always, and should not be used as an instrument for any kind of extraneous reward, whether political or otherwise.

In the interests of better civil service instead of worse, vote NO on Amendment No. Two.

Amendment No. Three is to permit a highway to be constructed over State lands in the Adirondacks. Inasmuch as the Association for the Protection of the Adirondacks approves, and the State Conservation Department does not oppose, the amendment may properly be carried.

Vote YES on Amendment No. Three.

Amendment No. Four will allow the State to turn over to New York City the West Fifty-third Street State Barge Canal Terminal.

The State has found the site unsuitable for a canal terminal, and the city needs the land for its West Side waterfront developments.

Vote YES on Amendment No. Four.

• • •

NOW we come to the New York City referendum—proposing a commission of seventeen persons to draft a new charter for the municipality.

The city unquestionably should abandon its present obsolete and detrimental "organic law." A modern and useful charter is a basic essential to good local government—but the pending proposal is no way in which to get a new charter.

In the first place, it is a Tammany scheme, railroaded politically through the Legislature, and as such it presupposes the perpetuation of Tammanyized city government. If the proposal is carried at the polls Mayor O'Brien—irrespective of the results of the mayoral election—will appoint this commission. If Mayor O'Brien is defeated he should not make "lame duck" appointments of such consequence. If he should be re-elected a better method of procuring charter reform should be followed.

In the second place, no special legislation is necessary to institute charter reform. Elected officials, UNDER EXISTING LAW, have the power as well as the obligation to do so.

The Tammany scheme should be defeated overwhelmingly.

VOTE NO ON THE CHARTER REVISION PROPOSAL.

A Library in Miniature

CRICKETS.

Questions.

1—To what order of insects do crickets belong?
2—Does a cricket leap or walk?
3—What is a katydid?
4—How does a cricket produce its chirp?
5—Why does a cricket chirp?
6—What is a Mormon cricket?
7—Are crickets destructive?

Answers.

1—Orthoptera, a zoological classification which includes cockroaches, mantids, grasshoppers, locusts and their allies.

2—It leaps. Orthoptera are divided into leaping and walking forms, the former being called "saltatory." The saltatory orthoptera include grasshoppers, both long and short horned, true locusts and crickets.

3—A variety of orthoptera closely allied to the grasshopper. Their name was given in reference to the curious strident sound which they emit and which was thought to resemble "Katy did."

4—By rubbing one forewing across the other. The under side of one wing is equipped with a rough saw-like covering which rasps across the projecting edge of the smooth wing.

5—Only the male chirps and his stridulating is a love song intended to attract the female. Succeeding in that, the cricket lowers his tone considerably. An entomologist has discovered that a cricket makes a full-tone slur downward from the fifth "D" above middle "C" in one-fiftieth of a second.

6—The so-called Mormon cricket is not a cricket at all, but a long-horned grasshopper. In 1848, when the Mormons were attempting to settle Great Salt Lake Valley, a horde of these "black crickets" threatened to devour all the crops, but were stopped by myriads of gulls, which appeared suddenly and devoured the insects. In 1913 a monument commemorating the incident was unveiled in Salt Lake City.

7—Yes. They eat clothes, rugs, furniture, meat, bread, and certain kinds do injury to vineyards and gardens.

Thwarting Romance by Law? -:- By Winifred Black

MOVIE FANS, don't go to Germany—not if you want to stay movie fans.

Germany is a nice, green, comfortable country, with plenty of rivers and deep, pleasant valleys and nightingales singing in the moonlight and good beer and the best sausages and pretzels in the world.

There is music in Germany, lots of it, all the time.

Everybody plays something.

The postman, if you please, plays the flute.

The grocer plays the drum and the man behind the counter at the drug store plays the piccolo.

And as for the fiddle—every other boy in high school is a violinist of sorts, and on Saturday nights and all day Sunday there is music in the air in Germany.

Good music, too, if you please. And the German moving pictures—have you seen them? They're very good, don't you think?

But Mr. Hitler is mad at the screen stars. He doesn't want any stars in Germany unless their names begin with H and end with r, it is said.

So he's made a brand new law about picture stars.

• • •

THEY aren't stars any more—not in Germany. They're just numbers.

Their names cannot be printed in big type and the name of the play must come first.

Big salaries for stars are out—in Germany. And woe be to anyone who tries to say that one pretty fraulein or one handsome herr is prettier or handsomer than anyone else.

Down with the movie fans—so says Mr. Hitler.

Now, isn't that just too silly of him?

What would you give for a girl who had never fallen in love with an actor, either on the screen or on the stage?

Not a snap of my finger, for my part.

• • •

KYRLE BELLEW, the handsome Englishman, said something to me once about matinee idols. He was a matinee idol himself, mind you.

Why, the girls used to lie in wait for him at the stage door and fairly tear him to pieces when he came out into the street after an afternoon of "The Romance of a Poor Young Man."

"They aren't crazy about me," said Kyrle Bellew. "They're crazy about romance, that's all.

"I'm always a hero in my plays. I'm poor but honest. I'm young but brave. I am humble but brilliant. I offer my life in defense of the lady of my choice. I defy tyrants. In short, I unfasten the wings of romance—they don't even know me, myself, but, ah! the hero of the play, that's different!

"If I had a daughter she'd bore me to death if she didn't have romance enough in her soul to fall in love with a hero once or twice.

"A faraway hero, of course—but a hero nevertheless."

• • •

NOW, Mr. Hitler, are you going to try to crush romance out of the German heart? You'll have to do a good deal of trying, I'm afraid.

The German fraulein hasn't those blue eyes for nothing, let me tell you.

New York American, October 27, 1933

assigned to one or two columns to the left of the cartoon. Columns and letters filled the remainder of the page. The *Washington Post* of Jan. 20, 1953 (Figure 3, page 276) reflected that makeup arrangement, although the use of white space between the columns represented a step away from tradition. Bohle found at the time of his 40-year look that many newspapers still were using this design.

BOLDER, MORE FLEXIBLE

Partly spurred by editorial page critique sessions at the annual meetings of the National Conference of Editorial Writers and by the needling of designers such as Arnold, editors in the 1960s and 1970s began experimenting with more flexible layouts. Wider columns and "cold type"—which could be pasted anywhere and at any angle on a page—opened new possibilities that not even the most skilled printer could have managed with unwieldy hunks of metal type. Contributing to the flexibility was the introduction of a few cartoons that were wider than they were high. This combination led to pages that, in their boldest form, looked like the Feb. 15, 1979, editorial page of the Boise *Idaho Statesman* (Figure 4, page 277). One problem with this page was that the long editorial was set in a very wide measure (26 picas, or about 4½ inches). Also, the lines contain more than 60 characters. A rule of thumb suggests that, for optimum newspaper reading, lines should contain the equivalent of about one and a half lower-case alphabets, or about 39 characters.[5]

Instead of always displaying the cartoon in the most prominent position, editors began experimenting with cartoons to illustrate written material. A page from the Aug. 7, 1979, *Houston Post* (Figure 5, page 278) provides an example of an article wrapped around a LePelley cartoon. Notice, too, how the editorials are indented from the left side of the page. A large amount of white space separates the articles and sets off the headlines. The page also illustrates the preference of some editors to slide the newspaper's masthead (the box that lists the ownership and the executives of the newspaper) to a lower corner of the page. Why, some editors wondered, should the most important spot on the page, the upper left corner, carry the same information every day? The bold labeling of the page as "Commentary" represents another trend among editors: an effort to help readers distinguish between news and opinion.

The next question editors asked themselves was why each editorial should be set in only the first column or in the first two columns—the traditional position. If the page is to be horizontal, why not spread the editorials into three or more columns? An example of this type of makeup is provided by the April 25, 1978, page of the *Louisville Times* (Figure 6, page 279). The editorial titled "Welfare 'Crackdown' Must Not Be Distorted" is dog-legged around the masthead, and the lead editorial covers four columns. Another innovation on this page is the specific labeling of each editorial as opinion. The next step toward flexibility was to display editorials from time to time in less prominent parts of the page, making them compete with other available material such as letters and columns. An example is the March 15, 1979, page of the *Norfolk* (Va.) *Ledger-Star* (Figure 7, page 280), which introduced this flexibility when it started the

FIGURE 3   WASHINGTON POST

The Washington Post

EUGENE MEYER, Chairman of the Board   PHILIP L. GRAHAM, President and Publisher
HERBERT ELLISTON .... Editor   CHARLES O. BOTHER .... Secretary   DONALD M. BERNARD, Advertising Director
J. R. WIGGINS ...... Managing Editor   JOHN W. SWEETERMAN, Business Manager   JOHN S. HAYES, President WTOP Radio-TV
AN INDEPENDENT NEWSPAPER   TUESDAY, JANUARY 20, 1953   PAGE 14

Inauguration Day

This is a great day for the American system of government, and a thrilling day for all good citizens of this Republic. Dwight D. Eisenhower will take the oath of office as President of the United States. That means a great change at the White House, not only in occupants, but also in parties. And it is all being done with order and consideration and cooperation, thanks in both the retiring and the incoming Presidents. The transition is something to create pride and awe in the breast of every American.

General Eisenhower will take over the Presidency in the plenitude of the country's power and prosperity. The office is a branch of the American trinity of branches of government. Let us give thanks to our forefathers for the political edifice they outlined. It is refreshing on this day of days to hark back to the Federalist to read what the founding fathers had in mind. Madison, Hamilton and Jay were seeking in the Federalist to secure ratification of the Constitution. Their basic assumption was that the very definition of tyranny consists of accumulating all powers in the same hands. Whether the hands were hereditary, self-appointed or elected—that made no difference. Thus the founding fathers had already set up a government in three separate and coequal departments in an effort to prevent the rise of tyranny.

The separation of powers upon which our Government rests makes it a tremendously difficult system to operate, because unless there is a considerable relation among the three, the branches could revolve in their respective orbits, and there would be chaos. A balance has somehow to be struck and maintained and be subject, as Dr. Johnson said about friendship, to constant repair in order to insure the functioning of government.

This constant and continuing need for balance calls for a qualification on the part of a successful President, second only to leadership. The qualification is diplomacy. Leadership is obvious enough as a prerequisite, but diplomacy is not often thought about. A President must do his part in getting along with his partners. Harmony between the White House and the judiciary was difficult till there had been general acceptance of a famous dictum of John Marshall, the country's third Chief Justice. "It is emphatically the province and duty of the judicial department," said the great Marshall, "to say what the law is," and when that statement had become axiomatic, the foundation of our constitutional liberties was well and truly laid.

The prime problem of American government as a day-to-day proposition lies in the relation between the President and Congress. Here there is need for a very high degree of diplomacy—of that kind of diplomacy which recognizes the rights under the organic law of both coordinates, yet seeks consciously to respect what in another connection a great jurist called "the law of the unenforceable." The jurist was talking about the behavior of people in a free society—how 95 percent of their actions are governed not by law but by a feeling of right conduct. The same thought could be applied to relations between a President and Congress under the American system. Ideally, one owes to the other a respect for its individuality and authority—that is to say, power at the other's expense is "an encroaching spirit" that gentlemen must resist. "It is one thing," as Alexander Hamilton said, "to be subordinate to the laws and another to be dependent on the legislative body."

It is said, by way of example, that the men on the Hill feel they are professionals in the business of government and must guide the "amateur in the White House." This kind of arrogance is intolerable to the spirit of the Constitution. The new President could respond to any such outcropping with weapons that would be more than salutary, at least in his initial period—the weapons of his vast public support and of his patronage. It is plain he harbors no idea of using a big stick. He is said to be very conscious of his own responsibilities in creating a smooth-working liaison with Congress. The evidence is the report of his purpose to set up a bipartisan council with which to take counsel on foreign affairs. This will show the President's good intent, and the way that the partnership is worked out will depend upon the conduct of the men involved.

If the new President shows this will to cooperate, then he can legitimately expect Congress to respect his constitutional right to the initiative. For the world of free men will depend upon the wise and swift exercise of the initiative in the conduct of American foreign relations. It was not always so. The framers of the Constitution did not envisage a rank for America of high mightiness. They based the organic law upon the feeling that America would be neutralist in a world of big powers. Even as late as the first edition of The American Commonwealth Bryce could write that "four fifths of the President's work is the same in kind as that which devolves on the manager of a railway." Now "the President's job is Atlas-like."

With power has come responsibility, and the need to be ready for sure and swift action. Congress must realize that the President's initiative must never be allowed to become palsied; that he must show that "vigor of government" within the "perfect security of freedom" which George Washington said was required of the management of the common interests of Americans. May the new President be aided by Almighty Providence in the discharge of the obligations which he will assume today!

Loyalty And Liberty

The country looks with hope to the great American who assumes the Presidency today for a revitalization of its traditional civil liberties. These liberties have sometimes been curtailed—needlessly curtailed—in the name of national security. They are, of course, a vital source of security. They constitute the real roots of American loyalty.

In the championship of civil liberties which he has promised, President Eisenhower can make no better beginning than to establish a Commission on Internal Security and Individual Rights—made up of distinguished citizens, as was the Nimitz Commission which President Truman vainly tried to set in motion—to advise the country and himself as to the effectiveness of its security precautions and the maintenance of its essential freedoms.

Security and freedom are not in conflict, they are, on the contrary, complementary. The American public needs the reassurance which such a commission could afford, that disloyalty is being checked without enfeebling democracy. The President needs the counsel of such a commission in maintaining a wise balance between national needs and individual rights.

Conserving Resources

It was characteristic of President Truman to make the conservation and development of natural resources as the subject of his final message to Congress. The subject is one respecting which he takes tremendous pride—and justly—in the record of his Administration. It is a subject with a long and highly creditable record of bipartisanship—a fitting subject for the final recommendations of a President about to turn over the reins of authority to his successor. And, finally, these natural resources, as the President observed, are a foundation upon which rest our national security, our ability to maintain a democratic society, and our leadership in the free world.

The conservation movement got its start under President Theodore Roosevelt in 1902 with the enactment of the reclamation laws. These laws have had the support of every President since then, regardless of party, resource development in a variety of forms was given great impetus during the 20 years of the F. D. Roosevelt and Truman Administrations, and, in particular, the accomplishments since 1945 rank Mr. Truman indeed how much this kind of conservation and development can mean in terms of living standards and general welfare. Some 1,200 new soil conservation districts have been formed during the past eight years, about 2,700,000 irrigated acres have been added to the Nation's farm lands; three million acres have been given flood protection; electricity has been brought to one and one-half million farms that didn't have it prior to 1945, making nearly 4 out of 10 American farms electrified.

This is a proud legacy to leave to one's successor. Mr. Truman leaves it with a dual admonition. "We have learned," he says, "that the mark of a well-managed land lies in the care a Nation gives to its rivers. The Tennessee Valley Authority stands as perhaps the greatest domestic achievement of the last two decades a symbol of what can be done through Federal-State cooperation, imaginative planning and decentralized, local administration. The rest of his warning to the Eisenhower Administration is that we must make sure that we safeguard the use of these resources for the benefit of all the people. Where the public moneys are invested, the resulting gains must accrue to the public, and not be diverted to the undue benefit of any private group."

Each generation holds the natural resources of the Nation in trust for its posterity. Mr. Truman can relinquish his trusteeship with a clear conscience. He spoke, in this final message to Congress, in behalf of the most vital interests of the American people.

Symbol Of Tradition

For all the revolutionary spirit which General Eisenhower displayed in spurning a top hat and buying a new homburg for his Inauguration, some devotees of reaction or tradition or just high revelry —whatever you like—have defied the new President and appeared, at least on the pre-Inaugural scene, in tall silk hats. Perhaps they are Democrats! Whoever they are, their defiance of the example of the man of the day is pardonable, and, indeed, even deserves our salute. After all, the high hat in different colors is the badge for high occasions, and what remains in the secular calendar of events could be higher than Inauguration? Even if you simply want something to do something with, after your rejoicing over the day's event (such as kicking your hat into the Potomac), what better object than a topper?

Some of the local stores report they have sold out of homburgs since the general announced his decision on their behalf, while the supply of toppers, in view of Ike's decision, is far from exhausted. But other occasions will come around. And the new President may then relent, for it is our surmise that his ukase was a sudden outburst of independence after acquiescence in ritual over many days, and he simply decided that for a change he would be himself.

The Law And Wilson

We reprint below for the benefit of our readers the statute which Senators have raised in connection with the nomination of Charles E. Wilson to be Secretary of Defense.

Whoever, being an officer, agent or member of, or directly or indirectly interested in the pecuniary profits or contracts of any corporation, joint-stock company, or association, or of any firm or partnership, or other business entity, is employed or acts as an officer or agent of the United States for the transaction of business with such business entity, shall be fined not more than $2000 or imprisoned not more than two years, or both.

This law was enacted in 1948.

Thanks To Neely

As Senator Case takes over the chairmanship of the Senate District Committee, it is important not to overlook the good work done by the retiring Democratic chairman, Senator Neely. The West Virginia legislator has exercised a conscientious stewardship over District affairs for the last two years. His insistence on punctual meetings of the District Committee was an index to his businesslike approach in getting things done. Particularly in his credit was the manner in which, with Senator Case's cooperation, he fought to see the local crime investigation through, against considerable odds. He also was a stalwart champion of home rule for Washington. In extending what we feel confident is the thanks of many Washingtonians, we are glad that Senator Neely intends to continue his progressive interest in District affairs in the new Congress.

Letters To The Editor

Acheson's Record

[text illegible]

— JULIAN F. WILLIAMS
Mount Rainier, Md.

Overflow Bait

[text illegible]

Arlington Roses

[text illegible]

— JAMES ROSE, JR.
Washington

Communists In Schools

[text illegible]

Missing Face Boxes

[text illegible]

"End Of Mob Murder"

[text illegible]

Eisenhower Maps Middle Road Course

By Marquis Childs

AFTER THE LONG drought, the Republican rejoicing is full of a fine fervor. But when the bunting comes down and the paraders go home, this Capital will see the beginning of one of the most interesting experiments in government in many, many years.

The outlines of that experiment are already evident. In essence, it is an effort to apply the management techniques of big industry to big government.

The wisecrack about the Eisenhower Cabinet consisting of eight millionaires and a plumber or, more accurately, a steamfitter, misses the real point. These businessmen now in Government have been handsomely rewarded for their ability. But money reward has been secondary to the fact of the power and the skills they have wielded as the managers of industry financed by thousands of investors large and small.

They will now be the managers of the far larger enterprises of Government. Often the past the complaint about the Government administrators has been that they never met a payroll. The men in the Eisenhower Administration have been responsible for meeting some very large payrolls.

But, with two or three exceptions, they have not met the voters at the polling booth. Republicans in Congress, who feel that through the years they put the political capital into this enterprise, look with skepticism on the experiment of managerial government. The Senate hitch over Charles E. Wilson's confirmation as Defense Secretary because of his General Motors stock indicates the relationship between the managers and the politicians may be difficult.

The new Administration is not, however, without its political managers and very skillful ones, indeed. They come out of the hard-boiled organization built up in New York State by Gov. Thomas E. Dewey. They also have roots in California, where Gov. Earl Warren has demonstrated how to build up a political following transcending the two-party system as we have known it in the past 20 years. Significantly, in this connection, it is in California and New York that the most populous States in the country, that the decay of the Democratic Party is most conspicuous.

THE AIM IS TO go down the middle of the road with a party having few resemblances to the old Republican Party. Thus a minimum of 10 percent, and perhaps nearer to 15 or 20 percent, of the following that has kept the Democrats in power—farmers, labor, minorities—will be permanently won over. This is the pattern evident behind many of the moves made since November 4, and it promises to become increasingly apparent as the new Administration takes over.

One of the able and successful members of the political team which will work toward the long-term goal is Senator Irving Ives of New York. Ives won reelection last fall by the huge plurality of 1,332,198. He carried New York City, which Eisenhower lost, by a plurality of 2743. In a speech in New York last week, Ives said, in effect, that the Republican Congress was Republican because of the personal popularity of General Eisenhower. The people, he said, were still progressive and there could be "no turning back of the clock of progress." Then Ives spoke of what is the biggest hazard faced by the new Administration:

"With a spirit of mutual helpfulness and cooperation the new Administration can and will succeed. Without it, failure is certain and the Republican Party is doomed to defeat in 1956."

A MEMBER OF the Senate Labor Committee, Ives is hoping to head a subcommittee that will study discrimination in industry and business. The political implications of this are obvious. The Republican majority is expected to agree on a compromise civil rights bill providing for a commission to educate and persuade employers that discrimination is not only unfair, but that it does not pay. This would be labeled as a first step and it would be taken by men like Ives as a trial of what can be achieved by a law without power of Federal punishment.

Thus the pattern will be developed if the able political managers working for the Eisenhower Administration can bring it off. They will have many resources, particularly in the honeymoon phase, and they will be working with some shrewd operators.

One of these is Gen. Lucius D. Clay, now retired, an old Eisenhower comrade with a unique influence although he will hold no office. Clay serves as a kind of bridge between the business community and Eisenhower's familiar military associations. A man of outstanding ability, as he demonstrated in his military career which concluded with his appointment as occupying chief in Germany. Clay is now chairman of the board and chief executive officer of the Continental Can Co. He is also on the board of the General Motors Corp, which gives him a link with top Eisenhower Cabinet officers.

The Washington Post

Registered in U. S. Patent Office
Published every day in the year by
The Washington Post Company

The Associated Press is entitled exclusively for the republication of all news dispatches credited to it or not otherwise credited to this paper and also the local news of spontaneous origin published herein. Rights of republication of all other matter herein are also reserved.

1515 L Street N.W. Washington 5, D.C.
Telephone National 6-4200

Offices of National Advertising Representatives
New York .... 30 East 42nd St., Room 822
Chicago .... 333 North Michigan Avenue
Detroit .... 1435 Guardian Building
Atlanta .... 30 Marietta St.
Philadelphia .... 1406 Batts Penn Square
Los Angeles .... 411 W. Fifth St.
San Francisco .... Russ Building
Miami Beach, Fla.—The Nat Whitzel Co.
London, England—Joshua B. Powers, Ltd.

CARRIER DELIVERY—WASHINGTON AREA
Daily and Sunday ...... Daily Only   Daily Only
One week $ .45   One week $ .35   One week $ .15
Daily and Sunday ....   Daily Only
Daily and Sunday ....   Daily Only
BY MAIL—PAYABLE IN ADVANCE
Daily and Sunday   Sunday Only   Daily Only

Entered as second-class matter at the
post office, Washington, D.C.

FIGURE 4 IDAHO STATESMAN

STATESMAN

Editorials

Robert B. Miller Jr., Publisher
Rod Sandeen, Managing Editor
Jim Dean, Asst. Managing Editor — Gary F. Sherlock, Advertising Director
Jim Boyd, Editor of Editorial Page — Russell W. Ford, Circulation Manager

The comments below represent the opinions of The Idaho Statesman. Columns, commentary, cartoons and letters appearing elsewhere on this page represent the opinions of the authors.

PAGE 6A — Thursday, February 15, 1979

"A Part of Life in Idaho"

Oil!

Oil! A few years ago you drove to the auto discount store, bought a can of it for 39 cents and poured it in your engine without a second thought. Today it threatens our economy, our security, our lifestyle.

The chaos in Iran serves to give us pause. A government crumbles half a world away, in a country peopled by individuals whose ways we don't understand and whose names we can't pronounce, and we tremble at the prospect of losing the vital link. Admit it. We as a nation are not driven by concern for the well-being of the people of Iran. The drama of recent happenings in that country does, of course, merit our interest. The overriding question, though, is what will happen to Iran's oil.

The Iranian hiatus illuminates the extent of our dependence. We've lost less than 3 percent, and here we are talking of closing service stations on Sunday, waiting lines at the pumps, dollar-a-gallon gasoline, even rationing. The latter is a remote possibility, but if 3 percent is enough to raise the specter of gas-rationing, what fears would stem from a cut of 6 percent? 12 percent?

It would be nice to think we could count on a steady supply of Mideast oil from other exporters. At the moment there appears to be no cause to fear further disruptions. We would be hugely surprised if, say, Saudi Arabia cut its oil shipments. But we were surprised when the Shah of Iran was overthrown. We were surprised again when the Iranian army withdrew its support of the Bakhtiar government. It is foolish to count on anything in the Mideast, because anything can happen there.

Iran underscores the perilousness of relying on other countries for a vital, not to mention dwindling, resource. Washington currently is agog with the lure of Mexican oil, and indeed there appears to be reason for hope. But Mexico's oil, as President Jose Lopez Portillo cautions, should not be viewed as a panacea for America's energy woes.

Mexico, in addition to oil, has a troubled economy, a population explosion, grinding poverty and epidemic unemployment, any one of which could threaten exports. And Mexicans aren't likely to forget overnight the decades of indifference displayed by their rich neighbor to the north. If we look to Mexico for salvation, we're apt to be looking for a good long time.

Mexico, and the Mideast as well, should be viewed only as temporary allies, and tenuous ones at that. If we are to survive and prosper in the long term, we must abandon illusions of salvation at the hands of foreign oil.

We realize the magnitude of what we are saying. A country nurtured and grown to maturity on oil cannot be weaned overnight. But oil, in addition to running the country, has fueled inflation, thrown our trade balance out of kilter, polluted our air and threatened our basic well-being. It is time to begin to look away from oil, foreign and otherwise. It is time to look to ourselves.

We're fond of calling America the most advanced nation on earth, yet we are almost wholly dependent on countries where people ride camels to work and justice amounts to cutting off hands with swords. We do not worship the god of technology, but we cannot believe that it is beyond this nation to become energy independent. If there is salvation, it is in the form of alternative energy sources, and those who scoff should take a closer look.

Solar energy is not some distant, unattainable goal. It is here. People are heating their homes with it — in this city and scores of others. If solar can work, and it does, it can be improved. And if we can heat our homes with the sun's energy, who is to say we can't use it to get from one place to another? Who is to say we can't solve the problems of nuclear power and develop other forms of alternative energy?

The challenges are great, but if this really is the most advanced nation in the world, it's time we started trying to prove it where it counts.

God help the queen

Queen Elizabeth, while visiting the Mideast, is being forced to abstain from wine with meals, wear dresses that cover her from wrist to ankles, and hide her face with scarves. In countries where women are considered insignificant, the queen is being treated as "an honorary man." When you stop and think about it, that's pretty big news. It takes something like this — the queen of England groveling — to make us realize how much the world has changed lately.

"I KNOW NOT WHAT COURSE OTHERS MAY TAKE...."

Legislature needs ethics code

John Corlett

The Lenaghen confirmation squabble brought out the long overdue need for a legislative code of ethics or a conflict-of-interest law. On this subject this column has been a voice crying in the wilderness for many years.

It may be many more years before the people elect a legislature attuned to the moral need for a code of ethics and a conflict-of-interest law, the latter to apply to public officials at all levels of government. The current Legislature is not about to upset a system that is predicated more on political and personal considerations than on the public welfare. This is a legislature that could seriously consider eliminating some of the disclosure provisions of the Sunshine Law, enacted by initiative.

The national Congress has made considerable strides in the disclosure field of elections, lobbying, and the personal financial arrangements and records of its members. The Senate and the House have their own ethics committees, albeit they have moved gingerly in coming down hard on violators, both of the law and of congressional ethics. But a start has been made.

The Sunshine Law of 1974 authorized the disclosure of election financing and activities and expenditures by lobbyists. The law has stood the test of need, although some of the more conservative Republican legislators still oppose it.

As long as Idaho remains a relatively small state and elects purely citizen, as opposed to professional, legislators, it hardly seems necessary for the Legislature to call for financial reports of its members.

As far as the Legislature is concerned, a code of ethics could include a conflict-of-interest provision, and that is vitally needed. The only effort to establish a code of ethics was made about 15 years ago, but it got short shrift, and there has been no effort since. Former Attorney General Tony Park urged the 1974 Legislature to pass a conflict-of-interest law, but it got nowhere.

A conflict of interest arises when a legislator's occupation or financial earnings could influence his vote on a particular law or issue. In other words it could be assumed he was voting for his own private gain, or for benefit of a firm with which he is employed or has a financial arrangement.

In the Lenaghan affair, Senate Majority Leader James Risch was said to have a conflict of interest in his opposition to PUC President Robert Lenaghan because his law firm had collected $17,000 in retainer fees from Idaho Power Company, which has rate increase filings before the Public Utilities Commission.

Under a code of ethics Risch would have been required to disclose his conflict of interest. With the public being given notice of that disclosure, Risch could vote or ask to be excused from voting, whatever his determination. The important point is that a disclosure was made from which the public could decide on the efficacy of any vote.

Without question a poll taken today would show the Legislature at a very low spot on the popularity scale for two reasons. One, it took no action in halting or reducing a 40 percent pay raise, and, two, its members are eating quite high on the hog at dinners at which lobbyists play host, about $20,000 worth in January alone. A friend of mine, disgruntled by the disclosure of the freebies going to the Legislature, said that if the Legislators "are so bad off maybe we better give them food stamps and low-cost housing."

The method used by the Legislature in getting its pay raise was unconscionable. There is a big question about freebies these days. A code of ethics ought to prohibit them, although the disclosure of expenditures by lobbyists at least informs the public about which legislators are accepting the freebies.

In another day, the public probably would have accepted the 40 percent pay raise with a measure of equanimity. But with President Carter calling for others to limit a pay increase to 7 percent, the Legislature could have followed suit.

The Legislature's credibility vanishes now that it is proposing only a 7 percent pay increase for state employees, counting the 5 percent incremental raise authorized by the last Legislature.

Only the Legislature creates the reasons for a code of ethics to inform and protect the public it represents.

(John Corlett is a retired Statesman political editor.)

Letters to the Editor

Government: no friend to NNC

Editor, The Statesman:

In 1941 I completed four years of study at NNC. Employed by the school, I earned my way. I helped build Morrison Hall. For two years I was night police on the campus. Consequently, I am very much interested in what become of Cady as well as the president she attacked in her editorial.

It was not academic leadership that helped me to know what was going on and solve my problems. I believe a man must be honest and blameless before God, create his own atmosphere and live in it. One's spiritual and academic orientation develops from within-out rather than without-in.

NNC was born to give young people Christian education. When it stops doing just that, it has ceased from doing that for which it was born. If the spiritual students of the 1930s were to walk down the road and meet the spiritual students of 1970s, would they know each other? If not, why not?

There is much to be learned from freedom of speech. Everyone will learn that he must walk on criticism or sink. It is futile to sail on praise alone. A person must learn to get power from criticism as well as praise.

Freedom of speech or freedom of the press is not the paramount bug gnawing at NNC's vine. It is the fact that they have accepted government money to run the school. The government is no friend to holiness.

A man was authorized to take a pig to market. On his way he stopped for a cup of coffee. Hanging the sacked pig on a peg with his hat, he ordered his hot coffee. An old maid came by with a pup. She pulled out the pig and placed the pup in the sack.

None the wiser, the man continued his journey. At the market he offers his pig for sale, but to his amazement, out popped a pup. With no sale for the pup, he starts homeward. Again he stops for that cup of coffee. And again the lady comes and changes the pig for the pup. Soon the man goes home with his sack. But what confusion — out wiggles the pig. The point is, don't take time for substitutes. One switch can get you off the track and it is doubtful whether the man with the little mustache ever gets the pig to market and may never even get the pig home. — GLENN STOUT, Boise

Nix negativism

Editor, The Statesman:

The last year or so, The Statesman has shown an interest in the local schools by writing and printing positive articles. I'm very disappointed, however, that Bruce Spence could only see the negative side of the meeting held at South Junior High between parents and school trustees on Jan. 25.

There were 150 people who attended that meeting for the purpose of finding out what we can do to help support funds for Boise schools. A small handful (two or three) voiced concern of "scare tactics." It is unfortunate that parents feel the scare tactics are coming from the schools. I, personally, feel that the parents who are most concerned, talk about it at home and to their friends and the anxiety or enthusiasm goes from parent to child, and from child to child.

We are not using "scare tactics," but if that is what it will take [to] help our schools — fine.

I just hope that everyone will do as suggested at that meeting and write to your legislator and tell them how you feel and that we want our quality education to continue. Our legislators have to know what we want in order to make decisions we elected them to make.

The headlines of Spence's article was not the primary feeling of those attending the meeting, but that is what thousands of Statesmen readers will think because of a handful of negative opinions.

It is unfortunate that the minority seems to be the loudest. — ILAINE TRACY, Boise

Urgent

Editor, The Statesman:

Any TV watcher knows about commercials, but I ponder the sensibility of some of them. Take, for instance the "Mr. Goodwrench" commercial, where a driver, in a GM sedan, looks down at the door, saying "You never had it so good!" as he pats it.

Rather silly, isn't it, or if this is a trend it may bring new ideas in every business. Can't you just imagine a commercial showing a man with his hand on a casket, saying "I'm sure going to feel snuggy in you!" Don't wait, friends. — ANDREW P. DEMBOWSKI, Boise

Kudos for Boise Rhodes Scholars

Editor, The Statesman:

I was pleased to read in The Statesman that Michael Hoffman of Payette (Boise State University), and Thomas A. Smith of Boise (Cornell University), had been successful in the 1978 competition for the American Rhodes Scholarships. I congratulate these young men on their achievement.

As a former Rhodes Scholar, and former secretary for the Idaho Rhodes Scholarships Selection Committee, I now have had an opportunity to look over the complete list of American Rhodes Scholars-elect for 1979. I have thought that friends of the new Idaho Scholars might be interested to know where, from the national standpoint, their election "fits."

According to the regulations of the Rhodes Trust, an American college student may make application for a Scholarship from either the state of his residence, or the state in which his sponsoring school is located. For the purposes of the annual Rhodes competition, the United States has been divided into eight districts: New England, Middle Atlantic, Southern, Great Lakes, Middle West, Gulf, Southwestern and Northwestern.

Only four scholarships may be awarded each year by a district selection committee.

At the Northwestern District interviews this year, Idaho's two candidates competed against young men and women representing Washington, Oregon, Montana, Wyoming, North Dakota and Alaska.

An analysis of the official complete list of Rhodes Scholars-elect indicates that, as in past years, eastern schools seem to exert a disproportionate influence on the competition. This year, 16 of the 32 scholarships made available to the United States went to students at eastern universities: Harvard, six; Yale, four; Princeton, two; Amherst, Cornel, Johns Hopkins and Wellesley, one each.

The current local success is indeed gratifying. I can recall only one previous instance of a double win by Idaho at the Northwestern District test. Boise State University's breakthrough, with the achievement of a Rhodes Scholarship "first," should afford particular satisfaction to the community. — ROBERT S. SMITH, M.D., Sun City, Ariz.

Taxes

Editor, The Statesman:

After reading Guest Opinion by Ken Robison on the editorial page of The Statesman on Dec. 22, it still becomes clearer that our politicians atd bereaucrats still do not want to look the monkey in the face on what the people have told them in the 1 percent in November. So I will take it upon myself to try and get it through their thick, "I am important" skulls.

Most of the Democrats and some of the Republicans, and all of the bureaucrats are liberal spenders, as long as it is some one else's money. Now here is what the people told you in November. Stop big government and reduce the spending. Do it in 1979, not in 1985.

Also they did not say to reduce property tax, then find some other way to tax the people.

Now, here is the way it can be done, if our legislature will put the people ahead of their desires, which is being a big shot, and wanting to be re-elected to something or other.

The first thing to do, is destroy at least half the state or federal bureaucratic agencies that are destroying the people of the United States and the states.

As The Statesman will only publish letters 300 or less long, watch for the second half at a later date if they publish this one, save this so you can continue the next. — DRADGER S. POWELL, Mountain Home

Anti-American

Editor, The Statesman:

Open letter to Sen. Frank Church.

Your speech sharply criticizing Saudi Arabia is the most anti-American we have heard for a long time and certainly the most anti-American we have ever heard come from the American Senate. Why do you seek to antagonize the friends of your country? Who or what influence causes you to make such utterances? Certainly not your conscience to which you attributed your Panama Canal stand.

A copy of this letter is going to the Idaho Statesman because Idaho's leading newspaper must be made aware that you will be challenged on any public utterance you make against the best interests of the United States. — M. E. THOMPSON, New Plymouth

Idaho Statesman, February 15, 1979

FIGURE 5   HOUSTON POST

Post/commentary

Woodway's impact

Houston, through the shock of Woodway Square, is once again alert to our need for a better building code. While this awareness lasts, we should press forward briskly but thoroughly. Through mayor and City Council, Houston should follow the best available principles of fire prevention. Our own Fire Department can provide the guidance.

It is the obligation of this city to offer those who live here and those who will move here the protection of adequate building codes. Houston is growing so rapidly that it is essential for high-rise buildings and wide-flung complexes to be built with smoke alarms, sprinkler systems, fire walls and fire-resistant or fire-retardant materials. Given time, anything will burn. The code should enable building inspectors and fire inspectors to insist upon the kind of construction that confines a blaze in a small area or keeps a small fire from becoming a holocaust. Houston fire officials have campaigned steadily for provisions that would strengthen the code. A few gains have been made. But not enough.

In the early 1970s a worldwide rash of high-rise building fires made headlines: two killed, 24 injured in Kushiro, Japan; five killed, 150 injured in the 41-story Avianca Tower in Bogota, Colombia; nine killed in a new old people's home in Atlanta. In 1974 180 people died in the blaze of a 22-story office building in Sao Paulo, Brazil. At the time, Houston was reviewing its building codes.

Fire Marshal Alcus Greer and H. E. Gilmore of the Fire Department's inspection division urged the city to require sprinkler systems in all future high-rise buildings. They also urged fire walls, smoke-alarm systems and retardant materials. Now, Houston does require fire alarms and public address systems in new high-rise buildings. Sprinklers must be installed in new retail sales and exhibit hall areas larger than 12,000 square feet, and in new hospitals and nursing homes. But our code still makes no requirement for sprinkler systems in high-rise buildings.

Many cities require smoke-alarm systems in every house, apartment and building built. They are cheap, easy to install. No house should be without at least one, preferably several. As the smoke alarms have been produced in quantity, they have improved in performance and gone down in price. Cities that have required them report a great reduction in the number of deaths by fire. Certainly our new city code should respect the advice of our Fire Department. In our gratitude that no one died in the Woodway Square holocaust, we should dedicate ourselves to the cause of a new and adequate building code for Houston's future.

No scapegoats

We cannot shout or bully the Organization of Petroleum Exporting Countries into selling us unlimited quantities of oil at pre-1973 prices. And for the United States or Americans to look upon OPEC as either unreasonable or an enemy may annoy them but hurts them not at all. We owe our present plight to our own lack of foresight and self-discipline, not to OPEC.

In 1978 the United States used energy equivalent to 1,842.4 million tons of oil. Japan used 358.5, West Germany 271.3, Britain 212.6 and Canada 206.8. In other words, we used more oil than Japan, West Germany, Britain, Canada, France and Italy combined. After the 1973-74 oil embargo, our allies' consumption stayed about the same or, in Britain, actually dropped. Our use of energy continued to grow. Though American technology and corporate investment helped develop OPEC's oil industry, we have bought the product at cheap prices, used it cheaply, wasted it unnecessarily — much as we did with our domestic oil.

W. W. Rostow, University of Texas professor of economics and history, writes: "We are in the fix we are in because we failed to change course." And, "In a mature democracy like ours, it is unwise to build policy on scapegoats." For us to make an adversary out of OPEC would only hurt the United States, our foreign policy, our economy, our people. Taken individually, many of the OPEC countries are important to us and our allies in our hopes for world stability. Venezuela, one of Latin America's few democracies, is an OPEC country. Its friendship is important to our relations with the entire hemisphere. Nigeria, Africa's largest nation, a large oil supplier, is essential to the stability of Africa. Saudi Arabia, long a friend, is essential to any lasting peace in the Middle East.

OPEC oil will not last. Many of its members expect their supplies to taper off after the 1980s. But they, too, have a growing need for energy as they rush to industrialize. Unless they are to lose all hope of modernization, they, too, must find alternate sources of energy. Instead of calling OPEC names and loudly resenting their refusal to sell us oil at 1973 rates, the United States and our allies should be working with OPEC on what is ultimately a shared problem.

The Houston Post

Written and edited to merit your confidence

Time for no-holds-barred look at Israel

Violations of faith mounting

By Joseph C. Harsch
Christian Science Monitor

Israel again has expressed its disapproval of American behavior. The Israeli government not only has officially rejected an American arrangement for observing the process of peace between Egypt and Israel in Sinai, but it has called the American plan a breach of President Carter's promises at Camp David.

This protest reached Washington along with reports that Israeli air forces were bombing a highway in Lebanon loaded with Sunday evening traffic going home from the beaches. The Israelis were using American planes for the attack in spite of the U.S. position that such American weapons are sold or given to Israel exclusively for the defense of Israel. Women and children were reported to be among the casualties.

There was an American protest about the use of American planes in that raid and a stiff U.S. protest on Israel's rejection of the truce observer force. Secretary of State Cyrus Vance denied the slightest breach of faith. But Israel paid little or no attention to the American protests.

This is not the first time that Israel has scolded the U.S. for doing things which the U.S. regards as being in the interests of the United States. Nor is it the first time Israel has used American weapons for what Washington regards as an aggressive purpose in violation of the terms of the original gift or sale.

The record is dotted with American protests against such use of American weapons. Israel is unimpressed and undeterred. It operates on the assumption that military action it undertakes is "defensive" in character.

I can't help feeling that somewhere, somehow, something is out of scale or proportion in this sort of thing, which has been going on for years. Israel is constantly complaining that Washington is not doing what it ought to be doing to Israel and for Israel. The president of the United States is lectured repeatedly for allegedly being insufficiently considerate of Israel and Israel's needs. What are the facts?

From the day the State of Israel came into being the United States has been its protector and its benefactor. American weapons have been its shield in all its wars. American economic aid has sustained its economy.

'Sooner or later we've got to take a stand'   *Christian Science Monitor*

Before the 1967 war the amount of aid was modest. According to an article in the current issue of Foreign Affairs (by Anne Crittenden of the New York Times) it amounted only to $1.5 billion 'over the first 18 years. Yet even this, she says, "represented the highest rate of assistance, on a per capita basis, that the United States had ever provided to any nation."

That was trivial compared to what came after the 1967 war when the level went to $500 million per year. Then it jumped again after the 1973-1974 war. That time it went up to an average of $2.5 billion per year.

Now, with the Camp David peace settlement between Egypt and Israel (which I can't help feeling is much to Israel's advantage), the United States is to pay even more. The regular annual aid is now up to $2.8 billion. In addition, the United States is to provide Israel an extra $4.8 billion over three years. This is to compensate Israel for the costs of moving its military installations and civilian settlements out of the Sinai peninsula and back to Israeli home territory.

There is no such thing as gratitude in foreign affairs. Nations act according to what they conceive to be their own best interests at any given time. No one should expect Israel to be grateful to the United States for its continued support at a level above historical precedent. But should it not be considerate of American interests, if only to protect its own standing in Washington?

It is not in the American interest to have American weapons used for killing Arabs with whom the United States has no quarrel.

It is not in the American interest to have Israel continue to plant settlements of Jews in occupied Arab territory in contravention of what the government of the United States considers to be right and conducive to peace. Washington believes they block progress toward an overall peace with the Arab countries.

I can't help feeling that Israel's country is singularly careless of American wishes and interests.

Leadership gap persists

Little America no match for big challenges

By Joseph Kraft

In thinking about the country's leadership problem, the first commandment is not to imagine a heroic past. No doubt there has recently taken place a diffusion of authority in America.

But the United States has never had a national elite. Nor, in peacetime at least, did the country ever need, nearly as much as it does now, a strong capacity to make decisions in one place.

A half-forgotten classic published in 1956 — *The Power Elite* by C. Wright Mills — provides a good guide to the once, present and future leadership of the United States. In that book, Mills advanced the theory that the country was run by a national alliance of corporate executives and labor barons who used as auxiliaries the political bosses and military brass.

Today such a view would evoke hoots of hysterical laughter. It is suggestive that of the more than 130 leaders invited by President Carter to the domestic summit at Camp David, only 10 came from the ranks of industrial corporations and industrial labor. There was only one person from organization politics, and not a single military man.

The fact is that the part of the country primarily concerned with producing goods — the group I have called Big America — has lost confidence and authority. Their place in the forefront has been taken by persons primarily concerned with improving the quality of life — a group I have called Little America. It is suggestive that 37 of the people invited to Camp David came from academia, the media and the clergy. Of the 10 mayors present, five were blacks.

The change in emphasis from Big America to Little America defines the recent diffusion of authority. The circle of people who can make things happen has grown wider. Connections between leaders and followers are attenuated. Isolated individuals, celebrities, count for more than those who wield the levers of economic power.

But if there has been a softening of the America establishment, it is not as though the system was ever very tight. To be sure, there have been identifiable power structures in many places. New York City had, and has, an establishment. So do Boston and Philadelphia and Richmond and Charleston and Memphis and Chicago and Detroit and Cleveland and Houston and Minneapolis and St. Louis and Denver and San Francisco and Los Angeles.

But the peculiar feature of this country — a quality that sets our national life apart from that of Britain and France and the Soviet Union and Japan — is that nobody ever put it all together here. There is not, and there never has been, a national establishment. There is not, and there never has been, a power elite.

One sign of the difference is that this country has no equivalent of what Oxford and Cambridge do in Britain or the *grandes ecoles* in France or the Communist Party in Russia or Tokyo University in Japan. The would-be elite on the East Coast of this country may go to the Ivy League schools. But in Michigan and in Texas and in California they go to excellent universities in Ann Arbor or Austin or Berkeley or Palo Alto. There is not, in the United States, even an institution for nationalizing an elite.

This hole in the system didn't matter much for most of our national life. The task of settling a continent and rapidly developing a modern economy was well left to the uncoordinated efforts of different power centers. In times of peril the country was slow to react, but once the challenge became dramatic — as in World War II — the response was overwhelming.

Now, however, a different kind of challenge confronts the United States. The country's industrial society, with its millions of jobs in major cities, is threatened. Part of the threat comes from excessive demands put upon the system by the environmentalists, consumer advocates and minority groups. Part comes from abroad in the form of dizzying rises in the price of oil and increasingly stiff competition in heavy industry from Japan, West Germany and other countries.

Meeting the so-called energy-economic crisis does not merely mean giving up joy-riding on Saturday night. It does not mean saving Chrysler or selling it off to foreigners. It means reindustrializing the country — laying down a new transport system and refurbishing such basic industries as steel and autos.

That task, of course, requires leadership. But it is not the kind of anti-system leadership offered by President Carter and Little America. It is a leadership rooted in Big America — but on a scale and in a detail such as we have never before known in this country.

'Woman of Steel'

Thatcher's program is simple, direct, but politically costly

By Robert Merry
Chicago Tribune

LONDON — Margaret Thatcher has been in power in Britain for more than 2½ months, and one thing is already clear. She is determined that, whatever the cost in popularity, the British people shall face up to the economic realities that surround them. One is that only through financial prudence and hard work will they get out of the mess they're in.

For any other British politician, such a task might take a lifetime. But Thatcher wants quick results. She has said she has no interest in governing a country that goes downhill all the time.

Each piece of legislation that has come from the Conservative government since the election May 3 has borne the Thatcher stamp. She is running the government just the way she wants.

In the election, it was put around that who better than a "woman of steel" could lead the country out of a sick economy into a land where there is a chance for individuals to prosper? With Thatcher's leadership, the Conservatives won their biggest victory since 1935.

If all goes well, Thatcher is in charge for the next five years. Generally, there is an eight- or nine-month "honeymoon" between a new government and the voters. Then the voters tend to become much more critical.

In Thatcher's case, the people agree that she is carrying out her election pledges. She has cut individual taxes just as she said she would. She is breaking up the bureaucrat-loaded government-owned industries by turning such things as the state airline and the aerospace industries into private companies with stocks offered to investors.

Controls on private industry imposed by the last Labor government are being lifted. British investors can now put more of their money in overseas companies. The only trouble with the tax cuts is that the government, to find the money for them, had to increase a sales tax known here as value added tax. This tax goes on everything, with the exception of food and other essentials of life.

The effect has been a considerable jump in the cost of living. An inflation rate of 18 percent is expected soon, compared to one of 14 percent at the moment. Rising costs lose votes. Already, opinion polls put the Conservatives 5 percent behind the opposition Laborites. Thatcher's personal rating has also suffered.

Thatcher is unworried. She understands that the big changes in policies necessary to move from a semi-socialist state to one which goes back to traditional conservative beliefs in free enterprise will be hard for the public to accept. She is prepared to wait.

In a major announcement, the government ordered all aspects of state spending cut by $6 billion.

Thatcher was still not satisfied. She called her ministers together and said government spending must be cut by a further $2 billion. Her arguments convinced her colleagues and they are now setting about trimming their budgets.

It is no secret that Thatcher does not think highly of the trade union leaders. Britain's stagnating economy, she thinks, can be laid at the doorstep of union leaders who refuse to back modernization of industry and yet insist on high wage demands.

So Thatcher has said that the closed shop law will be altered so that workers not desiring union shops can have their wishes met. Government money will be provided so that secret postal ballots can be held before official strikes are called.

There are no restrictions on wage bargaining, but Thatcher points out that if workers demand extravagant pay raises and so put their employers in a bind, the government will not bail the firms out. So modest wage increases mean that jobs will be preserved.

Thatcher believes her policies will help give back to Britons their self-respect. She says it is time to learn the mistakes of the past and to make sure they do not occur again. Margaret Thatcher has the gift of speaking in language that ordinary people understand. The message comes over loud and clear.

FIGURE 6 LOUISVILLE TIMES

Harsh reminder

Study shows much remains to be done to overcome housing bias

times opinion

While questions about its objectivity are legitimate, a national study by the U.S. Department of Housing and Urban Development still offers powerful evidence of widespread discrimination in the sale and rental of housing.

The discrimination is more subtle than it was, say, 15 years ago, when a black family may have been bluntly told it wasn't wanted.

These days, a house or apartment may suddenly be unavailable when a black inquires about it. A real estate agent may quote a higher price to a prospective black buyer. Or the black may in various sordid ways be "steered" to black areas.

Yet, as the study disclosed, blacks may be treated with such courtesy that they have no reason to suspect they are not getting the same information as their white counterparts.

HUD testers found considerable discrimination of this sort in Lexington and somewhat less in Louisville and Indianapolis. The objectivity of the blacks and whites who visited real estate offices separately and asked similar questions about listed properties is the key to the study's validity. If there was a predisposition to find bias, that will color the conclusions.

But the survey appears to have been designed to screen out subjective judgments. The fact that the results were much the same everywhere suggests that the overall findings are valid even if some individual reports were off base.

The findings are not surprising, in any case, at least not to blacks. Anyone who thinks racial antipathies are dead is insulated from reality. Real estate agents and their clients have the same biases as anyone else. Inevitably, sneaky methods have been devised for evading the 1968 Civil Rights Act, which prohibits discrimination in the sale and rental of most housing.

While the law can't extirpate the uglier instincts of human nature, it can, if enforced, at least guarantee that all citizens receive equal treatment when they decide to move to a new home in the suburbs or closer to jobs and schools.

One unavoidable conclusion is that fair housing has not become a reality because there have not been enough systematic and continuous efforts to crack down on those determined to keep it unfair.

There's no sure-fire remedy, particularly for discrimination that is often hard to detect and even more difficult to prove. But the severely unequal treatment for blacks makes it clear that several types of activity are necessary to combat it.

For instance, more frequent monitoring of the type designed by HUD would help provide evidence for court suits against flagrant violators. What's more important, real estate and rental agents would be deterred from discriminatory practices by the knowledge that "auditors" are checking on them.

A bill sponsored by Senator Mathias of Maryland, meanwhile, would strengthen the federal governments's ability to enforce the law. HUD must now attempt conciliation between landlord and tenant or a seller and prospective buyer. An individual can go to court if that doesn't work, although the time and cost involved make it difficult for most to do so.

The Mathias bill would allow the Justice Department to file suit on behalf of individuals and would sock the losing party with court costs, including attorney's fees. That, in itself, would tend to discourage real estate agents from politely neglecting to tell a prospective customer about houses for sale in white neighborhoods.

It would be encouraging, too, if leaders in the real estate business would try harder to persuade their colleagues that discrimination is not only illegal, but wrong. The Louisville Board of Realtors, for instance, might do more to publicize Article 10 of its code of ethics, which says that a Realtor ". . . shall not deny equal professional services" to or discriminate against any person.

There's been a general assumption among whites that the laws passed in the 1960s were the end of the civil rights battle. The pervasive pattern of racial bias shown in this latest report is a harsh reminder that much remains to be done.

UNCLE TOM'S CABIN
HOUSING DISCRIMI-NATION
ENGELHARDT

Engelhardt in The St. Louis Post-Dispatch

'Now here's something I'll bet would be just perfect for you folks'

Welfare 'crackdown' must not be distorted

times opinion

When Human Resources Secretary Peter Conn, at the behest of Governor Carroll, sent 20 investigators into Jefferson County a month ago to search for welfare abusers, he was neither acting on a hunch nor going on a wild goose chase.

The decision resulted from a year's study by caseworkers who had observed approximately 200 of the 345 abuse situations identified by the investigators and announced yesterday.

In fact, state officials believe the key to the identification was the attention of local workers, since they are closer to the situation than anyone in Frankfort.

Because of its legal arrangment, the welfare system is closely identified with the communities even though the money flows through Washington and Frankfort. Consequently, the best kind of monitoring is done locally, and who better to serve as gatekeeper than the individuals responsible for issuing food stamps and determining eligibility for aid to families with dependent children?

Although the Jefferson County attorney's office will prosecute the bulk of the cases, some of the biggest — involving alleged felonies — will go to the commonwealth's attorney.

In either case, the focus will be on penalizing those who have abused the system. In the past, the emphasis was on obtaining repayments, an often fruitless endeavor.

The human resources department's inspector general, William Burkette, believes that between 20 and 30 new cases may be identified in Jefferson County each month under the system announced yesterday. In addition, a welfare-reporting hotline, which will allow any person who observes a case of suspected fraud to report it, is expected to increase the number of cases for investigation.

The investigators are moving on to other counties now, to continue the work they started in Jefferson. However, they are to be available for return visits when local officials feel the need.

This program is not without merit, but it would be indeed tragic if the emphasis on cracking down on "cheats" turned sour, placing all legitimate welfare recipients under suspicion.

The clear intent at the moment is to assure responsible allocation of public funds. It must not be distorted so that it makes all welfare recipients live under a cloud of suspicion and turns their friends and relatives into stool pigeons.

The Louisville Times

opinion

BARRY BINGHAM JR.
Editor and Publisher

VAN A. CAVETT
Opinion Page Editor

WARREN BUCKLER
KEN LOOMIS
KEITH RUNYON
Associate Editors

TUESDAY, APRIL 25, 1978

Add 2 more victims to toll in Cold War

times opinion

The sketchy accounts of the downing of a Korean airliner in Russia last week raise more questions than they answer. The basic one — how the airliner came to have made a turn of almost 180 degrees and flown almost 1,800 miles off course — may never be explained satisfactorily.

Its flight took it into particularly sensitive Soviet territory, so it was natural that Russian aircraft soon appeared alongside. It is the events that followed that are in dispute.

What cannot be in dispute is that the Russians severely overreacted. There was no need to fire at an unarmed, civilian transport that should have been clearly recognizable as such to any experienced aviator. The equivalent of the old maritime shot across the bow should have been enough to warn the Korean pilot to land the Boeing 707.

Instead, the shots went into the plane, adding two more apparently innocent victims to the Cold War's toll. It was a shameful act.

letters to the times

'We cannot afford to cut off' Mall's 600 block

As the entire length of the River City Mall, including the 600 block, is perceived as part of the downtown, and all planning up to this point seems to exclude it, a comprehensive plan and sense of direction should be initiated for this area. This part of the downtown, including the movie-row area, has many fond memories of the time when it was alive and teeming with people.

With the emphasis primarily towards the river, we cannot afford to cut off from the spine — the 600 block needs to be considered. With its neighbors, the Macauley Theatre and nearby stores, and close proximity to our newspapers, the area is vital in being the anchor of all downtown rejuvenation efforts. If the problems of the 600 block can be corrected, then we will be helping to insure the success of the proposed Galleria, Performing Arts Center, Commonwealth Convention Center, Hyatt Regency Hotel and all future efforts.

The entire 600 block, including all tenants, property owners and interested parties, must get it together and work together, or nothing but continued decline looms ahead.

Other areas of the downtown must not continue to ignore each other, but must recognize each other and get a little closer, as the success of each depends on the other in these projects. The only competition should be for the success of Louisville as a whole, with the downtown as the nucleus.

The 600 block of the Mall, because of its outstanding theaters, offers an unusual opportunity to provide the Louisville community with a concentrated area to provide artistic and cultural activities, which are now almost totally lacking, while, at the same time, combating severe downtown deterioration. This deterioration of the area is definitely detrimental to the economic health and well-being of the entire downtown and regional area.

The Movie Row Foundation and Up-Downtown promotion have as their goal to give Louisvillians another chance to enjoy our palatial landmarks, while also enjoying fine entertainment, which includes family-type entertainment events. We need to get our people back on their feet again — not afraid to take the bus downtown to conduct their business, living and shopping.

FREDERICK G. BISBEE
2025 Brownsboro Rd., Louisville

Dedicated to religious drama

In light of your March 3 editorial opinion by Keith Runyon, "Troubled 600 can have a future — as a new kind of place to live, play, shop," I would like to inform you and The Louisville Times readers that the key to the survival of the 600 block of River City Mall is the public bending over backwards to utilize the things still there.

The Christian Workshop Community Theatre, a newcomer to the block, is now housed in the old Mary Anderson Theatre, and could attract far more patrons than it does if it received help from interested patrons or grants from arts foundations. Its budget allows it to continue only because of the interest Lincoln Federal Savings has in preserving some dignity in the use of this historic theatre.

On its meager budget, it is, of course, impossible for CWCT to make really noticeable changes to herald its presence. But we are there.

We are the only community theatre in this area dedicated to religious drama, in a town that is steeped in religious tradition. The media have for the most part been very encouraging, but at times we feel as though they skip over us in discussing revitalizing the mall. We feel we have much to offer. Give us the chance!

JAMES OLIVER LYTTLE
Producing-Director
The Christian Workshop
Community Theatre
612 River City Mall, Louisville

Keeneland: the best of racing

Since 1935, Keeneland has presented the best of racing with dignity and grace. All the big things and all the little things that are almost inconspicuous in a class operation, have been carefully tended at Keeneland for many years.

There is an entirely different feeling about the horses in the crowds at Keeneland. I suppose that's because to so many of those present, horses are really horses, fine and courageous animals with habits and temperaments of their own, and not just figures in a book or a racing sheet.

ISRAEL GOODMAN
201 York St., Louisville

Against taxes on automobiles

Regarding the Times opinion by Ken Loomis, "A better way — New laws would make it easier to collect auto tax". Have him check on other automobile taxes — sales tax on new cars, used cars, parts and tires, which go to the state, schools and other taxing bodies.

He failed to mention this revenue, which makes the personal property tax on automobiles look like petty cash. The agencies waste most of it.

He may not know this, but ex-Governor Wetherby had the personal property tax on household furnishings taken off the books. It produced as much revenue as the present car tax, and everything went along fine without it.

ROY R. OHLSON
3874 Darlene Dr., Shively, Ky.

Thanks U of L team

I would like to thank the University of Louisville basketball team and especially Steve Bugg for being so nice to me when I attended my first college game, the U of L-Tulane game. I think they should be ranked No. 1 in basketball and kindness.

JON GADDIS
12208 Brightfield Dr., Louisville

Correction

The April 20 letter by W. David Strait incorrectly gave his address as 1369 S. First St. It is 1396 S. First St. — Editor.

'A funny way for history to be made'

mary mcgrory

WASHINGTON — The world that [illegible]

That you might agree [illegible] Senate Majority Leader Robert C. Byrd worthy of the last speech before the vote on the second Panama Canal treaty.

Except it was never given. The world didn't hear the creak, the thump and the shuffle. It didn't even hear the speech. The speech was never given.

[illegible]

GEE, THANKS DAD... NOW I WON'T HAVE TO SMASH YOUR FACE...

Lynch in The Fort Wayne Journal-Gazette

[illegible]

NCEW EXCHANGE: Frank Callaham, The Ledger-Star, Norfolk, Va.

What gives ex-wives of servicemen a right to benefits?

To the Editor:

After reading a letter in the Open Forum March 6, I decided to express my opinion of the bill presently in Congress, HR 8284, sponsored by 2nd District Rep. G. William Whitehurst. The bill would allow former wives of military men, who were married as long as 20 years though now divorced, to continue to be eligible for military benefits.

THE LEDGER-STAR
OPEN FORUM

Whatever happened to the theory that the wife (not ex-wife) is entitled to these privileges for being the wife of an active duty or retired military person?

I am a government employee, a divorcee from a military man, and a taxpayer. For any ex-wife to retain her privileges after a divorce from a military man is unthinkable. It would seem a settlement is being bestowed upon her by the government and the taxpayers for services rendered. What services?

As a taxpayer, I feel this is a great injustice to the public. A military man performs a service to the public and deserves his privileges, but his ex-wife has earned nothing. The taxpayers shouldn't have to maintain these women in the manner in which they have become accustomed.

SUSAN RIPLEY

Chesapeake

Test-tube conception

To the Editor:

The Department of Health, Education and Welfare will soon decide whether or not test-tube fertilization of human life will be funded with American tax dollars.

We are mistaken if we think that experimentation on human life will not deeply affect us. Laboratory conception of human life will not always and necessarily be implanted and brought to the threshold of conscious human existence. Nor will a beautiful and animated Louise Joy Brown always be the result of in-vitro fertilization.

Many untold numbers of Louise Joy Browns will be fixed on glass slides, frozen in time, and collected, like delicate butterflies pinned to the backs of cards, all of them carefully labeled and studied; all of them mysterious and silent worlds of would-have-beens.

The conception of a human person should always be brought about by an act of human love and responsibility, in human tenderness and human unselfishness.

By comparison, everything else is as nothing.

SCILA HUDSON

Chesapeake

Stay home, Jimmy

To the Editor:

President Carter's frequent and seemingly total preoccupation with the Middle East problem leaves me greatly disturbed. I realize the importance of this attempt to achieve peace. But our economy and well-being are vital to such peace. And I cannot help feeling we Americans elected our president to solve OUR problems and not only those of the world.

No, this is not the view of an isolationist. It is only the concerned opinion of an American who has lived abroad and witnessed the bungled attempts at buying friendship and allegiance that our government has made.

Mr. Carter's aims are admirable but not enforceable. A firm stand by this country should be taken—and then retirement from the center of controversy.

PEGGY S. FERRELL

Chesapeake

THE LEDGER-STAR
Founded 1876
Published by Landmark Communications, Inc
Frank Batten, Chairman
Richard F. Barry III, President
Thursday, March 15, 1979

Perry Morgan, Publisher
Robert D. Benson, President
Frank Caperton, Executive Editor
Robert W. Dodson, Managing Editor

Opinion Page
George J. Hebert, Editor
Frank H. Callaham, Associate Editor
William H. Wood, Associate Editor

Browsing the Chrysler

Various forms of sea life are depicted on this 15-inch cameo glass plate by Emile Galle, Nancy, France. The piece, dating to 1900, is on display at Norfolk's Chrysler Museum.

Surry foul-up socks all of us

Some of the facts about the shutdown of five nuclear power plants, including two in Virginia, are a little confusing. We don't know how long it will take to fix them. Or how much it will cost. But one thing is certain:

You and I are going to pay for somebody else's mistake.

We're going to pay in increased costs of electricity. Vepco, which has been getting more than 50 percent of its power from nuclear units, will have to use more coal and oil. Coal- and oil-fired electricity is more expensive than nuclear-powered electricity. Consumers will make up the difference.

We're also going to pay more for gasoline. The shutdown of the five plants means that America will have to import an extra 200,000 barrels of oil each day. That's only a little more than two percent of the oil we're importing now. But, combined with the 900,000 barrels per day we're losing because of the Iranian chaos, it's enough to push up oil prices.

The shutdown of the nuclear plants is in no way analagous to the loss of the Iranian oil. The United States did not have much (if any) control over events in Iran. But the U.S. has control over the nuclear power industry, through the Nuclear Regulatory Commission (NRC).

And the NRC, which is supposed to protect the public interest, blew it.

Here's what happened: A Boston-based nuclear design and construction firm used a computer to figure out specifications for pipe systems at nuclear plants. The pipes had to be able to withstand a certain amount of stress. If they broke, and the water that cools the reactor leaked, nuclear fuel could burn out of the plant—releasing radioactivity.

The firm developed the computer figures. Pipes were designed according to those stress figures. Then the NRC ran

WILLIAM H. WOOD
An Opinion

checks on all safety systems—but never checked to see if the computer formula was accurate.

That formula was used for plants at Surry, and at plants in Pennsylvania, New York and Maine. The people who run those plants apparently never checked on the accuracy of the computer formula, either.

Finally, last December, engineers at the Pennsylvania plant, alarmed by discrepancies in their piping system, found out that the old computer formula was not consistent with current specifications for similar pipes.

And, last week, after further checking, they discovered that the old computer model was, in fact, in error. In devising that formula, the people with the Boston design firm had subtracted horizontal stress calculations from vertical stress figures—when they should have been adding them together! So, in some cases, the pipes were one-sixth as strong as NRC regulations said they should be.

Well, that's pretty stupid. Subtracting instead of adding. And it seems like somebody, either with the NRC or with Vepco, should have checked those figures before the plants were built.

There's a lesson to be learned from this. It's simple: No matter how sophisticated we become in dealing with nuclear power, we can never eliminate the human element. Humans are going to make mistakes, so, in something as potentially dangerous as nuclear power, the government has to set up a fail-safe procedure for checking and re-checking all figures.

If that means that the NRC has to be expanded, at greater cost to the taxpayers, so be it. The costs from this failure—not to mention the disastrous costs if those pipes had failed and the radioactive materials had been released—are far greater.

That's an important lesson to learn. The tragedy is that you and I will have to pay for it.

This may help when you go apply for your gasoline loan

WASHINGTON — As the price of gasoline keeps going up, people may have to resort to buying it on long-term credit.

The scene is the branch of Morgan Chemical Bank of America. Mr. Klingle is ushered toward the loan officer's desk.

"Can I help you, Mr. Klingle?"

"Yes sir, I would like to make a gasoline loan."

Art Buchwald

"Very good. How much gas were you going to buy?"

"A full tank. We want to attend our daughter's graduation."

The loan officer takes out a form.

"We don't usually advance money for a full tank of gasoline without some collateral. What were you planning to put up for the loan?"

"My house. It's in tiptop condition on an acre of land."

"And what else?"

"The house won't be enough?"

"Mr. Klingle, do you know what a full tank of gas costs these days? The bank demands more than just a house for collateral."

"I was afraid of that. What about my house and my 1980 Cadillac?"

"Are we talking about leaded or unleaded gasoline?"

Mr. Klingle said nervously, "Unleaded."

The loan officer looks at his chart. "That won't be sufficient. What else can you give as a guarantee you'll pay back the loan?"

"I have a hundred shares of IBM which is now selling at $340 a share."

"That just might do it. You'll have to leave the stock with us."

"I'll do that. I didn't know the bank demanded so much collateral for a gasoline loan."

"We consider these loans very high-risk ventures," the loan officer said. "When we first started giving them, people would take the money, buy the gas, use it up, and then default. Since there was nothing left in their tanks to recover, we've had to make sure that in the future we could get something else back in exchange. How long do you want to take to pay us back?"

"How much time do I have?"

The loan officer referred to his chart. "You can pay us over a period of 24 months, 36 months or string it out over four years. I am obliged under the 'truth in lending' law to advise you that we are permitted to charge 20 percent interest on gasoline loans. Of course, you can pay the loan back sooner, but there is a penalty."

"I think I'll be able to pay it back in 36 months providing my wife can get a job."

"All right. Here are the papers to fill out and these are for the gas station attendant to sign, attesting to the fact that he filled up your car with a full tank. When you bring in the deeds to your house, automobile, and the IBM stock, we will send the check directly to the gas station."

"Thank you very much, sir. You don't know what this gasoline loan means to me."

"Mr. Klingle, I wouldn't approve it if I didn't have faith in you. Besides, this bank believes people should have the good things in life today and not have to wait until they're old and gray before they can afford to buy a tankful of fuel."

Both men get up and shake hands. The loan officer says, "And don't forget—when you pay us back in 36 months we'll be happy to refinance another tank for you. Have a safe trip."

Not all of our wildlife is vanishing

A lot of earnest people are engaged these days, as for some time past, in efforts to save the wild birds and animals on our continent.

This is all to the good. No reasonable person would have it any other way. The bald eagles, the California condors, the black-footed ferrets and a number of other species which are still losing ground need all the allies they can get.

However, the record isn't all bad, and it would be wrong for Americans to feel under some wholesale indictment. I'm concerned that the angry zeal of some of the very conservationists who have helped improve things may be contributing to an unfair impression.

When I was growing up in Norfolk, a trip to Richmond held a special pleasure—the sight of wild animals gamboling right in the thick of the city's bustle. The gray squirrels living on the Capitol grounds had no parallel in Norfolk, where their habitat had been reduced to the protected acres of City Park.

Today there are squirrels almost eveverywhere hereabouts, to the point of a pesky surplus—in yards with bird feeders, for instance.

As a kid, the only uncaged opossums I ever saw were dead ones on rural

GEORGE HEBERT
An Opinion

roads. One night not long ago, a good-sized possum stalked nonchalantly through my headlight beam about a block and a half from my house in the built-up northern part of the city.

There are raccoons, too, in a nearby neighborhood, as columnist Guy Friddell has reported, and wild mallards aplenty (a pair came regularly to our door for crackers one summer), and doves and muskrats and herons and bitterns—all within blocks of the monoxide and roar of Hampton Boulevard. I went through early life thinking you had to trek deep into Dismal Swamp or Seashore State Park to see such things.

In those days, too, a bluejay was something you found in a book, or caught a glimpse of, perhaps, between Williamsburg and Richmond. Now, its range has dramatically expanded, and its bright plumage and raucous cries are a familiar part of urban Tidewater.

Almost as familiar are the nighttime and early morning rabbits—like the one I saw nibbling grass with great unconcern the other day in the median strip of one of our busiest city roadways.

The occasional, honking wedge of geese of a few decades back is now multiplied many times over. Sightings of Canada geese have been commonplace in the past few months. And within 45 minutes' drive of here, I made, one day this winter, an approximate count of 30,000 snow geese passing over—using the average number of

Opossums

birds in an incredible series of big V's flying from farm feeding areas to Currituck Sound. Not to mention, a week or two later in the same area, a flock of about 300 whistling swans.

In this part of the world at least, there is proof we must be doing something right.

Dogged president

Peace: On track

A Carter-orchestrated peace treaty between Israel and Egypt was thought at hand once before—in the euphoria that followed the historic Camp David summit last fall. A comprehensive formula was worked out there; the treaty itself, officials were saying, would be signed before Christmas.

But this didn't happen. Instead the two countries began moving apart. President Carter, doggedly pursuing his role as

FRANK CALLAHAM
An Opinion

peacemaker, initiated further moves in an attempt to bring the two sides back together. These, too, failed to erase the remaining differences.

Finally, Mr. Carter went the extra mile—literally—with his journey to Egypt and Israel. Even this seemed not enough, and the cautious language the leaders used as Mr. Carter prepared to leave Israel added up, in effect, to failure. But the dramatic breakthrough came as Mr. Carter made a final airport stop at Cairo and conferred with Egypt's President Sadat.

Now Egypt has agreed to a pact, the Israeli cabinet has voted yes and Israel's Prime Minister Begin is talking bullishly about winning approval from the parliament.

So a partial Mideast peace is at hand—again. What happened after Camp David invites caution, but this appears to be a genuine accord that is being established between Egypt and Israel.

Even if new obstacles do appear, however, Mr. Carter's performance has been commendable. Beset by troubles at home, some of them of his own making and others not, he has applied great energy and effort and, yes, pressure to bring the two Mideast countries together.

If the Israelis and the Egyptians do not carry through to conclusion the agreement that Mr. Carter put in motion—and kept in motion—then the failure will be the Mideast combatants', not the American peacemaker's.

These firemen turned off their hoses

Landmark News Service

For years the prophets and philosophers have glumly warned us that Americans are losing their moral fiber, their imperative to stand up for right, their sense of caring about their neighbor. We were reminded of this gloomy prediction several days ago by an outrageous incident in Montana.

As fire swept through the rural house of a Montana family the firemen suddenly turned off their hoses in midblaze and refused to extinguish the fire. It seems the firemen checked with their accounting office during the fire and discovered the family had not paid their $25 initiation fee and $15 annual fee for membership in the rural fire association. Given

Rosemary Yardley

this piece of news, the firemen promptly shut off the spigot and allowed the house to burn. The family, who had moved into the house ony hours earlier, claimed they weren't told by the seller about the fees. The fire was a total loss.

On hearing this disturbing story, we recalled how our forebears of an earlier America would have responded to the crisis. The earlier generation, including the frontiersmen who settled Montana, were a special breed that looked out for their neighbor. The first whiff of smoke would have brought wagonloads of friends and neighbors to the blaze where bucket brigades would work wearily into the night to put out the fire.

After the ashes had cooled and the ruins were surveyed, the neighbors would show up several days later, hammer in hand, to raise a new barn or house on the ruins of the other ones. All free of charge, of course.

While it's unfair to let a few rotten apples characterize the entire barrel, it does appear that some Americans have traded their values for a pile of ashes.

(Ms. Yardley is an editorial writer for the Greensboro Daily News.)

Norfolk Ledger-Star, March 15, 1979

practice of signing editorials. On the page shown here letters are given the most prominence at the top of the page.

READERS IN A HURRY

Although the bold, bright look still represents a major trend among American editorial pages, more and more editors are redesigning their pages with emphasis on providing information quickly to readers in a hurry. At least as early as 1978, the *Detroit Free Press* began using a hammer headline for editorials: a large capitalized word or two followed by a summary sentence that continued on to a second line. More recently the *Free Press* has placed the two elements on separate lines to allow for more characters in the first element (Figure 8, page 282). *The Oregonian* in Portland has allowed itself an even greater opportunity to tell readers what an editorial is about: one line that allows for several words and two or three lines to summarize the editorial (Figure 9, page 283). The *Plain Dealer* in Cleveland has tried to catch readers' attention with a take-out quotation from its lead editorial (Figure 10, page 284). The *Phoenix Gazette* has added what might be called a "nut graf" in the left margin of the editorial page (Figure 11, page 285).

All of these efforts seem directed toward providing readers with quick summaries, as well as sufficient information to know what an editorial is about. Bohle has called attention to and applauded these steps in a *Masthead* series titled "Designing the Editorial Page." "Successful design changes are not really so because they are prettier or more colorful or trendy," he has written. "They work because they are better at what they do: deliver information."[6]

A prime example of this trend, and of what Bohle was talking about, appears in changes made in the editorial and op-ed pages of the *Charlotte Observer*. Ed Williams, editor of the editorial page, said that the makeover was intended to increase the visual impact of the editorials, make the letters column look more lively and devise a format that gave readers more information.[7] (Before and after editorial pages appear in Figures 12 and 13, pages 286 and 287.) "The design changes work because they are reader-driven," Bohle concluded. "This redesign works because the headlines are better draws into the stories, the headlines introduce white space into what used to be a typically gray opinion page, the letters have better heads to draw in readers, and column grids are used better."[8] (In a critique dealing with letters, in a different issue of *The Masthead*, Bohle made a strong pitch for meaty, two-line heads on letters to attract readers better.[9])

Other suggestions have come from Ralph J. Turner of the W. Page Pitt School of Journalism at Marshall University: Letters and perhaps columns might be set ragged right to introduce white space and a varied look. A lead editorial might be tied to art through use of a box or tint block. Large initials, tint blocks, borders, reverse heads, spot color and even process color can "add 'color' and weight to the 'old gray mare.'"[10]

INNOVATIVE FEATURES

Editorials, columns, cartoons and letters—plus a Bible verse or short prayer and a "back when" column—have traditionally made up the American editorial page.

8A DETROIT FREE PRESS/WEDNESDAY, APRIL 26, 1978

in our opinion

Detroit Free Press
AN INDEPENDENT NEWSPAPER
JOHN S. KNIGHT, Editor Emeritus
LEE HILLS, Publisher
RALPH S. ROTH, President
LEE E. DIRKS, General Manager
KURT LUEDTKE, Executive Editor
JOE H. STROUD, Editor
FRANK ANGELO, Associate Executive Editor

ARMS: A new SALT agreement can work for our interests

SECRETARY of State Vance was being very careful in what he said publicly about his conversations with the Soviet Union out of concern for two parties to these discussions: the Soviet Union itself, and the United States Senate.

On his first arms control mission to Moscow, in the early days after the administration took office, the secretary of state tried to be frank and open with the press. The Soviet Union felt that he was too frank and open, too early in the negotiations, and stiffened its attitudes. So there is some legitimacy to his concern about talking, prematurely, about the bargaining that is going on over a new Strategic Arms Limitation Treaty.

Likewise, there is clearly an overriding need for care in putting together the agreement and presenting it as a package to the U.S. Senate. Even this week, Sen. Henry Jackson was on television, expressing his own very skeptical attitude on the agreement being sought. Even under the best of circumstances, the negotiations with the Senate will be as tough as the negotiations with the Soviet Union.

That is as it should be. On anything as momentous as an arms control agreement, the Senate would be defaulting on its duty if it did not take seriously its responsibility to "advise and consent" with the president. The new SALT agreement should work for the interests of the United States, or it should not be ratified. Indeed, it should not even be signed. The last thing this country needs is mere paper security, without the ceilings and safeguards that ought to be built into arms control arrangements.

Jackson

Vance

A tough, but necessary, bargaining process

But we remain convinced that it is possible to negotiate a treaty that puts effective ceilings on arms development and assures a close enough approximation of equity that it does not leave either side vulnerable. We believe the administration understands this and will act on it.

The United States does not attempt to negotiate such issues with the Soviet Union because we love or trust the Soviet government. There are many ways in which their interests are antithetical to our interests. But on the question of survival in a dangerous world, and on the issue of how to reduce the risk of nuclear war, it is possible to find major areas of mutual interest and to act on them.

The progress reported by Secretary Vance, and such details as are being released or leaked out, do not tell us much. This has been, and ought to be, a painstaking bargaining process. The proof will not be in fragments made public now, but in the agreement as a whole, presented and argued carefully before the United States Senate.

We hope the Senate will keep an open mind and reserve its ultimate judgment until the proposed agreement is put together. This is an effort vital to the security of the United States. It deserves a full hearing and full debate. It also deserves a measure of patience while the negotiators seek to answer all the potential questions they can.

GERALDS: The Legislature shirks its responsibility by delaying his expulsion

WHILE THE state Legislature drags its feet about kicking out convicted felon Monte Geralds, D-Madison Heights, its own credibility is crumbling, the state Constitution being mocked, and the tolerance of voters getting strained to the snapping point.

Rep. Geralds, since his conviction earlier this month of embezzling $24,000 from a law client, has clung tenaciously to his seat, despite a section of the Michigan Constitution declaring ineligible anyone "convicted of a felony involving a breach of public trust. . ." He has refused to resign now and has even announced he will seek re-election.

But his fellow legislators' response to Mr. Gerald's adamancy has been mild, to say the least. First, legislators said nothing would be done until Attorney General Frank Kelley ruled whether Mr. Geralds' crime constituted a breach of the public trust. Mr. Kelley then said it was his legal opinion that it was only a private breach. A vote on expelling Mr. Geralds was expected to follow the Kelley opinion, but, instead, more stalling tactics have ensued.

On Thursday, the House Policy Committee is scheduled to begin hearing testimony on the question of Mr. Geralds' expulsion. And there is no telling what other stumbling blocks to speedy action may be scattered by the Legislature before a vote on Mr. Geralds' worthiness for office finally takes place.

All of this is profoundly disturbing. Despite Mr. Kelley's ruling, it seems beyond dispute that Mr. Geralds, as a lawyer, did indeed violate his public responsibility to serve as an ethical officer of the court—which lawyers are. Moreover, the circumstances of his conviction point to a clear-cut case of the kind of unscrupulous behavior that destroys public trust in elected officials.

The Legislature's slowness in dealing with Mr. Geralds suggests a perhaps understandable reluctance on the part of elected officials to sit in judgment on a peer. But since the Michigan Constitution makes legislators "the sole judge" of their own conduct, only they can expel or reprimand a member. Under these circumstances, legislative inaction becomes intolerable.

Unfortunately, the present impasse gives the impression that no one in the Capitol gives a hoot about voter sensitivity. At the moment, Mr. Geralds is not even functioning as an active member of the House and needs an alternate to vote on pending legislation. If the Legislature doesn't act soon to rid itself of Mr. Geralds, the general cynicism about politicians is going to take over, and incumbents generally can be expected to suffer. This is a case where it is a political crime, at least, to do nothing.

FAIR LANE: The people have a victory in the fight to preserve nature

THE GREEN WEDGE of forest preserved by agreement between the Ford Land Development Corp. and an environmental group may seem small in size; but its 43 acres loom large as a legal precedent and as a symbol of how natural areas can be protected in the midst of rapid urban development.

The area preserved is an L-shaped tract containing an important stand of beech-maple forest and hundreds of varieties of plant life, including several endangered and threatened species. It is home for numbers of birds and small animals such as opossum, raccoons, rabbits, fox and woodchuck.

In years to come, motorists who pass it along busy Ford Road and Evergreen will have a moment's rare pleasure at the sight of the undisturbed woods. So will those who travel its footpaths. And Ford officials have the satisfaction of knowing their company has acted responsibly and generously to preserve one of the last forested remnants of the old Fair Lane estate.

The agreement, reached after the citizens' group sued the Ford Motor Co. subsidiary, leaves the company free to build on an adjoining 163 acres. But naturalists believe the preserved area is large enough to sustain itself in the midst of the surrounding development.

The suit was an important test of the state's Environmental Protection Act of 1970, which gave citizens the right to challenge potentially harmful development. The act has most often been used against possible polluters or projected uses of public lands. This is the first major victory involving a private company seeking to develop private land in a heavily urban area.

By the settlement, both the company and the court have recognized the people's right to influence the use of precious natural areas held in private ownership. That vital understanding should mean a great deal in future battles to save the dwindling green spaces of our region.

Housing is neighborhood's only hope

By BETTY De RAMUS
Free Press Editorial Writer

I USED TO KNOW the neighborhood as well as I know my own name. I knew the small boys who hid behind garbage cans to stone strolling girls with bricks. I knew who had set fire to Mr. Sam's garage, and who had half chopped down a tree.

It was some neighborhood. Mary Hill woke up there one morning seeing spirits streaking across her ceiling and dashed out into the October chill wearing only a fleece sweater and skin. The Kentuckians next door plucked a battered guitar and groaned songs about good-time women, until, finally, the oldest son bashed the guitar over his father's head. The Chicanos edged away from the blacks, afraid people would dump them into the same sooty pot, but it did no good: The Polish kids snubbed them anyway.

DeRamus

Vacant lots are no way to bring life back to a decimated neighborhood

Yet people, somehow, raised families there, without any gang fights or sermons from police, so it was ort of sad to read the other day that the neighborhood had never returned to life since urban renewal killed it.

Today only grass grows on the chunk of Fourth Street near Forest where the mountain people and the Chicanos and Mary Hill used to live. And for 10 controversial years, much of the surrounding community has been home only to a few die-hard residents, some missions and churches, bars and parked cars—while bureaucrats and citizen groups and courts have argued about what to do.

Officials and members of the University City "A" Citizens District Council want to build what they call the Calumet Project—102 units of townhouses and garden apartments—in the area bounded by Third, the Lodge Service Drive, Calumet and Prentis.

BUT SOME area residents, including people who bought and renovated some of the old Victorian townhouses stretching along Canfield between Second and Third, say the community isn't ready to rebuild. It needs to first rid itself of prostitutes or they will move into the new housing and run other residents out. These people, the preservationists, also are concerned with maintaining the area's architectural character, something new buildings could threaten.

I can almost sympathize with the preservationists because there is so little left in Detroit to preserve. Grand old neighborhoods have been sacrificed for freeways, historic homes razed to make space for gas stations. My old flat at 4738 Fourth had been lived in, according to folklore, by Henry Ford: It had ceilings that seemed as distant as the moon and huge cut-glass chandeliers. A perfect place for a college student to fall in love with books. But that didn't save it.

And I can sympathize, too, with the people who say this area should be cleaned up before anything else is built. I can sympathize, but I can't quite agree.

IT IS DEPRESSING walking those old cracked streets. The Midtown Theater where we used to see Saturday matinees is gone, though Greater King Solomon Baptist Church still flashes a sign reading, "Jesus Cares . . . Do You?" on Forest near Fourth.

But the bars are thriving, particularly Anderson's Gardens and the Willis Show Bar, padlocked under the state nuisance law, then unpadlocked by an Appeals Court decision. The Michigan Supreme Court will decide, some day, whether or not they can be closed on the grounds that prostitutes make dates with customers there. Meanwhile, even at midday, people flock inside—most of them young, white and male.

Yet despite all this, there is not much life to these streets. A boarded-up Dairy Foods concession sits, brooding, on the corner of Canfield and Third, King Solomon rules over barren land. Monday afternoon, a couple of elderly ladies chatted at a bus stop about lace-making; a prostitute paraded down the other side of Third in a fringed leather jacket. But they all seemed isolated figures on a mostly empty canvas.

The only thing that can bring this area to life is more housing. The land was cleared for that purpose. Henry Hagood, the developer, promises that the new townhouses and garden apartments will use brick and wrought iron so they blend in with existing structures in the neighborhood. I hope he is right.

Most of the housing projects built in this city—even the middle and upper class ones with fancy names—have had a bleak sameness about them. They have been the kind of places where you couldn't tell the front door from the back or find your own unit after you'd had a few drinks.

BUT MUCH AS I dislike new housing developments, seeing vacant lots where houses should be is a lot worse. Twice, I have been displaced, forced to pull up roots, because someone had other plans for the land. The corner of Farnsworth and John R became a parking lot near the science center; Fourth and Forest is nothing at all.

Prostitution? Yes, it's in the area. In this city, it is everywhere. I've lived here all of my life, and in every neighborhood prostitutes always strutted right around the corner on the main thoroughfare. A cleanup, if it ever comes, will need to take in the whole town. It's a sad but true fact that if people had to wait for prostitution to die before housing could be built, little would ever be constructed in Detroit.

I just hope that when Calumet is finally built—in maybe another 10 years or so—they won't call it a project.

Shabby!

from our readers

Calumet: To build or not to build?

WE GREATLY appreciated Tom Fox's coverage (Free Press, March 26) of the latest attempt of former suburbanites on West Canfield to block housing on the Calumet site, housing for which the community fought for over 10 years and that is desperately needed to give the area new life and hope after the massive destruction of urban renewal in the '60s.

If our courts of law permit West Canfield residents to win their misguided fight, it will be clear that a single block will be able to set aside the wishes of the majority of area people, the unanimous vote of Detroit's City Council and the entire government of the U.S., simply because it is an historic district.

It doesn't matter that Calumet land is outside West Canfield historical boundaries. West Canfield will control it. It doesn't matter that our elected officials designated the land for housing before West Canfield was declared historic, or that when West Canfield sought historical designation, its leader, Beulah Groehn, declared that her association saw no conflict with proposed Calumet housing and actually supported it.

If West Canfield wins, the American principle of equal justice and the self-determination of Detroit will be a nostalgic memory.

RONALD SEIGEL
Chairman and Director
United Community Ombudsman

I LIVE ON PRENTIS between Second and Third and do not want to see the Calumet housing project built for several reasons that were not considered in Tom Fox's article (Free Press, March 26).

The article assumes that prostitution plagues the neighborhood, but its existence there has not been a problem to me.

I don't want to see a housing project whose "focus will be inward, blocking off street traffic" in a neighborhood that has been characterized by openness, tolerance and communication among residents. I don't want to see the cheap, quickly built, quickly deteriorating, unsightly architecture that is characteristic of government projects.

Will the Canfield homes be adversely affected by the Calumet housing project?

I don't want to lose the wild-flower park that now exists. Those fields have an assortment of vegetation, wild flowers, herbs and interesting trees and even birds not usually found in the city. The beauty of these things can be enjoyed through the change of seasons. It's a little bit of country in the city.

LYN ORDON

Speaking too soon

I WAS SHOCKED to read article (Free Press, April 11) by L. Brooks Patterson, prosecuting attorney for Oakland County. I was not so much shocked by the content of his message, as it may well have merit, but by the fact that he has apparently utilized the Free Press for perhaps his own individual political gain at the expense of two individuals who, at this moment, stand presumed innocent of any criminal activity in the tragic homicide on March 20.

In our Anglo-American system of jurisprudence, trial should take place in the courts and not in the press. I would draw your attention and Mr. Patterson's specifically to Disciplinary Rule 7-107 of the Code of Professional Responsibility governing all lawyers, which specifically prohibits pre-trial publicity of this matter.

Subsection (B)1 of that portion of the code prohibits any lawyer associated with the prosecution or defense of a criminal matter, until the commencement of the trial or disposition without trial, from making or participating in making any extra-judicial statements, (that is, a statement not made in court), that a reasonable person would expect to be disseminated by means of public communication that relates to the character, reputation or prior criminal record of the accused. Clearly, an article in the Free Press could be reasonably expected to be disseminated by means of public communication.

Mr. Patterson's rashness in writing this would be inexcusable, and the Free Press' agreeing to publish it at this time was very bad judgment.

WALTER L. HARRISON
Grand Rapids

Intercepted Letters

SEN. EARL NELSON
Lansing
Dear Borrower:

LOANLINESS of the runner.

Pipeline Pete

Detroit Free Press, April 26, 1978

Figure 9   THE OREGONIAN

The challenge remains

*Failure of the governor's tax plan puts burden
on Legislature's leaders to respond fast to Measure 5's threat*

I f not this, what? That's the question asked here the other day, when the Legislature was preparing to meet in special session to consider Gov. Barbara Roberts' tax-reform package.

It's the question that remains now that her proposal has been consigned to history and Measure 5's ugly face still stares at the state.

Senate President John Kitzhaber aptly termed it "a failed session." The people deserved a chance to vote on Roberts' package, skeptical as they appeared about it.

Blame for the Legislature's failure to place that proposal on the ballot can be spread broadly. Roberts gambled heavily when she called a session with only shaky support for her plan. House Speaker Larry Campbell, locked in unblinking disagreement with the governor over an election date, blocked reconsideration of the plan after it initially failed in the House. A few of the plan's supporters, expecting a second vote, foolishly voted against the plan the first time because of the date dispute.

But Oregon can't afford to wallow in assigning blame. Neither should Oregonians indulge in the temptation to laugh away this legislative session as the latest evidence that government doesn't know what it's doing.

Measure 5 is no joking matter. It threatens devastating cuts to valuable state programs, including education, social services, corrections and many other governmental functions that people so take for granted that they forget that's where the bulk of their tax money goes.

In the Legislature, at least, that point — Measure 5's threat — is sinking in. Out of the wreckage of the spe-

cial session, moreover, has come a more focused interest by legislative leaders of both houses and both parties to set aside partisanship and, as Kitzhaber put it, work at "the common task at hand, which is stabilizing Oregon's fiscal picture."

Legislative leaders correctly understand that by rejecting the governor's response to Measure 5's billion-dollar bite into the state general fund, they have assumed the burden of finding a responsible alternative. They need to start moving.

They also need outside help, from community leaders, business and representatives of the various other constituencies state government serves. Government can't rebuild its credibility with a skeptical and increasingly hostile public all by itself. It must have an endorsement of its core effectiveness from outside.

So, if not a vote on Roberts' proposal, what? The legislative leaders' new cooperative venture to identify budget needs and how to raise the money to meet those needs must move promptly toward those goals.

The effort should aim at having replacement revenues for much of Measure 5's bite in place before the 1993 legislative session begins in January. Roberts must be a full player in that process.

The exercise will be painful and controversial. You don't cut budgets or raise taxes without affecting people. But this pain is nothing to the trauma that the next phase of Measure 5 will bring if left to itself.

If not this, what? Oregon cannot afford to allow the answer to be massive and destructive cuts in state services. One failure only underscores the need for ultimate success.

The Oregonian, July 5, 1992

Except for letters to the editor, those who wrote and drew for the editorial page essentially talked to one another, mostly about politics and government. It was a page that belonged to professionals. But as editors began to search for ways to enliven their pages and keep their readership, they came up with a variety of ideas for attracting more diverse views of more people to the page. The innovations have included guest columns and other contributions from knowledgeable persons, in-depth analyses, a question of the week, pro-con arguments on specific issues, and critiques of and comments on the press. To a large extent these have been made possible through the addition of more editorial space, notably the op-ed (opposite-editorial) page, which will be discussed later.

FIGURE 10   PLAIN DEALER

For the jobless, only more pain

Jobless Americans need not bother to look toward Washington for any recession-fighting help this winter. When the White House this week succeeded in blocking extended unemployment benefits for many of the nation's 8.4 million luckless job hunters, it marked a low point in social-policy cynicism.

The Bush administration, claiming that the chronically unemployed are merely a "lagging indicator" of the economy, sees no need to extend unemployment benefits to the jobless who exhaust their standard 26 weeks of payments. Bipartisan majorities in both houses of Congress recently backed a $6.4 billion benefits bill — the Senate by 65-35 and the House by 300-118 — but the Senate on Wednesday fell two votes short of the two-thirds majority needed to override President Bush's veto.

As families suffer, the White House will boost its budget-cutting image by pocketing the money that should have gone to aid the jobless. More than $8 billion, dedicated to the federal unemployment-insurance trust fund, will continue sitting idle in the Treasury. Hoarding the trust-fund money, rather than releasing it, helps disguise the enormity of the budget deficit.

Pretending to show its concern, the White House advanced an alternative that would have aided only 200,000 of the jobless, rather than the 1.1 million helped by Congress' plan. Worse, the White House relied on accounting gimmicks — the kind

"

Deaf to pleas for compassion, the White House has shortchanged the unemployed, many of whom are victimized by this year's economic slump.

that were supposedly forbidden by last year's deficit-reduction pact — to claim that it came up with a quick-fix $3.1 billion.

Too clever by half, the White House plan would shift future years' student-loan collections into this fiscal year, thus robbing future federal budgets. Even more illogically, it would accelerate a planned federal sell-off of unused broadcasting channels. Such a hurry-up sale would bring in only about $2 billion, rather than a potential $4.5 billion if Washington patiently drove a hard bargain.

Deaf to pleas for compassion, the White House has shortchanged blameless workers, many of whom are victimized by this year's economic slump. The position of the Bush administration, needlessly sacrificing its credibility, undercuts voters' faith in its promise of "kinder, gentler" social policies.

The Plain Dealer, October 18, 1991

Guest Columns

One of the first widely noted efforts to bring more non-journalists to an editorial page was a column called "In My Opinion," begun by the *Milwaukee Journal* in 1970. An early participant was Milwaukee's mayor, one of the *Journal*'s severest critics. Other participants included a radical student, a welfare worker, a policeman with a gripe about judges and a defense lawyer with a complaint about the police. Columns usually ran between 600 and 700 words and participants were not paid for their contributions. Editors of the paper reported that the column had helped the *Journal* build an image of journalistic fair play in an era of concern about too-powerful mass media.[11]

Board of Contributors

After I left *The Columbian*, the editorial page staff invited several literate, informed citizens in the community to serve on a board of contributors. From time to time they would write on a timely issue, sometimes local, sometimes state, national or international. The *Plain Dealer* in Cleveland reported having a board of contributors numbering 30.[12]

In-depth Page

Extra space also has allowed editors to use their pages for an in-depth look at issues. The *Tucson Daily Citizen* selected a local, national or international topic

FIGURE 11   PHOENIX GAZETTE

A beginning
President's health care plan

The politicians feel an irresistible urge to do something about health care this election year. Heaven help us.

The president's health care plan isn't wonderful, but it beats anything the Democrats have to offer.

Ever since Democrat Harris Wofford beat Republican Dick Thornburgh in Pennsylvania's Senate race, allegedly by thumping the health care drum, there has been a lot of hustle-bustling over at the White House in search of a plan for the president to endorse.

Unfortunately, any proposal that would address fundamental problems has been ruled politically unacceptable.

The Democrats aren't telling the truth about health care and the Bush administration isn't going to try, either — at least not in an election year.

The truth is that there is no free lunch, least of all in health care. As a good part of the world has discovered, when anything is free the demand for it will soon overwhelm the capacity of any government to provide it.

The result, as the president noted, is long waiting lists for surgery and shortages of high-tech equipment for the miracles of modern medicine.

Proponents of nationalized health care would have us believe that the same government that can't control the $390 billion it now spends on health care could do so if it were permitted to spend many billions more.

Those who want business to pick up the tab are just as guilty of ignoring basic economic facts. Mandated benefits translate into lower wages or fewer jobs.

The president's plan is a step, albeit a hesitant one, in the right direction. He is trying to move toward a market-driven health care system. That's the direction taken by the British government in 1989, and the way New Zealand and even Sweden are edging after years of socialized medicine.

The president's proposal would preserve individual choice, but make health care more accessible to those who can't afford it. He would help the uninsured by providing $100 billion in vouchers and tax breaks to the poor and middle class to buy insurance.

Poor and many middle class Americans would get tax credits and deductions worth up to $3,750 per family for the purchase of health care. The self-employed, for whom health care is prohibitively expensive, could take tax deductions equal to 100 percent of their monthly premiums.

Unfortunately, the president is hazy about where the money is coming from, offering to negotiate with Congress about the specifics.

Among other recommendations, Bush would provide for a "blue book" similar to those used for auto sales to help consumers determine how much various medical services should cost.

He would make insurance more affordable for small businesses through insurance pools and put a leash on malpractice litigation.

Another element of the Bush plan is flat, per-person grants to states for Medicaid recipients rather than payments on services provided. Medicaid payments to states would be capped and tied to population growth and inflation. That is not so much a cut in spending, however, as it is a shift to state and local governments.

Admittedly, the president's health care proposal is driven by election year politics, intended to deflect Democratic criticism that the president isn't attending to the problem. That is a poor climate in which to develop sound policies.

Opponents have attacked the president's plan as too limited in scope. Considering the damage the Democrats would do to health care, that's a recommendation.

The Phoenix Gazette, February 8, 1992

each day for analysis in depth. Staff writers wrote the stories if they were local, while material on national and international topics came from the wire services, reprints from other newspapers and other publications.[13] *USA Today* has experimented with tying editorials, guest columns, opposing opinions and "Voices from the USA" together around a single topic.

FIGURE 12 CHARLOTTE OBSERVER (BEFORE)

The Charlotte Observer

ROLFE NEILL, Chairman and Publisher
RICHARD OPPEL, Editor — JOHN LUBY, General Manager
ED WILLIAMS, Editor of the Editorial Pages — DOUGLAS CLIFTON, Managing Editor
JACK CLAIBORNE, TOM BRADBURY, JERRY SHINN, Associate Editors
Sunday, May 6, 1990

Editorials

A Crazy Way To Pick Judges

Surely N.C. Legislature Is Ready For Merit Selection

You're about to help elect North Carolina's judges. But unless you're a lawyer, chances are you won't have the slightest idea who's best qualified. We think the vote-in-the-dark method of selecting judges is nutty; when you see your ballot, we think you'll agree. It's time for the legislature to make judgeships appointive, rather than elective.

On Tuesday, for example, Mecklenburg Democrats will help decide whether Judge Gene Phillips or Assistant Attorney General Ellen Scouten will be their party's nominee for the state Court of Appeals. Some Mecklenburg voters — and we'll bet few of you know whether you're among them — will decide whether Judge Ken Griffin, Judge Robert Johnston or Julia Jones will be nominated for the two seats in District 26B.

In November, N.C. voters will decide who should sit on the state Supreme Court and Court of Appeals. You'll vote on who should be superior court judges from Manteo to Murphy — most of them people you haven't heard of before and won't hear of again until the next election.

The N.C. way of selecting judges, though nutty in principle, used to work pretty well because it was in fact a system of appointment. Most judges left office by death, retirement or resignation, and the governor appointed their successors, who seldom faced electoral opposition.

But that was when Democrats won every statewide election. Now the Republican Party is strong statewide, and judgeships have become partisan contests. That means voters make more choices, and in all but a few races they will do so ignorantly.

Judges, you see, are chosen in elections in which there can be no political debate. Their code of conduct prohibits it. They can't discuss anything voters might be interested in — the death penalty, rulings by other judges, what they'd do to drunk drivers or drug pushers. Candidates' backers, however, can say anything they like. Divorcing the candidate from responsibility for the campaign is a sure way to encourage irresponsibility. Recent judicial elections have been marred by slander, whispering campaigns and demagoguery. As competition intensifies, that will get worse.

Then there is money. Judges can't solicit contributions, so their supporters do. Judges are supposed to be independent and impartial, but they have lawyers raising money and soliciting endorsements for them and against them. What can lawyers expect when their candidate loses? Or wins: In Texas, a judge in a case involving the oil business may have received a big campaign donation from oil company lobbyists and lawyers. Such lawyer-judge coziness isn't what North Carolina needs.

There are many problems involved in creating a system of appointing judges, but they're the sort of problems legislators are elected to deal with. It's time for action in Raleigh.

Environmental Favoritism?

Rauch Industries Case Compromises State's Enforcement

Allowing Rauch Industries of Gastonia to violate environmental standards 91 times in 12 years without a fine or other sanctions is an outrage against the people of North Carolina.

Rauch

Officials of the N.C. Department of Environment, Health and Natural Resources deserve the condemnation they got from environmentalists this past week. The state has made it difficult for citizens to put much confidence in its environmental protection.

The lax enforcement not only has compromised the quality of N.C. water, air and soils; it also has embarrassed state Sen. Marshall Rauch, D-Gaston, the president of Rauch Industries, who is also chairman of N.C. Senate's tax-writing Finance Committee and a potential Democratic candidate for governor in 1992. The lack of fines or other punishment makes it look as if he got special treatment as a result of his political position, though state officials insist that was never the case.

Unlike many perennial polluters, who treat fines for environmental damage as a cost of doing business, Sen. Rauch "has always been a model of courtesy," said Don Follmer, a spokesman for the state's environmental resources department. "He was always very cooperative and tried to fix whatever was wrong."

Each time the state cited the company for inadequately treating its wastes, the company responded in ways it thought would solve the problem, Sen. Rauch said. Finally, when it became clear that the company would have to build its own waste-treatment plant, it spent $300,000 for a state-of-the-art facility that was in operation before news of the company's past violations was made public.

But by then the damage was done, not only to the environment but also to the senator's reputation. It now appears he would have been better off to have paid hefty fines.

"We are not proud of what has happened," Sen. Rauch said. In 40 years of doing business in Gaston County, his company's integrity and responsibility were never in question, he said. "Now we owe the people of the community an apology and we do apologize."

The state's environmental police should be equally as apologetic. They claim they are aggressive in prosecuting polluters and play no favorites. And, in fairness, it should be said that recent records show a sharp increase in fines and sanctions. But the Rauch Industries case still breeds suspicion that other violators have been getting off easy. The state should work hard to dispel that impression.

Some Capital Reservations

Need For More Jails, Parking Can Be Endless, Unless...

The Mecklenburg County Citizens Capital Budget Advisory Committee's report to the county commissioners last week included a couple of reservations that ought to be among the fundamental working premises of growing urban centers in the 1990s.

Committee member Ike Heard, noting the projected need for a new 1,837-bed county jail, which could cost as much as $130 million, warned against simply building an expensive "warehouse" for prisoners. Before undertaking such a project, he said, the county ought to study the possibility of a multi-use incarceration facility that would include counseling and services that, over time, might restrain the growth of the county's jail population. He also suggested building a new jail in stages. With increased emphasis on alternative sentences, the need for jail space might turn out to be less than current projections suggest.

And he said the county ought to explore the idea of a regional jail. That wouldn't be appropriate for people awaiting trial, who need to be near the courts. But if the state solves part of its prison-crowding problem by requiring counties to keep more misdemeanants in county jails instead of sending them to state prison, a regional facility for those prisoners might make sense.

Franklin McCain asked whether county government really wanted to keep building parking decks at prices ranging up to $10,000 per space. One alternative, he said, might be satellite surface parking with shuttle buses to take employees to their offices. As commissioner Rod Autrey noted, the longer the county continues to accommodate employees' cars, the longer it will be before car-pooling, van-pooling and real transit alternatives become a way of life in this community.

The county desperately needs more jail space, of course, and it may need more parking decks, too. But in a growing urban center, jails and parking decks — and roads, too — have this in common: They will fill up as fast as we can build them. They will consume more and more of our public capital, unless we challenge some old assumptions about how people get to and from work, about what we do with people awaiting trial, and about how we deal with misdemeanants.

Hunt Gave Money To Wrong School

The Observer Forum
Our Readers' Views

There's a lot of talk going on in political circles about how hard it is for Democrats to raise money for this year's Senate race.

I was surprised recently to learn Jim Hunt is still trying to use all the money he raised in 1984. I think Jim Hunt was very selfish when he took the last $100,000 of his campaign funds and set up a scholarship in his name at Wake Forest.

A much better gesture on Hunt's part would have been to set up the scholarship at a black public or private institution to, in part, make up for a gross error in the Goals and Policy Survey for North Carolina that was formulated in 1977 under Jim Hunt's leadership.

This survey, released with a lot of media attention, had a goal for North Carolina "opportunities for women." At no place did the survey mention opportunities for minorities. For six months I tried to find out from Jim Hunt how this grave error happened. He never told me.

A scholarship at a black institution would have been a most appropriate gesture for Jim Hunt to express appreciation for past and maybe future black support.

HARRILL JONES
Gastonia

Sports Before Police Safety

If you know someone who's close to Mayor Myrick, would you please ask him or her to suggest that if there's enough money left over from building the NFL football stadium it be used to buy proper equipment for our police officers. Specifically, it would be ever so thoughtful to spend a small amount of our tax money to provide our officers with flak jackets and updated weapons.

My daughter patrols some nightmarish areas at night, by herself. Fortunately, through the kindness and generosity of Charlotte Ford Tractor Co., she now has a flak jacket. Many other officers do not.

Because Charlotte is such a sports-oriented city, I would not presume to suggest that police safety should take precedence over the building of an NFL stadium. I'm only suggesting a possible way in which to spend any surplus funds we might end up with.

WILLIAM C. MARTIN
Concord

Editorial On Right Track

As one who has enjoyed riding the Amtrak Carolinian to Greensboro, Raleigh and Washington, I am pleased to see the return of this daytime train once again.

Your April 29 editorial "Swifter Passenger Trains" makes at least two important points — reducing travel time to make the trip competitive to auto travel and less polluting overall.

As you say, roads are like prisons — the more we build them (or add additional lanes), the quicker they are filled up. It just doesn't make sense.

Finally, let's hope our political hopefuls, local and statewide, are paying attention. The funds saved can be much better used for education, housing and health needs.

ARTHUR KORTHEUER
Charlotte

'Kiss Of Death' For Gantt

Gantt can pack it in now and save a bundle. His endorsement by The Charlotte Observer (April 29, "Harvey Gantt For The Senate") was the "kiss of death."

The Observer seldom, if ever, has endorsed the winner in a major campaign such as this.

HARRY GRIFFIN
Charlotte

Keep Drugs Off UNCC

Three cheers to the Mecklenburg County Police Department for the sting operation on April 25 that resulted in 21 drug arrests on the UNC Charlotte campus.

As a student residing in the dormitories at UNCC, I have witnessed repeated violations concerning the use of illegal drugs, with nothing more than a shrug of the shoulders from university officials.

The drug problem at UNCC is not unlike that at any other campus across North Carolina. I can only hope that operations such as the one at UNCC are a sign of things to come.

Drugs have no place in our society, and especially not in our schools. While they are the root of many of our problems, they are also the result of many problems such as illiteracy and poor education. This is one reason Gov. Martin and Lt. Gov. Gardner have been trying to enact Drug-Free School Zone legislation. Drugs do not belong on the campus where young minds are being educated to be the leaders of tomorrow.

CRAIG S. LEWIS
Charlotte

Law Not Always Right

Here is Reality 101 for you, Charlotte Observer editors (April 30, "Reality 101")! Because something is illegal does not mean the law is correct.

As to thinking we live in never-never-land, I ask you to reflect on your own college-age days. Did none of you stand up and protest against the Vietnam war, even if you were told it was illegal?

What happened to our brothers and sisters who were arrested had nothing to do with protecting innocent people; it is the politics of the anti-drug hysteria.

THOMAS WILLIAMS
Charlotte

Whom Can We Trust?

I have lived 20 years of "Reality 101." I know the law, but I think marijuana should be legal.

I should have the choice. But what The Observer failed to realize is the nature of the protest that you are criticizing. It is not the fact that our fellow students and friends were thrown in jail for breaking the law that annoys us, it is the manner in which the arrests were made.

We disagree with having fellow students buddy up to us and gain our trust as friends so that they can stab us in the back. It creates a paranoid society (campus) in which people walk around looking over their shoulder wondering who their friends are. Is this good?

MICHAEL FAUST
Charlotte

Write The Forum

We welcome letters. Please sign and include your address and daytime telephone number. Mail to Observer Forum, P.O. Box 32188, Charlotte 28232.

We edit letters for brevity, grammar and clarity, and we reject those published elsewhere. Because of the volume received, we cannot return letters not used. Editors, The Observer

Reexamine Clubs' Membership Policies

The subject of membership in private clubs has recently created a lot of interesting conversation in Charlotte.

Zimmerman

It's been amazing how many club members were not even aware of existing membership restrictions that result in discrimination. One thing that has come through in conversations is that most people want their clubs' membership policies examined and remedied.

Let's hope that will happen and we can proceed with our mission to be a world-class city by first becoming world-class citizens.

JOAN H. ZIMMERMAN
Charlotte

Didn't Mean To Offend

The writer is president of the board, Guild of Science Museums of Charlotte Inc.

This letter is in response to The Observer's April 18 editorial "Public Affairs, Private Clubs" and Kevin Siers' cartoon. The guild has been supporting and raising funds for the Nature Museum and Discovery Place for almost 30 years.

Our fund-raising efforts have included Collector's Corner, Haunted House, a nature booklet, the Christmas Plum, a cookbook and a Festival of Trees. We have raised more than $400,000 to support a variety of museum projects such as the JASON Project, Climbing Sculpture and "Dinosaurs" at Discovery Place. At the Nature Museum, we have supported the Owl's Nest, Dragonfly Puppet Theater and the Animal Room. Our scholarships provide classes and activities for needy children and adults.

We are proud of our past successes. We appreciate the support we have received from the friends of Discovery Place and the Nature Museum. The fund-raiser in question was designed to continue our support of Science Museums of Charlotte Inc.

If our guild embarrassed Myers Park Country Club or offended any member of the community, we apologize. We simply want to continue to support two of our community's treasures — the Nature Museum and Discovery Place. Our membership has always been open to anyone wishing to help the museums.

SYLVIA TARLETON
Charlotte

Negative Criticism Hurts

Time out! For the life of me, I can't understand why we take such pleasure in taking jabs at one another. I'm having trouble figuring out why The Observer is using so much space on negative reporting about a Discovery Place fund-raiser.

I recently went off the Discovery Place board after having served for more than 10 years. That organization has involved all sectors of this community in all of its activities. The board of directors and other Discovery Place support groups take their role of fiscal responsibility very seriously, and I applaud the guild for trying something new to raise money.

Woollen

All of the chastising of Discovery Place was surprising enough, but to then take on the business community and their club memberships was too much. Polly Paddock's column (April 23, "Private Clubs Compromise City's Class") offended me. I don't know of a time in Charlotte's recent history that there has been a need that was not addressed by the members of the business community, who were referred to as WASPS in her column.

In all the community activities in which I have been involved, I have never heard such comments. These are the people who are in the trenches of this community, solving problems, meeting needs, giving money, serving on boards, providing jobs, tutoring kids, cleaning up after Hugo — working to make Charlotte a great place for all to live.

Charlotte is a "world-class city" because it's made up of "world-class" people.

We have so much to celebrate in this city. There is simply no need for so much negative criticism. It makes me want to quit trying. Maybe I'll just go play golf.

VELVA W. WOOLLEN
Charlotte

The Charlotte Observer, May 6, 1990

FIGURE 13 CHARLOTTE OBSERVER (AFTER)

10A THE CHARLOTTE OBSERVER Friday, February 5, 1993 • • • •

The Charlotte Observer

ROLFE NEILL, Chairman and Publisher
RICHARD OPPEL, Editor **JOHN LUBY**, General Manager
GENE WILLIAMS, Executive Vice President
ED WILLIAMS, Editor of the Editorial Pages **JANE SHOEMAKER**, Executive Editor
TOM BRADBURY, JACK BETTS, Associate Editors **FRANK BARROWS**, Managing Editor

Editorials

Violence in schools

■ Gov. Hunt's school violence task force may help focus attention on the problem, but the state needs to move quickly.

While it may be true that violence in North Carolina schools is still relatively minor, any violence at all is too much violence. Gov. Jim Hunt is right to take violence in schools seriously and make its eradication a priority. Incidents of violence and weapons in schools are more than a threat to learning; they are a danger to life and limb.

Diamont

State Rep. David Diamont, a Surry County school teacher in real life, got a first-hand look at school violence last fall when he helped break up a fight. He makes a good point: "What good does it do to lower class sizes when kids are afraid to come to school?"

That's why Gov. Hunt appointed a School Violence Task Force this week to study the problem and make recommendations within 60 days. Mr. Hunt named Secretary of Crime Control and Public Safety Thurman Hampton to chair the panel with Attorney General Mike Easley and Superintendent of Public Instruction Bob Etheridge.

Giving such a high profile to the group will help focus public attention on the problem and perhaps prompt extraordinary cooperation with the panel's mission: find out what works and what doesn't.

Appointing a study commission may be a predictable reaction, but the School Violence Task Force in this case is a reasonable response. When the State Board of Education looked at school violence a year ago, it concluded it didn't know enough about the problem to take any action. It still doesn't.

But the panel can examine many approaches. Greensboro schools use airline-style metal detectors and require students to use see-through book bags to limit weapons. Other schools use security guards and video monitoring systems. Some schools have experimented with weapons-free zones; others have more flexibility to expel students who carry weapons or assign them to alternative schools.

The panel plans to conduct hearings across the state. It should listen to citizens like Rep. Diamont, who is working on a bill to provide grants to school systems to develop school violence programs. It should listen to students and parents who want the state to take proper steps to preserve schools as safe havens for learning. And it should listen carefully to concerns about transforming schools into armed prison camps aimed at keeping students in and violence out.

Public support is part of a delicate formula crafted to improve our schools and their performance. If we allow a small school violence problem to become a big one, that balance will collapse, and we will pour more of our resources into patrolling schools and less into teaching our children what they need to know.

Sell the Coliseum?

■ It's hard to imagine an offer good enough to justify selling one of the city's jewels, but the discussion could be useful.

Privatization of city services is a topic that can put even insomniacs to sleep. But the idea of selling the Charlotte Coliseum turns dull theory into lively controversy, showing that privatization is an emotional issue as well as a financial one.

Finance is the logical starting point, of course. Last year the Coliseum had an operating surplus of some $3.2 million, but it costs the taxpayers roughly $4 million for the annual payments on the remaining bond debt of $39 million. If the Coliseum were sold, the Auditorium-Coliseum-Convention Center Authority would no longer have the surplus to draw on for its other facilities. But if somebody were willing to pay the $75 million to $100 million that the authority's managing director thinks the Coliseum is worth, the city could retire the debt, stop making bond payments and have a tidy pot of money for other needs — and it would receive the taxes paid each year by the new private owner.

All that ought to be examined. What would be the impact for now and the foreseeable future on the city budget and the overall operations of the authority? Would the city be better off, worse off, about the same? What sale price would it take to make the deal not only positive, but attractive?

That is where the question becomes much more than an accounting issue. Mayor Richard Vinroot and City Manager Wendell White say the city should retain control of a major asset. City Council member Don Reid, on the other hand, thinks that governments have pushed into areas best left to private enterprise. Some of the Coliseum's benefits — such as its economic impact — would continue under private ownership. But proponents of continued city ownership argue that public control is important to preserving other benefits, such as attracting events that are good for the community but not profitable for the arena.

It's hard to imagine an offer good enough to justify selling one of the city's jewels. But this is a chance to stir up interest in talking more generally about what makes sense for local governments in a time of mounting needs and limited resources. The lessons will apply not only to the Coliseum, but to privatizing other services and facilities, and to the decisions about what new public investments to make.

For the record: Gov. Jim Hunt

School violence victimizes all

■ *From Gov. Jim Hunt's remarks Wednesday announcing a task force on school violence.*

We must build a brighter future for our youngsters, and we must keep them safe. We must keep our children safe in our streets, and safe in our schools.

Hunt

Every week, news reports tell another tragic story of school violence, and another tragic story of a child in danger. Just yesterday, a 17-year-old was sentenced to life in prison for murdering a young girl as she sat in a Randolph County classroom last year.

Last Monday, a star football player was shot in the corridors of a Richmond County high school. On Thursday, students were assaulted and robbed in the schoolyard of Sanderson High School, and a Raleigh police officer was wounded after a subsequent shoot-out.

Just as frightening are the reports of guns, knives and other weapons in the schools. In this school year alone, more than 100 Mecklenburg County students have been caught bringing weapons into school.

Our public schools cannot thrive surrounded by violence.

As governor — and as a parent and grandparent — I say enough is enough.

Our children cannot learn surrounded by violence. Our teachers cannot teach in classrooms surrounded by violence. Our public schools cannot thrive surrounded by violence. And our state cannot realize its potential in an environment of violence. In short, school violence victimizes all of us.

And we must all band together to fight it. All of us — elected officials, law enforcement officers, educators, parents, religious and community leaders — must join hands to stem the tide of school violence. It is our responsibility to make our schools safe. . . .

No state agency is now devoting its efforts and resources to fighting school violence. Today, that's changing.

We must develop a comprehensive approach to preventing violence in our classrooms and we must put the resources of state government squarely behind this effort.

I've asked my new secretary of crime control, Thurman Hampton, to make school violence his No. 1 priority. I've asked him to identify federal and state money in his department to target school violence, and to make school violence a fundamental part of the crime prevention plan he's drawing up. . . .

I'm looking to North Carolina's leading law enforcement officers and our top education officials to bring their unique perspectives and expertise to this critical task.

It's my hope that this task force will conduct hearings across North Carolina in the next 60 days — in places like Rockingham, Durham, Charlotte, Greensboro and Raleigh.

We must hear from local law enforcement officials, parents, students, teachers, school administrators, judges, legislators and others involved in the fight against school violence.

We must find out what local school systems are doing to fight violence in their classrooms. We must find out what works, and what doesn't.

We must develop a statewide approach to prevent school violence, and to make our classrooms safe again.

Kevin Siers

WE OWNERS FOUND HER COMMENTS UNACCEPTABLE, REFLECTING THE WORST KIND OF RACIAL STEREOTYPES...
DISPLAYING A SHOCKINGLY CALLOUS INSENSITIVITY...
TOTALLY DISREGARDING THE BEST INTERESTS OF BASEBALL...
FOCUSING ATTENTION ON OUR MINORITY HIRING PRACTICES!
MARGE SCHOTT SUSPENSION

The Observer Forum

Payroll tax would give poor a break

A city-county payroll tax is probably the best idea I've heard since I moved here.

Increasing the property tax hurts the same people consistently. Enacting a payroll tax would affect all people who work here and use services here, whether they live here or not, whether they own or rent.

At last — a tax that wouldn't increase the burden on the poor. How can we even think of increasing the sales tax on food or the property tax for those on fixed incomes?

ANN MARIE LLOYD
Charlotte

Snowboarders imperil traditional skiers

I'm infuriated that Sugar Mountain, last bastion of snowboard-less skiing in North Carolina, has now given in (Jan. 29, "More getting on board, finding it a fine way to get down a hill"). Snowboarding is rightly called "shredding" or "carving," because that's exactly what it does to the slopes, ruining them for normal skiing. North Carolina has enough trouble making and keeping its snow without having what little there is unmercifully scraped away.

Lambert

Most snowboarders I've encountered have been rude, out-of-control youngsters who have no consideration for traditional skiers — and who try to knock us off the slopes.

Snowboarding should be banned or at least partitioned from the rest of us.

BETSY LAMBERT
Charlotte

Snowboarding: Surfing on the slopes

I found Monte Mitchell's observance of carvers and shredders extremely pleasing.

Before moving to Hickory, I spent my mornings surfing at Huntington Beach, Calif. A relaxing peace, often coupled with an intense adrenaline rush, made it part of my life.

I have found snowboarding provides a similar experience. After the first couple of days, the pain and soreness will seem a small price for the pleasure.

GEOFFREY BICKEL
Hickory

Plan for your death, or system will decide

Every adult should read Ellen Goodman's column on the way death is prolonged (Feb. 2 Viewpoint, "Medicine and money"), then observe for an hour or so life in a nursing home. If people did these two things, they would sign documents to discourage their being "maintained" with tubes running in and out of their bodies.

The law seems to require that each person make for himself the decision not to be poked at and pulled at and denied the dignity needed at the end of life. If we do not tell our doctors what we want *before* we can no longer think clearly or speak up, the system will inflict on our poor selves every treatment it knows.

MARY F. OWEN
Boone

Military system unsuited for complaints

Accepting open homosexuality in the military would tax the system with special-interest rights, demands, harassment charges, special commissions, complaints of unequal treatment, quotas — all unavailable to the straight majority.

The sergeant has always intimidated the private, the lieutenant the sergeant, the captain the lieutenant, the major the captain. Does this system have room for insubordination or complaints? No! You either grin and bear the system for three or four years, or you incorporate the system for 20 years. As the wise colonel stated at the first of "Apocalypse Now": "When the system breaks down, we break down" — "we" meaning our nation.

CHARLIE WELLS
Charlotte

Clinton puts military at higher AIDS risk

Bill Clinton stands alongside the outstretched arm of the military with a syringe in his hand. The needle is tinged with AIDS, the syringe is full of homosexuality. The military's bloodstream is about to carry this disease to its heart. Why does Clinton want to reduce our strong soldiers to AIDS patients? Doesn't our nation have enough already?

GENE DODGE
Morrisville

Aren't my rights worth fighting for?

Please, President Clinton, stop the discrimination that prevents me from serving in my country's military. They say I am too short. They say my eyesight doesn't come up to standard. They say I am obese.

I wasn't part of an organization that contributed to your campaign, but I did vote for you knowing you held individual rights above all else. Now I trust you will be as concerned about *my* rights as you are about the homosexuals'.

RALPH DRAKE
Charlotte

Military is no place for social experiments

The military is not intended to be a microcosm of society. It is not a petri dish for liberal policy experiments. It exists only to protect our country.

MICHAEL D. ELLIS
Hickory

Just say no to homosexuality

If homosexuality were genetic, God would not have stated it as a specific deviant behavior. I see no reason for government to consider any action on this issue except to say no — just as we do with drugs!

ANNETTE COWAN
Charlotte

Gays' goals aren't 'a reach'

Mike Barnicle (Jan. 28 Viewpoint, "Gay activists ask too much") says that gays' "asking anything beyond tolerance, understanding, compassion and a respect for privacy is a reach." As a U.S. citizen I have the freedom of speech to state in this letter that I am gay. If I were in the military, however, such a public statement would cost me my job.

What Mr. Barnicle considers "a reach" for gays' goals is in fact just a request for the rights of every citizen guaranteed under the Constitution. This isn't asking too much, is it?

ODIE D. STUTTS
Rock Hill

"I KIND OF LIKE BEING JUST PLAIN ORDINARY CITIZEN GEORGE BUSH. DO I GET TO KEEP AIR FORCE ONE ?"

Gays would improve bonding of soldiers

The reasoning that homosexuals would interfere with the necessary bonding of men in combat is illogical. Homosexuals, men who are committed to men, seemingly would be of a *greater* benefit in protecting the lives of their fellow man.

Most homosexuals who join the services aren't looking for sexual fulfillment, only a chance to contribute and support America for what it represents: "liberty and justice for *all*."

GREGORY PLATIS
Charlotte

Where are military's 'Christian values'?

In response to " 'I don't think the president understands our position,' Fort Bragg soldier says" (Jan. 29):

Help me understand the logic in Sgt. Johnny Donoto's quote: "You try to bring your children up with Christian values. When they see the Army says it's OK to be gay, what are we doing?"

This is the same Army that's already doing such a great job of instilling Christian values in our children, by blasting people of other countries?

APARNA IYER
Matthews

Clinton following in JFK's footsteps

Many trivialize gay and lesbian rights by terming them "lifestyle issues." Millions of Americans know this is not true. President Clinton is wrestling with as profound an issue of civil rights as President Kennedy did with his stands against racial segregation. He must not bow to the forces of hate and fear. We must create a world where decent people are as disgusted by the beliefs behind the word "faggot" as they are by the beliefs behind "kike" and "nigger."

KEN SCHELL
Charlotte

Forum writers choose herd over individual

A criticism too often leveled at The Observer is that it is liberally biased and that its editorial staff is pursuing some "agenda." Even if this were true, it is more than amply compensated for: The daily dose of unstomachable illogic from demagogues in the Forum could be compiled into a book called "Mein Kampf."

In their preference for the herd mentality over individualism, these quarterwits are paradoxically un-American. The concept of *individuals*, in their *many and varied forms*, is what this country supposedly is all about. It is a poor reflection on this society and, indeed, on the whole of humanity, when even one of its citizens is intolerant in matters of religion, politics, ethnicity or sex.

THOMAS HENKEL
Lincolnton

■ Write the Forum

We welcome letters. Please sign and include your address and daytime telephone number.

We edit letters for brevity, grammar and clarity, and we reject those published elsewhere. Edited letters typically address a single idea and do not exceed 150 words. Because of the volume received, we cannot return letters not used.

— *Editors, The Observer*

The Observer Forum
The Charlotte Observer
Box 32188
Charlotte, N.C. 28232
Fax number: (704) 358-5022
Computer bulletin board: (704) 358-5072

The Charlotte Observer, February 5, 1993

Question of the Week

Some papers have posed a question of the week to help readers feel they can have a say. The *Milwaukee Journal* and the *Philadelphia Evening Bulletin* were among the first to try this. On the *Bulletin* a typical page contained 11 or 12 letters for readers, an editorial on the subject and an announcement of the next week's question. The *Intelligencer Journal* in Lancaster, Pa., has solicited readers' opinions on a public issue through a weekly "People's Poll," with a tabulation published on Saturday.

Pro-Con Arguments

One attempt to give readers the feeling that they are getting a fair debate on the issues, not just the newspaper's side, is the pro-con package developed in 1971 by editors of the *St. Petersburg* (Fla.) *Times*. They saw the feature as a way to "reduce reader resistance to persuasion" without reducing the newspaper's commitment to its own viewpoint. The package contained a question and an explanation of the issue, "yes" and "no" arguments, a brief editorial stating the *Times*' position, and a coupon on which readers could write their comments. They could then clip out the coupon and mail it to the newspaper.[14]

Alternative Opinion Page

The possibility of losing an alternative editorial voice when the competing newspaper folded was avoided, at least temporarily, in Shreveport, La., and Anchorage, Alaska. A full editorial page headed "Shreveport Journal" appears each day in *The Times* of Shreveport, and a half page headed "Anchorage Times" appears in the *Anchorage Daily News*.[15]

Opinions of Other Newspapers

To obtain different point of views, some newspapers make a point of reprinting all or parts of editorials from other newspapers. The *Globe and Mail* in Toronto, Ontario, carries a column titled "Other Voices," in which the writer cites and comments on items that have appeared in other newspapers.

Media Critics

The relatively few newspapers that have ombudsmen, media critics or reader advocates generally run their columns on the editorial page. These columns can help maintain a newspaper's credibility if the persons assigned to them are knowledgeable, fair and free to write what they wish. Other newspapers prefer to have their editors write the columns dealing with media affairs. These usually turn out to be more explanatory than critical. (The media criticism column is discussed in Chapter 15, "Other Types of Opinion Writing.")

Visual Illustrations

Most editorial page editors have not been innovative in using illustrative material to brighten their pages and reinforce the opinions offered on the editorial page.

Most stick with their regular syndicated cartoonists plus an illustrator (such as Geoffrey Moss, Eleanor Mill or Ranan Lurie). An editor now and then will think about presenting information in some manner other than the traditional paragraph. To help explain an editorial criticizing high concession prices at Atlanta's airport, the *Atlanta Constitution* printed a table comparing 12 sets of prices at the airport with those at malls and other airports (Figure 14, below). A few editors will ask for photographs to go with editorials, letters or other pieces. The *Detroit Free Press* ran a rear view of a woman receiving a breast X-ray to accompany a letter on that subject. Once in a while readers appreciate artwork that has no heavy editorial message. The *Akron Beacon Journal* reproduced a photograph from an art show to accompany some comments about the show that were written by one of the newspaper's editors. The *Coalfield Progress* of Norton, Va., from time to time publishes on its editorial page a picture labeled "A Coalfield Album," which might depict almost any non-news scene in the community.

Telecommunication Editorials

An innovation that has nothing to do with design and layout is the call-in editorial. A growing number of newspapers offer phone-in information services of various kinds—sports scores, weather, crossword puzzle hints, cultural events.

FIGURE 14   ATLANTA CONSTITUTION

Prices fly high at Hartsfield

ITEM	HARTSFIELD INTERNATIONAL AIRPORT	METRO MALLS AND AIRPORTS IN THE SOUTHEAST
Gum	$ .95	$ .25
Candy Bar	.95	.55
Cigarettes	2.94	1.49
Yogurt (regular)	2.35	1.54
Yogurt (super)	3.65	2.49
Cone (regular)	2.05	1.54
Cone (waffle) w/ toppings	3.60	1.94
Shake	3.75	1.11
Sundae	3.75	1.05
Coke (small)	1.00	.60
Coke (large)	1.50	.89
Coffee	1.00	.47

Source: Hartsfield International Airport

The Atlanta Constitution, February 19, 1992

In Vancouver, Wash., you also can request recorded summaries of editorials that have appeared in *The Columbian* during the previous week. (The voice sounds more like a radio announcer than an editorial writer.) Several newspapers offer abbreviated versions of their news and editorial product to facsimile (fax) subscribers. One of the first was the *Hartford Courant*. Editorials of major newspapers also are accessible through the various computer data bases.

OP-ED PAGES

The first opposite-editorial pages may have been produced by the *New York World* in the early 1920s. The executive editor, Herbert Bayard Swope, said he got the idea for an op-ed page when he found that, "in spite of our hard and fast principle," opinion kept creeping into the news columns. "It occurred to me that nothing is more interesting than opinion when opinion is interesting," he recounted later, "so I devised a method of cleaning off the page opposite the editorial page . . . and thereon I decided to print opinions, ignoring facts."[16] The page sparkled with the names of famous writers that Swope recruited: Alexander Woollcott, writing on books and theater; Harry Hansen, on books; Heywood Broun, on whatever he wished. Franklin Pierce Adams (better known as F.P.A.) wrote a witty, acerbic column called "The Conning Tower." The *World*'s op-ed page was heavily oriented toward the arts and culture. (A book on newspaper editing published in 1942 credited the Louisville *Courier-Journal*'s editorial page and "page opposite editorial," or "op-ed" page, with setting one of the outstanding examples in design for editorial pages.[17])

Although the idea and the name of the op-ed page have been around for a long time, the *New York Times* is generally credited with setting the example that has led to a substantial number of such pages in recent years. Harrison E. Salisbury, the first editor of the *Times*' op-ed page, said the idea emerged when editors were looking for something to attract readers from the *New York Herald Tribune*, which has just folded. A wider diversity of opinion was the immediate aim. The *Times* was also facing the need to raise subscription and advertising rates. The op-ed page was seen as an opportunity "to give the readers something extra for their extra money," Salisbury said. The *Times* moved its own columnists to the op-ed page, leaving room for more letters on the editorial page, and began to publish a variety of articles on the remainder of the page. Salisbury was given only three-quarters of a page; an advertisement occupied the remainder. He said he accepted the ad partly to anchor the page in the real world but also because he feared he would not have enough material to fill a whole page.[18]

Op-ed pages, with variations, were soon being added at many papers. The *Washington Post*, soon after the *Times*, created a page that was more closely integrated with the regular editorial page than was the *Times*'. The *Chicago Tribune*'s page, as described by *Los Angeles Times* press critic David Shaw, was "part of a continuing trend away from the single-mindedly conservative image the paper had for decades." When the *Los Angeles Times* joined the movement, according to Shaw, it deliberately planned a less intellectual page than that of the *New York Times*. Readers got enough reporting on social issues in the opinion columns and from the columnists. "I'd especially like us to give our readers a clear feeling of what it's really like to live in Southern California," the op-ed page editor was quoted as saying. "I want personal experience pieces, stories that tell how it feels to drive the freeway and to suffer a death in the family and to be out of work."[19]

Editors have devised a variety of ways to obtain contributions to the page. The *New York Times* and the *Los Angeles Times* generally solicit articles but will publish an occasional unrequested piece. An editor on the *Plain Dealer* in Cleveland reported 18 contributions in one day, five locally written, two of which he expected to use.[20] The Nashville *Tennessean* first tried for contributions from academic people, but they refused to be rushed, wrote like academics and didn't like to be edited. When the community's "movers and shakers" were asked to write, the result was usually "trite, turgid and never shaking," Lloyd R. Armour said. Finally the *Tennessean* turned to its own staff, with reporters and editors given enough time to write one or two articles a month. The goal was to have half the articles written by staff, half by outsiders.[21] The *Long Beach Press-Telegram* reported greater success with getting acceptable contributions from community organizations and faculty members. The paper found that publishing community-based writers prompted a welcome flow of unsolicited manuscripts.[22] The *Tulsa Tribune* set out to establish a base of contributors by contacting between 75 and 100 people who had been suggested by staff members. To the half that accepted, the *Tribune* sent out three postcards a week requesting columns (with four-week deadlines).[23]

Some newspapers pay for contributions, notably those that they solicit. (The *Plain Dealer* reported cancelling $40,000 worth of syndicated columns to provide funds to pay contributors.) For some newspapers, pay depends on who the contributor is. The *Long Beach Press-Telegram* reported paying writers that the paper solicited and local writers attempting to earn a living by their writing, but not politicians or people "who get to champion their favorite cause or point of view."

Among the newspapers whose op-ed pages were critiqued in *The Masthead*, the *Charlotte Observer* got the highest praise from Bohle. (Figure 15, page 292.) He liked the informative headlines, the ample use of white space and a 6-column grid that offers "more opportunities for sizing and displaying the art."[24]

CONCLUSION

The principal purpose of innovation, whether in layout, content or telecommunications, should be to encourage readers to think more deeply about more subjects. The purpose of page design is to get ideas across to readers by attracting them and then holding their attention long enough to stir their thoughts. The makeup of the page itself cannot carry a message to readers, but it can help set the tone of the page. If an editor has a flamboyant editorial style, a flamboyant style of typography will help reinforce the message. Conservative typography will help reinforce a conservative, reserved editorial style.

Whatever style an editor chooses, page design must serve two purposes. The first is to distinguish the opinion pages from the news pages. Readers need constantly to be reminded of this distinction. Editorial columns can be wider than news columns. Body type can be larger. Headlines can use different typefaces.

FIGURE 15 CHARLOTTE OBSERVER (OP-ED)

•••• THE CHARLOTTE OBSERVER Friday, February 5, 1993 **11A**

VIEWPOINT

Getting single moms off welfare

■ Help with day care, health care and child support can make the working world a better option.

By BARBARA R. BERGMANN
Los Angeles Times

In his address on welfare reform to the nation's governors this week, President Clinton said that most people on welfare were "aching for the chance to move from dependence to dignity." If Clinton is to help welfare mothers make that move in large numbers, he will have to go beyond forcing people on welfare into jobs.

Dignity does require work, but it also means being able to live in decent circumstances. Most of the jobs available to welfare mothers don't pay enough for that. More government help to working single mothers would also have to be provided.

The old liberal idea was that welfare benefits should be available without stigma and should be high enough to keep single parents and their children at a decent standard of living while the mothers stayed home. Clinton's speech is the last nail in the coffin of that idea.

The old conservative idea was to force people to take jobs by cutting off their benefits. Clinton continues to endorse the idea that welfare recipients should have to take jobs after getting benefits for two years. However, his main thrust in dealing with the welfare problem will be to structure policy so that welfare mothers are motivated to get jobs voluntarily. That means giving working single mothers more help from government, thus making work more attractive.

Dependence to dignity

As things now stand, welfare mothers have little incentive to take a job. For many of them, leaving welfare for work is more like a move from the frying pan to the fire than from dependence to dignity.

A single mother on welfare and Medicaid who is thinking about taking a job faces the need to buy child care, which can eat up a quarter of her new paycheck. If, as is likely, she is eligible only for low-paying jobs without health benefits, taking a job will make her situation worse, not better.

More government help with child care would improve the motivation for single mothers to work. Hillary Rodham Clinton has been interested in child-care programs developed in France, which has kept welfare dependence and child poverty far lower than here. In France, the central government and local governments combine to provide free, high-quality nursery schools to all toilet-trained children and subsidized care to infants and toddlers of many working parents.

The Head Start program would be a good base for a larger, more inclusive program here. It would have to be made into an all-day, all-year program if it were to enable single parents to work.

The Clinton administration's efforts to reform the health care system are also important to welfare reform. Women now feel they have to stay on welfare because many of the jobs available to them don't carry health benefits. If employers were required to give benefits, or if an alternative source of subsidized benefits were available, the incentive to stay on welfare would be reduced.

Safety net for children

Another way to help job-holding single mothers is to get them higher and more dependable child-support payments. Clinton will be examining a possible program of child-support assurance, based on an idea developed by Irwin Garfinkel, a former University of Wisconsin colleague of Health and Human Services Secretary Donna Shalala's. Greater efforts would be made to identify and find every child's father. Parents not living with their children would be assessed according to their ability to pay.

Federalizing the administration of child-support collections would end the evasion by fathers who skip from one state to another to avoid state-based enforcement efforts. If the poverty or unemployment of the father made it impossible to collect some minimum amount, the government would supply that minimum.

Child-support payments are of little benefit to mothers who stay on welfare, because the government uses most of the money to reimburse itself for welfare expenses. But mothers who go off welfare and hold jobs get to keep the support payments as an addition to their wages.

The United States spends more than $100 billion to support single mothers at home, in abject poverty.

Clinton has the drive, the ideas and the advisers to redirect money into new programs that supplement the work efforts of single mothers. This is the only way that "dignity" can be assured for these women and their children.

□□□

Barbara R. Bergmann is a professor of economics at American University.

ELEANOR MILL/Mill News Art Syndicate

Please don't inhale

■ Hillary Clinton's ban on smoking in the White House sends the right message.

New York Times

The mental picture is riveting: While a four-star fete goes on within, a senator, an ambassador or a captain of industry huddles in a doorway of the White House, cold and disgusted.

He or she is losing valuable ear time with movers and shakers, has missed a chance to confab with the president, and has gone head-to-head with the president's wife. And all because of the need for a smoke.

ANNA QUINDLEN

Since Hillary Rodham Clinton said she would ban smoking in the White House, there has been this irresistible image of people in evening clothes doing what smokers have learned to do in recent years — go outdoors, as though they were unruly pets. Or Secret Service agents wrestling a cigarette to the ground. Or alliances unraveling as frazzled envoys from heavy-smoking nations try to get through dinner without nicotine.

It may be the president's infamous allergies. Or it may be that Mrs. Clinton knows that, since Jan. 7, the arguments against public tobacco use have become considerably more powerful than aesthetics or annoyance.

That was the day the Environmental Protection Agency released a blistering report on secondhand smoke that classified it as a Group A carcinogen, as dangerous as benzene, arsenic and radon. The report noted that 3,000 nonsmokers die each year from secondhand-smoke lung cancer, and that smoking poses special risks to children.

(I have to stop here for the warning label on this column: The tobacco industry wants you to know that all of this is poor science and political hysteria. And if its executives don't want people to smoke around their children, you shouldn't draw any wild conclusions.)

We've come a long way

The evolution of attitudes toward smoking has been rapid and constant. In 1964, when the first Surgeon General's report linked lung cancer and smoking, more than 40% of adults smoked and could do so nearly everywhere; today the number is one in four, and smoking is banned in many offices, theaters and restaurants.

No one talks much about an outright ban on cigarettes for reasons ranging from the pragmatic to the political. We know from our experience with alcohol and drugs that a ban works poorly and leads inevitably to a contraband market.

We also know that there is scarcely a lobby in this country as rich and powerful as the tobacco lobby. After Mrs. Clinton clears the White House of secondhand smoke, it would be grand if she would get rid of secondhand smoking money, which is given in huge amounts to both political parties.

Making smoking expensive and uncomfortable has become a useful way to deal with a health risk in an open society. The members of Congress who wrote the blessed legislation banning smoking on domestic airline flights have moved on to banning smoking in places that provide federally financed services for children.

Children have no choice

But the EPA report gives us issues to think about that are more difficult than keeping smokers in one corner of a restaurant. If a mother was found to be putting a bit of benzene in baby's bottle, baby might wind up in a foster home.

But many babies live day after day surrounded by cigarette smoke and, according to health experts, at increased risk of asthma, bronchitis, pneumonia and ear infections.

Advocates for smokers like to talk about choice, a word that has become the clarion call for everything from abortion to schools. But one thing the secondhand smoke report made manifest is that parents who smoke are making a life-threatening choice, not just for themselves but for their kids.

You choose; we cough. A White House smoking ban is an obvious corollary to what we now know about cigarette smoking and what we all ought to do about it. And besides, the drapes won't smell.

□□□

Anna Quindlen is a columnist for The New York Times.

Why block peace for Bosnia?

■ Clinton administration is strangling a good and workable plan to end the bloodshed.

Washington Post Writers Group

WASHINGTON — Why is the Clinton administration blocking the best chance for peace in Bosnia? That chance is embodied in the peace plan offered by U.N. and European Community mediators Cyrus Vance and David Owen dividing Bosnia into 10 highly independent ethnic cantons.

CHARLES KRAUTHAMMER

The Europeans have endorsed the plan. The Croats have accepted it. But the Bosnian Serbs and Muslims have refused to sign. That prompted Vance and Owen to bring the plan to the United Nations and ask the Security Council to endorse and impose it.

Its fate now hinges on the United States. Without U.S. support, it dies. Secretary of State Warren Christopher has been killing it softly.

Q: Does the United States support the peace plan?

Christopher: Well, we've been supportive of the process in the hope that the parties would come into agreement on the process. That's as far as I'm prepared to go this afternoon. (News conference, Feb. 1.)

Mr. Christopher, it seems, is all for peace processes. Peace plans — the concrete stuff that can put an end to war and, alas, to peace processes — are quite another thing.

Christopher: We hope that the process can continue with the parties meeting here in New York, and (we'll) pursue the process as we have in the past. We've thought the process itself is desirable. . . . I found Mr. Vance and Mr. Owen quite understanding that we're in the midst of a policy process. As I say, I urged them to continue their process. (Remarks, same day, after meeting with Vance and Owen.)

Get past the process

This would all be comic were it not so tragic: For Bosnia, process means continued war.

Why is Christopher resisting?

"Some administration officials," reports The New York Times, "said (the plan) was flawed because it specifically abolishes the legitimate government of an internationally recognized state and replaces it with an ethnically based nine-member council that divides power among the Muslims now in power and the Croats and Serbs."

What is wrong with dividing power in an ethnically divided land? Muslims are Bosnia's largest minority but still a minority. What makes their sectarian, minority government so sacrosanct?

Does Christopher have a better idea for settling the conflict? If he does, what is it? More process?

Well, say the critics, the Vance plan is unenforceable. How do they know? And how enforceable is Bosnia's current unitary state? Totally unenforceable, short of massive Western military intervention to roll the Serbs and Croats out of Bosnia.

The Vance plan is at least potentially enforceable because it is realistic. Unlike the alternative, it recognizes the irreconcilable ethnic divisions in Bosnia. It gives up on the unitary state, a bloody fantasy that cannot be put right without enormous human costs, Western and Yugoslav. The new reference point is a different but real Bosnia: a country with a very loose central government where the ethnic groups live within highly independent provinces.

Plan of action

What to do?

1. Declare full U.S. support for the Vance-Owen plan.

2. Sponsor, with Russia, a Security Council resolution accepting the plan as the only basis for solving the war in Bosnia.

3. Announce Security Council measures to enforce the plan. First, European and Russian ground troops — it is their backyard — to ensure the separation of forces. Second, American air power to enforce disarmament.

4. Treat all parties according to their cooperation with the plan. If the Serbs resist, they get bombed. If they cooperate, sanctions are gradually lifted. If Muslims cooperate, they get the protection of Great Power troops. If they resist, they face total isolation.

'A bitter irony'

What is the alternative? The alternative being pushed by Bosnia hawks in the United States is punitive intervention — bombing the Serbs, arming the Muslims — to shore up the present Bosnia government and punish the Serbs. That might make us feel better, but at the cost of countless Yugoslav lives lost pointlessly in a prolonged war.

Punitive intervention is mindless moralism. What is our national interest in Bosnia? We have no interest in how the lines are drawn in Bosnia. Our only interest is that the lines be drawn, that the rival groups be secure behind them, and that the war end. That is what the Vance-Owen plan offers.

"It's the best settlement you can get, and it's a bitter irony to see the Clinton people block it," said Owen. "What do they want down there, a war that goes on and on?"

□□□

Charles Krauthammer is a syndicated columnist.

Gene Payne

NAW, HE'LL NEVER KICK THE HABIT
Fed. SPENDING
CONGRESS
PAYNE

The hunter's legacy

■ Bringing down his prey elicits a feeling of triumph, and for this hunter's son, remorse.

By STEVE STOECKEL
Special to The Observer

Today my father's ghost visited me again. As usual, it happened during hunting season, this time as I looked at a sporting goods ad. One second I'm reading about a sale on camouflage clothing, and the next moment I'm 11 years old, tramping behind my dad, bird hunting in the Everglades. My father, an eccentric, intelligent man with a Hemingway appetite for hunting and game fishing, has for the past month been patiently teaching me to shoot the .410 shotgun that I'm carrying so reverently today. The gun, one of about 20 my father owns, was given to him by his father, and is now mine.

Stoeckel

It's a gorgeous day, early morning, and my dad, always happiest when he's outdoors, is in a relaxed and humorous mood. Talking quietly, we hike through the scrubby grassland as the fog burns away; suddenly we flush a covey of birds. I raise my shotgun and pick one bird, leading it slightly, just as I have for all those tin cans my father has thrown for me, and, incredibly, I bring it down.

Conflicting feelings

I can't believe it — my first shot on my first hunt; my dad, who has shot and missed, laughs delightedly and squeezes the back of my neck — a gesture I can still feel so clearly to this day.

And so, Dad, here is your unintended legacy. Your only son is a vegetarian, and has been for 20 years. I don't own a gun, and the National Rifle Association nauseates me.

Later that night, as I eat the small bird that has been so carefully prepared for me, I have conflicting feelings about this memorable day. Mixed with the pride and affection is a pang of guilt for the life I've taken. I attempt to explain in my clumsy adolescent fashion and get only half of it out.

We never hunt again. My dad is neither callous nor incredibly understanding about it; he simply concludes — quite rightly — that my heart isn't in it. It would be years later, long after my dad died, before I could articulate my feelings about hunting.

And so, Dad, here is your unintended legacy. Your only son is a vegetarian, and has been for 20 years. I don't own a gun, and the National Rifle Association nauseates me. Your grandsons and I go hiking and camping in the woods every chance we get; like you, we're happiest outdoors, but unlike you, we don't need a gun as an excuse to be there.

You were absolutely right about hunting: It gets families outdoors together. It pays for conservation through its licensing fees, and it thins overabundant species. But its main purpose, its measure of success, is to put a bullet through the head or heart of a beautiful animal, ending its life.

Ancestral exhilaration

Hunters may spout all kinds of poetic nonsense about being out in a field with a gun and a dog, worshiping God's beauty and even the animals they intend to destroy, but I know their secret. I know why they are there. It is simply this: It feels good to kill animals. Any hunter who denies this is lying. Even that tiny bird's death sent a feeling of exhilaration through me; an inexplicable triumph, of connecting with my ancestors, who doubtless brought down much larger prey than mine.

To acknowledge these feelings is to understand a part of being human; to wallow in them at the expense of animals' lives is obscene. It wasn't always so, but the difference between a Plains Indian killing a bison for food and an insurance salesman mounting a deer head on his living room wall should be apparent to anyone.

So that, Dad, is the lesson I learned that day. At 42 (the same age you were then), I am far past the age of needing your approval, even after death. Yet I write this, hoping you'd understand.

□□□

Steve Stoeckel of Charlotte is an electronics technician by day and musician by night.

The Charlotte Observer, February 5, 1993

Heads can be centered instead of flush left. Sketches instead of photographs can be used. The page can be run in a distinctive and consistent position in the paper.

The second task of typography is to present a page that will attract readers. The makeup should say that this is an important page and that the editors have put a great deal of time, effort and thought into it. Thus the page should be deliberately, carefully and attractively laid out. It should have enough life to it that it is not always the same day by day, yet it also must have enough consistency in page design to suggest that the same editors, with the same editorial philosophy, are producing it each day.

If editors can meet those two criteria, they can design their pages in any manner they wish. In the end, what really counts is what they say on the pages.

The search for new ways to bring more, and more varied, viewpoints to the opinion pages also reflects an effort to keep the pages from becoming routine. Just as readers ought to be surprised from time to time by the appearance of an editorial page, so should they be surprised once in a while by the content. This means that editors must go beyond the traditional staff-written editorials, syndicated columns and cartoons, and letters to the editor. The possibilities are limited only by editors' imaginations and their ability to carry out their ideas, possibilities that may include the features discussed in this chapter—op-ed pages, guest columns, solicited contributions, boards of contributors, questions of the week, pro-con packages, visual illustrations and reprints from other publications as well as criticism of, and comment on, the press itself.

The purpose of all these efforts, of course, is to promote a greater exchange of ideas among readers and to convince readers that their newspaper is doing a thorough and responsible job of serving them. Even more important is actually to do a thorough and responsible job.

QUESTIONS AND EXERCISES

1. Examine the makeup of the newspapers in your area. Do you find it easy to distinguish editorial pages from news pages?

2. Does the liberal or conservative nature of the makeup reflect the liberal or conservative editorial policy of the page? Consider the size of headlines, the style of headline type, the use of white space or rules, the horizontal or vertical nature of the layout.

3. Does the makeup of a specific newspaper change from day to day or remain the same? If it changes, what principles seem to be operating in determining the layout—the relative importance of elements, the readership appeal of the elements or whim? Does the layout change so radically day by day that the page has a disjointed character?

4. What could be done to improve the design of the editorial pages in your area?

5. Which newspaper do you judge to have the best design? Why?

6. Which newspapers in your area have op-ed pages? How often do they appear? Is there a difference between the material that appears on the editorial page and the material on the op-ed page? What seems to be the policy in determining what goes where?

7. Does the editor of the op-ed page seem to be trying hard to bring contrary and different views onto the page? Does the page contain surprises?

8. What devices does the editor use to try to encourage more participation by more people in the opinion pages? A pro-con package? A question of the week? A guest columnist? An in-depth analysis? Articles by experts?

9. Do any of the newspapers have media critics? If so, how free do they appear to be to criticize the newspaper?

Chapter 19

The Editorial Page That May, and Must, Be

Truth crushed to earth, shall rise again;
The eternal years of God are hers
But, Error, wounded, writhes in pain,
And dies among his worshippers.

—WILLIAM CULLEN BRYANT [1]

Historians have been prophesying the death of the American editorial page since the passing of Horace Greeley. It is true that after the great days of personal journalism, the pages of many newspapers, reflecting the wishes of their corporate owners, became bland, anonymous and irrelevant to the interests of many readers. A principal theme of this book, however, has been that today editorial writers have increasing opportunities to speak out.

Changes in hiring practices, newspaper ownership and reading audiences have helped create these new opportunities. The changes are not without dangers. Newspapers in metropolitan areas, especially evening papers, are dying or merging with other papers. Newspaper circulation is not keeping up with the growth in family households. Readers spend less time with their newspaper and tend to believe that they get most of their news from television. Cable and new electronic systems threaten to cut even more into reading time. Newspapers and other media are being bought by conglomerates that are only incidentally interested in news and opinion; profits are their greatest, perhaps only, concern. Much of the media industry is not as prosperous as it was a few years ago.

In spite of these dangers, the immediate future looks reasonably bright for newspaper editorial writers, and the more distant future looks bright for journalists who can perform the editorial writing function, in whatever medium it is needed.

TODAY'S CHALLENGES

In recent years the demise of the old, prestigious newspapers has given some Americans the impression that newspapers are dying. In the next few decades, newspapers perhaps will be replaced by one or more electronic marvels, but for the immediate future newspapers are likely to continue to play a strong role in providing information and opinion in most communities. Except for problems resulting from the state of the economy, most newspapers have been reasonably, if not immensely, profitable. As long as newspapers exist, editorial pages are likely to exist.

But if writers and editors are to keep editorial pages timely, lively and informative, they cannot rest on tradition or past performance. Four areas in particular, all previously discussed in this book, need the attention of editorial writers and editors: the editorial page audience, the message of the page, other viewpoints and the messenger.

The Audience

Papers that serve large metropolitan areas may face problems providing efficient delivery service and identifying with many of their readers, but newspapers in small and medium-sized communities continue to provide services that readers find essential. In many instances these papers are the principal sources of community news, and they may be the only sources of local editorial comment. Still, neither news editors nor editorial page editors can count on readers sticking with them if they aren't meeting the needs of those readers.

One of the points made in this book is that editorial writers need to get out of the office and into the community if they expect to know what people are concerned about. They have to talk with business people, neighborhood groups, city officials, political leaders, educators, religious leaders, special interest groups, the unemployed and the handicapped. Writers benefit in two ways. They gain information about the community and come back to the office knowing more about what they are writing about. Also, members of the community who see them out and about come to recognize that these writers care about finding out what is really going on. So writers gain both knowledge and credibility.

The Message

An important key to editorial writing is knowing, or locating, the appropriate information needed for an editorial. You don't have to store all the facts you need in your head, but you do have to have a good idea of what you want and where you can get it—whether through an interview, a phone call, a data base, an encyclopedia, a current nonfiction best-seller or the merchant down the street. To know what to write about, you need to read widely, listen to what other people are talking about and keep up with the news.

Once writers have the information they need to back up what they want to say, they must present facts and ideas in a convincing manner. As we have noted several times, readers today do not want opinions jammed down their throats. They want information and help in forming their own opinions, but they also want the feeling that they are discovering truth for themselves. The successful editorial writer is likely to be the one who can make a point without antagonizing readers who hold other opinions. Respecting and recognizing the opinions of others does not necessarily mean that the writer must write in a dull, plodding manner. It is possible to present both sides of an issue in a bold, convincing way before revealing your conclusion about which side has the better argument. Readers ought to feel that they are wrestling with the issue right along with the writer.

We have noted that instant conversions of readers to the writer's point of view are rare. But the impact of an editorial page, and of an editorial policy on a specific topic, can become significant over a period of time. Consistent, reasonable editorial policies eventually are bound to influence the decision-making climate of a community.

Other Viewpoints

The most effective decision making results when all sides of an issue have been considered. One of the primary responsibilities of the editorial page editor, especially in a one-newspaper community, is to bring onto the page viewpoints that are as diverse as possible. Relying on the mail to bring letters and syndicated material is not sufficient. Editors have to seek out persons with differing ideas. To do this editors must know what issues must be discussed and who ought to be asked to discuss them.

An editor should try to give readers at least one surprise a day—an unexpected editorial position, a highly worthy letter, an incisive column or cartoon, a piece by an outsider with something unusual to say, even a different editorial page format.

The Messenger

One of the main contentions of this book is that, if today's editorial writers are given or can seize the opportunity, they have the qualifications and abilities to produce editorial pages that will attract, inform and persuade readers. Publishers and general managers, it seems to me, have more to fear from sitting on their editorial writers, and thus producing a boring editorial page, than from giving them room to experiment and speak out, even at the risk of antagonizing some members of the community. Whether writers are given this kind of freedom may depend on whether management believes that the purpose of an editorial page is to stimulate thinking or to impose a viewpoint.

The persons best suited for editorial writing are those who are well-educated, well-acquainted with people and ideas, skilled in digging out information and skilled in blending into a few hundred words their ideas, facts and conclusions. Aside from writing the editorial, the toughest part of being an editorial writer is keeping up with what is going on in the world. Unless a writer is assigned to a special subject area, almost anything at local, state, national or international levels is a potential topic. Consequently the editorial writer must constantly seek ideas, sources and information. This wealth of ideas and information can prove to be a valuable bargaining chip for the editorial writer in dealing with publishers, general managers and editorial boards. The informed person stands a better chance of making a case for an editorial position than someone who has a strong opinion but few facts to back it up.

Opportunities for editorial writers and editors to play a stronger role in making policy seem to have been enhanced, ironically, by the growth of group ownership. Major groups contend that editorial policy is set at the local level. In many instances publishers and general managers are more concerned with the business side than with news and editorial departments. Since groups tend to move their top managers from paper to paper, editorial page editors and writers may find that they have been on the paper longer, and have firmer roots in the community, than the publisher. They therefore should have a better grasp of what is going on in the community and be able to make a strong case for their points of view.

The trend toward concentrated ownership poses dangers, as well. Group executives could, if they wished, decide to impose uniform editorial policies on their papers. A group that is privately owned—that does not sell its stock on the market—may be able to decide for itself how to spend its money and how much financial risk it is willing to run, but a group that sells stock publicly may try to avoid any risks that might damage the value of that stock. Investors who buy stock in a company do so not because they are especially fond of the product the company produces; they are not likely to care whether the product is toilet paper or newsprint. Corporations that start with newspapers and expand into other areas may keep their original commitment to journalism; income from other properties, in fact, may make them stronger corporations that are better able to publish good newspapers. But the general profitability of newspapers and newspaper groups has made them attractive for acquisition by non-newspaper corporations.

Editorial staff members may not be able to do much about these changes. About all they can do is try to establish a strong tradition of editorial excellence in their community that stands a chance of persisting through changes in editors, publishers, general managers or owners. If readers have become accustomed to a good editorial page, they also may prove a source of support for continued excellence.

If a company is satisfied with producing a bad newspaper, editorial writers and members of a community can't do much about it. Except in some growing suburban areas, opportunities for starting competing papers are rare. Editorial writers can look for jobs elsewhere, but members of a community are stuck with whatever editorial product is sold to them.

One way to strengthen the position of editorial writers, and to improve a paper's relations with its readers, is to give those writers more public recognition. Publicizing individual writers may not appeal to publishers who perceive the editorial voice of a paper as being stronger than the voice of the individuals who put out the editorial product. But any loss in this perception may be more than offset by increased reader interest in the page and greater credibility for the page. Readers are likely to feel closer to the editorial page if they think of the editorial page staff members as real people.

If editorial writers are to be expected to do the best possible job, they must be sufficient in number to do that job. Working at bringing more readers into the page, sending editorial writers out of the office and asking staff members to write columns or bylined pieces require time. If publishers want readers to take their editorial pages seriously, they need to budget the personnel needed to make them serious pages. Adding another body will not solve all the problems of the editorial page, but additional personnel should help improve the product.

Publishers also need to budget amply for travel and other expenses that editorial writers incur if they get out to see what the world is like.

TOMORROW'S CHALLENGES

Newspapers that serve small and medium-sized communities are likely to persist and prosper no matter what happens in the technological revolution now under way. The form in which the paper is delivered may change drastically. It may be produced on a printer in the home, delivered by fax, appear on a television screen or wind up in a computer. Form may not make much difference to most people for most of their news, but they still are going to want some means of preserving portions of what they regard as news. Readers are likely to want a product of some kind that they can pick up and read when they want to. Perhaps the local printed paper will persist, if only because readers like to clip out and save items— about births, weddings, deaths, assassinations, wars and presidential elections.

Perhaps the greatest changes in the delivery of news will come in the multiplicity of different media and the diversity of channels within the media. In theory, this expanding technology could deliver an opinion product that is superior to that of most daily newspapers. The product would not be limited to the equivalent of six or 12 columns of type a day. The computer from which viewers would order written or spoken material could provide many times the number of syndicated columns that editors find space for now. It could offer all the letters to the editors—in their unabbreviated, unedited forms, maybe even delivered by the writers themselves from their home consoles. Editorial cartoons could be animated and in full color. You might be able to watch the artist draw the cartoon. Editorials, not limited to two columns of type, could be more numerous and either written or spoken. An editorial point could be emphasized through sketches, photographs or video.

Two-way interaction would offer viewers the opportunity to register instantly their reactions to an editorial, letter or cartoon. If moved to write a letter, a viewer could type one directly into the computer. The letter could be made instantly accessible to other viewers, just as messages are shared through computer bulletin boards. Letters, editorials and other material could be indexed by subject matter, location or other criteria for easy access.

This electronic marvel could become a true community forum.

The day that people get their information and conduct their business electronically may be a sad one for publishers and owners of newspaper printing plants. Unless they have diversified into electronics, they may find themselves with an outmoded product.

That day may be a sad one, too, for editors and editorial writers who love the printed word and the printed page. We will miss the art of page design, headline writing and type arrangement. After all these years of being able to hold a product fresh off the press, we may find it hard to comprehend that we have produced anything.

Sad as that prospect may seem to print journalists, they should have far less cause for despair than their associates who own the presses. Opinion, unlike printing, is a function that can be transferred from one medium to another. So can reporting and copy editing. These are functions that will be as much in demand in the telecommunications era as they are now. Skilled opinion writers, reporters and editors who can adapt to a new medium should not lack employment opportunities. The telecommunications era may even provide more jobs for editorial writers than the print era. Most communities are now limited to one print source of opinion. With multiple channels and direct access to the computer, editorial voices may proliferate.

Print journalists may shudder when they think about using their skills in television editorial writing as it exists, or doesn't exist, in most communities. Editorials are scarce, and many of those aired are thin, emotional harangues with as much complexity as a first-grade reader. News accounts are brief and superficial. Good film footage is often more important than good reporting and good writing. But opportunities for serious editorialists may expand in the multichannel era. While simpleminded editorials will remain for viewers who want them, other channels may provide viewers who are interested with substantive news and opinions.

Some editorial writers may want to practice up on their elocution so that they can deliver their own opinions to viewers. But some editorials will remain in written form, appearing on the screen or as computer print-outs. Whatever form editorials take, the opinion writers of the future will need all the skills that are necessary today. Writers will need knowledge about the local community and the world, the ability to recognize issues that merit analysis and opinion and the ability to communicate through writing; they will still need compassion, a sense of justice and the ability to reason. In short, their role will remain the same: helping the public to understand what is going on in the world.

CONCLUSION

If editorial pages are going to provide leadership in the coming years, editorial writers will have to possess some other qualities more difficult to identify than the skills of obtaining information and putting words on pages. They will need insight, if they are to perceive what is really going on in the world. They will need vision, to help them see what the future can be. They will need optimism, for surely one of the roles of the editorial page is to remind readers that solutions can be found for problems. They will need to retain faith in the "self-righting" process that John Milton wrote about in his defense of press freedom, *Areopagitica*— and maintain a conviction that, if all the facts and all the viewpoints are allowed to come forth in the marketplace of ideas, the right decisions will be made and the right actions will be taken. William Cullen Bryant expressed that faith in the poetic credo quoted at the beginning of this chapter.

If all this sounds like something out of an earlier, more naive era, let it be so. The editorial as a form had its origins in such an era, when writers such as Sam Adams and Thomas Paine thought that a pen and a little buckshot could free oppressed colonies from a dictator. It would be fitting for an editorial writer of today to possess the dedication to freedom and enlightenment that Milton, John Locke and Thomas Jefferson had. Two and three centuries later, these writers still look like good company to keep. If Milton could keep the faith when it looked as though the Puritans would never defeat King Charles, and Jefferson could keep the faith when it looked as though signers of the Declaration of Independence might be signing their own death warrants, surely 20th-century editorial writers can keep the faith in humanity's ability to perceive problems and deal with them. That hope may seem simplistic in an age of complexity and frustration, but life might not seem so complex and frustrating if people today had more of the confidence that editors of earlier days had in their ability to cope with life.

Perhaps the editorial page, with its emphasis on analyzing problems and seeking solutions to them, is an antique left over from the Age of Reason. Perhaps this page is one of the last voices of reason and enlightenment crying out in a dark, irrational world. But if it is, that is all the more reason for holding firm to the pursuit of truth.

References

Introduction

[1] David Shaw, "The Death of Punditry," in *Gannett Center Journal*, 3:1 (Spring 1989).

[2] Rosemary Yardley, "The Editorial Writer (2)," Ibid., p. 43.

[3] Kenneth McArdle, "The Real Pressure Is to Make Sense," *The Masthead*, 22:8–9 (Spring 1970).

[4] Shaw, "The Death of Punditry," pp. 2–3.

Chapter 1   The Editorial Page That Used to Be

[1] Rollo Ogden, ed., *The Life and Letters of Edwin Lawrence Godkin* (Westport, Conn.: Greenwood Press, 1972), p. 255.

[2] James Parton, "Prestige," *North American Review*, 101:375–76 (April 1866), in Frank Luther Mott, *American Journalism* (New York: Macmillan, 1941), p. 385.

[3] Isaiah Thomas, *The History of Printing in America* (New York: Weathervane Press, 1970), p. 508. (First appeared in 1810.)

[4] Wm. David Sloan, Cheryl Watts, and Joanne Sloan, *Great Editorials* (Northport, Ala.: Vision Press, 1992), p. 24.

[5] Ogden, *Life and Letters*.

[6] Michael Emery and Edwin Emery, *The Press and America*, 6th ed. (Englewood Cliffs, N.J.: Prentice Hall, 1988), pp. 66–68.

[7] Ishbel Ross, *Ladies of the Press* (New York: Harper & Brothers, 1936), p. 29.

[8] Ibid., p. 32.

[9] Ibid., p. 37.

[10] Roland E. Wolseley, *The Black Press*, 2nd ed. (Ames, Iowa: Iowa State University Press, 1990), p. 25.

[11] Ibid., p. 28.

[12] Allen Nevins, *American Press Opinion: Washington to Coolidge* (Boston: D.C. Heath, 1928), p. 111.

[13] Parton, "Prestige," p. 385.

[14] Edward P. Mitchell, *Memoirs of an Editor* (New York: Charles Scribner's Sons, 1924), p. 109.

[15] Harold E. Davis, *Henry Grady's New South* (Tuscaloosa: University of Alabama Press, 1990).

[16] Hal Borland, *Country Editor's Boy* (Philadelphia: J. B. Lippincott, 1970), pp. 156–69.

[17] Sally Foreman Griffith, *Home Town News: William Allen White and the Emporia Gazette* (New York: Oxford University Press, 1989), pp. 113–38.

[18] Harrison E. Salisbury, *Without Fear or Favor* (New York: Times Books, 1980), p. 26.

[19] Lincoln Steffens, cited in Justin Kaplan, *Lincoln Steffens* (New York: Simon and Schuster, 1974), p. 87.

[20] Upton Sinclair, *The Brass Check* (Pasadena: The Author, 1920), p. 22.

[21] Ibid., p. 14.

[22] Ibid., p. 15.

[23] Griffith, *Home Town News*, p. 138.

[24] Nathaniel B. Blumberg, *One-Party Press?* (Lincoln: University of Nebraska Press, 1954), p. 44.

Chapter 2   The Editorial Page That Should, and Could, Be

[1] Alexis de Tocqueville, "A Newspaper's Value," cited in *The Masthead*, 28:29 (Winter 1976).

[2] Robert Reid, "More Hell-Raising Editorials," *The Masthead*, 39:26–27 (Winter 1987).

[3] George P. Crist Jr., "Stimulating Public Awareness, Debate," *The Masthead*, 29:10 (Fall 1977).

[4] Brian Dickinson, "You Win Some, You Lose Some," *The Masthead*, 29:13 (Fall 1977).

[5] Tom Kirwan, "Save Crusades for Important Causes," *The Masthead*, 29:5–6 (Fall 1977).

[6] "A Death Foretold," *Lexington Herald-Leader*, Dec. 2, 1990.

[7] Buford Boone, cited in Johanna Cleary, "Lessons in Editorial Leadership," *The Masthead*, 40:46 (Summer 1988).

[8] Hazel Brannon Smith, ibid., pp. 49–50.

[9] Ed Williams, "Do We Shed Light or Generate Heat?" *The Masthead*, 29:8–9 (Fall 1977).

[10] Robert Reid, "Do Newspapers Crusade Too Much?" *The Masthead*, 29:4 (Fall 1977).

[11]Bernard Kilgore, "A Publisher Looks at Editorial Writing," *The Masthead*, 6:47 (Spring 1954).

[12]Paul Greenberg, "Tyerman Sums Up," *The Masthead*, 17:23 (Winter 1965).

[13]Philip Geyelin, "Who Listens to Your Bugle Calls?" *The Masthead*, 30:9 (Summer–Fall 1978).

[14]Elsa Mohn and Maxwell McCombs, "Who Reads Us and Why," *The Masthead*, 32:24 (Winter 1980–81).

[15]Lenoir Chambers, "Aim for the Mind—and Higher," *The Masthead*, 13:20 (Summer 1961).

[16]James J. Kilpatrick, "Editorials and Editorial Writing," *The Masthead*, 5:7 (Spring 1953).

[17]Jane E. Healy, "Healy Used Reporter's Approach to Win Editorial-Writing Pulitzer," *The Masthead*, 40:14–16 (Fall 1988).

[18]Symposium, "93 Ways to Improve the Editorial Page," *The Masthead*, 33:19 (Winter 1981).

[19]Neal R. Pierce, "For Best Results, Do Your Homework," *The Masthead*, 29:7 (Winter 1977).

[20]Thomas Williams, "New Role Seen for Editorial Page," *The Masthead*, 31:20 (Spring 1979).

[21]Symposium, "93 Ways," pp. 20–21.

[22]R. S. Baker, "The Editorial Writer, The Man in the Piazza," *Montana Journalism Review*, 15:18–19 (1972). (Reprinted by permission of the *Montana Journalism Review*.)

Chapter 3   **Anybody for Editorial Writing?**

[1]Robert H. Estabrook, "Why Editorial Applicants Aren't," *The Masthead*, 12:53 (Summer 1962).

[2]G. Cleveland Wilhoit and Dan G. Drew, "Portrait of an Editorial Writer, 1971–88," *The Masthead*, 41:6–7 (Spring 1989).

[3]Wilbur Elston, "The Editor Goes Status Seeking and Image Hunting," *The Masthead*, 15:1–18 (Fall 1963).

[4]William W. Baker, "A Lack of Communication," *The Masthead*, 15:21–22 (Fall 1963).

[5]Elston, "Status Seeking."

[6]Warren H. Pierce, "What Makes a Good Editorial Writer?" *The Masthead*, 10:23–24 (Spring 1958).

[7]David Manning White, "The Editorial Writer and Objectivity," *The Masthead*, 4:31–34 (Fall 1952).

[8]Hoke Norris, "The Inside Dope," *The Masthead*, 8:55–57 (Spring 1956).

[9]Pierce, "What Makes."

[10]Irving Dilliard, "The Editor I Wish I Were," *The Masthead*, 19:51–57 (Summer 1967).

[11]Frederic S. Marquardt, "What Manner of Editor Is This?" *The Masthead*, 19:57–58 (Summer 1967).

[12]G. Cleveland Wilhoit and Dan G. Drew, "Profile of the North American Editorial Writer," *The Masthead*, 31:8–13 (Winter 1979–89).

[13]Wilhoit and Drew, "Portrait of an Editorial Writer," p. 5.

[14]Morgan McGinley, "Minorities Key to Competitive Edge," *The Masthead*, 41:14 (Summer 1989).

[15]"Women, Minorities Hold Ground at Newspapers," *presstime*, 14:45 (September 1992).

[16]Jean Gaddy Wilson, "Only 68 Years to Go," *Press Women*, 51:1 (January 1988).

[17]Evelyn Trapp Goodrick, "Comparison of Women and Men on Editorial Page Staffs," *The Masthead*, 42:3–7 (Fall 1990).

[18]Symposium, "Miss/Mrs./Ms. Editorial Writer," *The Masthead*, 26:5–29 (Summer 1974).

[19]Jane Reid, "The NRA Held Its Fire," *The Masthead*, 26:5–10 (Summer 1974).

[20]Elisabet Van Nostrand, "The Problems are Neuter," *The Masthead*, 26:20–21 (Summer 1974).

[21]James H. Howard, "Feedback From Readers Helps Teach," *The Masthead*, 27:12 (Spring 1975).

[22]Donald L. Breed, "Why Publishers Rarely Write Own Editorials," *The Masthead*, 14:21 (Fall 1962).

[23]John H. Cline, "The Quest for 'Good Editorial Thinking,'" *The Masthead*, 18:17–18 (Fall 1966).

[24]Editor in the West, "Not in That Newsroom," *The Masthead*, 18:7–8 (Fall 1966).

[25]William D. Snider, "Try Law, Politics or Campus," *The Masthead*, 18:10–11 (Fall 1966).

[26]Ben H. Bagdikian, "Editorial Pages Change—But Too Slowly," *The Masthead*, 17:16 (Winter 1965–66).

[27]Jonathan W. Daniels, "The Docility of the Dignified Press," *The Masthead*, 17:8–14 (Winter 1965–66).

Chapter 4   **Preparation of an Editorial Writer**

[1]LeRoy E. Smith, "The Poll of Journalism Educators," *The Masthead*, 28:25–29 (Spring 1976).

[2]Robert B. Frazier, "What Do You Read, My Lord?" *The Masthead*, 14:10–16 (Summer 1962).

[3]Hugh S. Fullerton, cited in Jake Highton, "Perhaps It's Time to Abolish Journalism Schools," *The Masthead*, 40:33 (Winter 1988).

[4]Highton, "Perhaps It's Time," p. 33.

[5]Otis Chandler, cited in LeRoy E. Smith and Curtis D. MacDougall, "What Should Journalism Majors Know?" *The Masthead*, 27:28–32 (Spring 1975).

[6]Smith, "The Poll of Journalism Educators."

[7]Curtis D. MacDougall, "A Modern Journalism Curriculum," *The Masthead*, 28:30–34 (Spring 1976).

[8]Don Carson, "The Goal: Aiming for Perfection," *The Masthead*, 28:34 (Spring 1976).

[9]Anson H. Smith Jr., "Try an Inspiring Year at Harvard," *The Masthead*, 22:3–5 (Spring 1970).

[10]Sig Gissler, "A Sabbatical: Too Sweet to Be True?" *The Masthead*, 29:30–31 (Spring 1977).

11Anonymous, "Educational Opportunities," *The Masthead*, 44:28–29 (Spring 1992).

12Kenneth Rystrom, "An Editor Returns to Campus," *The Masthead*, 29:12–15 (Winter 1977–78).

13Terrence W. Honey, "Our Ivory Tower Syndrome Is Dead," *The Masthead*, 23:26 (Summer 1971).

14Frazier, "What Do You Read, My Lord?"

15Robert B. Frazier, "The Editorial Elbow," *The Masthead*, 15:5–16 (Summer 1963).

16James J. Kilpatrick, "Editorials and Editorial Writing," *The Masthead*, 5:1–3 (Spring 1953).

17Irving Dilliard, "The Editorial Writer I Wish I Were," *The Masthead*, 19:52 (Summer 1967).

18J. T. Johnson, "The Unconscious Fraud of Journalism Education," *Quill*, 80:31–34 (June 1992).

19Lawrence Krumenaker, "Get a Clue!" *Quill*, 80:35–37 (June 1992).

Chapter 5   Who Is This Victorian "We"?

1J. G. Saxe, in *The Press*, cited in *The Masthead*, 21:20 (Summer 1969).

2Fred C. Hobson Jr., "A We Problem," *The Masthead*, 18:18 (Spring 1966).

3Robert E. Kennedy, "(signed) The editorial writer," *The Masthead*, 42:23 (Summer 1990).

4Ernest C. Hynds, "Editorial Pages Remain Vital," *The Masthead*, 27:19 (Fall 1975).

5Robert U. Brown, "Shop Talk at Thirty," *The Masthead*, 17:38–39 (Fall 1965).

6Floyd A. Bernard, "There Has to Be a Corporate Opinion," *The Masthead*, 23:12 (Spring 1971).

7G. Cleveland Wilhoit and Dan G. Drew, "Portrait of an Editorial Writer," *The Masthead*, 41:4–11 (Spring 1989).

8Anonymous, "Editors Say More Leeway on Group-Owned Papers," *presstime*, 2:36 (May 1980).

9Calvin Mayne, "Gannett Company," in Symposium, "Yeah, What About That Monopoly of Opinion?" *The Masthead*, 26:14 (Fall 1974).

10Reese Cleghorn, "Knight Newspapers," in Symposium, "Yeah, What," pp. 18–19.

11Merrill Lindsay, "Lindsay-Schaub Newspapers," in Symposium, "Yeah, What," pp. 22–23.

12Daniel B. Wackman, Donald N. Gillmor, Cecilie Gaziano, and Everett E. Dennis, "Chain Newspaper Autonomy as Reflected in Presidential Campaign Endorsements," *Journalism Quarterly*, 52:411–20 (Autumn 1975).

13Brown, "Shop Talk at Thirty."

14Kennedy, "(signed) The editorial writer."

15George C. McLeod, "The Paper's Masthead Is the Byline," *The Masthead*, 23:13 (Spring 1971).

16Ann Lloyd Merriman, "No to Signed Editorials," *The Masthead*, 23:14 (Spring 1971).

17Michael J. Birkner, "Behind the Editorial 'We,'" *The Masthead*, 36:20 (Summer 1984).

18John J. Zakarian, "The Visiting Board Member," *The Masthead*, 43:19–20 (Summer 1991).

19Richard T. Cole, "Pursuing the Elusive Editorial Board," *The Masthead*, 42:24–25 (Summer 1990).

20George Neavoll, "We Who Live in Glass Houses," *The Masthead*, 41:11 (Fall 1989).

21Sam Reynolds, "Editorial Transubstantiation," *The Masthead*, 27:2 (Fall 1975).

22George J. Hebert, "Going Loose and Lively in Norfolk," *The Masthead*, 28:21–22 (Spring 1976).

23Warren G. Bovee, "The Mythology of Editorial Anonymity," *The Masthead*, 24:26–35 (Fall 1972) and 24:54–65 (Winter 1972). (Copyright 1972 by Warren G. Bovee.)

24Everett Ray Call, "Yes to Initialed Editorials," *The Masthead*, 23:16–17 (Spring 1971).

25Robert Schmuhl, "Accountability Through Initials," *The Masthead*, 39:31 (Winter 1987).

26Anonymous, "Report of the 1972 NCEW Continuing Studies Committee," *The Masthead*, 25:37–39 (Spring 1973).

27David V. Felts, "Roosevelt's 'I' or Victoria's 'We'?" *The Masthead*, 28:20–21 (Fall 1967).

28James Partin, *The Life of Horace Greeley* (New York: Publisher Unknown, 1855), p. 78.

29Kenneth Rystrom, "Would You Quit Over Editorial Stand?" *The Masthead*, 37:25–26 (Fall 1985).

Chapter 6   Relations with Publishers

1Meg Downey, "Editors and Publishers Should Fight," *The Masthead*, 42:18 (Winter 1990).

2Hugh B. Patterson Jr., "When Ownership Abdicates Its Responsibility, Newspaper Suffers," *The Masthead*, 14:16 (Fall 1962).

3Bernard Kilgore, "A Publisher Looks at Editorial Writing," *The Masthead*, 6:44 (Spring 1954).

4Ibid.

5Donald L. Breed, "The Publisher and the Editorial Page," *The Masthead*, 3:34 (Winter 1951).

6John Lofton, "Can Editorial Writers Afford to Deal With Their Publishers?" *The Masthead*, 3:1–8 (Winter 1951).

7G. Cleveland Wilhoit and Dan G. Drew, "Profile of the North American Editorial Writer, 1971–1979," *The Masthead*, 31:10 (Winter 1979–80).

8Robert T. Pittman, "How to Free Editorial Writers," *The Masthead*, 22:11 (Spring 1970).

9David Halberstam, *The Powers That Be* (New York: Alfred A. Knopf, 1979), p. 573.

10Ben H. Bagdikian, "Newspaper Mergers—The Final Phase," *Columbia Journalism Review*, 15:20 (March–April 1977).

11Jon G. Udell, *The Economics of the American Newspaper* (New York: Hastings House, 1978), p. 62.

[12]Donald L. Breed, "Why Publishers Rarely Write Own Editorials: It's a Tough Routine," *The Masthead*, 14:22 (Fall 1962).

[13]Suraj Kapoor, John Cragan and Irene Cooper, "Publishers' and Opinion-Page Editors' Political Perceptions: A Comparative Analysis," *The Masthead*, 42:7–14 (Winter 1990).

[14]G. Cleveland Wilhoit and Dan G. Drew, "Profile of an Editorial Writer, 1971–88," *The Masthead*, 41:4–11 (Spring 1989).

[15]Robinson Scott, cited in Kilgore, "A Publisher Looks."

[16]Wilhoit and Drew, "Profile of an Editorial Writer."

[17]Downey, "Editors and Publishers Should Fight."

[18]David Holwerk, "Conflicts Are Inevitable—and Even Desirable," *The Masthead*, 42:18 (Winter 1990).

[19]Kenneth McArdle, "The Real Pressure Is to Make Sense," *The Masthead*, 22:8–9 (Spring 1970).

[20]Kilgore, "A Publisher Looks."

[21]Hoke Norris, "The Inside Dope," *The Masthead*, 8:55 (Spring 1956).

[22]Frank W. Taylor, "Relations with the Publisher," *The Masthead*, 2:21 (Winter 1950).

[23]Houstoun Waring, "Fertilizer for the Grass Roots," *The Masthead*, 4:12 (Spring 1952).

[24]Nathaniel B. Blumberg, "Still Needed: A School for Publishers," *The Masthead*, 22:16 (Spring 1970).

[25]Alan Kern, "Publisher Conflicts Not Often a Problem," *The Masthead*, 42:20–22 (Spring 1990).

[26]Phil Duff, "'Yes, but . . .': Should the Publisher Be Involved in Civic-Political Affairs?" *The Masthead*, 37:3 (Summer 1985).

[27]Breed, "The Publisher," p. 47.

[28]Curtis D. MacDougall, "Our Opportunity to Educate or to Sabotage," *The Masthead*, 22:10 (Spring 1970).

[29]Sam Reynolds, "It's Time We Blew the Whistle," *The Masthead*, 29:45 (Winter 1977).

[30]Steve Parrott and Steve O'Neil, "Wall Between Editorial, News Necessary, Most Editors Agree," *The Masthead*, 41:16–18 (Spring 1989).

[31]Ibid.

[32]Patterson, "When Ownership Abdicates."

[33]Taylor, "Relations."

[34]Sevellon Brown III, "Setting Editorial Policy—Editors vs. Publishers," *The Masthead*, 7:22–24 (Summer 1955).

[35]Kilgore, "A Publisher Looks," p. 46.

[36]William H. Heath, "Editorial Policy," *The Masthead*, 19:66 (Summer 1967).

Chapter 7   **Relations with the Newsroom**

[1]Clifford E. Carpenter, "When Reporters Speak Up," *The Masthead*, 12:30–32 (Spring 1960).

[2]Steve Parrott and Steve O'Neill, "Wall Between Editorial, News Necessary, Most Editors Agree," *The Masthead*, 41:16–18 (Spring 1989).

[3]Edward M. Miller, "Take a Managing Editor to Lunch," *The Masthead*, 22:31–33 (Spring 1970).

[4]Parrott and O'Neill, "Wall Between," p. 16.

[5]Carpenter, "When Reporters Speak Up."

[6]William J. Woods, cited in Anonymous, "Policies and Politics," *The Masthead*, 11:43–44 (Summer 1959).

[7]Parrott and O'Neill, "Wall Between," p. 17.

[8]Desmond Stone, "How Does the News Staff Dissent?" *The Masthead*, 23:24–26 (Spring 1971).

[9]Rufus Terral, "In Conference," *The Masthead*, 3:30 (Summer 1951).

[10]Parrott and O'Neill, "Wall Between," p. 17.

[11]David H. Beetle, "Can a Paper Call on a Reporter for Bylined Opinion?" *The Masthead*, 11:69–71 (Spring 1959).

[12]Fred A. Stickel, "To the People of Oregon," *The Oregonian*, Nov. 1, 1992.

[13]Nathaniel B. Blumberg, "The Case Against Front-Page Editorials," *The Masthead*, 8:17–20 (Summer 1956).

[14]James J. Kilpatrick, "Why Not Throw Outworn Traditions Away?" *The Masthead*, 6:1–5 (Spring 1954).

[15]James C. MacDonald, "'News' and 'Opinion' Get All Mixed Up," *The Masthead*, 6:21 (Summer 1954).

[16]Symposium, "The Role of the Ombudsman/Media Critic," *The Masthead*, 28:3–15 (Spring 1976).

Chapter 8   **The Editorial Page Staff**

[1]Lawrence J. Paul, "Many Papers Wretchedly Understaffed," *The Masthead*, 24:1 (Spring 1972).

[2]Don Shoemaker, "Mine, by Damn, Mine," *The Masthead*, 3:10 (Fall 1951).

[3]G. Cleveland Wilhoit and Dan G. Drew, "Profile of the North American Editorial Writer, 1971–1979," *The Masthead*, 31:10 (Winter 1979–80).

[4]Wilbur Elston, "Writers Need Topics, Not Orders," *The Masthead*, 28:10 (Spring 1976).

[5]Shoemaker, "Mine."

[6]Michael Loftin, "Dodging the Daily Boulder," *The Masthead*, 35:6 (Summer 1983).

[7]Karli Jo Hunt, "Read, Read, Read, Clip, Clip, Clip," *The Masthead*, 35:9 (Summer 1983).

[8]Linda Egan, "A Resilient Bunch," *The Masthead*, 38:4 (Winter 1986).

[9]Paul, "Many Papers," pp. 1–3.

[10]John G. McCullough, "Consulting Some Other Oracles," *The Masthead*, 28:5–6 (Spring 1976).

[11]Hugh B. Patterson Jr., "When Ownership Abdicates Its Responsibility, News Suffers," *The Masthead*, 14:18 (Fall 1962).

[12]Pat Murphy, "Fie on the Conference," *The Masthead*, 28:8–9 (Summer 1976).

[13]Gilbert Cranberg, "Skull Sessions Over Lunch," *The Masthead*, 28:10–11 (Summer 1976).

[14]John Sanford, "Interruptions in Reno," *The Masthead*, 19:21–22 (Fall 1967).

Chapter 9   Relations with the Community

[1]Susan Hegger, "Credibility Depends on Being Fair and Appearing Fair," *The Masthead*, 44:9 (Summer 1992).

[2]Norman A. Cherniss, "In Defense of Virtue," *The Masthead*, 18:4 (Summer 1966).

[3]Symposium, "Proposition No. 1: To Be Involved?" *The Masthead*, 18:1–15 (Summer 1966).

[4]G. Cleveland Wilhoit and Dan G. Drew, "Portrait of an Editorial Writer, 1971–88," *The Masthead*, 41:4–11 (Spring 1989).

[5]Paul Greenberg, cited in Sue Ryon, "Editorial Writers Face Classic Dilemma," *The Masthead*, 42:32 (Winter 1990).

[6]David Boeyink, "Anatomy of a Friendship," *The Masthead*, 41:7 (Fall 1989).

[7]James J. Kilpatrick, "How the Question Came Up," *The Masthead*, 18:2 (Spring 1966).

[8]Ibid.

[9]Laird B. Anderson, "A Few Thoughts on the 'Ethics Thing,'" *The Masthead*, 41:9–10 Fall 1989).

[10]Don Lowery, cited in Ryon, "Editorial Writers Face."

[11]Lewis A. Leader, "Journalism and Joining Just Don't Mix," *The Masthead*, 44:5 (Summer 1992).

[12]Susan Hegger, "Credibility."

[13]Van Cavett, "If Your Paper Supports a Position, Then You Can, Too," *The Masthead*, 44:7–8 (Summer 1992).

[14]Charles J. Dunsire, "Stay Away from Causes That Could Become a Topic," *The Masthead*, 44:7 (Summer 1992).

[15]John Alexander, "Newspapers Took Different Roles as Corporate Citizens," *The Masthead*, 41:6–7 (Fall 1989).

[16]H. Brandt Ayers, "Does a Plane Ticket Buy Your Soul?" *The Masthead*, 28:3–4 (Winter 1976).

[17]John Causten Currey, "Is It Better to Nurture Ignorance?" *The Masthead*, 28:4–5 (Winter 1976).

[18]Smith Hempstone, "Self-Righteousness Gives Cold Comfort," *The Masthead*, 28:5–6 (Winter 1976).

[19]Richard B. Laney, "Code Gives No Real Guidance," *The Masthead*, 28:6–7 (Winter 1976).

[20]Robert Estabrook, "Those All-Expense Tours," *The Masthead*, 4:39–41 (Fall 1952).

[21]Catherine Ford, "Ethics Are Expensive, But They're Well Worth the Price," *The Masthead*, 41:4 (Fall 1989).

[22]Mark Clutter, "Don't Be Churlish," *The Masthead*, 12:5 (Spring 1960).

[23]Jack Craemer, "One Who Refuses Feels Lonely," *The Masthead*, 12:8 (Spring 1960).

Chapter 10   Nine Steps to Editorial Writing

[1]Vermont Royster, "Parsley and Pot-Boiled Potatoes," *The Masthead*, 8:38 (Fall 1956).

[2]George Comstock, Steven Chafee, Natan Katzman, Maxwell McCombs, and Donald Roberts, *Television and Human Behavior* (New York: Columbia University Press, 1978), pp. 318–28.

[3]*The Oregonian*, March 9, 1992.

[4]Werner J. Severin and James W. Tankard Jr., *Communication Theories* (New York: Hastings House, 1979), p. 248.

[5]Wilbur Schramm and William E. Porter, *Men, Women, Messages and Media*, 2nd ed. (New York: Harper and Row, 1982), pp. 110–11.

[6]Elsa Mohn and Maxwell McCombs, "Who Reads Us and Why," *The Masthead*, 32:21 (Winter 1980–81).

[7]W. Phillips Davison, James Boylan, and Frederick T. C. Yu, *Mass Media*, 2nd ed. (New York: Holt, Rinehart and Winston, 1982), p. 173.

[8]Alexis S. Tan, *Mass Communication Theories and Research* (Columbus, Ohio: Grid, 1981), p. 103.

[9]Schramm and Porter, *Men, Women*, p. 188.

[10]Tan, *Mass Communication*, p. 149.

[11]Henry M. Keezing, "Who Are Your Readers?" *The Masthead*, 8:47 (Spring 1956).

[12]James J. Kilpatrick, "Editorials and Editorial Writing," *The Masthead*, 5:6–7 (Spring 1953).

[13]James H. Rubin, "Supreme Court Voids 'Hate Crime' Statute," *The Oregonian*, June 23, 1992.

[14]Tan, *Mass Communication*, p. 140.

[15]Schramm and Porter, *Men, Women*, p. 196.

[16]Ibid.

[17]Tan, *Mass Communication*, p. 139.

[18]Davison, Boylan, and Yu, *Mass Media*, p. 190.

[19]*West Central Tribune*, Willmar, Minn., June 26, 1992.

[20]*Daily Tribune*, Hibbing, Minn., June 23, 1992.

Chapter 11   Nine Steps to Better Writing

[1]James J. Kilpatrick, "Editorials and Editorial Writing," *The Masthead*, 5:5 (Spring 1953).

[2]Vermont Royster, cited in Harry Boyd, "They Write by Ear," *The Masthead*, 8:31 (Fall 1956).

[3]R. Thomas Berner, "Let's Get Rid of Those Pesky Pronouns," *The Masthead*, 31:32 (Summer 1979).

[4]Galen R. Rarick, "The Writing That Writers Write Best—or Should I Say 'Better'?" *The Masthead*, 21:3–5 (Winter 1969–70).

[5]Rudolf Flesch, *The Art of Readable Writing* (New York: Harper & Bros., 1949), and *How to Test Readability* (New York: Harper & Bros., 1951).

[6]Francis P. Locke, "Too Much Flesch on the Bones?" *The Masthead*, 11:3–6 (Spring 1959).

[7]*Wall Street Journal*, "On the Other Hand," *The Masthead*, 7:20 (Fall 1955).

[8]*Milwaukee Journal*, date unknown.

[9]"Words Have Disabling Power," *Roanoke Times & World-News*, Aug. 23, 1992.

[10]Judy E. Pickens, ed., *Without Bias: A Guidebook for Nondiscriminatory Communication* (New York: John Wiley & Sons, 1982).

[11]Kilpatrick, "Editorials and Editorial Writing," p. 4.

Chapter 12   Subjects That Are Hard to Write About

[1]Creed Black, "Government Is Great, But—," *The Masthead*, 19:23 (Summer 1967).

[2]Lauren K. Soth, "How to Write Understandable Editorials About Economics," *The Masthead*, 6:19 (Winter 1954).

[3]*Greenville* (S.C.) *News*, Oct. 30, 1990.

[4]*Birmingham News*, Aug. 27, 1990.

[5]*Deseret News*, Salt Lake City, May 13–14, 1991.

[6]*Milwaukee Journal*, date unknown.

[7]*News-Sentinel*, Fort Wayne, Ind., Oct. 4, 1990.

[8]*Sun-Sentinel*, Fort Lauderdale, Fla., date unknown.

[9]Jenkin Lloyd Jones, cited in Francis P. Locke, "A Word for Afghanistanism," *The Masthead*, 19:33 (Summer 1967).

[10]*Atlanta Constitution*, Feb. 18, 1992.

[11]*Star Tribune*, Minneapolis–St. Paul, Feb. 18, 1992.

[12]*The Oregonian*, Portland, Ore., June 25, 1992.

[13]Aubrey Bowie, "The Arts Need Same Zeal as Sewers," *The Masthead*, 41:23 (Fall 1989).

[14]*Washington Post*, Feb. 25, 1992.

[15]*Washington Times*, Feb. 14, 1989.

[16]*Charleston* (W. Va.) *Gazette*, Aug. 2, 1991.

[17]*Times-Herald*, Newport News, Va., date unknown.

[18]D. Michael Heywood, "Health Care Can Be Lethal to Editorial Writing," *The Masthead*, 43:8 (Fall 1991).

[19]Anonymous, "AIDS and the Editorial Page," *The Masthead*, 40:6 (Winter 1988).

[20]*Detroit Free Press*, Feb. 14, 1992.

[21]*Salt Lake Tribune*, May 13, 1991.

[22]Michael McGough, "The Naked Public Triangle," *The Masthead*, 43:24–26 (Fall 1991).

[23]*Roanoke Times & World-News*, Feb. 23, 1988.

[24]*Daily News*, Newport News, Va., Feb. 3, 1991.

[25]*Free Lance–Star*, Fredericksburg, Va., Feb. 2, 1990.

[26]*Des Moines Register*, April 11, 1991.

Chapter 13   Subjects That Are Deceptively Easy or Neglected

[1]James E. Casto, "Holiday of Headaches," *The Masthead*, 35:15 (Fall 1983).

[2]David Jarmul, "Ain't Science Articles Fascinating?" *The Masthead*, 39:15 (Summer 1987).

[3]*Detroit Free Press*, Feb. 11, 1992.

[4]*Pittsburgh Post-Gazette*, Jan. 19, 1991.

[5]*Charlotte* (N.C.) *Observer*, April 18, 1990.

[6]Casto, "Holiday of Headaches."

[7]Lauren K. Soth, "From Alpha to Omega," *The Masthead*, 20:3 (Spring 1969).

[8]Richard B. Childs, "When You Can't Pass the Buck," *The Masthead*, 29:3–4 (Summer 1977).

[9]Jim Wright, "It Gets Tough to Give Thanks," *The Masthead*, 35:12 (Fall 1983).

[10]Kyle Thompson, "A Wish List on Christmas Day," *The Masthead*, 35:17 (Fall 1983).

[11]Ann Lloyd Merriman, "It Helps to Be Prepared," *The Masthead*, 35:6 (Fall 1983).

[12]Elissa Papirno, "The Holiday 'Problem,'" *The Masthead*, 35:13–14 (Fall 1983).

[13]Joanna Wragg, "Relying on Traditional Material," *The Masthead*, 35:9–11 (Fall 1983).

[14]*Courier-Journal*, Louisville, Ky., Feb. 14, 1992.

[15]Hoke Norris, "The Utility Editorial," *The Masthead*, 4:14 (Spring 1952).

[16]Jarmul, "Ain't Science Articles Fascinating?"

[17]*St. Petersburg* (Fla.) *Times*, date unknown.

[18]Albert B. Southwick, "Why Not More Nature Editorials?" *The Masthead*, 9:53–55 (Winter 1957–58).

[19]Ibid.

[20]Hal Borland, *An American Year* (New York: Simon and Schuster, 1946).

[21]Erwin Rieger, *Up Is the Mountain* (Portland, Ore.: Binfords and Mort, 1973).

[22]Ibid., pp. 17–21.

[23]*The Columbian*, Sept. 3, 1969.

[24]Ben H. Bagdikian, "Editorial Pages Changing—But Too Slowly," *The Masthead*, 17:20 (Winter 1965–66).

[25]Andy Rooney, "Editorial Pages Are Better Off Without Humor," *The Masthead*, 43:9 (Summer 1991).

[26]Nordahl Flakstad, "It's No Laughing Matter, But There's Still Room for Humor," *The Masthead*, 43:7–8 (Summer 1991).

[27]Rick Horowitz, "Call Me Irresponsible?" *The Masthead*, 43:8 (Summer 1991).

[28]Rena Pederson, "Give Readers a Break," *The Masthead*, 43:6 (Summer 1991).

[29]*Los Angeles Times*, date unknown.

[30]Mark L. Genrich, "Down With Fruitcakes," *The Masthead*, 39:5–6 (Spring 1987).

[31]Joseph Plummer, "Use It Selectively," *The Masthead*, 39:10 (Spring 1987).

[32]Dave Cummerow, "Takes a Deft Touch," *The Masthead*, 39:11 (Spring 1987).

[33]Shirl Short, "Consider the Audience," *The Masthead*, 39:8–9 (Spring 1987).

[34]*Kentucky Post*, March 11, 1986.

[35]*San Francisco Examiner*, July 7, 1991.

Chapter 14   **Editorials on Elections**

[1]Elizabeth Bird, "Kingmaker or Informer?" *The Masthead*, 40:35–36 (Summer 1988).

[2]Cited in "Candidate Endorsements—Who, When and Why: A Complaint and a Reply," *The Masthead*, 20:19 (Summer 1968).

[3]Bird, "Kingmaker or Informer?"

[4]Fred Fedler, Lownes F. Stephens, and Tim Counts, "Endorsement Surprises," *The Masthead*, 33:49 (Spring 1981).

[5]"Paid Ads or Endorsements?" Letter to the Editor, *Daily News*, Longview, Wash., date unknown.

[6]Cited in "Candidate Endorsements—Who, When and Why."

[7]Sylvan Fox, "New Day at Newsday," *The Masthead*, 33:41 (Summer 1981).

[8]Nelson Poynter, "Speaking of Elections: The Case for Endorsements," *The Masthead*, 25:20 (Spring 1973).

[9]Mary Ann Sharkey, "Give Each Candidate a Fair Hearing," *The Masthead*, 43:12 (Spring 1991).

[10]Thomas W. Still, "Readers May Overestimate Power of Endorsements," *The Masthead*, 43:15 (Spring 1991).

[11]Bird, "Kingmaker or Informer?"

[12]"Some Changes in the Editorial Page," *Los Angeles Times*, Sept. 23, 1973, part 6, p. 2.

[13]Hugh M. Culbertson and Guido H. Stempel III, "Public Attitudes About Coverage and Awareness of Editorial Endorsements," in Guido H. Stempel III and John W. Windhauser, eds., *The Media in the 1984 and 1988 Elections* (Westport: Greenwood Press, 1991), pp. 187–199.

[14]Frank Luther Mott, "Has the Press Lost Its Punch?" *The Rotarian*, Oct. 1952, p. 13.

[15]Nathaniel B. Blumberg, *One-Party Press?* (Lincoln: University of Nebraska Press, 1954), p. 11.

[16]George Comstock, Steven Chafee, Natan Katzman, Maxwell McCombs, and Donald Roberts, *Television and Human Behavior*, (New York: Columbia University Press, 1978), pp. 136, 319–328.

[17]Peter Clarke and Eric Fredin, "Newspapers, Television and Political Reasoning," *Public Opinion Quarterly*, 42:143–160 (Summer 1978).

[18]Fred Fedler, "To Endorse or Not to Endorse," *The Masthead*, 36:26 (Summer 1984).

[19]Kenneth Rystrom, "The Impact of Newspaper Endorsements," *Newspaper Research Journal*, 7:19–28 (Winter 1986).

[20]Kenneth Rystrom, "Apparent Impact of Endorsements by Group and Independent Newspapers," *Journalism Quarterly*, 62:449–453, 532.

[21]Fred Fedler, Ron F. Smith, and Tim Counts, "Voter Uses and Perceptions of Editorial Endorsements," *National Research Journal*, 6:20 (Summer 1983).

[22]Ruth Ann Weaver-Lariscy and Spencer F. Tinkham, "News Coverage, Endorsements and Personal Campaigning: The Influence of Non-Paid Activities in Congressional Elections," *Journalism Quarterly*, 68:442–43 (Fall 1991).

[23]Sharkey, "Give Each Candidate a Fair Hearing."

[24]Norman Blume and Schley Lyons, "The Monopoly Newspaper in a Local Election: The Toledo Blade," *Journalism Quarterly*, 45:286–92 (Summer 1968).

[25]Fedler, Stephens, and Counts, "Endorsement Surprises," pp. 48–49.

[26]Byron St. Dizier, "Republican Endorsements, Democratic Positions: An Editorial Page Contradiction," *Journalism Quarterly*, 63:581–586 (Autumn 1986).

[27]John J. Zakarian, "Speaking of Elections: Sacred Cows of the Highest Order," *The Masthead*, 25:3 (Spring 1973).

[28]St. Dizier, "Republican Endorsements."

[29]Robert J. White, "Endorsement Process Became an Election Issue," *The Masthead*, 43:6 (Spring 1991).

[30]Douglas J. Rooks, "Given a Chance, Candidates Take Issues Seriously," *The Masthead*, 43:14 (Spring 1991).

[31]Mindy Cameron, "Share the Process and Remove Presumptuous Arrogance," *The Masthead*, 43:8–9 (Spring 1991).

[32]Cecilie Gaziano, "Chain Newspaper Homogeneity and Presidential Endorsements, 1972–1988," *Journalism Quarterly*, 66:836–45 (Winter 1989).

[33]John C. Busterna and Kathleen A. Hansen, "Presidential Endorsement Patterns by Chain-Owned Papers, 1976–84," *Journalism Quarterly*, 67:286–94 (Summer 1990).

[34]Roya Akhavan-Majid, Anita Rife, and Sheila Gopinath, "Chain Ownership and Editorial Independence: A Case Study of Gannett Newspapers," *Journalism Quarterly*, 68:59–66 (Spring/Summer 1991).

[35]Nancy Q. Keefe, "Sins of Flesh Mean Less Than Failings of Spirit," *The Masthead*, 44:11 (Fall 1992).

[36]Clarence Page, "Opponents Shouldn't Define Character," *The Masthead*, 44:6–7 (Fall 1992).

[37]William E. Rone Jr., "Learn the Lesson of Nixon," *The Masthead*, 44:10–11 (Fall 1992).

[38]Peter Clarke, "Endorsement Editorials," *The Masthead*, 33:36–37 (Spring 1981).

[39]*Beaver County Times*, November 1, 1991.

[40]*Philadelphia Daily News*, October 25, 1991.

[41]*Scranton Times*, October 31, 1991.

[42]*Patriot News*, Harrisburg, Pa., October 20, 1991.

[43]*Tribune-Democrat*, Johnstown, Pa., October 20, 1991.

[44]*Pittsburgh Post-Gazette*, October 30, 1991.

[45]Calvin Mayne, "The Unendorsement of a Candidate," *The Masthead*, 22:21–26 (Spring 1970).

[46]Ronald D. Clark, "Benefits Go Beyond the Box Scores," *The Masthead*, 43:16 (Spring 1991).

[47]Stephen M. Kent, "Rating Job Performance at City Hall," *The Masthead*, 35:37–38 (Spring 1983).

[48]Clark, "Benefits Go Beyond."

Chapter 15   Other Types of Opinion Writing

[1]John Beatty, cited in Anonymous, "Broadcast Editorials: A Dying Breed in a Ripe Market," *Quill*, 80:37 (July/August 1992).

[2]William L. Rivers, *Writing Opinion: Reviews* (Ames, Iowa: Iowa State University Press, 1988), p. 24.

[3]Boyd A. Levet, "Editorials and the Business of Broadcasting," *The Editorialist*, 17:7 (Spring 1991).

[4]G. Donald Gale, "The Need for Broadcast Editorials," *The Masthead*, 40:37–38 (Spring 1988).

[5]Cited in Howard W. Kleiman, "Unshackled but Unwilling: Public Broadcast and Editorializing," *Journalism Quarterly*, 64:708 (Winter 1987).

[6]Gale, "The Need," p. 37.

[7]"Broadcast Editorials," p. 37.

[8]Gale, "The Need," p. 37.

[9]"Broadcast Editorials," p. 37.

[10]Elizabeth Krueger and James D. Fox, "The Effects of Editorials on Audience Reaction to Television Newscasters," *Journalism Quarterly*, 68:402–411 (Fall 1991).

[11]"Broadcast Editorials," p. 37.

[12]Cited in Kleiman, "Unshackled but Unwilling," p. 713.

13Gale, "The Need," p. 37.

[14]Robert Logan, "TV vs. Print," *The Masthead*, 37:11–25 (Summer 1985).

[15]Martha Sieleff, cited in ibid., pp. 17–18.

[16]Phil Johnson, cited in ibid., pp. 19.

[17]Lesley Crosson, cited in ibid., p. 21.

[18]William P. Cheshire, cited in ibid., pp. 16–17.

[19]Robert McCord, cited in ibid., pp. 15–16.

[20]KCBS-Radio, "Un-American Activities," Jan. 14, 1991.

[21]Richard Elam, "Editorialist Critique," *The Editorialist*, 14:6 (April/May 1988).

[22]Anonymous, "Critics Corner," *The Editorialist*, 10:14 (November–December 1983).

[23]Rivers, *Writing Opinion: Reviews*, p. 56.

[24]Laird B. Anderson, "Secrets of the Masters," *The Masthead*, 44:24 (Spring 1992).

[25]Hope Aldrich, "NEA Under Fire," *Santa Fe* (N.M.) *Reporter*, July 18, 1990.

[26]Joe H. Stroud, "Where Is Strategy to Make This City Whole?" *Detroit Free Press*, April 1, 1990.

[27]Frank Wetzel, "The Ombudsman: Merely a Public-Relations Gimmick?" *Seattle Times*, Sept. 19, 1988.

[28]Frank Wetzel, "Newspapers Should Separate Facts and Opinion," *Seattle Times*, Nov. 20, 1988.

Chapter 16   Letters to the Editor

[1]Peter G. Fradley, "Inclusiveness Is the Best Policy," *The Masthead*, 28:12–13 (Fall 1976).

[2]Barry Bingham Sr. in "Dear Sir You Cut! A Symposium on Letters to the Editor," *The Masthead*, 3:38 (Fall 1951).

[3]Diane Cole, "Letters to the Editor: Who Needs 'em? We Do," *The Masthead*, 44:7 (Spring 1992).

[4]Suraj Kapoor and Carl Botan, "Studies Compare How Editors Use Letters," *The Masthead*, 44:5–7 (Spring 1992).

[5]Keith Carter, "Successful Letters Column Requires Ongoing Effort," *The Masthead*, 44:10 (Spring 1992).

[6]Robert Bohle, "Just Running Letters Is Not Enough," *The Masthead*, 43:10–13 (Spring 1991).

[7]Charles VanDevander, "Building a Readers' Forum," *The Masthead*, 18:16 (Spring 1966).

[8]M. Carl Andrews, "How Letters to the Editor Influenced a Community," *The Masthead*, 13:24–26 (Spring 1961).

[9]Anonymous, "Interview Your Letter Writers," *The Masthead*, 17:31 (Spring 1965).

[10]James Dix, "Customers Love Crossfire," *The Masthead*, 20:22 (Fall 1968).

[11]Barney Waters, "Handling the Daily Mail," *The Masthead*, 22:47 (Fall 1970).

[12]Kapoor and Botan, "Studies Compare," p. 6.

[13]Carter, "Successful Letters Column."

[14]John R. Markham, "A Letter Is a Dangerous Thing," *The Masthead*, 5:18–19 (Fall 1953).

[15]James J. Kilpatrick, cited in ibid., p. 20.

[16]M. Carl Andrews, "Pity the Editor Without Letters," *The Masthead*, 20:12 (Fall 1968).

[17]Carol Suplee, "A Problem," *The Masthead*, 39:32 (Winter 1987).

[18]Hap Cawood, "Should Madmen, Illiterates Be Heard?" *The Masthead*, 28:15–16 (Fall 1976).

[19]Kapoor and Botan, "Studies Compare," p. 6.

[20]Waters, "Handling the Daily Mail," p. 45.

[21]Geoff Seamans, "The Feature You Love to Hate," *The Masthead*, 44:8–9 (Spring 1992).

[22]Charles Towne, "The Trouble with Letters Is Editors," *The Masthead*, 28:9 (Fall 1976).

[23]Seamans, "The Feature You Love to Hate."

[24]Wally Hoffman, "Keep a Balance," *The Masthead*, 40:5–6 (Spring 1988).

[25]Phil Fretz, "Don't Run 'em," *The Masthead*, 40:6 (Spring 1988).

[26]Frank Partsch, "Check 'em Out," *The Masthead*, 40:9 (Spring 1988).

[27]Robert A. Pierce, "In General," *The Masthead*, 40:7–8 (Spring 1988).

[28]Marc Franklin, "Letters and Libel," *The Masthead*, 40:10–13 (Spring 1988).

[29]Steve Pasternack, "Dear Editor—Print This at Your Own Risk," *The Masthead*, 36:5–6 (Spring 1984).

[30]Clifford E. Carpenter, "The Letter Litter, Its Dangers and Potentials," *The Masthead*, 19:80 (Summer 1967).

[31]Kapoor and Botan, "Studies Compare."

[32]Palmer Hoyt, "A Publisher Looks at Editorial Writing," *The Masthead*, 6:49 (Spring 1954).

[33]Franklin Smith, "Who Elected the Times?" *The Masthead*, 23:34 (Summer 1971).

[34]Andrews, "Pity the Editor Without Letters," p. 13.

Chapter 17   Columns and Cartoons

[1]Edwin M. Yoder Jr., "In 40 Years, a Sea Change," *The Masthead*, 38:12–13 (Fall 1986).

[2]Donald P. Keith, "Champions of Truth or Claques for Extremists," *The Masthead*, 19:60 (Summer 1967).

[3]Robert H. Estabrook, "Their Varied Views Are Important," *The Masthead*, 10:22–24 (Fall 1958).

[4]Mark Ethridge, "The Come-Back of Editorial Pages," *The Masthead*, 18:28–32 (Summer 1966).

[5]Yoder, "In 40 Years."

[6]Ethridge, "The Come-Back of Editorial Pages,"

[7]Yoder, "In 40 Years."

[8]Ernest C. Hynds, "Editorial Pages Remain Vital," *The Masthead*, 27:19–22 (Fall 1975).

[9]Sig Gissler, "Color Me Peeved," *The Masthead*, 19:5 (Spring 1967).

[10]Frank Wetzel, "Territorial Exclusivity Is Attacked," *The Masthead*, 30:3–4 (Winter 1978).

[11]Yoder, "In 40 Years."

[12]William F. Buckley Jr., "Major Complaint Erratic Scheduling," *The Masthead*, 27:5 (Winter 1975).

[13]Yoder, "In 40 Years."

[14]Buckley, "Major Complaint Erratic Scheduling."

[15]James J. Kilpatrick, "Life and Times With Cranberg Rule," *The Masthead*, 27:9–12 (Winter 1975).

[16]National News Council, "Nicaragua Government Information Service against Jack Anderson/United Features Syndicate (1977)," Complaint No. 101, March 22, 1977.

[17]Robert Schulman, "The Opinion Merchants," *The Masthead*, 32:21 (Spring 1980).

[18]Lauren Soth, "Conflicts of Interest by Political Writer, Editor," *Des Moines* (Iowa) *Register*, Nov. 29, 1973.

[19]National News Council, "Findings of the National News Council," *The Masthead*, 26:53 (Fall 1974).

[20]Schulman, "The Opinion Merchants."

[21]Draper Hill, "Cartoonists Are Younger—and Better," *The Masthead*, 38:14–17 (Fall 1986).

[22]Roger Van Ommeren, Daniel Rife and Don Sneed, "What Is the Cartoonist's Role?" *The Masthead*, 36:12–15 (Spring 1984).

[23]Ibid.

[24]Anonymous, "Getting Along With Your Cartoonist," *The Masthead*, 40:6–13 (Fall 1988).

[25]Thomas Gephardt, "A Gamble Paid Off," *The Masthead*, 40:7 (Fall 1988).

[26]Jim Borgman, "No Trench Warfare," *The Masthead*, 40:7–8 (Fall 1988).

[27]Dick Herman, "Facts Is Facts," *The Masthead*, 40:8–9 (Fall 1988).

[28]Paul Fell, "The Self-Imposed Limits of My Cage," *The Masthead*, 40:9 (Fall 1988).

[29]Charles J. Dunshire, "More Treasure Than Challenge," *The Masthead*, 40:11 (Fall 1988).

[30]David Horsey, "A Journalist, Not a Comedian," *The Masthead*, 40:12 (Fall 1988).

[31]Gephardt, "No Trench Warfare."

[32]Fell, "The Self-Imposed Limits."

[33]"Editorial Cartoonist Goes Audio/Fax," *Quill*, 80:4 (October 1992).

[34]A. Rosen, Discussion Session, American Press Institute, Columbia University, May 1972.

Chapter 18   Innovations in Makeup and Content

[1]Ralph J. Turner, cited in Anonymous, "Professor Gives Tips on Improving Appearance of Editorial Pages," *SNPA Bulletin*, January 3, 1990.

[2]Robert Bohle, "Most Pages Have Resisted Change," *The Masthead*, 38:18–21 (Fall 1986).

[3]Cited in Ibid.

[4]John E. Allen, *Newspaper Makeup* (New York: Harper and Bros., 1936), p. 332.

[5]Miles E. Tinker, *Legibility in Print* (Ames, Iowa: Iowa State University Press, 1963), pp. 74–107.

[6]Robert Bohle, "Does It Work?" *The Masthead*, 44:13–15 (Spring 1992).

[7]Ed Williams, "Dreaded Redesign Accomplishes Goals," *The Masthead*, 44:12–13 (Spring 1992).

[8]Bohle, "Does It Work?" pp. 13–14.

[9]Robert Bohle, "Just Running Letters Is Not Enough," *The Masthead*, 43:10–13 (Summer 1991).

[10]"Professor Gives Tips on Improving."

[11]Sig Gissler, "A Better Forum for Our Readers," *The Masthead*, 23:31–32 (Spring 1971).

[12]Dennis R. Ryerson, "Two Op-ed Pages in Cleveland," *The Masthead*, 36:10 (Fall 1984).

[13]Tony Tselentis, "Another Page, a Better Understanding," *The Masthead*, 23:33–34 (Spring 1971).

[14]Robert T. Pittman, "Ten Best Bets for Edit Pages," *The Masthead*, 26:34–38 (Summer 1974).

[15]"Byline," *Washington Journalism Review*, 14:10 (July/August 1992).

[16]E. J. Kahn, Jr., *The World of Swope* (New York: Simon and Schuster, 1965), p. 260.

[17]Norman J. Radder and John E. Stempel, *Newspaper Editing: Makeup and Headlines* (New York: McGraw-Hill, 1942), pp. 332–33.

[18]Harrison E. Salisbury, "An Extra Dimension in This Complicated World," *The Masthead*, 23:29–31 (Spring 1971).

[19]David Shaw, "Newspapers Offer Forum to Outsiders," *Los Angeles Times*, Oct. 13, 1975.

[20]Ryerson, "Two Op-ed Pages."

[21]Lloyd R. Armour, "Let the Staff Write Them," *The Masthead*, 36:6–7 (Fall 1984).

[22]John J. Fried, "From the League and the Campus," *The Masthead*, 36:9–10 (Fall 1984).

[23]John Drummond, "Idea From a Critique Group," *The Masthead*, 36:11 (Fall 1984).

[24]Bohle, "Does It Work?"

Chapter 19   The Editorial Page That May, and Must, Be

[1]William Cullen Bryant, "The Battle-Field," *Poems* (Philadelphia: Henry Altemus), p. 124.

Bibliography

Editorial Writing and Editorial Pages

Babb, Laura Longley, ed., *The Editorial Page* [of the *Washington Post*]. Boston: Houghton Mifflin (1977).

Hulteng, John L., *The Opinion Function: Editorial and Interpretive Writing for the News Media*. Hayden Lake, Idaho: Ridge House Press (1973).

Kreighbaum, Hillier, *Facts in Perspective: The Editorial Page and News Interpretation*. Englewood Cliffs, N.J.: Prentice-Hall (1956).

MacDougall, Curtis D., *Principles of Editorial Writing*. Dubuque, Iowa: Wm. C. Brown (1973).

Rivers, William L., *Writing Opinions: Reviews*. Ames, Iowa: Iowa State University Press (1988).

Rivers, William L., Bryce McIntyre, and Alison Work, *Writing Opinions: Editorials*. Ames, Iowa: Iowa State University Press (1988).

Sloan, Wm. David, *Pulitzer Prize Editorials: America's Best Writing, 1917–1979*. Ames, Iowa: Iowa State University Press (1980).

Sloan, Wm. David, Cheryl Watts, and Joanne Sloan, *Great Editorials: Masterpieces of Opinion Writing*. Northport, Ala.: Vision Press (1992).

Stonecipher, Harry W., *Editorial and Persuasive Writing: Opinion Functions of the News Media*. New York: Hastings House (1979).

Waldrop, A. Gayle, *Editor and Editorial Writer*. 3rd ed. Dubuque, Iowa: Wm. C. Brown (1967).

Press Criticism

Bagdikian, Ben H., *The Effete Conspiracy and Other Crimes of the Press*. New York: Harper & Row (1972).

Blumberg, Nathaniel B., *One-Party Press?* Lincoln: University of Nebraska Press (1954).

Efron, Edith, *The News Twisters*. Los Angeles: Nash (1971).

Ghiglione, Loren, ed., *The Buying and Selling of America's Newspapers*. Indianapolis: R.J. Berg (1984).

Irwin, Will, *The American Newspaper*. Ames, Iowa: Iowa State University Press (1969). (First appeared in *Colliers*, January–July 1911.)

Isaacs, Norman A., *Untended Gates*. New York: Columbia University Press (1986).

Lee, Martin A., and Norman Solomon, *Unreliable Sources*. New York: Carol Publishing Group (1990).

Seldes, George, *You Can't Print That*. Garden City, N.Y.: Garden City Publishing (1929).

Seldes, George, *Lords of the Press*. New York: Julian Messner (1938).

Sinclair, Upton, *The Brass Check: A Study of American Journalism*. 8th ed. Pasadena: The Author (1920).

Cartoonists

Block, Herbert, *The Herblock Gallery*. New York: Simon and Schuster (1968).

Block, Herbert, *Herblock's State of the Union*. New York: Simon and Schuster (1972).

Editors of the Foreign Policy Association, *A Cartoon History of United States Foreign Policy, 1776–1976*. New York: William Morrow (1975).

Lendt, David L., *Ding: The Life of Jay Norwood Darling*. Ames, Iowa: Iowa State University Press (1979).

Miller, Frank, *Frank Miller Looks at Life*. No publisher, no date.

Nelson, Roy Paul, *Cartooning*. Chicago: Henry Regnery (1975).

Salzman, Ed, and Ann Leigh Brown, *The Cartoon History of California Politics*. Sacramento: California Journal Press (1978).

Columnists and Writers

Abell, Tyler, ed., *Drew Pearson Diaries, 1949–1959*. New York: Holt, Rinehart and Winston (1974).

Allen, Robert, and Drew Pearson, *Washington Merry-Go-Round*. New York: Liveright (1931). Published anonymously.

Alsop, Joseph, with Adam Platt, *I've Seen the Best*. New York: W. W. Norton (1992).

Anderson, Jack, and James Boyd, *Confessions of a Muckraker*. New York: Random House (1979).

Burner, David, and Thomas R. West, *Column Right: Journalists in the Service of Nationalism*. New York: New York University Press (1988).

Chadakoff, Rochelle, ed., *Eleanor Roosevelt's My Day*. New York: Pharos Books (1989).

Childs, Marquis, *I Write from Washington*. New York: Harper and Brothers (1942).

Childs, Marquis, and James Reston, *Walter Lippmann and His Times*. New York: Harcourt, Brace (1959).

Davis, Richard Harding, *The Notes of a World Correspondent*. New York: Charles Scribner's Sons (1911).

Delaplane, Stanton, *The Little World of Stanton Delaplane*. New York: Coward-McCann (1959).

Driscoll, Charles B., *The Life of O. O. McIntyre*. New York: Greystone Press (1938).

Fuller, Edmund, ed., *The Essential Royster*. Chapel Hill: Algonquin Books (1985).

Harris, Sydney J., *Leaving the Surface*. Boston: Houghton Mifflin (1968).

Kaplan, Justin, *Lincoln Steffens*. New York: Simon and Schuster (1974).

Kilpatrick, James J., *The Foxes' Union*. McLean, Va.: EPM Publications (1977).

Klurfled, Herman, *Behind the Lines: The World of Drew Pearson*. Englewood Cliffs, N.J.: Prentice-Hall (1968).

Krock, Arthur, *Memoirs: Sixty Years on the Firing Line*. New York: Funk and Wagnalls (1968).

Kurth, Peter, *American Cassandra: The Life of Dorothy Thompson*. Boston: Little, Brown (1990).

Lippmann, Walter, *Early Writings*. New York: Liveright (1970).

Meyer, Karl E., *Pundits, Poets, & Wits: An Omnibus of American Newspaper Columns*. New York: Oxford University Press (1990).

Nichols, David, ed., *Ernie Pyle's America: The Best of Ernie Pyle's 1930s Travel Dispatches*. New York: Random House (1989).

Pilat, Oliver, *Pegler: Angry Man of the Press*. Boston: Beacon Press (1963).

Pilat, Oliver, *Drew Pearson: An Unauthorized Biography*. New York: Harper's Magazine Press (1973).

Pyle, Ernie, *Ernie Pyle in England*. New York: Robert M. McBride and Co. (1941).

Pyle, Ernie, *Brave Men*. New York: Henry Holt (1944).

Reston, James, *Sketches in the Sand*. New York: Alfred A. Knopf (1967).

Riley, Sam G., *The Best of the Rest: Leading Newspaper Columnists Select Their Best Work*. Westport: Greenwood Press (1993).

Ross, Ishbel, *Ladies of the Press*. New York: Harper and Brothers (1936).

Royster, Vermont, *A Pride of Prejudices*. New York: Alfred A. Knopf (1967).

Sanders, Marion K., *Dorothy Thompson*. Boston: Houghton Mifflin (1973).

Steel, Ronald, *Walter Lippmann and the American Century*. Boston: Little, Brown (1980).

von Hoffman, Nicholas, *Left at the Post*. Chicago: Quadrangle Books (1970).

Watson, Emmett, *Digressions of a Native Son*. Seattle: Pacific Institute (1982).

Yoder, Edwin M., Jr., *The Night of the Old South Ball*. Oxford, Miss.: Yoknapatawpha Press (1984).

Editors and Publishers

Barrett, James Wyman, *Joseph Pulitzer and His World*. New York: Vanguard Press (1941).

Becker, Stephen, *Marshall Field III*. New York: Simon and Schuster (1964).

Bigelow, John, *William Cullen Bryant*. Boston: Houghton Mifflin (1890).

Bower, Tom, *Maxwell: The Outsider*. New York: Viking (1992).

Bowman, Charles A., *Ottawa Editor*. Sidney B.C.: Gray's Publishing (1966).

Braddon, Russell, *Roy Thomson of Fleet Street*. London: Collins (1965).

Brenner, Marie, *House of Dreams: The Bingham Family of Louisville*. New York: Random House (1988).

Brown, Francis, *Raymond of the Times*. New York: W. W. Norton (1951).

Carlson, Oliver, *Brisbane*. Westwood, Conn.: Greenwood Press (1937).

Carlson, Oliver, *The Man Who Made News: A Biography of James Gordon Bennett*. New York: Duell, Sloane and Pearce (1942).

Carter, Hodding, *Where Main Street Meets the River*. New York: Rinehart (1952).

Chandler, David Leon, with Mary Voeltz Chandler, *The Binghams of Louisville*. New York: Crown Publishers (1987).

Chaney, Lindsay, and Michael Cieply, *The Hearsts: Family and Empire: The Later Years*. New York: Simon and Schuster (1981).

Coblentz, Edmund D., ed., *William Randolph Hearst: A Portrait in His Own Words*. New York: Simon and Schuster (1952).

Cochran, Negley D., *E. W. Scripps*. Reprint. Westport, Conn.: Greenwood Press (1972).

Cox, James E., *Journey Through My Years*. New York: Simon and Schuster (1946).

Crockett, Albert Stevens, *When James Gordon Bennett Was Caliph of Bagdad*. New York: Funk and Wagnalls (1926).

Crouthamel, James L., *James Watson Webb*, Middletown, Conn.: Wesleyan University Press (1969).

Daniels, Jonathan, *They Will Be Heard: America's Crusading Editors*. New York: McGraw-Hill (1965).

Daniels, Josephus, *Tar Heel Editor*. Chapel Hill: University of North Carolina Press (1939).

Daniels, Josephus, *Editor in Politics* Chapel Hill: University of North Carolina Press (1941).

Davis, Harold E., *Henry Grady's New South*. Tuscaloosa: University of Alabama Press (1990).

Duncan, Bingham, *Whitelaw Reid: Journalist, Politician, Diplomat*. Athens, Ga.: University of Georgia Press (1975).

Fyfe, Hamilton, *Northcliffe: An Intimate Biography*. New York: Macmillan (1930).

Gies, Joseph, *The Colonel of Chicago* [Robert McCormick]. New York: E. P. Dutton (1979).

Greeley, Horace, *The Reflections of a Busy Life*. 2 vols. Reissued. Port Washington, N.Y.: Kennikat Press (1971).

Grayson, David, *American Chronicle: The Autobiography of Ray Stannard Baker*. New York: Charles Scribner's Sons (1945).

Griffith, Sally Foreman, *Home Town News: William Allen White and the Emporia Gazette*. New York: Oxford University Press (1989).

Haines, Joe, *Maxwell*. Boston: Houghton Mifflin (1988).

Hale, William Harlan, *Horace Greeley: Voice of the People*. New York: Harper and Brothers (1950).

Hearst, William Randolph, Jr., with Jack Casserly, *The Hearsts: Father and Son*. Niwot, Colo.: Roberts Rinehart Publishers (1991).

Hinshaw, David, *A Man from Kansas: The Story of William Allen White*. New York: G. P. Putnam's Sons (1945).

Johnson, Gerald W., *An Honorable Titan: A Biography of Adolph S. Ochs*. New York: Harper and Brothers (1946).

Kahn, E. J., Jr., *The World of Swope* [New York World]. New York: Simon and Schuster (1965).

Kansas City Star Staff, *William Rockhill Nelson*. Cambridge: The Riverside Press (1915).

Leapman, Michael, *Arrogant Aussie: The Rupert Murdoch Story*. Secaucas, N.J.: Lyle Stuart (1985).

Linn, W. A., *Horace Greeley*. New York: D. Appleton and Co. (1903).

Lundberg, Ferdinand, *Imperial Hearst*. New York: Equinox Cooperative Press (1936).

Marberry, M. M., *Vicki* [Victoria C. Woodhull]. New York: Funk and Wagnalls (1967).

Marcosson, Isaac F., *"Marse Henry": Biography of Henry Watterson*. New York: Dodd, Mead (1951).

Martin, Harold H., *Ralph McGill, Reporter*. Boston: Little, Brown (1973).

McKabe, Charles R., ed., *Damned Old Crank: A Self-Portrait of E. W. Scripps*. New York: Harper and Brothers (1951).

Meeker, Richard H., *Newspaperman: S. I. Newhouse and the Business of News*. New Haven: Ticknor and Fields (1983).

Mills, George, *Harvey Ingham and Gardner Cowles, Sr.* [Des Moines Register and Tribune]. Ames, Iowa: Iowa State University Press (1977).

Mitchell, Edward, *Memoirs of an Editor*. New York: Charles Scribner's Sons (1924).

Moscowitz, Raymond, *Stuffy: The Life of Newspaper Pioneer Basil "Stuffy" Walters*. Ames, Iowa: Iowa State University Press (1982).

Munster, George, *Rubert Murdoch: A Paper Prince*. New York: Penguin Books (1985).

Nye, Russell B., *William Lloyd Garrison and the Humanitarian Reformers*. Boston: Little, Brown (1955).

Ogden, Rollo, *The Life and Letters of Edwin Lawrence Godkin*. 2 vols. Reprint. Westport, Conn.: Greenwood Press (1972).

Parton, J., *The Life of Horace Greeley*. New York: Mason Brothers (1855).

Patner, Andrew, *I. F. Stone: A Portrait*. New York: Pantheon (1988).

Pfaff, Daniel W., *Joseph Pulitzer II and the Post-Dispatch*. University Park, Pa: Pennsylvania State University Press (1991).

Rosebault, Charles J., *When Dana Was the Sun*. Reprint. Westport, Conn.: Greenwood Press (1971).

Seitz, Don Carlos, *James Gordon Bennett*. Reprint. New York: Beckman (1974).

Sharpe, Ernest, *G. B. Dealey of the Dallas News*. New York: Henry Holt (1955).

Smith, Rixey, and Norman Beasley, *Carter Glass*. New York: Longmans, Green (1939).

Steele, C. Frank, *Prairie Editor: The Life and Times of Buchanan of Lethbridge*. Toronto: Ryerson Press (1961).

Steffens, Lincoln, *Autobiography of Lincoln Steffens*. New York: Harcourt, Brace (1931).

Stern, J. David, *Memoirs of a Maverick Publisher*. New York: Simon and Schuster (1962).

Stoddard, Henry Luther, *Horace Greeley*. New York: G. P. Putnam's Sons (1946).

Storke, Thomas L., *California Editor*. Los Angeles: Westernlore Press (1958).

Suggs, Henry Lewis, *P. B. Young: Newspaperman: Race, Politics and Journalism in the New South*. Charlottesville, Va.: University Press of Virginia (1988).

Swanberg, W. A., *Citizen Hearst*. New York: Charles Scribner's Sons (1961).

Swanberg, W. A., *Pulitzer*. New York: Charles Scribner's Sons (1967).

Swanson, Walter S. J., *The Thin Gold Watch: A Personal History of the Newspaper Copleys*. New York: Macmillan (1964).

Tebbel, John, *The Life and Good Times of William Randolph Hearst*. New York: E. P. Dutton (1952).

Thomson, Lord, of Fleet, *After I Was Sixty*. London: Nelson (1975).

Tifft, Susan E., and Alex S. Jones, *The Patriarch: The Rise and Fall of the Bingham Dynasty*. New York: Summit Books (1991).

Trible, Vance C., *The Astonishing Mr. Scripps: The Turbulent Life of America's Penny Press Lord*. Ames, Iowa: Iowa State University Press (1992).

Villard, Oswald Garrison, *Fighting Years: An Autobiography*. New York: Harcourt, Brace (1939).

Waldrop, Frank C., *McCormick of Chicago*. Englewood Cliffs, N.J.: Prentice-Hall (1966).

Wall, Joseph Frazier, *Henry Watterson: Reconstructed Rebel*. New York: Oxford University Press (1956).

Watterson, Henry, *"Marse Henry": An Autobiography*. 2 vols. New York: George H. Doran (1919).

Wells, Evelyn, *Fremont Older*. New York: Appleton-Century (1936).

White, William Allen, *Autobiography*. New York: Macmillan (1946).

Whited, Charles, *Knight: A Publisher in the Tumultuous Century*. New York: E. P. Dutton (1988).

Williamson, Samuel T., *Frank Gannett*. New York: Duell, Sloan and Pearce (1940).

Wilson, R. Macnair, *Lord Northcliffe: A Study*. Philadelphia: J. B. Lippincott (1927).

Newspapers

Andrews, J. Cutler, *Pittsburgh's Post-Gazette*. Reprint. Westport, Conn.: Greenwood Press (1970).

Anonymous, *The History of The Times: "The Thunder" in the Making 1785–1841*. Vol. 1. New York: Macmillan (1935).

Anonymous, *The History of The Times: The Tradition Established 1841–1884*. Vol. 2. New York: Macmillan (1939).

Anonymous, *The History of The Times: The Twentieth Century Test 1884–1912*. Vol 3. New York: Macmillan (1947).

Anonymous, *The History of The Times: The 150th Anniversary and Beyond 1912–1948*. Vol. 4. New York: Macmillan (1952).

Anonymous, *The Lee Papers: A Saga of Midwestern Journalism*. Kewanee, Ill.: Star-Courier Press (1947).

Ayerst, David, *The Manchester Guardian*. Ithaca, N.Y.: Cornell University Press (1971).

Baker, Thomas Harrison, *The Memphis Commercial Appeal*. Baton Rouge: Louisiana State University Press (1971).

Baehr, Harry W., Jr., *The New York Herald Tribune Since the Civil War*. New York: Octagon Books (1972).

Berger, Meyer, *The Story of the New York Times*. New York: Simon and Schuster (1951).

Bruce, Charles, *News and the Southams*. Toronto: Macmillan of Canada (1968).

Canham, Erwin D., *Commitment to Freedom: The Story of the Christian Science Monitor*. Boston Houghton Mifflin (1958).

Catledge, Turner, *My Life and The Times*. New York: Harper and Row (1971).

Chamberlain, Joseph Edgar, *The Boston Transcript: A History of the First Hundred Years*. Boston: Houghton Mifflin (1930).

Chapman, John, *Tell It to Sweeney: An Informal History of the New York Daily News*. Garden City, N.Y.: Doubleday (1961).

Claiborne, Jack, *The Charlotte Observer*. Chapel Hill: University of North Carolina Press (1986).

Cohen, Lester, *The New York Graphic*. Philadelphia: Chilton Books (1964).

Conrad, Will, Kathleen Wilson, and Dale Wilson, *The Milwaukee Journal: The First Eighty Years*. Madison: University of Wisconsin Press (1964).

Copley, *The Copley Press*. Aurora, Ill.: Copley Press (1953).

Crouthamel, James L., *Bennett's New York Herald and the Rise of the Popular Press*. Syracuse, N.Y.: Syracuse University Press (1989).

Dana, Marshall N., *The First Fifty Years of the Oregon Journal*. Portland, Ore.: Binfords and Mort (1951).

Dyar, Ralph E., *News for an Empire: The Story of the Spokesman-Review*. Caldwell, Idaho: Caxton Printers (1952).

Edelman, Maurice, *The Mirror: A Political History*. New York: London House and Maxwell (1966).

Gottlieb, Robert, and Irene Wolf, *Thinking Big: The Story of the Los Angeles Times: Its Publishers and Their Influence on Southern California*. New York: G. P. Putnam's Sons (1977).

Goulden, Joseph C., *Fit to Print: A. M. Rosenthal and His Times*. Secaucus, N.J.: Lyle Stuart (1988).

Hooker, Richard, *The Story of an Independent Newspaper: One Hundred Years of the Springfield Republican*. New York: Macmillan (1924).

Kelly, Tom, *The Imperial Post*. New York: William Morrow (1983).

King, Charles, *The Ottaway Newspapers: The First 50 Years*. Campbell Hall, N.Y.: Ottaway Newspapers (1986).

Kluger, Richard, *The Paper: The Life and Death of The New York Herald Tribune.* New York: Alfred A. Knopf (1986).

Lyons, Louis, *Newspaper Story: One Hundred Years of the Boston Globe.* Cambridge, Mass. (1971).

MacNab, Gordon, *A Century of News and People in the East Oregonian.* Pendleton, Ore.: East Oregonian Publishing Co. (1975).

McClure, Kevin Michael, *The Great American Newspaper: The Rise and Fall of the Village Voice.* New York: Charles Scribner's Sons (1978).

Nevins, Alan, *The Evening Post: A Century of Journalism.* New York: Boni and Liveright (1922).

O'Brien, Frank M., *The Story of the Sun.* Reprint. Westport, Conn.: Greenwood Press (1968).

Perkin, Robert L., *The First Hundred Years: An Informal History of Denver and The Rocky Mountain News.* Garden City, N.Y.: Doubleday and Company (1959).

Price, Warren C., *The Eugene Register-Guard.* Portland, Ore.: Binfords and Mort (1976).

Pritchard, Peter, *The Making of McPaper.* Kansas City., Mo.: Andrews, McMeel and Parker (1987).

Pugnetti, Frances Taylor, *Tiger by the Tail: Twenty-Five Years with the Stormy Tri-City Herald.* Pasco, Wash.: Tri-City Herald (1975).

Rice, William B., *The Angeles Star: 1851–1864.* Berkeley: University of California Press (1947).

Roberts, Chalmer, *The Washington Post: The First 100 Years.* Boston: Houghton Mifflin (1977).

Roberts, Chalmer, *In the Shadow of Power: The Story of The Washington Post.* Cabin John, Md.: Seven Locks Press (1989).

Robertson, Charles L., *The International Herald Tribune: The First Hundred Years.* New York: Columbia University Press (1987).

Robertson, Nan, *The Girls in the Balcony: Women, Men and The New York Times.* New York: Random House (1992).

Root, Waverley, *The Paris Edition: 1927–1934.* San Francisco: North Point Press (1989).

Ross, Margaret, *Arkansas Gazette: The Early Years 1819–1866.* Little Rock: Arkansas Gazette Foundation (1969).

Salisbury, Harrison, *Without Fear or Favor: An Uncompromising Look at The New York Times.* New York: Times Books (1980).

Talese, Gay, *The Kingdom and the Power* (The New York Times). New York: World Publishing (1969).

Tebbel, John, *An American Dynasty: The Story of the McCormicks, Medills and Pattersons.* Garden City, N.Y.: Doubleday (1947).

Veblen, Eric, *The Manchester Union Leader in New Hampshire Elections.* Hanover, N.H.: University Press of New England (1975).

Wendt, Lloyd, *The Wall Street Journal.* Chicago: Rand McNally (1982).

Williams, Harold A., *The Baltimore Sun: 1837–1987.* Baltimore: John Hopkins University Press (1987).

Index

NAMES

NEWSPAPERS, MAGAZINES AND BROADCAST STATIONS

ABOUT THE AUTHOR

Kenneth Rystrom has spent 20 years in the newspaper business, 17 of them writing and editing editorials for the *Register* in Des Moines, Iowa, and *The Columbian* in Vancouver, Washington. He has been a professor of communication studies at Virginia Polytechnic Institute and State University since 1984. He received his bachelor's degree from the University of Nebraska–Lincoln, his master's degree from the University of California–Berkeley and his Ph.D. from the University of Southern California.

Professor Rystrom has been recognized for his contributions to journalism, journalism education and scholarship. For his contributions to journalism and journalism education, he has been awarded a life membership in the National Conference of Editorial Writers, an organization for which he has also served as president. For his scholarly work in journalism, he received the Henry W. Grady Award in both 1992 and 1993.